LAW'S IMPUNITY

When faced with those who act with impunity, we seek the protection of law. We rely upon the legal system for justice, from international human rights law that establishes common standards of protection, to international criminal law that spearheads efforts to end impunity for the most heinous atrocities. While legal processes are perceived to combat impunity, and despite the ready availability of the law, accountability often remains elusive. What if the law itself enables impunity?

Law's Impunity asks this question in the context of the modern Private Military Company (PMC), examining the relationship between law and the concepts of responsibility and impunity. This book proposes that ordinary legal processes do not neutralise, but rather legalise impunity. This radical idea is applied to the abysmal record of human rights violations perpetrated by the modern PMC and the shocking absence of accountability. This book demonstrates how the law organises, rather than overcomes, impunity by detailing how the modern PMC exploits ordinary legal processes to systematically exclude itself from legal responsibility. Thus, *Law's Impunity* offers an alternative to conventional thinking about the law, providing an innovative approach to assess and refine the rigour of legal processes in the ongoing quest to end impunity.

Volume 56 in the series Studies in International Law

Studies in International Law

Recent titles in this series

The Interception of Vessels on the High Seas: Contemporary Challenges to the Legal Order of the Oceans
Efthymios Papastavridis

Integration at the Border: The Dutch Act on Integration Abroad and International Immigration Law
Karin de Vries

An Equitable Framework for Humanitarian Intervention
Ciarán Burke

Democratic Statehood in International Law: The Emergence of New States in Post-Cold War Practice
Jure Vidmar

International Law and the Construction of the Liberal Peace
Russell Buchan

The OIC, the UN, and Counter-Terrorism Law-Making: Conflicting or Cooperative Legal Orders?
Katja Samuel

Statelessness: The Enigma of the International Community
William E Conklin

The Reception of Asylum Seekers under International Law: Between Sovereignty and Equality
Lieneke Slingenberg

International Law and Child Soldiers
Gus Waschefort

The Contractual Nature of the Optional Clause
Gunnar Törber

Non-State Actors in International Law
Edited by Math Noortmann, August Reinisch and Cedric Ryngaert

For the complete list of titles in this series, see 'Studies in International Law' link at www.hartpub.co.uk/books/series.asp

Law's Impunity

Responsibility and the Modern Private Military Company

Hin-Yan Liu

• HART •
PUBLISHING
OXFORD AND PORTLAND, OREGON
2017

Hart Publishing
An imprint of Bloomsbury Publishing Plc

Hart Publishing Ltd
Kemp House
Chawley Park
Cumnor Hill
Oxford OX2 9PH
UK

Bloomsbury Publishing Plc
50 Bedford Square
London
WC1B 3DP
UK

www.hartpub.co.uk
www.bloomsbury.com

Published in North America (US and Canada) by
Hart Publishing
c/o International Specialized Book Services
920 NE 58th Avenue, Suite 300
Portland, OR 97213-3786
USA

www.isbs.com

First published in hardback, 2015
Paperback edition, 2017

British Library Cataloguing-in-Publication Data
A catalogue record for this book is available from the British Library.

ISBN: PB: 978-1-50991-839-3
HB: 978-1-84946-516-8

Typeset by Compuscript Ltd, Shannon
Printed and bound in Great Britain by
Lightning Source UK Ltd

To my wife, Agnieszka, with love and gratitude

Preface

It has become cliché to open a commentary addressing the modern Private Military Company (PMC) with the now infamous Blackwater incident at Nisour Square, but this book did in fact grow as a reaction to that atrocity. Between the media headlines and ensuing public scandal there simmered troublesome, yet nebulous, allegations of impunity in the aftermath of what was single bloodiest incident involving American PMCs in Iraq. It was this incident that ignited my own outrage and was to become the driving force behind this project. As the media limelight soon dimmed, many commentators turned their attention towards other aspects of the PMC phenomenon: the status of military contractors under international law; the relationship between the PMC contractor and the disparaged traditional mercenary; the legitimacy of privatising, commodifying and outsourcing military services, especially where these are the source of material profit; in addition to the overarching questions concerning the role and function of the State in an era where its monopoly on the legitimate use of force appears to be under assault.

The private military industry was, and continues to be, an area of intrigue for a cadre of academics, journalists and activists who produce a deluge of books, articles and reports expounding on the various challenges posed by the modern PMC. Yet, the core allegations of impunity for private military atrocities continue, and somewhat paradoxically considering their gravity, receive little more than superficial attention. In particular, where the PMC excites legal controversy, or at least reveals ambiguity within the underlying law, the general approach has been to put the matter firmly to rest by pointing to the potential applicability of existing law to cover the situation in question. This was unfortunate because this potential applicability in theory never translated into the law being applied in practice: it may even be that this approach was pernicious, insofar as it veiled the initial controversy with the appearance of resolution.

Faith in the legal system to address and remedy the allegations of impunity levelled at the PMC continued unwavering in spite of the absence of supporting evidence, and even in spite of mounting evidence to the contrary. It became increasingly clear that the law, despite the appearance of being able to regulate the activities of the PMC, was not being deployed to this end. This suggested either that the law was incapable of acting in such a manner, or that it was complicit in continuing the impunity enjoyed by the PMC. Either way, it was clear that a fundamentally different approach to the issues was necessary.

At a superficial level, it may be argued that the case is now closed even in a literal sense. As I write this, a US District Court has recently handed down convictions for four of the members of the Blackwater team responsible for the Nisour Square massacre. This provides an obvious retort to the central claim in this book that the law is not doing its job properly—it may have taken a long time, but the legal processes did what they were supposed to and held those responsible to account. It is a strange coincidence that this project took the same length of time as the *US v Paul Slough* saga took to unfurl, and some would argue that the project became obsolete at the moment of its completion as a result. The difficulty with this line of argumentation, however, is that the case is likely to be appealed so the convictions may not be firm. As to the project itself, the realisation that the law might have iatrogenic effects significantly broadened both its scope and application. While the focus remains very much upon the modern private military company as a way of developing the ideas and testing various claims, the direction of the project shifted from being another commentary on the contemporary privatisation of security and military force towards building new tools with which to measure subtle effects. As one of the examiners quipped during my viva, this is not so much a book about the private military company—one would not turn to it seeking to learn more about the phenomenon or to understand more about how it operates. Rather, it has grown from those roots into a book that seeks to raise questions about the ability and efficacy of the law to regulate emerging practices. It aims to use the challenges raised by the private military company as a platform from which to launch an enquiry about how the law might in fact be the source of the very problems it is applied to redress.

The origin of this project was a dissertation written at University College London and subsequently published in the *Journal of Conflict and Security Law*. As is often the case, more questions were raised than answered in this process, and these were convincing enough for Penny Green to agree to supervise my PhD at the Law School of King's College London, and I remain grateful to her for giving me such an excellent opportunity. Dr Christopher Kinsey became my second supervisor after the internal upgrade process and has made significant contributions to the aspects of the book tackling the private military company phenomenon and we continue to work together on questions raised by mercenary activity. At King's, I was fortunate enough to find myself in a friendly and engaged doctoral community which helped to ease the solitude of thesis writing. In particular, I am thankful for the friendship of Harry Nikolaidis, John Charney, Henrique Carvalho, Christine Schwobel, Bryan Druzin, Fabiana di Lorenzo, Wang Peng and Jingyi Peng. I would also like to thank my examiners, Professors Nigel White and Mervyn Frost for their insightful suggestions for developing the thesis into this monograph.

I would also like to gratefully acknowledge the generous support that this project received from the Social Sciences and Humanities Research Council of Canada for the Doctoral Fellowship, the King's Annual Fund for the King's Continuation Scholarship and the Government of Alberta for the Sir James Lougheed Award of Distinction. I am also thankful first to the Max Weber Programme and later the Academy of European Law at the European University Institute for the space and support they offered at critical junctures.

Finally, and most importantly, I would like to thank James Sims, without whose considerable help this project could not have begun, and my wife, Agnieszka, whose tolerance and understanding made it possible to finish.

Hin-Yan Liu
December 2014
Il Laghino, Florence

Contents

Abbreviations

API	Protocol Additional to the Geneva Conventions of 12 August 1949, and relating to the Protection of Victims of International Armed Conflicts (Protocol I). 8 June 1977.
APII	Protocol Additional to the Geneva Conventions of 12 August 1949, and relating to the Protection of Victims of Non-International Armed Conflicts (Protocol II). 8 June 1977.
ATCA	Alien Tort Claims Act 1789 (United States) 28 U.S.C. paragraph 1350
CAT	United Nations Convention Against Torture and Other Cruel, Inhuman or Degrading Treatment or Punishment. A/RES/39/46. 10 December 1984
CIA	Central Intelligence Agency
CPA	Coalition Provisional Authority
DC	District of Columbia (United States)
DoD	Department of Defense (United States)
ECHR	European Convention on Human Rights. 3 September 1953.
FCO	Foreign and Commonwealth Office (United Kingdom)
GC III	Convention (III) relative to the Treatment of Prisoners of War. 12 August 1949
GC IV	Convention (IV) relative to the Protection of Civilian Persons in Time of War. 12 August 1949
HRL	Human Rights Law
ICC	International Criminal Court
ICCPR	International Covenant on Civil and Political Rights. 16 December 1966
ICJ	International Court of Justice
ICL	International Criminal Law
ICoC	International Code of Conduct
ICRC	International Committee of the Red Cross
ICTR	International Criminal Tribunal for Rwanda
ICTY	International Criminal Tribunal for the former Yugoslavia
IHL	International Humanitarian Law
ILC	International Law Commission
IMT	International Military Tribunal
JAB	*Jus ad Bellum*
JCE	Joint Criminal Enterprise

JIB	*Jus in Bello*
MOD	Ministry of Defence (United Kingdom)
MEJA	Military Extraterritorial Jurisdiction Act 2000 (United States) Public Law 106–523 114 Stat 2488
MNF	Multinational Force
OAU	Organisation of African Unity
OHCHR	Office of the High Commissioner for Human Rights
PMC	Private Military Company
PMSC	Private Military and Security Company
PTO	Perpetration Through an Organisation
SCSL	Special Court for Sierra Leone
SFOR	Stabilisation Force in Bosnia and Herzegovina
SOFA	Status of the Forces Agreement
TNC	Transnational Corporation
TVPA	Torture Victim's Protection Act 1991 (United States) Public Law 102-256, 106 Stat 73
UCMJ	Uniform Code of Military Justice 2006 (United States). Public Law 109-364 120 Stat 2083
UK	United Kingdom
UNGA	United Nations General Assembly
UNGAR	United Nations General Assembly Resolution
UNHRC	Human Rights Council
UNSC	United Nations Security Council
UNSCR	United Nations Security Council Resolution
US	United States
USAID	United States Agency for International Development

Table of Cases

International Criminal Tribunal for Rwanda

International Military Tribunal

The Netherlands

New Zealand

Privy Council

South Africa

Special Court for Sierra Leone

United Kingdom

United States

Table of Instruments and Legislation

International

Organisation of African Unity

United Kingdom

United States

Introduction

AT THE CORE of this book is a radical idea: the law creates and maintains situations of impunity. This is an idea that is difficult to articulate and argue, let alone accept, given the fundamental assumption that ordinary legal processes function precisely to assert responsibility and to impose accountability. The purpose of this book is to erode this assumption by proposing an alternative approach to the law that views ordinary legal processes as an integral part of the problem. In doing so, this approach demonstrates that situations of impunity need not be deliberately cultivated by any specific legislator who seeks to shield a particular actor or activity from legal control. Rather, situations of impunity can be the default consequence of the repetitive exclusion from the processes that are relied upon to allocate responsibility. This approach does not, of course, discount more traditional avenues to situations of impunity which arise from the lack of political will, the effects of prosecutorial discretion, and extra-legal settlements. As these more overt routes are well known, however, these will only be discussed in passing. Here the focus is to elucidate the systemic defects of ordinary juridical processes which are both more imperceptible, and potentially more pervasive.

This book explores the question by analysing the relationship between the law and its processes and the concept of impunity through the challenges posed by the modern Private Military Company (PMC). This is because the PMC has been demonstrated to be potentially governed by a plethora of applicable laws that should have assigned responsibility to the PMC and imposed accountability for its actions. Yet, the observed persistence of PMC impunity raises questions as to how the law has failed to fulfil these expectations and in doing so, asks what role the law itself plays in creating and maintaining the structures of impunity that benefit the PMC.

The problem of PMC impunity was initially framed by what I term the orthodox legal approach. This sought to explain the lack of PMC responsibility and the failure to impose accountability for its actions by the dearth of applicable laws that govern the industry. The implicit assumption underlying this approach is that impunity cannot persist where legal processes function, so PMC impunity must necessarily subsist within the *lacunae* in existing laws or between the current reaches of different bodies of law. Viewing law and impunity as mutually exclusive, the orthodox legal approach would suggest that overcoming PMC impunity would be a simple matter of filling in the gaps within the law and bridging the gulfs between different systems of the law. Yet, the recidivist practices of the industry, which continue to be embroiled within allegations of impunity despite the potential regulation by current law and the introduction of new laws, challenge the validity of the orthodox approach. The persistence of PMC impunity in the face of potentially applicable law suggests that legal processes are themselves implicated within the structures that organise impunity for the industry. This would mean that more law, at least by itself, cannot provide the solution as the orthodox legal approach might suggest.

An original approach to the issue of PMC impunity is adopted here which inverts the orthodox legal approach. Instead of seeking to demonstrate that impunity arises from the gaps within or between existing laws, I argue that it is the *law itself that creates and maintains the structures of impunity* that are enjoyed by the PMC. The structure of this argument is similarly reversed, taking impunity as the point of departure for exploration, rather than the conclusion that the argument works towards. This reversal is necessary because the question is not whether PMCs enjoy impunity, but instead asks how that impunity is legally structured, organised and applied to the industry. This approach promises to reinvigorate the debate surrounding the question both by examining the nature of impunity and by broadening the field of analysis. I will also demonstrate that the response made through the orthodox legal approach can only be counterproductive by showing how legal processes inherently generate PMC impunity and how the functioning laws can be suspended or circumvented to prevent accountability. The response fuelled by the orthodox legal approach can only entrench PMC impunity because it will continue to develop and refine the very laws that are the source of the problem.

The argument is made by developing the concept of legalised impunity which comprises of two complementary dimensions: passive impunity which is generated by the structural and organisational characteristics inherent within the ordinary legal process; and active impunity whereby this ordinary legal process is circumvented or suspended. As such, this book seeks to develop an analytical framework through which to study the ways in which impunity is structured and to understand how its processes operate. This illuminates the limitations of the law for overcoming impunity in order to open the debate concerning the appropriate legal reaction to new actors and emerging practices. While it is the law's creation of impunity for the PMC that will be discussed at length in this book, both its framework and its approach will be capable of broader application in situations where the law appears to struggle in according responsibility or ascribing accountability in novel situations.

But what is the PMC and why focus on it in this context? The PMC is the latest manifestation of organised mercenary activity because it provides personnel for direct participation in hostilities through the for-profit business model. Thus, the emergence of the PMC and the subsequent prosperity of the industry has challenged our contemporary understanding of how armed force may be organised, the purposes towards which coercive violence may be deployed, and has significantly undermined the mechanisms of responsibility that govern the conduct of hostilities. These can be expressed by emphasising the three inherent characteristics that distinguish the PMC which are signified by each component of the term. First, the *private* military company underscores the mercenary origins of the industry and concern whether violence can lawfully or legitimately be used by private actors or be deployed in pursuit of private purposes. Second, the private *military* company emphasises its proximity to armed conflict and its ability to inflict severe harm in a direct manner. Third, the private military *company* stresses its juridical personhood which is legally separate and independent from the association of natural persons of which it is composed.

These three distinguishing features of the PMC are shown to frustrate the dominant bodies of law that regulate the fields of activity within which they operate: Human Rights Law (HRL), International Humanitarian Law (IHL) and International Criminal Law (ICL). First, HRL was formulated to protect the individual in their hierarchical relationship against State power. The private dimension of the PMC suggests, at least formally, a horizontal relationship between the PMC and its victims because State action is absent, thereby excluding the applicability of HRL to its activities. Despite the control over coercive force by the PMC and the concomitant risks of violating HRL principles, the private nature of the PMC undermines its capacity to bear HRL obligations, let alone its ability to be accountable for any actual violation. Second, the military nature of PMC activities suggests that IHL, which governs the conduct of hostilities, would act as operative law. But because IHL was conceived and developed during an era when the State possessed the monopoly over the legitimate use of force, it only created obligations for, and regulated the conduct of, States within armed conflict. Furthermore, the subsequent expansion of IHL to encompass non-international armed conflict and to embrace certain categories of non-State actor neither explicitly addressed the PMC nor implicitly regulated its conduct. Thus, the orientation of both HRL and IHL towards State action thwarts their unambiguous regulation of the PMC. Third, ICL was developed to impose individual criminal responsibility for those most responsible for egregious international crimes. The jurisdiction of ICL is exclusively over natural persons because it was developed by the International Military Tribunal at Nuremberg as a counter-reaction to previous forms of collective criminal responsibility. The result is that the PMC cannot be liable under current manifestations of ICL because of its juridical corporate personhood, and even the susceptibility of PMC contractors is diminished because the focus of ICL is on those who are the most responsible for the worst crimes.

The response forwarded by the orthodox legal approach has been to bridge the gap between HRL and IHL on the one hand and the PMC on the other. One approach in this vein attempted to connect PMC activity with that of the State, while another sought to clarify specific industry obligations under HRL and IHL in order to forge a direct link with the PMC. In relation to ICL, the response was to highlight the ability of individual PMC contractors to bear ICL responsibilities even when the PMC remained immune to its provisions. This enabled the orthodox legal approach to posit that the PMC did not operate within a legal black hole, but instead to show that PMC activity is regulated by a wide range of potentially applicable law. The shortcomings and inadequacies of this response were strikingly demonstrated in the recidivist practices of the PMC industry, thereby anchoring the need to take a new tack on the issue. The book is structured as follows:

Chapter one develops the concept of impunity and begins by exploring its indeterminate and contested nature. After identifying the core themes that underlie impunity, the chapter dissects the passive and active dimensions of legal impunity that provide the theoretical framework for analysing the function of the law within PMC impunity. Passive impunity, on the one hand, concerns structural characteristics inherent within the law and is further divided into six sections. The first concerns the compartmentalisation of law that is evident in the split of legal regulation among separate juridical fields for any activity. The second considers the overextension of law as it seeks to regulate armed conflict. The third analyses the tendency of the law towards hegemony that magnifies any failure of the law to regulate the activities of the PMC activities. The fourth discusses the legal nature of irresponsibility. To do so, it segregates the component concepts of responsibility in the law to demonstrate that impunity inheres within the legal preoccupation with role responsibility and the downplaying of outcome responsibility. The fifth is concerned with the function played by the law in the denial of wrongdoing: because the law is instrumental in recognising and categorising harm, it becomes vulnerable to manipulation that seeks to deny or downplay the very existence of a wrong. The sixth explores the role played by the law with regard to the polar opposite of denial, assertion, and how impunity might arise as a result of the claims the PMC is able to make through the consequences of legal recognition.

The active dimension of impunity, on the other hand, concerns legal exceptionalism which occurs by suspending or circumventing the ordinary legal process, and may be seen as a more orthodox view of impunity. These concern the retrospective mechanisms of amnesty and pardon, and the atemporal device of immunity. The chapter considers whether IHL can broadly be considered as an active impunity mechanism before examining states of exception whereby the legal paradigm is partially or completely suspended. The contribution of this chapter is that it unifies disparate expressions of the inadequacies and shortcomings of law in order to form the passive dimension of impunity, demonstrating in the process the creation of impunity through ordinary juridical processes. The flaws in legal architecture are structured alongside the orthodox understanding of impunity as the absence of law in order to present an integrated and nuanced theoretical framework of legalised impunity.

Chapter two studies the modern PMC by painting a contemporary portrait of the industry and its activities by examining the functions they fulfilled in the conflicts in Iraq and Afghanistan. The factual basis of the claim that the PMC enjoys impunity for its actions will be made by demonstrating that PMCs have allegedly perpetrated a range of atrocities in these conflicts, repeatedly and without accountability. This is further underscored by evidence of persistent recidivism and PMC involvement within different categories of violation. Accountability considerations will be shown to focus upon issues of fiscal waste and fraud, despite widespread evidence that the industry has been involved with serious human rights abuses. The judicial and legislative responses to these allegations of impunity will also be shown to be inadequate. This raises the debate between the two UN Special Rapporteurs on the Use of Mercenaries who respectively considered the PMC as a criminal enterprise and as a potentially legitimate business. The PMC industry is then considered in greater detail, from the emergence of Watchguard International, the first modern PMC, and the pressures that sustain the industry and which foster its growth. The remainder of the chapter is devoted to categorising the types of entity that are potentially encapsulated within the term 'Private Military Company'. After illustrating the flexibility of PMCs and the diversity of their services, the main typologies that have been developed to understand the industry are analysed. These typologies sustain two broad effects: they distract attention away from the fact that the PMC industry provides organised private violence that is clearly criminal within other contexts; and that the organisation of this violence potentially raises the severity level of its activities to the plane of international crime. In order to redress these effects, a revised typology is proposed that seeks to emphasise the criminality of the PMC. This typology will adapt the IHL principle of distinction and focus both upon the level of violence offered or controlled by a PMC, and the directness with which their services engage, or their contractors participate, in armed conflict. The main contribution of this chapter is this revised typology which underscores the aberrantly violent nature of the PMC within the predominantly civilian context of the corporation.

Chapter three examines the treatment of mercenary activity under international law, arguing that the law has both failed to marginalise the individual mercenary or criminalise the broader practices of mercenarism. Thus, this chapter demonstrates the passive dimension of impunity in operation. First, although the capability of the law in criminalising organised private violence is demonstrated in its approach to the threat posed by maritime piracy, its treatment of mercenary activity failed to adopt this model. Mercenaries are then shown to have been historically prevalent, but to have gradually declined with the rise and eventual domination of the modern State. Before examining mercenary activity in law, the difficulty in differentiating between mercenaries and soldiers is considered. The chapter then showcases the difficulty of defining a mercenary in law, arguing that a restrictive definition fosters impunity by isolating the stigma into a category that has no practical application. Laws seeking to marginalise the individual mercenary are shown to run against both the history and purpose of IHL, which in turn raises questions for its purported customary international humanitarian law status. The alternative approach of criminalising the practice of mercenarism is shown to be limited to the specific historical context of decolonisation and the struggle for political self-determination, thereby limiting its contemporary relevance. This context also restricted the scope of international support such that mercenarism failed to crystallise into an international crime. Ultimately, the failure of law to decisively determine the status of mercenary activity enabled the emergence of the PMC, and these legal ambiguities continue to facilitate the claims of the industry in distancing themselves from allegations that they engage in unlawful activities. The contribution of this chapter is in overturning the questionable consensus that mercenaries and mercenary activity are unlawful, at least under international law. This close examination reveals that mercenaries and mercenarism were subjected to separate legal regimes which pursued distinct purposes and were mired in practical problems of application.

Chapters four and five examine in detail the structure of legalised impunity as it relates to the PMC. Chapter four first lays the groundwork for analysing passive impunity by setting out the developments that led to the recognition of the corporation as a juridical person before moving to discuss a range of important consequences this led to under contract law. Chapter four then departs from the predominant focus upon *Jus in Bello* (JIB) conduct considerations to account for PMC impunity for 'violations' of *Jus ad Bellum* (JAB) decision to use force. The contemporary focus upon the conduct of the PMC industry by commentators has skewed the frame of debate, largely obscuring the question of whether the PMC should be operating in the first instance. The contemporary neglect of the JAB dimension will foster PMC impunity because it will neither be responsible for violations of the prohibition of the threat or use of force, nor be accountable for what would amount to acts of corporate aggression. Passive impunity is also demonstrated through a number of barriers which obstruct the application of the doctrine of command responsibility to PMC contractors. Chapter five then examines the active impunity mechanisms that suspend ordinary laws from applying to the PMC or its contractors. It begins by framing the nature of the corporation and illustrating that the criminal law does not apply to the corporate juridical person, thereby immunising the PMC from indictment. To examine the operation of active impunity in greater detail, recourse is made to the jurisprudence of US federal courts. This is both because there is extant legislation that has been deployed by victims of PMC activities, and because of attempts to amend legislation to close the perceived *lacunae* in the laws that regulate their activity. In criminal law, the exemption of the PMC itself is accompanied by significant discrepancies between soldiers and PMC contractors in their indictment. This difference suggests that the latter category benefit, at least in a relative sense, from active impunity mechanisms. Active impunity is also shown to operate within the civil remedies that are purportedly available under the Alien Tort Claims Act and the Torture Victim's Protection Act. These are the centrepieces of US legislation that have been utilised by victims of human rights violations at the courts and initially appear to overturn allegations of impunity by providing a clear avenue for suit. A closer examination, however, reveals a range of impunity paradoxes operating in tandem to prevent the success of PMC victims using these laws. The contribution of this chapter is that it reveals the operation of the legalised impunity mechanisms that effectively protect the PMC and its contractors from responsibility and liability. By clearly demonstrating that the ordinary legal processes contribute to and create powerful situations of impunity, I argue that the efficacy and appropriateness of the orthodox legal approach is undermined.

Chapter six discusses the future of PMC impunity through analysing, and extrapolating from, the nascent mechanisms that are emerging on the international plane to regulate PMCs. This examination reveals that these regulatory mechanisms are in fact informed by starkly divergent approaches to the issue of responsibility. These mechanisms are shown to be divided upon their temporal orientation towards responsibility: one primarily establishes prospective standards while the other focuses upon ensuring retrospective accountability. This bifurcation of responsibilities within the very mechanisms that are being developed to regulate the industry is likely to structure PMC impunity into the future because blind spots result from taking such a narrow focus. The chapter then charts the preference for self-regulation in the United Kingdom, as a precursor to similar developments at the 'international' level which is then outlined, before turning its attention to the international legal approaches to the issue. Chapter six then proposes to incentivise robust self-regulation, given the current dominance of this approach for regulating PMC activities, by developing forms of collective responsibility for self-regulatory bodies. The chapter concludes by providing four dimensions along which to measure the adequacy and efficacy of developing regulatory regimes that can be readily applied beyond the narrow PMC issue. The contribution of this chapter is to show the existence of impunity for PMC activity beyond the areas that are currently under scrutiny and to suggest that the regulatory regimes that seek to overcome impunity have instead incorporated its structure within them.

This book is liable to face an uphill struggle by trying to articulate an issue which has received much recognition, to give some form to the imperceptible and to do all of this against the grain of accumulated and entrenched orthodoxy. Three points need to be made clear at the outset to avoid misunderstanding and overreach. First, this book is not intended as an outright assault upon the law or the way ordinary legal processes function. Rather, the aim here is to illuminate a systemic flaw within juridical processes that, identified, may be remedied through restructuring that may be capable of strengthening and adapting the law in face of emerging challenges. Second, while the book's claim is broadly phrased to reflect the possibility that similar effects may occur in other domains, the intent here is not to condemn all law, and certainly not to do so based upon such a limited case study. Indeed, the effects identified in this book, where they occur, are likely to be found at the margins of the law and in particular where it is extended in attempts to regulate new actors or activities. The third is to answer Susanna Lindroos-Hovinheimo's observation that splitting a dichotomy is not necessarily helpful because such an approach fails to differentiate between the degrees of the effect and overlooks aspects that might be salvaged or remediated.[1] By considering in depth the particular challenges wrought by the modern Private Military Company (PMC), whose characteristics have repetitively excluded its activity from legal regulation, this book tries to identify the factors involved in generating and maintaining impunity.

[1] S Lindroos-Hovinheimo, 'Is Law Necessarily Unjust' (2009) 6 *No Foundations—Journal of Extreme Legal Positivism* 69, 85–86.

1

Law's Impunity

I. INTRODUCTION

THE PRESENT CHAPTER lays the theoretical groundwork for this book by dissecting the contested concept of impunity in order to elucidate its architecture and to express the manifold ways in which the law both generates and sustains impunity. Implicit within the orthodox legal approach is the assumption that impunity arises solely from the absence of law, either at the fringes of the legal system or entirely external to it. Thus, the orthodox legal approach considers impunity to be the antithesis of, and overcome by, the law: impunity can only occur either where there is a lack of legal process, or where the law has predetermined impunity by providing exemptions to its processes. The dominance of this approach obfuscates the more radical argument that is proposed here, that impunity is *created* by the law.

In order to demonstrate this idea, the theoretical structure of impunity is carefully developed here to bridge the gap between the orthodox legal approach to PMC impunity as an *effect* of the law, and the more radical argument that the impunity enjoyed by the PMC is a *creation* of the law. To make this argument, this chapter demonstrates that the law organises impunity through two complementary mechanisms. In the passive dimension, the structural properties and characteristics that are integral to the law are shown to generate impunity. In the active dimension, impunity is indicated within the suspension of the ordinary juridical process as well as in situations where it is exempted altogether. Roughly framed then, the law can create impunity both through formal and factual restrictions imposed upon *access* to accountability procedures (passive). Where there is at least nominal access to such procedures, impunity can arise in obstacles erected which limit the probability, or even the possibility, of securing substantive remedies through those accountability procedures (active).

This chapter begins by exploring different approaches to the concept of impunity to distil its core characteristics. It becomes clear that the concept of legal impunity is primarily retrospective and is concerned with the lack of accountability for (usually harmful) outcomes. These are traditionally segregated into de jure and de facto forms of impunity that loosely correspond to the proposed dimensions of active and passive impunity.

Part of the contribution of this chapter is to highlight the fundamental role played by the law in *both* forms of impunity: that all impunity is really de jure because it is legally structured. The otherwise myopic view of impunity neglects the strong structural forces within the passive dimension of impunity which preclude or foreclose the very possibility of responsibility and accountability.

The chapter examines the passive dimension of impunity which is demonstrated to be primarily legal in nature, despite its traditional association with de facto impunity. This perspective confers the advantage of creating a different set of criteria for regulatory mechanisms to avert impunity: if de facto impunity is recognised to possess legal roots, this suggests that their solutions may also be found in the legal realm. The passive dimension of responsibility unifies four disparate critiques of the law. First is the juridification of warfare, the processes in which legal rules and mechanisms began to regulate recourse to and conduct within armed conflict. The severe nature of armed conflict challenges the ability of law to articulate, categorise and ascribe meaning to these activities and their consequences, potentially rendering them extra-juridical, but the law has extended to govern even these activities. Second is the tendency of law towards overreach and its susceptibility to capture, which are expressed in the dark sides of law. The consequent failures are magnified by the dominance of law as an arbitration and regulation regime that has efficiently crowded out possible alternatives. Third is the generation of irresponsibility through the multifarious nature of the concept of responsibility. The different component concepts that weave together to constitute the idea of responsibility, enable the real possibility of claiming to be responsible while simultaneously disavowing responsibility: this is best illustrated by the divorce between role (being responsible) and outcome (accountable for) forms of responsibility. The passive impunity dimension is then reconciled with the discourse on interpretive denial. Unlike literal denial where the facts themselves are contested, interpretive denial concerns the reclassification of the facts: the meaning attributed to them is redefined. Interpretive denial enriches the concept of impunity because it is able to account both for impunity and its effects. To complete the concept of interpretive denial in the context of impunity, this chapter then proposes the complementary idea of interpretive assertion. As a counterpart to interpretive denial, interpretive assertion aspires to form affinities with virtuous actors and actions, contributing to the prospect of impunity by distorting the context within which accountability analyses and responsibility evaluations occur.

Then, the active dimension of impunity is analysed to explicate the mechanisms that suspend ordinary legal processes. This involves the practices of pardon, amnesty and immunity, and inheres within states of exception that alter the entire legal paradigm. The active dimension of impunity is rooted problematically within the exercise of sovereign power that serves simultaneously as the source of law and the authority for war.

While the explicit mechanisms that suspend the ordinary legal process for PMC activity are considered here, this framework provides the basis for chapter five, which demonstrates the methods through which the jurisprudence developed by the courts operate in interlocked fashion to exempt PMCs and their contractors from assertions of legal liability.

The contribution of this chapter is thus to reverse the orthodox legal approach towards impunity, thereby paving the way to addressing the question of PMC impunity in particular. Inverting the orthodox legal approach provides new insights into the persistence of PMC impunity by revealing the fundamental role played by the law. This close relationship between law and impunity cannot be perceived in attempts that seek to extend the application of existing laws to the PMC, and which consider how the existing legal framework might accommodate for the challenges posed by the industry. Thus, the crux of the problem of PMC regulation and accountability is that there is too much potentially, *but ambiguously*, applicable law. The impunity enjoyed by PMCs arises simultaneously from their assertion of legal existence and legitimate operation without being accompanied by sufficiently robust oversight and accountability mechanisms. The attempts made in this chapter which seek to recognise the manner in which the law itself creates and maintains impunity will specifically provide insight for the regulation of the PMC industry, but should also be sufficiently generalisable as a perspective with which to approach any situation of apparent and persistent impunity. Opening up the possibility for the law itself to be the culprit should justify deep examinations into the role played by the law with relation to any situation of impunity, and restrict tenuous extensions of existing legal principles in attempts to govern contemporary and emerging challenges.

II. THE CONTESTED CONCEPT OF IMPUNITY

The question of impunity is both persistent and perplexing, as an early UN report addressing the impunity of perpetrators of human rights violations underlines:

> From the origins of mankind until the present day, the history of impunity is one of perpetual conflict and strange paradox: conflict between the oppressed and the oppressor, civil society and the State, the human conscience and barbarism; the paradox of the oppressed who, released from their shackles, in their turn take over the responsibility of the State and find themselves caught in the mechanism of national reconciliation, which moderates their initial commitment against impunity.[1]

[1] EH Guissé and L Joinet, 'Progress Report on the Question of Impunity of Perpetrators of Human Rights Violations pursuant to Sub-Commission Resolution 1992/23' (UNESC, 1993) E/CN.4/Sub.2/1993/6 para 1, p 4.

While the term 'impunity' appears to hold a specific legal meaning, it is difficult to extract either a universally acceptable definition or an authoritative source from which to derive such a meaning, since 'these terms have become so ubiquitous that their respective meanings are deemed obvious'.[2]

A useful point of departure is Amnesty International's approach, which despite its derivation from the specific context of officially-sanctioned 'disappearances' policies, aids our understanding of what might be meant by the term impunity:

> Literally, impunity means exemption from punishment. More broadly, the term conveys a sense of wrongdoers escaping justice or any serious form of accountability for their deeds. Impunity can arise at any stage before, during or after the judicial process.[3]

The presumption of a judicial process of accountability can be deduced from this definition. In other words, the ordinary juridical process is understood as *the* mechanism of accountability: impunity arises in situations where that process is disrupted. This underscores the orthodox legal approach to PMC impunity since it views the ordinary juridical process as being necessary and sufficient to hold PMCs and their contractors to account. From this perspective, impunity would be averted by unfettered judicial accountability mechanisms.

Building upon this definition, Amnesty International delineated two versions of impunity: legal and practical.[4] The first version maps roughly onto the active dimension of impunity proposed here: 'Legal impunity arises from laws, decrees, or other official measures providing that certain officials, classes of officials, or others carrying out official duties will not be brought to justice'.[5] This is, however, a narrower approach on two accounts. First, this conception is grounded in the assumption that the ordinary juridical process is both necessary and sufficient to impose responsibility, a contention which is challenged by the passive dimension of impunity proposed here. This leads to the idea that impunity is *exceptional*, rather than being the default position as is argued in this book. Second, this conception of impunity is applied exclusively to 'officials, classes of officials or others carrying out official duties'.[6] While the

[2] M Penrose, 'Impunity—Inertia, Inaction, and Invalidity: A Literature Review' (1999) 17 *Boston University International Law Journal* 269, 273.

[3] Amnesty International, '"Disappearances" and Political Killings: Human Rights Crisis of the 1990s: A Manual for Action' (1994) 184.

[4] ibid.

[5] ibid.

[6] ibid. It should be noted that even where human rights violations are restricted to those committed by the State or its agents, whether directly or indirectly, that 'mercenaries, paramilitary groups, death squads, and private militias, etc' have been included in an early UN consideration of impunity: Guissé and Joinet, 'Progress Report on the Question of Impunity of Perpetrators of Human Rights Violations pursuant to Sub-Commission Resolution 1992/23' (n 1) 9, p 5.

purpose of such limitations may be to assert the role played by policy, or accords primacy to State action that is consistent with the human rights paradigm, it unnecessarily and arbitrarily confines the range of beneficiaries who enjoy impunity to those possessing or exercising official power.

Turning to the second version, practical impunity is understood to 'stem from weaknesses in the judicial system and from actions of officials which hinder or obstruct the course of justice'.[7] This practical impunity broadly correlates with the passive dimension of impunity because it addresses the defects of the ordinary juridical process. The conception of practical impunity, again, is narrower than the passive dimension of impunity proposed here because it asserts that a fully functioning legal system would be able to avert situations of impunity.

Part of the strength of Amnesty International's definition is that it merges the concepts of legal and practical impunity to create a broader and holistic picture that is internally coherent. While it may suffer from excessive narrowness, these restrictions are justifiable because it was developed within the context of 'disappearances' and political killings. Of particular interest, however, is the claim that 'Ending impunity is fundamentally a matter of political will'.[8] The inference here may be the recognition that legal processes alone are insufficient to tackle impunity, or perhaps even suggesting that the legal process itself is implicated in generating impunity.

Looking beyond this conception of impunity, other definitions cluster around the nodes of exemption or freedom from punishment for criminal actions, or injustice arising from a lack of available remedy to the victims of such actions. For instance, Christopher Joyner offers:

> Impunity … means exemption or freedom from punishment and connotes the lack of effective remedies for the victims of crimes. Within the context of human rights law (HRL), impunity implies the lack or failure to apply remedies for victims of human rights violations.[9]

This focus upon lack of punishment for the perpetrator and remedy for the victim is reminiscent of the processes of denial which is addressed later in this chapter.[10] A broader definition is required which removes the potential for such circularity. The definitional connection between the alleged criminal action and the failure to punish or provide effective remedies for them needs to be broken. One useful method of doing this might be to take a step back to before a determination of the action was made which might involve the removal of the *possibility* of being held to account. For instance,

[7] Amnesty International, '"Disappearances" and Political Killings' (n 3) 185.

[8] ibid.

[9] C Joyner, 'Redressing Impunity for Human Rights Violations: The Universal Declaration and the Search for Accountability' (1997) 26 *Denver Journal of International Law and Policy* 591, 595–96.

[10] S Cohen, *States of Denial: Knowing About Atrocities and Suffering* (Polity, 2001) 76–116.

UN Special Rapporteur Louis Joinet offers the following definition in his Final Report on the question of impunity:

> 'Impunity' means the impossibility, de jure or de facto, of bringing the perpetrators of human rights violations to account—whether in criminal, civil, administrative or disciplinary proceedings—since they are not subject to any inquiry that might lead to them being accused, arrested, tried and, if found guilty, convicted.[11]

This broader definition is more appropriate, because of its ability to address and account for broader structural and systemic barriers that prevent the alleged perpetrators from being questioned in the first place. In a subsequent revision of this definition, his focus turns towards punishment and reparation by replacing 'convicted', above, with 'sentenced to appropriate penalties, and to making reparations to their victims'.[12] The focus upon the punitive and reparative purposes of the revised definition may obscure the core aspects of impunity. Thus, Louis Joinet's earlier definition will be adopted as the working definition for this thesis.

III. THE PASSIVE AND ACTIVE DIMENSIONS OF LEGAL IMPUNITY

With this background in mind, this section seeks to differentiate between the dimensions of impunity in order to refine the concept and understand its sources. The existing definitions treat impunity as a *consequence* arising from averting or subverting the ordinary legal process, thereby conflating the concept of impunity with general lawlessness. In order to make the argument that legal processes generate impunity and therefore precede the consequences, rather than simply avoid them, a new model is necessary that is capable of conceptually segregating these interwoven assumptions. The proposed model conceptualises impunity as comprising of complementary passive and active dimensions integral to the operation of the law.

The passive dimension, associated with de facto impunity, operates where the accountability and remedy mechanisms inherent within the ordinary juridical process fail to adequately or appropriately structure responsibility. The active dimension, associated with de jure impunity, concerns the circumvention or suspension of the ordinary juridical process.

[11] L Joinet, 'Question of the Impunity of Perpetrators of Violations of Human Rights (Civil and Political Rights): Final Report Prepared by Mr. L. Joinet, pursuant to Subcommission Resolution 1995/35' (UNESC, 1996) E/CN.4/Sub.2/1996/18 9.

[12] L Joinet, 'Question of the Impunity of Perpetrators of Violations of Human Rights (civil and Political Rights): Revised Final Report Prepared by Mr. L. Joinet, pursuant to Subcommission Decision 1996/119' (UNESC, 1997) E/CN.4/Sub.2/1997/20/Rev.1 17.

It is best demonstrated through official exemptions from the ordinary application of the law that is manifest in pardons, amnesties and immunities and where the ordinary juridical paradigm is subverted, as in states of exception. Together, the contribution of this model is that it highlights the defects of the ordinary system of legal responsibility that underlie both types of impunity: the active dimension operates to suspend their operation while the passive concerns systemic failures integral to the ordinary juridical system itself.

This categorisation emphasises several important characteristics of impunity. First, while impunity has hitherto been understood as an *omission* from necessary action the active dimension of impunity illustrates that impunity can also arise from the action itself.[13] Second, since active forms of impunity are forms of deliberate action, they are necessarily both narrow and specific: a pardon or an amnesty, for example, is the result of a discrete action that exculpates a certain defined set of actions (narrow) from subsequent punishment (specific). As such, it constitutes exceptions to ordinary treatment and is readily identifiable where it occurs. This can be differentiated from forms of impunity that arise as default: the amorphous, imperceptible and pervasive forms of impunity that occur systematically which characterise the passive dimension. The third is that this categorisation recognises the exceptional nature of active impunity, thereby segregating the more readily visible forms of impunity to develop a conceptual space within which to acknowledge ordinary and systemic tendencies that generate passive impunity.

An objection to this model might be raised from the consequentialist perspective as there may be little difference between impunity, in the general sense, and amnesty. Both the acts of amnesty or pardon and the omissions that create impunity lead to a situation where punishment is withheld or where the remedy is insufficient. By rolling together amnesty and pardon with impunity, Charles Harper describes a useful understanding of consequentialist approach:

> Impunity is the means by which persons accused of crimes against humanity escape being charged, tried and punished for criminal acts committed with official sanction in time of war or dictatorial rule. Impunity can be achieved through amnesty laws passed or decreed by governments under whose authority the crimes were committed or by a successive government. It can result from presidential pardons given to convicted criminals who remain unpunished. Impunity can also occur by default—the deliberate lack of any action at all.[14]

[13] M Cherif Bassiouni, 'Searching for Peace and Achieving Justice: The Need for Accountability' (1996) 59 *Law and Contemporary Problems* 9, 19.

[14] C Harper, 'From Impunity to Reconciliation', *Impunity: An Ethical Perspective* (World Council of Churches Publications, 1996) viii–ix.

Differentiating between an act of amnesty and the omission that results in impunity, despite the quasi-identical consequences, is necessary to recognise the divergent pathways through which impunity can arise.[15] The question may then shift to whether there are any differences in the perception or understanding between instances of active impunity such as pardon and amnesty, and passive impunity that arises from the failure to take action. While the effects may broadly be the same at the superficial level, the derived meaning may differ considerably.

The basis for differentiating between active and passive dimensions of impunity goes back to the idea of the exceptional nature of the act of pardon or amnesty, and also therefore by implication, the ordinary nature of impunity resulting from omission. This differentiation is crucial: pardon and amnesty have the effect of exculpating the actor of the (legal) guilt of an act which has been previously found to be unlawful, thereby carving an explicit exception to ordinary rules. In other words, acts of pardon and amnesty may be interpreted as creating limited states of exception to the ordinary juridical process, or alternatively states of denial relating to the resultant harm. The same, however, cannot be said for situations in which the same effects are created by the failure to take action: passive impunity by omission is anything but clear-cut since there is no unequivocal determination of criminality or blameworthiness in the first place. This lack of substantiated infringement presents a serious obstacle to claims of impunity, which can be readily be deflected with the credible counter-claim that there was no wrongdoing. Thus, allegations of impunity of the latter kind arise out of the operation of ordinary structural or systemic forces: neither processes of exception or denial are implicated because the process is not clearly demarcated.

Finally, passive impunity subtly restricts the area open to debate because it circumscribes the sphere within which the law operates at an anterior stage. In other words, active impunity mechanisms that suspend the application of the law are not necessary if the law has not, or indeed cannot, recognise either the offender or the harm in question in the first place. This reveals the residual role of active impunity mechanisms because these can only operate after the relevant laws are made and when its processes are functioning. Thus, passive impunity mechanisms largely pre-empt recourse to active impunity mechanisms because these constrain the field within which the law functions. After all, there can be no exception or suspension of something which does not exist.

[15] It should be noted that Harper envisages that the 'lack of any action at all' is 'deliberate', thereby implying that intentionality lies behind the generation of impunity by omission. While this would certainly be a more odious source of impunity, the idea of passive impunity here requires neither intent, nor other forms of teleological purpose. Instead, and more ominously, the 'lack of any action at all' arises as a default of the system itself.

IV. PASSIVE IMPUNITY: STRUCTURAL CHARACTERISTICS OF THE ORDINARY LEGAL PROCESS

While the active dimension of impunity is readily apparent either in explicit provisions or as the consequence of jurisprudential decisions, passive impunity mechanisms operate more subtly because these embody forms of impunity arising as a structural feature of the law itself. Within the context of armed conflict, passive impunity may arise from four interrelated characteristics of the law.

First, there is legal compartmentalisation and segregation of the entire enterprise into the different spheres that regulate recourse to, and conduct within, warfare respectively. This leads to divergent approaches to regulating interrelated activities, leading in turn to different modalities and forms of legal responsibility. Second, the law may be substantively overstretched in its capacity to grasp the significance of warfare and to account for its attendant atrocities. This effect is further magnified by the gradual extension of the law and legal processes into the field of organised violence famously thought to be an extension of politics by Clausewitz. Third are the 'dark sides' of law, in which over-reliance upon legal processes to govern conduct in armed conflict ultimately amplifies its subsequent failure to fulfil expectations. The spread of legal processes into other domains, and their subsequent dominance as the overarching framework crowds out alternative approaches to the issues, thereby entrenching legal failures within expanded contexts. Fourth, the legal obsession with individual responsibility fails to accommodate for collectively produced outcomes. This leads to legal determinations of guilt sounding hollow because it fails to recognise that the total outcome is *greater* than the sum of its individual contributory parts. This last aspect is developed through the lens of responsibility where the concept of responsibility is dissected by focusing upon the relationship between role and outcome responsibilities. The separation of these concepts of responsibility is shown to generate passive impunity because legal processes over-emphasise individual role responsibility to the neglect of collective outcome responsibility.

The insidious nature of passive impunity can be illustrated by juxtaposing it against the complementary active dimension of impunity. Not only is the active dimension easily perceptible because it requires the explicit suspension of the ordinary legal order, but because of the action that underlies it, active impunity can also be more simply resolved by removing the suspension and thereby reinstating the ordinary legal order. Passive impunity, however, is both harder to perceive and considerably more difficult to rectify. The dissociation of responsibility is an intrinsic characteristic of the existing legal system itself and a systematic remedy would require fundamental reappraisal and reorganisation. Viewed from a different perspective, the passive dimension of impunity can be understood as the default position since it only requires the ordinary system of law to function, whereas the active dimension of impunity requires at least an exception to operate.

A. Compartmentalisation of Law

A significant source of passive impunity is the distorting and excluding effects introduced through the process of segregating the legal regulation of an activity overall into separate juridical fields. This separation into functionally independent juridical fields, which constitute only a segment of the former whole, obscures the holistic overview by focusing in on particular criteria and characteristics while minimising or entirely excluding the consideration of others. Thus, the overall picture involved in the allocation of responsibility is distorted in this process of selective focus and exclusion of certain (arguably arbitrary) aspects while largely overlooking others. Knock-on impacts follow, as such approaches alter both the modality and form of responsibility that ultimately affect the very meaning and scope of legal responsibility.

To ground this idea, the example of the differentiating between the legal spheres of *Jus ad Bellum* (governing the legality of war, henceforth JAB) and *Jus in Bello* (governing the conduct of warfare, henceforth JIB) is given.[16] In this vein, Michael Walzer writes that 'The moral reality of war is divided into two parts … we say that a particular war is just or unjust … [and] we say that the war is being fought justly or unjustly'.[17] This example neatly demonstrates that considerations of responsibility are isolated exclusively within their specific juridical context that ignores ulterior factors.[18] The division between the laws regulating recourse to war and the laws that regulate the conduct of warfare bisects and curtails the range of considerations taken into account in the process of ascribing legal responsibility. This permits the inescapable observation that the overall responsibility in relation to both war and warfare, and the harms it generates, has been

[16] The juridification of war is discussed in greater depth in the following section. On the long historical distinction drawn between JAB and JIB, see Y Dinstein, *War, Aggression and Self-Defence* (Cambridge University Press, 2011) 65–84.

[17] M Walzer, *Just and Unjust Wars: A Moral Argument with Historical Illustrations* (Basic Books, 2006) 21.

[18] Framed in Walzer's terminology, this allows for three possibilities in which responsibility is under-recognised: an unjust war fought justly; a just war fought unjustly; and an unjust war fought unjustly. In the former two situations, injustice is perceived only within one sphere (JAB and JIB respectively) despite the overall effect those wars being tainted by injustice. In the last situation, despite the possibility that injustice is recognised within both JAB and JIB spheres, the loss of the overall perspective suggests that sight will be lost as to the total injustice which can only be articulated in JAB and JIB terms rather than holistically.

lost through this legal compartmentalisation.[19] Unfolding this observation reveals the extent to which this responsibility, insofar as it has ever existed as a totality, has been dispersed. Restricting the legal context distorts the responsibility calculus by determining the factors that are considered, including the range and nature of possible candidate entities that can be ascribed responsibility, the particular form of responsibility at stake, and the legally imputed meaning of that responsibility. This distortion obscures the burden of certain types of responsibility that should be borne by certain types of entities, generating impunity in the process. This suggests that the initial division between JAB and JIB leads to serious ramifications in terms of responsibility and the creation of impunity.

The distortion is threefold. First, there is the substantive scope because JAB is invoked only in connection with assessments of the legality of the war. Because JAB does not look beyond whether the decision to initiate or participate in an armed conflict is lawful, it effectively exculpates those who decide on the recourse to war of the responsibility for any unlawful conduct within the hostilities. The responsibility calculations for any unlawful conduct is displaced into the sphere of JIB instead, despite the observation that any conduct within armed conflict is necessarily preceded by the decision to initiate hostilities, which suggests JAB responsibility as a precondition for JIB assessments. The basic observation is that isolation of the decision to go to war within the JAB sphere insulates those who bear this responsibility from the burden of much greater responsibility for the harms arising from the conduct of the hostilities. The ramifications, however, are much greater because this reveals JAB to generate a species of role responsibility which arise from fulfilling the obligations attached to a particular social function. Impunity will be generated insofar as this is detached from the ascription of causal outcome responsibility causing the harmful consequences of fulfilling those obligations.

These effects are reflected in JIB because those bearing responsibility for the conduct of hostilities are relieved from bearing responsibility for the prior consideration of whether they are fighting a just or unjust war. From the JIB perspective, then, those who bear responsibility for the lawful conduct of hostilities are immunised from bearing responsibility for pursuing an aggressive war provided that they comply with the requirements imposed by international humanitarian law (IHL). This becomes the equivalent of pursuing unlawful ends through lawful means, and as the ultimate objective remains unlawful the entire pursuit is tainted. This reveals that the disconnect between role and outcome forms of responsibility is also replicated within JIB because the assessment of responsibility for those involved in the conduct of hostilities is focused upon fulfilment

[19] This distinction is so ingrained that it is reflected in the very language employed to describe these activities, which must be expressed separately.

of obligations (compliance with IHL) rather than the effect of the outcome (the harms caused by fighting an aggressive war).

Second, there are differences in the locus of responsibility. JAB involves collective forms of responsibility that centre upon the State, coupled simultaneously with the emerging potential for penal sanctions to be imposed on certain individuals as a crime of aggression.[20] Similarly, State responsibility for violations of JIB can be deduced from Rules 149 and 150 of Customary International Humanitarian Law,[21] which is similarly complemented by individual criminal responsibility for war crimes captured in Rules 151–155.[22] There is unequal emphasis in terms of State and individual responsibility, however, despite the apparent parity between JAB and JIB which places a heavier burden on individuals involved in the conduct of hostilities while shielding those who make the decision to go to war. From the JAB perspective, this is apparent from the long-standing liability of the aggressor State for restitution, compensation or satisfaction,[23] when juxtaposed against the deferral of the International Criminal Court's (ICC) exercise of jurisdiction over the crime of aggression under Article 5(2) of the Rome Statute.[24] By contrast, individual criminal responsibility for war crimes is well established, existing alongside State responsibility and the obligation to make full reparations in relation to such violations.[25] It is, however, the translation of serious violations of IHL into the substantive scope of international criminal law that places a disproportionate burden of responsibility on to the individuals who are engaged in the conduct of hostilities relative to the responsibility borne by the State. Comparing the individual criminal responsibility, it is clear that a disproportionate burden falls upon the participants in armed conflict compared with the State or its officials who make the determination to go to war. This is readily apparent from the substantive scope of the Rome Statute, and again by the deferred jurisdiction concerning the crime of aggression by the ICC.

Finally, these effects channel conclusions towards different forms of legal responsibility and assign different meanings to the transgressions.

[20] Dinstein, *War, Aggression and Self-Defence* (n 16) 109–18 and 124–12, respectively; ICC, 'The Crime of Aggression' (11 June 2010, Resolution RC/Res 6 of the Kampala Review Conference). See also C McDougall, *The Crime of Aggression under the Rome Statute of the International Criminal Court* (Cambridge University Press, 2013).

[21] J-M Henckaerts and L Doswald-Beck, *Customary International Humanitarian Law*, vol I (Cambridge University Press, 2009) ch 42.

[22] ibid 43. It is clear that: 'The obligation of an aggressor State to indemnify the victims of aggression (for the violation of [JAB]) must not be confused with the independent liability of a Belligerent Party to pay compensation for breaches of [JIB]': Dinstein (n 16) 111.

[23] Dinstein (n 16) 109–18.

[24] ibid 131–34. As is well known, after the Kampala Review Conference, the earliest exercise of jurisdiction over the crime of aggression by the ICC is in 2017: McDougall, *The Crime of Aggression under the Rome Statute of the International Criminal Court* (n 20) 281–335.

[25] Henckaerts and Doswald-Beck, *Customary International Humanitarian Law*, vol I (n 21) 530–31 and 537–50 respectively.

That the State is primarily responsible for JAB, at least until the ICC attains jurisdiction over the crime of aggression, leads to acts of aggression largely taking the form of civil wrongs.[26] While in practice, this may be beneficial from the perspective of receiving reparations, the impression is that breaches of JAB are not sanctioned with the full force of law.[27] Conversely, despite IHL providing for State responsibility for breaches,[28] the traction gained by international criminal law leads to the focus for transgressions on individuals for criminal liability. The broad separation into violations of JAB as collective civil wrongs and violations of JIB as individual criminal wrongs contorts the forms of responsibility ordinarily attached to these types of activities and their derived meaning. More specifically, this grounds the argument that the compartmentalisation engendered by the law promotes impunity: high-ranking State officials are insulated from legal indictment for waging aggressive war, which filters down to diffuse allegations of aggression at a more general level. Instead, lower-ranking officers and soldiers are left to shoulder criminal responsibility for misconduct within hostilities. This leads to the reality that they are more likely to be punished for transgressions than more senior personnel for theirs, which is suggestive of impunity. More importantly, this leads to the perception that those who violate JAB are criminals, while both language and law fail to articulate and comprehend the wrong of those who initiate aggressive war. Impunity is created in the disproportionate ascription of responsibility made possible through the compartmentalisation of law.

Under certain situations, exemplified by the PMC in contemporary times, this trend becomes reversed. As discussed in depth in chapter four, the myopic concentration upon the obligations under, and compliance with, IHL in relation to the PMC obscures the possibility of suggesting that they engage in acts of aggression. In limiting the assessment of their legality solely within the realm of JIB, the PMC enjoys impunity in relation to JAB. This is because its potential to violate the requirements imposed by JAB through its formal and functional independence from belligerent States is not matched with the potential to bear responsibility for acts of

[26] This can be deduced both from the reparative nature of State responsibility, and the reluctance of the international community to accept the criminal responsibility of States: Dinstein (n 16) 110 and 114–16 respectively.

[27] The payment of reparations may impose responsibility for the damages caused by an aggressor State for an unlawful war, but may also oppose the post-war goal of reconstruction and reconciliation. This is not to mention that excessive payments, such as in the paradigmatic case of those imposed on Germany in the Treaty of Versailles, have the potential to fuel resentment and foster further conflicts: ibid 112–13.

[28] Art 91 of the Protocol Additional to the Geneva Conventions of 12 August 1949, and relating to the Protection of Victims of International Armed Conflicts (Protocol I), 8 June 1977, provides that 'A Party to the conflict which violates the provisions of the Conventions or of this Protocol shall, if the case demands, be liable to pay compensation. It shall be responsible for all acts committed by persons forming part of its armed forces'.

aggression. This example suggests that the compartmentalisation of law facilitates impunity in both directions.

B. Impunity Through the Juridification of War

There is a sense of inevitability that surrounds claims of impunity for atrocities: that broadly the law is neither able to grasp the nature of these events nor to attribute significance to them. Hannah Arendt's famous claim that '[h]anging Goring is certainly necessary but totally inadequate. For this culpability ... transcends and destroys all legal order'[29] captures this sentiment. If she is correct, individual criminal responsibility is *necessary*, but not *sufficient* to overcome impunity beyond a certain scale of action and organisation. Martti Koskenniemi interpreted this to mean 'that sometimes a tragedy may be so great, a series of events of such political or even metaphysical significance, that punishing an individual does not come close to measuring up to it'.[30] Referring to the Eichmann trial, Karl Jaspers suggested that the charges 'stand outside the pale of what is comprehensible in human and moral terms' and that '[s]omething other than law [was] at stake here—and to address it in legal terms [was] a mistake'.[31] In a similar vein, Gerry Simpson asks: 'Law seems to belong to the everyday of traffic violations and house sales. Could it be of any help in understanding the metaphysics of evil?'[32] Approaching from a different perspective, Scott Veitch presents this tension as 'the *asymmetry* between suffering and responsibility for its production'.[33] The common denominator among this range of opinion is the sense that the law is incapable of comprehending, let alone contributing to, the understanding of atrocity. Thus, any reliance upon the law to allocate responsibility for such events inevitably generates passive impunity because it is substantively incapable of accomplishing this task.

Despite this sentiment, the law's tendency towards hegemony leads to what Gerry Simpson has termed the juridification of war.[34] This is the process through which the understanding of organised warfare has evolved from being a political activity, echoing Carl von Clausewitz, to being a juridical activity regulated by the forces of law.[35] Indeed, from a historical

[29] Quoted in M Koskenniemi, *Politics of International Law* (Hart Publishing, 2011) 172.
[30] ibid.
[31] ibid.
[32] G Simpson, *Law, War and Crime: War Crimes Trials and the Reinvention of International Law* (Polity, 2007) 83.
[33] S Veitch, *Law and Irresponsibility: On the Legitimation of Human Suffering* (Routledge-Cavendish, 2007) 7. Emphasis original.
[34] Simpson *Law, War and Crime* (n 32) 140–56.
[35] ibid 132–33; 140–43.

perspective, understanding war as a *legal* activity has extremely recent roots: war was initially perceived as a type of natural disaster beyond the control of mankind which only gradually transformed into the litmus test for State sovereignty in modern times.[36]

The juridification of warfare developed through a twofold process that paralleled the separate strands of JAB and JIB. Taking JAB first, the prohibition of the threat or use of force on the international plane that was enshrined in 1945 within the Charter of the United Nations was preceded by the 1928 Kellogg-Briand Pact—its purpose elucidated by its formal title, the General Treaty for the Renunciation of War.[37] The effect of these developments was to transform the hitherto sovereign right to wage war into a criminal act, with narrow exceptions. From the perspective of JIB, it became clear from the first international attempts to regulate the conduct within armed conflict in the 1868 St Petersburg Declaration that not all the means and methods of its pursuit would henceforth be tolerated.[38] This recognition quickly snowballed, culminating with the various Hague and Geneva Conventions and more specific treaties adopted subsequently. Thus, both the resort to (JAB) and conduct within (JIB) armed conflict gravitated towards the juridical sphere, or depending upon your perspective, the regulation of law extended to cover armed hostilities.

The nature of armed conflict, however, did not significantly alter to accommodate for this shift towards juridification. A concomitant expectation arose with the juridification of warfare: the law that purports to regulate armed conflict should also act as the ultimate arbiter of conflicts arising from the conduct of armed hostilities. The necessary corollary of this expectation is the additional burden placed upon the law, especially the criminal law, both to determine responsibility for breaches of JAB and JIB and to impose appropriate punishment for perpetrators and remedy for victims. The size of this task, coupled with the ontological severity of the activity involved, fundamentally questions whether the law would be capable of averting impunity in this area.

In the terminology adopted by Gerry Simpson, the law suffers from a lack of proportion that takes two forms.[39] The first is that 'it was discovered

[36] Dinstein (n 16) 75–79. Reinforcing the shift to recognising human influence in previously 'natural events', see P Green and T Ward, *State Crime: Governments, Violence and Corruption* (Pluto Press, 2004) 52–67. This shift is considered below in the context of outcome responsibility in the passive dimension of impunity.

[37] Dinstein (n 16) 85–109.

[38] G Solis, *The Law of Armed Conflict: International Humanitarian Law in War* (Cambridge University Press, 2010) 49–51.

[39] It should be noted that Simpson is dealing specifically with criminality in international law and not the field of armed conflict.

in the 1940s that there was no legal language available to confront the horrors of mass atrocity'.[40] Attempts to resolve this led to the second form,

> [a]s law began to cover the field with procedure and precedents, the crimes themselves threatened to disappear in a welter of process … 'Genocide', 'crimes against humanity' and 'serious violations of human rights', in the face of our best intentions, became terms of technical art to be debated and reinvented.[41]

This lack of proportion reinforces the sense of inappropriateness and inadequacy that pervades the application of law to situations of atrocity that this section opened with.

Furthermore, a more insidious problem associated with the inability of law to articulate the language of atrocity may be its vulnerability to the category of 'interpretive denial' enunciated by Stanley Cohen.[42] While this will be addressed in greater detail later in this chapter, this is the process through which '[b]y changing the words, by euphemism, by technical jargon, the observer disputes the cognitive meaning given to an event and re-allocates it to another class of event'.[43] As Cohen himself notes, '[p]owerful forms of interpretive denial come from the language of legality itself'.[44] This potential is clearly magnified in the current context owing to the aforementioned lack of precedent without which 'the law in some of the early war crimes trials … seemed incapable of dealing with the exceptional nature of administrative massacre'.[45] The inherent potential for interpretive denial within the law is increased with organised violence by the processes of extending and creating of legal categories to capture, categorise and define atrocity, and through the employment of legal mechanisms to punish and remedy it.

C. Impunity within the 'Dark Sides' of Law

The question of whether the law is capable of grasping the significance of warfare and sanctioning its breaches is related to the tendency of law towards hegemony: this over-reliance upon the law amplifies the potential effects of its failure. In this vein, David Kennedy has argued that: 'Like the vocabulary of human rights, humanitarian law can crowd out modes of evaluation … *Occupying the field, the humanitarian vocabulary can channel attention to a limited range of questions*'.[46] The dominance of IHL and HRL

40 Simpson (n 32) 83.
41 ibid 84.
42 Cohen, *States of Denial* (n 10) 7–8, 105–09.
43 ibid 8.
44 ibid 107.
45 Simpson (n 32) 84.
46 D Kennedy, *The Dark Sides of Virtue: Reassessing International Humanitarianism* (Princeton University Press, 2005) 300. Emphasis added.

considerations has effectively marginalised or obscured other relevant factors in the judgement calculus relating both to the resort to and conduct within armed conflict. In addition to marginalising competing factors, the specific bias towards the laws of war in situations of armed conflict and other complex environments creates too narrow a focus within the law itself, again as David Kennedy writes:

> [W]e overlook the far more important contribution made by other legal rules to the incidence of violence ... By contesting and promoting only the institutions, principles, and rules of the United Nations humanitarian law system, we can make these background rules, whatever their consequences for the incidence of violence, seem matters of fact rather than points of choice.[47]

Thus, despite the laudable intentions and some substantial benefits of juridifying warfare, this process marginalises competing paradigms and suffers from excessive myopia. The cumulative effect for claims of impunity arises from the exclusion of alleged wrongs that do not register within law, and specifically do not constitute violations of IHL or HRL. Scott Veitch has underscored the difficulty with the law acting as the final arbiter of injury:

> [I]f the law can recognise some damages as injuries—if law sets some standard or test for ascertaining which damages will count as injuries—then the law also defines, by exclusion, that which will count as damage, but not injury. *Such suffering is, legally speaking, legitimate.*[48]

The entrenched dominance of IHL is thus twofold: first because the law excludes non-legal considerations; and second because the *lex specialis* status of IHL within armed conflict further refines and enhances this effect.[49] This significantly restricts the field of grievances that can be claimed within armed conflict: only wrongs that run contrary to IHL will be recognised as injury, as opposed simply to 'legitimate' damage that do not. It is the failure to recognise damage as injury outside of the established categories recognised by law that give rise to *inarticulable* allegations of impunity: the denial of responsibility is coupled with the deprivation of the language that can express the grievance. Accountability and punishment become foreclosed where the law simultaneously denies competing frameworks of consideration and denies the existence of an injury or the

[47] ibid 305.

[48] Veitch, *Law and Irresponsibility* (n 33) 86. Emphasis added. Thus, according Veitch's distinction, by definition 'injury' are harms that are recognised by the law, while 'damage' are harms to which the law is blind. This suggests that the initial categorisation is critical, since responsibility need not be considered, let alone established, for 'damage'.

[49] As Yoram Dinstein summarises, 'in the event of an international armed conflict, the [Law of International Armed Conflict] norms—as *lex specialis*—prevail over the *lex generalis* of human rights': Y Dinstein, *The Conduct of Hostilities under the Law of International Armed Conflict* (Cambridge University Press, 2010) para 56. See generally ibid 23–26.

occurrence of a wrong.[50] Other concepts need to be explored before this idea can be developed later in this chapter.

New vulnerabilities of the law further compound these difficulties in the context of armed hostilities which are expressed by David Kennedy: 'The new law of force nevertheless still exhibits the dark sides … Its institutions are also subject to capture by states, by ideologies, by other agendas'.[51] This is especially pertinent with regards to the international law that purportedly serves to prohibit the use of force and to regulate all instances of organised violence that do arise. It is essential to recognise that the law which regulates armed conflict is created, interpreted and enforced (when it is) predominantly by powerful States in the pursuit of their own interests. Within IHL, this can be seen with the primacy of 'military necessity' criterion upon which the legal principles are predicated.[52] In the words of Yoram Dinstein: '[The Law of International Armed Conflict (LOIAC)] amounts to a checks-and-balances system, intending to minimize human suffering *without undermining the effectiveness of military operations*'.[53] This reveals the structural weakness of IHL: especially when phrased as LOIAC, the humanitarian considerations that are inscribed within the law are, with narrow exceptions, superseded by countervailing interests of military necessity. While it is important not to lose sight of the dual benefits of IHL, that it seeks to stymie total war and that it 'has the immense advantage that it has been accepted by states as law which can be respected, even in war',[54] these diametrically opposing forces that shape IHL underline Kennedy's concern. This area of law is particularly susceptible to capture because IHL asserts to constrain the actions of States during times of emergency and vulnerability and because IHL is accepted by States to do so.

D. The Irresponsibility of Law

Before proceeding to consider the fourth aspect of passive impunity concerning the legal preoccupation with individual responsibility to the

[50] Indeed, the failure to frame a grievance within the language of the law may prevent the expression of that grievance owing to the monopoly that the law holds.

[51] Kennedy, *The Dark Sides of Virtue* (n 46) 296.

[52] Military necessity is one of the four core principles of the law of armed conflict: Solis, *The Law of Armed Conflict* (n 38) 258–69.

[53] Dinstein, *Conduct of Hostilities* (n 49) 5. Emphasis added. Note also the seemingly subtle difference in terminology. 'LOIAC must be predicated on a subtle equilibrium between the two diametrically opposed stimulants of military necessity and humanitarian considerations'. This is different in terms of emphasis from IHL, which at least nominally prioritises humanitarian concerns: ibid.

[54] M Sassòli, 'The Implementation of International Humanitarian Law: Current and Inherent Challenges' (2007) 10 *Yearbook of International Humanitarian Law* 45, 59 and 50 respectively.

consequent neglect of collective outcomes, it is necessary to develop the intertwining concepts that constitute the idea of responsibility. In particular, the relationship between ascription and demarcation of responsibility through the architecture of law must be explicated in order to demonstrate that under certain circumstances, the law both creates and perpetrates *irresponsibility*.[55] Because many of the definitions of impunity considered above are intricately associated with the concept of accountability[56]—the concept of impunity defined as the failure of accountability—a connexion must be forged between these two concepts within the passive dimension of impunity. Thus, the passive dimension is concerned with the deficiency or failure of responsibility attribution, in this case by legal processes, to appropriately determine the responsibility for a given effect.

E. Impunity within the Multifarious Character of Responsibility

Up until this point, a short-cut has been adopted by treating the concept of responsibility as a unitary and monolithic concept, but as James Crawford and Jeremy Watkins suggest:

> One of the complications that besets any treatment inside or outside of the law comes from the ambiguities in the term itself. 'Responsibility' has a bewildering array of meanings, each of which occupies a distinctive role in legal and moral reasoning.[57]

In order to recognise the dissociating processes of responsibility, however, it is necessary to separate out the converging concepts that together constitute the polycentric character of responsibility. Thus, the dissociation of responsibility does not concern the dissolution of responsibility: rather it arises from a disproportionate focus on one component of responsibility to the neglect of its other components. This bias makes it possible simultaneously to be responsible and irresponsible in relation to the same event, provided that these concern different aspects of the concept, and it is necessary to dissect these concepts of responsibility to reveal the process underlying irresponsibility. Indeed, the argument may even be made that the converging concepts that combine to inform the concept of responsibility can be deployed in theoretically incompatible ways. This is particularly evident when the extension of one type of responsibility is

[55] Building upon Veitch (n 33).

[56] Joinet is concerned with the 'impossibility … of bringing the perpetrators of human rights violations to account', Joinet, 'Question of the Impunity of Perpetrators of Violations of Human Rights (Civil and Political Rights)' (n 11) 9; whereas Harper focuses upon the exclusion of accountability: Harper, 'From Impunity to Reconciliation' (n 14) viii–ix.

[57] J Crawford and J Watkins, 'International Responsibility' in S Besson and J Tasioulas (eds), *The Philosophy of International Law* (Oxford University Press, 2010) 283.

proposed to bridge a 'responsibility gap' created by a deficit of another form of responsibility.[58]

The point of departure is the typology of responsibility proposed by HLA Hart, not least because it serves as the basis for subsequent approaches.[59] Hart recognised that the term 'responsibility' encapsulated a range of interconnected concepts, usefully categorising responsibility under four distinct heads: role responsibility, causal responsibility, liability responsibility and capacity responsibility.[60] The primary focus here is on the relationship between the two former categories. For example, any over-emphasis on role responsibility diverts attention away from causal responsibility: this in turn generates passive impunity because of the deficit of outcome responsibility relating to the consequences that arise from the responsible fulfilment roles that generate those consequences.

Role responsibility is one of the most important forms of responsibility, in the words of HLA Hart:

> [W]henever a person occupies distinctive place or office in a social organisation, *to which specific duties are attached* to provide for the welfare of others or to advance in some specific way the aims or purposes of the organisation, he is properly said *to be responsible for the performance of these duties*, or for what is necessary to fulfil them.[61]

Role responsibility is thus hermetically isolated from other forms of responsibility and both introspective and self-referential in character. Hart appears to derive the obligations of role responsibility from the performance of duties appropriate to virtuous relationships. In other words, as the 'aims and purposes of the organisation' are *presumed* to be beneficial, the *fulfilment* of role responsibility will (at least be assumed to) create positive outcomes. This beneficial presumption, however, has neither been grounded nor justified: more importantly, there do not appear to be barriers against role responsibilities where the fulfilment of which would

[58] This idea is being developed in the author's current work in relation to responsibility for autonomous weapons systems: H-Y Liu, 'Refining Responsibility: Differentiating Two Types of Responsibility Issues Raised by Autonomous Weapons Systems' in N Bhuta et al (eds), *Autonomous Weapons Systems—Law, Ethics Policy* (Cambridge University Press, 2015). For a more general approach to the 'responsibility gap', see A Matthias, 'The Responsibility Gap: Ascribing Responsibility for the Actions of Learning Automata' (2004) 6 *Ethics and Information Technology* 175.

[59] The historical background of the concepts of responsibility has been omitted due to space constraints. It is assumed that the understanding of responsibility is shared insofar as it has been incorporated or adopted into current legal, and to some extent moral, thinking.

[60] HLA Hart, *Punishment and Responsibility: Essays in the Philosophy of Law* (Oxford University Press, 2008) 211–12.

[61] ibid 212. Emphasis added.

lead to the creation of harm.[62] It is this disjuncture of role responsibility from causal or outcome responsibility that enables the 'virtuous' (in terms of acting role responsibly) generation of systematic harm.

The necessary corollary to Hart's conception of role responsibility is the seriousness with which the actor addresses his role:

> A responsible person is one who is disposed to take his duties seriously; to think about them, and to make serious efforts to fulfil them. To behave responsibly is to behave as a man would who took his duties in this serious way.[63]

Peter Cane argues that Hart's conception of role responsibility is too narrow, since it is primarily retrospective. Instead, Cane suggests that '[b]eing a responsible person involves taking seriously the prospective responsibilities, *whatever they are*, attaching to *whatever activity* one is engaged in at any particular time'.[64] The underlying problems with both of these conceptions are, again, that there are no limitations upon the role or activity that is performed per se, and that they are unhinged from the consequences of fulfilling the role. Rather than remedying this problem, Cane's broadening of role responsibility through the addition of the prospective element only magnifies the separation with outcome responsibility insofar as it places extra emphasis on the role at the expense of the outcome.

Furthermore, the separation between the two forms of role responsibility envisaged by HLA Hart has been largely overlooked. Another important aspect of legal role responsibilities is that legal activities are divided up in such a way as to provide an impermeable barrier to the transfer of responsibility across juridical fields.[65] Put differently, how an equivalent physical act registers in law differs according to the legal context; that is whether that act has been legally authorised and thus ties into aspects of positive impunity. The two examples offered by Veitch are particularly instructive in our present context.[66] First, the deliberate infliction of physical harm registers as assault under the criminal law. Yet, the deliberate infliction of physical harm does not register as assault, or indeed as other forms of injury in the context of a boxing match or the surgeon's activities in the professional context of the operating theatre. Second, in the international sphere and relating to the discussion concerning the compartmentalisation

[62] eg Adolf Eichmann's situation whereby fulfilment of a bureaucratic role facilitated the outcome of industrialised slaughter. His counsel, Dr Servatius argued along the lines 'that his client was nothing more than a cog in the machine. He did not physically perpetrate the atrocities. His activities had the outward appearance of legality and he had merely obeyed orders': H van der Wilt, 'Joint Criminal Enterprise: Possibilities and Limitations' (2007) 5 *Journal of International Criminal Justice* 91, 104.

[63] Hart, *Punishment and Responsibility* (n 60) 213.

[64] P Cane, *Responsibility in Law and Morality* (Hart Publishing, 2002) 32. Emphasis added.

[65] Veitch (n 33) 78.

[66] ibid.

of law above, a State opting to deploy legally sanctioned military force is absolved from liability for the potentially large-scale violation of human rights, provided that the actions in question satisfy certain legally prescribed requirements such as those of proportionality and military necessity. Analogous to active impunity mechanisms, legal authorisation may immunise activities that would otherwise be criminal in the absence of such legal authorisation. The question of role responsibility thus plays a neglected part in determining applicable active impunity mechanisms and in the recognition of denial mechanisms.

The cardinal position of role responsibility in law is best demonstrated by the criminal law principle of individual culpability. For international criminal law (ICL), the International Criminal Tribunal for the former Yugoslavia (ICTY) Appeals Chamber clearly expressed this in *Tadic*, 'the foundation of criminal responsibility is the principle of individual culpability: nobody may be held criminally responsible for acts or transactions in which he has not personally engaged or in some other way participated'.[67] Antonio Cassese further separates this into two notions: that 'nobody may be held accountable for criminal offences perpetrated *by other persons*', and that 'a person may only be held criminally liable if he is somehow *culpable* for any breach of criminal rules'.[68] Because the imposition of criminal responsibility is limited to personal engagement and individual culpability, the sanction of law is restricted exclusively to the role played by the individual, thereby isolating their liability from the overall criminal outcome of their actions.

Responsibility for the outcome or consequence was termed 'causal responsibility' by Hart, who considered it as a synonym for '"caused" or "produced" or some other causal expression in referring to consequences, results, or outcomes'.[69] It is thus characterised by its retrospective character: in order to be causally responsible for an outcome, the relevant action or omission must necessarily have preceded it. Furthermore, Hart also noted that 'it is clear that in this causal sense not only human beings but also their actions or omissions, and things, conditions, and events, may be said to be responsible for outcomes'.[70] This opens the door to two directly relevant effects: first, that abstract juridical (and other) entities may be ascribed responsibility for the outcomes they produce; and second, that there may be a discrepancy to the meaning, and the possibility and type of sanction, attached to causal responsibility that is dependent upon the type of entity in question.

67 *Prosecutor v Tadic (Appeals Chamber)* [1999] ICTY Appeals Chamber IT-94-1-A [186].
68 A Cassese, *International Criminal Law* (Oxford University Press, 2008) 33. Emphasis added.
69 Hart (n 60) 214.
70 ibid.

While the first effect is uncontentious, whether a human or some other entity is deemed causally responsible bears significant effect upon its interpretation. Hart, although considering this view is mistaken, thought that: 'It is sometimes suggested that, though we may speak of a human being's action as responsible for some outcome in a purely causal sense, we do not speak of a person, as distinct from his actions, as responsible for an outcome, unless he is felt to deserve censure or praise'.[71] The implication underlying this view is that while responsibility for outcomes may subsist in all manner of entities or events, causal responsibility is only informative and largely remains neutral. Only when human beings fall within this category do ideas of praise or punishment for outcomes emerge. With this understanding, juridical persons may be bear causal responsibility *without* the concomitant culpability that would arise where the result was effectuated by natural persons, raising the spectre of interpretative denial in addition to passive impunity.

This understanding of causal responsibility creates significant effects in relation to the juridification of warfare discussed above. This process signalled a shift from armed conflict being understood as natural disasters beyond the remit of law to armed hostilities being a human activity which *prima facie* may be susceptible to legal regulation.[72] The impact of shifting armed conflict into the sphere of human activity upon the understanding of causal responsibility is that it ceases to be neutral and matter-of-fact: it may now be judged with 'censure or praise'. The judgement of the cause and conduct of armed conflict became possible because warfare was recognised as a human creation and a human activity capable of appropriate reward and punishment. In this context, the introduction of the corporation into armed conflict may signal a reversion. While the corporation has juridical personhood, it remains an abstract entity which enables it to be causally responsible for outcomes only in the limited neutral matter-of-fact manner devoid of meaning. In other words, the idea that the corporation is involved in the outcomes of armed conflict precludes the possibility of 'censure or praise' because it removes such conduct out of the human sphere. This potentially creates discrepancies between our understandings of armed conflict as a human activity governed by juridical processes, and those of hostilities being an ulterior force beyond human intervention and judgement. More broadly, this approach may also implicitly undergird the reluctance in many jurisdictions to recognise corporate criminal responsibility because, independent of the difficulty surrounding appropriate means of punishment,[73] corporations are understood to bear causal outcome responsibility only in the descriptive sense.

[71] ibid 214–15.
[72] Y Dinstein (n 16) 75–77.
[73] J Coffee, '"No Soul to Damn: No Body to Kick": An Unscandalized Inquiry into the Problem of Corporate Punishment' (1981) 79 *Michigan Law Review* 386.

Finally, it is necessary to make a terminological clarification. The term 'outcome responsibility' will supplant Hart's category of causal responsibility here because the emphasis is placed upon the consequence or outcome, rather than the relationship between cause and effect. This shift in focus is necessary because the contention made here is that the disjuncture between responsibility for the cause and responsibility for the effect is the source of this type of passive impunity.[74]

While the potential for irresponsibility subsists in each aspect of responsibility, it is not predominantly found in either form. By combining the previous two sections, however, it is clear: first, that role responsibility may be a component of causal responsibility; and second, that irresponsibility arises in the space between the two forms of responsibility. A different way of seeing this effect is through the lens of 'obligations of result' (outcome responsibility) and 'obligations of diligent conduct' (role responsibility) requirements imposed upon the State, and the emphasis of international law on the latter.[75]

First, role responsibility may be a component aspect of conditions and events that constitute outcome responsibility. In other words, the fulfilment of the role may contribute to those actions that together cause the outcome, and vice versa, and failure to recognise this relationship may lead to irresponsibility. The isolation, or over-emphasis, of role responsibility may be extremely hazardous in that it may exclude consideration of the consequences, or the outcome responsibility, consequent to fulfilling the role in question. In the words of Scott Veitch:

> Here, then, is a key insight: breach of the responsibilities attached to the role will be irresponsible, but their fulfilment will not be … The bureaucrat who is just doing his or her job; the professional fulfilling his or her role; the weapons manufacturer merely producing components; the judge who is only applying the law; the minister who is merely fulfilling the offices of state; the soldier who is carrying out orders: in all such cases, role responsibility, at least in terms of the most common and predominant cultural expectations, has the same effects. *It segregates responsibility for role from responsibility for consequences; it legitimates the separation of intention from ultimate outcomes and does indeed, offer the presumption of these persons' actions as both responsible* and *blameless*. The fact that these forms are so very occasionally found to be deeply problematic—with such headline-making cases of an Eichmann or the East German border guards—merely shows up the fact that … they *do* carry the weight of justification that sees the question of responsibility successfully measured by role.[76]

[74] T Honore, *Responsibility and Fault* (Hart Publishing, 2002) 27, 31–32; Cane, *Responsibility in Law and Morality* (n 64) 105–11.

[75] H Tonkin, *State Control Over Private Military and Security Companies in Armed Conflict* (Cambridge University Press, 2011) 59–64.

[76] Veitch (n 33) 48–49. Emphasis mine.

The problem Veitch identifies is one that arises out of the division of labour, a division that segregates and compartmentalises responsibility. As individual roles are carved out of the whole and spheres of activity are defined around each role, the measurement of success or failure at a given task becomes narrowly defined as success or failure in the individual fulfilment of the role itself. The underlying assumption is that the culmination of the success of each individual role component will lead to the successful outcome of the broader labour as a whole. Scott Veitch goes on to offer a startling conclusion arising from this process:

> And thus we come to the most profound implication: the perpetuation of harm and suffering may come about *not* through so many broken promises, but rather through something far more disturbing, its opposite—*promises fulfilled, bargains kept and jobs well done.*[77]

While this has been a sociological analysis until this point, these effects are exacerbated and compounded by the operation of the law. This is because 'legal categories define forms of acting that simply *are* constitutive of role responsibilities'.[78] In other words, an essential aspect to the operation of the law is to prescribe a certain mode or sphere of action dependent on the legal role being fulfilled: the operation of the law entrenches role responsibility.

There is, however, an important corollary; that legal categories defining certain roles also have as 'one of their key purposes is precisely to *circumscribe* the range of rights and obligations that attach to the role … Across the range of legal activities, then, roles are defined in ways that both create and limit liabilities'.[79] Situating the corporation into this context, it becomes immediately obvious that their role, defined by law, is the generation of economic profit.[80] The 'best interests of the corporation' principle that was entrenched in the United States by the Supreme Court in *Dodge*[81] legally obliged company directors to put the financial interests of the shareholder above all countervailing considerations. In the corporation, the disjuncture between role and outcome responsibility is heavily accentuated because responsibility for fulfilling the role of generating material profit is entirely segregated from the outcome responsibility for adverse or harmful consequences, leading Joel Bakan to label it as the externalising machine.[82] Crucially, this segregation of responsibilities is mandated by the law. This is because the law requires role responsibility

[77] ibid 50. Emphasis original.
[78] ibid 74. Emphasis original.
[79] ibid 75. Emphasis original.
[80] See generally J Bakan, *The Corporation: The Pathological Pursuit of Profit and Power* (Constable & Robinson, 2005) 35–39.
[81] *Dodge v Ford Motor Company* (1919) 204 Mich 459 (Michigan Supreme Court).
[82] Bakan, *The Corporation* (n 80) 3.

to trump conflicting considerations, including those of responsibility for adverse outcomes. The space for passive impunity is clear: irresponsibility that leads to impunity for outcome responsibility is generated by the exclusive legal focus upon unfettered role responsibility.[83]

Furthermore, Veitch points to two ways in which 'legal ordering replicates the features of the division of labour' that characterise the dispersal of responsibility.[84] The second is considered below within the context of denial while the first is addressed here:

> [W]ithin the realm of legal regulation, legal rights and duties attaching to particular roles are ways of dividing up the juridical field itself ... This field is not only constituted by way of jurisdiction at a general level ... but is itself made up of a plethora of smaller jurisdictions pertaining to all manner of legal roles, from courts and legislatures, to corporations and clubs ... in other words, legal roles work to demarcate the boundaries of responsibility in ways that are facilitated by the division of competencies, rights and obligations.[85]

Although this is not symptomatic of a fragmentation process, as responsibility never initially constituted a platonic whole,[86] the mosaic of role responsibilities arising from the division of rights and obligations further isolate role from outcome responsibility. In addition, the division of roles creates layers of role responsibilities that in turn lead to the potential for overlapping regulatory mechanisms: Scott Veitch gives the example that a medical doctor will simultaneously be subjected to laws that govern duties towards patients, standards of professional conduct and criminal and fiscal liabilities.[87] Myopic focus on role responsibility thus opens the door for non-legal regulatory mechanisms which relegate legal regulation to a residual position. Taking the medical doctor example, fulfilment of professional standards of conduct *implies* fulfilment of the role responsibilities attendant to being a doctor and suspends initial doubt over fulfilment of other duties for that role. Chapter six will show that this assumption may be poorly grounded and illustrate the hazards associated with the possibility of according primacy to non-legal regulatory mechanisms in relation to PMCs.

The dominance of role responsibility is readily demonstrated in the doctrine of command responsibility, discussed further in chapter four, which the ICTY developed into a separate crime of omission largely independent and distinct from the substantial crimes committed by the subordinates.[88]

[83] 'Unfettered' is crucial here; negative impunity may be restrained if limitations were imposed upon types of permissible role.
[84] Veitch (n 33) 75.
[85] ibid.
[86] ibid 76.
[87] ibid.
[88] C Meloni, 'Command Responsibility Mode of Liability for the Crimes of Subordinates or Separate Offence of the Superior?' (2007) 5 *Journal of International Criminal Justice* 619, 625–26.

Pre-Trial Chamber II of the ICC in *Bemba* reconfirmed that 'a superior may be held responsible for the prohibited conduct of his subordinates for *failing to fulfil his duty* to prevent or repress their unlawful conduct' and further clarified 'that the criminal responsibility for omissions is incurred only where *there exists a legal obligation to act*'.[89] This suggests that 'the superior who has done everything materially possible to prevent or punish the commission of crimes by his subordinates should not be held responsible if, notwithstanding his appropriate exercise of control, crimes have been committed'.[90] Plainly put, a commander who has fulfilled the obligations attaching to his role is absolved from legal liability for the criminal actions of his subordinates. This remains the case where the criminal outcomes caused by his subordinates occur *despite* the fact that he fulfilled his duty to prevent or punish such conduct. Thus, the consequences of his subordinates' actions are divorced from the responsibility of the commander.

It is now possible to return to the third aspect of passive impunity. The question concerns the tension between individual and collective modes of liability, and whether legal mechanisms with their focus upon the former, are appropriate or even capable of accounting for organisational or collective effects that characterise, inter alia, armed conflict.[91] Highlighting the problem, Kirsten Ainley has argued 'that responsibility for war crimes lies not with individual perpetrators alone but also in significant measure *with collectives and with those individuals who did not commit crimes but did contribute to harm*'.[92] This observation is premised upon the argument that legal processes allocate more than the fair share of the responsibility to individual perpetrators for the consequences of collective action because these processes focus upon ascribing and apportioning individual responsibility.[93] It is the gulf between individual role responsibility, on the one hand, and collective outcome responsibility on the other, that is the source of this aspect of passive impunity. The inadequacies of the legal mechanisms that purport to bridge this gulf indicate the structural tendency of the law to generate this form of impunity.

First, it should be noted that the term 'impunity' is itself heavily loaded in the sense that it presupposes particular actors, assumes specific situations, and prescribes certain types of redress. For example, the aforementioned

[89] *Prosecutor v Bemba (ICC Pre-Trial Chamber)* [2009] ICC Pre-Trial Chamber II ICC-01/05-01/08 [405]. Emphasis added.

[90] Meloni, 'Command Responsibility Mode of Liability for the Crimes of Subordinates or Separate Offence of the Superior?' (n 88) 628.

[91] Tracy Isaacs outlines these tensions in a wider sense outside of the context of armed conflict, which are addressed in greater depth in the relevant book chapters: see T Isaacs and R Vernon (eds), *Accountability for Collective Wrongdoing* (Cambridge University Press, 2011) 6–10.

[92] K Ainley, 'Excesses of Responsibility: The Limits of Law and the Possibilities of Politics' (2011) 25 *Ethics & International Affairs* 407, 409. Emphasis added.

[93] ibid 410–14.

definitions by both Joinet and Harper hinge upon punishing the *persons* responsible for violating human rights to rectify situations of impunity. These presumptions create special difficulties, however, because of the collective dimension inherent within the perpetration of egregious harms. Antonio Cassese expresses this difficulty:

> International crimes … share a common feature: they tend to be expression of collective criminality, in that they are perpetrated by a multitude or persons … When such crimes are committed, it is extremely difficult to pinpoint the specific contribution made by each individual participant in the criminal enterprise or collective crime.[94]

One consequence may be that impunity, in the legal sense, is inevitable owing to the absurdity and meaninglessness of attempting to place responsibility for collective egregious harms which are *organisational* outcomes, upon *individuals* through a concept of individual responsibility.[95] This supports Ainley's perspective, such that indicting individuals may amount to nothing more than a show trial: a surplus of responsibility is necessarily allotted to the individual because the collective outcome is greater than the sum of the component individual responsibilities. This holds true also for more benign organisational effects, where responsibility may be diffused, as Jorge Vinuales suggests for example, 'it is not clear who should be responsible for apparent possible violations such as an inadequate supply of water or the ramifications of an excessively heavy debt burden'.[96] In this sense, the victim-orientated understanding of impunity propounded by Joyner may be more appropriate since the focus has been shifted away from (legal mechanisms of) punishment towards (political processes of) restitution and reconciliation.[97]

The dominance of individual responsibility for international crimes is a recent phenomenon which Gerry Simpson has situated within its historical context by emphasising the oscillation between the poles of collective and individual responsibility.[98] It must be stressed at this point

[94] Cassese, *International Criminal Law* (n 68) 189; similarly: 'Responsibility is not a zero sum game; in most situations of atrocity, no single perpetrator (or even small group of perpetrators) can be considered completely responsible … Individuals act within complex contexts to which many others contribute'; Ainley, 'Excesses of Responsibility' (n 92) 413.

[95] While ICL attempts to punish those *most responsible*, the indictment of even the most culpable individuals may remain insufficient.

[96] J Vinuales, 'Impunity: Elements for an Empirical Concept' (2007) 25 *Law and Inequality: A Journal of Theory and Practice* 115, 118.

[97] Joyner, 'Redressing Impunity for Human Rights Violations: The Universal Declaration and the Search for Accountability' (n 9); similarly, Kirsten Ainley has advocated that mechanisms of political responsibility should be reintroduced to parallel legal mechanisms of accountability, in part because 'courts are not the optimal forums in which to determine the institutional and societal reforms required to prevent similar violence in the future': Ainley (n 92) 422–27.

[98] G Simpson, 'Men and Abstract Entities: Individual Responsibility and Collective Guilt in International Criminal Law' in A Nollkaemper and H van der Wilt (eds), *System Criminality in International Law* (Cambridge University Press, 2009) 78.

that these historical perspectives on collective responsibility concern the State exclusively, so their application to other types of organisations or juridical entities, such as corporations, remains tangential. The infamous dictum of the International Military Tribunal (IMT) at Nuremberg, which gave rise to the pre-eminence of individual criminal responsibility, that 'Crimes against international law are committed by men, not by abstract entities' must be contextualised.[99] The criminalisation of the German State at Versailles, and the subsequent failure and abandonment of the collective mode of liability, suggest that 'Nuremberg was a riposte not only to conventional international law with its relentless focus on states' "civil" liability but also to the state crime model pursued without much success at Versailles'.[100] Henry Stimson, then US Secretary of War, revealed the purpose of adhering to individual responsibility in what were then to become to Nuremberg Trials:

> We should always have in mind the necessity of punishing effectively enough to bring home to the German people the wrongdoing done in their name, and thus prevent similar conduct in the future, without depriving them of the hope of a future respected German community … Remember, this punishment is for the purpose of prevention and not for vengeance.[101]

Seen from a different angle, the balance that was struck at Nuremberg is instructive since it reveals the bias *against* collective responsibility perceived to be necessary in the interests of peace. In other words, Nuremberg and its successor tribunals are based upon, and propound, an ideology favouring prospective peace over retrospective justice in its focus upon 'those who bear the greatest responsibility'.[102] While striking this balance may be essential for reconciliation in factual terms it is a poor footing upon which to base the exclusivity of individual responsibility for international crimes. This is especially the case where this leads either to excesses of responsibility that characterise show trials, or to inadequacies relating to the result that indicate impunity. Furthermore, what is often neglected is that the 'abstract entities' within the contemplation of the Tribunal was

[99] *Trial of the Major War Criminals before the International Military Tribunal*, vol 1 (IMT, 1947) 223; Furthermore, it is clear that the 'abstract entities' in the context of Nuremberg was the State. This raises questions as to the broader applicability of this assertion over other systems or organisations; see J Kleffner, 'The Collective Guilt of Organised Armed Groups for System Crimes' in Nollkaemper and van der Wilt (eds), *System Criminality in International Law* (n 98).

[100] Simpson, 'Men and Abstract Entities' (n 98) 80.

[101] Cited in E Mendes, *Peace and Justice at the International Criminal Court: A Court of Last Resort* (Edward Elgar Publishing, 2010) 5.

[102] See eg Article 1(1) of the Statute of the Special Court for Sierra Leone (http://www.rscsl.org/Documents/scsl-statute.pdf. While Errol Mendes does not frame the balance between *prospective* peace and *retrospective* justice in such explicitly temporal terms, seeing these trends in such light illuminates the systematic prejudice towards impunity for past actions. This potentially links the aforementioned practices of amnesty and pardon to the balance struck between individual and collective responsibility: ibid 1–7.

the *State*, rather than any other juridical entity or organisation, such as the corporation. This persistent legacy of Nuremberg, however, continues to frustrate the development of corporate criminal responsibility that is considered in depth in chapter five.

Although Gerry Simpson notes a vein of hybridity between collective and individual modes of responsibility in the post-War approach to the defeated Axis powers,[103] there are now signs that the pendulum is again swinging away from individual responsibility. There is growing recognition that: 'Individuals who transgress fundamental norms of international law often are not acting on their own initiative or for their own cause … individuals do what they do because they act on behalf, or as a part, of a state or other larger collective entity'.[104] Similarly, Immi Tallgren writes:

> It seems that instead of being exceptional acts of cruelty by exceptionally bad people, international crimes are typically perpetrated by unexceptional people often acting under the authority of a state, or, more loosely, in accordance with the political objectives of a state or other entity.[105]

Antonio Cassese, as cited above, reiterated this point and has acknowledged collective criminality as the common denominator for ICL crimes: groups of people acting in unison or following a policy.[106]

Indeed, the collective dimension of criminality that was expressed in the Nuremburg Charter itself is often overlooked. Article 6 empowered the Tribunal 'to try and punish persons who, acting in the interests of the European Axis countries, whether as *individuals* or as *members of organizations*'.[107] This was further reinforced by Article 9 which empowered the IMT to designate a group as a criminal organisation.[108] The effect of such determination by the IMT, however, was restricted to empowering competent national authorities to try *individuals* for membership of such a declared *criminal organisation* by providing the unchallengeable factual basis for such trials at lower courts. In other words, while the Charter for the IMT explicitly provides for the criminalisation of organisations, this mechanism was devised as a short-cut for the prosecution of the *individuals* as members of such groups, and not the group per se.[109] This recognition of group criminality

[103] Simpson (n 98) 81–82; see also A Gattini, 'A Historical Perspective: From Collective to Individual Responsibility and Back' in Nollkaemper and van der Wilt (n 98).

[104] Nollkaemper and van der Wilt (n 98) 4.

[105] I Tallgren, 'The Sensibility and Sense of International Criminal Law' (2002) 13 *European Journal of International Law* 561, 575.

[106] Cassese (n 68) 189. It is collective criminality that separates ordinary crimes from terrorist acts. The former are motivated by individual gain while the latter are motivated by organisational or collective goals: ibid 167.

[107] Emphasis added.

[108] Note that the criminal prosecution of organisations as juridical entities was not intended: van der Wilt, 'Joint Criminal Enterprise: Possibilities and Limitations' (n 62) 94; the focus upon collective guilt had arguably undermined the outcome of Nuremberg, ibid 95.

[109] For an overview of the bifurcated approach at Nuremberg, see van der Wilt (n 62) 93–95.

in the Nuremburg Charter itself at sub-State levels erodes the assertion that international crimes are committed only by men, and not abstract entities. Instead, the Nuremburg Charter appears to strike a delicate balance, *recognising* the potential for collective criminality of sub-State organisations but only *punishing* individual members of criminal organisations. If this is indeed the case, it is clear that impunity is created with regard to the collective and that responsibility is over-ascribed to the individual—a worrying precedent to establish.

The hybridity of the IMT between individual and collective responsibility has been lost with the subsequent tribunals, and ICL now operates to attach responsibility exclusively to individuals. Seen from this perspective, the major flaw of ICL is in adopting the approach of domestic criminal law which is structured to punish the individual direct perpetrator for criminal harm: an approach that sees only individual connections and is largely blind to organisational relationships.[110] Even relating to criminal law mechanisms that seek to bridge the gap, such as Joint Criminal Enterprise (JCE), Antonio Cassese writes: '[JCE] denotes a mode of criminal liability that appears particularly fit to cover the criminal liability of *all participants* in a common criminal plan',[111] and as such, only individuals are under the contemplation of JCE. This approach is not suitable for assessing large-scale harms, such as those that are characteristic of ICL, because these may constitute more than a criminal plan: instead, these may be the expression of a policy and require the cumulative effort of a larger collective to perpetrate. As Hannah Arendt reflected upon the trial of Adolf Eichmann: 'The prosecution, unable to understand a mass murderer who had never killed … was constantly trying to prove individual murder'.[112] The failure to recognise the schism between the planner and the perpetrator that has been driven by organisations underpins the apparent incoherence of this idea. In this sense, the burgeoning Perpetration Through an Organisation (PTO) doctrine is an improvement in attempting to connect the clean hands of the leaders, planners and instigators with the international crime committed through an organisational, rather than an individual, nexus. Unfortunately, however, the adoption of this concept on the international plane remains controversial.[113] Thus, while ICL seeks to punish those individuals most responsible for international crimes, it inappropriately deploys the mechanism used to punish ordinary crimes. In doing so, ICL fails to recognise that the instigators, commanders and

[110] S Ratner, 'The Schizophrenias of International Criminal Law' (1998) 33 *Texas International Law Journal* 237, 251; Ainley (n 92) 410–14.

[111] Cassese (n 68) 191. Emphasis added.

[112] H Arendt, *Eichmann in Jerusalem: A Report on the Banality of Evil* (Penguin, 1994) 215 (2006 edition).

[113] T Weigend, 'Perpetration through an Organization' (2011) 9 *Journal of International Criminal Justice* 91.

leaders who should bear the greatest responsibility also have the cleanest hands in relation to the actual criminal outcomes made possible through organisational distancing.

> The collective dimension raises another type of problem in relation to passive impunity. Not only are juridical entities precluded from criminal responsibility through active impunity mechanisms discussed in chapter five, but the structures of organisation operate to diffuse responsibility for its individual members. Hannah Arendt articulated this:
>
> Today we ought to add the latest and perhaps most formidable form of such domination: bureaucracy or the rule of an intricate system of bureaus in which no men, neither one nor the best, neither the few nor the many, can be held responsible, and which could properly be called rule by Nobody.[114]

Thus the 'bureaucracy', or perhaps more specifically the group or organisation, is the system that dissociates individual responsibility: a suggestion that is reflected in the paradox of shared responsibility in turn rooted in 'the problem of many hands'.[115] Stating the obvious, this is the inverse proportionality between organisational size and complexity vis-a-vis individual responsibility for the outcome that creates an a priori problem for seeking to arraign individuals for the effects of the collective. Interestingly, Maurice Punch takes this argument to the logical conclusion by claiming 'that there are no "individuals" in organisations and that organisations commit "crimes"'.[116]

The combination of these complementary effects creates an impunity paradox. Individuals within an organisation, who as natural persons are capable of bearing criminal responsibility, become entirely subsumed within the juridical status of the organisation and have their individual responsibility dissociated by it to the extent that they cannot be held as perpetrators of the crime. Conversely, the organisation as a juridical entity could be considered as being responsible for the crime as the perpetrator but is precluded from bearing criminal responsibility because of the legacy of Nuremberg.

[114] H Arendt, *On Violence* (Harcourt Publishers, 1970) 38. She continues by saying: 'If … we identify tyranny as government that is not held to give account of itself, rule of Nobody is clearly the most tyrannical of all, since there is no one left who could even be asked to answer for what is being done'. This points to the severe dispersal of responsibility made possible through organisations.

[115] M Bovens, *The Quest for Responsibility: Accountability and Citizenship in Complex Organisations* (Cambridge University Press, 1998) 45–52. While many hands may dilute individual responsibility, the contribution to this result of 'many minds' has often been ignored.

[116] M Punch, 'Why Corporations Kill and Get Away with It: The Failure of Law to Cope with Crimes in Organisations' in Nollkaemper and van der Wilt (n 98) 42. In the context of this thesis, what is particularly striking about his analysis is that it exclusively concerns benign civilian corporations, in contradistinction to militarised corporations, such as arms manufacturers and PMCs.

The tension between the modalities of individual and collective responsibility remains in international law, however, as evident in the contemporaneous cases of *Milosevic*[117] at the ICTY and *Genocide Case*[118] at the International Court of Justice (ICJ).[119] A common denominator of these cases (aside from both these trials taking place at The Hague in early 2006) is the indictment for genocide in the former Yugoslavia: the former sought to impose individual responsibility (albeit through the mechanism of JCE), while the latter attempted to hold Serbia collectively responsible for the act.[120] As is well known, Milosevic died before the ICTY issued a final verdict, but the ICJ held that although Serbia had not committed genocide, largely because it lacked the necessary *dolus specialis* required under the Genocide Convention, it had failed in its obligation to prevent genocide.[121] As Dermot Groome notes, however, these parallel processes were detrimental to a satisfactory outcome: the ICJ neglected to consider the evidence presented by the prosecution before the ICTY in the Milosevic trial 'upon which a reasonable trial chamber *could* be satisfied beyond reasonable doubt that Milosevic had committed the crime of genocide'.[122]

In light of the tension between individual and collective responsibility for the Srebrenica genocide, the bifurcated approach at The Hague rendered a singularly unsatisfactory outcome. While the *dolus specialis* for the crime of genocide *could* have been established by the ICTY, Milosevic's death prevented a conclusive ruling. That evidence before the ICTY, however, could potentially have tipped the balance at the ICJ to that Serbia had committed genocide, rather than failing in its obligation to prevent it.[123] It is arguable that, through either process, the attribution of responsibility was disproportionate such that the outcome misses the point. Even in the hypothetical scenario where Milosevic was found to be guilty by the ICTY, such a verdict sounds hollow because the commission of genocide requires a collective effort for which he, as an individual, is necessarily the most visible and thus likely to be the scapegoat.[124] Conversely, had the ICJ

[117] *Prosecutor v Milosevic* [Trial not completed] ICTY IT-02-54.

[118] *Genocide Case* [2007] ICJ 91, 2007 ICJ Rep 43.

[119] Simpson (n 32) 66; Ainley (n 92) 419–21.

[120] Ainley (n 92) 421.

[121] The ICJ found 'that the acts committed at Srebrenica … were acts of genocide' *Genocide Case* (n 118) [297]. The ICJ went on to find that Serbia 'violated its obligation to prevent the Srebrenica genocide' as well as its obligation to punish genocide: ibid 438 and 450, respectively.

[122] D Groome, 'Adjudicating Genocide: Is the International Court of Justice Capable of Judging State Criminal Responsibility' (2007) 31 *Fordham International Law Journal* 911, 914. Emphasis original.

[123] The ICJ explicitly stated that it had to make its own determinations despite the ICTY having tested relevant allegations, *Genocide Case* (n 118) [212].

[124] This remains a possibility at the ICTY, *Prosecutor v Mladic* [At trial] ICTY IT-09-92; this is because he would bear an excess of responsibility: see Ainley (n 92).

determined that Serbia was collectively guilty such a verdict would have failed to appropriately proportion responsibility to its leaders who had planned, organised and overseen the genocide. This tension between the mandate and jurisdiction of the ICJ and the ICTY revolving around State and individual responsibility was expressed in the Separate Opinion by Judge Tomka, who concluded that the '[ICJ] and the ICTY have two different missions but one common objective'.[125] This common objective, however, may be frustrated by the mutual opposition between the divergent missions of the two Courts.

ICL has developed a few mechanisms to bridge the gap between individual criminal responsibility and collectively produced outcomes. These can be categories broadly into two groups: hierarchical (command responsibility and the defence of superior orders) and complicity (joint criminal enterprise and perpetration through an organisation) mechanisms. These mechanisms share a common weakness of bias towards role responsibility, and are undermined by their overextension in seeking to reconnect role and outcome responsibilities which potentially violates of the cardinal principle of 'individual culpability and criminal responsibility'.[126]

The primacy of individual role responsibility over collective outcome responsibility is readily evident in the doctrine of command responsibility.[127] The modality of this form of responsibility is debatable, as Chantal Meloni asks, 'is the superior to be held criminally responsible for the crimes committed by his subordinates "*as an accomplice*", or for a separate offence of omission, consisting of the dereliction of his duty to control, prevent or punish?'.[128] Command responsibility initially adhered to the former modality whereby the commander was held responsible through complicity; an approach which implied that the superior actively and directly participated in the crimes of his subordinates.[129] That the commander was charged with the principle crime committed by his subordinates was confirmed by the watershed Trial Chamber judgment in *Delalic*.[130] The ICTY gradually distinguished between direct modes of

[125] Separate Opinion of Judge Tomka *Genocide Case* (n 118) [73]. The ICJ itself 'observes that the duality of responsibility continues to be a constant feature of international law': ibid 173.

[126] Meloni (n 88) 633; Cassese (n 68) 33–35.

[127] Command responsibility has a customary international law basis: r 152 for crimes pursuant to orders, and r 153 for failure to prevent or punish: Henckaerts and Doswald-Beck (n 21) 556, 558, respectively; see also Judgment *Prosecutor v Delalic (Trials Chamber)* [1998] ICTY Trial Chamber IT-96-21-T [333, 343]. Beyond ICL, command responsibility has also been codified in arts 86 and 87 of API, art 1(1) of Annex to Hague IV and art 4(2)(a) of GC III. Although also referred to as 'superior responsibility', I will use 'command responsibility' to emphasise the military dimension of the doctrine.

[128] Meloni (n 88) 620. Emphasis original.

[129] ibid 621–22.

[130] *Prosecutor v Delalic (Trials Chamber)* (n 127) [331–333].

responsibility under Article 7(1) of the ICTY Statute and that of superior responsibility embodied within Article 7(3). In *Halilovic*, the Trial Chamber differentiated between these two provisions by holding that the latter consisted of the failure to fulfil the role of a commander:

> The commander *is responsible for the failure to perform an act required by international law*. This omission is culpable because international law *imposes an affirmative duty* on superiors to prevent and punish crimes committed by their subordinates ... the Tribunal *does not mean* that the commander *shares the same responsibility* as the subordinates who committed the crimes, but rather that because of the crimes committed by his subordinates, the commander *should bear responsibility for his failure to act*.[131]

It is clear that command responsibility arises from the role played by the commander rather than attaching to the outcome of the crimes committed by the subordinates. The ICTY reaffirmed this in *Oric* where the Trial Chamber determined that 'superior criminal responsibility is characterised by the *mere omission* of preventing or punishing crimes committed by others'.[132] This reasoning effectively transformed command responsibility into a separate crime of omission for failure to discharge a duty which is detached and functionally independent from the crimes of the subordinates.[133] The limitation of commander responsibility to a 'dereliction of duty offence', rather than connecting directly with the crimes committed by the subordinates is evident in the sentence of two years imprisonment, rather than the 18 requested by the prosecutor and also in the lower *mens rea* threshold required.[134]

Although command responsibility originated as a mechanism to connect the role responsibility of military superiors to the outcome responsibility over their subordinates, the ICTY has severed this connection in *Oric*. Only by holding the commander responsible for the fulfilment of obligations attached to their role and by isolating this role responsibility, could the individual criminal responsibility of superiors be re-established. The consequence is that commanders who do not order or otherwise participate directly in the commission of the crimes of their subordinates can only be charged with omission offences that are unrelated to the severity of the crimes. The contribution of superiors to international crime will be greatly underestimated by circumscribing commander responsibility strictly to their role.

[131] *Prosecutor v Halilovic (Trials Chamber)* [2005] ICTY Trials Chamber IT-01-48-T [54]. Emphasis added.

[132] *Prosecutor v Oric (Trials Chamber)* [2006] ICTY Trial Chamber IT-03-68-T [293]. Emphasis added.

[133] Meloni (n 88) 626.

[134] *Prosecutor v Oric (Trials Chamber)* (n 132) [158]; Meloni (n 88) 621 and 631 respectively.

One final point of comparison between individual and State responsibility should be made.[135] Individual command responsibility was established by the ICTY Trial Chamber in *Delalic* upon the criterion of 'effective control',[136] while only the lesser threshold of 'overall control' needed to be fulfilled for collective State responsibility to be established per the ICTY Appeals Chamber in *Tadic*.[137] This reinforces the idea that passive impunity mechanisms function to shield the individual against liability for collectively generated harms. Not only is primacy accorded to role responsibility, which is isolated from the outcome, but the higher threshold for individual responsibility will prevent a relationship of control from being established in many cases.

F. Law's Denial: Determining Damage, Injury and Wrong

While the previous sections have tackled the ways through which passive impunity arises from the misallocation of responsibility and the generation of irresponsibility, this section targets an anterior stage whereby responsibility considerations are forestalled. Impunity that arises from the pre-emption of the very possibility of responsibility can occur in instances where harm is either not appropriately registered, or is categorised in a manner that renders the remedies inadequate or unavailable. Broadly speaking, the law is able to pre-empt responsibility in two ways: first, through its process of filtering the criteria that are to be taken into consideration; and second, in the meaning that the law ascribes to harm.

The former effect works picks up on the second of Scott Veitch's ways whereby legal ordering mirrors the division of labour, addressed above. Legal responsibilities are contextualised as constituting 'one part of the division of labour of responsibility practices across a whole range of normative forms and relationships'.[138] Veitch makes this argument by appealing to Neil MacCormick's work:

> The special sort of [juridical] reasoning is one which *leaves aside* any general and abstract deliberation on what in a given context it would be best or would all things considered right to do or not to do. *Where law is appealed to, all things are not considered*.[139]

[135] B Bonafé, 'Finding a Proper Role for Command Responsibility' (2007) 5 *Journal of International Criminal Justice* 599, 618, note 63.

[136] *Prosecutor v Delalic (Trials Chamber)* (n 127) [378]. This is addressed in greater depth in ch 4.

[137] *Prosecutor v Tadic (Appeals Chamber)* (n 67) [145].

[138] Veitch (n 33) 76.

[139] N MacCormick, 'Argumentation and Interpretation in Law' (1995) 9 *Argumentation* 467, 470. Emphasis added.

While it is trite to note that all systems of dispute resolution impose a mechanism for selecting what factors to take into account, the peculiarity of law is that its processes confer legitimacy. As Veitch writes, 'the juridical field comprises processes of systematisation, formalisation, rationalisation and universalisation, which play a vital role in asserting and maintaining the distinctiveness and legitimacy of the force of law'.[140] This ties into the tendency of law towards hegemony discussed above: the effect of its weaknesses become magnified and entrenched because its processes of determination marginalise competing frameworks of analysis. Thus, while the juridical process is shown to be only one of a range of mechanisms through the division of labour that allocate responsibility, its relative dominance leads to schizophrenic results:

> [G]iven the way in which legal roles function to *limit* responsibilities attaching to them, and do so in reasonably clear and authoritative terms, we can see that they provide ways of both asserting *and* denying responsibilities.[141]

To clarify, the ability of the law to assert responsibility arises from the aforementioned legitimacy and force of law. Responsibilities that have been determined by juridical processes assume a superior status to responsibilities ascribed through other mechanisms. Conversely, responsibilities that lack the force of law have their claims to responsibility eroded.[142]

In order to situate this discussion into the context of impunity, consider the juridical process of labelling harm.[143] Passive impunity may arise where harm is either not recognised or where it is inappropriately labelled, leading to responsibility for such harm being precluded or diluted respectively. Scott Veitch puts it thus:

> What registers in law as a wrong? This question has a deceptively simple answer: *what registers in law as a wrong is a breach of the law*. Strictly speaking, then, it is not any particular loss—physical suffering, economic harm, or whatever—that registers as such, *but rather only that suffering or harm that is given legal cognisance*.[144]

This tautology of law in the recognition of harm is striking. It needs to be placed in relation to one of the three initial questions raised at the outset as to whether the law was capable of capturing and articulating large-scale harms brought within the remit of law through the juridification of war. If such harms are not within the contemplation, or the comprehension, of the law then impunity arises because the very possibility of responsibility for these harms has been precluded. As Veitch recognised, a new dimension

[140] Veitch (n 33) 77; The force of law may be usurped by non-legal processes in states of exception, however: G Agamben, *State of Exception* (University of Chicago Press, 2005) 38–39.
[141] Veitch (n 33) 77. Emphasis original.
[142] But see Agamben, *State of Exception* (n 140) 2.
[143] Veitch (n 33) 85–96.
[144] ibid 92. Emphasis added.

of irresponsibility has been introduced by 'this "double silencing" that constitutes the more profound sense of irresponsibility … it constitutes the disappearance of the *possibility* of responsibility'.[145] Thus, a more insidious form of passive impunity is generated through this initial preclusion of responsibility which precedes the juridical process.

While Scott Veitch focuses upon the ability of the harm to fit within legal categories, Stanley Cohen approaches this question from the perspective of denial. Although he develops three themes of denial, it is Cohen's conception of 'interpretative' denial that holds the most relevance for present purposes. Interpretative denial does not contest the factual basis of a claim; 'Rather, they are given a different meaning from what seems apparent to others'.[146] In other words, this process operates 'by changing the words, by euphemism, by technical jargon, the observer disputes the cognitive meaning given to an event and re-allocates it to another class of events'.[147] While all three forms of interpretative denial[148]—euphemism, legalism and denial of responsibility—all operate in the context of PMCs, it is denial from legalism that forms the current focus.

Converging with Veitch's approach, Cohen writes that '[p]owerful forms of interpretative denial come from the language of legality itself',[149] and that 'interpretive denials are not fully-fledged lies; they create an opaque moat between rhetoric and reality'.[150] The contribution made by the denial discourse is that it reveals the juridical process as simply a framework for interpreting facts, whereby '[t]he harm is cognitively reframed and then reallocated to a different, less pejorative class of event'.[151] This enables a more nuanced approach through which the *magnitude* of harm can be contested.[152] Scott Veitch's model of legal harm recognition is binary: a harm is either recognised by the law or it is not. The perception of impunity may, however, also arise in the disparity between the severity of the harm that has been suffered and the severity of the harm that has been registered in law. Any lack of proportion between these types of harm dilutes responsibility, giving rise to passive impunity. The contribution of Stanley Cohen's model is that it allows for precisely such readjustment and re-evaluation because while it may not be possible for the law to not register a great harm as harm, it is possible for the law to re-categorise that great harm as a lesser wrong. This lesser wrong may be registered

[145] ibid 90.
[146] Cohen (n 10) 7.
[147] ibid 8.
[148] ibid 105–09.
[149] ibid 107.
[150] ibid 108.
[151] ibid 106.
[152] See eg the critique presented in M Krygier, 'Compared to What?' (2009) 34 *Australian Journal of Legal Philosophy* 241.

in law, in Veitch's sense that it is a breach of the law, but this will not adequately or proportionally reflect the magnitude or scale of the initial harm. Responsibility is not so much denied as it is deflected or diluted such that irresponsibility arises from the lack of proportion between the large scale of the harm and the lesser scale of the wrong that the law recognises. This disparity gives rise to passive impunity, as responsibility for the harm is dissociated because that responsibility becomes attached to a lesser wrong.

Finally, interpretive denial may provide a conduit between passive and active forms of impunity because (retrospective) accountability mechanisms are particularly vulnerable to interpretive denial processes. While active impunity, as discussed below, operates by suspending the application of the ordinary juridical process, interpretive denial operates in an analogous manner by altering the meaning that is subsequently ascribed to an act through that juridical process. In other words, while interpretive denial does not literally suspend the ordinary legal process, the effect of reallocating categories of meaning results in a similar effect.

G. Law's Assertion: Legitimacy, Legality and Rightfulness

Stanley Cohen's concept of interpretive denial may only capture half of this overall effect and may usefully be complemented by the concept of 'interpretive assertion' proposed here. While interpretive denial seeks to neutralise allegations of wrongdoing, the idea of interpretive *assertion* seeks instead to ascribe legitimacy and rightfulness through similar mechanisms made available through the plasticity of language and interpretation. From this perspective, interpretive denial falls along the negative dimension in distancing vices while interpretive assertion lies along the positive dimension in seeking proximity with virtues through similarly nefarious means. The difference can be subtle because concepts may be intertwined and work towards the same overall purposes and generate their effects together. Yet, the hitherto unrecognised concept of interpretive assertion is a necessary component in the legitimation enterprise: distance and distinction from unsavoury connotations and unfavourable associations may be necessary in the quest for legitimacy, but it is an entirely insufficient basis upon which to complete the enterprise. Denying wrongdoing is not the same as asserting rightfulness.

Where interpretive denial generates impunity by under-recognising the type of harm or intensity of injury, it shares the characteristic of filtering the criteria to be taken into consideration with interpretive assertion. In this sense, interpretive denial can arise from the adoption of specific formal appearance or arrogation of certain types of organisation which are capable of altering the legal categorisation, and hence the legal meaning, of an activity. This can occur through the use of other legal statuses that lend legitimation, and through the use of rhetoric that is more commonly found within other spheres of activities which are unambiguously permissible. In these, and other, ways entities and activities are able to assert greater legitimacy of existence and operation that lead to claims of rightfulness. Thus, interpretive assertion cloaks entities and activities in legitimacy through fluid transitions in translation, despite reality remaining substantively unchanged. To provide a concrete example in the context of this book, which is discussed in greater depth in chapter four, interpretive denial in relation to the PMC would be to distance its mercenary roots and diminish its association with mercenary activities while interpretive assertion would point to its juridical corporate personhood to underscore claims to legitimate and legal basis of existence and operation.

The impact of interpretive assertion upon the existence and perpetuation of impunity, however, is less direct and concrete than is the case with interpretive denial. Where the latter is predominantly employed in redefining the understanding or meaning of consequences that have already taken place, the former opens the possibility for more pervasive, but critically prospective, forms of impunity. In other words, while interpretive denial is a useful mechanism to avoid the full force of retrospective accountability, interpretive assertion skews the frame of reference by altering the nature and scope of prospective standards against which (future) behaviour is understood and evaluated. As such, interpretive assertion does not generate impunity in a directly identifiable sense, but rather facilitates the adoption of more apparently benign forms and couches activities in loftier language. In summary, interpretive assertion alters the presumptions that lie beneath the framework for ascribing responsibilities and thus operates in a much more subtle manner than interpretive denial which seeks to directly neutralise specific allegations.

The potential power of interpretive assertion—proclamations in which potentially ungrounded claims are made—can be underscored by psychological research that reveals the immense impact of intuitive predispositions on the final outcome of decisions.[153] Some context is necessary to illustrate the insidiousness of interpretive assertion in this regard and its impact on impressions. Daniel Kahneman has showcased many of the psychological mechanisms involved in the process of human decision-making. He underscores in particular the ordinarily smooth and continuous flow of impressions, intuitions, intentions and feelings from fast, automatic and non-voluntary processes that subsequently become accepted and endorsed by the voluntary cognitive processes associated with the subjective experience of agency, choice and concentration.[154] This suggests that

[153] D Kahneman, *Thinking, Fast and Slow* (Penguin, 2012) pts 1 and 2.
[154] ibid 24. See also 20–21 for a brief outline of the two different mental systems involved.

decisions which appear to be rationally concluded are, in reality, heavily influenced almost to the point of being determined by unconscious intuitive psychological processes. Thus, the stage is set for the translation of a range of intuitive prejudices into rationally-condoned choices.

The invocation of psychological research in the context of interpretive assertion is important because of the mechanism that Kahneman calls, 'what you see is all there is (WYSIATI)' which 'represents only activated ideas. *Information that is not retrieved … from memory might as well not exist*'.[155] WYSIATI lends force to the initial connotations invoked through allusions made by borrowing language and form, especially at first glance and to the unsuspecting. Insofar as controversial actors seek proximity with the benign and the virtuous through the assertions made possible by ambiguities within interpretation, the frame of reference with regard to their activities can be altered. The alteration of the context in which their activities are considered is further affected by WYSIATI: only the information associated with that new context will be retrieved, and therefore relevant, to the assessment of both the actor and its activities. Put into concrete terms in the context of this book, interpretive assertion that the PMC is a legitimate corporate entity conjures up information associated with business entities.[156] Filtered through the WYSIATI mechanism, the PMC is then understood by the intuitive mental system as a business corporation and analysed as such, thereby entirely ignoring the potentially controversial nature of the mercenary activities that the PMC engages in. If this is subsequently accepted and endorsed by the rational and conscious mental system, the interpretive assertion transformation is complete.

While this suggests that interpretive assertion can be made through explicit channels, the possibility for interpretive assertion to be made implicitly through imitation should also be considered. The idea here is that while the adoption of certain forms or identities can constitute interpretive assertions; it need not be such a blunt instrument. Instead, interpretive assertions can arise within the connotations made by conveying a certain impression. The style of language used to communicate or assuage concerns is an obvious form of interpretive assertion insofar as it draws associations, and increases the perceived proximity, with desirable outcomes. An example of this, discussed in greater detail in chapter six, is the illusion created by the International Code of Conduct for Private

[155] Emphasis added. The intuitive and automatic system seeks to maintain 'coherence in the story it manages to create. The amount and quality of the data on which the story is based is largely irrelevant. When information is scarce … [the intuitive system] operates as a machine for jumping to conclusions'. WYSIATI leads in particular to overconfidence in the judgement or decision, renders decision-making vulnerable to the way in which information is framed, and encourages statistical facts regarding an outcome to be ignored: ibid 85–88.

[156] Legitimacy may be extended subtly through 'the associative machine' that primes us towards certain conclusions in ambiguous contexts: ibid 50–58.

Security Providers of an international treaty. Despite the explicitly non-legally binding nature of this Code, and the obviously non-State nature of the instrument, it co-opts the language, form and approach of international legal processes. While the conscious, rational mental processes may register this subtle allusion as attempts to ascribe legitimacy to the PMC-industry, the automatic, unconscious mental processes, like with optical illusions that continue to confound after they are known to be illusions,[157] cannot overcome the basic association. Insofar as the rational mental system condones the suggestion made by the unconscious mental system, interpretive assertion will prevail.

One final point needs to be made with regard to the possible consequences of interpretive assertion: the potential for the entity or activity subjected to critique to assimilate, and thereby neutralise, that critique. This has occurred in contemporary art practice, where art practices critical of their own institutions (such as museums and galleries) have been appropriated by those institutions themselves.[158] In the process of displaying these institutionally critical art practices within the very institution that are being critiqued, the critique espoused by those practices has become engulfed and neutralised. Similar processes can be seen with the PMC industry adopting human rights rhetoric in regulatory mechanisms developed in reaction to allegations of human rights abuse: the very vocabulary of the critique has become absorbed by the target against which it was deployed, neutralising its relevance and effect in the process. While the assimilation of both the language and concerns of human rights in PMC regulation takes place at a later stage, this course has been set earlier by interpretive assertions that draw the PMC closer to the corporation that lead to the acceptability of forms of corporate social responsibility, despite its martial activities.

V. ACTIVE IMPUNITY: LEGAL EXCEPTIONALISM

Where passive impunity concerns characteristics that are inherent to the ordinary legal process, active impunity mechanisms suspend that ordinary legal process to create a more explicit form of impunity. There are four main mechanisms through which active impunity operates: pardon, amnesty, immunity and states of exception. The last category is considered afterwards as it shifts the paradigm entirely away from the legal realm by completely suspending the ordinary juridical process. While the idea of sovereign power serves as the lynchpin of legal exceptionalism, active impunity mechanisms are not restricted to such overt manifestations. The suspension of ordinary legal processes may also arise where the courts have developed

[157] ibid 26–28.

[158] I owe this point to conversations with Agnieszka Mlicka, who proposed this parallel with the idea of interpretive assertion.

the jurisprudence in a manner which renders the law similarly impracticable or inapplicable, or where the application of the law is withheld from certain categories of actors.[159]

A. Pardon, Amnesty and Immunity

Pardon and amnesty can be differentiated from immunity in its origins, effects and temporal scope.[160] Geoffrey Robertson explains the sources, categories and purposes of pardons and amnesties:

> Every state has power … to pardon those who offend against its laws. A pardon offered or proclaimed to a whole class of offender is described as an amnesty … Pardons and amnesties have been used since time immemorial, benevolently (as a measure of forgiveness to those who have already suffered some punishment for their crimes), politically (to bring an end to civil wars and insurrections, legally (to absolve convicts who later appear innocent), and even festively (to celebrate a ruler's birthday).[161]

Authority relating to the effect of pardon comes from the Privy Council in *Phillip*[162] where Lord Justice Ackner approvingly cited the High Court of New Zealand

> that the effect of a pardon was to *remove the criminal element of the offence* named in the pardon, but *not to create any factual fiction*, or to raise the inference that the person pardoned *had not in fact committed the crime* for which the pardon had been granted.[163]

The Privy Council had a further opportunity to elaborate upon the temporal aspect of pardon, on appeal, where Lord Justice Woolf said:

> However while a pardon can expunge past offences, a power to pardon cannot be used to dispense with criminal responsibility for an offence which has not yet been committed. This is a principle of general application which is of the greatest importance. The state cannot be allowed to use a power to pardon to enable the law to be set aside by permitting it to be contravened with impunity.[164]

[159] To be clear, there need not be any teleological intention or coordination behind the development of such jurisprudence. Instead, all that matters is the overall effect.

[160] In this regard, the US Supreme Court affirmed the 'crucial distinction between a right not to be tried and a right whose remedy requires the dismissal of charges': *Midland Asphalt Corp v US* (1989) 489 US 794 (US Supreme Court) 801. Furthermore, the US Supreme Court has consistently held that immunity is a protection against the burden of litigation: 'The entitlement is an immunity from suit rather than a mere defence to liability; and like an absolute immunity, it is effectively lost if a case is erroneously permitted to go to trial': *Mitchell v Forsyth* (1985) 472 US 511 (US Supreme Court) 525–27, 526. Emphasis omitted.

[161] G Robertson, *Crimes Against Humanity: The Struggle For Global Justice* (Penguin, 2006) 296–97. For an early example, see Indemnity and Oblivion Act 1660.

[162] *Phillip (Lennox) v DPP* [1992] 1 AC 545 (Privy Council).

[163] ibid 557. Emphasis added.

[164] *Attorney-General of Trinidad and Tobago v Lennox Phillip* [1995] 1 AC 396 (Privy Council) 411.

It can be deduced from this speech that both pardon and amnesty constitute mechanisms of the active dimension of impunity because they absolve ordinary legal liability, and crucially that they are exclusively retrospective.[165] Pardon and amnesty are incapable of bearing prospective application since this would violate the narrow and exceptional nature of these mechanisms of exoneration which would have the potential to degenerate into less distinct forms of passive impunity. Seen from this perspective, pardons and amnesties may be categorically differentiated from other passive forms of impunity because although they may converge in effect, they diverge in both origin and purpose.

The divergence between the active and passive impunity mechanisms is also illustrated in the conflicted treatment of pardons and amnesties under international law.[166] From the IHL perspective, Rule 159 of the International Committee of the Red Cross (ICRC) Study on Customary International Humanitarian Law[167] reiterates the earlier obligation under Article 6(5) of Additional Protocol II (APII) to the Geneva Conventions which applies only to non-international armed conflicts:

> At the end of hostilities, the authorities in power shall endeavour to grant the broadest possible amnesty to persons who have participated in the armed conflict, or those deprived of their liberty for reasons related to the armed conflict, whether they are interned or detained.[168]

The formulation in the ICRC Study is identical, apart from the additional 'exception of persons suspected of, accused of or sentenced for war crimes'[169] necessary in order to recognise the countervailing obligations imposed by Rule 158.[170] Although requirements such as these which apply amnesty in an expansive and liberal sense have not gained prominence in the emerging discipline addressing *Jus Post Bellum*, it does echo Alexander Hamilton's main justification in *The Federalist* No 74 that 'in seasons of insurrection or rebellion there are often critical moments when a well-timed offer of pardon to the insurgents or rebels may restore the

[165] Similarly, under the US Constitution, 'Because the power to pardon is given only for "offenses against the United States," the crime must precede the pardon; it may not be anticipated. Otherwise the power that allows presidential clemency for the consequence of a violation would be a power to dispense with the observance of the law': W Duker, 'The President's Power to Pardon: A Constitutional History' (1976) 18 *William and Mary Law Review* 475, 526.

[166] Robertson, *Crimes Against Humanity* (n 161) 301–12.

[167] Henckaerts and Doswald-Beck (n 21) 611–14.

[168] Protocol Additional to the Geneva Conventions of 12 August 1949, and relating to the Protection of Victims of Non-International Armed Conflicts (Protocol II), 8 June 1977.

[169] Henckaerts and Doswald-Beck (n 21) 611.

[170] Rule 158 obliges States to investigate and prosecute alleged war crimes committed by their nationals, armed forces, or on their territory and within their jurisdiction: ibid 607–11.

tranquillity of the commonwealth'.[171] This is a contention which is further supported by the Commentaries to the Additional Protocols to the Geneva Conventions.[172] Thus, pardons and amnesties are understood to play both restorative and preventative roles, especially in the context of non-international armed conflicts such as insurrections and rebellions.

It should be noted, however, that while Article 6(5) of APII is prima facie an example of active impunity insofar as amnesty is encouraged for the purposes of reconciliation, this view is not strictly correct. The ICRC's interpretation of this provision was communicated to the Prosecutor of the ICTY as follows:

> Article 6(5) of Protocol II is the only and very limited equivalent in the law of non-international armed conflict of what is known in the law of international armed conflict as 'combatant immunity' … In non-international armed conflicts, no such principle exists, and those who fight may be punished, under national legislation, for the mere fact of having fought, even if they respected international humanitarian law. The 'travaux preparatoires' of [Article] 6(5) indicate that this provision aims at encouraging amnesty, ie, a sort of release at the end of hostilities, *for those detained or punished for the mere fact of having participated in hostilities. It does not aim at an amnesty for those having violated international humanitarian law.*[173]

In other words, Article 6(5) of APII is concerned with exonerating those punished under domestic law for IHL-compliant actions in the context of non-international armed conflicts that would have been lawful in international armed conflicts because it seeks to provide a parallel to the privileged belligerency status. As such, it is the functional equivalent of Article 43(2) of API which provides that '[m]embers of the armed forces of a Party to a conflict … are combatants, that is to say, they have the right to participate directly in hostilities', which grants immunities for IHL-compliant actions in international armed conflicts.

The divergence in temporal scope between these provisions should be noted: the 'combatant immunity' provided under API for international armed conflicts is atemporal, encompassing all IHL-compliant activity.

[171] A Hamilton et al, *The Federalist Papers* (Oxford University Press, 2008) 365–66. It must be noted, however, that Alexander Hamilton was arguing for the powers of pardoning to be reposited in a single person for reasons of expediency in order to be able to act swiftly and decisively in its exercise.

[172] 'The object of this sub-paragraph is to encourage gestures of reconciliation which can contribute to reestablishing normal relations in the life of a nation which has been divided': ICRC, *Commentary on the Additional Protocols of 8 June 1977 to the Geneva Conventions of 12 August 1949* (Martinus Nijhoff, 1987) para 4618.

[173] As quoted in D Cassel, 'Lessons from the Americas: Guidelines for International Response to Amnesties for Atrocities' (1996) 59 *Law and Contemporary Problems* 197, 218. Emphasis added.

The amnesty provided for in APII for non-international armed conflicts, however, is purely retrospective, meaning that the applicability of the amnesty is not determined at the time of the conduct in question. This disparity places direct participants in non-international armed conflicts into a vulnerable position. This is because the (domestic) law criminalising their activity, even where the actions in question are entirely consistent with IHL, remains unless it is lifted at the *discretion* of the State within which the conflict is occurring, and then only at the cessation of hostilities. Put differently, while the formal equality of combatants in international armed conflicts, as expressed in 'combatant immunity', guarantees exemption from ordinary criminal laws provided that their actions comply with IHL, the default position with amnesty under APII is that of prosecution under domestic law, despite their potential compliance with IHL.

This divergence in treatment along international and non-international armed conflict lines is likely to have a significant bearing on the prosecution of suspected mercenaries both because contemporary armed conflicts are predominantly non-international in character and because mercenaries are more likely to become engaged in this type of conflict.[174] The contempt for mercenary activities by State authorities, which is best illustrated by the OAU Convention definition of a 'mercenary',[175] make it unlikely for those authorities to exercise their discretion over amnesty under Article 6(5) of APII in the aftermath of conflict. Clearly, this renders suspected mercenaries particularly susceptible to prosecution exclusively upon the basis of their participation in the armed conflict, regardless of their compliance to IHL.[176] The ramifications depend upon the perspective taken of post-conflict amnesty. Where such amnesty is seen as an exemption of ordinary juridical processes the vulnerability of suspected mercenaries to such an arbitrary mechanism is accentuated and justifies

[174] Since mercenaries are legally defined as external to the State, those that would otherwise be defined as mercenaries in international armed conflicts are likely to be incorporated into the armed forces or be sent on official duty and thus cease to be mercenaries under art 47(2)(e) and (f) of API. The suspicion of being a mercenary has been used to persecute refugees and other visible minorities, with the Libyan conflict providing a recent example: UNHCR, 'UNHCR Fears for the Safety of Refugees Caught in Libya's Violence' *UNHCR* www.unhcr.org/4d6393e06.html. The overlap between mercenaries and PMC contractors extends these effects to such personnel as well.

[175] Under art 1 of this Convention, a 'mercenary' is any person external to the State who seeks to overthrow or undermine the independence, territorial integrity or normal working institutions of an OAU government or to frustrate a recognised liberation movement: OAU Convention for the Elimination of Mercenarism in Africa 1977 (OAU CM/817 (XXIX) Annex II Rev 1) art 1.

[176] This argument has internal consistency with the denial of prisoner-of-war status under art 47(1) of API, addressed in greater depth in ch 3. For a contemporary illustration, see esp the punishment of accused mercenaries in Libya: H Al-Shalchi, 'Libya Military Court Jails Accused Foreign Mercenaries' *Reuters* (4 June 2012) www.reuters.com/article/2012/06/04/us-libya-trial-ukrainian-idUSBRE8530QY20120604.

uniform application. Seen from the equivalence perspective between international and non-international armed conflict, however, this vulnerability is justified: the liability for prosecution under domestic laws arising from the discretionary application of post-conflict amnesty can be considered to be equivalent to the explicit denial of privileged belligerency status expounded in Article 47 of API for international armed conflicts.[177]

ICL adopts a different emphasis which is concerned with the removal of pardons, amnesty and immunity.[178] The view adopted by ICL is that these active impunity mechanisms may be applicable to ordinary crimes which may be perpetrated in the course of armed conflict, but against which privileged combatants are either immunised under API or may be subsequently granted amnesty under APII. These cannot, however, apply with international crimes as Geoffrey Robertson writes:

> The sea change in the international community's approach to amnesty, from regarding it as a blessing of forgiveness to reproaching it as the curse of impunity, has turned on the dawning realisation of the unacceptability of amnesties for the 'authors' of crimes against humanity ... amnesties cannot absolve the political and military leaders for genocide, torture, crimes against humanity and grave breaches of international and humanitarian law.[179]

The limitations imposed by ICL upon amnesties are traditionally explained by according precedence to the obligation to prosecute international crimes. This trumps attempts to exempt their perpetrators from punishment: 'international law now imposes an *erga omnes* obligation on states to investigate and prosecute crimes against humanity, even if this means rejecting or annulling amnesty laws and taking some risk of counter-revolution'.[180] The limits upon amnesty that ICL imposes may be explained from two different approaches; those of severity and responsibility. First, the active impunity afforded by amnesty provisions may be limited by the severity of the crimes that they seek to absolve. In other words, the force of amnesty may be limited only to exonerating ordinary crimes, and fail to have sufficient power or force to shield against the magnitude of international crimes. The second approach focuses upon the level of responsibility borne by those who seek the aegis of amnesty. The protective force of amnesty provisions may be excluded from protecting those who bear the greatest responsibility for international crimes. As Geoffrey Robertson puts it, 'The rule against impunity that has crystallised in international law is a norm which denies the legal possibility of pardon to those who bear

[177] See ch 3 for a detailed analysis of the legal treatment of mercenaries under international law.

[178] The ICRC Study on Customary International Humanitarian Law, r 158 exemption embodied within r 159, above, illustrates the limiting role played by ICL in process.

[179] Robertson (n 161) 304.

[180] ibid 311.

the greatest responsibility for crimes against humanity'.[181] This is supported by the position of the UN Human Rights Committee relating to the prohibition of torture found in Article 7 of the International Covenant on Civil and Political Rights (ICCPR):

> The Committee has noted that some States have granted amnesty in respect to acts of torture. Amnesties are generally incompatible with the duty of States to investigate such acts; to guarantee freedom from such acts within their jurisdiction; and to ensure that they do not occur in the future.[182]

Thus, the active impunity provided by pardoning and amnesty mechanisms is gradually losing force, especially when these are deployed to protect those most responsible for serious international crimes. Although the protective force of such measures against prosecution has been left unresolved for the ICC, there are strong arguments for the prima facie incompatibility of pardons and amnesties with the Rome Statute, which will only be allowable in exceptional circumstances when accompanied by other mechanisms of justice.[183]

The other form of active impunity arises from the practice of according immunity under international law which has a similar effect of suspending the application of (usually domestic) laws to certain categories of actor.[184] In this sense, immunity may appear prima facie to be analogous to the aforementioned grant of pardon or amnesty. There are important differences in their characteristics, however, based upon the underlying principles, rationale and the temporal scope of immunities. It should be noted at the outset that immunities are deployed in theory to protect the State and are based upon sovereign equality:[185] the concomitant protection of individuals is justified only insofar as they represent or are acting on behalf of the State.[186]

While the broad subject of immunities is beyond the scope of this thesis, certain characteristics require elaboration owing to their theoretical

[181] ibid 309.

[182] UN Human Rights Committee, 'Compilation of General Comments and General Recommendations Adopted by Human Rights Treaty Bodies' (1997) HRI/GEN/1/Rev.3.

[183] See generally C Stahn, 'Complementarity, Amnesties and Alternative Forms of Justice: Some Interpretative Guidelines for the International Criminal Court' (2005) 3 *Journal of International Criminal Justice* 695.

[184] See generally I Brownlie, *Principles of Public International Law* (Oxford University Press, 2008) 323–48. The general operation of IHL falls within this category, as it exempts privileged belligerents from prosecution for violent domestic crimes.

[185] This is expressed in the maxim: 'par in parem non habet jurisdictionem': ibid 325.

[186] For the purposes of this discussion, I leave aside the legal technicalities between immunity *ratione personae* (personal immunity) and immunity *ratione materiae* (functional immunity). Briefly, the former attaches to the person of a State official irrespective of conduct in both public and private conduct but lasts only for the duration of the appointment. The latter attaches to the role of a State official and only prevents prosecution of conduct in the course of official duties. See also Mendes, *Peace and Justice at the International Criminal Court* (n 101) 174.

bearing both upon the laws of armed conflict and those governing military operations.[187] First, it should be noted that immunities are atemporal, and so are capable of being prospective in nature. Thus, unlike pardon and amnesty, immunities may apply to acts that may not yet have happened or for actions for which responsibility has yet to be ascribed (in other words, where the physical act may have taken place but its legal significance has yet to be determined). Second, because immunities in theory protect the State and the principle of sovereign equality, they are capable of being waived by the beneficiary State.[188] This supports the contention that the purpose behind the practice of immunity is to indicate the forum in which claims against State officials are heard rather than to create impunity, and to prevent domestic laws from tampering with international politics. This is a point that will be revisited in the context of Status of the Forces Agreements (SOFAs) below. The point made here with regard to temporality, however, is that the potential for prospective immunity remains contingent upon the possibility of subsequent revocation if the beneficiary State decides to waive that immunity. Aside from this narrow exception, however, immunities differ significantly from pardons and amnesties in that they provide a *carte blanche* for certain actors to engage in conduct beyond the application of law, based upon the sovereign equality of States.

Here lies a crucial point: immunities are especially significant in the generation of impunity because they attach to State officials and others who claim to act on behalf of the State. Describing the power of those within the apparatus of the State to determine both the content and significance of the law, Penny Green and Tony Ward write:

> [T]he other obvious difference between 'robber bands' and 'states without justice' is that states claim the power to determine what is 'just', who is the robber and who is the tax-collector … If states define what is criminal, a state can only be criminal on those rare occasions when it denounces itself for breaking its own laws.[189]

The rarity with which a State condemns itself is underscored by the highly aberrant decision recently handed down by a Dutch appeals court which ruled that the Netherlands, *qua* State, was responsible for three hundred Srebrenica deaths.[190] The point to be made about immunities, however, is that they go beyond the structural determination of legality but rather that

[187] T Gill and D Fleck (eds), *The Handbook of the International Law of Military Operations* (Oxford University Press, 2011) 94–109; 143–19.

[188] An example of immunity waiver is explicitly provided by art 5 of the CPA Order 17 in Iraq: C Lehnardt, 'Individual Liability of Private Military Personnel under International Criminal Law' (2008) 19 *European Journal of International Law* 1015, 1031.

[189] Green and Ward, *State Crime* (n 36) 1.

[190] D Bilefsky and M Simons, 'Netherlands Held Liable for 300 Deaths in Srebrenica Massacre' *New York Times* (16 July 2014) www.nytimes.com/2014/07/17/world/europe/court-finds-netherlands-responsible-for-srebrenica-deaths.html

immunities constitute an additional hurdle. In other words, a State may in the first instance pre-empt the criminality of its officials by defining its laws in a favourable manner to exclude them or their actions (structural determination). Immunities are available as an additional step where these earlier attempts have failed to absolve official behaviour.

In the context of armed conflict, the practice of immunity is particularly significant because such agreements are usually negotiated for members of, and those accompanying, foreign forces under Status of Forces Agreements (SOFAs). These are considered essential to prevent members of the occupying power from being embroiled within domestic legal disputes.[191] These are also unlike the forms of immunity discussed above because

> SOFAs are based on the assumption that the presence of foreign personnel is in the interest of the host state as well as the sending state. Each SOFA is unique because this kind of agreement is negotiated on a case-by-case basis.[192]

Thus, the foundation of SOFAs is in perceived *benefit* to, rather than in the *sovereignty* of, the State such that their particular terms are not dependent upon an official nexus with the State.[193]

The question of immunities has significant bearing upon the PMC because discrepancies arise between national armed forces and PMC contractors with regard to the sources and extent of immunity that their personnel enjoy. Members (including civilian members) of national armed forces enjoy functional immunity derived from their status as organs of a sovereign State even in the absence of special SOFAs.[194] Functional immunity does not (and arguably should not), however, apply to private companies and their employees[195] such that any immunity that contractors actually enjoy must necessarily be derived through SOFA mechanisms. This discrepancy is magnified by the fact that 'SOFAs have become one of the most relevant international sources of immunity for private contractors … PMSC employees are often included under the scope of these arrangements' provided that they are employed by or operating on behalf of the State.[196] The result is that although PMCs cannot benefit from functional immunity as they are not organs of the State, SOFAs are negotiated to ensure their immunity from the application of the domestic laws of the host State. In other words, SOFAs that grant PMC immunity create a strong and ungrounded form of active impunity. SOFAs elevate the PMC

[191] M Frulli, 'Immunity for Private Military Contractors: Legal Hurdles or Political Snags?' in F Francioni and N Ronzitti (eds), *War by Contract: Human Rights, Humanitarian Law, and Private Contractors* (Oxford University Press, 2011) 451–54.
[192] ibid 451–52.
[193] See generally ibid 448–69.
[194] Gill and Fleck, *The Handbook of the International Law of Military Operations* (n 187) 144–45.
[195] ibid 145.
[196] Frulli, 'Immunity for Private Military Contractors' (n 191) 451.

above the application of domestic law although they do not perform official functions, upon the presumption that its activities are of perceived benefit to the States involved.

The SOFA immunity issue with specific regard to PMCs has been further refined in the context of the Iraq conflict.[197] In June 2004, just before the transfer of authority to the Iraqi Interim Government, the Coalition Provisional Authority (CPA) issued Order 17 granting all contractors immunity from domestic Iraqi law.[198] Order 17 was clearly an instrument of immunity because it acknowledged an ordinary domestic legal system in operation within the territory which the Authority temporarily administered, but carved out an exception by suspending the application of that ordinary juridical system with regards to a circumscribed group of actors.[199] This perspective is reinforced by section 4(3), which provides that 'Contractors shall be immune from Iraqi legal process with respect to acts performed by them pursuant to the terms and conditions of a Contract or any sub-contract thereto'.[200] Micaela Frulli notes the conditional wording of the subsection is reminiscent of that used to describe the functional immunity enjoyed by State officials, and argues on this basis that immunity provided to contractors 'should only cover acts performed in the regular course of duty and not when exceeding their powers'.[201] Drawing this analogy justifies a restrictive interpretation of the functional immunity that potentially strengthens the accountability of PMC contractors. The fact that Order 17 immunity is contingent upon contractual provisions is particularly alarming because this is unhinged from the 'official function' criterion that forms the lynchpin for functional immunity. In other words, although the purpose of subjecting Order 17 immunity to contractual terms and conditions may have been to create symmetry with the 'official function' requirement on functional immunity, conditioning the exemption on contractual provisions fails to provide for this and does not place any restrictions per se on the scope of Order 17 immunity. This is because there is no requirement for contractual provisions to mirror strictly 'official functions', and even where such requirements were put

197 For the background prior to CPA Order 17, see Gill and Fleck (n 187) 102–04; Tonkin, *State Control Over Private Military and Security Companies in Armed Conflict* (n 75) 169.

198 s 2(1) of the Order provides: 'Unless provided otherwise herein, the [Multinational Force], the [Coalition Provisional Authority], Foreign Liaison Missions, their Personnel, property, funds and assets, and all International Consultants shall be immune from Iraqi legal process': Coalition Provisional Authority, 'CPA Order 17: Status of the Coalition Provisional Authority, MNF—Iraq, Certain Missions and Personnel in Iraq' www.iraqcoalition.org/regulations/20040627_CPAORD_17_Status_of_Coalition__Rev__with_Annex_A.pdf.

199 A waiver of the immunity exists under s 5; these have reportedly never been used: Lehnardt, 'Individual Liability of Private Military Personnel under International Criminal Law' (n 188) 1031.

200 Coalition Provisional Authority, 'CPA Order 17' (n 198).

201 Frulli (n 191) 456.

in place, these would be advisory at best given the principle of the freedom of contract.[202] Two further points need to be made. First, in relation to the passive dimension of impunity above, the emphasis that section 4(3) placed upon the fulfilment of contractual role responsibility serves to further alienate outcome responsibility, thereby contradicting the goal for overcoming immunity provisions. Second, although beyond the scope of this chapter, there are ramifications that arise from Article 64 of the Fourth Geneva Convention (GC IV) which imposes limitations upon the extent to which an occupying power may change or circumscribe the domestic law of the territory which it is occupying.[203]

While Order 17 has been subjected to heavy criticism for extending immunity from domestic Iraqi laws to contractors, this is in fact common practice for occupying forces, according to Major General Tim Cross, the most senior British uniformed officer in Iraq during the Coalition Provisional Authority.[204] He stated that the need for such immunity is twofold. First, it is to ensure the harmony of applicable laws, and in most cases to *raise* the legal standards operative in the zone of occupation to an international standard. Second, the immunity prevents domestic actors from using the domestic law to wreak havoc among the occupying forces, either by passing specialised laws against those forces, or indicting members of the occupying forces in domestic courts. Interpreting this common practice differently, another way of viewing Order 17 is that the grant of immunity for foreign persons in the territory of Iraq is an assertion of sovereign power by the CPA. The exclusion of aliens involved with the reconstruction process from the operation of ordinary Iraqi laws unequivocally established the supremacy of the CPA.

Seen in this light, Order 17 and other SOFA laws of its ilk are far from being immunity practices de jure. Instead, their operation simply excludes the applicability of domestic laws to the occupying forces (and certain categories of civilian aliens), which are in theory still subjected to the laws of the occupying power, albeit extraterritorially.[205] Furthermore, because the domestic legal system in the Iraq context was arguably below international

[202] See ch 4 for a detailed discussion of the limitations of enforcing ulterior interests or requirements under contract law.

[203] Art 64 provides: 'The penal laws of the occupied territory shall remain in force, with the exception that they may be repealed or suspended by the Occupying Power in cases where they constitute a threat to its security or an obstacle to the application of the present Convention'. See generally A Roberts, 'Transformative Military Occupation: Applying the Laws of War and Human Rights' (2006) 100 *American Journal of International Law* 580.

[204] Personal communication, 5 November, 2010

[205] This extraterritoriality may breed impunity de facto, as practical barriers associated with gathering evidence make the reality of applying the law more difficult. Furthermore, questions of jurisdiction make the reality of applying the law more difficult. In this regard, note the restrictive interpretation of art 2(1) of the ICCPR by the US government. It considered that the ICCPR 'would apply only to individuals who were both within the territory of a State Party and within that State Party's jurisdiction': 'Human Rights Committee Consideration

standards in terms of protecting fundamental rights, immunity from the applicability of these laws might be considered to further, rather than hinder, the process of justice. Indeed, this might account for Doug Brooks' curious critique of the lapse of immunity as a move which 'throws the DoD contractors under the bus, as pretrial detention and incarceration in Iraq are "way below" global standard'.[206] While the standard of protection of fundamental rights in the domestic Iraqi legal system may have indeed been questionable, suspending the operation of domestic law may generate impunity for violations of human rights or other criminal activity which cannot be justified.

As a postscript for immunity, it was the perceived abuse of PMC contractor immunity under Order 17 in the aftermath of the Blackwater scandal at Nisour Square, described in chapter two, that was a major reason behind the official end of US involvement in December 2011. Although CPA Order 17 was only in effect from June 2004 until December 2008 when the UN mandate for the Multi-National Force (MNF) elapsed, Iraqi objection was such that the SOFA which took effect in January 2009 explicitly revoked any claim to contractor immunity.[207] Prosecution of PMC contractors under Iraqi law subsequently commenced with Daniel Fitzsimons who was convicted of killing two other PMC contractors.[208] The immunity

of Reports Submitted by States Parties under Article 40 of the Covenant: Fourth Periodic Report United States of America' paras 504–05. This is manifestly more restrictive than the Human Rights Committee's interpretation of the ICCPR requiring State Parties 'to respect and to ensure the Covenant rights to all persons who may be within their territory and to all persons subject to their jurisdiction': 'General Comment No. 31: The Nature of the General Legal Obligation Imposed on States Parties to the Covenant' para 10.

[206] This immunity lapsed with the return of power to the Iraqi government: G Ratnam and V Gienger, 'Iraq-U.S. Accord Wipes Out Contractor Immunity (Update1)' *Bloomberg* (20 November 2008) www.bloomberg.com/apps/news?pid=newsarchive&sid=a_bhi85h5LLg. Doug Brooks is a lobbyist for the PMC industry, as the president of the trade organisation, ISOA.

[207] Article 12 states unequivocally that 'Iraq shall have the primary right to exercise jurisdiction over United States contractors and United States contractor employees': 'Status of the Forces Agreement' *New York Times* (21 October 2011) http://topics.nytimes.com/top/news/international/countriesandterritories/iraq/status-of-forces-agreement/index.html?scp=8&sq=Nouri%20al-Maliki%20immunity&st=cse.

[208] M Schmidt, 'Immunity Gone, Contractor in Iraq Sentenced to Prison' *New York Times* (28 February 2011) www.nytimes.com/2011/03/01/world/middleeast/01iraq.html?scp=6&sq=SOFA%20iraq&st=cse. Although this is a sign that PMC contractors may no longer be beyond Iraqi law, this case indicates that while 'ordinary' crimes will be tried, serious allegations of international crimes perpetrated by contractors may remain excluded; and J Meikle, 'British Contractor Jailed in Iraq for Colleagues' Murders' *The Guardian* (28 February 2011) www.guardian.co.uk/world/2011/feb/28/british-contractor-jailed-iraq-murders. See also Ratnam and Gienger, 'Iraq-U.S. Accord Wipes Out Contractor Immunity (Update1)' (n 206); and J Risen, 'End of Immunity Worries U.S. Contractors in Iraq' *New York Times* (1 December 2008) www.nytimes.com/2008/12/01/world/middleeast/01contractors.html. It is curious that the first prosecution concerned inter-contractor violence. This suggests that impunity for alleged misconduct against Iraqis remains largely intact despite the removal of Order 17.

of PMC contractors remained a sticking point that resulted in the official end of US involvement in December 2011, as discussed in greater detail in chapter two. As a hallmark of a SOFA is the perceived benefit of the presence of aliens to the host State, the implication of Iraq refusing to agree a SOFA that immunises PMC contractors signals a trenchant rejection of PMCs.

B. International Humanitarian Law

It may be argued from the foregoing that the entire juridical regime of IHL constitutes an active impunity mechanism. This contention accrues importance in the PMC context because of IHL's treatment both of mercenaries and civilians directly participating in armed conflict that is examined in chapter three, and thus its consequences upon the legal regime binding PMC contractors.

Recall Charles Harper's description that, 'Impunity can be achieved through amnesty laws passed or decreed by governments under whose authority the crimes were committed or by a successive government.'[209] Aside from the initial specification requiring amnesty laws to be passed by government,[210] the purpose and operation of IHL is precisely to exculpate otherwise criminal actions committed by members of the armed forces under State authority. Another way of putting this is that IHL embodies the specific authorisation of a category of actions in the context of armed conflict which would otherwise amount to criminal violence. According to Yoram Dinstein, the fundamental distinction between combatants and civilians under the law of international armed conflict that privileges certain categories of persons is driven by a specific motivation:

> The goal is to ensure in every feasible manner that international armed conflicts be waged solely among the combatants of the belligerent Parties. Lawful combatants can attack enemy combatants or military objectives, causing death, injury and destruction. In contrast, civilians are not allowed to participate actively in the fighting: if they do, they lose their status as civilians. But as long as they retain that status, civilians 'enjoy general protection against dangers arising from military operations'.[211]

From this passage, IHL can broadly be understood as a law of immunity. Individuals fulfilling the requirements set out by IHL, for instance those

[209] C Harper (ed), *Impunity: An Ethical Perspective* (World Council of Churches Publications, 1996) viii–ix.

[210] If Charles Harper's concept of government can be interpreted loosely, then the creation of the laws by government fits the definition perfectly; IHL is the creation of a collection of states which have agreed to abide by the commitments that are imposed by that legal corpus. Thus, IHL may be understood as a creation of a number of governments acting in unison.

[211] Dinstein, *The Conduct of Hostilities under the Law of International Armed Conflict* (n 49) 27.

enumerated under Article 4 of the Third Geneva Convention (GC III) defining prisoner-of-war status, are classified as lawful combatants. IHL then operates to shield these individuals from the ordinary operation of the law. Yoram Dinstein elaborates an illustrative scenario:

> At bottom, warfare by its very nature consists of a series of acts of violence … ordinarily penalised by the criminal codes of all countries. When a combatant, John Doe, holds a rifle, aims it at Richard Roe (a soldier belonging to the enemy's armed forces) with an intent to kill, pulls the trigger and causes Richard Roe's death, what we have is premeditated homicide fitting the definition of murder in virtually all domestic penal codes. If, upon being captured by the enemy, John Doe is not prosecuted for murder, this is due to one reason only. [The law of international armed conflict] provides John Doe with a *legal shield, protecting him from trial and punishment, by conferring upon him the status of prisoner of war.* That is not to say that the shield is available unconditionally. If John Doe acts beyond the pale of lawful combatancy, [the law of international armed conflict] removes the protective shield. Thereby, it subjects John Doe to the full rigour of the enemy's domestic legal system, and the ordinary penal sanctions provided by that law will become applicable to him.[212]

Taking these points together, what first appeared as the broad law of immunity needs to be refined, and there are three aspects to the suspension of ordinary law by IHL. First, it applies only to a defined and clearly identifiable category of persons who are theoretically in a position of consensual reciprocal danger.[213] The point is that IHL attempts to segregate privileged combatants by their consent to be mutually-subjected to attack. In juxtaposing privileged combatants with morally innocent civilians, and this is the second point, this distinction might well be justified. The restrictions placed upon privileged combatants—the 'pale of lawful combatancy'—attempt to isolate the armed conflict away from the sphere of civilian life. Put differently, IHL carves out a legal space free from the operation of ordinary domestic laws in which privileged combatants may engage in armed conflict amongst themselves in the hope that the civilian population might be largely spared.[214] This is how IHL protects civilians from the general dangers associated with armed conflict.[215] Thus, the third point is that the potential for immunity created by such a legal space in which the privileged combatants may engage in armed conflict is far from creating

[212] ibid 31. Emphasis added.

[213] This is clearly the idealised situation since the consensual dimension is eroded by the presence of the draft and the reciprocity of danger is challenged by the increasingly asymmetric nature of modern warfare.

[214] Direct, indiscriminate, and disproportionate attacks against civilians are prohibited: Dinstein (n 49) 115–23.

[215] API, art 48 encapsulates the Basic Rule of distinction 'In order to ensure respect for and protection of the civilian population and civilian objects'. The protection of civilians and civilian objects is further elaborated in arts 51 and 52 of API respectively.

a situation of impunity. Rather, the suspension of ordinary domestic laws with regard to the privileged belligerents seeks to provide a more rigorous legal mechanism for the protection of the civilian population. Civilians are thus protected from attack, either directly,[216] or indiscriminately,[217] with the possibility of civilian collateral damage being acceptable subject to the principle of proportionality.[218]

Finally, it is essential to note that any potential immunity effect of IHL in suspending ordinary laws is quite fragile in application. IHL clearly defines its criteria for inclusion within the immunity and removes its protections if these criteria are no longer fulfilled. The immunity effects of IHL hold in both directions. Not only are privileged combatants who exceed the 'pale of lawful combatancy' stripped of IHL's shield against prosecution in domestic legal systems but civilians who cease their abstinence and participate directly in hostilities also cannot claim the shield of IHL and may be subjected to prosecution in the domestic legal system for actions which would otherwise be immunised by the status of privileged belligerency.[219] To clarify, in both scenarios above, it is only the immunity that would otherwise be accorded by IHL that is removed with the result of subjecting individuals to prosecution for ordinary domestic crimes. This is categorically different from the prosecution for war crimes, which are instead serious violations of IHL itself.[220] Indeed, ICL operates to limit the active impunity effects of IHL by holding breaches of IHL as a matter of international crime. IHL therefore only exempts a certain category of action from the ordinary juridical process. Thus, the clearly defined rights and obligations delineated from IHL might be understood as a special category of immunity laws that are justified upon its separation and protection of civilians from armed conflict.

Thus, the rationale and purpose of IHL justify its operation to exempt a circumscribed sphere of activity from the ordinary legal process, and importantly does not constitute a bare active impunity mechanism. Its *lex specialis* status in situations of armed conflict suggests that it supplants, rather than suspends, the ordinary legal process. As IHL shields only privileged belligerents from legitimate acts of violence that comply with

[216] Dinstein (n 49) 115–16. Not only is direct attack prohibited under IHL (see arts 50–52 of API to the Geneva Conventions, 1977), but it constitutes a category of war crime under the Rome Statute of the International Criminal Court, art 8(2)(b)(i)–(ii).

[217] ibid 116–19.

[218] ibid 29.

[219] ibid.

[220] Confirmed by customary international humanitarian law: J-M Henckaerts and L Doswald-Beck, *Customary International Humanitarian Law*, vol II (Cambridge University Press, 2005) 568–611.

its criteria, the exclusion of civilians directly participating in hostilities, including PMC contractors, from its protection is consistent and justified.

C. States of Exception

While instances of pardon and amnesty, and the practices of immunity exculpate certain actors and actions from the ordinary juridical process, which otherwise continues to operate, something quite different happens within states of exception whereby the entire architecture of ordinary law may be suspended, or where this suspension becomes permanent, abolished. This short section illustrates this different category of positive impunity.[221]

The maxim, *inter arma enim silent leges*,[222] attributed to Cicero, neatly captures the notion that that armed conflict triggers states of exception where the ordinary juridical process simply ceases to apply. Obviously, such a move focuses power within executive branches of government, unfettering decision-making processes from ordinary procedures of checks and balances.[223] Thus, states of exception can be differentiated since the entire system of ordinary law has been suspended, or as Giorgio Agamben puts it, 'The state of exception is not a special kind of law (like the law of war); rather, insofar as it is a suspension of the juridical order itself, it defines law's threshold or limit concept'.[224]

The paradigmatic state of exception is warfare which is exemplified in *Korematsu* in the US[225] and *Liversidge v Anderson* in the UK[226] which concerned failed challenges against the legality of executive-authorised detention during the Second World War. These cases illustrated the broad reach of states of exception, which suspended the guarantees against

[221] See further Agamben (n 140).

[222] 'In times of war the laws are silent'.

[223] Such as human rights guarantees. The ECHR, art 15(1) illustrates this:

In time of war or other public emergency threatening the life of the nation any High Contracting Party may take measures derogating from its obligations under this Convention to the extent strictly required by the exigencies of the situation, provided that such measures are not inconsistent with its other obligations under international law.

The ability to temporarily suspend human rights obligations is also found in ICCPR, art 4 and the American Convention on Human Rights, art 27 (the ICESCR does not have such a provision due to the aspirational and largely unenforceable nature of economic, social and cultural rights). The guarantee of certain rights cannot be derogated from (ECHR, art 15(2) stipulates: 'No derogation from Article 2, except in respect of deaths resulting from lawful acts of war, or from Articles 3, 4 (paragraph 1) and 7 shall be made under this provision').

[224] Agamben (n 140) 4.

[225] *Korematsu v United States* (1944) 323 US 214 (US Supreme Court).

[226] *Liversidge v Anderson* (1942) 1942 AC 206 (HL).

arbitrary detention.[227] Similarly, Dean Acheson, the former US Secretary of State, famously said during the Cuban Missile Crisis that:

> I must conclude that the propriety of the Cuban quarantine is not a legal issue. The power, position and prestige of the United States had been challenged by another state; *and law simply does not deal with such questions of ultimate power—power that comes close to the sources of sovereignty*.[228]

Most recently, the ordinary legal system has been displaced by the threat of terrorism.[229] It is clear that these forms of active impunity have a common root in sovereign power, and where this power is exercised as a state of exception the entire ordinary juridical process is quite simply suspended. This led Carl Schmitt to define the sovereign as 'he who decides on the state of exception':[230] whoever held the power to suspend the ordinary juridical process must possess a power anterior to the law.

It may, however, make little sense to consider this a form of active impunity because the ordinary process of the law itself is suspended because it instead appears to pre-empt the law itself.[231] As Schmitt himself acknowledged, however, 'Because the state of exception is always something different from anarchy and chaos, in a juridical sense, an order still exists in it, even if it is not a juridical order'.[232] In this sense, it can be understood as a more fundamental and pervasive form of active impunity.

VI. CONCLUSION

This chapter has united disparate strands of critique that hint at the inadequacies of the law to create a framework for identifying and investigating impunity. This model demonstrates that the law creates and structures impunity for activities at the fringes of the juridical order that can be best

[227] The threat of terrorism has refined the erosion of these guarantees, referring to the USA PATRIOT Act: 'What is new about President Bush's order is that it radically erases any legal status of the individual, thus producing a legally unnamable and unclassifiable being … it is entirely removed from the law and from judicial oversight'. Agamben (n 140) 3–4.

[228] D Acheson, 'Law and Conflict: Changing Patterns and Contemporary Challenges—Panel: Cuban Quarantine: Implications for the Future: Remarks' (1963) 57 *American Society of International Law Proceedings* 13, 14. Emphasis added.

[229] Under the ECHR, however, the ability of the State to derogate from its obligations is overseen by the ECtHR and claims to derogation have been found to be flawed: *A and Others v UK* [2009] ECtHR GC 3455/05 [190]. For poignant examples as to how exceptional laws become normalised and entrenched, see C O'Cinneide, 'Strapped to the Mast: The Siren Song of Dreadful Necessity, the United Kingdom Human Rights Act and the Terrorist Threat' in M Gani and P Mathew (eds), *Fresh Perspectives on the 'War on Terror'* (ANU Press, 2008).

[230] Agamben (n 140) 1.

[231] ibid 32–33.

[232] ibid 33.

represented by the legal regulation of organised violence. The benefit of this model is that it can reveal the subtle generation and maintenance of impunity that subsists within the ordinary legal process, and that it complements the form of impunity produced by the more overt suspension of the ordinary legal order. In doing so, this model illustrates the core contribution of the law itself towards situations, and possibly systems, of impunity. This suggests that more law, or laws that are more refined, will not neutralise those effects but will instead serve to perpetuate impunity.

While this model has been developed to analyse PMC impunity in particular, adopting this approach within other contexts of persistent impunity is likely to reveal similar legal barriers, reinforcing the idea that the law is not, per se, the panacea capable of overturning impunity. Instead, the law may harbour iatrogenic effects such that increasing the scope and substantial reach of legally processes will expand and entrench allegations of impunity within these areas.[233] Finally, although this chapter has concentrated upon the ways in which the law contributes towards the generation of impunity, it has overlooked the possibility that legal processes may have improved access to justice for victims and functioned appropriately as a dispute resolution and accountability mechanism.[234] In this sense it is worth reiterating that legalised impunity functions primarily at the fringes of the legal order where its processes struggle to grasp the nature and significance of the activities at stake. This is well expressed by Gerry Simpson who noted that the sphere of law operated well to regulate everyday transactions and only began to struggle with serious atrocity.[235]

[233] This idea is adapted from Ben Bowling's application of iatrogenesis to transnational criminology. While Bowling's argument concerned the perpetuation of crime through measures designed to fight crime, this idea is adapted to argue that legal measures adopted to overcome impunity instead perpetuate that impunity: B Bowling, 'Transnational Criminology and the Globalisation of Harm Production' (British Society of Criminology Conference 2010, 'Human Rights Human Wrongs: Dilemmas and Diversities in Criminology').

[234] The admitted imbalance presented in this chapter is justified because it is developing a counter-intuitive idea that seeks to balance the discussion with regard to the role played by the law and legal processes in the ascription of responsibility, and in combating impunity.

[235] Simpson (n 32) 83.

2

The Modern Private Military Company

I. INTRODUCTION

THIS CHAPTER PROVIDES some background related to the development and characteristics of the modern PMC. It begins by providing a contemporary picture of the industry to illustrate the role the PMC plays in contemporary armed conflict and some of the problems that this raises. The chapter then highlights the factual allegations of impunity and the recidivist nature of the PMC industry which continues to fulfil key functions despite being embroiled in continuous controversy. Examining the question of accountability for PMC activities reveal that these considerations are biased towards focusing on fraud and fiscal waste, to the neglect of overcoming alleged impunity for violations of human rights (HRL) and international humanitarian law (IHL) engendered by their activities. This raises the tension between the alleged criminality of the PMC and the legitimacy that is claimed for the industry, which is neatly revealed by juxtaposing the positions of the two former UN Special Rapporteurs for the Use of Mercenaries.

The chapter then steps back to situate the PMC within its historical context. First, the origins of the PMC are identified in Watchguard International before the chapter moves to consider the historical pressures that drove the privatisation of military services. Contemporary trends that are likely to secure the future of the industry are then highlighted to suggest a smooth continuum of development for the PMC industry. The main contribution of this chapter lies in its proposed typology for the private military industry that seeks to overcome some of the issues raised by definitions and classifications. An overview of the existing typologies shows that these fail to recognise the departure from the *civilian* nature of the corporation signalled by, and an attribute of, the PMC. Thus, the revised typology is proposed to emphasise the specific *military* characteristics of the PMC, as defined by their provision of organised violence and the direct nature of their involvement within armed hostilities by adapting the IHL principle of distinction. This emphasis distinguishes the PMC as a fundamentally different type of corporation, whose activities raise particular and elevated risks that justify greater oversight and closer regulation because of the grave nature of potential harm it can cause.

II. A CONTEMPORARY OVERVIEW OF THE MODERN PRIVATE MILITARY COMPANY

The official end to the Iraq War offers a useful demarcation point because it was military contracting in the Iraq and Afghanistan conflicts that spurred the enormous growth of the PMC industry and it was their controversial activity in these conflicts which sparked criticism, attracted outrage and illustrated the impunity that PMCs and their contractors enjoy in some situations of armed conflict and instability.[1] It is particularly telling that President Barack Obama, speaking at Fort Bragg on 15 December 2011 to mark the official end of Iraq War said:

> Nearly forty-five hundred Americans made the ultimate sacrifice … We also know that these numbers don't tell the full story of the Iraq War, not even close. *Our civilians have represented our country with skill and bravery*. Our troops have served tour after tour of duty with precious little dwell time in between. Our guard and reserve units stepped up with unprecedented service.[2]

As with most speeches, the points of interest lie in what is not said, and I want to raise three brief points. The first relates to the invisibility of PMC contractors, as indicated by their general exclusion from official casualty figures as compiled data encompass only the causalities suffered by military personnel.[3] This closely relates to the second point which is that the contribution of contractors in Iraq, and presumably extended to other contexts as well, is similarly masked. Precise figures are notoriously difficult to obtain, especially since the criteria upon which they are reached

[1] Human Rights First, 'Private Security Contractors at War: Ending the Culture of Impunity' www.humanrightsfirst.org/wp-content/uploads/pdf/08115-usls-psc-final.pdf.

[2] BBC, 'US Flag Ceremony Ends War in Iraq' *BBC* (15 December 2011) www.bbc.co.uk/news/world-us-canada-161921051. Emphasis added.

[3] BBC, 'Iraq War in Figures' *BBC* (14 December 2011) www.bbc.co.uk/news/world-middle-east-11107739. Figures for contractor casualties are harder to track down as there is no official record and many PMCs are reluctant to provide such information. An indication is given by organisations such as Iraq Body Count and iCasualties, but unlike the military they do not have access to complete records and have access and resource limitations. According to figures of the United States Department of Labor, over 1000 contractors have died and more than 12, 000 have been injured between 2003 and 2007 in Iraq alone: J Gómez del Prado, 'Report of the Working Group on the Use of Mercenaries as a Means of Violating Human Rights and Impeding the Exercise of the Right of People to Self-Determination' (UNHRC, 2008) A/HRC/7/7 paras 42–43. An official, albeit incomplete, compilation of civilian casualties is kept through claims made under the Defense Base Act; summary reports can be found at: www.dol.gov/owcp/dlhwc/lsdbareports.htm.

vary but it can, however, be confidently asserted that contractor numbers overtook those of their military personnel counterparts in 2007 in Iraq.[4] The presence of military contractors in theatre has the effect of artificially suppressing the statistics on the size of the military involvement. Their support also enables the military to disproportionately weigh their personnel towards the 'tip-of-the-spear' activities, allowing them to focus upon the combat arms because military contractors can fulfil backstage supporting roles. The combined effect allows for a larger and more focused military presence than is reported in the official figures, leading to the erosion of democratic control and oversight because the size and characteristics of the overall military presence are obscured.[5] The third point illuminated in Barack Obama's speech is that when PMC contractors are mentioned, they are shrouded in ambiguity. The brief mention of civilians fails to conjure the images of civilian intelligence operators participating in the torture at Abu Ghraib,[6] and of heavily armed civilian contractors firing upon and massacring Iraqi civilians, which occurred with alarming regularity from released contact reports and most visibly at Nisour Square,[7] that form a core part of the picture of PMC operations in that conflict.

A final point should be stressed in relation to the official end of the Iraq War and the role played by PMCs. The central issue concerns immunity, a practice which was examined in greater depth in chapter one, for US troops and contractors. These are usually negotiated under a Status of Forces Agreement (SOFA),[8] and it was the refusal of Iraqi authorities to grant immunity from domestic law to remaining US troops after the end of 2011 (when the existing SOFA terminated) that ultimately precipitated the US withdrawal.[9] While the grant of immunity under agreed SOFA

[4] C Miller, 'Contractors Outnumber Troops in Iraq' *Los Angeles Times* (4 July 2007) http://articles.latimes.com/2007/jul/04/nation/na-private4.

[5] See eg N Rosemann, 'The Privatization of Human Rights Violations—Business' Impunity or Corporate Responsibility? The Case of Human Rights Abuses and Torture in Iraq' (2005) 5 *Non-State Actors and International Law* 77, 83–84.

[6] P Chatterjee, 'Outsourcing Intelligence in Iraq: A CorpWatch Report on L-3/Titan' (CorpWatch 2008) www.corpwatch.org/article.php?id=15253; 'Abu Ghraib Inmates Sue US Firms' *BBC* (1 July 2008) http://news.bbc.co.uk/1/hi/world/americas/7482617.stm.

[7] See section below on indiscriminate and disproportionate use of force in Iraq. An overview of the Nisour Square incident can be found in J Glanz and A Rubin, 'From Errand to Fatal Shot to Hail of Fire to 17 Deaths' *New York Times* (3 October 2007) www.nytimes.com/2007/10/03/world/middleeast/03firefight.html?scp=3&sq=nisour%20square%20blackwater&st=Search.

[8] See generally 'Status of the Forces Agreement' *New York Times* (21 October 2011) http://topics.nytimes.com/top/news/international/countriesandterritories/iraq/status-of-forces-agreement/index.html?scp=8&sq=Nouri%20al-Maliki%20immunity&st=cse. It should be noted that immunity from Iraqi domestic law is not intended to create a situation of impunity. Rather, US laws are considered to apply under US jurisdiction.

[9] T Arango and M Schmidt, 'Iraqis Say No to Immunity for Remaining American Troops' *New York Times* (4 October 2011) www.nytimes.com/2011/10/05/world/middleeast/iraqis-say-no-to-immunity-for-remaining-american-troops.html?_r=1&scp=1&sq=Nouri%20al-Maliki%20immunity&st=cse1; see also P van Buren, 'Immunity: Disastrous Decisions in

terms for foreign troops is by no means extraordinary, it was arguably the prior conduct and the consequent reputation of PMC contractors that scuppered the prospects for renewed SOFA immunity, as Tim Arango and Michael Schmidt report:

> Immunity strikes a deep nerve among ordinary Iraqis because it would mean that American troops could not be prosecuted in Iraq. The issue evokes some of the worst horrors of the war here, from the Abu Ghraib prison scandal to the killing of civilians by Blackwater mercenaries … For Iraqis, [immunity] evoked memories of mercenaries operating with impunity and sometimes killing civilians.[10]

In this context, it may be incongruent for the US to continue pursuing immunity protections for the contractors who will remain in Iraq,[11] especially since it was the actions of Blackwater contractors at Nisour Square that strengthened Iraqi insistence to end legal immunity in the first place.[12] Terry Gill and Dieter Fleck have noted that although PMC contractors are often not regulated by SOFAs, it is often in the interest of the relevant States to put their regulation on such terms, and that this is especially relevant outside the context of armed conflict since PMC contractors will no longer possess the special status of persons accompanying the armed forces.[13] But whether legal immunity for PMC contractors is really required for their continued enjoyment of impunity is another question:

> American security contractors, thousands of whom are flooding into the country to support an expanded State Department mission, are technically subject to Iraqi law, but none have ever been held criminally liable in Iraq. Even now, the United States government occasionally, and secretly, removes contractors from the country when they are accused of crimes.[14]

The point is that, even without de jure immunity, contractors are accorded broad de facto immunity. It is important to note that while the highly-touted Fitzsimmons conviction under domestic Iraqi law suggests that this broad claim is not strictly accurate,[15] the conviction only signaled a narrow category of exception for violence perpetrated *between contractors*.

2007 Return to Haunt 2012' *Huffington Post* (4 November 2011) www.huffingtonpost.com/peter-van-buren/blackwater-shootings-2007_b_1066135.html; T Gill and D Fleck (eds), *The Handbook of the International Law of Military Operations* (Oxford University Press, 2011) 102–04.

[10] Arango and Schmidt, 'Iraqis Say No to Immunity for Remaining American Troops' (n 9).

[11] E Slavin, 'U.S. Pursuing Legal Protections for Contractors Still in Iraq' *Stars and Stripes* (14 December 2011) www.stripes.com/news/u-s-pursuing-legal-protections-for-contractors-still-in-iraq-1.163465.

[12] J Risen, 'End of Immunity Worries U.S. Contractors in Iraq' *New York Times* (1 December 2008) www.nytimes.com/2008/12/01/world/middleeast/01contractors.html.

[13] Gill and Fleck, *The Handbook of the International Law of Military Operations* (n 9) 492–93.

[14] Arango and Schmidt (n 9).

[15] Contractor immunity in Iraq lapsed on 1 January 2009. M Schmidt, 'Immunity Gone, Contractor in Iraq Sentenced to Prison' *New York Times* (28 February 2011) www.nytimes.com/2011/03/01/world/middleeast/01iraq.html?scp=6&sq=SOFA%20iraq&st=cse.

Iraqi criminal law has yet to operate against PMC impunity in a broader sense to account for violence perpetrated against local civilians.

Indeed, Nils Rosemann, Desk Officer for Human Security and Business at the Swiss Federal Department of Foreign Affairs responsible for spearheading the Montreux Document and the International Code of Conduct discussed in chapter six, has argued in 2005 in relation to the increasing privatisation of military services in the form of PMCs, 'that impunity is another *intended goal* by the private engagement in Iraq'.[16] Although the argument he presents is both a narrower and weaker version of the one that is being developed here, he illustrates the ways in which impunity was sought and secured through the law by drawing an analogy with Guantanamo Bay:

> In order to torture in Guantanamo Bay, the U.S. tried to create a non-legal, non-territorial free zone of international law. By introducing a formerly unknown type of unlawful combatant, the U.S. is claiming that International Humanitarian Law which protects prisoners of war, is not applicable … With Guantanamo as a rehearsal there came another legal loophole this time in Iraq. There, detainees are either members of the armed force of the conflicting party or criminals or criminalised civilians, to whom [IHL] is applicable. *In order to escape the framework of international law again, certain duties are shifted to military and security corporations such as governing and protecting prisons as well as the interrogations.* In this way, private companies became able to do things government forces found unacceptable and deniable, such as torture.[17]

The ascription of *intent* to circumvent the law inherent in Rosemann's view may be difficult to sustain as evidence of an overt and explicit policy may be lacking and is at any rate unavailable. There are, however, serious grounds to support a diluted form of his assertion: that the use of PMCs has *resulted* in the circumvention of the law which gives rise to allegations of impunity for egregious abuses. Indeed, it should be noted that the International Court of Justice (ICJ) recognised as 'a well-established rule of a customary nature … [that] a party to an armed conflict shall be responsible for all acts by persons forming part of its armed forces'.[18] Yet, this default position of State responsibility may neither apply directly nor uniformly to the activities of PMCs because of their separate status from State armed forces. States are able to circumvent this rule by contracting PMCs, rather than deploying their own armed forces, thereby disconnecting this

[16] Rosemann, 'The Privatization of Human Rights Violations' (n 5) 85. Emphasis added.

[17] ibid. Emphasis added.

[18] *Armed Activities* [2005] ICJ 908, 2005 ICJ Rep 168 [214]; the question of State responsibility has been the subject of lively debate; see H Tonkin, *State Control Over Private Military and Security Companies in Armed Conflict* (Cambridge University Press, 2011); O de Schutter, 'The Responsibility of States' in S Chesterman and A Fisher (eds), *Private Security, Public Order* (Oxford University Press, 2009); C Lehnardt, 'Private Military Companies and State Responsibility' in S Chesterman and C Lehnardt (eds), *From Mercenaries to Market: The Rise and Regulation of Private Military Companies* (Oxford University Press, 2007).

a priori assumption of State responsibility. As such, the use of PMCs by States to fulfil military roles should operate as a rebuttable presumption that the rules of State responsibility have been subverted. This presumption can be overturned, for example, by the treatment of PMCs as forming part of the armed forces of the State to avert the potential impunity for their actions or by other forms of analogous action that reconnect the State's responsibility for PMC activities.

III. IMPUNITY FOR PRIVATE MILITARY COMPANY INVOLVEMENT IN ATROCITIES

In order to justify the point of departure of this book, that the impunity enjoyed by the PMC and its contractors is a legal *creation*, rather than merely a legal *effect*, it is necessary to provide an overview of recent work done in this area.[19] In 2000, PMC industry lobbyist Doug Brooks pronounced that 'what worries the international community enough to shy away from utilizing PMCs is the *potential* harm that they do, *not any particular past incident*'.[20] While this claim may not even have been justifiable when it was made, ensuing events have certainly overtaken Brooks, who has since dropped this claim.[21] The catalogue of alleged 'past incidents' is now both long and varied, such that I will provide only three of the more prominent examples that have received extensive media coverage and for which documentation is more readily available.[22] Within the examples given, there is no attempt here to provide a systematic catalogue of human rights abuses perpetrated either by the highlighted PMC or within the operational context under consideration. Instead, reporting on the transgressions of the PMC industry is left to others, and the examples given

[19] But see generally J Glanz and A Lehren, 'Growing Use of Contractors Added to Iraq War's Chaos—Iraq War Logs—WikiLeaks Documents' *New York Times* (23 October 2010) www.nytimes.com/2010/10/24/world/middleeast/24contractors.html.

[20] D Brooks, 'Messiahs or Mercenaries? The Future of International Private Military Services' (2000) 7 *International Peacekeeping* 129, 135. Emphasis original; he continues to claim that 'there are remarkably few examples of PMCs abusing their authority … PMCs still fear legal action from their home states … and, thus far, have proven to be more observant of international laws of war and human rights than the forces they have faced in combat': ibid 143, note 13.

[21] D Brooks and J Shevlin, 'Reconsidering Battlefield Contractors' (2005) 6 *Georgetown Journal of International Affairs* 103.

[22] Substantiating claims of PMC abuse can be particularly challenging owing to their private corporate status which provides a claim to confidentiality. There are strong disincentives for whistleblowing since they, rather than the alleged offenders, are the ones to be punished by the PMC. This was the fate of Ben Johnston and Kathryn Bolkovac who blew the whistle in the DynCorp sex-trafficking scandal: see L Wayne, 'America's For-Profit Secret Army' *New York Times* (13 October 2002) www.nytimes.com/2002/10/13/business/america-s-for-profit-secret-army.html.

here are only intended to provide an indication of PMCs being repeatedly embroiled in abuses without adverse consequences.

It is particularly unfortunate to note that the issues of unaccountability continue to pervade the industry. Many authors continue to provide examples of PMC contractors falling between the gaps of the law,[23] despite many of these issues being brought to prominence almost a decade earlier.[24] Furthermore, all the examples concern allegations of serious, and seemingly systematic, misconduct that potentially amount to international crimes.[25] This makes the persistent failure to hold the PMC and its contractors accountable and the recidivism of the private military industry in these regards particularly striking. The following three sections sketch examples of criminal PMC behaviour, and the legal cases arising from the first two examples are analysed in greater depth in chapter five.[26]

A. Perpetration and Collusion in Torture: Abu Ghraib Prison

The prisoner abuse scandal at Abu Ghraib has been well publicised after the media broke the story in 2004. Pratap Chatterjee has charted the background of contractor involvement in the scandal,[27] and the official US Army investigation found that 'US civilian contract personnel (Titan Corporation, CACI, etc…) … and local contractors do not appear to be

[23] L Dickinson, *Outsourcing War and Peace: Preserving Public Values in a World of Privatized Foreign Affairs* (Yale University Press, 2011) 40–68. Most of the contributions from the PRIV-WAR project address various aspects of PMC accountability: see F Francioni and N Ronzitti (eds), *War by Contract: Human Rights, Humanitarian Law, and Private Contractors* (Oxford University Press, 2011); and F Ntoubandi, 'South Africa: The Regulatory Context of Private Military and Security Services' in C Bakker and M Sossai (eds), *Multilevel Regulation of Military and Security Contractors: The Interplay Between International, European and Domestic Norms* (Hart Publishing, 2012).

[24] PW Singer's work is considered to be the seminal analysis in the area: PW Singer, *Corporate Warriors: The Rise of the Privatized Military Industry* (Cornell University Press, 2004); United Kingdom Foreign and Commonwealth Office, *Private Military Companies: Options for Regulation* Green Paper (2001–02, HC 577); House of Commons Foreign Affairs Committee, *Private Military Companies* (2001–02, HC 922).

[25] The two former examples could classify, inter alia, as war crimes: O Quirico, 'The Criminal Responsibility of Private Military and Security Company Personnel under International Humanitarian Law' in Francioni and Ronzitti (eds), *War by Contract: Human Rights, Humanitarian Law, and Private Contractors* (n 23) 431.

[26] The third example concerning DynCorp in Bosnia was just one episode of Dyncorp's sex-trafficking and prostitution ring activities, continuing for at least a decade: D Isenberg, 'It's Déjà Vu for DynCorp All Over Again' *The Huffington Post* (6 December 2010) www.huffingtonpost.com/david-isenberg/its-dj-vu-for-dyncorp-all_b_792394.html. The notion of passive impunity may account for the lack of any legal action taken against either DynCorp or its contractors involved with sex-trafficking. Indeed, the only cases arising from Bosnia were those brought by the whistleblowers for wrongful termination of employment.

[27] Chatterjee, 'Outsourcing Intelligence in Iraq' (n 6).

properly supervised within the detention facility at Abu Ghraib'.[28] A subsequent official report raised allegations that 'contractor personnel were "supervising" government personnel',[29] indicating the confusion between the purportedly segregated roles played by soldiers and contractors at the prison that implicated contractor involvement at various levels. The Fay Report also underlined the jurisdictional discrepancy between soldiers and contractors operating at Abu Ghraib: 'Some of the employees at Abu Ghraib were not Department of Defense (DoD) contractor employees. Contractor employees under non-DoD contracts may not be subject to the Military Extraterritorial Jurisdiction Act' (MEJA).[30] As MEJA initially covered only DoD contractors,[31] this meant that PMC contractors were somewhat arbitrarily subjected to MEJA jurisdiction on the basis of its contract.

Aside from this jurisdictional imbalance, there are indications that human rights abuse allegations, and indeed pending law suits, fail to signal opprobrium against the companies or their conduct. A recurring theme from this set of examples is that lucrative contracts are renewed or awarded to PMCs even in the direct aftermath of their engagement in publicised atrocities, and CACI and Titan are no exception. A contemporary report noted that:

> Despite demands by human rights groups in the US that the two companies be barred from further contracts in Iraq ... CACI International has been awarded a $16 million renewal of its contract. Titan, meanwhile, has been awarded a new contract worth $164m.[32]

Finally, *Saleh v Titan*, considered in greater depth in chapter five, underscores PMC impunity in the Abu Ghraib saga. The majority decision of the Court of Appeals for the District of Columbia, which dismissed all claims against Titan/L-3 and CACI, stands because the US Supreme Court denied the plaintiff's petition in June 2011.[33] This decision stands in

[28] A Taguba, '"Taguba Report": Article 15-6 Investigation of the 800th Military Police Brigade' (2004) 26.

[29] G Fay, 'Fay Report: AR 15-6 Investigation of the Abu Ghraib Detention Facility and 205th Military Intelligence Brigade' (2004) 51.

[30] ibid 50.

[31] Public Law 106–523, s 3267(1). This Act was subsequently broadened in 2004 to remove the DoD nexus requirement, but crucially only 'to the extent such employment relates to supporting the mission of the Department of Defense'. The perhaps tenuous nexus between the Blackwater contractors working for the US State Department and the MEJA requirement to support the DoD mission may prove to be a point raised on appeal: J Stewart and S Gray, 'The Blackwater Trial: Part 2—Legal Issues' http://justsecurity.org/16807/blackwater-trial-part-2-legal-issues/. For the latest amendment drive, see C Doyle, 'Civilian Extraterritorial Jurisdiction Act: Federal Contractor Criminal Liability Overseas' www.fas.org/sgp/crs/misc/R42358.pdf.

[32] P Beaumont, 'Abu Ghraib Abuse Firms Are Rewarded' *The Guardian* (16 January 2005) www.theguardian.com/world/2005/jan/16/usa.iraq.

[33] For an overview, see Center for Constitutional Rights, 'Saleh et Al' http://ccrjustice.org/Saleh-v-Titan.

stark juxtaposition, recognised by the Court of Appeals for the DC Circuit itself, that while American servicemen have already been subjected to and convicted by criminal court martial in conjunction to their roles at Abu Ghraib, no criminal charges were made against the contractors *despite* the federal government possessing jurisdiction to do so.[34] A civil suit brought by the victims against also failed, but on points of jurisdiction rather than on lack of substantive merit.[35] The recent rejection of a sister case, the last opportunity for the victims to secure compensation, would mean that the evidence of CACI's involvement in the torture at Abu Ghraib would never be considered in open court.[36] As chapter five suggests, these cases were dismissed for legal technicalities at the expense of considering their substantive merits.

An interesting postscript indicating industry recidivism with regard to acts of torture is provided by the collusion of the PMC industry in the CIA extraordinary rendition programme whereby terrorist suspects are flown to 'black sites' where more rigorous interrogation methods, often amounting to torture, could take place.[37]

B. Indiscriminate and Disproportionate Use of Force: Iraq

The second example concerns the disproportionate and unprovoked use of force by PMC contractors in predominantly civilian areas and often unprovoked in Iraq.[38] The most high-profile incident is the Nisour Square massacre in September 2007, where Blackwater contractors killed 17 Iraqi civilians, and wounded many more.

[34] *Saleh v Titan* (2009) 580 F3d 1 (United States Court of Appeals for the DC Circuit) 2.

[35] *Al-Shimari v CACI* (2009) 657 FSupp2d 700 (US District Court for the Eastern District of Virginia, Alexandria Division) 728.

[36] K Hawkins, 'CACI's Forgotten Role in Abu Ghraib (I)' *Huffington Post* (29 August 2013) www.huffingtonpost.com/katherine-hawkins/cacis-forgotten-role-in-a_b_3830280.html; K Hawkins, 'CACI's Forgotten Role in Abu Ghraib (II)' *Huffington Post* (9 September 2013) www.huffingtonpost.com/katherine-hawkins/cacis-forgotten-role-in-a_1_b_3847081.html.

[37] Although Titan/L-3 and CACI were not directly implicated, the involvement of other PMC companies indicates the recalcitrant nature of the industry more broadly: I Cobain and B Quinn, 'How US Firms Profited from Torture Flights' *The Guardian* (31 August 2011) www.guardian.co.uk/world/2011/aug/31/us-firms-torture-flights-rendition; a large cache of documents concerning these operations is due to be released: P Chatterjee, 'CIA "Rendition" Contractors Data Cache To Be Released' (*Corp*, 22 May 2012) www.corpwatch.org/article.php?id=15730. To illustrate the multi-faceted activity engaged in by PMCs, Computer Sciences Corporation, which is heavily implicated in the rendition programme, was also found to be 'one of the NHS's worst-performing IT contractors': B Quinn, 'Computer Sciences Corporation Could Retain £1bn in Health Contracts' *The Guardian* (6 March 2012) www.guardian.co.uk/society/2012/mar/06/computer-sciences-corporation-retain-health-contracts.

[38] Human Rights First, 'Private Security Contractors at War' (n 1) 1–3, 6–9. This is addressed in greater detail in ch 5.

It is easy to dismiss the event as a solitary aberration that was overexposed by the media because it is rarely contextualised. Instead, Nisour Square should be viewed as being embedded within a repetitive and consistent operational style within a culture of impunity.[39] In the period between January 2005 and December 2007, there are 4448 pages of US State Department escalation of force reports by private contractors, giving an indication as to the bare minimum number of such incidents.[40] Two preceding Blackwater incidents suggest that the approach adopted at Nisour Square may have been condoned and routine and the lack of subsequent action constituted a form of default impunity. In February 2005, Blackwater contractors were not punished for issuing false statements in the aftermath of an incident where over 70 bullets were unjustifiably fired at an Iraqi's car because the official did not want to lower the morale of the contractors.[41] In May 2007, Blackwater contractors were involved in the fatal shooting of an Iraqi driver, and in a separate incident, triggered a furious battle in an Iraqi town leading to reports of a number of deaths.[42] During another incident in September, just before the Nisour Square massacre, the *Albazzaz* case records another fatal contact at Watahba Square, also in Baghdad.[43] Situated within this type of operational record, Blackwater's conduct at Nisour Square is hardly surprising.

The *Paul Slough* case is often cited to allay the charges of impunity for the Nisour incident because it resulted in criminal convictions in the US Federal District Court after a drawn-out legal saga.[44] The following excerpt, taken from *Paul Slough* illustrates both the operational style and the distinctly military nature of these formally corporate activities:

> The defendants … were security guards employed by Blackwater Worldwide ('Blackwater'), a private company that provided security services to U.S. government employees operating in Iraq … On September 16, 2007, the defendants were part of a Blackwater Tactical Support Team answering to the call sign

[39] The immunity provided by CPA Order 17 will be considered in greater detail in ch 3.

[40] On file with the author. Escalation of force reports record instances where force is used (usually involving shots fired). These reports are likely to grossly underestimate the real number of incidents; contacts are not always recorded and those that are may be lodged with other agencies or fall within the jurisdiction of other States: Human Rights First (n 1) 9–14.

[41] The consequence of the engagement is not documented since the contractors vacated the scene; see M Kelley, 'Falsehoods in Iraq Shooting Unpunished' *USA Today* (2 April 2009) www.usatoday.com/news/world/iraq/2009-04-01-blackwater_N.htm.

[42] S Fainaru and S al-Izzi, 'U.S. Security Contractors Open Fire in Baghdad' *Washington Post* (27 May 2007) www.washingtonpost.com/wp-dyn/content/article/2007/05/26/AR2007052601394.html.

[43] *In re XE Services* (2009) 655 FSupp2d 569 (US District Court Eastern District of Virginia, Alexandria Division).

[44] *US v Paul Slough* [2009] US District Court for the District of Columbia Criminal Action No.: 08-0360, 677 FSupp2d 122; M Apuzzo, 'Former Blackwater Guards Convicted in Iraq Shooting' *The New York Times* (22 October 2014) www.nytimes.com/2014/10/23/us/blackwater-verdict.html.

> 'Raven 23,' whose function was to provide *back-up fire support* for other Blackwater personal security details operating in Baghdad. The Raven 23 convoy consisted of four vehicles … *The defendants were armed with machine guns, grenade launchers, rifles and pistols.*
>
> Shortly before noon on September 16, 2007, Raven 23 received a message that a vehicle-borne improvised explosive device ('VBIED') had detonated in the vicinity of a compound in which U.S. officials were meeting with Iraqi officials. The Raven 23 convoy subsequently took up positions in [Nisour] Square, a traffic circle located just outside the International Zone in downtown Baghdad, to secure an evacuation route for the American officials and the Blackwater team providing their security … Soon after the Raven 23 vehicles entered the traffic circle, *a shooting incident* erupted, during which *the defendants allegedly shot and killed fourteen persons and wounded twenty others* … The government contends that the dead and wounded were unarmed civilians who were the victims of unprovoked violence by the defendants. The defendants maintain that they came under attack by insurgents and that their actions constituted a legitimate response to a mortal threat.[45]

Judge Urbina subsequently dismissed the indictment against all of the defendants on the basis of tainted evidence, as the compelled statements violated the Fifth Amendment protection against self-incrimination under *Garrity*.[46] From one perspective, the case appears to be a straightforward affirmation of constitutional rights on its face, but the main legal flaw arose out of an inevitable paradox which essentially immunised the Blackwater personnel from legal suit. This was obvious to the lawyers involved within the case at the time, who realised that the

> issue was that the guards, as government contractors, were obligated to give an immediate report of what they had done, but the Constitution prevents the government from requiring a defendant to testify against himself, so those statements could not be used in a prosecution.[47]

This meant that much of the evidence collected in the direct aftermath of the incident could not be used in the subsequent case.

Investigators also had a sense that their case was being undermined by the State Department itself, with Matt Apuzzo reporting that its agents 'had gathered up shell casings, trying to clean up the scene to protect Blackwater', and in particular one agent recalled in court testimony that other State Department officials had said, 'We've got enough to get these

[45] *US v Paul Slough* (n 44).

[46] *Garrity v New Jersey* (1967) 385 US 493 (US Supreme Court).

[47] M Wald, 'U.S. Lawyers Knew about Legal Pitfalls in Blackwater Case' *New York Times* (2 January 2010) www.nytimes.com/2010/01/02/us/02legal.html?_r=4&ref=blackwater_usa.

guys off now'.[48] When this allegation is combined with the State Department according limited immunity in exchange for statements about the shooting,[49] the picture suggests official attempts at extending both de jure and de facto impunity for Blackwater over this incident.

The Court of Appeals for the District of Columbia has overturned Judge Urbina's judgment, finding that the question of tainted evidence was not treated with appropriate levels of differentiation.[50] As the US Supreme Court refused to intervene,[51] this led to the case being remanded back to the District Court for retrial. Yet, because of the tainted evidence in relation to the team's sniper, Nicholas A Slatten, his case was not reinstated because the government itself moved to dismiss the indictment without prejudice to possible later reindictment.[52] While prosecutors had intended to renew charges against Slatten with untainted evidence, they had missed the deadline for the five-year statute-of-limitations for manslaughter.[53] This left the prosecutors with the option of charging for first-degree murder, which has no statute-of-limitations but higher burdens of proof, accounting for the apparent aberration in the jury verdict where Slatten was convicted of murder, while the other three members of the team were convicted instead for voluntary manslaughter.[54]

This detail is necessary to suggest that the murder charge was a quirk of circumstance rather than prosecutorial strategy; that the multiple setbacks that the case experienced had scuppered the prospect for more serious charges to succeed as evidenced by the default charges for manslaughter; and that the prosecution may have been conservative with its charges. Indeed, while the prosecutors may bear some of the blame for letting the statute-of-limitations elapse in relation to Slatten, the lengthy and unpredictable nature of the case itself seems to predispose it towards this conclusion. And if there is substance behind the reports that the investigation was sabotaged, the prosecution may have had little choice other than to charge conservatively to maintain any prospect for success: this is even more so if some of their more compelling evidence had to be disregarded because it had been procedurally tainted. In other words, the convoluted nature of this legal saga may have diluted the ultimate outcome, such that

[48] M Apuzzo, 'Trying to Salvage Remains of Blackwater Case' *The New York Times* (11 May 2014) www.nytimes.com/2014/05/12/us/trying-to-salvage-remains-of-blackwater-case.html.

[49] ibid.

[50] *US v Paul Slough* [2011] US Court of Appeals for the District of Columbia No. 10-3006, 641 F3d 544.

[51] *Paul Slough v US* [2012] US Supreme Court 11-591, 132 SCt 2710.

[52] *US v Paul Slough* (n 50).

[53] Apuzzo, 'Trying to Salvage Remains of Blackwater Case' (n 48).

[54] M Apuzzo, 'Blackwater Jurors Urged to Give Iraqis Justice' *The New York Times* (27 August 2014) www.nytimes.com/2014/08/28/us/in-closing-blackwater-prosecutor-says-us-court-levels-the-playing-field.html. The fifth member of the team had pleaded guilty and played the role of the star witness.

the convictions that eventuated were relatively light considering the gravity of the substantive allegations made against the conduct of the Blackwater contractors.

The prospect for passive impunity, even in face of the successful convictions, is clear not least in the propensity for interpretive denial. The gruesome consequences at Nisour Square were arguably unprovoked, according to the admission of Jeremy P Ridgeway, a member of that the Blackwater convoy who pleaded guilty to voluntary manslaughter:

> [A]t least six members of the Raven 23 convoy, … opened fire with *automatic weapons and grenade launchers on unarmed civilians* located in and around [Nisour] Square in central Baghdad, killing at least fourteen people, wounding at least twenty people, and assaulting but not injuring at least eighteen others. *None of these victims was an insurgent*, and many were shot while inside of civilian vehicles that were attempting to flee from the Raven 23 convoy. *One victim was shot in his chest, while standing in the street with his hands up.*[55]

Given such a factual admission by a member of the team involved in the incident, the manslaughter charges appear incongruent to the actions, and fail to reflect their gravity. Indeed, as these facts indicate unprovoked and grossly disproportionate use of force, even convictions of murder would appear to be inadequate. The relative lack of proportionality between the actions and the conviction indicate the presence of passive impunity.

Indeed, while these convictions have been lauded as having achieved accountability at Nisour Square,[56] there are a several reasons why this might be inadequate. First, the Nisour Square incident is only one of a multitude of recorded and unrecorded incidents involving PMCs which never made it to the courts (and which were often never investigated), and one of scores of shootings that directly involve Blackwater.[57] The high profile of the Nisour Square incident shrouds all of PMCs and contractors involved in the other incidents with impunity. Second, the shooting had little adverse effect on Blackwater, as the US State Department renewed the Blackwater contract seven months after Nisour Square, and the US government remains dependent upon its contractors despite not being able to manage them effectively.[58] Third, Jeremy Scahill draws attention to the fact that

> Just as with the systematic torture at Abu Ghraib, it is only the low level foot-soldiers of Blackwater that are being held accountable. [Erik] Prince and other

[55] *US v Jeremy P Ridgeway (Factual Proffer in Support of Guilty Plea)* (US District Court for the District of Columbia) [4]. Emphasis added.

[56] New York Times Editorial Board, 'A Verdict on Blackwater' *The New York Times* (22 October 2014) www.nytimes.com/2014/10/23/opinion/a-verdict-on-blackwater.html.

[57] Apuzzo, 'Former Blackwater Guards Convicted in Iraq Shooting' (n 44).

[58] New York Times Editorial Board, 'A Verdict on Blackwater' (n 56); 'Blackwater's Impunity' *The New York Times* (16 May 2008) www.nytimes.com/2008/05/16/opinion/16fri2.html.

> top Blackwater executives continue to reap profits from the mercenary and private intelligence industries.[59]

Scahill summarises poignantly:

> While the Blackwater verdict is an important and rare moment of accountability in an overwhelmingly unaccountable private war industry, it does not erase the fact that those in power—the CEOs, the senior officials, the war profiteers—walk freely and will likely do so for the rest of their lives.[60]

Unfortunately, these convictions are singular exceptions of retrospective accountability that fail to alter the system through which such atrocities are perpetrated. In other words, arraigning a handful of PMC contractors after the fact through an unpredictable and untested legal system cannot be considered to compensate for developing stricter management and accountability.[61] That this accountability stopped at the very lowest levels, and failed to hold those who establish, perpetuate and profit from the systems within which PMC contractors work hints at scapegoating. Indeed, these verdicts may prove to be a distraction to reforming the regulatory and oversight structures within which the PMC operates.

Finally, it should be noted that the convictions have not drawn a clear line under these cases. Because novel legal issues have been raised, the *Blackwater* case is expected to go through appellate courts for at least another year. In particular, the legalistic matter of whether the Justice Department had the jurisdiction to bring the case could unravel the entire case.[62] It is quite possible that, despite the apparent success in securing the convictions of these former Blackwater contractors for an egregious atrocity, these may subsequently be overturned through jurisdictional hair-splitting.[63] Thus, David Isenberg's conclusion, written in 2007, still resonates:

> PMC personnel in Iraq have shot their weapons in hundreds of incidents but to date not a single contractor has been prosecuted. Either every single use of force

[59] J Scahill, 'Blackwater Founder Remains Free and Rich While His Former Employees Go Down on Murder Charges' *The Intercept* (22 October 2014) https://firstlook.org/theintercept/2014/10/22/blackwater-guilty-verdicts/4.

[60] ibid.

[61] In this light, the claim by the *New York Times* Editorial Board is worrying: 'Following the Blackwater debacle, there has been a sensible international response to the problem. More than 600 private security contractors have pledged to abide by a code of conduct that in theory should encourage more professional, ethical behavior': The New York Times Editorial Board (n 56). Academi, the successor corporate entity of Blackwater, is a member of both the International Stability Operations Association and the International Code of Conduct (to which the article refers). This fundamentally questions whether this is a 'sensible international response'.

[62] Apuzzo (n 44).

[63] The question of Blackwater's contract with the US State Department could be considered as supporting the DoD mission, as required by the extended version of MEJA, was considered as a question of fact for the jury. This led to the whole trial proceeding despite lingering uncertainty as to whether the court had jurisdiction over the case at all. Stewart and Gray, 'The Blackwater Trial: Part 2—Legal Issues' (n 31).

has been beyond reproach or someone is looking the other way. Effective public accountability, despite the increase in the number of new laws and regulations on the books that at least theoretically apply to PMCs, is still lacking.[64]

C. Sex-Trafficking and Prostitution Rings: Bosnia

The third example is taken from before the Iraq conflict to show that PMC misconduct is neither temporally nor geographically confined. DynCorp's involvement with sex-trafficking in the Balkans was revealed by whistleblowers, who were subsequently fired for so doing.[65] Hollywood has since taken over, and the film *The Whistleblower* provides a fictionalised plight of Kathryn Bolkovac's character in the fiasco, but she has also documented the experience.[66]

DynCorp was contracted to provide logistical support by the Stabilisation Force (SFOR) in Bosnia, and its contractors were found by Human Rights Watch to have 'engaged in trafficking-related activities. Evidence indicated that some civilian contractors employed on U.S. military SFOR bases in Bosnia and Herzegovina *engaged in the purchase of women and girls*'.[67] DynCorp contractors enjoyed de facto impunity since none of the contractors implicated in trafficking-activities faced prosecution in the US, a fact confirmed by both the US Department of Justice Criminal Division and DynCorp itself.[68] David Isenberg reports of DynCorp's recidivism with regard to sexual slavery:

> [I]n October 2004 it was revealed that DynCorp contract workers operating at Tolemaida Air Base in Colombia distributed a video in which they could be observed sexually violating underage girls from the town of Melgar ... Nonetheless, the Lawyers' Collective of Colombia has not learned of any criminal investigation undertaken in relation to these acts involving minors.[69]

Continuing this trend, DynCorp was subsequently embroiled within yet another sexual slavery and child prostitution scandal, this time in relation

[64] D Isenberg, 'A Government in Search of Cover: Private Military Companies in Iraq' in Chesterman and Lehnardt (eds), *From Mercenaries to Market* (n 18) 93.

[65] Wayne, 'America's For-Profit Secret Army' (n 22). While Bolkovac won a wrongful termination case, she remains blacklisted: Isenberg, 'It's Déjà Vu for DynCorp All Over Again' (n 26); See also Human Rights Watch, 'Hopes Betrayed: Trafficking Women and Girls to Post-Conflict Bosnia and Herzegovina for Forced Prostitution' (Human Rights Watch, 2002) vol 14, no 9 (D) 54–56.

[66] K Bolkovac and C Lynn, *The Whistleblower: Sex Trafficking, Military Contractors, and One Woman's Fight for Justice* (Palgrave Macmillan, 2011).

[67] Human Rights Watch, 'Hopes Betrayed' (n 65) 5. Emphasis added. See also ibid 62–67; in particular, David Isenberg reports that 'the company's Bosnia site supervisor filmed himself raping two women. A number of employees were transferred out of the country, but with no legal consequences for them': Isenberg (n 26).

[68] Human Rights Watch (n 65) 67.

[69] Isenberg (n 26).

to 'dancing boys' in Afghanistan in 2009.[70] Furthermore, DynCorp was one of the private firms that profited from operating the aforementioned CIA rendition flights, indicating broader apathy with regard to human rights.[71]

DynCorp itself did not suffer adverse consequences from these episodes: it subsequently won a major UK MoD contract;[72] key contracts relating to policing post-Saddam Iraq;[73] and received US government money in Haiti.[74] The UN Working Group on the Use of Mercenaries has noted that, despite this public record for human rights abuse, DynCorp 'won a contract to support the Defense Logistics Agency (the largest logistics combat support agency of the [US DoD]) in managing supplies at seven sites in Afghanistan' in June 2013.[75] Thus, the failure of market-based regulatory mechanisms for PMCs is poignantly illustrated by DynCorp, where a single firm may repeatedly violate a plethora of rights with impunity and proceed to be rewarded by lucrative governmental contracts without suspension or punishment.

Indeed, DynCorp has been, and continues to be, a long-time member of the PMC industry trade association, International Stability Operations Association (ISOA).[76] As David Isenberg notes, 'ISOA's Code of Conduct clearly states "Signatories shall respect the dignity of all human beings and strictly adhere to all applicable international humanitarian and human rights laws"'.[77] Furthermore, despite DynCorp's record of involvement in sexual slavery and child prostitution, the company has been a Signatory Company of the International Code of Conduct (ICoC) since its inception.[78] It is interesting to note that the ICoC itself explicitly prohibits its

[70] 'US Embassy Cables: Afghan Government Asks US to Quash "Dancing Boys" Scandal' *The Guardian* (2 December 2010) www.theguardian.com/world/us-embassy-cables-documents/213720; Isenberg (n 26).

[71] Cobain and Quinn, 'How US Firms Profited from Torture Flights' (n 37).

[72] J Wilson and K Maguire, 'American Firm in Bosnia Sex Trade Row Poised to Win MoD Contract' *The Guardian* (29 November 2002) www.guardian.co.uk/uk/2002/nov/29/military.politics.

[73] Barnett, 'Scandal-Hit US Firm Wins Key Contracts' *The Guardian* (13 April 2003) www.guardian.co.uk/world/2003/apr/13/iraq17.

[74] J Johnston, 'Blacklisted Contractor Continues Receiving Government Money through Haiti Contracts' *The Hill* (2 December 2011) http://thehill.com/blogs/congress-blog/foreign-policy/196851-blacklisted-contractor-continues-receiving-government-money-through-haiti-contracts.

[75] Working Group on the Use of Mercenaries, 'Report of the Working Group on the Use of Mercenaries as a Means of Violating Human Rights and Impeding the Exercise of the Right of Peoples to Self-Determination' (UNGA, 2013) A/68/339 para 34.

[76] DynCorp's membership of ISOA can be accessed at: www.stability-operations.org/members/?id=18827238.

[77] Isenberg (n 26).

[78] DynCorp has been a Signatory Company since 9 November 2010: ICoC, 'The International Code of Conduct for Private Security Service Providers: Signatory Companies' para 168 www.icoc-psp.org/uploads/Signatory_Companies_-_August_2013_-_Composite_List2.pdf.

Signatory Companies from engaging in sexual exploitation and abuse or gender-based violence, human trafficking, slavery and forced labour, and the worst forms of child labour.[79]

IV. THE QUESTION OF ACCOUNTABILITY

The stagnation of the accountability question is most keenly sensed by the International Institute of Humanitarian Law focusing on the impact of PMCs in IHL as the topic of its thirty-fifth Round Table in 2012.[80] It is a question that continues to occupy academic conferences, evident through the presence of a Regulation Panel on an interdisciplinary PMC conference hosted at King's College London[81] and the proceedings on this topic hosted at Chatham House in 2008 and 2011.[82] That questions of PMC accountability still pervade academic discourse evince the persistent lack, or failure, of legal accountability mechanisms. This in turn suggests a more fundamental underlying problem, raising the spectre of a systemic defect. Thus, rather than recount the orthodox legal approach of PMC activities falling through the gaps in the law and how the law may be better refined to prevent such occurrences in the future, the persistence of the accountability question justifies a structural examination into the role that the law itself plays in the creation and maintenance of the system of impunity enjoyed by the PMC and its contractors.

The UN Working Group on the Use of Mercenaries has noted the 'alarming resurgence of the use of mercenaries in armed conflict—'often in new and novel ways'.[83] Although Faiza Patel, then the Chair-Rapporteur, began by highlighting that the '[recent events in Africa clearly demonstrate that the problems posed by mercenaries are still a live issue', it was clear that her main concern stemmed from the PMC industry when she

[79] Swiss Federal Department of Foreign Affairs, 'International Code of Conduct for Private Security Service Providers', arts 35–41.

[80] International Institute of Humanitarian Law, 'XXXVth Round Table: Private Military and Security Companies' www.iihl.org/iihl/Documents/Draft%20Agenda%20Internet%20Sanremo%202012%20%20%2831%2005%202012%29-1.pdf.

[81] 'Beyond Iraq and Afghanistan: Researching Today's Private Military and Security Industry' (King's College London, 18 November 2011).

[82] E Wilmshurst, 'Chatham House International Law Discussion Group Private Military and Security Companies' www.chathamhouse.org/sites/default/files/public/Research/International%20Law/il220108.pdf; I Ralby, H Tonkin and E Wilmshurst, 'Regulation of Private Military Security Companies in Armed Conflict: Meeting Summary International Law Programme' www.chathamhouse.org/sites/default/files/public/Research/International%20Law/071011ralby&tonkin.pdf.

[83] UN Working Group on the Use of Mercenaries, 'Alarming Rise in Mercenary Activities Calls for Attention' *UN Working Group on the Use of Mercenaries* (1 November 2011) www.ohchr.org/EN/NewsEvents/Pages/DisplayNews.aspx?NewsID=11558&LangID=E.

> noted that these companies continue to undertake an ever-larger range of activities in an increasing number of countries around the world. It is difficult to gauge the extent of the private military and security industry worldwide, with estimates varying from $20 billion to $100 billion per year.[84]

It is, however, the projected figures that create the most concern:

> Ms Patel recalled that spending on contracts and grants in Iraq and Afghanistan is expected to exceed *$206 billion* in 2011, according to the August 2011 report by the US Commission on Wartime Contracting. Also, in 2010, the number of contractor employees hired by the US Departments of Defense and State and USAID exceeded 260,000, in contrast with the 9,200 contractors hired by the US military during the first Gulf War. 'This is the tip of the iceberg, because private military and security companies also operate in a variety of other situations *ranging from drug eradication programs in Colombia to post-conflict reconstruction programs*,' she said. 'And it is not just governments who take advantage of their services, *but also NGOs, private companies and the United Nations*.' For the Working Group, '*the potential impact of the widespread activities of private military and security companies on human rights means that they cannot be allowed to continue to operate without adequate regulation and mechanisms to ensure accountability*.'[85]

It is clear that accountability for PMC activity, compounded by the size of the industry and the military services it provides, continues to be a fundamental and pervasive issue that has not been rectified. The Chair-Rapporteur 'welcomed all national efforts to regulate private military and security companies, but regretted *that none have yet come close to achieving full accountability for human rights violations*'.[86] This conclusion on the status of domestic regulation is particularly stark when placed in context because the Working Group has over the past few years conducted missions to Afghanistan,[87] United States,[88] Equatorial Guinea,[89] South Africa,[90] Iraq,[91] Somalia[92] and

[84] ibid.

[85] ibid. Emphasis added. Rather than the growth of the PMC industry being a symptom of the campaigns in Iraq and Afghanistan, it is clear from the projected figures that the PMC industry will undergo another boom that will accompany the withdrawal of State forces from these regions. For early indications for Iraq alone, see K Brown, 'With Troop Exit, a Civilian Phase for the U.S. in Iraq' *Bloomberg* (24 October 2011) www.bloomberg.com/news/2011-10-24/with-troop-exit-a-civilian-phase-for-the-u-s-in-iraq.html; D Rasor, 'Out of Iraq: What Will the War Service Industry Do Now?' *Truthout* (26 October 2011) www.truth-out.org/out-iraq-what-will-war-service-industry-do-now/1319637699.

[86] UN Working Group on the Use of Mercenaries, 'Alarming Rise in Mercenary Activities Calls for Attention' (n 83). Emphasis added.

[87] S Shameem, 'Mission to Afghanistan' (UNHRC, 2010) A/HRC/15/25/Add.2.

[88] S Shameem, 'Mission to the United States of America' (UNHRC, 2010) A/HRC/15/25/Add.3.

[89] AB de Pérez, 'Mission to Equatorial Guinea' (UNHRC, 2011) A/HRC/18/32/Add.2.

[90] A Nikitin, 'Mission to South Africa' (UNHRC, 2011) A/HRC/18/32/Add.3.

[91] J Gómez del Prado, 'Mission to Iraq' (UNHRC, 2011) A/HRC/18/32/Add.4.

[92] Working Group on the Use of Mercenaries, 'Mission to Somalia' (UNHRC, 2013) A/HRC/24/45/Add.2.

Honduras[93] all of which are heavily engaged with various forms of mercenary activity within the mandate of the Working Group.[94]

Newer figures have been released by the UN Working Group in 2013: 'Estimates suggest that global demand for private contract security services is increasing and will increase 7.4 per cent annually to $244 billion by 2016'.[95] The industry is also beginning to morph in order to adapt to the end of the conflicts in Iraq and Afghanistan, because as Stuart Bowen, the special inspector general of Iraq reconstruction, has said, 'The opportunities in this field are shaped by the unpredictable rhythm of when a fragile state will fail'.[96] There are even suggestions that the companies that branch out into other areas could have an even more profitable decade ahead as, for example, oil companies increase their operations.[97] As the UN Working Group noted, there is also significant PMC involvement in maritime security to protect commercial shipping,[98] which is becoming a growing market for the industry. These trends away from the model of contracting developed for the conflict in Iraq and Afghanistan may exacerbate attempts to subdue the industry with regulation into the future. As Sarah Percy has recently suggested, 'the [PMC] industry is agile and innovative, and has responded swiftly to changing market pressures. As a result, regulators at all levels have often been stuck in lengthy negotiating processes while the target of their regulation is rapidly changing form'.[99]

Illustrating significantly different accountability concerns, in the specific context of the United States, the independent and bipartisan Commission on Wartime Contracting in Iraq and Afghanistan was created by Congress in 2008 to give a *fiscal* account of the PMC industry.[100] In particular, it was concerned about the extent of the reliance of the Federal Government on contractors, with waste, fraud and (financial) abuse in contingency contracting and with the extent to which those who were

[93] Working Group on the Use of Mercenaries, 'Mission to Honduras' (UNHRC, 2013) A/HRC/24/45/Add.1.

[94] See also C Bakker and M Sossai (eds), *Multilevel Regulation of Military and Security Contractors: The Interplay Between International, European and Domestic Norms* (Hart Publishing, 2012).

[95] Working Group on the Use of Mercenaries, 'Report of the Working Group on the Use of Mercenaries as a Means of Violating Human Rights and Impeding the Exercise of the Right of Peoples to Self-Determination' (n 75) 29; see more generally ibid 29–33.

[96] A Fifield, 'Contractors Reap $138bn from Iraq War' *Financial Times* (18 March 2013) www.ft.com/intl/cms/s/0/7f435f04-8c05-11e2-b001-00144feabdc0.html#axzz2jmIpbQhn.

[97] ibid.

[98] Working Group on the Use of Mercenaries (n 75) 36–37. See generally Working Group on the Use of Mercenaries, 'Mission to Somalia' (n 92).

[99] S Percy, 'Regulating the Private Security Industry: A Story of Regulating the Last War' (2012) 94 *International Review of the Red Cross* 941, 941–42.

[100] Creation authorised by the National Defense Authorization Act (NDAA), s 841 for Fiscal Year 2008, Public Law 110–181. For the mandate of the Commission, see s 841(c)(3). As the Commission has terminated, its website is frozen but it continues to contain its reports: www.wartimecontracting.gov/.

responsible for such misconduct was held financially or legally responsible. The type of accountability sought by the Commission is especially telling because it was concerned with, and limited to, economic matters with the view, presumably, of making wartime contracting more efficient and streamlined in the future. That the Commission was uninvolved with issues of human rights accountability highlights the different accountability concerns at stake. Although the activities of this Commission *do not* concern responsibility for alleged violations of human rights or humanitarian law, its damning Final Report reveals an industry characterised by pervasive irresponsibility and blanketed in impunity in a broad sense. The opening paragraph of the Executive Summary summarises succinctly the extent of financial loss:

> At least $31 billion, and possibly as much as $60 billion, has been lost to contract waste and fraud in America's contingency operations in Iraq and Afghanistan. Much more will turn into waste as attention to continuing operations wanes, as U.S. support for projects and programs in Iraq and Afghanistan declines, and as those efforts are revealed as unsustainable.[101]

Interestingly, the scathing criticism issued by the Commission has exacerbated oversight problems, having made leadership of the Special Inspector General for Afghanistan Reconstruction (SIGAR) extremely unpopular.[102] This is also likely to stifle the creation of the proposed post of Special Inspector General for Overseas Contingency Operations (SIGOCO), who would have been a permanent officer with a mandate to oversee all overseas contingency operations, that was recommended by the Commission owing to the 'need for a top oversight official who is 'capable of going and looking wherever the U.S. military is operative'.[103]

The uncertainty of governmental oversight of the PMC industry in purely fiscal matters is expressed both in the broad range as well as in the absolute figures of unaccountable funds themselves. This uncertainty suggests more sinister implications behind the Commission's Final Report: the general inability of governmental agencies to oversee and enforce military contracts.[104] The central role conceived for contractual

[101] Commission on Wartime Contracting, 'Transforming Wartime Contracting: Controlling Costs, Reducing Risks. Final Report to Congress' (2011) 1 www.wartimecontracting.gov/docs/CWC_FinalReport-highres.pdf.

[102] J Rogin, 'McCaskill: The Afghan Oversight Office Is Rudderless' [2011] *Foreign Policy: The Cable* http://thecable.foreignpolicy.com/posts/2011/11/02/mccaskill_the_afghan_oversight_office_is_rudderless.

[103] ibid.

[104] Further accountability and scrutiny of wartime contracting practices have been hampered by a bizarre decision by the Commission to seal its internal records from the public for 20 years until 2031: N Hodge, 'Panel's War-Waste Records Sealed as Work Ends' *The Wall Street Journal* (30 September 2011) http://online.wsj.com/article/SB10001424052970204226204576603060868379444.html; a similar situation has plagued the United Kingdom Ministry of Defence: see N Hopkins, 'MoD Spent £600m on Consultants' *The Guardian* (17 November

monitoring and oversight within the ICoC[105] in the purported protection of human rights and humanitarian law is likely to translate the failure of fiscal oversight unearthed by the Commission into a lack of accountability for serious violations in the future. The ICoC is addressed in greater depth in chapter six, but the deficiencies relating to enforcement can be raised now. The ICoC, concluded on 9 November 2010, is significant for both appearing to be the favoured form of industry regulation at present, and for its attempt to uphold human rights and international humanitarian law through the incorporation of these provisions as contractual terms.[106] According to a DCAF policy document, 'The ICoC uses contractual mechanisms to impose human-rights-compliant standards *directly on the companies themselves, regardless of where they are operating*'.[107] Anne-Marie Buzatu clarifies that the use of contractual mechanisms would not only have the benefit of being enforceable through the law of contract, but would also enhance the ability to monitor and oversee the conduct of companies through the contractual nexus, and furthermore that it would incentivise such oversight.[108] The problems associated with this approach are threefold.[109] First, the encapsulation of human rights and humanitarian laws into contractual provisions significantly understates their normative significance and neutralises their normative force, thereby collapsing dimensions of complexity into the binary possibility of contractual fulfilment or breach. Second, the victims of alleged violations of fundamental rights and protections lose their standing to challenge PMC conduct because these have become contractual terms, and only parties to the contract may enforce their rights under the contract. The necessary corollary to this revelation is that the party contracting services with the PMC may be hesitant to enforce the human rights and humanitarian law provisions. This is because the reflected glare of negative limelight upon the contracting party is unlikely to incentivise that party to enforce those provisions. This may account for Judge Silberman's observation in *Saleh* that neither were criminal charges made '*nor did the government pursue any contractual*

2011) www.guardian.co.uk/uk/2011/nov/17/mod-consultants-specialists-fats. The systematic failure to rein in spending on contractors has ironically fed back into the system to create another round of MOD personnel cuts: N Hopkins, 'Ministry of Defence to Cut Further 3,000 Civilian Jobs' *The Guardian* (26 January 2012) www.guardian.co.uk/uk/2012/jan/26/ministry-of-defence-job-cuts.

[105] This is discussed in greater detail in both chs 4 and 6.

[106] Christopher Kinsey suggests that the industry would prefer regulation, but not of the type that would hinder its business activities. Personal communication, 9 March 2012. See further the discussion on contractual enforcement of human rights in ch 4.

[107] DCAF is the Geneva Centre for the Democratic Control of Armed Forces: A-M Buzatu and B Buckland, 'Private Military & Security Companies: Future Challenges in Security Governance' (DCAF, 2010) Working Paper DCAF Horizon 2015 Working Paper No 3 23.

[108] Personal communication with the author, 18 October 2010 during the IPOA Annual Summit, Washington D.C.

[109] This summarises the arguments presented at length in ch 4.

remedies against either contractor'.[110] The third point is that, considering the additional disincentive in the second point, the Commission's finding of the appalling fiscal oversight during the Iraq and Afghanistan campaigns, there is no evidence that contractual monitoring and oversight for human rights and humanitarian law is going to fare better. Indeed, early indications with relation to allegations of human trafficking by PMCs in war zones (this time in Iraq and Afghanistan) suggest at best that limitations of resources and jurisdictional questions prevent adequate oversight. At worst, these practices are indicative of impunity:

> 'Zero prosecutions,' said Martina Vandenberg, a lawyer and former Human Rights Watch investigator, 'suggests zero effort to enforce the law.' The State Department reported recently that allegations of contractors' employees procuring commercial sex acts were 'well publicized' but that no contractors have been prosecuted and no contracts terminated.[111]

On the other hand, there are two strong theoretical reasons that support the inclusion of human rights standards into contractual provisions. The first is that human rights standards will become incorporated into role responsibility as a factor for consideration, thus removing the question of violation from the realm of outcome responsibility, as previously explained in chapter one. The efficacy of this approach is necessarily predicated upon the weight allocated to this criterion, but part of 'a job well-done' in theory would include compliance with human rights standards. The second benefit is that enforcement mechanisms become built in by the possibility of contractual enforcement.[112] Hence, human rights standards cease to only prescribe prospective responsibilities and the prospect of retrospective responsibility emerges, as considered in chapter five. In practice, however, this type of enforcement is likely to breach the *nemo iudex sua causa* rule of natural justice: not only is it unlikely to be in the interests of either contractual party to enforce such a provision, but it will also be inadequate in terms of independence and impartiality.

V. MODERN PRIVATE MILITARY COMPANY: CRIMINAL ENTERPRISE OR LEGITIMATE BUSINESS?

The modern PMC has bifurcated opinion about the status of these entities: are these criminal enterprises or legitimate businesses? On the one hand,

[110] *Saleh v Titan* (n 34) 2. Emphasis added.

[111] N Schwellenbach and C Leonnig, 'U.S. Policy a Paper Tiger Against Sex Trade in War Zones' *Washington Post* (18 July 2010) www.washingtonpost.com/wp-dyn/content/article/2010/07/17/AR2010071701401_pf.html. Indeed, even were contracts to be terminated, such a response would arguably be insufficient given the gravity of the transgressions. See the analysis in ch 4.

[112] This suggestion conflicts with the second point raised and is clearly a theoretical reason, requiring both the will and resources of the contracting party to succeed.

PMCs trade in organised violence which is prohibited internationally and criminalised domestically within all jurisdictions, and profiting from the organisation of violence is a hallmark of criminal entities. On the other hand, PMCs have been able to lawfully adopt the corporate form. This may suggest that the activities of the PMC are not unlawful per se, a claim which can be reinforced by the apparent willingness of PMCs to subscribe and adhere to relevant standards, a prima facie signal of the goodwill of at least a section of the industry.

These poles are best represented by the opposing stances of the only two UN Special Rapporteurs on the Use of Mercenaries. Enrique Ballesteros considered the PMC phenomenon 'was leading to situations where the state was being *supplanted* by private actors in what constituted its basic raison d'être'.[113] Thus, he proposed the expansion of the definition of mercenarism to encompass the activities of private companies[114] and sought the criminalisation of mercenarism.[115] Ballesteros continued by providing concrete examples of the link between mercenaries and terrorists as well as other organised criminals: 'Mercenaries now participate in trafficking in persons, drugs and weapons, in the commission of terrorist acts and the settling of criminal scores, as well as in organized crime'.[116] Thus Ballesteros' position is that the PMC is simply a revival of criminal mercenarism. This is a sentiment most aptly described by Musah as 'nothing but the old poison of vagabond mercenaries in new designer bottles'.[117] Based upon this assumption, many commentators[118] have analysed the PMC phenomenon through the framework of mercenarism from the historical use of mercenaries and resultant creation of 'free companies'

[113] V-Y Ghebali, 'The United Nations and the Dilemma of Outsourcing Peacekeeping Operations' in A Bryden and M Caparini (eds), *Private Actors and Security Governance* (LIT & DCAF, 2006) 217.

[114] E Ballesteros, 'Report on the Use of Mercenaries as a Means of Violating Human Rights and Impeding the Exercise of the Right of Peoples to Self-Determination' (2003) E/CN.4/2004/15 para 43.

[115] The proposed crime of mercenary activity is broad and multi-faceted: 'In this crime, the mercenary who participates directly in the commission of the crime must be considered a perpetrator with direct criminal responsibility. It must also be borne in mind that mercenary activity is a complex crime in which criminal responsibility falls upon those who recruited, employed, trained and financed the mercenary or mercenaries, and upon those who planned and ordered his criminal activity': ibid 43(c).

[116] E Ballesteros, 'Report on the Use of Mercenaries as a Means of Violating Human Rights and Impeding the Exercise of the Right of Peoples to Self-Determination' (2001) E/CN.4/2001/19 paras 50–61.

[117] Singer, *Corporate Warriors* (n 24) 44.

[118] J Zarate, 'The Emergence of a New Dog of War: Private International Security Companies, International Law, and the New World Disorder' (1998) 34 *Stanford Journal of International Law* 75, 81–91; Singer (n 24) 19–23; T Milliard, 'Overcoming Post-Colonial Myopia: A Call to Recognize and Regulate Private Military Companies' (2003) 176 *Military Law Review* 1, 5; D Whyte, 'Lethal Regulation: State—Corporate Crime and the United Kingdom Government's New Mercenaries' (2003) 30 *Journal of Law and Society* 575, 575–577.

in medieval Europe.[119] This book argues that while the traditional historical understanding of mercenarism may be useful to understand the emergence and activity of the PMC, it constitutes only a part of the picture and fails to capture the essence of the modern PMC. Rather, the PMC phenomenon is more than merely a reincarnation of the medieval mercenary. Its legal corporate form provides an additional dimension of support for both its legitimate existence and right to operate by availing the modern PMC with both interpretive denial and assertion, leading ultimately to claims of industry self-regulation to become widely endorsed.

Ballesteros' successor, Shiasta Shameem, tentatively broke ranks with the position held by her predecessor when she said that 'the Special Rapporteur advocates that the United Nations undertake a debate on the fundamental question of the role of the State with respect to the use of force'.[120] In arriving at this suggestion, she emphasised that the lack of State interest and support for international anti-mercenarism instruments may arise from the fact that 'Member States and the United Nations itself employ entities that may be identified as mercenaries under the current definition'.[121] Thus she acknowledged that the control of force need not necessarily be a responsibility of the State, and she envisaged three possible outcomes arising from her proposed debate.[122] First, States would reclaim responsibility for their armed forces and be precluded from contracting services to non-State entities. This approach could require a renewed mercenary definition to encompass all non-State entities providing military-related services, and would need to create an effective mechanism to prohibit all States from using such services. Second, the reverse situation was considered in which all military functions will be privatised and outsourced from the State to private entities. The lack of standing armed forces of States would necessitate the contracting of military services as the situations demand, but importantly, this would negate the mercenary phenomenon because this would then become the standard method of procuring armed force. Finally, there is the prospect for an intermediate route where the State would retain a relatively small standing military core that would be supplemented by outsourcing for services as the need arises. This is the position that Western States, such as the UK and the US have adopted. Crucially, this position renders anti-mercenary instruments superfluous provided that the State was to be held responsible for the violations of human rights and international humanitarian law committed by

119 A Mockler, *New Mercenaries* (Sidgwick & Jackson, 1985) 9–10; Singer (n 24) 23–26.
120 S Shameem, 'Report on the Question of the Use of Mercenaries as a Means of Violating Human Rights and Impeding the Exercise of the Right of Peoples to Self-Determination' (2005) A/60/263 para 61.
121 ibid 47.
122 ibid 52.

the company. The practicalities of responsibility and accountability would have to be firmly established and an appropriate judicial forum agreed upon to address alleged grievances.[123]

Shameem highlights the intrinsic practical difficulties of renegotiating the control over organised force, as it is increasingly States or supra-State organisations which employ PMC services, despite their historically pejorative status as mercenaries:

> In terms of the current definition of a mercenary, *many of these companies can be classified as mercenaries or employing mercenaries*, although they themselves do not define their activities in that way. Moreover, as noted above, such companies are under contract with Member States, non-governmental organizations and, increasingly, the United Nations, to provide security, logistical support and training in conflict and post-conflict contexts, for example, in Iraq and Afghanistan.[124]

The corporate juridical form of the PMC may also provide the underlying organisational structure for both criminals and criminal activities. In other words, the corporate form not only legitimates activities that would otherwise be criminal, but also provides the criminal enterprise with the efficient corporate business framework with which to pursue its criminal agendas.

Thus, although former Secretary-General of the UN, Kofi Annan, considered in June 1998 that 'the world may not be ready to privatise peace',[125] this situation has shifted seismically in the ensuing years. The question is why the only two Special Rapporteurs on the Use of Mercenaries were capable of holding such disparate responses to the same challenge? Similarly, how has the UN gone from hesitating to employ PMCs despite its urgent 'need for skilled soldiers to separate fighters from refugees in the Rwandan refugee camps at Goma'[126] in 1998, to contracting for their services on an increasingly regular basis only a few years later?[127] The following sections will outline the pressures behind the privatisation of military services to account for their conception and success, and to show that PMCs only recently grew from mercenary roots recently.

[123] See eg art 29: J Gómez del Prado, 'Report of the Working Group on the Use of Mercenaries as a Means of Violating Human Rights and Impeding the Exercise of the Right of Peoples to Self-Determination with the Draft of a Possible Convention on Private Military and Security Companies (PMSCs) for Consideration and Action by the Human Rights Council' (UNGA, 2010) A/HRC/15/25.

[124] Shameem, 'Report on the Use of Mercenaries 2005' (n 120) 48. Emphasis added.

[125] UN Secretary General, 'Secretary-General Reflects on "Intervention" in Thirty-Fifth Annual Ditchley Foundation Lecture' (1998) 8.

[126] ibid.

[127] But not for services that involve the potential use of lethal force. See generally ÅG Østensen, *UN Use of Private Military and Security Companies: Practices and Policies* (DCAF, 2011) 3.

VI. WATCHGUARD INTERNATIONAL: THE CONCEPTION OF THE MODERN PRIVATE MILITARY COMPANY

The modern PMC was created in a very specific set of historical and political circumstances in order to address certain important challenges. Christopher Kinsey provides an insightful look at its formative stages:

> Since the setting up of the first [PMCs] the term has been synonymous with mercenaries. Such a claim was justified in the early days when there were strong links between these two groups of actors. Watchguard, for example, employed mercenaries to launch a military operation against Qadaffi in 1970 … Since then, the industry has changed beyond recognition. Instead of being perceived as guns for hire, many in the international community now recognise that [PMCs] can make a valuable contribution to international peace and security through training and other areas of expertise.[128]

Kinsey claims that, despite an inauspicious beginning as little more than a loosely affiliated band of criminal mercenaries, time is '[c]hanging the industry's image from guns for hire to agents of democracy'.[129] Two problems emerge from these claims: first that such a teleological progression cannot be assumed or so easily asserted; and second that the conditions present when, and for which, the PMC was created is likely to have a lasting effect upon its structure and modus operandi. An exploration into the history and early development of the PMC will be instructive for understanding its structure, its purposes and its outlook.

Watchguard International, the very first modern PMC, was established by Colonel David Stirling, the founder of the Special Air Service (SAS) in North Africa during the Second World War.[130] Stirling was concerned over the 1962 coup in Yemen, reflecting the position of the British government whose agents were already considering possible courses of action. The conclusion was that

> [i]t would take too long to establish a team of agents in the area, while getting permission to deploy the SAS was also ruled out. The only alternative action appeared to be the unofficial use of mercenaries and former SAS soldiers.[131]

[128] C Kinsey, 'Private Security Companies: Agents of Democracy or Simply Mercenaries?' in T Jäger and G Kümmel (eds), *Private Military and Security Companies: Chances, Problems, Pitfalls and Prospects* (VS Verlag fur Sozialwissenschaften, 2007) 87. The longer historical perspective offered by Kinsey reveals the contradictions inherent in utilising mercenary forces. In the 2011 Libyan conflict, Colonel Gaddafi was heavily criticised for employing mercenaries to defend his flailing regime to the point that the Security Council issued Resolutions radically departing from previous mercenary measures in an attempt to deprive him of purchased foreign military support: see H-Y Liu, 'Mercenaries in Libya: Ramifications of the Treatment of "Armed Mercenary Personnel" under the Arms Embargo for Private Military Company Contractors' (2011) 16 *Journal of Conflict and Security Law* 293.

[129] Kinsey, 'Private Security Companies' (n 128) 87.

[130] ibid 88–91.

[131] ibid 89.

Interestingly, the ex-SAS officer approached for the job, Lieutenant Colonel Jim Johnson, would go on to found another early PMC, Control Risks Group.[132] The ensuing successes accomplished by the initial small team of ex-SAS servicemen in training and equipping local warriors in Yemen convinced Stirling that this was a viable path to combine the 'national interests of the British Government with his commercial interests through Watchguard International and heralded the 1967 formalisation of the company in the Channel Islands'.[133] A biographer of Stirling's noted these motivating factors in the formation of Watchguard:

> Stirling knew roughly the cost of using a mercenary force and he felt there was scope for setting up a private force whose main function would be to have a *controllable political effect*, but which must *produce an operating profit; politics was the driving force but it had to be financially viable* ... Stirling conceived the idea of forming a commercial company to operate in areas of paramount interest to the highest national figures—the heads of state.[134]

This explicitly indicated Stirling's desire to circumvent the political checks and balances built into the decision to deploy coercive force, thereby undermining accountability and the rule of law. Indeed, Stirling himself said that: 'The organisation was designed to tackle really important military objectives which could not be tackled officially because of questions in the House of Commons. *The British government wanted a reliable organisation without any direct identification*'.[135]

Thus, the fledgling PMC was employed to diversify the tools of covert operations available to the British government. Crucially, however, the organisation was the first to try to formalise its relationship for the government, adopting a corporate business model.[136] The adoption of the business model gave Watchguard more autonomy. Whereas previous types of covert operators tended to have informal, and thus more dependent, ties with the State the independent existence of the PMC necessarily reduced the control by the State to mere influence. The adoption of the corporate model was to become a crucial innovation for the PMC, imbuing the organisation with a permanent and independent identity that must have been an important factor for both political deniability and economic profitability. Thus, the birth of Watchguard heralded a new form of covert operator, one which was easier to plausibly deny while simultaneously being more difficult to control. PMC independence from strict

[132] ibid.
[133] ibid.
[134] A Hoe, *David Stirling: The Authorised Biography of the Founder of the SAS* (Warner Books, 1992) 369. Emphasis added.
[135] Although this never happened: C Kinsey, *Corporate Soldiers and International Security: The Rise of Private Military Companies* (Routledge, 2006) 47. Emphasis added.
[136] ibid 46–47.

governmental policy enabled it to pursue its own interests and have its own motivations for acting.

Whatever is said about the origins of these companies, it is obvious that narrow State and commercial interests prevail in directing the course of their activities. As Kinsey notes:

> Clients for the company fell into two groups; countries the British Government could support overtly and countries the government would like to help but could not be seen to assist because of political problems it would cause. In relation to the latter group, the British government could always deny any knowledge about Watchguard's involvement with such countries if it became public.[137]

The former category of clients is relatively unproblematic because overt governmental action indicates public interest and political accountability for the intervention, and the PMC effectively acts as a State organ.[138] The latter category, however, is problematic on three levels. First, the 'political problems' associated with the countries requiring assistance suggest that the government, in its desire to provide aid, acts upon private interests not consonant with its public functions. This is a strong indicator that the government is exercising its powers inappropriately. Second, the implicit purchase of 'plausible deniability' for the government, along with the actual contracted military services from the PMC, creates suspicion and distrust for the government and undermines the rule of law by obfuscating transparency and accountability mechanisms necessary for political accountability.[139] Third, these effects are exacerbated because PMCs provide military labour for purchase. Revealing this contradiction is the fact that 'Stirling intended the company to provide services that would prevent the violent overthrow of a government, while not trying to exert political influence'.[140] Political influence is inseparable from physical coercion and any entity which is capable of providing such services will acquire commensurate political influence. Thus, in terms of foreign policy in the post-Cold War era, the evolution of PMCs became a useful development for Western governments. The challenges raised by the desire to maintain global influence in the face of increasing constraints that arise from a combination of international law, ethical policy, media accountability and rising costs of military intervention meant that the privatisation of security was not initially a contentious issue, at least in the United Kingdom.[141]

[137] Kinsey (n 128) 90–91.

[138] Tonkin, *State Control Over Private Military and Security Companies in Armed Conflict* (n 18) 80–122.

[139] See eg S Gul, 'The Secretary Will Deny All Knowledge of Your Actions: The Use of Private Military Contractors and Implications for State and Political Accountability' (2006) 10 *Lewis and Clark Law Review* 287.

[140] Kinsey (n 128) 91.

[141] Kinsey, *Corporate Soldiers and International Security* (n 135) 58–59.

VII. HISTORICAL PRESSURE TOWARDS MILITARY PRIVATISATION

It is necessary at this point to consider the underlying reasons driving the privatisation of military labour that has enabled corporations to provide services that have hitherto been considered as core governmental functions.[142] The contemporary resurgence of private forces cannot be understood without acknowledging the political context and historical changes which fostered its emergence and growth: the modern PMC is an entity of its time. PW Singer argues that the development of the PMC resulted from two main factors associated with the end of the Cold War which 'produced a vacuum in the market of security ... feeding both the supply side and the demand side. Global threats became more varied, more capable, and more dangerous, while the traditional responses to insecurity and conflict were at their weakest'.[143] The culture of outsourcing and privatisation during the Reagan-Thatcher administrations accompanied these developments and imbued the privatised military industry with the economic logic and rhetoric that encouraged the perception of military services as legitimate business.

The PMC phenomenon was fuelled on the supply side by the flood of military labour into the market that resulted from mass demobilisation at the end of the Cold War. In certain cases, whole military units essentially transferred into the private sector after their official disbanding. For example, the South African 32 'Buffalo' Battalion transformed into Executive Outcomes under the unit's second-in-command, Eeben Barlow, in 1989.[144] Moreover, the surplus of military labour was accompanied by an analogous flood of military equipment onto the market, so 'that anyone with enough cash can find a private supplier of almost any type of weapon at a bargain price'.[145] The result of the demobilisation at the end of the Cold War was that both military experience and equipment were not only available to purchase but also at a relatively low price, increasing potential profitability. This resulted in organised private forces that could be both better trained and equipped than their State counterparts, in turn

[142] Even the core advocates of privatisation admit that the military should remain within the public sphere. eg William Niskanen, the chairman of the Cato Institute, is quoted to hold this opinion: see J Bakan, *The Corporation: The Pathological Pursuit of Profit and Power* (Constable & Robinson, 2005) 113–14. Milton Friedman himself held the opinion that the military was one of a handful of services that should be provided by the government: see interview in J Abbott and M Achbar, *The Corporation* (In 2 Film, 2006). It should also be noted that the 'inherently governmental' concept should not be utilised as a guide to contracting practices in armed conflict: Commission on Wartime Contracting, 'Transforming Wartime Contracting' (n 101) 2; see also art 9 of the Draft Convention which prohibits the delegation or outsourcing of inherently State functions: Gómez del Prado, 'Draft Convention' (n 123).

[143] Singer (n 24) 49.

[144] E Barlow, *Executive Outcomes: Against All Odds* (Galago, 2008).

[145] Singer (n 24) 54.

jeopardising the ability of States to maintain internal order and challenging the State-centric international system regulating the prohibition of the threat or use of force. Together, these trends suggest that the PMC drove a self-perpetuating cycle the fuelled the growth of the industry.

First, the end of the Cold War also brought about a drastic shift in both the nature of actual armed conflict as well as the emerging threats challenging the stability of the State. While the opposing superpowers of the Cold War had been able to impose order and exert global influence through the grant of military aid, the end of the Cold War thawed these frozen tensions. The high incidence rate of civil wars which could in part be attributed to the failures of governance associated with the withdrawal of patronage from the superpowers. This may have led many post-colonial states to structural readjustments 'which opens up new spaces for private military actors to operate. Transnational criminals, economic insurgents, warlords for profit, armies of child soldiers, and brutalised civilians are all found in these zones of conflict and lawlessness'.[146] As State authority weakened in many of these countries, indicated by the atrophy of State institutions, their legitimacy to power was challenged by non-State actors rushing to fill the vacuum. Insurgency forces, State forces and interested third parties became potential employers of PMCs.

General Sir David Richards, then the incoming UK Chief of the General Staff, noted the second factor when he suggested that there might be a 'virtuous congruence' relating to the style of the threat emerging from both State and non-State actors: 'there is a good case for believing that even state-on-state warfare will be similar to that we will be conducting against non-state groupings'.[147] Thus, it appears that the nature of warfare post-Cold War has shifted towards low-intensity internal conflicts, regardless of the type of adversary faced. This shift away from State-orientated 'total war', which peaked with the two World Wars and ended with the fall of the Berlin Wall, reopened the field of armed conflict to market forces. In other words, while 'total States' are a prerequisite to the conduct of 'total war',[148] which precluded the ready marketisation of armed force,[149]

[146] ibid 50–51.

[147] D Richards, 'Twenty-First Century Armed Forces—Agile, Useable, Relevant' (Annual Defence Lecture, Chatham House, 17 September 2009) 8.

[148] On the point that total war is required to create the total State, and conversely that only total States can wage total war, see M Centeno, 'Limited War and Limited States' in D Davis and A Pereira (eds), *Irregular Armed Forces and their Role in Politics and State Formation* (Cambridge University Press, 2003) 82–95.

[149] It is interesting to note that, even in the paradigmatic examples of total war such as World War Two, there were still spaces in which entities which could arguably be considered as private military contractors could operate. A good example of such a combat group is the 1st American Volunteer Group of the Chinese Air Force, known as the 'Flying Tigers'. This group comprised heavily of ex-US servicemen and was recruited with presidential sanction. See generally D Ford, *Flying Tigers: Claire Chennault and His American Volunteers, 1941-1942* (HarperCollins-Smithsonian Books, 2007).

the retrogression to less intense forms of armed conflict allows for the re-entry of private entities onto the battlefield. Moreover, the varied nature of post-Cold War security threats has been observed where

> [t]o succeed, we must examine rigorously what capacities we need and where we must rebalance our investment in Defence—and rebalance we must, not from one service to another but from one type of conflict to another, for we simply can't afford to retain a full suite of capability for all eventualities.[150]

Put differently, the unconventional small-scale nature of security threats, coupled with a lower level of resources allocated to State defence budgets will combine to favour a security strategy where only the core armed services are retained directly by the State, to be supplemented by targeted outsourcing to the private sector in reaction to specific threats.[151] As David Richards reiterated, 'successful armed forces adapt and transform at a pace greater than their potential enemies'.[152] It is this necessity of adaptation that is seen as the logic driving the shift towards hiring PMCs.

The third factor cultivating the growth of the PMC is the broader environment of outsourcing and privatisation.[153] This is not easy to demonstrate as it is a pervasive influence. The gradual infiltration of the private sector into the core governmental competency area of defence has been convincingly demonstrated by Naomi Klein when she examined the attempts by then US Secretary of Defence, Donald Rumsfeld, to implement the parallel reforms for the Pentagon that he had done during his extensive experience in the private sector:

> Where corporations unburdened themselves of geography-bound factories and full-time workers, Rumsfeld saw the army shedding large numbers of full-time troops in favour of a small core of staffers propped up by the cheaper temporary soldiers from the Reserve and the National Guard. Meanwhile, contractors from companies such as Blackwater and Halliburton would perform duties ranging from high-risk chauffeuring to prisoner interrogation to catering to health care. And where corporations poured their savings on labour into design and marketing, Rumsfeld would spend his savings from fewer troops and tanks on the latest satellite and nano-technology from the private sector.[154]

[150] Richards, 'Twenty-First Century Armed Forces' (n 147) 1.

[151] On the question of whether States should produce and retain military resources 'in-house' or purchase it from the market, see J Cockayne, 'Make or Buy? Principle-Agent Theory and the Regulation of Private Military Companies', *From Mercenaries to Market: The Rise and Regulation of Private Military Companies* (Oxford University Press, 2007) 196–216. Cockayne suggests that whilst the option of purchase may be available, the purveyor of force has a tendency to be a bad agent to the hiring principal.

[152] Richards (n 147) 1.

[153] See generally D Harvey, *A Brief History of Neoliberalism* (Oxford University Press, 2007).

[154] N Klein, *The Shock Doctrine: The Rise of Disaster Capitalism* (Penguin, 2008) 283–85.

The expression of this doctrine, and its specific relatedness to the privatisation of military services, is found in a speech given by Rumsfeld to the Pentagon on 10 September 2001:

> The topic today is an adversary that poses a threat, a serious threat, to the security of the United States of America. This adversary is one of the world's last bastions of central planning. It governs by dictating five-year plans. From a single capital, it attempts to impose its demands across time zones, continents, oceans and beyond. With brutal consistency, it stifles free thought and crushes new ideas. It disrupts the defense of the United States and places the lives of men and women in uniform at risk ... The adversary's closer to home. It's the Pentagon bureaucracy. Not the people, but the processes. Not the civilians, but the systems. Not the men and women in uniform, but the uniformity of thought and action that we too often impose on them.[155]

Rumsfeld continued this speech by advocating that the Pentagon pursue an agenda of modernisation implemented through privatisation. Klein reported the reactions of Rumsfeld's audience: 'the only thing standing in the way of Rumsfeld's bold vision of outsourcing the army was the small matter of the US Constitution, which clearly defined national security as the duty of government, not private companies'.[156] The very fact that Rumsfeld was capable of announcing plans for such reform, however, is indicative of the culture of privatisation cultivating the rapid growth of the PMC industry.[157]

This direct privatisation of the military constituted only a part of the infiltration of military companies into the provision of governance. The end of the Cold War sent arms manufacturing companies scrambling for an alternative business model because the defence budgets which comprised the lion's share of their revenue were being slashed. 'At Lockheed [Martin] and its fellow arms manufacturers, a strategy emerged to aggressively pursue a new line of work: running the government for a fee'.[158] The role of public government in the provision of security was under a pincer attack: the modern role of a State to provide security was being eroded from within its very institutions while the challenge of the private sector was brought to bear.

[155] D Rumsfeld, 'DOD Acquisition and Logistics Excellence Week Kickoff—Bureaucracy to Battlefield. U.S. Department of Defense, Office of the Assistant Secretary of Defense (Public Affairs)' (2001) paras 1–4 www.defenselink.mil/speeches/speech.aspx?speechid=430.

[156] Klein, *The Shock Doctrine* (n 154) 287.

[157] There are arguably two distinct, but interlinked, periods of rapid expansion for the PMC industry. The first was signalled by the successes of Executive Outcomes where the end of the Cold War left a security gap filled by the private sector. The second wave was launched by the 2003 Iraq War where Rumsfeld's drive towards privatisation for the Pentagon meant that the use of contractors in support of the military operations increased rapidly.

[158] Klein (n 154) 293.

The PMC phenomenon was therefore fostered in the broad context of shifting and emergent threats, the widespread availability of military men and materiel, and the cultural preference for the private provision of public goods and services. This is not to say that the specific form of the PMC would not have emerged without the confluence of these factors. Rather the point is that the speed at which these changes have occurred and have become embedded has been spurred by these background conditions. While the private provision of force had always been available, albeit in a limited fashion, the settled consensus was that it was criminal in modern times. It was the confluence of these varied factors that were able to raise an implicit challenge to this stance.

VIII. CONTEMPORARY TRENDS AND FUTURE TRAJECTORIES TOWARDS MILITARY PRIVATISATION

While other commentators have revealed the reasons surrounding the initial drive towards the privatisation of military services in the modern era, I would like to elaborate upon the likely trajectory of military privatisation into the near future. I will begin by highlighting recent developments that militate against the private provision of organised force before turning to consider the reasons why the private military industry will continue to prosper.

The aforementioned US Commission on Wartime Contracting[159] began its Final Report to Congress with a sobering message that squarely contradicted the claims that contractors are more efficient, even in purely financial terms. It reported that a sum between \$31 billion and \$60 billion had been either wasted or lost through fraud in the US operations in Iraq and Afghanistan alone, and that more waste is likely to materialise with the as US involvement dwindles.[160] Furthermore, the Commission has been reported to suggest that these figures are 'conservative'.[161] In an opinion for *The Washington Post*, the co-chairs of the Commission, Michael Thibault and Christopher Shays, put this figure into context, 'At least one in every six dollars of U.S. spending for contracts and grants in Iraq and

[159] Formally known as 'The Commission on Wartime Contracting in Iraq and Afghanistan: A Bipartisan Legislative Commission Established to Study Wartime Contracting'. The Commission was created by Congress in 2008 under Public Law 110-181.

[160] Commission on Wartime Contracting (n 101) 1. The Commission elaborate in the Report that 'at the mid-range of the estimate, this amounts to \$12 million every day for the past 10 years': ibid 32.

[161] R Lardner, 'Military Spending Waste: Up To \$60 Billion In Iraq, Afghanistan War Funds Lost To Poor Planning, Oversight, Fraud' *Huffington Post* (30 August 2011) http://www.huffingtonpost.com/2011/08/30/military-spending-waste_n_942723.html.

Afghanistan over the past decade … has been wasted'.[162] Furthermore, 'Outright fraud consumed something like 5–9% of that $206bn total … while waste was estimated to be as high as 20% of the total'.[163] While such allegations of tax-dollar waste in military contracting have been made before,[164] this Report will have greater impact because the scathing critique was issued by an official and politically-balanced Commission established by Congress. A backlash against military contracting is conceivable when what might be in hindsight referred to as the 'private military bubble' bursts with the realisation that '[t]en years of war in Iraq and Afghanistan have seen the United States using too many contractors for too many functions with too little forethought and control'.[165] This backlash might be reinforced by the fact that, the Report specifically recommended to '[p]hase out use of private security contractors for certain functions' that might be described as inherently governmental.[166]

Developments which may operate in either direction are the deep budget cuts to the Ministry of Defence, which will severely reduce the size of the armed forces in the United Kingdom, in part through large numbers of compulsory redundancies.[167] On one hand, there will be a surplus of military labour generated by redundancies, which holds the potential to increase the pool of contractors in a similar fashion to military downsizing at the end of the Cold War. On the other hand, as British military spending constricts, less money would be available for contracting PMCs which would constrain a large sector of the market.[168] Other factors influencing the future of military contracting would hinge upon whether the Ministry of Defence would scale down its operations in proportion, because this would decrease the demand for contracting military services. One effect

[162] C Shays and M Thibault, 'Reducing Waste in Wartime Contracts' *Washington Post* (29 August 2011) www.washingtonpost.com/opinions/reducing-waste-in-wartime-contracts/2011/08/26/gIQAyqQhlJ_story.html

[163] P Chatterjee, 'Military Contractors' Mercenary Motives' *The Guardian* (31 August 2011) www.guardian.co.uk/commentisfree/cifamerica/2011/aug/31/us-military-contractor-waste?INTCMP=SRCH.

[164] R Greenwald, *Iraq for Sale: The War Profiteers* (Disinformation, 2006).

[165] Commission on Wartime Contracting (n 101) 38.

[166] Recommendation 3 ibid 61.

[167] The army is to be reduced by a fifth, with the navy and air force suffering significant losses also: see N Hopkins, 'War in Whitehall and an Uncertain Future for Armed Forces' *The Guardian* (1 September 2011) www.guardian.co.uk/politics/2011/sep/01/war-whitehall-armed-forces?INTCMP=SRCH. See also N Hopkins, 'Defence Cuts: More Compulsory Redundancies to Come' *The Guardian* (1 September 2011) www.guardian.co.uk/uk/2011/sep/01/defence-cuts-compulsory-redundancies.

[168] An interesting postscript is provided by the UK MoD: initial overspending on external civilian consultants led to a budgetary deficit resulting in the termination of the employment of 3000 civilian MoD employees. The circle may be completed as the services of these personnel need to be re-acquired through expensive external contracts: Hopkins, 'MoD Spent £600m on Consultants' (n 104); Hopkins, 'Ministry of Defence to Cut Further 3,000 Civilian Jobs' (n 104).

may be that the redundant personnel from the British forces would seek PMC employment elsewhere, harking back to medieval times when 'Free Companies' composed of soldiers from Britain moved to the Italian city-states in search of employment at the end of the Hundred Years War.[169]

Events that favour growth in the PMC sector include the developing Responsibility to Protect doctrine operationalised for the first time in the 2011 Libya conflict.[170] Industry lobby groups have persistently argued in favour of PMCs undertaking humanitarian roles and this doctrine may help to create a potential post-'War on Terror' market for the industry.[171] Another advantageous effect is the high cost of modern military operations,[172] which may dissuade future direct State intervention. This is combined with increasing, but low-intensity, volatility in many strategic regions within the operational competence of PMCs. Merging these three factors creates a situation where PMCs may prosper, and there are indications from Libya that the companies are already getting involved, especially for the provision of security to the oil industry.[173]

Finally, there is the demand from transnational corporations (TNCs) for the provision of security, particularly in the extractive industry sector.[174] Historical examples of the close, but highly obfuscated, links between the private military and extractive industries have been documented. The difficulty involved in obtaining and verifying relevant information, however, has combined with the historical legacy of mercenaries engaged in the protection of extraction sites that have perpetuated the myth and misconception.[175] As the extractive industries move into increasingly volatile regions, the demand for PMC (security) services is bound to increase as illustrated by the quiet successes of Control Risks and Global Rescue in

[169] Singer (n 24) 23–24; N Bicanic and J Bourque, *Shadow Company* (Purpose Built Films, 2006).

[170] Peace and Security in Africa 2011 (S/RES/1970); The Situation in Libya 2011 (S/RES/1973).

[171] Brooks, 'Messiahs or Mercenaries?' (n 21) 134–36; D Brooks and M Chorev, 'Ruthless Humanitarianism: Why Marginalizing Private Peacekeeping Kills People' in A Alexandra, D-P Baker and M Caparini (eds), *Private Military and Security Companies: Ethics, Policies and Civil-military Relations* (Routledge, 2008).

[172] A Stratton, 'Libya Campaign May Cost UK £260m' *The Guardian* (23 June 2011) www.guardian.co.uk/politics/2011/jun/23/libya-campaign-has-cost-uk-260m?INTCMP=SRCH.

[173] K Fahim and M de la Baume, 'Head of French Security Company Killed in Libya' *New York Times* (12 May 2011) www.nytimes.com/2011/05/13/world/africa/13benghazi.html?_r=1&scp=1&sq=Pierre%20Marziali&st=cse.

[174] D Shearer, *Private Armies and Military Intervention* (Oxford University Press, 1998) 43–45; G Cleaver, 'Subcontracting Military Power: The Privatisation of Security in Contemporary Sub-Saharan Africa' (2000) 33 *Crime, Law & Social Change* 131, 139–43.

[175] R Abrahamsen and M Williams, *Security Beyond the State: Private Security in International Politics* (Cambridge University Press, 2010) 122–71. The authors note the shift in PMC engagement with the extractive industry, tending towards training State militaries and consigning direct protection to non-military Private Security Companies: ibid 124–25.

protecting their Libyan clients.[176] Similarly, the threat to shipping posed by Somali piracy may create a lucrative market for armed security.[177]

IX. TOWARDS A DEFINITION AND TYPOLOGY FOR THE MODERN PRIVATE MILITARY COMPANY

In the first report of the UN Open-ended Intergovernmental Working Group to consider Private Military and Security Companies in December 2012, Marcia VJ Kran, the Director of the Research and Right to Development Division of the Office of the High Commissioner for Human Rights, opened by noting that:

> [T]he issues at hand were complex, starting with the very definition of private military and security companies, which were engaged in a variety of activities and provide a broad range of services internationally and domestically. In this regard, she recalled that discussions during the first session underscored the importance of a clear definition of the term 'private military and security companies', with some suggesting the need to distinguish the activities of private military companies, on the one hand, and those of private security companies on the other.[178]

This suggests that the definition of what constitutes a PMC remains problematic a full decade after the rapid expansion of the industry that was sparked by the conflict in Iraq. It is equally striking that the categorisation of the industry remains unsettled, despite all of the work and attention that has been focused upon the industry in the intervening time. Yet, the effect of uncertain definitions and categories is not merely an academic problem, but suffuses into practical policy and regulatory issues. It is difficult to conceive how a rigorous discussion concerning appropriate standards, regulation, oversight and accountability can begin when the contours of the PMC that constitutes the threat are not even agreed upon or fully understood.

The porous boundaries that attempt to segregate the various categories of actors in these areas create uncertainties both regarding the legal

[176] D Mitchell, 'Libyan Extraction: How Companies Get Employees out of Global Hotspots' *CNN* (3 March 2011) http://money.cnn.com/2011/03/03/news/international/libya_protests_company_rescues.fortune/index.htm. This shift into the provision of 'security services' to private business interests by the PMC industry underscores the difficulties inherent with the language used to describe the activities of the industry.

[177] K Manson and R Wright, 'Somali Pirates Spawn Lucrative Security Trade' *Financial Times* (8 February 2012) www.ft.com/cms/s/0/410d1b40-45b0-11e1-acc9-00144feabdc0.html#axzz1lqtpHUhU.

[178] A Minty, 'Report of the Open-Ended Intergovernmental Working Group to Consider the Possibility of Elaborating an International Regulatory Framework on the Regulation, Monitoring and Oversight of the Activities of Private Military and Security Companies on Its Second Session' (UNGA, 2012) A/HRC/22/41 para 4.

treatment as well as the types of roles played by the contractors themselves. José Luis Gómez del Prado, then Chairperson-Rapporteur of the UN Working Group on the Use of Mercenaries, illustrates these points well. With regard to legal categorisation, he observed that:

> In zones of armed conflict the employees of transnational private military and security companies, *contracted as civilians but armed as military personnel*, operate in these 'grey zones' with *uncertainties as to whether their status is that of a combatant or of a civilian* … These new modalities have replaced to a certain extent the use of traditional individual mercenaries.[179]

Later in the same report, he underscores the uncertainties under which PMC contractors often operate:

> Although they were not specifically recruited to take part in hostilities, their contracts did not specify either that they would receive military training and would be militarily armed. *Recruited in their respective countries from all over the world as 'private security guards' to provide protection, most of them have in fact taken part in an internal low-intensity armed conflict.*[180]

Together, these observations point to the contradictions that underlie the modern PMC which frustrate attempts to define and categorise the industry, necessary precursors to regulation. What is particularly clear in these comments is the divergence between form and function embodied by the PMC: the use of civilian status to organise military activities. These categories are further obfuscated because of the industry's overlap with the commercial security sector. The possibility for the PMC industry to seek refuge within the commercial security industry can be seen with the strategic labelling, for example in the ICoC, that PMCs are Private Security Providers. Furthermore, this trend is likely to increase insofar as the PMC shifts focus to cater for private commercial interests, such as the shipping and extractive industries, where the provision of security may appear more justifiable.

The Draft Convention proposed by the UN Working Group on the Use of Mercenaries provides a useful starting point for considering definitions. Article 2(a) of the Draft Convention stipulates: 'Private Military and/or Security Company (PMSC): refers to a corporate entity which provides on a compensatory basis military and/or security services by physical persons and/or legal entities'.[181] This wide definition, which encompasses

[179] Gómez del Prado, 'Report of the Working Group on the Use of Mercenaries' (n 3) 25. Emphasis added.

[180] ibid 38. Emphasis added.

[181] Gómez del Prado (n 123) 24. Furthermore, both military and security services are defined in the following subsections:

> (b) Military services: refers to specialized services related to military actions including strategic planning, intelligence, investigation, land, sea or air reconnaissance, flight operations of any type, manned or unmanned, satellite surveillance, any kind of

activities related to the provision of coercive force, justifies the broad approach to the PMC industry taken here. While there may be possible errors associated with over-inclusion, this is necessary to capture all facets of the diverse and dynamic industry.

The potential spectrum of the PMC industry is immense, so a definition needs to be developed. A *Private Military Company* is considered expansively here: a PMC is a private company providing military services for the purposes of private profit. Thus, the PMC possesses three critical components, emphasising each of its constituent words. Taking these in reverse, first the *company* component is stressed. The PMC is a juridical person, having a separate and independent legal identity to the natural persons constituting or involved with it. This corporate status of the PMC simultaneously shields natural persons from different forms of liability and imbues it with claims of legitimate existence and a right to operate. Second, the PMC renders inherently *military* services. This is defined broadly such that it encompasses all activities ranging from direct participation in hostilities to the logistical and administrative support involved in the projection of organised violence. This breadth captures any company associated with the military in order to subject them to close scrutiny and is justified to prevent companies from evading classification as a PMC that might facilitate their circumventing PMC scrutiny and regulation. Third, it is a *private* entity. The PMC neither possesses nor exercises public power or authority and is driven by the motive of private profit by selling military services for material gain. It is the sale of the means of coercive force for private gain which informs much of the moral condemnation levelled against both the mercenary as well as the PMC.

Finally, the euphemistic tone of the 'Private Military Company' and of 'contractor' for their employees may constitute a form of interpretive denial identified by Stanley Cohen that 'mask, sanitize and confer respectability … deny or misrepresent cruelty or harm, giving them neutral or respectable status'.[182] This approach will be adopted in greater detail in chapter three, which addresses the problematic nature of defining the 'mercenary' and the subsequent ability of the PMC industry to distance itself from its mercenary roots. The focus here will be on the nature of the contemporary industry itself and in categorising the various types of company that constitute the PMC industry.

knowledge transfer with military applications, material and technical support to armed forces and other related activities.

(c) Security services: refers to armed guarding or protection of buildings, installations, property and people, any kind of knowledge transfer with security and policing applications, development and implementation of informational security measures and other related activities.

[182] S Cohen, *States of Denial: Knowing About Atrocities and Suffering* (Polity, 2001) 107.

A. Existing Typologies for the Private Military Company Industry

While the expansive definition of a PMC provided above demarcates the broad category of entities that are encompassed within the term, a refined typology is necessary to systematically differentiate between the various types of, and services offered by, these companies. The difficulties that plague attempts to categorise these companies should be noted at the outset, such that Christopher Kinsey has reiterated the preference to categorise companies upon the services they offer rather than the companies themselves.[183] Although classification upon the nature of the services provided remains the best approach, difficulties remain because the provision of services within the PMC industry are dependent upon market forces, and as such are malleable to demand. The broader structural realities of the industry must be considered, as Naomi Klein illustrates:

> Made possible by the September 11 attacks, the war in Iraq represented nothing less than the violent birth of a new economy ... since every possible aspect of both destruction and reconstruction has been outsourced and privatized, there's an economic boom when the bombs start falling, when they stop and when they start up again—a closed profit-loop of destruction and reconstruction, of tearing down and building up.[184]

She provides Lockheed Martin as an example of the blurring boundaries between civilian companies, arms manufacturers and military companies:

> Lockheed Martin has gone furthest in this direction. In early 2007, it began 'buying companies in the $1,000bn-a-year healthcare market,' according to The Financial Times, and it also snapped up the engineering giant Pacific Architects and Engineers. The wave of acquisitions signified *a new era of morbid vertical integration* in the disaster capitalism complex: in future conflicts, *Lockheed is poised to profit not only from making the weapons and fighter jets but from rebuilding what they destroy, and even from the treating the people injured by its own weapons.*[185]

Thus, the drive towards profitability leads to the consolidation of a diverse range of activities within the auspices of a single corporation which challenges the very conception of the PMC. Indeed, attempts to classify the PMC industry have been compounded by the expansion, contraction and refocus of the PMCs in question.[186]

With the additional profitability factor, militarised corporations in the broader sense no longer need to provide military goods or services directly because it may prove both more lucrative and more expedient to concentrate on providing services away from the controversial 'tip-of-the-spear'.

[183] Kinsey (n 135) 9.
[184] Klein (n 154) 381.
[185] ibid. Emphasis added.
[186] Kinsey (n 135) 9–10.

There are indications that the larger security companies are moving away from the provision of such controversial services: as an industry insider had commented, the profits are no longer from 'the guys with the guns and wrap-around sunglasses', but from proactive security provision and other robust services.[187] What should be recognised from the conglomeration of the PMC industry is that market forces dictate the type of services that are offered. Thus, neither structural shifts nor normative boundaries can be inferred from the contemporary retreat from the provision of offensive military-style services that were previously offered, for example, by Executive Outcomes. Instead, all that this reveals is the current lack of market demand, and therefore low profitability, associated with providing these services in the contemporary market-place. Effective typologies and regulatory mechanisms will need to be mindful of the distinct possibility that these demands resurface in the future, leading to the re-emergence of PMCs providing services once thought beyond the pale.

Returning to PMC typologies, these can be differentiated upon the number of dimensions that they employ, and two-dimensional models are preferable because these reduce the amount of ambiguity in comparison to one-dimensional typologies. A critical overview of the main typology models that have been applied to the PMC follows. The neutral stance towards the PMC industry that can be deduced from these models ignores the objectionable nature of its two core characteristics; their trade in organised violence and their direct participation in hostilities. These characteristics form the two dimensions upon which a revised typology is constructed. This proposed typology recognises the intrinsically military nature of the services they provide and the concomitant nature of the threat they pose. This in turn justifies the necessity for strict oversight and rigorous regulatory mechanisms to be adopted for the industry.

B. One-Dimensional Typologies

One of the earliest and most influential models of PMC classification has been PW Singer's tripartite 'tip-of-the-spear' typology which concentrates upon the nature of the services the company provides.[188] This model functions by mapping a company onto a metaphorical one-dimensional 'spear' that represents the theoretical battlespace, such that the position of a company within this typology depends upon its proximity to actual combat. Companies which offer combat, or 'tip-of-the-spear' services, are known as Military *Provider* Firms (MPF). Military *Support* Firms (MSF)

[187] Interview with G4S Advisor, 22 January 2010.
[188] Singer (n 24) 88–100.

and Military *Consultant* Firms (MCF) are positioned toward the spear shaft and provide other services short of direct participation in hostilities, but are nevertheless of a military nature. This basic differentiation which separates companies according to the level of force which they are likely to use has been developed and refined by other commentators who have also linked this to the other effects raised by the PMC. Despite the numerous strengths of this typology, it has been criticised for failing to distinguish between the specific activities, such as coercive violence, which are of particular concern and because it does not account for the possibility that a single company may offer services within each subdivision.[189] The latter objection may be allayed by simply considering the specific service under analysis separately. For example, a PMC may be a MPF in a particular instance, while under different circumstances it might function as a MCF, even within the same operation.

To remedy this potential weakness, Deborah Avant has approached the classification of PMCs through the contract as an analytical unit as opposed to that of the type of company.[190] This seemingly minor alteration neutralises the problem of PMC flexibility where one firm may play numerous roles simultaneously or transform between roles. In other words, the company is seen simply as a PMC and is defined subsequently according to the type of service it is contracted to provide, allowing for the full recognition of the multi-faceted nature of the services offered by PMCs. This approach may be criticised for focusing upon contractual formalities at the possible expense of overlooking the actual activities in which a PMC is engaged. A contract may be vague or inaccurate, as suggested by José Luis Gómez del Prado above, or the activities of a PMC may simply exceed its contractual obligations. Yet, while a PMC may be most accurately classified based upon its activities, the contract may be a useful heuristic which confers the additional benefit of ascertaining role responsibilities in a prospective manner and as evidence to what types of activities a PMC should be engaged in.

A refined version of this one-dimensional typology is proposed by Thomas Jäger and Gerhard Kümmel by adding a lateral aspect to PW Singer's 'spear'.[191] This model emphasises that the 'spear shaft' is much

[189] B Sheehy, J Maogoto and V Newell, *Legal Control of the Private Military Corporation* (Palgrave Macmillan, 2009) 17–18.

[190] D Avant, *The Market for Force: The Consequences of Privatizing Security* (Cambridge University Press, 2005) 16–22.

[191] The addition of a lateral dimension suggests that this is in fact a two-dimensional model. Yet, the additional information that is yielded does not help to classify any particular PMC, but rather illustrates the economic distribution of the PMC industry at large: T Jäger and G Kümmel, 'PSMCs: Lessons Learned and Where to Go from Here' in Jäger and Kümmel (eds), *Private Military and Security Companies: Chances, Problems, Pitfalls and Prospects* (n 128) 457–62, 460–61.

wider than the 'spear tip' when judged upon the financial turnover and specialisation of the industry as a whole. Thus, while the PMC industry is still classified along one dimension, a broader characteristic is acknowledged. This dimension of weight gives an idea to the relative size of each of the three components of the PMC industry. From this typology, the industry currently appears to be primarily providing support and consultancy services over the direct provision of force. Jäger and Kümmel suggest that this is evidence for the increasing legitimacy of the industry since services involving direct participation constitute only a small minority of PMC interests.[192] The industry itself mirrors this suggestion as it perceives the shift of PMCs away from MPFs towards MCFs and MSFs as providing support for their assertion of legitimacy and associated right of existence and operation.

This is a logical extension of the argument that MPFs are little more than thinly veiled mercenary bands, because of the distinction this creates from the illegitimacy of mercenaries and MPFs that in turn implies that MCFs are unproblematic. This is erroneous because the objection towards mercenary activity is wider than the acts of the individual mercenary, as Enrique Ballesteros observes:

> [I]t is clear that mercenary activity is not limited to the agent who actually commits the criminal act. He is merely the one who executes a wrongful act. In reality, before a mercenary is recruited and before he commits a wrongful act, *there has to be an operation which has been conceived, planned, organised, financed and supervised by third parties*; the latter may be private groups … which, through covert operations, decide on illegal action against a state or against the life, liberty, physical integrity and safety of persons, and involve mercenaries in that action.[193]

The difficulty with Singer's typology, and its adaptation by Jäger and Kümmel, is that the models imply that a shift 'down' the 'spear shaft' away from direct provision of force results in the increased legitimacy of the PMC industry. The 'tip-of-the-spear' typology does not correspond directly to a scale of legitimacy, or conversely, of criminality because all of the activities engaged in by the industry relate to the projection of organised violence, albeit in often indirect and diffused ways.

A similar approach has been advocated by Kevin O'Brien, whose typology provides an alternative set of characteristics upon which to categorise the industry based upon the company's *intention to alter the strategic*

192 It must be underscored, however, that this is only the contemporary distribution of the industry, and that changes in market pressures may swiftly alter this distribution.

193 E Ballesteros, 'Report on the Use of Mercenaries as a Means of Violating Human Rights and Impeding the Exercise of the Right of Peoples to Self-Determination' (1995) E/CN.4/1995/29 para 92. Emphasis added. This is also reflected in the broad nature of the criminalisation of mercenarism in the regional and international conventions: see ch 3.

environment.[194] Thus for O'Brien, *Military Operations* is used for 'private actors intended to alter the strategic environment', which included all forms of active or passive operational support and advisory services.[195] *Military-Support Operations*, on the other hand, do not seek to alter the strategic environment and include services such as logistics.[196] His third and fourth categories remain unnamed and revolve around security provision and non-lethal local services respectively.[197] The strength of O'Brien's model is its ability to accurately define what was hitherto referred to as services of a military nature. Engaging with the idea of altering the strategic environment enables a more nuanced approach to categorising the services offered by PMCs. Furthermore, it is preferable over the *active—passive* distinction often forwarded by commentators in favour of the PMC industry, such as Doug Brooks, discussed below. The weaknesses of O'Brien's model, however, are twofold: first because it is premised upon activities *intended* to alter the strategic environment, such that the actual outcome is ignored; and second, there are the obvious difficulties associated with proving motivation. This latter point is further exacerbated by the juridical personhood of the corporation, as well as its reality as an association of natural persons, that complicate determining requisite motivation.

From the perspective of the PMC industry pursuing its interest in establishing its legitimacy and right to operate, Doug Brooks has forwarded a model of the PMC industry similar to PW Singer's. Interestingly, he labels the industry the PMC the 'Military Service Provider', perhaps attempting to deploy Stanley Cohen's interpretive denial mechanisms.[198] In Brooks' model, there is the Non-lethal Service Provider, Private Security Companies, Private Military Companies (Passive) and Private Military Companies (Active).[199] By distinguishing non-lethal service providers, however, Brooks implicitly recognises that the default position of Military Service Providers is trade in lethal services. It is also arguable that the category of Non-lethal Service Provider is a contradiction when applied to the Military Service Provider because their services release soldiers for active deployment in hostilities, or who alternatively act as 'force multipliers' when they engage in training or support roles for militaries. By ignoring this effect, Brooks' model implicitly suggests that there is a legitimate field of activity for Military Service Providers that is distinguished from

[194] K O'Brien, 'What Should and What Should Not Be Regulated?' in Chesterman and Lehnardt (eds), *From Mercenaries to Market: The Rise and Regulation of Private Military Companies* (n 18) 29–48, 40–41.

[195] ibid 40.

[196] ibid 41.

[197] ibid.

[198] Cohen, *States of Denial* (n 182) 105–09.

[199] Sheehy, Maogoto and Newell, *Legal Control of the Private Military Corporation* (n 189) 19.

illegitimate activities, upon an assumption of allegiance with the State. Brooks' model thus trends towards Kinsey's, but applies more formal and less rigorous criteria as to what constitutes public interest. Similarly, James Davis proposes definitions based upon a scale of legitimacy, but has limited his categorisation to entities which provide combat roles only. This categorisation is separated into Regular Foreign Unit, Auxiliary Foreign Unit, Foreign Volunteer and Private Military Company, with declining levels of legitimacy.[200] Again, it is clear from this classification that Davis conceives of legitimacy as a factor of proximity with the State, implicitly supporting the Weberian notion of the State as the legitimate monopoly holder over the use of force.

C. Official Typologies

Official typologies also only employ one dimension, but they are specifically preoccupied with the question of industry legitimacy. Thus, the Working Group on the Use of Mercenaries

> is of the opinion that States must make a clear distinction between those private companies which offer security services in strict compliance with imperative norms, regulations and accountability, such as respect for the principle of the State's monopoly on the use of force, and those recruiting, training, hiring, or financing mercenaries to operate in zones of armed conflict, whose activities should be criminalised.[201]

This suggests that the Working Group, which succeeded the Special Rapporteurs, is following Shiasta Shameem's position over that of Enrique Ballesteros. It is unclear how the Working Group has resolved this debate and why it moved away from the presumption, expressed by Enrique Ballesteros, that PMCs are criminal organisations. The UK stance, as reflected in the Green Paper published by the Foreign and Commonwealth Office (FCO), has a preoccupation with the respectability and legitimacy of the PMC. The Paper divides the private provision of force abroad into six categories: mercenaries, volunteers, servicemen enlisted in foreign armies, defence industrial companies and private military companies.[202] The context, however, is imperative because the Report was requested in the direct aftermath of the Sandline International 'Arms to Africa' scandal

[200] J Davis, *Fortune's Warriors: Private Armies and the New World Order* (Douglas & McIntyre, 2002) 74; Sheehy, Maogoto and Newell (n 189) 18–19.

[201] Working Group on the Use of Mercenaries, 'Report of the Working Group on the Use of Mercenaries as a Means of Violating Human Rights and Impeding the Exercise of the Right of Peoples to Self-Determination' (UNGA, 2007) A/62/301 para 66.

[202] United Kingdom Foreign and Commonwealth Office, *Private Military Companies: Options for Regulation* (n 24) 9.

involving the shipment of arms to Sierra Leone in contravention of a UN arms embargo.[203]

The significance of these latter two approaches is the implicit acceptance of a legitimate sphere of private military activity in which the PMC may operate. There is palpable concern that potential regulation addressed at the PMC will also incidentally affect what the FCO terms 'Defence Industrial Companies', or arms manufacturers, since

> the services provided with the equipment may in some circumstances not be very different from those which a private military company might supply. Arms suppliers may for example arrange *to supply people to operate the equipment … In extreme cases this might involve combat missions*.[204]

As the FCO noted in its conclusions for instance, '[a] blanket ban would deprive British defence exporters of *legitimate business—services are often a necessary part of export sales*'.[205] Even aside from such a strong reaction, various advocates for the privatised military industry stress that the competitiveness of the defence sector on the international market would be jeopardised should regulations be imposed on the export of such services.

This leads to the international, albeit primarily Western, consideration of the modern PMC crystallised in the Montreux Document[206] which is not intended to increase the legitimacy associated with employing PMCs.[207] The Private Military and Security Company is understood as being

> private business entities that provide military and/or security services, irrespective of how they describe themselves. Military and security services include, in particular, armed guarding and protection of persons and objects … maintenance and operation of weapons systems; prisoner detention; and advice to or training of local forces and security personnel.[208]

The Document alludes to the potential inappropriateness of contracting for PMC services which could lead to their employees becoming directly involved in hostilities.[209] Otherwise it appears that the Document considers utilising PMCs as unproblematic so long as there is 'respect for relevant national law, international humanitarian law and human rights law'.[210] While this may be laudable on its face, these areas of law are woefully

[203] House of Commons Foreign Affairs Committee, *Private Military Companies* (n 24) 1. See generally T Spicer, *An Unorthodox Soldier: Peace and War and the Sandline Affair* (Mainstream Publishing, 2000).

[204] United Kingdom Foreign and Commonwealth Office (n 24) 9. Emphasis added.

[205] ibid 71. Emphasis added.

[206] Montreux Document on Pertinent International Legal Obligations and Good Practices for States Related to Operations of Private Military and Security Companies during Armed Conflict 2008.

[207] ibid 5.

[208] ibid 6.

[209] ibid 12.

[210] ibid 13; in contradistinction to the Draft Convention which prohibits the delegation or outsourcing of inherently governmental functions in art 9: Gómez del Prado (n 123).

inadequate both in defining specific obligations and in submitting the PMC to effective regulation, as chapter six explores.[211]

Finally, I was able to obtain the UK Ministry of Defence Policy which recognised three categories of services provided by the Private *Security* Company industry (the emphasis is necessary in relation to Category C below): Category A Risk Consultancy/Un-armed Defensive Services 'Predominantly concerned with minimising the operational risk to clients operating overseas'; Category B Armed Defensive Services 'who provide armed defensive security services'; Category C Armed Offensive Services which 'may be termed Private Military Companies and includes those companies prepared to take on contracts which could have an impact on the security and political environment of the state through violent force'.[212] The MoD policy document repeatedly emphasises that 'The MOD *does not* contract, or allow MOD Contractors to sub-contract, for Armed Offensive Services … or with companies that sell, or have previously sold, these services'.[213] While this commitment against Armed Offensive Services is laudable, this typology falls foul of the wide grey zone existing between offensive and defensive activities. This difficulty is illustrated by the direct participation in hostilities of PMC contractors providing defensive services to legitimate military targets.[214]

D. Two-Dimensional Typologies

The common problem plaguing one-dimensional typologies is their inability to capture the nuanced characteristics of the PMC industry because its activities within the military realm encompass support, consulting and provider roles in PW Singer's typology. The proposed typology refines this concept before providing the additional dimension of proximity to hostilities by adopting the idea of direct participation.

The advantage of two-dimensional typologies is illustrated by the analytical framework offered by Christopher Kinsey. This placed PMCs along two intersecting axes representing the international environment, drawing an intrinsic connection between the levels of force used and the

[211] Amnesty International, 'Amnesty International Public Statement on the Montreux Document on Pertinent International Legal Obligations and Good Practices for States Related to the Operations of Private Military and Security Companies during Armed Conflict' www.amnesty.org/en/library/asset/IOR30/010/2008/en/5bca5962-99de-11dd-bf88-f59215f3db50/ior300102008en.pdf.

[212] Private Security Companies (PSC)—MOD Policy. Version of 23 February 2012. On file with the author. Paragraphs 3108–12.

[213] ibid paras 3110 and 3111. Emphasis original.

[214] J Gómez del Prado, 'Private Military and Security Companies and the UN Working Group on the Use of Mercenaries' (2008) 13 *Journal of Conflict and Security Law* 429, 444.

purposes for which it is deployed. The *y-axis* is labelled as *Means of securing the object* along a continuum of lethality at the top to non-lethality at the bottom, whereas the *x-axis* concerns the *Object to be secured* spanning the spectrum between private interests on the left and public purposes to the right.[215] The four resultant quadrants possess very different characteristics. The vertical axis concerning the level of lethality vaguely corresponds with PW Singer's tip-of-the-spear typology. Thus on the left side of the vertical axis representing private objectives, the actors involved tend to be grouped in the bottom-left quadrant. This is because only low levels of potential lethality can be justified in pursuit of private objectives. That said, historically, there have been some actors which were willing to use high levels of lethal force in service of private ends, including mercenaries, privateers and a small section of early PMCs acknowledged to have been so engaged. Thus on the left side of the vertical axis, while a position near the bottom is relatively unproblematic, this rapidly changes towards illegitimacy and criminality as the level of contemplated lethality increases. On the right side of the vertical axis are the two quadrants concerned with the use of force according to public authority or in defence of the State (although Kinsey's narrow definition can conceivably be expanded to include broader notions of public service, such as humanitarian intervention and Responsibility to Protect, as potentially legitimate objectives to be pursued by the use of force). The right side of the vertical axis is dominated by State institutions, but PMCs have made a notable entry into this area. For instance, what Singer classifies as a MCF is placed in the bottom-right corner of Kinsey's model, and MPFs are considered by Kinsey to fall within the top-right quadrant.

Christopher Kinsey appears to suggest that the only problematic entities are those falling within the top-left quadrant where lethal force may be employed for private ends. While his model connects PW Singer's typology to a conception of the objective for which such force is employed, it may lead to two highly misleading conclusions. First, the bottom-left quadrant assumes the unproblematic employment of force for private ends, provided that it is relatively non-lethal. Such a connection ignores the problems associated with the diffusion, and eventual dissolution, of the State monopoly over the use of force. Such erosion may subsequently lead to the provision of increasingly lethal force in service of private interests. Second, it assumes that lethal force in service of public authority or in defence of the State is also unproblematic. In specifying these criteria, it simultaneously allows lethal force to be employed subject only to formal constraints, while providing immunity for PMCs which are considered to fall into this quadrant. Thus, from one perspective, a PMC such

[215] Kinsey (n 135) 8–33.

as Executive Outcomes or Sandline International may be seen to be providing a public service, while from another viewpoint they are perceived to provide lethal force for profit. Both views have strong merits, which Kinsey's classification skews in favour of legitimate operation. To be fair, Kinsey does stipulate in his explanation of the model that PMCs offering lethal services may be considered legitimate if they work for recognised governments or are sanctioned by the international community. What is overlooked, however, is that the need to resort to private forces to secure the stability of a government is a very strong indication that the legitimacy underlying its power has been eroded.

X. PROPOSED TYPOLOGY: SEGREGATING CIVILIAN AND MILITARY CORPORATIONS ON THE PRINCIPLE OF DISTINCTION

While the typologies examined above established frameworks with which to categorise PMCs, they collectively fail to account for the *military* nature of their services. In other words, the existing typologies do not recognise the watershed that has been signalled by the PMC because the corporation was previously an exclusively *civilian* entity. The United Kingdom House of Commons Foreign Affairs Committee had alluded to the implicit civilian nature of corporations when it stated: 'We recommend that private companies be expressly prohibited from direct participation in armed combat operations, and that firearms should only be carried—and if necessary used—by company employees for the purposes of training or self-defence'.[216] Again, because PMCs control and exert organised violence and directly participate in hostilities, a revised typology that underscores the emerging distinction between *civilian* and *military* corporations is required. In addition, this proposed typology has the benefit of recognising the heightened threats posed by the latter category that serves as justification for more rigorous regulatory mechanisms.

To begin this process, the juridical corporate status of the PMC means that it must be appropriately contextualised within the broader corporate business environment. Here, Carlos Ortiz's contributions are significant.[217] He places the PMC at the intersection between three interlocking spheres of commercial activity: the corporate security sector; conglomerates taking on outsourced state tasks; and established non-security corporations.[218] Ortiz further emphasises 'how the contemporary business

[216] House of Commons Foreign Affairs Committee (n 25) 108; this requirement is reiterated in art 8 of the Draft Convention which requires the prohibition and illegality of the direct participation in hostilities by PMCs and their contractors: Gómez del Prado (n 123).

[217] C Ortiz, 'The Private Military Company: An Entity at the Centre of Overlapping Spheres of Commercial Activity and Responsibility' in Jäger and Kümmel (n 128) 55–67.

[218] See fig 2: ibid 67.

environment renders the private military industry very fluid, in which mergers and acquisitions shift the PMC capabilities of firms across different corporate identities and sectors'.[219] While Ortiz begins the process of situating the PMC within the corporate context, his analysis unfortunately adopts a neutral perspective that fails to recognise the emergence of the *military* corporation embodied within the PMC.

The underlying assumption that corporations are civilian in nature is evident in the writings of even Maurice Punch, a vocal critic of the current state of corporate criminal responsibility, although PMC activity is not considered within his analyses of corporate violence and corporate killing.[220] Instead, his conceptions of corporate killing remain governed by the implicit civilian nature of the corporation and the indirect, predominantly negligent or reckless, manner in which it operates. Maurice Punch expresses this limited conception well in an introduction to corporate killing:

> This is obviously not to suggest that there is a direct comparison between the excesses of an army in a war zone and a legitimate corporation under normal circumstances. Business managers clearly cannot be placed in the same category as dictatorial leaders who sponsor mass violence … and executives do not share the 'bloody hands' experiences of front-line soldiers or paramilitaries.[221]

Furthermore, Punch refers to the 'palpable and convincing evidence that corporations "kill"' from "avoidable deaths in the workplace" to "serious accidents and disasters"'.[222] The point here is not to criticise the approach adopted by the fields of white collar and corporate crime, but rather to illustrate that the PMC is spearheading a new type of *military corporation*. Unlike the classic conception of the corporation envisaged by Punch, this new type of corporation is exactly capable of causing severe harm in a direct fashion which is inherent from its control of organised violence.

Approaching from a different perspective, the unspoken assumption that corporations are civilian entities leads to concomitantly limited conceptions of corporate harm, risk and intention. This is characterised by the diffused action and dissociated responsibility that is inherent with organisational activity, such as that undertaken by corporations. In turn, these may indicate the boundaries of appropriate corporate activity which

[219] ibid.

[220] M Punch, 'Suite Violence: Why Managers Murder and Corporations Kill' (2000) 33 *Crime, Law & Social Change* 243; M Punch, 'Why Corporations Kill and Get Away with It: The Failure of Law to Cope with Crimes in Organisations' in A Nollkaemper and H van der Wilt (eds), *System Criminality in International Law* (Cambridge University Press, 2009).

[221] Punch, 'Why Corporations Kill and Get Away with It' (n 220) 56. Punch's presumption here may obviously be rebutted with the operations of the PMC.

[222] ibid 57. It is interesting to note that deaths from both omissions and actions, respectively, are within the contemplation of corporate killing.

are breached where corporations are capable of perpetrating severe and direct harm through violence. Furthermore, assuming the civilian nature of the corporation perpetuates the imperceptibility of a distinct category of military corporation that emerged with the modern PMC.[223] Recognising the fundamental difference between civilian and military corporations would justify a radically different evaluation of corporate criminality. This may, in turn, feed back to reinvigorate the debate over civilian corporation criminality.

A. Adapting the Principle of Distinction

The typology proposed here is adapted from the principle of distinction under IHL, such that its strict application would necessitate the prior satisfaction of the severity threshold for classification as an armed conflict.[224] This threshold for 'hostilities' is essential for differentiating between situations of lawful belligerency which meet those requirements and those constituting unlawful armed violence that fall short.[225] It is clear from this perspective that the organised armed violence offered by PMCs may simply be classified as criminal activity under domestic laws in situations where the severity threshold is not met within the meaning of IHL.[226] This underlines the strong dimension of criminality for PMCs which operate in situations of violence that do not amount to 'hostilities'. This is further supported by the explicit loss of protection from direct attack for civilians who participate directly in hostilities, and because IHL 'neither prohibits nor privileges civilian direct participation in hostilities … [they] are not exempted from prosecution for violations of domestic and international law they may have committed'.[227] Applied to PMC contractors in international armed conflicts, unless they have been incorporated into the armed forces de jure or de facto, in which case they are disqualified as civilians as

[223] The term 'military' is used here as a short-cut for 'combatant' and in order to apply the idea of mutual exclusivity with 'civilian'. Adopting the expansive term 'military' is also preferable since a revised typology of the PMC should not be limited to the narrower category of 'combatant'.

[224] C Greenwood, 'The Scope of Application of Humanitarian Law' in Gill and Fleck (n 9) 45–56.

[225] Similarly, it should be noted that the use of armed force does not presuppose the existence of 'hostilities': N Melzer, 'Fifth Expert Meeting on the Notion of Direct Participation in Hostilities' 44 and 49 www.icrc.org/eng/assets/files/other/2008-05-report-dph-2008-icrc.pdf.

[226] The minimum level of severity required before IHL applies may be counter-productive since otherwise criminal acts may be absolved of their criminality by virtue of intensifying the violence.

[227] N Melzer, 'Interpretive Guidance on the Notion of Direct Participation in Hostilities Under International Humanitarian Law' (ICRC, 2009) Publication Ref 0990 17.

members of an organised armed group under responsible command, they are to be considered as civilian.[228] For non-international armed conflicts, the assumption of a continuous combat function is the yardstick for armed group membership, and the theoretical possibility for PMCs to become independent parties to a non-international armed conflict should be noted in this context.[229] With this in mind, the principle of distinction will be adapted in theory to create a typology that can differentiate between military corporations and civilian corporations that is capable of recognising the former categories' heightened risks for criminality.

B. The Severity of Harm Dimension: Control and Exercise of Violence

A new distinction between military and civilian corporations[230] may be proposed along the lines of the 'Basic Rule' in Article 48 of API that requires adherence to the cardinal principle of distinction.[231] The advantage of this taxonomy derives from the mutually exclusive relationship between the members of armed forces and civilians.[232] The question of participation in a *levée en masse* 'which refers to the inhabitants of a non-occupied territory who, on the approach of the enemy, spontaneously take up arms to resist the invading forces' can be excluded for present purposes.[233] Although it is theoretically conceivable that a PMC could act in such a capacity, it is generally precluded by its third-country status and its permanent existence, which together contradict the spontaneous characteristic of a *levée en masse*. Aside from this limitation, the strict separation and mutual exclusivity of the principle of distinction is a suitable basis upon which to distinguish between civilian and military corporations.

An advantage of adopting the division between civilians and combatants inheres within the possibility of conversion (provided it is not constant and repetitive) between the two categories. With regards to natural persons, Yoram Dinstein explains that: 'A civilian may convert himself into a combatant. In fact, every combatant is formerly a civilian: nobody is born a combatant. In the same vein, a combatant may retire and become a

[228] ibid 39.
[229] ibid 39–40.
[230] While the principle of distinction segregates combatants from civilians, I have substituted the former term with military to avert confusion related to privileged or unprivileged belligerency that may affect the analysis of the PMC.
[231] This is also reflected in r 1 of the Customary International Humanitarian Law Study: J-M Henckaerts and L Doswald-Beck, *Customary International Humanitarian Law*, vol I (Cambridge University Press, 2009) 3–8.
[232] For the distinction in international armed conflict, see Melzer, 'Interpretive Guidance on the Notion of Direct Participation in Hostilities Under International Humanitarian Law' (n 227) 20–26. For the distinction in non-international armed conflict, see ibid 27–36.
[233] Melzer (n 227) 25.

civilian'.[234] Applying this idea to the typology, the a priori position of all corporations, including potential PMCs, are that they are civilian entities. This presumption may then be overturned if there is evidence that these companies engage in military activities.

One approach focuses upon the question of whether a particular corporation could be a legitimate military objective per Article 52(2) of API. A problem rapidly arises as this criterion blurs the lines between civilian objects and legitimate military targets, since the foundational criterion is military necessity. This is evident from the *Commentaries*, which suggest that there would be no barrier to prevent civilian objects from being attacked which have nothing to do with military operations per se, since all that is required is that an object 'makes an effective contribution to military action … the destruction, capture or neutralisation which … offers a definite military advantage'.[235] This approach may also be criticised because it is accompanied by the concomitant expectation that legitimate military targets may be considered as analogous to privileged combatants. Defined in Article 43 of API, privileged combatants have a right to directly participate in hostilities, with the corollary that they may be legitimately subjected to direct attack. The association between privileged belligerency and susceptibility to direct attack may be relied upon as evidence supporting the legitimacy of PMCs. Thus, distinguishing military corporations on the grounds of being legitimate military targets not only casts too wide a net owing to the possibility of civilian corporations satisfying both of the criteria, but also risks an antecedent presumption of legitimacy for military corporations. With regard to PMCs in this category, such a determination might lead to an a priori claim that their contractors are privileged belligerents on the grounds that they may be legitimately targeted in armed conflict: a claim which is contentious at best, and erroneous at worst.

Rather than distinguish this dimension upon susceptibility to direct attack, activity within the military realm serves as the *x-axis* and may be delineated according to the level of violence controlled or organised by the company.[236] This spectrum broadly adopts the approach of the aforementioned one-dimensional typologies in categorising the PMC industry. Rather than simply importing a one-dimensional typology, however, it is necessary to combine *control* with the *organisation* of violence on this

[234] Y Dinstein, *The Conduct of Hostilities under the Law of International Armed Conflict* (Cambridge University Press, 2004) 28.

[235] ICRC, *Commentary on the Additional Protocols of 8 June 1977 to the Geneva Conventions of 12 August 1949* (Martinus Nijhoff, 1987) para 2018.

[236] Another way of approaching this axis is by comparison with Nora Karsten's 'Mandate of the entity' criterion for command responsibility: N Karsten, 'Distinguishing Military and Non-Military Superiors Reflections on the Bemba Case at the ICC' (2009) 7 *Journal of International Criminal Justice* 983, 1000–01.

axis. Applying the idea to Singer's typology, this recognises the similarity between the provision of violence by the MPF and the organisation of violence embodied within the MCF, in turn appropriately distancing MSFs. In short, the greater the level of violence exercised or organised by a company, the higher it will rank on the *x-axis*.

C. The Proximity of Harm Dimension: Direct Participation in Hostilities

The nuance imported into the revised typology is provided by the additional dimension of proximity to the harm caused. This *y-axis* is justified because it differentiates between *organising* violence and *perpetrating* the violence. Applying Singer's categories again, the difference between MPFs and MCFs is that the former directly impart violence while the latter only organised it. Furthermore, increased proximity to the harm justifies a different, more rigorous, approach to the concept of corporate criminal responsibility with regard to entities that are high on this axis because their effects are causally direct.

The direct participation in hostilities criterion will be employed to create the framework for this axis.[237] This framework is appropriate both because of the primacy that IHL accords to the protection of civilians,[238] and because it concerns the exception to this protection 'unless and for such time as they take a direct part in hostilities'.[239] In other words, this approach is premised upon a rebuttable presumption of protected civilian status depending on specific conduct. This approach is more precise because it segregates the civilian sphere between those that do, and those that do not, directly participate in hostilities.[240] It is also preferable to the blunter tool of segregating combatant from civilian because it recognises the trend towards civilianising armed conflict. Factually, this standard is appropriate since it sets quite a relatively high threshold before inclusion into the category. This is useful in order to eliminate those companies that are not unambiguously PMCs, but which have been caught in the net of other taxonomies.[241] The drawback to this approach is that it would not be possible to categorise a PMC *qua* corporation as a civilian because this category only applies to natural, as opposed to juridical, persons. Attempting

[237] Melzer (n 227).

[238] ibid 11–12.

[239] Rule 6: Henckaerts and Doswald-Beck, *Customary International Humanitarian Law*, vol I (n 231) 19–24. This is also found in both Additional Protocols: see Melzer (n 227) 5.

[240] Melzer (n 227) 12.

[241] On the basis of this taxonomy, the vast majority of PW Singer's MSFs and MCFs will be excluded and the unambiguously MPF will be included: a categorisation mirrored for the contractors themselves.

to infer the civilian nature of a corporation from the cumulative status of its constituent natural persons is likely to flounder both due to the trend towards corporate conglomeration and owing to the internal distribution of personnel. Since this book argues that the disparity of treatment in law between natural and juridical persons is unsustainable, however, direct parity may be achieved with the insertion of 'object' behind either civilian or military to designate either a civilian or military corporation.[242] Thus, the *y-axis* ensures the differentiation between corporations that provide either the means or the organisation of violence from those that offer the actual exercise of violence.[243] Importantly, this separates Singer's MCFs from MPFs and questions the refusal to recognise corporate criminal responsibility where the entity lies high on this axis.

D. Combining the Revised Typology

The typology formed by combining these axes is one which is capable of accounting for the relationship between potential severity of harm and the proximity of the entity to that violence, providing a gauge for the level of overall violence. Applying this typology at the macro-level of the corporation illustrates its predominantly civilian nature by its concentration at the lower reaches of both axes (lower left quadrant). Thus, employing these dimensions segregates military corporations that cluster at the upper reaches of these axes (upper right quadrant). Utilised at a micro-level that focuses upon military corporations alone, this typology separates the PMCs which exercise or organise high levels of violence from those that are largely unconcerned with the application of violence, as well as PMCs which directly apply violence from those that are further removed. Rigorous oversight and regulatory mechanisms will be justified for entities falling within the upper right quadrant at any level of analysis and should justify overturning the assumption that corporations cannot be held criminally responsible.

XI. CONCLUSION

This chapter has examined the modern PMC from a standpoint at end of the Iraq conflict. It has shown that impunity has persistently shadowed

[242] This may be unsatisfactory owing to possibility of confusion terminologically: 'civilian objects' and 'military targets' are labels used in conjunction with targeting considerations addressed above.

[243] Another way of approaching this axis is by comparison with Nora Karsten's 'Rationale of the entity' criterion for command responsibility: Karsten, 'Distinguishing Military and Non-Military Superiors Reflections on the Bemba Case at the ICC' (n 236) 1001–13.

the immense growth of the industry and that existing accountability mechanisms predominantly concern fraud and fiscal waste rather than breaches of HRL and IHL. This skews the concept of impunity by side-lining these serious violations which were raised in the debate between the PMC as a criminal enterprise or as a legitimate business. This in turn indicates a gradual shift towards the perception of legitimacy despite continuing allegations of abuse. This chapter explored the broader contexts that fostered the creation of the industry, the pressures that encouraged its rapid growth, and has charted the trends that support the military outsourcing into the future. Finally, the chapter found that existing typologies of the private military industry overlooked the radical departure from the hitherto civilian nature of the corporation. The contribution of this chapter is the proposed typology, adapted from IHL principles which reassert the distinction between the civilian and military spheres. Recognising these challenges presented by the PMC industry justifies a reappraisal concerning their contemporary acceptance as a legitimate business entity with predominantly civilian modes of organisation. Instead, this strongly grounds the claims made for stricter regulatory regimes that are necessary to overcome allegations of impunity in the future.

3

Law's Failure to Marginalise and Criminalise Mercenary Activity

I. INTRODUCTION

THE ORIGINS OF the PMC were situated, and closely intertwined, within the context of modern mercenary activity. Christopher Kinsey notes that,

> [s]ince the setting up of the first [PMC] the term has been synonymous with mercenaries', and continues by asserting that '[s]uch a claim was justified in the early days when there were strong links between these two groups of actors'.[1]

Referring to Alan Hoe's work, Kinsey then gives the example of Watchguard, the first PMC, employing mercenaries to launch a military operation against Gaddafi in 1970.[2] The mercenary roots of modern PMCs raise the key question of how PMCs were able to incorporate as independent legal entities, because corporations cannot legally be formed to pursue unlawful purposes. Crucially, however, objections to incorporation on this ground can only be valid if mercenaries were criminals or if mercenary activity was unlawful. Thus, in order to make the transition from loosely affiliated groups of individual mercenaries to a corporate entity possessed of juridical personhood, it was necessary to demonstrate two things. First, it has to be shown that mercenary activity was not, strictly speaking, unlawful. Second, it was necessary to demonstrate either that the contractors employed by the PMC could not be categorised as mercenaries in the legal sense of the term, or alternatively that being a mercenary is legally unproblematic.

The aim of the present chapter is to illustrate two things. First, this chapter will show that the law failed either to marginalise or criminalise mercenary activity, which are interrelated but distinct processes. On the one hand, marginalising processes operate either by removing privileges that

[1] C Kinsey, 'Private Security Companies: Agents of Democracy or Simply Mercenaries?' in T Jäger and G Kummel (eds), *Private Military and Security Companies: Chances, Problems, Pitfalls and Prospects* (VS Verlag fur Sozialwissenschaften, 2007) 87.

[2] ibid; A Hoe, *David Stirling: The Authorised Biography of the Founder of the SAS* (Warner Books, 1992) 410.

might otherwise accrue, or by rendering categories of activities unlawful. This is the approach adopted by IHL in the context of mercenaries. On the other hand, criminalising processes employ the stronger measures of criminal law to prohibit an activity. With mercenarism, this is expressed through the specific international conventions that outlaw such activity. Second, this chapter will reveal how the exceptionally high thresholds required for the legal definition of mercenary have the practical effect of excluding the vast majority of PMC contractors from its ambit. The restrictive legal definition enables the deployment of interpretive denial mechanisms: PMC contractors and industry supporters can confidently point to the legal definition of mercenary to distance themselves from any unsavoury connotations, not to mention from legal liability.

Thus, this chapter discusses the concept of passive impunity arising from the subtle failure of law to limit the initial conditions that fostered the emergence of the PMC. The prospect for passive impunity is introduced by the law's inability to recognise the challenges posed by mercenaries adopting the aegis of corporate legal personhood to cloak their activities in appearance of legitimate business interests. Indeed, the cynical tone of the last sentence underscores the extent to which objections against PMC incorporation are difficult to make. Fulfilling minimal formal legal requirements, the PMC enjoys the full benefits of corporate legal personality. As described below in chapters five and six, however, these benefits are not accompanied by any legal recognition of the novel forms of activities that PMCs engage in, nor does the concomitant harm that they may produce. The overall result is that the law is not attuned to the emergence of the PMC as a new form of corporation potentially requiring new regulatory tools. As we shall see, the best demonstration of this legal blindness is perhaps the lack of legal limitations encumbering the PMC to the extent that there are no clear prohibitions on private actors directly engaging in hostilities,[3] implicitly opening the door for the corporate provision of organised violence.[4]

[3] See esp the opinion of Faiza Patel on behalf of the UN Working Group on the Use of Mercenaries, and the ICRC for the position under IHL: A Minty, 'Report of the Open-Ended Intergovernmental Working Group to Consider the Possibility of Elaborating an International Regulatory Framework on the Regulation, Monitoring and Oversight of the Activities of Private Military and Security Companies on Its Second Session' (UNGA, 2012) A/HRC/22/41 paras 16 and 20, respectively. It is interesting to note that this lack of clear legal prohibition exists in spite of strong disapproval for private actors to engage in combat activities, and that PMCs should not be contracted by States to participate directly in armed hostilities. See also UN Working Group on the Use of Mercenaries, 'Submission by the Working Group on the Use of Mercenaries as a Means of Impeding the Exercise of the Right of Peoples to Self-Determination' (UN Human Rights Council, 2012) A/HRC/WG.10/2/CRP.1 paras 9–12.

[4] A critical distinction needs to be made here between PMCs deciding not to offer direct participation in hostilities services, and the legal prohibition over PMCs providing such services. PMCs may refrain from offering such services for a myriad of reasons, but the option to do so remains insofar as there is no clear legal prohibition over the possibility.

Together, these failures of the law indicate the operation of passive impunity. The ordinary legal process is incapable of limiting or preventing the threat and harm posed by mercenaries, and as a result, of not curtailing the range of corporate activities, by PMCs. Furthermore, even where laws do exist that seek to regulate such activities, these laws often trigger the reverse effect. This is because the scope of these laws is usually restricted to narrow categories of actors and activities that facilitate the ability of PMCs to exclude themselves from these categories. In turn, this exclusion can be offered by PMCs as evidence of their status as lawful entities engaged in legitimate activities and grounds claims for the sufficiency of light self-regulation governed by the industry itself.

The legality question hanging over mercenary activity is made more contentious by the divergent legal approaches that complicate attempts to provide a comprehensive answer. As we will see, one set of approaches sought to restrict or regulate mercenary activity by means of criminalisation. Yet, this set of approaches treats mercenary activity in a tangential manner as a means towards other ends. First, certain limited forms of mercenary activity were made unlawful under domestic laws protecting the State interest in neutrality. These domestic laws proliferated as neutrality increased in both acceptance and importance, thereby rendering an illusion that States objected to those forms of mercenary activity. Second, and much later, other forms of mercenary activity were condemned as a regional international crime in order to protect the right of self-determination of peoples in the modern era of decolonisation. Here, objections to mercenary activity were conflated with the perception that such activity frustrated the right of peoples to self-determination, and was therefore criminalised accordingly within this context.

Another approach was directed at mercenaries per se, but ineffectively sought their marginalisation. Pursued under the rubric of IHL, the effect appears to be limited to discouraging mercenaries. As discussed below, mercenaries found to satisfy the stringent legal definition are denied the right to privileged belligerency status in international armed conflicts. This approach, as we will see, is heavily nuanced, ascribing a limited set of consequences to a diminutive set of actors. And while this approach appears to be targeted specifically against the mercenary, however, a strong undertone suggests that it is not actually the mercenary that is the source of objection. This is because this approach developed from the same context and concerns as the perceived detrimental impact of mercenaries upon the right of peoples to self-determination, implying that these attempts at marginalisation serve the protection of that right.

Taken together, the divergent nature and interests pursued by the existing laws against mercenaries and mercenary activity challenge the contention, championed by Sarah Percy, that a strong norm exists against mercenary activity.[5] Although these laws may be confluent in their effect in restricting aspects of mercenary activity, the disparate purposes served by these laws and their different approaches to the mercenary question undermine the claim that a strong unitary norm exists.

This diversity of mercenary laws generates a great deal of ambiguity that in turn ground the diametrically opposed claims of legitimacy and criminality made by the proponents and critics of the PMC industry respectively. The existing patchwork of laws that is potentially, but not unambiguously, applicable to the mercenary activity bolsters the claim made by proponents of the orthodox legal approach that PMCs are sufficiently regulated, with the effect of forestalling the development of a robust regulatory mechanism for PMCs. The analysis in this chapter will demonstrate the deficiency of this orthodox legal approach by showing both the restricted nature of those measures tangentially regulating mercenary and by underscoring the inapplicability and ineffectiveness of those that do target mercenary activity directly.

This chapter will begin by illustrating existing international law's capacity to criminalise organised *private* violence by looking at the unequivocal stance adopted by the international community against maritime piracy. Despite its historical origins, the provisions that criminalise maritime piracy have been reiterated in contemporary treaties. Together this suggests that the objectionable characteristics of maritime piracy have been relatively stable, and that operable definitions and enforceable legal provisions can be crafted around these characteristics. After examining the model of maritime piracy, the chapter turns to address mercenary activity. A brief history of mercenarism is provided to complement the contemporary account provided in chapter two in order to show that mercenaries were almost ubiquitous until their sharp decline in the modern era. The contemporary pejorative status of mercenaries is then examined. In particular, this chapter will highlight the difficulties raised by attempts to differentiate between forms of organised violence. Examining these difficulties both reveals the challenge of drafting a definition that describes the mercenary, and questions the justifiability of condemning mercenarism if such activities cannot be convincingly and consistently differentiated. The chapter concludes with a discussion of the legal measures deployed against mercenary activity that reveal their confused and conflicting approaches. An examination of IHL's approach illustrates that recent measures adopted to marginalise the individual mercenary contradict both the direction and purpose of IHL itself. Similarly, the laws developed to criminalise mercenarism are shown to pursue narrow contexts that now

[5] S Percy, 'Mercenaries: Strong Norm, Weak Law' (2007) 61 *International Organization* 367; S Percy, *Mercenaries: The History of a Norm in International Relations* (Oxford University Press, 2007).

confine them to obsolescence. Together, this has hindered the proposals to develop an international crime against mercenarism and has limited the utility of the recently framed crime of aggression under the Kampala Review Conference for the Rome Statute.

Chapters four and five continue from these developments to show how PMCs are able to exploit and entrench these legal failures. As this chapter will demonstrate, mercenary activity is not unlawful per se, and even if it were, PMCs can easily claim that they are not engaged with mercenary activities in the legal sense. This neutralises the barrier of illegality for the PMC to incorporate, enabling the PMC to exploit the impunity mechanisms presented in chapter one. Chapter four illustrates two other instances of passive impunity enjoyed by the PMC associated with circumscribed spheres of responsibility: excluding the PMC from the possibility of responsibility under *Jus ad Bellum* and the prospect for corporate aggression, and criteria governing command responsibility largely excluding the PMC and its contractors from liability under the doctrine. Chapter five analyses the complementary active impunity mechanisms provided by the aegis of juridical personhood affording the possibility of interpretive denial for prospective harms and by exempting legal responsibility for alleged criminal acts. Chapter five then provides a detailed analysis of US Federal Court jurisprudence relating to the PMC in order to demonstrate the operation of intertwined active impunity mechanisms benefitting the PMC.

II. MARITIME PIRACY: *HOSTES HUMANI GENERIS*

The forceful criminalisation of maritime piracy attests to the capability of the law to appropriately articulate the problem raised by organised *private* forces and to rigorously regulate such activities. This capacity indicates that the difficult and contrived legal treatment of mercenaries does not arise from the *inability* of the law to address such problem, and raises the question over the divergent path pursued in the legal treatment of mercenaries.

The maritime pirate was, and continues to be, the paragon of organised private force because they were neither owned nor under the authority of the State.[6] Yet, the historical use of pirates remained widespread because of the benefits they conferred both to the State and segments of society, as Janice Thomson notes:

> There simply is no question that piracy was a legitimate practice in the early European state system. Pirates brought revenue to the sovereign, public officials,

[6] See Table 1.1 for a useful categorisation: J Thomson, *Mercenaries, Pirates, and Sovereigns: State-Building and Extraterritorial Violence in Early Modern Europe* (Princeton University Press, 1994) 8.

> and private investors. They weakened enemies by attacking their shipping and settlements. They supplied European markets with scarce goods at affordable prices. They broke competing states' trade monopolies.[7]

Despite this utility, the response to the practice of maritime piracy gradually coalesced into the first international criminal law, attaining the status of *hostes humani generis*—enemies of humankind.[8] Broken down, this legal development on the treatment of pirates encompasses a twofold departure from the existing legal system which makes this development compelling.

The first departure arises from that fact that 'if piratical acts are divorced from state authority, and therefore responsibility, they do not come under the rubric of international law, which deals only with sovereign states'.[9] Thus, international *criminal* law, 'a body of international rules designed both to proscribe certain categories of conduct … and to make those *persons* who engage in such conduct criminally liable'[10] was spawned to capture the individuality of maritime piracy, eroding the exclusivity of the State's personhood under international law.

The second departure is that maritime piracy constituted one of the rare exceptions to territorial jurisdiction, creating an *erga omnes* obligation. As Antonio Cassese writes:

> All states of the world were empowered to search for and arrest pirates on the high seas; they were also empowered to bring them to trial, regardless of the nationality of the victims and of whether the proceeding state had been directly damaged by piracy.[11]

Indeed, this position has crystallised to the extent that, 'under customary international law, *piracy* constitutes the only case where states are undoubtedly authorized to exercise universal jurisdiction'.[12] The crystallisation of piracy into one of the earliest international concerns is evidenced in the jurisprudence of the Alien Tort Claims Act (ATCA),[13] passed by the first US Congress in 1789 and discussed at length in chapter five. Here, the US Supreme Court in the seminal case of *Sosa*, considered that maritime piracy was one of the Blackstonian trilogy of identifiable violations of the law of nations which constituted a sufficient threat on the international

[7] ibid 107–08.

[8] '[P]irates were regarded as enemies of humanity (*hostes humani generis*) in that they hampered freedom on the high seas and threatened private property': A Cassese, *International Criminal Law* (Oxford University Press, 2008) 28.

[9] Thomson, *Mercenaries, Pirates, and Sovereigns* (n 6) 108.

[10] Cassese, *International Criminal Law* (n 8) 3. Emphasis added.

[11] ibid 28.

[12] A Cassese, 'When May Senior State Officials Be Tried for International Crimes? Some Comments on the Congo v Belgium Case' (2002) 13 *European Journal of International Law* 853, 857

[13] 28 U.S.C. para 1350.

sphere to warrant a judicial remedy, presumably to stave off inter-State conflict.[14] In the words of Souter J for a unanimous Court on this point:

> There was, finally, a sphere in which these rules binding individuals for the benefit of other individuals overlapped with the norms of state relationships. Blackstone referred to it when he mentioned three specific offenses against the law of nations addressed by the criminal law of England: violation of safe conducts, infringement of the rights of ambassadors, and piracy … It was this narrow set of violations of the law of nations, admitting of a judicial remedy and at the same time threatening serious consequences in international affairs, that was probably on minds of the men who drafted the [ATCA] with its reference to tort.[15]

In addition to the unequivocal criminalisation of maritime piracy under customary international law, the crime of piracy is expressed in contemporary international treaties such as the 1958 Convention on the High Seas,[16] which was later incorporated into the 1982 Convention on the Law of the Sea.[17] The latter Convention provides, in Article 100, the duty of cooperation to repress piracy both on the high seas and other areas beyond the jurisdiction of any State. It is, however, the clarity of the definition that is illuminative for present purposes, especially when juxtaposed against international law's convoluted attempt to define a mercenary discussed below. The pertinent aspects of the definition are provided in Article 101:

> Piracy consists of any of the following acts:
>
> (a) any *illegal* acts of violence or detention, or any act of depredation, committed for *private* ends by the crew or the passengers of a *private* ship or a *private* aircraft, and directed:
> (i) *on the high seas*, against another ship or aircraft, or against persons or property on board such ship or aircraft;
> (ii) against a ship, aircraft, persons or property in a place *outside the jurisdiction of any State;*
>
> (b) any act of *voluntary* participation in the operation of a ship or of an aircraft with knowledge of facts making it a pirate ship or aircraft;
>
> (c) any act of *inciting or of intentionally facilitating* an act described in subparagraph (a) or (b).[18]

[14] Fletcher, *Tort Liability for Human Rights Abuses* (Hart Publishing, 2008) 153–57; the imposition of universal jurisdiction for pirates may have been pragmatic: 'Originally, hostis humani generis might have had a purely procedural meaning—pirates were subject to universal jurisdiction because no single state could claim jurisdiction': ibid 155.

[15] *Sosa v Alvarez-Machain* (2004) 542 US 692 (US Supreme Court) 715.

[16] Convention on the High Seas 1958 (Treaty Series) 11, arts 14–22.

[17] Convention on the Law of the Sea 1982, arts 100–107.

[18] ibid. Emphasis added. Interestingly, the definition of piracy may now be in doubt: B Vergakis, 'Piracy Definition in Dispute as Piracy Trial Looms' *Huffington Post* (16 April 2012) www.huffingtonpost.com/huff-wires/20120416/us-prosecuting-pirates/. The definition of 'piracy' has recently been considered at length in the US courts: *US v Dire* [2012] US Court of Appeals for the Fourth Circuit 11-4310—11-4317; see also *US v Said* [2012] US Court of Appeals for the Fourth Circuit 10-4970, that was heard together with and applied the holding in *Dire*.

From this text, the key characteristics of piracy can be distilled into two dimensions of concerns: the prohibition of acts of private violence, and the sphere of action beyond the territoriality of the State. The emphasis upon the first dimension concerning the private nature of the violence is clear from the requirements that piracy needs to be perpetuated from a private ship or aircraft with the purpose of furthering private ends. The second dimension is evident from the need for the relevant actions to take place either on the high seas or beyond the jurisdiction of any State. Thus, the international fear reflected in the criminalisation of piracy can be understood as a threat of violence that does not emanate from any particular State in areas that are beyond the inter-State system. Again, Antonio Cassese writes that:

> [P]iracy was (and is) not punished for the sake of protecting a *community* value: all states were (and are still) authorized to capture on the high seas and bring to trial pirates in order to safeguard the *joint interest* to fight a common danger and a consequent (real or potential) damage.[19]

Maritime piracy thus represents the clear paradigm of organised private violence. Yet, while the pirate was universally condemned, a mere piece of parchment was able to differentiate its sovereign-sanctioned counterpart: the privateer. Often indistinguishable from the pirate, the privateer could be identified by the grant of a *Letter of Marque and Reprisal* by a sovereign.[20] Hence, the key factor differentiating the pirate by legitimating the privateer was the possibility of attributing responsibility for the privateer's actions to a sovereign, by definition impossible for acts of piracy. The subsequent confusion between pirates and privateers resulted in the Declaration of Paris which abolished the latter practice.[21] That the paragon of organised private force, maritime pirates, constituted a threat to the system of nation States is shown by the willingness of the States themselves to agree to desist from utilising privateers.

A useful comparison can be made between the abolition of privateering arising from the criminalisation of maritime piracy and the present mercenary question. On one hand, like maritime pirates, mercenaries are also neither owned by nor under the authority of the State, exposing them to the possibility of analogous criminalisation. On the other hand,

[19] Cassese (n 8) 12.

[20] See generally Thomson (n 6) 22–26.

[21] The corollary to abolishing piracy was the abolition of privateering made in the Declaration Respecting Maritime Law, Paris 1856. It should be noted, however, that the power to issue Letters of Marque and Reprisal still exists. Perhaps the most notable is the 'War Powers' clause of the US Constitution, where art 1, s 8 provides that Congress shall have the power '[t]o declare War, grant Letters of Marque and Reprisal, and make Rules concerning Captures on Land and Water'; see also Thomson (n 6) 69–76.

like privateers, mercenaries can be, and often are, employed by the State to further its purposes. Drawing these approaches together, international law should have both criminalised mercenaries who operate outside of the State system and prohibited States from engaging in the practices of mercenarism, if the legal treatment of mercenaries adopted the approach taken against the maritime pirate and the privateer. The broad effect would be the international prohibition of mercenarism and the criminalisation of the individual mercenary, following the privateer and pirate precedent. A broader historical background is required before this analysis can proceed.

III. SOLDIERS OF (MIS-) FORTUNE: A BRIEF HISTORICAL BACKGROUND OF MERCENARY ACTIVITY

This section provides an overview of mercenarism by charting the historical prevalence of this practice through its demise in the modern era. While chapter two highlighted the mercenary roots of the modern PMC through its origins in Watchguard International, this section situates these contemporary developments in the broader historical context. This contextualisation will demonstrate that mercenary activity was a widely accepted, if not the dominant, form of legitimately organised violence employed by the sovereign State. This long historical perspective underscores the difficulties in identifying the distinguishing characteristics of organised private violence. This difficulty, in turn, challenges the indignant moral response to the scourge of mercenarism and subsequently pervades the inconsistencies of the subsequent legal response.

The practice of mercenarism is a notably ancient tradition that extends into prehistory. PW Singer has suggested that '[h]iring outsiders to fight your battles is as old as war itself … In some eras, these private entrants into conflicts were individual foreigners, brought in to fight for whichever side bid the highest, known as "mercenaries" in common parlance'.[22] Peter Tickler provides early evidence, recorded by Xenophon, of the failed use of mercenaries by Cyrus in 401 BCE.[23] Similarly, Alexander Gillespie comments on the involvement of mercenaries 'being noted in various epochs, at least as early as 2200 BCE' and that 'the earliest records of mercenaries record them as being unreliable and dangerous "locust swarms

[22] PW Singer, *Corporate Warriors: The Rise of the Privatized Military Industry* (Cornell University Press, 2004) 19, and generally 19–39.

[23] P Tickler, *The Modern Mercenary: Dog of War, or Soldier of Fortune?* (Patrick Stephens, 1987) 15, as cited in J Zarate, 'The Emergence of a New Dog of War: Private International Security Companies, International Law, and the New World Disorder' (1998) 34 *Stanford Journal of International Law* 75, 82–83.

[which] covered the land"'.[24] Indeed, as Juan Zarate notes, the presence of foreigners on the battlefield was ubiquitous from antiquity until the modern era.[25] Furthermore, the use of mercenaries was not exclusively a classical or even European practice; Edward Kwakwa has provided historical examples of widespread mercenary activity on the African continent and the Middle East and has documented their persistence in these regions into the modern era.[26]

Although the term 'mercenary' conjures images of individual soldiers hiring themselves out individually as 'free lances', the fluctuating nature of conflict, and therefore of employment, led to the formation of 'companies': these 'were organisations designed to facilitate their employment as a group … They would travel together in search of work, usually in the form of new campaigns to fight, and support themselves along the way by blackmailing towns and villages'.[27] Although individual mercenaries continued to be pervasive, the development of the 'Free Companies' grew to prominence in the early-modern Europe. These included the Grand Catalan Company, which established an independent duchy for over six decades after a betrayal, and the infamous Italian *condottieri*,[28] which were so famously castigated by Niccolo Machiavelli.[29] At the apex of pre-modern military entrepreneurship was Albrecht von Wallenstein, 'who through the private military business became the wealthiest man in all of Europe', rivalling the imperial power of the House of Hapsburg and thwarting the expansion of the Swedish Empire in the process.[30] These notable examples highlight mercenarism historically as a widely adopted and profitable practice.

Reflected in this historical context, the development of the modern PMC can be considered as simply the latest iteration in the process of consolidating organised private forces. The loose associations of individual mercenaries, such as those under the leadership of Bob Denard and Mike Hoare in Katanga, gradually gave way to the formation of the first PMC. Under David Stirling, Watchguard International regularised employment and formally opened up the possibility to tender for government contracts. This early model of the PMC in turn paved the way for the giant PMCs of today to dominate government contracting, opening the possibility for future iterations to refine private military contracting organisations.

24 A Gillespie, *History of the Laws of War: Combatants and Captives*, vol 1 (Hart Publishing, 2011) 13.

25 See generally, Zarate, 'The Emergence of a New Dog of War' (n 23) 81–91.

26 E Kwakwa, 'The Current Status of Mercenaries in the Law of Armed Conflict' (1990) 14 *Hastings International & Comparative Law Review* 67, 75–76.

27 Singer, *Corporate Warriors* (n 22) 24.

28 Zarate (n 23) 83–86.

29 N Machiavelli, *The Prince* (P Bondanella tr, Oxford University Press, 2005) ch 12.

30 PW Singer, 'The Ultimate Military Entrepreneur' (2003) Spring *Military History Quarterly* 6, 6 and 11–13.

The consequence arising from this perspective is that the ownership and control of organised armed forces by the State can be seen as a historical aberration, clearly asserted by Janice Thomson:

> The contemporary organisation of global violence is neither timeless nor natural. It is distinctively modern. In the six centuries leading up to 1900, global violence was democratised, marketised, and internationalised. Nonstate violence dominated the international system. Individuals and groups used their own means of violence in pursuit of their particular aims, whether honour and glory, wealth, or political power. People bought and sold military manpower like a commodity on the global market. The identity of the suppliers and purchasers meant almost nothing.[31]

This historical organisation of violence was subsequently reversed by the 1648 Peace of Westphalia that ended the Thirty Years' War in Europe. More than a mere peace treaty, it both consolidated the nation State system of governance and cemented the modern State as the holding the exclusive entitlement to organise violence. This latter arrangement found expression in Max Weber's famous definition of a State as 'a human community that (successfully) claims the *monopoly of the legitimate use of physical force* within a given territory'.[32] Charles Tilly capped this line of thought by convincingly demonstrating that State-making and war-making were iterative, mutually reinforcing, processes.[33] Indeed, Mary Kaldor adopts the State monopoly over the legitimate use of violence as the litmus test for failed States:

> One of the key characteristics of failing states is the loss of control over and fragmentation of the instruments of physical coercion. A disintegrative cycle sets in which is almost the exact opposite of the integrative cycle through which modern states were established ... Effectively, the 'failure' of states is accompanied by a growing privatisation of violence.[34]

Despite the asserted supremacy of the nation State and its monopoly over legitimate violence in the modern era, it was not incongruous for the State to resort to external forces. Indeed, States tolerated mercenary activity, in a broad sense, and foreign fighters continued to be widely utilised by States to bolster their regular forces post-Westphalia.[35] In apparent anticipation of this dissonance, Max Weber himself recognised that State monopoly

[31] Thomson (n 6) 3.

[32] M Weber, *From Max Weber: Essays in Sociology* (HH Gerth and C Wright Mills eds, Routledge and Kegan Paul, 1946) 78. Emphasis original.

[33] C Tilly, *Coercion, Capital and European States, A.D.990-1990* (Blackwell, 1992); C Tilly, 'War Making and State Making as Organised Crime' in P Evans, D Rueschemeyer and T Skocpol (eds), *Bringing the State Back in* (Cambridge University Press, 1985).

[34] M Kaldor, *New and Old Wars: Organized Violence in a Global Era* (Polity, 2001) 92.

[35] As a FCO report noted, the wide dictionary definition of mercenary 'would include many people engaged in legitimate activities, for example Gurkha troops in the British and Indian Armies, troops in the British Army who have been recruited in Commonwealth countries, loan service personnel, the French Foreign Legion and the Swiss Guard in the Vatican': United Kingdom Foreign and Commonwealth Office, *Private Military Companies: Options for Regulation* Green Paper (2001–02, HC 577) 6.

went beyond mere *ownership* of organised armed force to encompass the possibility of delegating the State's *authority* to use force.[36]

The possibility for States to avail themselves of martial services offered by mercenaries and other private purveyors of organised violence raises questions relating both to the pejorative status of mercenaries and to the claims that organised private violence has been eliminated, criminalised or at least marginalised. Given this context, can it be possible to distinguish between legitimate (in the Weberian sense) and criminal forms of mercenarism? Furthermore, if affirmative, could such a distinction remain tenable in light of the positive impunity mechanisms discussed in chapter one?

To examine this question, the following section discusses the pejorative connotations associated with mercenarism. This then sets the stage to illustrate the difficulties inherent in attempting to differentiate mercenary characteristics, in moral terms, and how this has affected the way in which these connotations have become subsequently reflected in law.

IV. THE PEJORATIVE STATUS OF MERCENARIES

Niccolo Machiavelli famously wrote 'that mercenaries cause nothing but damage'.[37] This impression appears to have lasted until the present day, and the unsavoury character of mercenaries is well illustrated by its contemporary rhetorical use. Noam Chomsky, for instance, refers to a network of 'terrorist mercenary states' (which the US employs to further its interests abroad in diplomatically sensitive areas).[38] In addition to succinctly communicating the abhorrence of the activities branded under this label, Chomsky's intentional usage of the term 'mercenary' within this negative context underscores the deep-seated repugnance associated with mercenarism. But what is perhaps most striking about Chomsky's usage of 'mercenary' is that it can contribute towards the stigma, even when used in conjunction with the term 'terrorist'.[39]

[36] 'Specifically … the right to use physical force is ascribed to other institutions or to individuals only to the extent to which the state permits it. The state is considered the sole source of the "right" to use violence': Weber, *From Max Weber* (n 32) 78.

[37] Machiavelli, *The Prince* (n 29) 44.

[38] N Chomsky, *Understanding Power: The Indispensable Chomsky* (Vintage, 2003) 4–6; I have elaborated upon the definitional impasse surrounding the use of the term 'mercenary' elsewhere: H-Y Liu, 'Mercenaries in Libya: Ramifications of the Treatment of "Armed Mercenary Personnel" under the Arms Embargo for Private Military Company Contractors' (2011) 16 *Journal of Conflict and Security Law* 293, 302–04.

[39] If Chomsky's term 'terrorist mercenary states' were deconstructed, it would reveal that several incompatible concepts were forging together towards rhetorical ends. As discussed below, a terrorist is in part defined by his political, ideological or religious motivations, while a mercenary is characterised by his material or monetary motivation. This suggests that terrorists and mercenaries are mutually incompatible concepts. Furthermore, as both terrorists and mercenaries are understood to be individuals, it would be incongruous to describe a State as either, let alone both.

Reflecting these negative connotations, the former UN Special Rapporteur on the Use of Mercenaries, Enrique Ballesteros, has painted the individual mercenary as a war-mongering and greed-driven criminal in an official report:

> Generally speaking, mercenaries are former soldiers who compulsively identify themselves with the job of making war, pretend to be fanatical practitioners of an ideological option and are intrinsically intolerant or violent persons. However, the aggravating factor is that their participation is linked to the bloodier aspects of a conflict and to the most criminal violations of human rights. Moreover, financial considerations and the desire for illicit gain through looting which is associated with their participation may be decisive in extending the duration of the conflict. The mercenary's interest lies not in peace and reconciliation, but in war, since that is his business and livelihood.[40]

Critics draw upon this image to stigmatise the modern PMC as a revival of mercenarism. This sentiment is neatly captured by A-F Musah as 'nothing but the old poison of vagabond mercenaries in new designer bottles'.[41] While it is clear that the derogatory image of mercenarism continues to be invoked by those wishing to stigmatise such activity, it is necessary to delve deeper and explore the justifiability of the reasons underlying this position.

A useful point of departure point is the UK Foreign and Commonwealth Office report that associates mercenarism with negative events in the modern era:

> In modern times mercenaries have a bad reputation, so much so that the word has become almost a form of abuse. This is based partly on the experience of the 60s and 70s when, starting with the Congo, mercenaries were associated with instability and secessionist movements. They were also involved both in a number of attempted coups and in human rights abuses.[42]

Although the modern stigmatisation of mercenaries can be traced to the perception that their activities frustrated the exercise of the right of self-determination during the decolonisation period,[43] these have been mixed together with other negative images of mercenaries that persist from before this period, confusing the sources and bases of the objections.

[40] E Ballesteros, 'Report on the Use of Mercenaries as a Means of Violating Human Rights and Impeding the Exercise of the Right of Peoples to Self-Determination' (1995) E/CN.4/1995/29 para 27.

[41] Singer (n 22) 44.

[42] United Kingdom Foreign and Commonwealth Office, *Private Military Companies: Options for Regulation* (n 35) 32.

[43] The best evidence of this is the formation of the 'UN Working Group on the Use of Mercenaries *as a means of violating human rights and impeding the exercise of the right of peoples to self-determination*' (emphasis added) which was established in July 2005 under the authority of the Commission on Human Rights in Resolution 2005/2. The Working Group succeeded the role of the Special Rapporteur of the same name, previously appointed by the Commission on Human Rights in its Resolution 1987/16.

An earlier, and independent, line of objection centred upon the market aspect of mercenarism. This contended that mercenary practices equated to the commodification of human lives and the sale of humanity, such that lethal military services should not be the subject of open trade.[44] The parliamentary debates of the UK illustrate these concerns in relation to employing mercenaries in the American War of Independence and the Crimean War.[45] In the former, the Duke of Richmond thought that the various treaties made by the UK with the Landgrave of Hesse for the provision of troops were 'a downright mercenary bargain, for the taking into pay a certain number of hirelings, who were bought and sold like so many beasts for slaughter'.[46] Adamantly echoing these sentiments, Lord Camden asked:

> Is there one of your lordships, who does not perceive most clearly, that the whole is a mere mercenary bargain for the hire of troops on one side, and the sale of human blood on the other; that the devoted wretches thus purchased for the slaughter are mere mercenaries, in the worst sense of the word. This point once granted, look then on the present treaties in their naked and true light.[47]

Subsequently, Sir Edward Bulmer-Lytton drew upon this strand of objection in the context of the Crimean War, saying that he 'did not see how, if they repudiated the detestable practice of slave dealing, the principle could be different on the banks of the Elbe from that which took place on the banks of the Congo'.[48] Thus, the stigma of mercenary activity was enhanced by drawing the explicit analogy with slave-trading,[49] especially when the unique nature of the ban on the slave trade was emphasised:

> It was the first in which blatantly moral impulses were a key factor … it was the first to criminalise international commerce in a particular 'commodity'; and it

[44] Percy, *Mercenaries* (n 5) 152–53; and ibid 160–61 respectively; this line of argumentation is sustained in M Sapone, 'Have Rifle With Scope, Will Travel: The Global Economy of Mercenary Violence' (1999) 30 *California Western International Law Journal* 1. For a more theoretical perspective of the limits of what can be sold as a commodity, see MJ Radin, 'Market-Inalienability' (1986) 100 *Harvard Law Review* 1849; MJ Radin, *Contested Commodities: Trouble with Trade in Sex, Children, Body Parts and Other Things* (Harvard University Press, 2001).

[45] Alexander Gillespie notes that Crimea was the last army of foreigners raised to fight a war under the British flag; clearly he discounts units of continuous existence such as the Gurkha regiments: Gillespie, *History of the Laws of War* (n 24) 47.

[46] Cobbett's Parliamentary History, 'Debate in the Lords on the Duke of Richmond's Motion for an Address to Countermand the March of the German Troops' (1776) 16 George III 1193.

[47] ibid 1223.

[48] 'Hansard Parliamentary Debates' (Cornelius Buck, 1854) Hansard Parliamentary Debates 433.

[49] The strategy of analogising mercenaries with slaves is more conceptually coherent than Noam Chomsky's conflation of mercenaries with terrorism because both are treated as hapless victims of unrestricted markets. The difficulty in this line of argumentation, however, is that the mercenary is treated as an innocent victim. This is inharmonious with the modern portrait of the mercenary as the perpetrator of violence that limits its support of contemporary objections to mercenarism.

> was the first to evolve into a far more ambitious regime aimed at the criminalisation of all activity involving the production, sale, and use of that 'commodity' in every country.[50]

Although the slave trade does not technically fall within the notion of international crime,[51] Ethan Nadelmann argues that the prohibition of the slave trade has crystallised into a 'global prohibition regime' alongside maritime piracy.[52] The close intersections between mercenary activity, the prohibition of maritime piracy and the slave trade potentially justify the stigmatisation that it bears. Yet, it should be clear that the taint of mercenarism is informed by several distinct, and perhaps conflicting grounds, that raise difficulties in coherently distinguishing mercenary activity from other forms of organised armed force.[53] These difficulties are elaborated in the following section, and are reflected in the inconsistent attempts to address mercenary activity in law, below.

Beyond the problems of distinguishing mercenary characteristics, the pejorative status of mercenaries gives rise to tangential effects. The negative aura of mercenary activity was recently deployed in the context of the Libyan armed conflict in 2011.[54] Because foreigner status constitutes a core characteristic of the mercenary, this stigma is subject to xenophobic hijack.[55] In the Libyan context, the accusation of mercenary activity has plagued the black African population and Human Rights Watch has documented widespread arbitrary arrests within that specific demographic,[56]

[50] E Nadelmann, 'Global Prohibition Regimes: The Evolution of Norms in International Society' (1990) 44 *International Organization* 479, 497. Interestingly, parallels can be drawn between the complete criminalisation of all activity involved with the slavery 'commodity' with that which underpinned the OAU and UN international mercenary conventions, which similarly forbade all activity related to the practices of mercenarism; for the discussion on maritime piracy, see ibid 486–91.

[51] On the basis that customary law does not provide for the criminalisation of the slave trade and because they are not committed against States, these offences generally fall within the ambit of ordinary crimes. Cassese (n 8) 12.

[52] Nadelmann, 'Global Prohibition Regimes' (n 50) 491–98.

[53] A further objection to mercenary activity that serves the interests of State neutrality is considered in depth below as it informs one of the norms against mercenary activity in law: see esp J Lobel, 'The Rise and Decline of the Neutrality Act: Sovereignty and Congressional War Powers in United States Foreign Policy' (1983) 24 *Harvard International Law Journal* 1.

[54] The arms embargo imposed by the Security Council in Resolution 1970 included the novel term, 'armed mercenary personnel', which as a significant departure from previous terminology added further confused the treatment of mercenaries under international law: Liu, 'Mercenaries in Libya' (n 38).

[55] Despite the contention that '[h]istorically, foreign soldiers were common': Percy, *Mercenaries* (n 5) 52. Referring to the difficulties of categorising mercenaries on motivational grounds, CAJ Coady places emphasis upon the affiliational, or alien, status of the mercenary which would exacerbate these effects: CAJ Coady, *Morality and Political Violence* (Cambridge University Press, 2008) 206.

[56] Human Rights Watch, 'Libya: Stop Arbitrary Arrests of Black Africans' *Human Rights Watch* (4 September 2011) www.hrw.org/news/2011/09/04/libya-stop-arbitrary-arrests-black-africans; see also L Moreno-Ocampo, 'Statement to the United Nations Security

and the United Nations High Commissioner for Refugees (UNHCR) feared for the safety of visible-minority refugees being persecuted as suspected mercenaries in the conflict.[57]

The derogatory stance adopted against mercenaries is reflected in other reports that highlight the human rights abuses suffered by individuals suspected of being mercenaries.[58] Precedent for the abuse of suspected mercenaries can be found in the Angolan Trials of 'Colonel Callan' and his men in June and July 1976. George Lockwood, an international observer at the trials, after analysing the question whether the crime of being a mercenary existed in international or domestic law at the material time said that: 'In my opinion, the crime of being a mercenary did not exist in Angolan law and the defendants therefore were unjustly convicted on that count'.[59] A significant difference in the Libyan situation is, of course, that the crime of being a mercenary and crimes associated with the practice of mercenarism can now be found in relevant international laws that bind Libya, a State Party to both the United Nations (UN) and Organisation of African Unity (OAU) Mercenary Conventions.[60] Furthermore, Libyan engagement with the question of mercenary activity is underscored by the representation of one of its nationals within the UN Working Group on the Use of Mercenaries.[61] These facts, however, do not appear to militate against the likelihood of especially harsh treatment for suspected mercenaries.[62]

Rather than resolve this issue, even within the Libyan context, these provisions of international law may have the perverse effect of removing

Council on the Situation in Libya, pursuant to UNSCR 1970 (4 May 2011)' www.icc-cpi.int/NR/rdonlyres/0BDF4953-B5AB-42E0-AB21-25238F2C2323/0/OTPStatement04052011.pdf. More recently, Syrian President al-Assad deployed similar tactics when he referred to 'foreign mercenaries' allegedly involved in the fight against his regime; Syria had previously mentioned that 12 foreign terrorists had been killed in Syria, blurring the categories and demonstrating the rhetorical effect of the mercenary label: I Black, 'Syria's Bashar Al-Assad Vows to Display Captured Foreign Mercenaries' *The Guardian* (16 May 2012) www.guardian.co.uk/world/2012/may/16/syria-bashar-assad-vows-display-mercenaries?INTCMP=SRCH.

57 UNHCR, 'UNHCR Fears for the Safety of Refugees Caught in Libya's Violence' *UNHCR* www.unhcr.org/4d6393e06.html.

58 M Chulov and D Smith, 'Libya: Gaddafi's Army of Mercenaries Face Backlash' *The Guardian* (2 September 2011) www.guardian.co.uk/world/2011/sep/02/libya-gaddafi-army-mercenaries-backlash?INTCMP=SRCH.

59 G Lockwood, 'Report on the Trial of Mercenaries: Luanda, Angola-June, 1976' (1976) 7 *Manitoba Law Journal* 183, 197. On this view, there is a distinct possibility that the minimal protections accorded by Common Article 3 to the Geneva Conventions has been breached, see art 3(1)(d).

60 International Convention against the Recruitment, Use, Financing and Training of Mercenaries 1989 (A/RES/44/34); OAU Convention for the Elimination of Mercenarism in Africa 1977 (OAU CM/817 (XXIX) Annex II Rev 1) with no reservations entered for either.

61 Between 2005–11, 1 of the 5 members of the UN Working Group of Mercenaries was a Libyan national. This may account for the unusually quiet stance of the Working Group with regard to the Libyan situation: see esp Liu (n 38) 300–01.

62 H Al-Shalchi, 'Libya Military Court Jails Accused Foreign Mercenaries' *Reuters* (4 June 2012) www.reuters.com/article/2012/06/04/us-libya-trial-ukrainian-idUSBRE8530QY20120604.

barriers to the abuse of suspected mercenaries. This is because these two binding international conventions provide authority to criminalise the practice of mercenarism, thereby increasing the stigma attached to the practice. Yet, there are three particulars of both the UN and OAU Convention that further exacerbate these problems: the criminalisation of a *status*, deviating from the orthodoxy of criminalising *actions*; the low signatory rates, indicative of the lack of an international norm to the point of potentially providing implicit international support for mercenary activity;[63] and crucially, that the use of mercenaries specifically in the Libyan context may actually be in frustration of a national liberation movement envisaged in the two conventions.[64] These three factors are likely to militate against the availability of fair trial to suspected mercenaries by the Rebel authorities, leading to a process which may verge upon victor's justice.

This book, following other commentators who have viewed the PMC phenomenon through the lens of mercenarism, is premised upon the assumption that PMCs are direct descendants of the mercenary lineage.[65] These writers have concentrated upon the historical use of mercenaries and resultant creation of 'free companies' in medieval Europe,[66] which subsequently declined with the emergence of citizen armies serving increasingly powerful States. This raises the question as to whether mercenary activity can appropriately be distinguished from other forms of organising armed force, and if so, whether this separation can be sustainable. In addition to the alien status of the individual discussed above, the objection to mercenarism appears to be primarily founded upon the material motivation and the voluntary willingness of the individual to readily resort to violence.

V. THE MORAL MERCENARY AND THE PROBLEM OF DIFFERENTIATING ORGANISED VIOLENCE

Tony Lynch and AJ Walsh argue that the strong and unfavourable connotations associated with the term 'mercenary' is unfounded for the simple reason that '[i]t is no easy matter to distinguish on moral grounds between mercenarism as a professional activity and the activities of national

[63] I have developed this argument elsewhere: see H-Y Liu, 'Leashing the Corporate Dogs of War: The Legal Implications of the Modern Private Military Company' (2010) 15 *Journal of Conflict and Security Law* 141, 148.

[64] There are, however, a plethora of problems surrounding the self-determination and State sovereignty debate that are beyond the scope of the present chapter: see G Robertson, *Crimes Against Humanity: The Struggle For Global Justice* (Penguin, 2006) 164–71.

[65] Zarate (n 23) 81–91; Singer (n 22) 19–23; T Milliard, 'Overcoming Post-Colonial Myopia: A Call to Recognize and Regulate Private Military Companies' (2003) 176 *Military Law Review* 1, 5.

[66] A Mockler, *New Mercenaries* (Sidgwick & Jackson, 1985) 9–10; Singer (n 22) 23–26.

armed forces'.[67] Furthermore, they contend that a 'certain kind of anti-mercenarism ... which extols *inter alia* the virtues of a citizen's willing subordination of his or her personal interest to the communal good' underlies the unfounded denigration of mercenaries.[68] Thus, if Lynch and Walsh are correct, attempts to segregate and marginalise the mercenary are necessary to assert the legitimacy of the State, and the legality of the State's allocation of force. This suggests that the dividing line between the soldier and the mercenary, characterised by a tight nexus with the State, will necessarily break down where the State owns or allocates mercenary forces.

While few extol the virtues of mercenarism,[69] it is important to emphasise that the core characteristics used to define the mercenary are incapable of objectively distinguishing him from other martial actors. Aside from this hegemonic assertion, it becomes difficult to differentiate the mercenary from the national soldier on more objective grounds that express moral objection. This difficulty becomes reflected in the perplexed legal definition and treatment of the mercenaries. The only clarity appears to be that State affiliation neutralises adverse allegations of an individual being a mercenary, and that the State may utilise armed forces that would under other circumstances be considered as mercenary forces without unfavourable consequences.

A. Motivational Objections

The cardinal objection to mercenarism is that it is an economically motivated activity: mercenaries participate in armed hostilities for material gain.[70] This is readily apparent from the two ordinary meanings for 'mercenary' given by the *Oxford Dictionary of English*: first, the adjectival form meaning 'primarily concerned with making money at the expense of ethics'; and second, as a noun meaning 'a professional soldier hired to serve in a foreign army' and a 'person primarily motivated by personal gain'.[71] While economic motivation 'is the crux of the matter' for those

[67] T Lynch and AJ Walsh, 'The Good Mercenary?' (2000) 8 *Journal of Political Philosophy* 133, 133.

[68] ibid 134.

[69] See notably C Fabre, 'In Defence of Mercenarism' (2010) 40 *British Journal of Political Science* 539; In his analysis, CAJ Coady points to the support of St Thomas More and his Utopians for mercenary soldiers to avert the need to send citizens into battle. Aside from such pragmatic interests, there are few credible supporters of mercenary activity: Coady, *Morality and Political Violence* (n 55) 205.

[70] Many commentators agree that pecuniary motives form a central, albeit problematic, characteristic of mercenarism: Zarate (n 23) 18; HC Burmester, 'The Recruitment and Use of Mercenaries in Armed Conflicts' (1978) 72 *American Journal of International Law* 37, 37; Singer (n 22) 41; Thomson (n 6) 26.

[71] 'Mercenary' in *Oxford Dictionary of English*, Second Revised Edition (Oxford University Press, 2003).

seeking to marginalise mercenaries,[72] the Diplock Report duly noted the dangers of utilising motivation to define mercenaries:

> [A]ny definition of mercenaries which required positive proof of motivation would … either be unworkable, or so haphazard in its application as between comparable individuals as to be unacceptable. Mercenaries, we think, can only be defined by reference to what they do, and not by reference to why they do it.[73]

The aberrant nature of specifying a dominant motivation is particularly striking when it is juxtaposed alongside maritime piracy, which only requires voluntary participation or acts of inciting or of intentionally facilitating the impugned actions.[74] Despite the problems associated with characterising mercenary activity upon motivation,[75] these 'remunerative motives' constitute only the first of three objections to mercenarism that are premised upon the question of appropriate killing motives, which also include 'right intention' and 'armed reluctance'.[76]

The problem of motivation can be further broken down into three constituent issues. First, an individual's desire for financial gain is problematic in that actual motivation is necessarily uncertain and typically rests upon an array of relevant factors. Thus, the critique of mercenarism 'is not that they do things for money, but that money is the *sole* or the *dominant* consideration'.[77] While the castigation of mercenaries rests primarily upon their desire for material gain,[78] the hypocrisy arises in the lack of structural guarantees that prevent career soldiers in national armies from being predominantly motivated by competitive remuneration.[79] In addition, the presence of countervailing motives, such as residual patriotism, effectively nullifies the effect of the remuneration critique for soldiers

[72] ICRC, *Commentary on the Additional Protocols of 8 June 1977 to the Geneva Conventions of 12 August 1949* (Martinus Nijhoff, 1987) para 1807.

[73] Committee of Privy Counsellors, *Report of the Committee of Privy Counsellors Appointed to Inquire into the Recruitment of Mercenaries* (Cmnd 6569, 1976) para 7.

[74] The Convention on the Law of the Sea (n 17) art 101(b) and (c). There is no provision for the crime of 'being a pirate'; that is, piratical status is not prohibited but rather only acts of piracy.

[75] The commentaries to art 47 of API note that 'the concession made by this article is not without importance, for it is not the task of humanitarian law to make distinctions based on the motives which induce a particular person to participate in an armed conflict': ICRC, *Commentary on the Additional Protocols of 8 June 1977 to the Geneva Conventions of 12 August 1949* (n 72) 573.

[76] Lynch and Walsh, 'The Good Mercenary?' (n 67) 142.

[77] ibid 136. Emphasis original.

[78] Financial motivation can be problematic because it is individualistic and because it suggests an amoral approach with few limitations: J Pattison, 'Just War Theory and the Privatization of Military Force' (2008) 22 *Ethics & International Affairs* 143, 146.

[79] The difficulties of recruiting an all-volunteer force mean that the terms of employment and specifically pay, must be sufficiently lucrative in the armed forces to sustain the required number of personnel: see S Armstrong, *War Plc: The Rise of the New Corporate Mercenary* (Faber and Faber, 2008) 208–44.

but remains inapplicable to mercenaries.[80] Again, an appeal to linguistics reveals the shared roots of the mercenary and the soldier: as the UK Foreign and Commonwealth Office noted, the etymology of related terms such as 'soldier' which is derived from 'solde' meaning 'pay' and the meaning of a 'commission' was essentially a contract to hire men.[81]

Second, there is ambiguity in the relation between the economic motivation and the relative level of remuneration to be received. Jean de Preux noted in the ICRC Commentary to the Additional Protocols that 'as all soldiers of all armies receive a remuneration for maintaining themselves and their families, it was necessary, in order to be consistent, to specify that this remuneration should be substantially higher than that of the members of the army'.[82] Specifying that an individual should receive 'substantially higher' levels of remuneration to qualify as a mercenary obfuscates the motivational criterion. Could an individual who is primarily motivated by the material reward for directly engaging in hostilities, but only receives remuneration on a par with other members of that army be characterised as a mercenary? Another way of approaching the question is to ask whether the individual's economic motivation can be deduced absent evidence of his receiving 'substantially higher' levels of remuneration.

The third issue concerns the locus of the motivation. Applying principles discerned from the Just War Tradition, a 'just cause' combined with the 'right intention' are required for legitimate participation in hostilities.[83] The Just War Tradition is, however, strongly divided upon whether it is the sovereign or the combatant who should make the final determination regarding the justice of a cause or the righteousness of an intention. While a detailed consideration of this is beyond the scope of this book, it is sufficient to note that the decision to engage in hostilities might prudently be alienated from the individual participating in hostilities because this would reflect the dividing line between the traditional doctrines of *Jus ad Bellum* (JAB) and *Jus in Bello* (JIB). Indeed, the treatment of mercenaries is already differentiated along such lines in law. With regard to JAB, the crime of aggression inheres within '[t]he *sending* by or on behalf of a *State* of … mercenaries'[84] which locates the just cause criterion within the sovereign and beyond the mercenary. While the right intention requirement is likely to remain with the individual, this only constitutes a part of the legitimate participation in hostilities calculus. This broader perspective raises the question whether it could be legitimate for a just cause to be

[80] Lynch and Walsh (n 67) 136–37; James Pattison, however, notes that it is not the absence of a suitable motive that is problematic, but rather the presence of an unsuitable motive, Pattison, 'Just War Theory and the Privatization of Military Force' (n 78) 146.

[81] United Kingdom Foreign and Commonwealth Office (n 35) 14, fn 1.

[82] ICRC (n 72) 1807.

[83] Lynch and Walsh (n 67) 138.

[84] See Definition of Aggression 1974 (A/9631), art 3(g). Emphasis added. This has been incorporated verbatim into the Rome Statute as art 8 *bis* 2(g).

pursued through individuals with questionable intention, including pecuniary motivation.

The difficulty of distinguishing mercenaries upon their motivation is exacerbated by the potentially serious consequences of being identified as a mercenary. The punishment which flows from this status, as Henry van Deventer elaborates, can be severe: 'If whether one is a mercenary or not turns on motivation, then motivation can be a life or death issue, for the person found to be a mercenary will be subject to the death penalty'.[85] Despite this strong basis for reconsideration, CAJ Coady advocates that a refined motivation element should be retained within the mercenary definition. He asserts that the motivation characteristic is essential for our *moral* evaluation of mercenarism, even if *legal* implementation is problematic.[86] In her attempt to retain the economic motivation criterion, Sarah Percy argues that motivation needs to be considered together with the foreign aspect of being a mercenary in a holistic manner.[87] It appears that economic motivation perseveres as the lynchpin in the definition of a mercenary, despite this analysis demonstrating that attempts to distinguish mercenaries from soldiers on motivational grounds have both floundered and led to adverse consequences.

B. Armed Reluctance Objections

Another objection against the mercenary arises from the perspective of armed reluctance. As Lynch and Walsh put it, 'A necessary element of an appropriate killing motive … is that it is done reluctantly—a just person only engages in the use of deadly force as a method of last resort'.[88] Thus, this objection is premised upon the assumption that mercenaries engage in lethal violence voluntarily and uninhibitedly. The armed reluctance objection is raised against mercenaries in particular because, unlike the national soldier who receives his wages regardless of whether he is actually required to participate in hostilities or not, the eagerness of the mercenary to fight is implied through his pay being dependent upon his active deployment.[89] On this basis, the claim is that the mercenary desires to fight because it is the source of his livelihood.

[85] H van Deventer, 'Mercenaries at Geneva' (1976) 70 *American Journal of International Law* 811, 815. Even with the gradual abolition of capital punishment, the consequences remain severe.

[86] Coady (n 55) 207–11. Coady notes that, despite the difficulty of establishing such motivation, it is often employed in legal determinations.

[87] This shifts the focus to the question of State control, Percy, 'Mercenaries: Strong Norm, Weak Law' (n 5) 371–72.

[88] Lynch and Walsh (n 67) 141.

[89] The freedom with which mercenaries engage in violence, and their positive desire to do so, is thus intricately linked to their pecuniary motivation, above.

This objection ignores three strong interests held by mercenaries that militate towards armed reluctance. First, the mercenary is especially prone to risk-aversion because he must survive in order to receive his pay. While this is true also for national soldiers, the importance of receiving his pay is elevated for mercenaries because the material reward is his primary motivation. Second, in order to generate the maximum amount of remuneration from armed conflict, the historical focus was to take prisoners that would command ransom instead of killing the adversary.[90] This is related to the third point, that the mercenary has no incentive to inflict lethal violence per se, and indeed might prudently refrain from participating too vigorously in hostilities provided that he is paid. This is because the mercenary does not have motives that are more powerful than the material rewards he will receive, unlike religious or nationally motivated zealots:

> Mercenaries have been castigated for their *reluctance* to engage in battle. And as [Geoffrey] Trease notes, the death knell for the medieval mercenaries came with the appearance of the religious warrior, breathing 'fire and slaughter' in the name of *religious ideologies*.[91]

Indeed, Machiavelli himself paradoxically castigated the *condottieri* for fighting near blood-less battles, providing accounts of large 'battles' between mercenary forces concluded without bloodshed.[92] Although CAJ Coady challenges the factual underpinnings of these claims, he questions whether 'the relative nonbelligerency of mercenaries … would constitute a decisive objection to their use'.[93] In this light, the pecuniary motivation of mercenaries may even be virtuous!

A different form of the armed reluctance argument refocuses the issue away from individual behaviour towards the collective organisation and deployment of force best seen through the problems associated with aggression.[94] At one end of this spectrum, the objection against purchasing private forces is founded upon their ability to circumvent the democratic resistance to the use of armed force, thereby removing a major barrier to the initiation of hostilities.[95] Aligned with this objection is the argument that the availability of military labour for purchase undermines

[90] Singer (n 22) 24–25.

[91] Lynch and Walsh (n 67) 142. Emphasis added.

[92] Machiavelli's claims have been contested by modern historians: see Coady (n 55) 212.

[93] ibid.

[94] See generally, S Sayapin, 'The Definition of the Crime of Aggression for the Purpose of the International Criminal Court: Problems and Perspectives' (2008) 13 *Journal of Conflict and Security Law* 333.

[95] While this is primarily a concern in democracies, an associated issue for non-democratic societies is that private forces can be hired to maintain the status quo. Relating directly to mercenaries, their foreign status distances them from local allegiances, and their economic motivation overshadows ulterior motives making them useful props for undemocratic regimes. A vestigial example of this are the Vatican's Swiss Guards.

the effectiveness of conscientious objectors.[96] Where diminished resistance leads to acts of aggression, difficult to justify under even the most favourable circumstances, the private nature of both the means and the ends towards which it is perpetrated becomes an aggravating factor. Thus, the availability of alternative sources of military labour dilutes the State monopoly, making the prospect of armed conflict more likely.

At the other end of the spectrum is the question of where responsibility is located with regard to acts of aggression. While the sovereign traditionally bears responsibility for acts of aggression, the alleged lack of armed reluctance by mercenaries implies that they might be more susceptible to perpetrating such acts such that responsibility for aggression may fall upon them. Thus, similar to the locus question concerning 'just cause' and 'right intention' above, does responsibility for acts of aggression remain in the sovereign or might it shift to the individual mercenary? As mentioned above, the international consensus for the crime of aggression as expressed in Article 3(g) of UNGA Resolution 3314[97] and subsequently reaffirmed verbatim in Article 8 *bis* 2(g) of the Rome Statute, externalises this responsibility away from the individual mercenary. International law thus treats mercenaries not as the aggressors, but rather as the as the implements of aggression. This position is evident in the context of the 2011 Libyan conflict where UNSC Resolutions 1970 and 1973 included 'armed mercenary personnel' within the ambit of the arms embargo.[98]

Under this traditional paradigm, which is justifiable where the State holds the Weberian monopoly over the legitimate use of force, the State and its agents are responsible for acts of aggression. Where this monopoly becomes eroded, however, a significant *lacuna* may be created because the deployment of armed force outside the framework of the State will circumvent this system of attributing responsibility, leading to impunity for aggression. In addition, the use of proxies lowers the level of control exercised by the State or its agents over organised armed force,[99] erecting another obstacle for responsibility mechanisms. In summary, the introduction of private forces into a responsibility system tailored for State monopoly simultaneously erodes the resistance to the use of force and the prospect of accountability for such acts.

[96] CAJ Coady points to the utility in conscientious objection in democratic societies regardless of whether the war waged is just: see CAJ Coady, 'Objecting Morally' (1997) 1 *Journal of Ethics* 375, 384; M Sandel, *Justice: What's the Right Thing to Do?* (Penguin, 2010) 76–91. Michael Sandel points to the availability of hiring a replacement for individuals subjected to the Union draft during the US Civil War. While military conscription is particularly odious, the removal of individuals who could employ replacements from the draft process effectively removed a strong barrier from suing for peace.

[97] Definition of Aggression (n 84).

[98] Peace and Security in Africa 2011 (S/RES/1970); The Situation in Libya 2011 (S/RES/1973); for an analysis of these Resolutions, see Liu (n 38).

[99] See further Liu, 'Leashing the Corporate Dogs of War' (n 63) 165.

Thus, having pondered the question of the moral mercenary, Lynch and Walsh conclude:

> In the end, the contemporary abhorrence of mercenarism reflects not so much a well-founded moral disgust, even … prudential good sense; instead it reflects all too often both the interests in power and wealth of that 'class of statesmen' … and the demands of an emergent citizenry.[100]

If Lynch and Walsh are correct, there are no coherent objections against the mercenary. Instead, the impulse to delegitimise mercenarism appears to pursue the consolidation of the State's Weberian monopoly over the use of force. The rest of this chapter will demonstrate this agenda in the law purporting to regulate mercenary activity.

VI. MERCENARIES AND MERCENARISM IN THE LAW

The rest of this chapter builds upon the material presented above by examining the treatment both of individual mercenaries and the broader practice of mercenarism under international law. The problems with pinning down the repugnant characteristics of mercenary activity discussed above have become reflected in the notoriously difficult legal definition. Beyond the definition, mercenary activity is subject to schizophrenic treatment by international law. On the one hand, IHL seeks to marginalise the individual *mercenary*: it discourages such activity by explicitly denying the *right* to privileged belligerency status by removing the legal shield to lawful acts of violence committed in international armed conflict. On the other hand, other international laws seek to criminalise the broader practice of *mercenarism*: two existing international conventions make it a *crime* both to be a mercenary, and more significantly, to engage in the support or use of mercenaries. The fundamental divergence in aim, subject and consequence of legal treatment highlights the unstable, inconsistent and incoherent attempt to regulate mercenary activity. Furthermore, the availability of the 'softer' and more limited approach of IHL takes the wind out of the sails of 'harder' and broader attempts to criminalise mercenarism that is found in the international conventions. Looking ahead to chapter six, the bifurcation in legal treatment is replicated with respect to the regulatory mechanisms developed for PMCs, likely with similar results.

Before exploring these different approaches and their consequences in more detail, it is necessary to elaborate upon the definitional difficulties that confound the legal reaction to mercenary activity that severely undercut the efficacy of both approaches under international law.

[100] Lynch and Walsh (n 67) 134.

A. The Definitional Impasse

Unlike the clearly defined problem of maritime piracy that plagued the international arena, the issues raised by mercenary activity are considerably more opaque. An initial, and persistent, difficulty arises with what is definitionally encompassed by the terms surrounding mercenary activity, and why. This has been neatly articulated in a Foreign and Commonwealth Office report:

> [T]he problem of definition is not merely one of wording. The internationally agreed definitions have been shaped to suit the agendas of those drafting them and are not necessarily very useful. The fact is that there are a range of operators in this field who provide a spectrum of military services abroad. It is possible to devise different labels according to the activities concerned, the intention behind them and the effect they may have; but in practice the categories will often merge into one another. If the Government were to conclude that it was desirable to regulate this activity then choosing the right definitions will be an important challenge.[101]

While the discussion above has shown mercenarism TO be conceptually complex and that a precise definition remains elusive, this need not preclude the possibility of identifying the constellation of characteristics deemed to constitute the concept 'mercenary' that can form the basis for a workable legal definition.[102] The image of the mercenary has been sketched as a natural person who is employed to directly participate in hostilities which are external to his home State for the purpose of economic gain. The true picture is, however, much more difficult to paint: '[t]he mercenary's multiple and complex identity as well as his changing nature seem to have made him as elusive target even for the legislator'.[103]

Somewhat counter-intuitively, Sarah Percy has argued that the weaknesses of the law are indicative of a strong norm against mercenarism.[104] She claims that the problems of the legal definition are significant because they codify an established social norm which holds that mercenary activity is intolerable:

> [P]art of the reason states pursued a clear yet unworkable definition is because that definition reflected and publicised exactly what they felt to be problematic about mercenaries: their financial motivation and their status as fighters outside state control. Law is a public declaration that the international system considers … the use of mercenaries, to be wrong.[105]

[101] United Kingdom Foreign and Commonwealth Office (n 35) 16.

[102] Despite the aforementioned moral objections as the law may be capable of greater refinement to overcome such objections.

[103] D Kritsiotis, 'Mercenaries and the Privatization of Warfare' (1998) 22 *Fletcher Forum of World Affairs* 11, 18.

[104] Percy, 'Mercenaries: Strong Norm, Weak Law' (n 5) 378–81; Percy, *Mercenaries* (n 5) 169–79.

[105] Percy, 'Mercenaries: Strong Norm, Weak Law' (n 5) 387.

Expounding upon this line of reasoning, Percy points out that there were viable alternatives to creating codified legal provisions specifically targeting the issue of mercenaries. The harmonisation of existing domestic and international law had been successful in curbing other international problems caused by armed non-State actors, such as hijacking and hostage-taking.[106] These approaches, however, would not have had the explicit effect of stigmatising mercenarism that the development of specific provisions would develop and advertise. In other words, Percy argues that the *utility* of the legal definition was sacrificed as a compromise struck in favour of a strong declaration condemning mercenarism. This argument, however, is undermined by the difficulties faced in describing coherent objections to mercenary activity as discussed above, and in the contradictions and tautologies in the ensuing legal response as described below.

Turning to the law itself, the commonly agreed standard international definition of mercenarism is expressed in the six cumulative requirements of Article 47(2) of API:[107]

> A mercenary is any person who:
>
> (a) is specially recruited locally or abroad in order to fight in an armed conflict;
> (b) does, in fact, take a direct part in the hostilities;
> (c) is motivated to take part in the hostilities essentially by the desire for private gain and, in fact, is promised, by or on behalf of a Party to the conflict, material compensation substantially in excess of that promised or paid to combatants of similar ranks and functions in the armed forces of that Party;
> (d) is neither a national of a Party to the conflict nor a resident of territory controlled by a Party to the conflict;
> (e) is not a member of the armed forces of a Party to the conflict; and
> (f) has not been sent by a State which is not a Party to the conflict on official duty as a member of its armed forces.

These six criteria can usefully be divided in half, such that subsections (a) through (c) articulate the positive characteristics of a mercenary, and subsections (d) to (f) provide for exculpating circumstances. The interaction between the two halves is particularly interesting: an individual may possess all of the odious characteristics associated with the mercenary by ticking the first half of the list, yet avoid being labelled a mercenary in the legal sense through any of the State affiliations in the second half of the list.

While it is likely that the substance of subsection (c) would be most difficult to prove, given the qualification that material compensation must

[106] ibid 385.

[107] With 171 State Parties at the time of writing, API constitutes the most widely accepted international definition of 'mercenary'. For a useful analysis, see Y Dinstein, *The Conduct of Hostilities under the Law of International Armed Conflict* (Cambridge University Press, 2010) 57–59.

be 'substantially in excess' of payment to similar members of the armed forces, subsection (e) constitutes the most simple avenue for a State to hire individuals who otherwise would be branded as mercenaries. A startling example was provided by Sandline International, whose contractors were incorporated into the Papua New Guinean Defence Force as 'Special Constables' and issued with passports.[108] While the direct purpose of this was to circumvent section 200(1) of the country's constitution forbidding the use of mercenaries by bringing Sandline contractors within the ambit of section 200(2) exceptions,[109] this move conferred the additional benefit of excluding Sandline contractors from the international legal definition of a mercenary. This example demonstrates the relative ease by which States can sidestep the legal definition to avail themselves of foreign military assistance without tripping up on international law's attempt at regulating mercenaries.[110]

Geoffrey Best quipped at the operational difficulty of this definition that: '[A] mercenary who cannot exclude himself from this definition deserves to be shot—and his lawyer with him!'[111] More prosaically, Henry van Deventer echoed the difficulties in defining a mercenary by discussing the drafting stages of this definition:

> The central element of being a mercenary seemed to be that he is an individual who is motivated to fight by the desire for gain … but it is fruitless to attempt to lay down any standard that would turn on the level or method of compensation … The foreign character of the mercenary was also regarded as important … a person who is a national of the state in the armed forces of which he serves cannot be a mercenary … It also seemed to be a characteristic of the mercenary … that

[108] See generally V Newell and B Sheehy, 'Corporate Militaries and States: Actors, Interaction, and Reactions' (2006) 41 *Texas International Law Journal* 67, 74–75.

[109] 200. RAISING UNAUTHORIZED FORCES.

(1) It is strictly forbidden to establish, organize, equip, train or take part in or associate with a military or para-military force, or to organize or take part in military or para-military training, except such as is provided for by this Constitution, or to plan, prepare for or assist in the raising or training of such a force or in such training.

(2) Subsection (1) does not prevent–

  (a) the establishment of a reserve, auxiliary or special force (by whatever name known) as part of the Defence Force; or

  (b) the establishment of civilian components of the Defence Force, or the establishment or recognition of non-combatant units or organizations within, attached to or associated with the Defence Force, in accordance with an Act of the Parliament.

(3) An Act of the Parliament may provide that Subsection (1) does not apply to the armed forces of any other country specified in or under the Act, or to the civilian components of, or to the non-combatant units or organizations whether attached to or associated with such forces.

[110] It is evident that some delegations recognised this loophole when drafting the definition. As Henry van Deventer reports from the deliberations, 'all a party to the conflict had to do was to integrate "mercenaries" in its armed forces and they would cease to be mercenaries for legal purposes': van Deventer, 'Mercenaries at Geneva' (n 85) 813.

[111] G Best, *Humanity in Warfare: Modern History of the International Law of Armed Conflicts* (Methuen, 1980) 328, note 83.

> he is specially recruited to fight in a particular conflict. There seemed to be a contradiction in terms in speaking of a mercenary recruited for long-term service … [i]n that event, he seemed to be a lawful combatant.[112]

These three characteristics together represent subsections (a) to (c) of the Article 47 definition. While there was some deliberation about the content expressed in subsection (e) of Article 47, '[t]his was as far as consensus seemed to go'.[113] This lack of consensus over the key traits of the mercenary emphasises the amorphous nature of what is actually abhorred in the mercenary, in turn reflecting the difficulties associated with identifying the attributes of the mercenary discussed above.

Enrique Ballesteros, the first UN Special Rapporteur on the Use of Mercenaries, also highlighted the fact that 'as an instrument of international humanitarian law, *the Protocol does not legislate on mercenaries themselves*, but on their possible involvement in an armed conflict. It restricts itself *to regulation of a specific situation*'.[114] The suggestion is that the concern and the target of Article 47 of API is not the mercenary per se, but is instead confined within a narrow and specific context. Ballesteros continued to summarise that

> The loopholes and shortcomings in the international legislation are compounded by the fact that the domestic legislation of most States does not criminalize mercenary activity. *A mercenary may become a social outcast, but the law can take no action against him.*[115]

While the restrictiveness of the mercenary definition has attracted attention, its consequences have been largely been neglected. By recourse to the maxim, *expressio unius est exclusio alterius* (the expression of one thing excludes the other), the six cumulative characteristics that serve to demarcate the 'mercenary' as a particular and problematic actor may instead be interpreted as implicitly exculpating from any hint of wrongfulness all those who fall short of the definitions. This manipulation of the legal definition can be seen in a letter written by Sir Antony Parsons, then the UK Permanent Representative to the UN General Assembly:

> There now exists an internationally agreed definition of this term; it is not necessary therefore to rely upon encyclopedias. The agreed definition is contained in article 47 of [API]. *From the terms of that definition, it is clear that no person who took part in the recent conflict on the side of the United Kingdom could properly be described as a 'mercenary'.*[116]

[112] van Deventer (n 85) 813–14.

[113] ibid.

[114] E Ballesteros, 'Report on the Use of Mercenaries as a Means of Violating Human Rights and Impeding the Exercise of the Right of Peoples to Self-Determination' (2003) E/CN.4/2004/15 para 38. Emphasis added.

[115] ibid. Emphasis added.

[116] G Marston, 'United Kingdom Materials on International Law 1982' (1982) 53 *British Yearbook of International Law* 337, 418. Emphasis added. The broadly pejorative status of the mercenary is, however, implicit in such attempts to distance oneself from the mercenary.

The mechanism of interpretive denial identified by Stanley Cohen is at the core of this ability to counter-intuitively employ this restrictive definition in order to distance or exclude activity that would otherwise be defined as mercenarism.[117] Cohen, however, only raises a weaker form of interpretive denial in the presence of 'definitional battles' taking place 'because law is a "plastic medium of discourse"'.[118] Yet, the restrictive definition of a mercenary belies a stronger form of interpretive denial that was not raised by Cohen. The cumulative nature of the definition readily provides for multiple escape routes from the mercenary label in a strict legal sense. This ease of exclusion *precludes* the very possibility of contesting that definition. In other words, the form of interpretive denial operating here arises from the *lack of ambiguity* of the legal definition of a mercenary, in the sense that the Article 47 definition has placed this beyond contestation, whereas the interpretive denial identified by Cohen *relies upon* the semantic ambiguity inherent in definitions.

Thus, this detailed legal definition provides an impregnable defence for those individuals who satisfy the bulk of the impugned characteristics and would fall likely foul of other frameworks for determining mercenary status. The unassailability of this legal definition is further anchored by its apparent international legitimacy, as expressed in the broad ratification of the API, and because it stipulates the mercenary status in what can be claimed to be unambiguous terms.

Thus, the approach of international law to define the mercenary achieves the diametrically opposite effect. Rather than separating out a category of actors to be marginalised or criminalised, the pejorative sting of this label has been entirely neutralised because it cannot be applied in reality. This definition enables the modern PMC to assert its legitimacy by distancing itself from its mercenary roots, in addition to the other layers of interpretive denial presented in chapter five.

B. The Departure in Definitional Approach

The attempts to legally define a 'mercenary' constitute a significant departure insofar as they target the *actor* rather than the *action*. This is revealed again by juxtaposing the definition of a mercenary against the aforementioned definition of maritime piracy. In criminalising maritime *piracy* (the action), there is no attempt in the convention to define the *pirate* (the actor). Instead the focus remains on defining the impugned actions of *piracy*, and the identity of those engaged in piratical acts remains legally irrelevant.

[117] S Cohen, *States of Denial: Knowing About Atrocities and Suffering* (Polity, 2001) 105–09.
[118] ibid 106.

Thus, mercenaries are penalised for *who they are*, departing from the orthodox approach of criminalisation for *what they do*. Indeed, the consequence of being a mercenary under Article 47 of API, namely the denial of the right to be a combatant or a prisoner-of-war, can be reached in more direct fashion without needing to rely upon the concept of mercenary at all. The mercenary can be treated like any civilian who directly participates in hostilities, as unprivileged belligerents.[119] Civilians who participate directly in hostilities become lawful targets of attack for the duration of their participation,[120] and can 'be prosecuted for their mere participation in hostilities, even if they respect all the rules of international humanitarian law'.[121] Seen in the context of consequences, the attempt to define the mercenary is essentially superfluous and targeting the actor rather than the action appears even more aberrant.

In part, this attempt to define the *mercenary* (the actor) rather than *mercenarism* (the action) is the source of the motivation conundrum. As Jean de Preux noted in the Commentaries, the definition in Article 47 included a motivational requirement in spite of the fact that 'it is not the task of humanitarian law to make distinctions based on the motives which induce a particular person to participate in an armed conflict'.[122] In terms of legal treatment, the mercenary shares company with the terrorist, who is also defined in part by his motivation. As Antonio Cassese writes:

> Another element unique to terrorism regards *motive*. The criminal conduct is not taken for a personal end … It is based on political, ideological, or religious motivations. Motive is important because it serves to differentiate terrorism as a manifestation of *collective criminality* from criminal offences … that are instead indicative of *individual criminality*.[123]

This juxtaposition reveals a potential paradox in the law's attempt to penalise motives. If the correct treatment of mercenaries is to deny their right to privileged belligerency, the implication is that their mere participation in hostilities constitutes unlawful activity, in turn rendering them susceptible to criminal prosecution. The result of mercenary activity is thus similar to terrorist activity insofar as these both describe violence activities subject to criminal prosecution. As mentioned above, both the terrorist and the

[119] K Dörmann, 'The Legal Situation of "Unlawful/Unprivileged Combatants"' (2003) 85 *International Review of the Red Cross* 45, 46. In light of this uncontroversial position, it is difficult to understand the proposition forwarded by some commentators 'that PMSC personnel should enjoy protections and privileges additional to those afforded civilians—for example it is suggested they should enjoy the right to participate directly in hostilities without losing the protections that civilians enjoy from attack': J Cockayne, 'Private Military and Security Companies', *The Oxford Handbook of International Law in Armed Conflict* (Oxford University Press, 2014) 627.

[120] Dörmann, 'The Legal Situation of "Unlawful/Unprivileged Combatants"' (n 119) 46.

[121] ibid 70.

[122] ICRC (n 72) 1791.

[123] Cassese (n 8) 167. Emphasis original.

mercenary are defined by their motivation. Yet, and this is the key point, the motives of the mercenary and the motives of the terrorist are diametrically opposed and mutually exclusive: the mercenary is motivated solely by the prospect for personal gain, while the terrorist is impelled to violence for selfless causes. Thus, in addition to the problems associated with describing and determining motivation in legal definitions, the contribution of motive is questionable beyond semantic labelling.

Part of the tautology of defining the mercenary can be seen in this light and there may be another paradox in relation to the mercenary if Cassese is correct. If external motivation is the lynchpin of collective criminality, such that this is the characteristic that ontologically elevates an ordinary crime into the realm of an international crime, then the internal motivation criterion for personal gain of the mercenary becomes superfluous.[124] In other words, the requirement that mercenaries are motivated by personal profit neither distinguishes nor contributes to the determination of individual criminality of the mercenary. This exacerbates the existing difficulties with defining mercenarism as an international crime addressed below.

Furthermore, while there are few analogies to this type of approach, the attempt to define the mercenary as a criminal status in the international conventions discussed below is reminiscent of the concept of the 'criminal organisation' that emerged and withered at Nuremberg.[125] Under Article 9 of the Nuremberg Charter, the IMT was empowered to declare that a particular group or organisation was a criminal organisation, which then opened the possibility for the trial of individuals for membership within that criminal organisation under Article 10. The legal definition of mercenary, insofar as it penalises a status, may be analogous to the approach of criminalising organisations. The analogy is that categorisation as a mercenary is similar to that of being a member of a declared criminal organisation because the penal label attaches not to any particular action, but rather to an affiliation or status. As the Nuremberg judgment stressed:

> A criminal organisation is analogous to a criminal conspiracy in that the essence of both is cooperation for criminal purposes. There must be a group bound together and organised for a common purpose. The group must be formed or used in connection with the commission of crimes denounced by the Charter.[126]

[124] Indeed, the personal pecuniary motive of the mercenary suggests that mercenarism is ontologically an *individual* crime because unlike the terrorist, the mercenary engages in violence precisely for personal gain rather than any other ulterior motive. This reveals the contradictions inherent in attempting to frame an *international* crime of mercenarism.

[125] N Jørgensen, 'Criminality of Organisations under International Law' in A Nollkaemper and H van der Wilt (eds), *System Criminality in International Law* (Cambridge University Press, 2009) 202–06.

[126] Office of the United States Chief of Counsel for Prosecution of Axis Criminality, *Nazi Conspiracy and Aggression*, vol Opinion and Judgment (United States Government Printing Office, 1946) 86 www.loc.gov/rr/frd/Military_Law/pdf/NT_Nazi_Vol-I.pdf.

The status of being a mercenary in the general sense, however, clearly exceeds the limitations placed upon the criminal organisation, simply because they cannot all be bound together as a group and organised towards a particular purpose. Indeed, as the Nuremberg judgment recognised, even the approach adopted for criminal organisations 'is a far-reaching and novel procedure. Its application, unless properly safeguarded, may produce great injustice'.[127] This is clearly a concept that must be applied restrictively and is inappropriate as an analogy for the treatment of mercenaries.

C. Different Definitions

The legal definition of mercenary has created an abstract category that possesses no practical application. This has neutralised the stigma of the mercenary label because the legal definition is predominately used to deny, rather than to ascribe, mercenary status. In this context, the contemporary departure embodied within the concept of 'armed mercenary personnel'[128] should be seen as an attempt to salvage the distain of mercenarism.[129] The overreaction of the Security Council, however, is evident in several inconsistencies of this new approach. First, while the term appears in several places in Resolutions 1970 and 1973, these documents do not provide any definition or guidance as to its meaning or effect. Furthermore, the use of this new term signals an explicit departure, suggesting that previous notions cannot aid its interpretation. Second, there are ambiguities inherent within the new term. It is uncertain whether 'mercenary' in the term acts as an adjective or a noun.[130] It may be: tautological because mercenaries are persons who are armed; or superfluous since the aim may be to circumscribe the flow of armed personnel, regardless of the presence of mercenary motives.[131] Third, the term 'armed mercenary personnel' is over-inclusive because of the aforementioned absence of definition and the terminological inconsistencies. While the restrictive legal definition in Article 47 can be deployed as a tool of denial,[132] the breadth of this term instead facilitates the persecution of foreigners. In Libya, this resulted in the victimisation of refugees and the persecution of sub-Saharan migrant workers as suspected mercenaries.[133] The fourth point resurrects the

[127] ibid 85.
[128] *Peace and Security in Africa* (n 98); *The Situation in Libya* (n 98).
[129] Liu (n 38) 297–302.
[130] See the *Oxford English Dictionary* definitions above which elaborate upon these disparate meanings of 'Mercenary' (n 71).
[131] Liu (n 38) 303.
[132] Cohen, *States of Denial* (n 117) 101–16.
[133] UNHCR, 'UNHCR Fears for the Safety of Refugees Caught in Libya's Violence' (n 57); Human Rights Watch, 'Libya: Stop Arbitrary Arrests of Black Africans' (n 56).

question over whether mercenaries are the implements or the perpetrators of aggression. The approach adopted by the Security Council suggests that the former perspective is adopted because 'armed mercenary personnel' is included within the terms of an arms embargo that otherwise circumscribes military materiel.[134] This holds conceptual implications related to responsibility because such categorisation as a means and method of warfare further dehumanises the mercenary. This in turn may erode the perceived autonomy of the mercenary, and their concomitant ability to bear responsibility. The fifth point relates directly to the modern PMC because the ambiguity inherent within the Security Council's approach may have been intended to be sufficiently flexible to embrace PMC activity in Libya.[135] This contention is supported by the broad nature of the proscribed arms embargo that covers 'technical assistance, training, financial or other assistance, related to military activities or the provision, maintenance or use of any arms and related materiel', of which 'armed mercenary personnel' constitutes only a subset.[136] In this context, the UN Security Council may be attempting to bridge the gap between activities that are purely 'mercenary' and the wider operations of the PMC, reinvigorating the approach by coining a new term.

While the difficulties associated with identifying and segregating the mercenary persist in the law, their subsequent treatment diverges significantly depending upon the legal approach that is adopted. This ambiguity of treatment provides further cover for those seeking to avoid the stigma of mercenarism. The following section will illustrate that the determination of mercenary status under IHL results only in the loss of the *right* to be a privileged combatant, rather than the more extreme possibility of an outright *denial* of this status,[137] introducing further interpretive denial mechanisms. The result is that mercenaries are only discouraged under IHL because individuals who are found to have fulfilled the legal definition only become susceptible to prosecution. In other words, IHL only marginalises mercenaries in not directly penalising them.[138] It is only in the context of the two international conventions that criminalise mercenarism that fulfilling the definitional requirements equates to the commission of a criminal offence. Yet, the availability of the lenient approach adopted by IHL removes the impetus for States to subscribe to the more severe international conventions, perhaps accounting for their low ratification rates.

[134] Liu (n 38) 310–14.
[135] ibid 314–16.
[136] *The Situation in Libya* (n 98).
[137] ICRC (n 72) 575.
[138] A different way of expressing this is that IHL removes a privilege or benefit rather than imposing a burden or punishment.

VII. INTERNATIONAL HUMANITARIAN LAW AND THE MARGINALISATION OF MERCENARIES

The approach adopted by IHL is neatly encapsulated within Rule 108 of the ICRC Study of Customary International Humanitarian Law: 'Mercenaries, as defined in API, do not have the right to combatant or prisoner-of-war status. They may not be convicted or sentenced without previous trial'.[139] While the customary nature of this rule may be questionable,[140] as discussed below, it is clear that the contemporary IHL approach is to *discourage* mercenaries through the explicit removal of privileged combatancy status embodied within Article 47(1) of API. This is only a weak form of marginalisation, however, because it only *affirms* the unprivileged belligerency status of civilians directly participating in hostilities that is, as discussed above, the status quo of suspected mercenaries.

Furthermore, because the treatment of mercenaries under IHL hinges upon the question of privileged belligerency, discrepancies are introduced relating to their treatment contingent upon the classification of the armed conflict as international or non-international.[141] This opens the possibility for the argument that mercenaries are *only* marginalised in the context of international armed conflicts. The implication is that mercenaries are not objectionable in non-international armed conflicts because they are not mentioned, defined, nor subjected to any special treatment in the relevant law. The result is that the use of mercenaries in non-international armed conflicts becomes an issue for domestic law. As illustrated in the Angolan trials discussed below, the treatment of suspected mercenaries becomes contingent upon the vagaries of national approaches and suspected mercenaries are especially vulnerable to persecution. Taken together, the approach adopted by IHL to marginalise mercenaries is both weak and inconsistent.

Yet, the denial of privileged combatancy status to mercenaries is only a contemporary development. Historically, mercenaries were accorded prisoner-of-war status upon capture: they were treated no differently when compared to other enemy nationals,[142] and some reports even indicate that suspected mercenaries received preferential treatment.[143]

[139] J-M Henckaerts and L Doswald-Beck, *Customary International Humanitarian Law*, vol I (Cambridge University Press, 2009) 391–95.

[140] For a broad critique of the Study, see D Turns, 'Weapons in the ICRC Study on Customary International Humanitarian Law' (2006) 11 *Journal of Conflict and Security Law* 201, 202–03.

[141] Henckaerts and Doswald-Beck, *Customary International Humanitarian Law*, vol I (n 139) 395. The contemporary classification of armed conflict remains dependent upon normative decisions: see N Berman, 'Privileging Combat—Contemporary Conflict and the Legal Construction of War' (2004) 43 *Columbia Journal of Transnational Law* 1, 16–17.

[142] Kwakwa, 'The Current Status of Mercenaries in the Law of Armed Conflict' (n 26) 85.

[143] J Cotton, 'The Rights of Mercenaries as Prisoners of War' (1977) 77 *Military Law Review* 143, 151, note 44.

The parity of treatment enjoyed by the mercenary arose from the blindness of the law on this question. Indeed, neither of the historical streams that together constitute IHL provided more than an implicit recognition of the mercenary problem until the advent of Article 47 of API in 1977.[144]

The following analysis deals only with international armed conflicts occurring between States and does not address non-international conflicts where belligerents are largely subject to relevant domestic law,[145] and into which international law does not interfere with regards to the status of belligerents.[146]

A. The Laws of Neutrality and the Hague Conventions

The earliest legal limitations imposed upon the participation of foreign individuals in armed conflict arose from the law of neutrality.[147] This, as Stephen Neff explains, comprised of 'two fundamental obligations: the duty of abstention … and the duty of impartiality'.[148] While these obligations existed early on under international law,[149] their expression was primarily within domestic law and it was the US Neutrality Act of 1794 that 'was the first domestic law in the world to deal specifically with the problem of hostile expeditions against foreign countries'.[150] The purpose of this legislation for the US was to avoid being dragged into the Napoleonic Wars: the 1794 Neutrality Act prevented belligerents from recruiting on US territory and limited the voluntary participation of American nationals in foreign conflicts.[151] In particular, the 'act prevented "citizens or inhabitants of the United States from accepting commissions or enlisting in the service of a foreign state"'.[152] The firm position adopted by the

[144] The lack of other IHL provisions directed at mercenaries undermines the contention of the ICRC Study of Customary International Humanitarian Law that mercenaries 'do not have the right to combatant or prisoner-of-war status' that this chapter opened with. Henckaerts and Doswald-Beck (n 139) 391–95.

[145] Again, the discrepancy between the treatment of mercenaries under IHL and the position adopted by various domestic laws contributes to the confusion surrounding mercenaries. This may be exacerbated where the domestic laws result from the ratification of the UN and OAU Mercenary Conventions.

[146] A Cassese, 'Mercenaries: Lawful Combatants or War Criminals?' (1980) 40 *ZaöRV* 1, 5.

[147] See generally Y Dinstein, *War, Aggression and Self-Defence* (Cambridge University Press, 2011) 25–29.

[148] S Neff, *War and the Law of Nations: A General History* (Cambridge University Press, 2005) 191.

[149] Lobel, 'The Rise and Decline of the Neutrality Act' (n 53) 16.

[150] ibid 2.

[151] Neff, *War and the Law of Nations* (n 148) 193; Thomson (n 6) 77–79.

[152] Thomson (n 6) 78. Similarly, Attorney General Richard Rush confirmed that it would be unlawful for a vessel to 'be fitted out, furnished, or armed, within the waters of the United States, and there be sufficient grounds for believing that it is done with intent' to employ it in the service of a foreign sovereign or State in order to participate in hostilities against another

1794 Act is revealed in the criminalisation of certain activities as violations of neutrality that exceeded the substantial requirements of international law at the time.[153] Furthermore, it served as a legislative exemplar because its template was globalised through transplantation into other the domestic laws, indicating that 'U.S. neutrality practices became "the standard of conduct which is now adopted by the community of nations"'.[154]

While the 1794 Act appeared to set a strong face against foreign military service by American nationals, and thus implying that mercenary activity was henceforth criminalised, it in fact pursued another purpose, that of 'strengthening the authority of central government vis-a-vis its citizens, particularly with respect to warfare'.[155] Jules Lobel continues:

> In order to ensure that control Congress enacted a statute which had as its object 'to repress and punish all enterprises of private war, one of the last relics of medieval barbarism'. By outlawing private warfare, the Act would insure that national policy would be made by the government acting through Congress, and not by the acts of individuals.[156]

In other words, the objection was not foreign military service per se, but rather the repercussions it had for the authority of government and the foreign relations of the State.[157] As Janice Thomson writes, 'the issue was the extent to which the nation-state could or should be held accountable for the actions of its citizens beyond its borders'.[158]

This position is readily evident in Attorney General Bradford's 1795 Breach of Neutrality Opinion,[159] which has been much discussed recently as one of the few historical documents making reference to the Alien Tort

foreign sovereign or State with which the US was at peace: R Rush, 'Neutrality (Opinion of 27 July 1816)' (1852) 1 *Official Opinions of the Attorneys General of the United States* 190, 190. Examples of this were confirmed by Attorney General Hugh Legare with respect to the 1818 Neutrality Act: H Legare, 'Violation of Neutrality and Act of Congress of 1818 (Opinion of 8 January 1842)' (1852) 3 *Official Opinions of the Attorneys General of the United States* 741, 739–41; and by Attorney General Reverdy Johnson: R Johnson, 'Violation of the Neutrality Act of 1818 (Opinion of 28 April 1849)' (1852) 5 *Official Opinions of the Attorneys General of the United States* 92. It is also clear that these legislative restrictions apply only to natural persons; Attorney General Charles Lee confirmed: 'That an enemy may come into the territory of a neutral nation, and there purchase and thence remove any article whatsoever, even instruments of war, is a law of nations, long and universally established': C Lee, 'Neutrality (Opinion of 10 December 1795)' (1852) 1 *Official Opinions of the Attorneys General of the United States* 61, 61.

153 Lobel (n 53) 16.

154 Thomson (n 6) 79–84; see esp Table 4.2 detailing the legal restrictions on foreign military service.

155 Lobel (n 53) 24.

156 ibid 25.

157 See ch 4 for a contemporary example related to PMC recruitment activities in Chile: see J Gómez del Prado, 'Mission to Chile' (UNHRC, 2008) A/HRC/7/7/Add.4 paras 55–68.

158 J Thomson, 'State Practices, International Norms, and the Decline of Mercenarism' (1990) 34 *International Studies Quarterly* 23, 43–45.

159 W Bradford, 'Breach of Neutrality (Opinion of 6 July 1795)' (1852) 1 *Official Opinions of the Attorneys General of the United States* 57.

Claims Act.[160] The event in question concerned US citizens joining an attack made by a French fleet on a British colony in Sierra Leone, providing a classic example of the potential for States to become embroiled in the consequences of private violence. Despite Bradford's uncontroversial opinion that 'the United States being in a state of neutrality relative to the present war, such acts of hostility committed by a citizen are an offence against this country, and punishable by the laws of this country',[161] there was little that the US was bound to do. This was because, aside from crimes committed on the high seas which are within the jurisdiction of US federal courts, 'the transactions complained of originated or took place in a foreign country, [so] they are not within the cognizance of our courts; nor can the actors be legally prosecuted or punished for them by the United States'.[162] All that the US was bound to do had already been done by the President, who had issued warnings to all US citizens and had declared that those who rendered themselves liable to punishment for engaging in these activities would not be protected by the US in subsequent proceedings.[163] Attorney General Bradford's Opinion thus confirms the contention that neutrality legislation is concerned solely with the attribution of private acts of violence to the State. Further support for this argument can be found in *Wiborg*,[164] which concerned a successor Act, the US Neutrality Act 1917. In that case, the US Supreme Court held that the government had no preventative power over citizens joining foreign armies, as long as they did so *outside* of American territory.[165]

Beyond the US, more evidence that neutrality legislation was enacted in pursuit of State interests, rather than to express abhorrence against mercenary activity, can be found in the UK Foreign Enlistment Act 1870.[166] The Diplock Report specifically concluded that 'these provisions are not concerned with mercenaries', and were thus constrained to analysing the mercenary question through sections 4–7 of that Act providing for 'Illegal Enlistment' instead.[167] In this regard, it must be stressed that the

[160] Curtis Bradley, 'Attorney General Bradford's Opinion and the Alien Tort Statute' (2012) 106 *American Journal of International Law* 509.

[161] Bradford, 'Breach of Neutrality' (n 159) 58.

[162] ibid.

[163] ibid 59.

[164] *Wiborg v US* (1896) 163 US 632.

[165] The Diplock Report concurred with this position for UK law: 'No administrative action can stop a United Kingdom citizen from volunteering for service as a mercenary once he is abroad': Committee of Privy Counsellors, *Report of the Committee of Privy Counsellors Appointed to Inquire into the Recruitment of Mercenaries* (n 73) 16. Note that '[e]veryone has the right to leave any country, including his own, and to return to his country' under art 13(2) of the Universal Declaration of Human Rights 1948 (UNGAR 217 A (III)).

[166] Foreign Enlistment Act 1870 (33&34 Vict Ch 90). This Act supplanted the earlier 1819 Act which proved ineffective against the outfitting of *The Alabama* in the UK for the Confederate forces: see Committee of Privy Counsellors (n 73) 7, para 24.

[167] Committee of Privy Counsellors (n 73) 7, para 24. The legal defects of these sections are detailed in ibid 7–10, paras 26–39.

circumscribed offences under section 4 the 1870 Act only concern *enlistment* and *recruitment*. Thus *service* in foreign forces is in no way limited by the statute. Indeed, while the Diplock Report 'would recommend the abolition of any statutory offence by a United Kingdom citizen of enlisting as a mercenary',[168] and had 'considered whether it would be appropriate to make *service* as a mercenary a statutory offence in place of enlistment',[169] it recommended against so doing. As the 1870 Act remains the sole piece of UK legislation regulating these activities, a later Foreign and Commonwealth Office report concluded that '[a]lthough successive governments have deplored the activities of mercenaries, no effective legislation exists to prevent either their recruitment or their participation in conflict'.[170]

A contemporary postscript to this discussion on domestic neutrality laws can be found in recent Swiss legislation in reaction to Aegis, a British PMC, effectively moving its headquarters from London to Basel in 2010.[171] Justice Minister Simonetta Sommaruga was reported to have said that it was important to know what companies were getting up to abroad when they took advantage of Switzerland's good reputation when the bill was proposed,[172] suggesting that Switzerland's concern is that it would become adversely affected by corporate activities abroad. The enacted legislation bans direct participation in hostilities, and the recruitment, training and supplying of such personnel both in Switzerland and abroad.[173] Interestingly, the legislation also prohibits '[a]ctivities that undermine Switzerland's traditional neutrality and its foreign policy aims, including the respect of humanitarian law',[174] indicating again that Switzerland is not so much concerned about mercenaries, or PMC contractors more broadly, per se. Rather, the legislation seeks to keep Switzerland's neutrality status unsullied and to maintain a good international reputation that might otherwise be threatened by association with the unsavoury activities of PMCs based in the country.[175]

[168] Committee of Privy Counsellors (n 73) 11, para 44.

[169] ibid 12, para 46. Emphasis added.

[170] United Kingdom Foreign and Commonwealth Office (n 35) 20, para 61.

[171] U Geiser, 'Mercenary Companies to Face Ban' *swissinfo.ch* (23 January 2013) www.swissinfo.ch/eng/swiss_news/Mercenary_companies_to_face_ban.html?cid=34803074. Aegis became 1 of 20 such firms based in Switzerland operating in conflict regions. It is worth noting the similarity between Switzerland's new law and South Africa's legislative response to Executive Outcomes' activities, as both were host States of prominent PMCs: Liu (n 63) 149–53; see also R Talijaard, 'Implementing South Africa's Regulation of Foreign Military Assistance Act' *Private Actors and Security Governance: Geneva Centre for the Democratic Control of Armed Forces* (LIT & DCAF, 2006).

[172] Geiser, 'Mercenary Companies to Face Ban' (n 171).

[173] 'Mercenary Services Outlawed by Parliament' *swissinfo.ch* (24 September 2013) www.swissinfo.ch/eng/politics/Mercenary_services_outlawed_by_parliament.html?cid=36968406.

[174] ibid.

[175] Switzerland might be hypocritical in this regard, however, given its long history as Europe's main supplier of mercenaries and with its citizens continuing to furnish the

Turning to international law, while the Hague Conventions generally regulate the conduct of hostilities, the 1907 Hague Convention V specifically concerns the rights and duties of neutrals.[176] Like domestic neutrality legislation, Hague V does not specifically address the question of mercenaries; rather its provisions regulate third-Party nationals to the armed conflict. In other words, Hague V regulates individuals, of whom mercenaries may constitute a subset, who are foreign to the armed conflict in question.[177] In that regard, Article 17 nullifies the protective status of neutrality where an individual either commits acts that are either hostile to or favour a belligerent Party.[178] This denial of the preferential treatment for neutrals upon their active participation is, however, entirely consistent with underlying principles which create and justify the principle of neutrality.

Furthermore, as the provisions of Hague V concern the broader institution of neutrality, they go beyond the mere individual. Article 4 stipulates: 'Corps of combatants cannot be formed nor recruiting agencies opened on the territory of a neutral power to assist the belligerents'.[179] This obligation is, however, limited by Article 6 which stipulates that: 'The responsibility of a neutral Power is not engaged by the fact of persons crossing the frontier separately to offer their services to one of the belligerents'.[180] Thus, it is clear from the foregoing that Hague V does not seek to marginalise the military activity of foreigners. First, it does not disprivilege foreigners participating in the conflict, but rather only removes the protections afforded to neutrals. Second, it only prevents neutral States from organising forces on its own territory. Third, the movement of individuals seeking to participate in hostilities is not impeded. Indeed, the international laws of neutrality only 'imposes certain limitations on the recruitment and exit of volunteers from neutral territory … the character of the origin and exit must not amount to the organisation of a hostile expedition'.[181]

Vatican's Papal Guard. In this vein, it may be argued that both Switzerland's legislation and its sponsorship of the Montreux Process and Document and the International Code of Conduct can be interpreted in terms of legitimating a particular type of Private Security Company activity. This legitimation agenda is pursued actively through the development of the Document and the Code, and passively by prohibiting so-called 'mercenary firms'.

[176] Hague Convention (V) Respecting the Rights and Duties of Neutral Powers and Persons in Case of War on Land 1907; Hague Convention (XIII) Concerning the Rights and Duties of Neutral Powers in Naval Warfare 1907 is beyond the scope of this book because mercenaries are generally considered to fight on land.

[177] Dinstein, *War, Aggression and Self-Defence* (n 147) 27.

[178] ibid. The requirement for strict parity of treatment is provided by art 17(b) which mandates that a neutral voluntarily enlisting in the armed forces of a Party to the armed conflict shall not be treated more severely than a national of the parties to the conflict.

[179] ibid.

[180] ibid.

[181] I Brownlie, 'Volunteers and the Law of War and Neutrality' (1956) 5 *International & Comparative Law Quarterly* 570, 571.

It is, however, necessary to contextualise the approach from the neutrality perspective. During the 1907 Diplomatic Conference 'a German proposal for a total ban on the service of foreigners in national militaries' was rejected in favour of the approach finally adopted in Hague V.[182] Furthermore, both the 1899 and 1907 sets of Hague Law concerning 'what makes a formal combatant … did not give consideration to issues such as nationality or motivation for fighting in the armies of choice'.[183] Any remaining doubt over the regulation of Hague Laws over the military service of foreign nationals are dispelled by their consequences: the 'decisions of 1899 and 1907 helped *facilitate a free-flow of foreign individuals* that became part and parcel of the practice of warfare in the coming decades'.[184] While Hague Law does not touch specifically upon mercenaries, its lax treatment of foreign nationals to an armed conflict suggests that they were not discouraged.

B. Geneva Law and Belligerency Status

At the Open-ended Intergovernmental Working Group meeting in 2012, the ICRC representative noted that

> while international humanitarian law prohibited the outsourcing of certain activities to PSMCs, such as the command of prisoner of war camps and civilian internment camps, as well as the exercise of an occupying power, *it did not explicitly prohibit the direct participation of any private persons in hostilities.*[185]

Turning to Geneva Law then, support for the contention that mercenaries potentially enjoy privileged belligerency status can even be inferred by the wide net cast by Article 4(A) of the 1949 GC III, provided of course that those requirements are fulfilled. Opinion on the question of privileged belligerency, however, is divided due to the lack of explicit reference to mercenaries in the four 1949 Geneva Conventions. John Cotton, writing before the conclusion of Article 47 of API, has relied upon the broad sense and inclusive nature of Article 4(A) to conclude that mercenaries are

[182] J Cockayne, 'The Global Reorganization of Legitimate Violence: Military Entrepreneurs and the Private Face of International Humanitarian Law' (2006) 88 *International Review of the Red Cross* 459, 474.

[183] Gillespie (n 24) 59.

[184] ibid 60. Emphasis added.

[185] The unwieldy full title of the Working Group is: 'open-ended intergovernmental working group to consider the possibility of elaborating an international regulatory framework on the regulation, monitoring and oversight of the activities of private military and security companies': Minty, 'Report of the Open-Ended Intergovernmental Working Group to Consider the Possibility of Elaborating an International Regulatory Framework on the Regulation, Monitoring and Oversight of the Activities of Private Military and Security Companies on Its Second Session' (n 3) 20. Emphasis added.

likely to be entitled to prisoner-of-war status upon capture.[186] Indeed, the lynchpin for this protection is the recognisable alignment of an individual combatant with a Party to the hostilities, which is further reinforced by the protections expanding to embrace previously ambiguous categories of combatants.[187] A further safety net is provided in Article 5(2) of GC III stipulating that in cases of doubt concerning the categorisation of a captured belligerent under the provisions of Article 4(A), prisoner-of-war status is to be conferred until a competent tribunal has determined his status. In other words, the default position is the rebuttable presumption of prisoner-of-war status. Cotton continues his argument by referring to Article 16 of GC III, which mandates equal treatment of prisoners-of-war without distinction upon non-exhaustive grounds including nationality.[188] Thus, under GC III, mercenaries can be presumed to benefit from prisoner-of-war status, unless this position is factually overturned by a competent tribunal, and cannot be treated differently from other prisoners-of-war.[189]

There may, however, be flaws with Cotton's approach. First, as other commentators have argued, the necessary alignment of a combatant with a Party to the conflict at the core of privileged belligerency may serve to differentiate armed bands acting for private, rather than public, purposes.[190] Thus, the provisional prisoner-of-war status to enumerated groups that are characterised by a close nexus to the State may be justified by the public nature of their participation in hostilities. While mercenaries who fight on behalf of a State and otherwise fulfil the requirements may remain protected under GC III, it is questionable whether mercenaries in the broader sense will be so covered. Second, Cotton's assertion regarding the applicability of the non-discrimination clause is contingent upon the *prior* determination of prisoner-of-war status. In other words, Article 16 operates to prevent differential treatment among those *accorded protection* as prisoners-of-war. If mercenaries are found initially to fall outside lawful belligerency, they would not benefit from this non-discrimination provision.

John Cotton's analysis is particularly useful because it considers the status of mercenaries immediately prior to the 1977 Diplomatic Conference which concluded API.[191] While the Geneva regime was not clear on the

[186] Cotton, 'The Rights of Mercenaries as Prisoners of War' (n 143) 155.

[187] ibid 156–57.

[188] ibid 158.

[189] The ambiguity introduced by this body of law prior to the conclusion of API challenges the ICRC Study on Customary International Humanitarian Law's conclusion that mercenaries should be denied the right to lawful combatancy or prisoner-of-war status: Henckaerts and Doswald-Beck (n 139) 391–95.

[190] T Mallison and S Mallison, 'The Juridical Status of Irregular Combatants under the International Humanitarian Law of Armed Conflict' (1977) 9 *Case Western Reserve Journal of International Law* 39, 50; Berman, 'Privileging Combat' (n 141) 9–10.

[191] Cotton (n 143) 165–66.

status of mercenaries, Cotton demonstrated the potential, and indeed the likelihood, that mercenaries would be treated as privileged combatants and without discrimination. This conclusion levels three challenges to the customary basis of the aforementioned Rule 108 of the ICRC Study.[192] First, Rule 108 reverses the treatment of mercenaries against the inclusive humanitarian grain of Geneva Law.[193] Second, because the Rule is premised upon Article 47 of API, the denial of privileged combatancy status is relatively recent. Insufficient time may have elapsed for the provision to have crystallised into customary law, especially because it cuts against the grain both of previous treatment and of the general humanitarian purpose of IHL. Third, the status of *Additional Protocol* I to the Geneva Conventions, suggests that it is supplementary to Geneva Law. Although it is widely ratified, there may be instances where GC III rather than API will apply. Indeed this potential is explicitly recognised by Jakob Kellenberger in the foreword to the Study: 'While the Geneva Conventions enjoy universal adherence today, this is not yet the case for other major treaties, including the Additional Protocols'.[194]

Mercenaries are first addressed, *expressis verbis*, in Article 47 of API, apparently as a consequence of contemporary developments arising out of the Congo and Angola, discussed in detail below. Writing before the conclusion of API, Robert Cesner and John Brant considered that 'the only moral and practical way to confront the mercenary phenomenon is to withdraw certain protections ordinarily afforded to uniformed combatants'.[195] This presaged the effect of Article 47, as Henry van Deventer observed,

> [t]he consequence of being a mercenary, it was widely asserted, should be that the individual is denied the status of combatant and of a prisoner of war, that is to say that he can be tried as a common criminal for having unlawfully taken part in hostilities.[196]

During its drafting stages, harsher proposals were forwarded whereby the status of being mercenary per se would engender prosecution even in the absence of any actual harm caused.[197] Some delegations attempted to go even further by imposing an *obligatory* denial, rather than the current denial of the *right* to privileged belligerency status for mercenaries: this

192 Henckaerts and Doswald-Beck (n 139) 391–95.

193 GC III, art 4 had been gradually broadened to grant privileged belligerency to groups like commandos and paratroopers, whose status was previously unclear: see Cotton (n 143) 157.

194 Henckaerts and Doswald-Beck (n 139) xvi.

195 R Cesner and J Brant, 'Law of the Mercenary: An International Dilemma' (1976) 6 *Capital University Law Review* 339, 340.

196 van Deventer (n 85) 814.

197 Ibid.

result would have led, paradoxically, to a violation of humanitarian law should a State Party desire to extend prisoner-of-war status to mercenaries pursuant to a wider humane philosophy.[198] These proposals, however, can properly be understood only in the context of the development of the mercenary-specific conventions which seek to criminalise the practice of mercenarism per se, discussed in the next section, and demonstrate the subtle cross-fertilisation between IHL and the mercenary-specific conventions.

In addition to the incoherence of API demonstrated above in relation to its definitional problems, its approach to mercenaries is also inconsistent with the broad corpus of IHL. First, the explicit creation of a new class of 'unlawful' (read 'unprivileged' for consistency here) combatants in Article 47 that is unhinged from the fundamental distinction between combatant and civilian has been argued by several commentators as representing a departure from customary international law.[199] Again, this conclusion challenges the validity of Rule 108.[200] While the ICRC Study purported to establish the denial of privileged combatancy status to mercenaries under customary international humanitarian law, the effect of this Rule instead contradicts the very foundation of that legal regime. Second, this departure is superfluous as the existing legal regime would have generated the identical outcome. As Henry van Deventer explained, where captured mercenaries in international armed conflicts fulfilled the criteria established under Article 4 A(2) of GC III, 'they would be entitled to prisoner-of-war treatment. If they did not meet these standards, then mercenaries would be treated like other civilians who had taken up arms, that is to say, as "unprivileged belligerents"'.[201] Thus, Article 47 of API contributes nothing but definitional difficulties and controversies and its existence detracts from the simplicity and consistency of GC III to the determination of combatancy status.

The marginalising effect of Article 47 is further eroded by both its weakness and its narrowness. Taking its weakness first, API specifically separates out mercenaries alongside spies, under Article 46, as unprivileged belligerents.[202] Drawing the analogy with spies, however, implies that this loss of privileged belligerency status is an only additional risk undertaken

[198] ICRC (n 72) 575, para 1795.

[199] Y Dinstein, *The Conduct of Hostilities under the Law of International Armed Conflict* (n 107) 51; Cesner and Brant, 'Law of the Mercenary' (n 195) 340.

[200] Henckaerts and Doswald-Beck (n 139) 391–95.

[201] van Deventer (n 85) 811.

[202] Curiously, Richard Baxter's consideration of unprivileged belligerency, published in 1951 (prior to the conclusion of API in 1977), considers only spies, guerrillas and saboteurs—mercenaries are conspicuously absent from his analysis: see R Baxter, 'So-Called Unprivileged Belligerency: Spies, Guerrillas, and Saboteurs' (1951) 28 *British Year Book of International Law* 323, 333–42. Does the exclusion of mercenaries in this article imply that they are not considered as unprivileged belligerents?

by these actors. Crucially, the loss of this status does not attract criminal liability per se. As the Dutch Special Court of Cassation, in the 1949 *Flesche* case, stated 'espionage … is a recognised means of warfare and therefore is neither an international delinquency on the part of the State employing the spy nor a war crime proper on the part of the individual concerned'.[203] It is worth noting that, despite the removal of privileged belligerency status, mercenaries remain within the fundamental protections accorded by IHL through the residual Article 75 of API.[204] The efficacy of IHL's approach is further hindered because its effects exclusively target the individual within international armed conflict. Because Article 47 deals myopically with the *individual* mercenary himself, it is blind to the wider contexts that foster, facilitate or otherwise further mercenary activity. Juxtaposition with the mercenary-specific conventions, discussed in detail below, reveal this limitation.

These conventions instead criminalise the *institution* of mercenarism and capture a wider pool of participants including those who aid, abet, counsel and procure mercenaries. In other words, while the former provision only denies the individual privileged belligerency status, the latter conventions provide for criminal prosecutions of mercenaries *qua* their status as mercenaries, in addition to their liability for any other crimes.[205] Seen in this light, it is clear that the discouragement of mercenaries under Article 47 is far from the criminalisation of mercenarism, suggesting that the IHL approach is overly narrow in failing to tackle the supply and support aspect of mercenarism practices. In this regard, the ICRC Study's reliance upon these purportedly harmonious treaties to ground the customary international humanitarian law status of denying mercenaries prisoner-of-war status cannot be unjustified.[206] This is because the purported harmony of the OAU and UN Conventions in discouraging mercenaries by denying privileged belligerency status is a tangential effect to the primary goal of these conventions to criminalise broader mercenarism practices.

Finally, it is worth noting that despite mercenaries being involved predominantly in non-international armed conflicts and other types of violence falling short of armed conflict categorisation, IHL only speaks to mercenaries embroiled within international armed conflict. As Antonio Cassese neatly summarises:

> [I]t is clear, therefore, that current international law does not make provision for the phenomenon of mercenarism in its present manifestations … mercenaries

[203] Holland, Special Court of Cassation, 1949, [1949] AD 266, 272. Dinstein (n 199) 211. See generally Baxter, 'So-Called Unprivileged Belligerency' (n 202) 329–33.

[204] Cassese, 'Mercenaries' (n 146) 24.

[205] K Fallah, 'Corporate Actors: The Legal Status of Mercenaries in Armed Conflict' (2006) 88 *International Review of the Red Cross* 599, 610.

[206] Henckaerts and Doswald-Beck (n 139) 391.

> participating in armed conflicts operate almost exclusively within the framework of civil wars and wars of national liberation. Current international law in fact ignores the status of those participating in such wars ... Therefore, international law ultimately leaves it to national law which ... protects mercenaries as long as they fight alongside, and on behalf of the established government, while considering them as 'outlaws' and bandits if they fight on behalf of the insurgents.[207]

The effects of this schism are far more than academic, as

> the major impact of the stigma of 'mercenarism' ... [has been] to mobilise domestic political support for summary criminal proceedings levelled against mercenaries—such as the trial of mercenaries in Angola in 1976, or the more recent trial of Simon Mann in Equatorial Guinea—sometimes entailing violations of the fundamental guarantees in fact accorded to such individuals by Common Article 3 and Article 75 of [API].[208]

Thus, not only is the *lex specialis* of IHL weak in its treatment of mercenaries, but may also be criticised for its incoherent approach and for fostering inequitable outcomes.

Beyond these critiques, however, Article 47 arguably has the opposite effect of discouraging mercenaries for three reasons. The first claims that IHL has monopolised the questions that govern the reaction to mercenaries, building up upon David Kennedy's observation hat 'humanitarian law can crowd out modes of evaluation ... Occupying the field, the humanitarian vocabulary can channel attention to a limited range of questions', discussed in chapter one.[209] The aforementioned difficulties with definition and other failures, secondly, are magnified by the monopoly of the law over the question of mercenaries because recourse to the law is often definitive. Together, then, IHL both restricts the range and scope of issues to be considered in relation to mercenaries and stifles further conversation on the appropriateness of its approach. Third, IHL unjustifiably skews the analysis by only targeting the individual mercenary, thereby ignoring the structures that support and sustain these activities. This is important in this context, especially if it is the *use* of mercenaries that is being considered, because the individual mercenary is often the last and most fungible part of the operation. If mercenaries are being *used*, others have devised and planned the operation, secured funding and other necessary support, and recruited and trained the soon-to-be mercenaries. The individual mercenary is therefore only the most visible and replaceable manifestation of a much larger operation, suggesting that the mercenary is neither the most culpable nor the most efficient target of sanction.

[207] Cassese (n 146) 6.

[208] Cockayne, 'Private Military and Security Companies' (n 119) 630.

[209] D Kennedy, *The Dark Sides of Virtue: Reassessing International Humanitarianism* (Princeton University Press, 2005) 300.

Kennedy's observation may be particular apt for the mercenary question:

> [H]umanitarian rules may well criticise too little—relying for their implementation on the agreement of the military and political establishments which collectively promulgate them. *Waging war within the rules may so little constrain the use of force that adherence to humanitarian rules will do more to legitimate than contain force.*[210]

Considering the failure of IHL to adequately marginalise mercenaries, it is necessary to consider the efficacy of the other approaches adopted by international law toward these ends. The following section considers the development, significance and limitations of mercenarism as a criminal offence under international law.

VIII. THE INTERNATIONAL CRIME OF MERCENARISM?

In 1976, the Diplock Report concluded that '[t]o serve as a mercenary is not an offence under international law'.[211] While this correctly expressed international law as it then stood, 1977 proved to be a watershed year both for legal attempts to discourage mercenaries and the criminalisation of mercenarism under international law.[212] The former, concerning the conclusion of Article 47 of API, has already been discussed above. The latter emerged from the first (regional) international instrument that specifically targeted mercenary activity as a crime, later supplemented by a truly international convention, albeit with severely limited uptake. Yet, Faiza Patel was able to state on behalf of the UN Working Group on the Use of Mercenaries in 2012 that 'although there were indications of strong disapproval of the involvement of private actors in combat activities, *there was no clear international prohibition*'.[213]

International initiatives to criminalise mercenarism were not, however, restricted only to these conventions. Despite mercenarism failing to crystallise into an international crime in its own right, certain types

[210] ibid 296–97. Emphasis added.

[211] Committee of Privy Counsellors (n 73) 10. Interestingly, this statement might have been the expression of a political stance associated with the involvement of British nationals in the Angolan War of Independence resulting in their trial as mercenaries. This trial led to the subsequent execution or imprisonment of many of these individuals in the famous Luanda Trials of 1976 held by the recently victorious MPLA. This event likely catalysed the African reaction to mercenarism as expressed in the OAU Convention: P Mourning, 'Leashing the Dogs of War: Outlawing the Recruitment and Use of Mercenaries' (1981) 22 *Virginia Journal of International Law* 589, 601–05; and generally Cesner and Brant (n 195); Lockwood, 'Report on the Trial of Mercenaries' (n 59); L Green, 'The Status of Mercenaries in International Law' (1978) 9 *Manitoba Law Journal* 201.

[212] See generally Gillespie (n 24) 80–86.

[213] Minty (n 3) 16. Emphasis added.

of mercenary activity constituted a distinct component of the crime of aggression to become incorporated into the Rome Statute through the 2010 Review Conference at Kampala.

While a raft of initiatives have been directed toward criminalising mercenary practices under international law, it remains unclear whether such activity constitutes an international offence beyond the jurisdiction of States Party to the conventions. The partisan nature and approach of these conventions raise a question mark over conclusions that mercenarism in a broad sense has been unequivocally criminalised. To pre-empt the conclusion of this chapter, Katherine Fallah writes; 'in singling out mercenaries as a specific actor in armed conflict, [API] and the mercenary-specific conventions deliver a firm message that mercenarism … is *at least discouraged* under international law'.[214] Firm foundations for conclusions beyond this position, however, are difficult to find.

A. Momentum towards Criminalising Mercenarism

Although the first international instrument that explicitly referred to the *crime of mercenarism* was the 1976 Draft Luanda Convention,[215] it was not until 1977 that the OAU concluded its Convention for the Elimination of Mercenarism in Africa.[216] As these were both regional instruments, the first and only truly international instrument providing for the criminalisation of mercenarism was the 1989 UN International Convention against the Recruitment, Use, Financing and Training of Mercenaries.[217]

The idea that mercenarism might be an international crime in its own right began to be discussed in earnest in 1961 when the UN first considered the issue of mercenarism within the problematic context of the Katangese secession.[218] The Security Council urged 'that measures be taken for the immediate withdrawal and evacuation from the Congo of all Belgian and other foreign military and para-military personnel … and mercenaries'.[219] These calls were reiterated by the UN throughout the 1960s.[220] In 1968, towards the end of this conflict and around the beginning of the Nigerian Civil War, the declarations by the OAU that the use of mercenaries was

[214] Fallah, 'Corporate Actors' (n 205) 610. Emphasis added.

[215] The text is reproduced in Mourning, 'Leashing the Dogs of War (n 211) 615–18, app II; and M Hoover, 'The Laws of War and the Angolan Trial of Mercenaries: Death to the Dogs of War' (1977) 9 *Case Western Reserve Journal of International Law* 323, 404–06, app VIII.

[216] CM/817 (XXIX) Annex II Rev.1.

[217] A/RES/44/34.

[218] ICRC (n 72) 572, para 1789.

[219] The Congo Question 1961 (S/4741).

[220] See The Congo Question 1960 (S/4387), 1960 (S/4405), (S/4426), (S/5002); Question Concerning the Democratic Republic of Congo 1964 (S/6129), (S/RES/226), (S/RES/241).

a punishable criminal act[221] were echoed by the UN. General Assembly Resolution 2465 '[d]eclares that the practice of using mercenaries against movements for national liberation and independence is punishable as a criminal act and that the mercenaries themselves are outlaws'.[222] Indeed, the Commentaries to Article 47 of API reaffirm that 'since 1968 the United Nations General Assembly has adopted a firm position stating that the practice of employing mercenaries against national liberation movements is a criminal act and the mercenaries themselves are criminals'.[223] A raft of subsequent General Assembly Resolutions supported this view.[224]

These purported crimes were, however, extremely narrow, being restricted exclusively to activity in opposition to what the General Assembly had established as the legitimate right of 'liberation movements' entitled to use 'all the necessary means at their disposal'.[225] Furthermore, this restrictive formulation served as the common denominator which often became even more circumscribed in particular applications, as General Assembly Resolution 3103 illustrates:

> The use of mercenaries by colonial and racist regimes against the national liberation movements struggling for their freedom and independence from the yoke of colonialism and alien domination is considered to be a criminal act and the mercenaries should accordingly be punished as criminals.[226]

It is clear from such provisions that it is not mercenarism practices that are objectionable per se. Instead, it is the use of mercenaries exclusively in opposition to the exercise of peoples to self-determination that is unconscionable. Thus, there are two interrelated implications: first, that mercenary

[221] OAU, 'Resolution of the Third Extra Ordinary Session of the Council of Ministers Held in Addis Ababa, Ethiopia, from 5 to 10 September 1964' EMC/Resolution 5 (III) www.issafrica.org/uploads/FCOM_1964XX.PDF; OAU, 'Resolutions and Declarations Adopted by the Fourth Ordinary Session of the Assembly of Heads of State and Government Held in Kinshasa, Congo, from 11 to 14 September 1967' AHG/Resolution 49 (IV)–AHG/Resolution 52 (IV) AHG/St. 1 (IV) and AHG/St. 2 (IV) www.issafrica.org/AF/RegOrg/unity_to_union/pdfs/oau/hog/eHoGAssembly1967.pdf.

[222] Implementation of the Declaration on the Granting of Independence to Colonial Countries and Peoples 1968 (A/RES/2465(XXIII)) at point 8.

[223] ICRC (n 72) 572, para 1790.

[224] Declaration on the Granting of Independence to Colonial Countries and Peoples 1960 (A/RES/1514(XV)); Question of Territories under Portuguese Administration 1968 (A/RES/2395(XXIII)); Implementation of the Declaration on the Granting of Independence (n 222), 1969 (A/RES/2548(XXIV)), (A/RES/2708(XXV)); Report of the Special Committee to Investigate Israeli Practices Affecting the Human Rights of the Population of the Occupied Territories 1970 (A/RES/2727(XXV)); Basic Principles of the Legal Status of the Combatants Struggling against Colonial and Alien Domination and Racist Regimes 1973 (A/RES/3103(XXVIII)); Drafting of an International Convention against Activities or Mercenaries 1979 (A/RES/34/140).

[225] Implementation of the Declaration on the Granting of Independence 1970 (A/RES/2708(XXV) (n 224).

[226] Basic Principles of the Legal Status of the Combatants (n 224) at point 5.

activity is generally unproblematic and does not usually attract legal censure outside of these contexts; and second, that the purported criminalisation of mercenarism may instead express the importance of the right of peoples to self-determination, especially in the era of decolonisation, rather than opprobrium against mercenarism.

Seen in this context, rather than formulating a general international crime of mercenarism, the purpose of such General Assembly Resolutions may instead be to express the abhorrence of using mercenaries only within the specific context of the post-colonial era. James Taulbee has captured this sentiment well:

> Whatever their effectiveness in individual conflicts, the mercenary has become the symbol of racism and neocolonialism within the Afro-Asian bloc. No matter who the mercenaries served, the scenario has always been the same: white soldiers of fortune fighting black natives.[227]

This context accounts for the contingent nature of the UN Economic and Social Council mandate that established the UN Special Rapporteur and subsequent Working Group addressing the issue of mercenaries.[228] The emphasis is placed upon 'the need for strict observance of the principles of … political independence … and self-determination of peoples, enshrined in the Charter of the United Nations' and 'the legitimacy of the struggle of peoples and their liberation movements for their independence, territorial integrity, national unity and liberation from colonial domination, apartheid, foreign intervention and occupation'.[229] Before recalling the relevant General Assembly and Security Council Resolutions to this effect, the Commission on Human Rights Resolution states in unequivocal terms:

> [T]hat the activities of mercenaries are contrary to fundamental principles of international law, such as non-interference in the internal affairs of States, territorial integrity and independence, and seriously impede the process of self-determination of peoples struggling against colonialism, racism and *apartheid* and all forms of foreign domination.[230]

The General Assembly expressed its support for this position, inter alia by reiterating this passage verbatim.[231] When the Commission on Human

[227] J Taulbee, 'Myths, Mercenaries and Contemporary International Law' (1985) 15 *California Western International Law Journal* 339, 342.

[228] Their full titles are also indicative of this mandate and their specific purpose: 'Special Rapporteur on use of mercenaries *as a means of impeding the exercise of the right of peoples to self-determination*' and 'Working Group on the use of mercenaries *as a means of violating human rights and impeding the exercise of the right of peoples to self-determination*'. Emphasis added.

[229] Commission on Human Rights Resolution 1987/16. 9 March 1987.

[230] ibid. Emphasis original.

[231] Use of Mercenaries as a Means to Violate Human Rights and to Impede the Exercise of the Right of Peoples to Self-Determination 1987 (A/RES/42/96).

Rights replaced the Special Rapporteur with the current Working Group, self-determination remained at the core of the mandate.[232]

The context of self-determination may also account for the initiative and rigour with which the OAU pursued the criminalisation of mercenarism.[233] In 1972, the OAU received the report of its Council of Ministers' Committee of Legal Experts which similarly sought to criminalise mercenarism.[234] This was not to be officially endorsed by the Organisation until the Libreville conference in 1976 that yielded the aforementioned Convention in 1977.[235] This turning point in 1977 was precipitated by events in Luanda, Angola.[236]

B. The Luanda Crucible of the International Conventions Criminalising Mercenarism

The background to the June 1976 trial of 13 white mercenaries in Luanda, Angola has been well documented due in part to the presence of international observers and counsel.[237] The Popular Movement for the Liberation of Angola (MPLA) had declared Angolan independence in November 1975, but conflict continued; in January 1976, mercenaries fighting for the rival National Front for the Liberation of Angola (FNLA) movement entered Angola and subsequently escaped, or were killed or captured.[238] This led to the Luanda trial before an Angolan Tribunal.[239] The indictment charged the defendants:

> [F]or the crime of being mercenaries and for crimes against peace, committed … in a mercenary war of aggression carried out with the aim of extinguishing the

[232] OHCHR 'The use of mercenaries as a means of violating human rights and impeding the exercise of the right of peoples to self-determination' Human Rights Resolution 2005/2, 7 April 2005, para 12. Interestingly, the self-determination context persists with the expansion of the mandate to cover PMC activities, at subparagraph (e): 'To monitor and study the effects of the activities of private companies offering military assistance, consultancy and security services on the international market on the enjoyment of human rights, particularly the right of peoples to self-determination'.

[233] The OAU had considered the mercenary problem since 1964. The OAU's approach, however, considered the use of mercenaries by the Congolese government in opposition to the rebels: Cassese' (n 146) 11–12.

[234] Draft Convention on the Prevention and Suppression of Mercenarism 1972 (CM/433/RevL, Annex 1).

[235] OAU Mercenary Convention (n 60).

[236] Cassese (n 146) 14.

[237] Hoover, 'The Laws of War and the Angolan Trial of Mercenaries' (n 215) 324–29; Cassese (n 146) 14–21; Cesner and Brant (n 195) 341–55.

[238] Cassese (n 146) 14–15.

[239] For a reproduction of the trial records, see Hoover (n 215) 352–81. The trial was observed by an International Commission of Enquiry on Mercenaries convened by the Angolan government: Lockwood (n 59). The counsel for the American defendants also wrote about the trial: Cesner and Brant (n 195).

> independence of the country, enslaving, oppressing, and dividing the Angolan People and pillaging the natural resources of the territory for the benefit of foreign, neo-colonialist and imperialist interests.[240]

Disposing of the 'crimes against peace' charge, Robert Cesner, who was the chief defence counsel representing the American defendants in the trial, and John Brant noted that this can only be tried by a Tribunal of International Composition under the London Agreement of 1945.[241] Reflecting this uncontroversial position, the Angolan Tribunal declined to make reference to this charge in the final indictment.[242]

This left the alleged 'crime of being mercenaries'.[243] It is worth noting two points in this charge. First, this purported crime is much narrower in scope than the subsequent OAU Convention, importing vagueness about the nature of the criminal. The charge in the Luanda trial is directed only at the suspected mercenaries themselves, whereas the OAU Convention provides for the indictment of 'the individual, group or association, representative of a State and the State itself' in the crime of mercenarism.[244] The focus on the mercenaries themselves seems to indicate an approach similar to that adopted by IHL, discussed above, ignoring other entities involved in mercenary operations. Second, this purported crime is framed within an extremely limited context that does not indicate any general objection to mercenarism in a broader sense. If visualised as a Venn diagram, the charge of 'being a mercenary' is the largest set: subsumed entirely within this is the more specific subset of 'being a mercenary in a mercenary war of aggression'. In turn, the extremely specific subset of 'being a mercenary in a mercenary war of aggression with the aim of extinguishing the independence of the country' is entirely within this narrower set. In other words, the probability is necessarily lowered when a possible event is specified in greater detail. Thus, the rhetoric of the charge sacrifices real legal efficacy as being a mercenary is only criminal in the extremely narrow context and circumstances defined in the charge. This presumably adds to the burden of the prosecution who will then have to demonstrate the existence of the exact context for the charge to succeed.

The primary flaw of this charge, however, is whether this purported crime existed at the material time. Under domestic Angolan law at the time, 'no mention is made of "being a mercenary"'.[245] Reliance was then placed upon the aforementioned General Assembly Resolutions as well as

[240] Hoover (n 215) 352–53.
[241] Charter of the International Military Tribunal 1949, art 6(a).
[242] Cesner and Brant (n 195) 342–44.
[243] The tautology of criminalising status should be noted here. If 'being a mercenary' were indeed a criminal offence, this indictment could be reduced to 'the crime of being a criminal'!
[244] OAU Mercenary Convention (n 60), art 1(2).
[245] Cesner and Brant (n 195) 349.

those propounded by the OAU, but as Cesner and Brant stressed: 'these declarations are by their terms nothing more than a collective group of resolutions seeking to define the problem of mercenary activity ... These resolutions, taken collectively, are declarations rather than laws'.[246] To allay possibilities of biased opinion in this regard, given that Cesner acted as the chief defence counsel for the American defendants, this point was reiterated by George Lockwood, who observed the trial as a member of the International Commission of Enquiry on Mercenaries:

> The most compelling argument in support of the position that the crime of being a mercenary existed in Angolan law at the time the alleged offences was committed is based on the [UN Resolutions numbers 2395, 2465, 2548, and 3103].[247]

Lockwood also elaborates upon the impossibility that the burgeoning international crime of being a mercenary, as evidenced in the accumulation of UN Resolutions to this effect, could have become incorporated into the domestic law of Angola for the purposes of the trial:

> The argument in support of the legality of the crime of being a mercenary is that [the UN Resolutions] form part of ... the Common International Law ... Angola, by an act of sovereignty, then incorporated that law into its own internal law when it became independent ... The difficulty with this line of argument is that Angola is not a member of the United Nations nor is there any internal law which evidences the desire of the State to incorporate the crime of being a mercenary into its own laws.[248]

Seen from this perspective, the question of whether the OAU declarations or UN Resolutions evidence the existence of a crime of being a mercenary under international law is moot for the purposes of the Luanda trial if there was no basis for this crime under domestic Angolan law at the material time. Thus, while the trial appeared to be 'fair in the procedural sense ... [t]he questions which remain, however, revolve around the legality of the charges. Specifically, under International Law or the law of Angola, can the status of "being a mercenary" constitute a punishable crime?'.[249] This led Hugh Byatt, the official British observer, to condemn the Luanda trial as a show trial conducted for political purposes.[250]

It was, paradoxically, the contentious legal foundations of the Luanda trial that catalysed Angolan efforts to criminalise mercenarism. To that end, Angola convened representatives from over 40 States as the International

[246] ibid. Furthermore, UNGA Resolutions are generally considered non-binding.
[247] Lockwood (n 59) 196.
[248] ibid 196–97.
[249] Cesner and Brant (n 195) 345.
[250] H Byatt, 'Sentences Passed on British Mercenaries in Angola, Part, The Trial of British Mercenaries in Angola June/July 1976'; see also for the British response, E Rowlands, 'Angola (Mercenaries)'HC Deb 12 July 1976, vol 915 cols 44–49.

Commission of Enquiry on Mercenaries and charged it with the task of drafting of a convention that outlawed mercenarism:[251] the 1976 Draft Luanda Convention.[252]

The preamble of the Luanda Draft Convention specified its purpose 'to codify in a single text and to develop progressively the rules of international law which have developed in order to prevent and suppress mercenarism' in response to the perceived 'development of new rules of international law making mercenarism an international crime'.[253] The explicit recognition that *new* rules are criminalising mercenarism is particularly instructive: echoing the Diplock Report,[254] the opinion of the drafting Commission was that being a mercenary was not a contemporaneous offence under international law.[255]

The Luanda Draft Convention adopted a broader approach than both the indictment of the Luanda trial and IHL because it targeted the practice of *mercenarism* rather than the individual *mercenary*. Under Article 1, perpetrators of the crime of mercenarism included 'the individual, group or association, representatives of state and the State itself' who engage in an array of activities that supported the practice of mercenarism. Again, the crime is tightly drafted because the purpose for these activities is 'the aim of opposing by armed violence a process of self-determination'. The initial question over the legality of the charge during the Luanda trial was unequivocally settled: Article 5 explicitly provided for the crime of 'being a mercenary' independent of any other crimes he may have committed, creating the free-standing crime of mercenarism. One further point about the Draft Convention should be made: Article 4 states that: 'Mercenaries are not lawful combatants. If captured they are not entitled to prisoner of war status', the approach that was subsequently incorporated into Article 47 of API,[256] and contentiously espoused by the ICRC as Rule 108 of customary international humanitarian law.[257]

Luanda was only a draft convention, however, and it was not until the 1977 OAU Convention for the Elimination of Mercenarism in Africa,[258] which came into force in 1985, that a binding international instrument became available to criminalise mercenarism. It can only apply to African States that have ratified the instrument because of its status as a regional

[251] Mourning (n 211) 603.

[252] OAU CM/817 (XXIX) Annex II Rev.1, app II. Produced by the International Commission of Inquiry on Mercenaries, June 1976. The text is reproduced in ibid 615–18, app II; and Hoover (n 215) 404–06, app VIII.

[253] Mourning (n 211) 616.

[254] Committee of Privy Counsellors (n 73) 10.

[255] This conclusion echoes the hesitation of commentators on the Luanda trial upon the legality of the indictment.

[256] Mourning (n 211) 603.

[257] Henckaerts and Doswald-Beck (n 139) 391–95.

[258] OAU CM/817 (XXIX) Annex II Rev 1 (1977).

convention.[259] Some semblance of continuity and coherence among the international instruments addressing mercenaries is evident in the almost identical definitions adopted: Article 1(1) is, aside from minor alterations related to material compensation, identical to that of Article 47(2) of API.

The Luanda roots of the OAU Convention are, however, readily evident. The crime of mercenarism under Article 2 closely follows the text of Article 1 of the Draft Convention, and thus suffers from the same restrictions. Similarly, Article 3 of the OAU Convention deprives mercenaries of privileged combatancy status and Article 4 establishes the independent crime of mercenarism. The OAU Convention does, however, exceed the Luanda Draft Convention in a subtle manner: Article 2(3) explicitly provides for the punishment of *juridical* persons for the commission of the crime of mercenarism; an extension which is appropriate because groups, associations and the State can perpetrate this crime. While Article 3 of the Luanda Draft Convention provided the mechanics for punishing States and their officials, the reference to juridical persons by the OAU Convention may enlarge its jurisdiction even further to encompass the corporation.[260] A final noteworthy aspect of the OAU Convention is its creation of a hypocritical double standard:[261] because the crime of mercenarism only exists in the context of 'the aim of opposing by armed violence a process of self-determination stability or the territorial integrity of another State' under Article 2, States may continue to engage in mercenarism practices in pursuit of all other purposes. In other words, the effect of the OAU Convention is only to criminalise mercenarism practices that challenge the right of peoples to self-determination and undermine the stability of the State.

Turning to the truly international arena, it was not until 1980 that the UN considered drafting an instrument to criminalise mercenarism.[262] This had its roots in the Nigerian Draft Convention,[263] but it took a further nine years to negotiate what would become the 1989 International Convention against the Recruitment, Use, Financing and Training of Mercenaries.[264] The definition of a mercenary under Article 1 is diluted: the requirement

[259] Currently at 30 State Parties according to the ICRC. Available at: www.icrc.org/applic/ihl/ihl.nsf/States.xsp?xp_treatySelected=485&redirect=0.

[260] This may have repercussions for PMCs; however, because of the restrictive definition of 'mercenary' upon which the broad range of impugned activities hinge and the stipulated purposes for which they must act, PMCs and their contractors are likely to evade the terms of this convention.

[261] Liu (n 63) 146.

[262] Drafting on an International Convention against the Recruitment, Use, Financing and Training of Mercenaries 1980 (A/RES/35/48).

[263] Mourning (n 211) 619–25, app III. See also the analysis of the Draft Convention at ibid 605–08.

[264] UN Mercenary Convention (n 60). The Convention came into force on 20 October 2001.

to directly participate in hostilities has been removed and an additional category of mercenary has been created that focuses upon the overthrow of a government and undermining the constitutional order or territorial integrity of a State. Article 2 provides for the criminalisation of broad mercenarism practices and Article 3 confirms that a 'mercenary ... who participates directly in hostilities or in a concerted act of violence ... commits an offence' under the Convention. This formulation is significant: by removing the direct participation in hostilities requirement from the initial definition of a mercenary, the inchoate and accessory dimensions of the offence are accentuated.[265] The safeguard to persecuting mercenaries under this definition who have not perpetrated concerted acts of violence or directly participated in hostilities has been instead relegated to Article 3. Finally, although Article 1(2) defines a separate category of mercenary in the context of destabilising States, reference to national liberation movements and the right of peoples to self-determination were removed. The UN Convention is thus more operable, broader in scope and not confined to a geographical region or historical movement, although the shadow of Luanda may persevere. The efficacy of the UN Convention is, however, significantly hampered by its low ratification rates.[266]

Thus, although the crime of mercenarism can be said to exist, its application is heavily restricted.[267] First, there are the definitional hurdles: the strict definition of a mercenary that hinders both conventions is further exacerbated under the OAU Convention by the required purposes which the actions must pursue. Second, there is the issue of geographical coverage: it is only applicable on the territory of State Parties because the offence is treaty based. Third, because of the regional basis of the OAU and the low ratification rate of the UN Convention, it is clear that international support for the crime of mercenarism is extremely limited. This suggests that the likelihood that mercenarism will develop into a general international crime will be marginal.

[265] This is especially because the UN Convention does not seek to target the individual mercenary, but rather to stymie their 'recruitment, use, financing and training' as its title suggests.

[266] Currently at 33 State Parties according to the ICRC. Available at: www.icrc.org/applic/ihl/ihl.nsf/Treaty.xsp?documentId=D5EDD61038ECF47FC12563CD002D6E50&action=openDocument. In 2005, Caroline Holmqvist noted that not a single Western power had acceded to the UN Convention: C Holmqvist, *Private Security Companies: The Case for Regulation* (SIPRI, 2005) 44 http://books.sipri.org/files/PP/SIPRIPP09.pdf. In 2004, the New Zealand Mercenary Activities (Prohibition) Bill was passed to allow the country to accede to the Convention: see Pl Goff, 'Mercenaries Bill Passed' www.beehive.govt.nz/node/20211.

[267] The difficulty of criminally accusing suspects 'of being mercenaries' is illustrated in *Kaunda v The President of the Republic of South Africa* [2004] Constitutional Court of South Africa CCT 23/04 2, 7–8. Here, 15 men were arrested in Zimbabwe alleged to be mercenaries involved in the attempted coup of Equatorial Guinea. The criminal charges that eventuated, however, all related to firearms and immigration offences. See generally A Roberts, *The Wonga Coup: Simon Mann's Plot to Seize Oil Billions in Africa* (Profile Books, 2006).

C. An International Crime of Mercenarism?

The final step of creating a free-standing international crime of mercenarism was pursued, but ultimately failed. Crimes associated with mercenarism were included in the 1991 Draft Code of Crimes against the Peace and Security of Mankind produced by the International Law Commission (ILC).[268] Article 23(1) of the Draft Code continued the shift in focus away from targeting the individual mercenary to tackling the problem by limiting the support for the practice, an approach that started with the UN Convention. Thus, the Draft Code addressed problem from the perspective of the *hiring State*:

> An individual who as an agent or representative of a State commits or orders the commission of any of the following acts:
>
> — recruitment, use, financing or training of mercenaries for activities directed against another State or for the purpose of opposing the legitimate exercise of the inalienable right of peoples to self-determination as recognized under international law.

To reiterate, the crime of mercenarism under the Draft Code, therefore, is committed *not* by the individual mercenary, but rather by State officials who engage their services.[269] This follows the approach of the UN Convention and explains why the definition of mercenary under Article 23(2) no longer included the 'direct participation in hostilities' requirement.[270] This is because the crimes of 'recruitment, use, financing or training' of mercenaries can be complete prior to any actual participation in hostilities by the mercenaries themselves.[271] In other words, the crime envisaged by the ILC was not strictly that of mercenarism, but rather was transformed into the crime of 'recruitment of mercenaries'.[272] The Commission was divided: several members held the opinion that 'the acts originally dealt with in Article 23 could be prosecuted as crimes linked to aggression, in

[268] ILC, *Yearbook of the International Law Commission 1991*, vol II, Part II (UN 1994) 97. The Draft Code was a precursor to the Rome Statute for the International Criminal Court.

[269] The Draft Code does not go as far to provide for criminalising the State itself, thus departing from approach adopted in the OAU Convention that explicitly provided jurisdiction over juridical persons.

[270] Fallah (n 205) 610. The definition adopted by the ILC of a mercenary is essentially a reproduction of that provided for under the UN Convention. That the Draft Code adopts the approach of the UN Convention, noteworthy for its low ratification rates, may have been a reason behind its failure.

[271] It may, however, be argued at a general level that if a mercenary is defined in part by his direct participation in hostilities, then the 'recruitment, use, financing or training' of mercenaries will remain inchoate because the relevant individuals cannot be characterised as mercenaries prior to their direct participation in hostilities.

[272] The Special Rapporteur had sought to eliminate the crime of recruiting mercenaries which was supported by some members of the Commission, ILC, *Yearbook of the International Law Commission 1995*, vol II, pt II (UN 1998) 27–28.

so far as they involved the participation of agents of the State, or as acts of international terrorism': others cautioned against its exclusion from the Draft Code, despite the limited acceptance of the UN Convention 'in the light of its historical significance, particularly in parts of Africa, and the ideological aspect of the crime as a means of preserving a model of colonialism'.[273] At any rate, the proposed crime of recruiting mercenaries was subsequently dropped from the ILC Draft Code in the second reading in 1995.

Comoros and Madagascar subsequently proposed the specific crime of 'mercenarism' at the Rome Conference, but it failed to garner enough support to be included in the Rome Statute.[274] The exclusion of the crime of mercenarism from the Statute, however, does not per se prevent its inclusion into other substantive provisions as demonstrated through the Kampala Review Conference process discussed below. It is important to note that there were no structural or formal barriers against incorporating the crime of mercenarism into the Rome Statute. Instead, Article 8(2)(b)(xxvi) criminalises as a war crime '[c]onscripting or enlisting children … into the national armed forces or using them to participate actively in hostilities',[275] demonstrating the potential for mercenarism to be criminalised analogously as a war crime. Thus, the exclusion of the crime of mercenarism from the Rome Statute is not the result of practical issues, but likely arises from the lack of international support at the proposal.

Consequently, the ICC does not hold jurisdiction over crimes related to mercenary activity per se. It is clear, however, that although there is no specific reference to mercenary activity within the Rome Statute, the relevant individuals will remain subject to prosecution at the ICC for the perpetration of any of the substantive crimes within its jurisdiction. In such instances, status as a mercenary might become an aggravating factor at the sentencing stage. This approach is arguably more coherent and consistent than those adopted by IHL or the mercenary-specific conventions discussed above because they focus upon alleged criminal conduct alone.

D. Mercenarism and the Crime of Aggression

There may now be scope for the ICC to consider some mercenary-related activity as a result of the 2010 Kampala Review Conference. Amendments

[273] ibid.

[274] UN, 'Proposal Submitted by the Comoros and Madagascar'.

[275] Indeed, this provision was deployed in the first ICC case against Thomas Lubanga Dyilo and resulted in its first conviction, 'ICC Finds Congo's Lubanga Guilty' *BBC* (14 March 2012) www.bbc.co.uk/news/world-africa-17364988. This suggests that criminalising mercenarism along similar lines could be workable for an international court.

were adopted at Kampala to include the definition of the crime of aggression in the Rome Statute and to initiate a regime to establish the jurisdiction of the Court over this crime.[276]

With regard to mercenarism, however, the initial question over aggression was raised by Janice Thomson: 'Should an individual act of violence against another nation-state or its citizens be interpreted as a private act, and therefore criminal, or as an act of the nation-state, and therefore an act of aggression?'[277] This question is especially pertinent regarding the activities of mercenaries because they are characterised by their prima facie private nature. This in turn makes the attribution of responsibility for their activities to the State more problematic, as discussed in chapter four.

The approach adopted by the international community was expressed in Article 3(g) of General Assembly Resolution 3314, which provides that '[t]he sending by or on behalf of a State of armed bands, groups, irregulars, or mercenaries' constitutes an act of aggression.[278] The ICJ in *Military and Paramilitary Activities* considered that this reflected customary international law,[279] and subsequently applied the provision in *Armed Activities*.[280] It was this definition that was incorporated verbatim into Article 8(2)(g) *bis* of the Rome Statute at Kampala,[281] paving the way for the ICC to establish jurisdiction of the crime of aggression.[282]

Crucially, through the 'sending' requirement, this approach treats mercenaries as the implements of aggression by States rather than as aggressors per se.[283] Thus, the implication is that inter-State aggression was the source and subject of concern both within the General Assembly and at the Kampala Conference, and not mercenarism. The superfluous nature of including mercenaries in a definition of aggression was noted

[276] ICC, 'The Crime of Aggression'; ICC, 'Depository Notification: Adoption of Amendments on the Crime of Aggression' http://treaties.un.org/doc/Treaties/2010/06/20100611%20 05-56%20PM/CN.651.2010.pdf. See generally for the background, Preparatory Commission for the International Criminal Court, 'Historical Review of Developments Relating to Aggression' paras 398, 399, 412, 417, 418.

[277] Thomson, 'State Practices, International Norms, and the Decline of Mercenarism' (n 158) 44.

[278] Definition of Aggression (n 84).

[279] *Military and Paramilitary Activities* (1986) 1986 ICJ Rep 14 (ICJ) [195], Judge Ago, however, expresses reservations about this status in his separate opinion: ibid 7. These reservations may, however, be allayed by their incorporation into the Rome Statute.

[280] *Armed Activities* [2005] ICJ 908, 2005 ICJ Rep 168 [146].

[281] ICC, 'The Crime of Aggression' (n 276); ICC, 'Depository Notification' (n 276).

[282] Art 15 *bis* and *ter* stipulate the conditions for the exercise of jurisdiction over this crime. It is important to note that individual criminal responsibility for the crime of aggression and State responsibility for unlawful instances of inter-State force exist in parallel and are not mutually exclusive: Dinstein (n 147) 110.

[283] The ICJ held that the DRC was not responsible for armed attacks against Uganda because the ADF were not armed bands or irregulars sent by or on behalf of the DRC within the meaning of UNGAR 3314: *Armed Activities* (n 280) [146]. A parallel approach was adopted by the Security Council in the Libyan embargo: UNSCRs 1970 and 1973 (2011).

much earlier by Paul Mourning, who argued that 'the use of mercenaries is irrelevant to the question of aggression since the actions of the attacking State would constitute aggression regardless of the nationality of the troops involved'.[284] It could be argued, however, that the nationality of the troops perpetrating the acts of aggression may be indicative or relevant in determining the identity of the aggressor because attributability is the fundamental concern. In this sense, aggression can be considered as the other side of the neutrality coin when it comes to mercenaries. While the neutrality laws discussed above protected States from being saddled with responsibility for the violence perpetrated by their nationals in a private capacity, including mercenaries within an international definition of aggression provides a widely-agreed means by which such responsibility can be attributed to the State under certain circumstances.

Approaching the mercenarism issue exclusively from the perspective of aggression, however, risks overlooking the potential for mercenarism to be used outside of the international plane and will be blind to mercenarism practices within non-international armed conflict or in pursuit of private ends.[285] The limitations inherent within this approach are clearly demonstrated in the context of the Security Council response in Benin and the Seychelles. In Benin, the Security Council was only able to condemn 'the act of armed aggression perpetrated against [Benin]' and to reaffirm the condemnation of 'any State which persists in permitting or tolerating the recruitment of mercenaries and the provision of facilities to them'.[286] The Council then reaffirmed its condemnation of 'the use of international mercenaries to destabilise States and/or to violate their territorial integrity, sovereignty and independence'.[287] The subtle balance is instructive: because the armed aggression has been perpetrated by non-State actors that had not been sent by a State, it fails to constitute an act of aggression under the definition provided by Article 3(g) of Assembly Resolution 3314. Thus, the Council's condemnation of mercenarism had to be detached from aggression and refocused instead on the State nexus.

Likewise, in the context of the Seychelles, the Council condemned 'the recent mercenary aggression against the [Seychelles]'.[288] Strictly speaking, this is a paradox: only States and their agents can commit acts of aggression and mercenaries can only be the implements, rather than the perpetrators, of acts of aggression: 'mercenary aggression' is impossible in contemporary international law. Although the Council subsequently

[284] Mourning (n 211) 594–95.

[285] This critique is similar to the one levelled above against IHL's treatment of mercenaries being restricted to international armed conflicts through art 47 of API.

[286] Benin 1977 (S/RES/405).

[287] Benin 1977 (S/RES/419).

[288] Seychelles 1981 (S/RES/496).

registered that this act was 'prepared and executed from South Africa',[289] because the mercenaries were not *sent* by or on behalf of South Africa, it could not be considered an *act* of aggression within the definition. Thus, while the Council was concerned about the 'danger which mercenaries represent for all States, particularly small and weak ones, and for the stability and independence of African States',[290] the international community's answer to the question posed by Janice Thomson is clear: private acts of violence are not interpreted as an act of the State and therefore are not categorised as aggression outside of the narrow circumstances where they are actually sent by or on behalf of the State. Interpretive denial lurks again in the background:[291] because mercenarism is generally excluded from the legal definition of acts of aggression, this implies that the ontological category of the threat posed is diminished. This form of denial will be accentuated by the crime of aggression at the ICC which retains the identical definition. This both hampers the practical ability of the Court to restrain mercenarism through this provision, and enables those who engage in mercenary activities to exclude themselves from these provisions with the effect of further diluting the objections raised by the critics of mercenarism.

IX. CONCLUSION

This chapter has shown that the laws purporting to discourage or marginalise mercenaries and to criminalise the practices of mercenarism have largely failed. The core problem has been that the restrictive legal definition of a mercenary can be easily evaded. In turn, this provides for interpretive denial: the pejorative legal status of the mercenary can be retained in the law because it cannot apply in practice.

But even in situations where this definition is satisfied, *being* a mercenary is not actually unlawful outside of extremely narrow contexts. The result is that the law has failed to marginalise the individual mercenary. Similarly, while an international crime of mercenarism can be said to exist, it only applies within the territory of the State Parties to the two specific conventions. These conventions are, however, hampered by their geographical restrictions, low ratification rates, and the fact that the crime restrictively defines both the mercenary and the purposes for which the mercenary activity is deployed. The lack of support for criminalising mercenarism meant that it failed to crystallise into an international crime within the Rome Statute, so the ICC does not have any special jurisdiction

[289] Seychelles 1982 (S/RES/507).
[290] ibid.
[291] Cohen (n 117) 105–09.

over these actors. While the crime of aggression tangentially encompasses mercenaries, the context signals that mercenarism is not the core concern, and the requirement that they must be sent by a State significantly curbs its applicability

Together, these failures constitute a form of passive impunity, paving the way for the formation of the modern PMC. Had this position been different, for example if the definitions were operable and the laws clearer in their castigation of mercenarism, it would be possible to show that the actors or the activities were unlawful. That would have prevented the possibility for the modern PMC to become incorporated, because a juridical corporation cannot be lawfully incorporated to pursue unlawful purposes, or at the very least this would have circumscribed their sphere of legal activity accordingly. Beyond enabling their existence and operation, these failures of the law enabled the modern PMC to distance itself from their mercenary origins and activities though an act of euphemistic interpretive denial:[292] the appropriate (legal) term became 'Private Military Company', not mercenary band; they provided 'security' and 'consultancy services', and did not offer mercenary services; their members were employees called 'contractors', not mercenaries. Finally, the distance created by the modern PMC from its mercenary roots was entrenched by a final aspect of interpretive denial, the mechanism that Cohen terms 'magical legalism'.[293] The PMC could not possibly be engaging in mercenary or illegal activities precisely because a corporation *cannot by legal definition* be formed to pursue illegal activities. In turn, these possibilities for interpretive denial undermine the case for robust, independent and enforceable regulation but instead facilitate the acceptance of voluntary self-regulatory mechanisms.

The corporate status of the PMC distorted the perceptions and understandings associated to it: after all, if corporations were legitimate legal entities that operated in the civilian sphere, then arguing that human rights law and the laws of war applied to its activities became increasingly untenable. Thus, at the root of the far-reaching consequences branching from the origins and development of the modern PMC is the failure of the law to marginalise and criminalise mercenary activities examined in this chapter.

[292] ibid 107.
[293] ibid 108.

4

Passive Private Military Company Impunity

I. INTRODUCTION

THIS CHAPTER EXAMINES the structures of legalised impunity enjoyed by the PMC. Building upon the failure of law to marginalise individual mercenaries or to criminalise mercenarism practices in the 1960s and 1970s, as demonstrated in chapter three, private military activities gradually became organised around the corporate model. This process culminated in the formation of the PMC as a fully-fledged corporation replete with independent juridical personhood. This corporate form of organising violence presented particular challenges to the laws that protect human rights and regulate armed conflict. This is because these areas of law presuppose certain types of actor and presume the existence of specific characteristics before they can be engaged, both of which the corporate form undermines. Thus, this chapter reveals the source of legalised impunity within the novel formula presented by the PMC in adopting a civilian structure to engage in military activities: it is this corporate status through which the PMC provides military services that is at the source of both impunity mechanisms identified within this book. This combination undermines both the ability of the law to articulate the harms that PMCs produce and the applicability of the laws that are designed to regulate the sphere within which they operate.

This chapter demonstrates how the lack of legal objections towards mercenary activity provides powerful, yet largely imperceptible, forms of passive impunity to the PMC. As alluded to in chapter one, passive impunity mechanisms are more difficult to identify because these prevent or suppress the very processes that would ordinarily bring instances of impunity to light. The reliance placed upon legal processes further obscures this imperceptibility insofar as these processes are stymied by passive impunity mechanisms. Instead, passive impunity must be inferred from the shadows; in the discrepancies between alleged and observed violations and the subsequent absence of investigation, oversight and accountability. Passive impunity can be inferred where no laws are available to impugn a particular category of action, and where lack of legal recognition or articulation pre-empts responsibility, both prospectively and retrospectively, because the interaction is beyond legal comprehension. Chapter five continues this analysis to discuss the complementary active impunity mechanisms, which suspend the application of potentially relevant laws, made available to the PMC owing mainly to its ability to project force through a corporate facade.

This chapter begins by charting the developments that led to the legal recognition of the corporation as an independent entity possessing juridical personhood. This discussion highlights in particular the curious notion that what is essentially an abstract concept can be afforded equal legal rights to physical human beings, and at times even at their expense. The independent juridical personhood of the corporation that transformed the provision of private military services is then viewed through the lens of interpretive denial and interpretive assertion to illustrate how the corporate form sterilises the perception of the PMC. This facilitates the claims to legitimacy of the PMC both to exist and to provide military services, and ultimately leads to the possibility for advocates of the PMC to press for light forms of self-regulation.

Three examples of passive impunity mechanisms are then presented in sequence. First, the passive impunity mechanisms made available through contract law are discussed because the corporate form of the PMC facilitates its ability to provide military services through contract. While this appears unproblematic at first flush, a deeper analysis reveals issues that arise both from contract law's exclusive focus upon the parties to the contract and from the formal equality between the PMC and the State contractual relations forged through contractual relations. The potential for contract law to promote passive impunity are exacerbated by the fact that developing soft law mechanisms aimed at regulating PMC activity place contractual enforcement of human rights in the keystone position.

Second, this chapter continues by departing from the ordinary debate about impunity for PMC *conduct* within the spheres of human rights law and *Jus in Bello* (JIB) that has preoccupied the attention of industry commentators. Instead, it considers the *Jus ad Bellum* (JAB) ramifications raised by the industry because the question remains whether the PMC should have been operating in the first instance, even if the PMC operates in full accordance with all applicable rules derived from human rights and IHL obligations. JAB issues may be straightforward insofar as PMCs contract to provide services for States alone, but they become increasingly complex where PMCs act either on behalf of non-State entities or on their own accord. This raises the spectre of impunity for the violation of the prohibition of the use of force or for acts of aggression, even where the conduct of hostilities itself is lawfully executed. The law is shown to be incapable of articulating what amounts to corporate aggression because the legal approach within JAB has bifurcated to impose either State responsibility or individual criminal responsibility for its breach. Focusing on the PMC reveals the potential problems of blindly adhering to the categorical separation of JAB and JIB as separate and independent legal spheres, suggesting that the reasons underlying the firm division need to be re-evaluated.

This chapter concludes by discussing passive impunity mechanisms exemplified within the doctrine of command responsibility. This doctrine exemplifies passive responsibility for the PMC for three reasons: because it is a form of role responsibility separate from outcome responsibility; that it functions to connect individual criminal responsibility for collectively produced harms; and because it is not a mode of direct liability. Recourse to this doctrine demonstrates the two ways in which the PMC undermines the legal presumption that organisations controlling violence must be hierarchically structured. First, the civilian status of PMC contractors elevates the standards applied under the doctrine which is unjustified because of their engagement with military services, and second, the horizontal relationship between contractors negates the requisite hierarchical relationship of control that serves as the lynchpin of the doctrine. This demonstrates that the very structure of law dissociates responsibility from the PMC and illustrates how legal processes organise PMC impunity.

II. THE PATH TO CORPORATE JURIDICAL PERSONHOOD

The question 'can a corporation be a legal person? … gives rise to a ready answer—law can and does accord to the corporation a separate status'.[1] The principle of independent existence for the corporation and the complete separation from its members has become 'the cornerstone of company law'.[2] But historically, it was not the legal status of the company that differentiated it from other forms of business organisation, as Paddy Ireland has argued:

> Today, of course, 'company' is usually used as a diminution of 'incorporated company', denoting an enterprise of a particular *legal status*—one which has incorporated and become subject to the rules of company law … For much of the eighteenth and nineteenth centuries, rather than referring to an enterprise with a particular *legal status*, the term 'company' was an abridgement of 'joint stock company', denoting an association of a particular *economic* type.[3]

The purpose of this section is not to delve into the history and intricacies of company law, but rather to elucidate the key developmental milestones

[1] C Wells, *Corporations and Criminal Responsibility* (Oxford University Press, 2001) 76.

[2] P Ireland, 'Capitalism without the Capitalist: The Joint Stock Company Share and the Emergence of the Modern Doctrine of Separate Corporate Personality' (1996) 17 *The Journal of Legal History* 41, 41.

[3] ibid 42. Emphasis added.

in the process towards the legal recognition of corporate juridical personhood. This sketch is necessary because the abstract device of separate and independent juridical personhood is a significant source of both passive and active impunity enjoyed by the modern PMC.

Corporate juridical personhood, however, gives rise to two contradictory effects. On one hand, Sara Seck notes that

> [c]uriously, it is international criminal law's preference for individual responsibility for mass crimes such as genocide that has opened the door to recognition of the legal responsibility of the corporation—a collective—for egregious human rights violations, while keeping the legal door closed where less serious human rights violations are concerned.[4]

Thus, the very potential for corporate responsibility for international crimes is arguably premised upon the juridical personhood status of the corporation. On the other hand, the possibility of corporate responsibility for international crimes that has been made possible by corporate juridical personhood acts as both a factual and legal shield for the individual criminal responsibility of the natural persons constituting that corporation.

The extension of the 'person' as a legal category beyond the individual natural human being raises fundamental questions concerning its characteristics. In particular, it challenges the concept of personhood because of the legal innovation of the corporation: an association of natural persons incorporated into a body which subsequently possesses independent identity and which is capable of enjoying rights and being subjected to duties. Indeed, John Dewey has suggested in an influential article 'that "person" might be used simply as a synonym for a right-and-duty-bearing unit'.[5] Furthermore, the consequences attached to such an understanding are that they 'must be social in character, and they must be *such* social consequences as are controlled and modified by being the bearer of rights and obligations, privileges and immunities'.[6] Thus, the lynchpin of personality in law may be distilled to the ability of an entity to benefit from rights and discharge obligations that are prescribed by the law: personhood is clearly a circular and self-referential concept. Support for this view is provided for through the common law concept of *filius nullius*, literally a son of nobody, through which an illegitimate son was denied specific legal rights despite the uncontested nature of his physiological existence.[7]

[4] S Seck, 'Collective Responsibility and Transnational Corporate Conduct' in T Isaacs and R Vernon (eds), *Accountability for Collective Wrongdoing* (Cambridge University Press, 2011) 140–41. Unfortunately, however, this door has subsequently been closed because the Rome Statute recognises only the individual criminal responsibility of natural persons under art 25.

[5] J Dewey, 'The Historic Background of Corporate Legal Personality' (1925) 35 *Yale Law Journal* 655, 656.

[6] ibid 661. Emphasis original.

[7] ibid 656. Other obvious differences concern disparities of treatment based upon age, sex and, historically, race.

In other words, 'for the purposes of law the conception of "person" is a legal conception; put roughly, "person" signifies what law makes it signify'.[8] This is the legal conception of personhood that illustrates the disparity of rights and obligations delineated by the law between natural and legal persons.

Considering the uncertainties raised by the creation of juridical persons in law and the issues arising from the recognition of corporations as juridical persons, its origins may be somewhat startling. In the United States, this legal recognition was expressed in *Santa Clara* in which Chief Justice Waite pronounced *before argument* for the Supreme Court that:

> [t]he court does not wish to hear argument on the question whether the provision in the Fourteenth Amendment to the Constitution, which forbids a State to deny to any person within its jurisdiction the equal protection of the laws, applies to these corporations. We are all of opinion that it does.[9]

The brevity with which corporate juridical personality was affirmed and the fact that this position had been reaffirmed by the Supreme Court in numerous cases since suggest that the decision in *Santa Clara* was uncontentious and did not signal innovation.[10] The context of the Fourteenth Amendment, which was intended to protect newly freed slaves after the Civil War, however, suggests that this conclusion was incongruous with this purpose: these constitutional rights were intended to afford protection to natural persons. Indeed, the fabrication of juridical personhood avails corporations of a range of constitutional rights in the US, where a narrow majority of the Supreme Court recently overturned two precedents to hold that the First Amendment prohibited governmental measures controlling expenditures of a political nature for corporations.[11]

It was not only in the United States that the corporation was accorded personhood in law. This principle has been unchallenged in the United Kingdom since it was established by the House of Lords in the 1897 case of *Salomon*, per Lord Chancellor Halsbury: 'it seems to me impossible to dispute that once the company is legally incorporated it must be treated like any other independent person with its rights and liabilities appropriate to itself'.[12] The *Salomon* case, however, only cemented the legislative shift. Paddy Ireland noted the subtle linguistic shift from section 3 of the 1856 Joint Stock Companies Act, which enabled persons to 'form themselves

[8] ibid 655.

[9] *Santa Clara County v Southern Pacific Railroad* (1886) 118 US 394 (US Supreme Court) 396. The Supreme Court went on to hold that only the state that grants the charter for incorporation can tax and regulate that corporation.

[10] M Horwitz, 'Santa Clara Revisited: The Development of Corporate Theory' (1985) 88 *West Virginia Law Review* 173, 173–74.

[11] *Citizens United v Federal Election Commission* [2010] US Supreme Court 08-205, 558 US.

[12] *Salomon v A Salomon* (1897) [1897] AC 22 (HL) 30.

into an incorporated company', to section 6 of the 1862 Companies Act which allowed persons 'to form' an incorporated company, leading him to conclude thereafter that: 'Companies, the [United Kingdom 1862 Companies] Act implied, were now made not *of* people but *by* them, in much the same way that a chair or table might be made by a carpenter'.[13] This signalled the shifting legal perception of the corporation from an association of natural persons to a distinct and independent entity.

While this is the contemporary position, the concept of juridical personality ascribed to corporate bodies is historically rooted in *personae fictae*, or the 'fiction theory', that was proclaimed by the Catholic Church in the thirteenth century. This was intended to apply to ecclesiastical bodies which were 'but a name and an incorporeal *res*' which crucially *could not be punished* because '*nomina sunt juris et non personarum*; they have neither a body nor a will'.[14] The persistence of recognising the 'right-and-duty-bearing unit' character of these corporate bodies while simultaneously denying their capability to bear responsibility for their adverse consequences pervades later understandings of corporate personhood. Even at this initial stage, however, the paradox of juridical personality is readily apparent insofar as the fiction theory of ecclesiastical bodies grants their recognition as independent rights-*but-not-duty* bearing units. The duties which are concomitant to their rights are asymmetrically curtailed because of the presumed impossibility of sanction or punishment for their wrongdoing. From the fiction theory of incorporation, this challenges the understanding of how juridical persons can be understood as a unit capable of bearing rights or duties at all for the simple reason that they possess neither a body nor a will.

Fiction theory was gradually replaced when the 'concession theory' of juridical personality grew alongside the rise of the State.[15] Fuelled by the drive of the State towards hegemony, all associations were prohibited apart from those that derived their existence and powers directly from the State, thereby cementing its sovereign authority further.[16] The re-conception of the juridical personality as an entity which explicitly derives its existence and power from the State connects juridical persons and organised violence in a fundamental fashion.[17] Thus, even the powerful mercantile

[13] Ireland, 'Capitalism without the Capitalist' (n 2) 47.

[14] Dewey, 'The Historic Background of Corporate Legal Personality' (n 5) 665.

[15] State control over companies is illustrated by the Bubble Act 1720 (6 Geo I, c 18) which prohibited all Joint Stock Companies that were not authorised by Royal Charter: see J Bakan, *The Corporation: The Pathological Pursuit of Profit and Power* (Constable & Robinson, 2005) 5–8.

[16] Dewey (n 5) 666.

[17] Approached from this perspective, the modern PMC may be considered the paragon rival to the State insofar as it organises private armed forces in the form of a corporate juridical person outside of the concession theory. Thus, the form of dissociated violence proposed by Mary Kaldor may be further refined to the effect that violence organised along the lines of the juridical person further exacerbates the degenerative cycle: M Kaldor, *New and Old Wars: Organized Violence in a Global Era* (Polity, 2001) 92.

corporations such as the East India Company, which were notable in their possession of armies, navies and territories that rivalled those of the State, derived their exercise of sovereign powers from the very State charters that underpinned their existence.[18] There were, however, jurisdictional variations that challenged any claim to the universality of the concession theory. The formation of corporations historically differed between civil and the common law jurisdictions: in the former, corporations 'seem to have been created by the mere act, and voluntary association of their members; provided such convention was not contrary to law' while in the latter, 'the king's consent is absolutely necessary to the erection of any corporation, either impliedly or expressly given'.[19]

To complicate things further, there are two versions of the concession theory of corporate juridical personality.[20] The strong version conceives of juridical incorporation as a privilege *granted* by the sovereign State: '[L]imited liability is a privilege. It is a privilege healthy as tending to the expansion of opportunities and commerce, but it is open to abuse'.[21] The weak version is premised upon the claim that 'corporation owes its *legal* existence and powers to the grant of corporate status from the state'.[22] The justifiability of regulatory interference by the State depends in part on which version is applied. The understanding of juridical personality as a privilege granted by the State may emphasise the susceptibility of the juridical person to constraining regulation by the State, but the theory itself is debatable. On the one hand, the privilege of juridical personality can be understood as an emanation of State power. This justifies strong regulatory interference by the State to constrain the power of the State itself, in a narrow sense, and to ensure that sovereign power is constrained in a broader sense. This claim is enhanced through the possibility of abuse that accompanies the right accorded by the State. On the other hand, the 'concession theory's endowment of the corporation with an independent life could conceivably imbue it with inviolable rights and thereby serve to restrict regulatory efforts'.[23] In other words, the bonds of reciprocity between the juridical person and the State which created and recognised it as a distinct entity may be appropriately severed.

[18] J Thomson, *Mercenaries, Pirates, and Sovereigns: State-Building and Extraterritorial Violence in Early Modern Europe* (Princeton University Press, 1994) 35–41. See generally N Robins, *The Corporation That Changed the World: How the East India Company Shaped the Modern Multinational* (Pluto Press, 2006).

[19] W Blackstone, *Commentaries On The Laws Of England*, vol 1 (Clarendon Press, 1765) 460.

[20] S Bottomley, 'The Birds, the Beasts, and the Bat: Developing a Constitutionalist Theory of Corporate Regulation' (1999) 27 *Federal Law Review* 243, 247.

[21] Per Cooke J *Nicholson v Permakraft Ltd* (1985) 3 ACLC 453 (New Zealand CA) 459.

[22] Bottomley, 'The Birds, the Beasts, and the Bat' (n 20) 247. Emphasis original.

[23] R Romano, 'Metapolitics and Corporate Law Reform' (1984) 36 *Stanford Law Review* 923, 933.

For present purposes, the emphasis is upon the shift from the concession theory of the corporation to the contemporary 'independent entity' perspective. While, mercantile companies had historically exercised sovereign powers, including the control of organised military forces, these had existed under the concession theory paradigm which effectively meant that they were emanations of the State that granted their charter. The competition 'to attract valuable incorporation business to their jurisdictions by jettisoning unpopular restrictions from their corporate laws' ensured the subsequent dilution of and departure from concession theory: these included the removal of rules that stipulated narrow corporate purposes, limited durations of existence and fixed geographical locations.[24]

The key point here is that the delegation of sovereign power to the corporation ended because these liberating measures signalled the end of the concession theory of incorporation. Without the narrowly defined and time-limited charter that positively empowered the corporation the delegated use of armed force, the modern corporation has since become exclusively civilian.[25] Under this analysis, it would not be objectionable if a State incorporated a modern PMC under the concession theory as such explicit authority would unambiguously subject the PMC to State responsibility.[26] The explicit grant of delegated sovereign power to the PMC would enable tight regulation by the State since the charter could be easily amended or revoked, and furthermore would incentivise close supervision because the State would accrue responsibility for PMC activity.[27] Thus, it is not the corporate form of the PMC per se that is objectionable. Rather, impunity is generated from the departure from the concession paradigm towards the independent entity status of the corporation. This

[24] Bakan, *The Corporation* (n 15) 14.

[25] Under art 1(8) of the US Constitution, Congress possesses the power to grant Letters of Marque and Reprisal; see generally T Cooperstein, 'Letters of Marque and Reprisal: The Constitutional Law and Practice of Privateering' (2009) 40 *Journal of Maritime Law and Commerce* 221. That this process does not correspond to the modern PMC is supported by W Nagan and C Hammer, 'The Rise of Outsourcing in Modern Warfare: Sovereign Power, Private Military Actors, and the Constitutive Process' (2008) 60 *Maine Law Review* 429, 444–56. In particular, 'PMCs … are not supported by traditional, appropriate sources of authority, even though national sovereigns are a key part of the process of assigning sovereign power to them': ibid 448.

[26] H Tonkin, *State Control Over Private Military and Security Companies in Armed Conflict* (Cambridge University Press, 2011) 55–59.

[27] The ILC Draft Articles suggest that where PMCs are specifically empowered by the State to exercise its sovereign authority, the State may be attributed liability for the consequences per art 5: ILC, *Yearbook of the International Law Commission 2001*, vol II, pt II (UN, 2007) 42–43. A residual situation is provided by art 8, which concerns factual action on the instructions of, or under the direction or control of the State: ibid 47–49. The concession theory of the corporation would enable the attribution of State responsibility for any adverse effects and would therefore be an unproblematic basis upon which to organise the PMC. See the discussion in ch 5 on State responsibility.

is because State authority and control over the PMC is alienated without the development of new rules and mechanisms to attribute responsibility. Thus, the present manifestation of the corporate form generates passive impunity because it provides for the asymmetric ascription of rights without responsibilities: the term 'Limited liability company' encompasses it all, but extends far beyond its intended purposes of restricting only the flow of financial liabilities.

A. Interpretive Denial for the PMC arising from its Corporate Juridical Personhood

Understood in this context, the modern PMC amalgamates two characteristics inappropriately to avail it of overlapping interpretive denial mechanisms: the law's failure to marginalise or criminalise mercenary activity and the appropriation of the status of the civilian corporation respectively.[28] As mentioned in chapter three, they fall outside the strict legal definition of mercenary and operate beyond the narrow contexts of objectionable forms of mercenarism, enabling PMCs to distance themselves from these unsavoury activities. This is complemented by the euphemistic label afforded by the classification of the PMC as a (civilian) corporation.[29] The euphemism engaged here hides the military nature and activity of the PMC behind the veil of the civilian corporation. Further neutralisation occurs with the removal of its military connotations, such as the adoption of other labels such as 'Private *Security* Company', and other references to organised force provision. For example, the self-regulatory framework of the International Code of Conduct concluded by a consortium of PMCs themselves and discussed in depth in chapter six, is for 'Private *Security Service Providers*',[30] and the main US trade association for these companies is called the 'International Stability Operations Association'.[31] Interpretive denial culminates in the deployment of a mechanism Stanley Cohen terms 'magical legalism'[32] which enables the argument 'that crime is necessarily an *ultra vires* act of a corporation; liability cannot be imputed to a corporation because a corporation cannot legally be formed for the purposes of committing a crime'.[33] Finally, to segue into chapter six, the strong claim

[28] See the analysis in ch 3 and the revised typology in ch 2 respectively.
[29] S Cohen, *States of Denial: Knowing About Atrocities and Suffering* (Polity, 2001) 107.
[30] www.icoc-psp.org/. Emphasis added.
[31] http://stability-operations.org/. This organisation was renamed on 19 October 2010, originally 'International Peace Operations Association'.
[32] Cohen, *States of Denial* (n 29) 108.
[33] Seck, 'Collective Responsibility and Transnational Corporate Conduct' (n 4) 143–44. This is taken to extremes in many jurisdictions where a corporation cannot by definition commit a crime.

to legality through the corporate form itself constitutes a justification for light regulation because the nominal equality in legal status enables the PMC industry to indignantly challenge unequal regulation in relation to other corporations. In short, the corporate status of the PMC obscures their military nature, which remains readily evident in light of the facts presented in chapter two. This in turn justifies differentially lax treatment of the PMC in relation to the armed forces of the State, despite the parity in the roles they play.

B. Interpretive Assertion for the PMC arising from its Corporate Juridical Personhood

While the adoption of the corporate mantle forged a perceived distinction between the PMC and the unsavoury connotations associated with mercenaries, this same act also drew the PMC towards the more benign sphere of profit-driven corporate activity. In doing so, the entire frame of reference against which PMC activity is gauged has shifted seismically. At this broad level, there are three effects of interpretive assertion made by the PMC in its adoption of the corporate juridical form. First, the PMC is able to claim legitimate existence and a stable and independent identity conducive to forging contractual relations. The ramifications of this observation are considered in greater detail in the following section.

Second, the primary concerns within which the PMC become embroiled shift from the military realm, with its attendant hazards of international humanitarian and human rights abuses, to the civilian sphere that spark more mundane concerns. This shift shields the PMC from the prospect of human rights abuse allegations because corporate activity is associated with trade and the provision of goods and services. Applying the 'what you see is all there is' (WYSIATI) concept introduced in chapter one, the question of human rights is less likely to be raised in such a context as relevant information becomes unlikely to be retrieved in this context. A good example of this is provided by the independent and bipartisan Commission on Wartime Contracting created by the US Congress in 2008 whose mandate was to examine the extent of waste, fraud and abuse in the context of contingency contracting in Iraq and Afghanistan.[34] The context of corporations and contracts may have influenced this mission, making it clear that the prime concern was to improve the functional efficiency of contractors while minimising financial waste. The potential for military contractors to be engaged in violations of international humanitarian and

[34] Commission on Wartime Contracting, 'Transforming Wartime Contracting: Controlling Costs, Reducing Risks. Final Report to Congress' (2011) www.wartimecontracting.gov/docs/CWC_FinalReport-highres.pdf.

human rights law, despite the Commission's vigilance for 'abuse' (understood purely in terms of financial abuse), was clearly rendered invisible.

Third, even where human rights concerns are included within the frame of reference, such as in the PMC-industry specific regulatory mechanisms discussed in chapter six, such concerns become subsumed as only one of a range of relevant considerations to be taken into account. This relegates the importance of human rights concerns to compete against other issues, and may become a pertinent consideration insofar as it positively affects material profit or public relations.

Taken together, the interpretive assertion made possible to the PMC by the adoption of the corporate juridical form alters the context in which private military activities are considered. With its formal status as a corporation, the PMC is able to divert attention away from activities with human rights implications and thereby avoid some scrutiny in this area. Any attention that cannot be diverted is minimised by balancing against other, apparently equal, concerns.

III. PASSIVE IMPUNITY FOR THE PMC UNDER CONTRACT LAW

A critical aspect of the passive impunity mechanisms enjoyed by the PMC that flows from its adoption of the corporate form, and through the consequent possibilities for interpretive denial, is the reliance placed upon softer forms of regulation when compared with the armed forces of the State. While the potential for impunity inherent in this approach is explored in greater detail in chapter six, it is readily evident in the attempts of developing self-regulation that the foreground contract law mechanism is the primary means through which PMC behaviour is regulated. This reliance upon contractual mechanism to incorporate and enforce human rights standards constitutes the logical end-point in treating PMCs as no more and no less than an ordinary corporation, providing a powerful passive impunity mechanism shielding the PMC.

This section challenges the possibility and prudence of relying upon contractual provisions to ensure that PMCs protect and promote human rights in the course of their operations. While few commentators to date have considered the regulatory potential of contract law in this regard,[35]

[35] Scholars that have, however, generally discuss specific contractual issues arising from military contracting practice, but have not considered the role that contract law might play in the protection of human rights more broadly: see eg S Schooner, 'Contractor Atrocities at Abu Ghraib: Compromised Accountability in a Streamlined, Outsourced Government' (2005) 16 *Stanford Law & Policy Review* 549. The notable exception is L Dickinson, 'Contract as a Tool for Regulating Private Military Companies' in S Chesterman and C Lehnardt (eds), *From Mercenaries to Market: The Rise and Regulation of Private Military Companies* (Oxford University Press, 2007). Dickinson, however, advocates for an expanded role for contract by highlighting its potential.

a critical analysis is necessary here because the framers of developing initiatives aimed at regulating the PMC have positioned contractual mechanisms as the centrepiece of their efforts. Notably, the Montreux Document suggests as good practice for States '[t]o include contractual clauses and performance requirements that ensure respect for relevant national law, international humanitarian law and human rights law by the contracted PMSC'.[36] In a similar vein, the International Code of Conduct (ICoC) requires that 'Signatory Companies will make compliance with this Code an integral part of contractual agreements with Personnel and subcontractors'.[37] Anne-Marie Buzatu expresses the faith that the ICoC has invested into contractual mechanisms in no uncertain terms: 'The ICoC uses contractual mechanisms to impose human-rights compliant standards *directly on the companies themselves, regardless of where they are operating*'.[38] While recourse to contract law holds the potential to circumvent significant jurisdictional hurdles affecting other regulatory efforts,[39] the increased reliance placed upon contract law to regulate PMC activities within the substantive scope of international humanitarian, human rights and criminal law is likely to magnify both the potential and problems inherent within contract law itself.

Laura Dickinson seeks to demonstrate the potential of contract law in this area when she argues that contracts are 'the vehicle of military privatisation', and so could import 'the norms and values of public international law into the "private" sector'.[40] In particular, she suggests that '[c]ontracts could be drafted to explicitly extend relevant norms of public international law to private contractors, provide for enhanced oversight

[36] Montreux Document on Pertinent International Legal Obligations and Good Practices for States Related to Operations of Private Military and Security Companies during Armed Conflict 2008, pt II, para A.IV.14 and 15.

[37] Swiss Federal Department of Foreign Affairs, 'International Code of Conduct for Private Security Service Providers' paras 18–23. Henceforth the ICoC.

[38] A-M Buzatu and B Buckland, 'Private Military & Security Companies: Future Challenges in Security Governance' (DCAF, 2010) DCAF Horizon 2015 Working Paper No 3 23. Emphasis original. Buzatu, who has been influential in the development of the ICoC through her work at the Geneva Centre for the Democratic Control of Armed Forces (which is itself under mandate from the Swiss government convening the ICoC initiative to facilitate its development), had emphasised her view that contract law mechanisms are integral to the protection of human rights in the PMSC context because of the direct legal enforceability of contractual provisions. Personal communication, 19 October 2010, Washington, DC.

[39] See esp C Bakker and M Sossai (eds), *Multilevel Regulation of Military and Security Contractors: The Interplay Between International, European and Domestic Norms* (Hart Publishing, 2012); L Cameron and V Chetail, *Privatizing War: Private Military and Security Companies under Public International Law* (Cambridge University Press, 2013).

[40] Note, however, that it is only the weaker possibility of norms and values that can be incorporated, rather than the stronger possibility of binding obligations and legal duties: Dickinson, 'Contract as a Tool for Regulating Private Military Companies' (n 35) 218. See generally L Dickinson, 'Public Law Values in a Privatized World' (2006) 31 *Yale Journal of International Law* 383; and L Dickinson, *Outsourcing War and Peace: Preserving Public Values in a World of Privatized Foreign Affairs* (Yale University Press, 2011) 69–101.

and enforcement, and include more specific terms such as carefully drafted training and accreditation requirements':[41] this advice appears to have been heeded by those drafting both the Montreux Document and the ICoC. Among the benefits of implementing relevant human rights and IHL rules as contractual provisions is the possibility of direct enforcement through contract law, thereby avoiding the hurdle of demonstrating that the PMC functions as an extension of government in order to satisfy the State action requirement.[42] The thrust of Dickinson's argument is that reform of the PMC contracting process is required, and she accepts that the reform of the contractual terms themselves can only serve as one avenue of PMC industry regulation reform among many.[43] Indeed, Dickinson's treatment of contract law as a regulatory tool for PMCs is devoted to overcoming the inertia associated with contractual reform, and with providing supporting evidence that contemporary PMC contracting practices are woefully inadequate.

This section takes up this debate by emphasising the shortcomings of contract law in adequately fulfilling the regulatory roles recently urged upon it by soft law instruments seeking to regulate the PMC industry. The aim of highlighting the inadequacies of contract law in this context is not to undercut Dickinson's proposals for contractual reform, but rather to re-evaluate the ability for contract law to carry the regulatory burden entrusted to it, and in particular to play the role that soft law has cast for it. In this regard, the general lack of debate about the merits and failures of contract law for regulating PMCs does not bode well for the regulatory efficacy of soft law mechanisms which rely upon its functioning.

The impetus of this section rests upon the characteristics of contract law that result in it microscoping towards the minutiae of bipartite agreements rather than telescoping to the cosmos of concerns beyond mere contractual provisions (as human rights law does). This inward-looking quality of contract law, discussed in the following section, undermines its usefulness as a mechanism to take into consideration effects that are beyond contractual terms, including issues of human rights and IHL. Even to the extent that contractual provisions are made to encompass humanitarian and human rights concerns, the egocentric nature of contract law transmutes those concerns into sterile terms whose sole force arises from the fact that they were subject to agreement by the contracting parties. Put in other words, when viewed through the lens of contract law, the protection and promotion of human rights need not have meaning, purpose or effect beyond that intended and agreed upon by the contracting parties.

41 Dickinson (n 35) 218.

42 ibid 220–21. Satisfaction of the State actor requirement, however, may accord immunity from certain types of legal suits leading to a Catch-22 situation. This is discussed further in ch 5.

43 ibid 237.

The immediate and pervasive effect of contract law's myopia is twofold. First, the range of responsibilities and obligations borne by the parties to the contract are limited because all considerations that are not expressly incorporated as contractual terms are excluded. Second, contract law confines the range of entities to which obligations are owed to the contractual parties only. Thus, the overall effect is that contract law curtails both the content and scope of responsibility.

Invoking contract law as a regulatory mechanism for the PMC industry introduces incidental issues that militate against its success. These can be grouped into three broad categories: the privity of contracts limits the likelihood of enforcement; the horizontality defining contractual relations circumvents existing responsibility mechanisms reliant upon hierarchies and effective control; and the remedies available under contract law are inappropriate responses to breaches of international humanitarian, human rights and criminal law.

A. Freedom of Contract and its Consequences

In sketching out the contours of contract law for this section, it is important to emphasise that the freedom of contract is the fundamental underlying concept: 'The notion is that parties … should have an *unhindered right to enter legally binding arrangements*, without regard as to whether the terms of the agreement seem to others to be wise or fair'.[44] Thus,

> [t]he basic ideal of contract law, freedom of contract, indicates that contract law is an area in which *parties can set their own rules, creating rights and obligations that apply only to the contracting parties, and only because of the contract that they have entered*.[45]

This concept informs the justification that agreements should be enforced, and while it has been expressed through competing analytical frameworks,[46] these nuances detract from the central point that contract law concerns the protection of consensual agreements between the contracting parties.[47]

[44] B Bix, *Contract Law: Rules, Theory, and Context* (Cambridge University Press, 2012) 11. Emphasis added. The UNIDROIT Principles, art 1.1 (Freedom of Contract) provides that 'The parties are free to enter into a contract and to determine its content': M Bonell, *Unidroit Principles in Practice: Caselaw and Bibliography on the Unidroit Principles of International Commercial Contracts* (Transnational Publishers, 2006) 69–70. The commentary states that 'The principle of freedom of contract is of paramount importance in the context of international trade'.

[45] Bix, *Contract Law* (n 44) 110. Emphasis added.

[46] For an overview, see ibid 132–36.

[47] There remain distant limits, generally concerning the prohibition of impermissible choices, beyond which there is wide consensus that agreements cannot and should not be enforced: Craswell, R, 'Promises and Prices' (2011) 45 *Suffolk University Law Review* 735, 746. For a concise discussion of freedom of contract, see Druzin, B, 'Restraining the Hand of Law' (2014) 117 *West Virginia Law Review* 100, 130.

The historical evolution of contract law itself further underscores its exclusive focus of enforcing consensual agreements. Jay Feinman sketches the traditional image of contract law: during the eighteenth century 'contractual liability was not sharply differentiated from liability arising out of nonconsensual situations, such as injury (tort) or status relations. Contractual obligation arose not solely or even principally from agreement, but from implied community standards of behaviour'.[48] Indeed, David Ibbetson provides supporting historical evidence that the different claims available in medieval times were a mixture of the modern categories of contract, tort and property.[49] At this developmental stage, the most that could be said was that an assortment of rules on different types of contracts existed, still far from what could be identified as a law of contract.[50]

This traditional image eventually gave way to the '[c]lassical contract law [which] conceived of contract as a field of private ordering in which parties created their own law by agreement' that is more familiar today.[51] It is interesting to note the emergence of contract law as a distinct discipline, as Feinman puts it:

> Classical theorists saw real, objective differences between contract law, in which *liability was imposed only through the consent of the parties*, and other private law fields, in which liability was imposed for causing injury to another (tort) or for violating another's entitlement (property).[52]

Stephen Hedley phrases this succinctly when he writes that 'the Victorians *invented* the idea that the law will enforce contracts as such'.[53] The upshot of this brief historical overview is to demonstrate that contract law was carved out as a distinct legal area relatively recently in order to pursue and protect business and consumer transactions, and thus was designed largely for commercial work.[54] The developmental trajectory of contract law underscores the idea that it is exclusively concerned with only the narrow set of issues that revolve around how consensual agreements are concluded and

[48] He anchors this position by writing that: 'The world view reflected in eighteenth century beliefs about contract law emphasized the relations between the individual and the community … In contrast to later times, individuals themselves had limited ability to define standards through contract': J Feinman, 'Critical Approaches to Contract Law' (1982) 30 *UCLA Law Review* 829, 831.

[49] D Ibbetson, *A Historical Introduction to the Law of Obligations* (Oxford University Press, 1999) 1–10. For the gradual emergence of contract law, see ibid 21–23.

[50] S Hedley, 'Keeping Contract in Its Place—Balfour v Balfour and the Enforceability of Informal Agreements' (1985) 5 *Oxford Journal of Legal Studies* 391, 402.

[51] Feinman, 'Critical Approaches to Contract Law' (n 48) 831–32.

[52] ibid 832. Emphasis added. Michael Moore suggests that 'one might think contract law to be defined by its function of getting people to keep their promissory obligations, obligations that are distinct from the non-promissory obligations dealt with by criminal law and torts': M Moore, *Placing Blame* (Oxford University Press, 2010) 20.

[53] Hedley, 'Keeping Contract in Its Place' (n 50) 402. Emphasis original. For a broader historical perspective, see Ibbetson, *A Historical Introduction to the Law of Obligations* (n 49) ch 11 'Foundations of the Modern Law of Contract'.

[54] Hedley (n 50) 402.

enforced, and with remedying breaches to contractual terms. This characterises contract law as egocentric and inward-looking, unconcerned with issues external to the contractual terms or third parties to the contract.

In addition to curtailing the content and scope of responsibilities, a cynical view of the freedom of contract might be that it allows the parties to inscribe only the responsibilities that are sufficiently beneficial (or at least those which are benign) as to be agreeable to both parties. Because contractual terms are up for negotiation between both parties, attempts such as that made by the ICoC to mandate that 'Signatory Companies will adhere to this Code, *even when the Code is not included in a contractual agreement* with a Client',[55] will be futile under contract law. Bluntly put, a client of a PMC will not be able to rely on the provisions of the ICoC directly unless those provisions have been explicitly incorporated into the contractual agreement.

Another related difficulty concerning the clarity of contractual obligations arises in the particular context of PMC contracts because flexibility can be useful or 'necessary to cope with the exigencies and security concerns inherent in the sorts of environments where PMCs are likely to be used'.[56] Laura Dickinson reports particular problems with current US practice whereby PMC contracts 'possess so few guidelines, requirements, or benchmarks that they effectively contain no meaningful evaluative criteria whatsoever'.[57] Diluting contractual specificity further is the practice of the US in procuring PMC services through 'blanket purchase agreement', effectively an open agreement under which particular services can be requested subsequently as the need arises.[58] The foundational notion of freedom of contract empowers the conclusion of such vague and open-ended agreements because neither formal nor substantive requirements can be mandated, provided of course that the contract is lawfully concluded. This remains the case even if these turn out to be difficult to monitor and assess and thus almost impossible to enforce.

This gives rise to a broad conceptual objection to protecting human rights through contract law. Where the norms and principles of human rights become incorporated into bilateral agreements, contract law transmutes these principles into contractual terms. This gives rise to three intolerable consequences. First, the meaning and purpose of human rights norms and principles are lost in translation as they are reduced to sterile contractual terms. The underlying concepts that compel the protection of human rights are collapsed into the confines of the contractual agreement,

[55] Swiss Federal Department of Foreign Affairs, 'International Code of Conduct for Private Security Service Providers' (n 37) 19. Emphasis added.
[56] Dickinson (n 35) 220.
[57] ibid.
[58] ibid 221 and 224.

thereby losing both their context as well as their content. The second is the tension between the sources of the rights: whereas human rights are the expression of 'the inherent dignity and … the equal and inalienable rights of all members of the human family',[59] contractual rights arise from the conclusion of voluntary bipartite relations. This incompatibility can be seen through the prism of contract law, which is only capable of upholding human rights protection on the basis of bilateral consensus. In the conversion to contractual provisions, the inherent dignity of the individual that is the source of universal and inalienable nature of human rights is replaced by a vision of rights that has the agreement of two parties as its origin. Third is the issue of consequences: a violation of human rights is ontologically different from a breach of contract. This perspective reveals the poverty of employing contract law to protect human rights because it is incapable of articulating the wrong at stake. In short, human rights cease to be *human* rights, but are sterilised into contractual rights.

B. Doctrine of Privity and its Limitations

A converging approach to this conclusion can be charted through the doctrine of privity. Despite the possible effects of a contract or its performance upon third parties, under English contract law (and transplanted to many common law jurisdictions), the doctrine of privity stipulates that the terms of a contract can neither impose obligations nor confer benefits to a third party.[60] While the imposition of duties through contractual agreement upon a third party absent his consent would amount to 'an unwarranted infringement' of his liberty and justifiably remains unaltered,[61] this rule controversially prevented third parties from asserting the benefits they would receive by virtue of contractual performance. This rule was conclusively established only as recently as 1861,[62] culminating in the famous exposition by Viscount Haldane LC that

> in the law of England certain principles are fundamental. One is that only a person who is a party to a contract can sue on it. Our law knows nothing of a *jus quaesitium tertio* [a right of action exercisable by a third party] arising by way of contract.[63]

[59] Preamble of the Universal Declaration of Human Rights 1948 (UNGAR 217 A (III)) para 1.

[60] Law Commission, *Privity of Contracts: Contracts for the Benefit of Third Parties* (Law Com No 242, 1996) para 2.1. Perhaps shockingly, the Law Commission notes that the privity doctrine had the effect of immunising parties to the contract from third-party tort claims arising from negligence in performing the contract prior to *Donoghue v Stevenson* [1932] AC 562 (HL).

[61] ibid (n 60) 2.1.

[62] *Tweddle v Atkinson* (1861) 1 B&S 393 (QBD).

[63] *Dunlop Pneumatic Tyre Co Ltd v Selfridge & Co Ltd* [1915] AC 847 (HL) 853.

A line of historical cases prior to 1861 that *allowed* a third party to enforce a contractual provision made to benefit, and intended to be enforced, by him question the apparently firm foundations of this doctrine under the common law.[64] Furthermore, the appropriateness of this doctrine has been undermined by its dilution through statute in recent times.[65] Yet, it is worth noting two persistent points despite these challenges: first, that the contractual parties retain the power to determine the content and scope of third parties to enforce contractual terms;[66] and second, that the standing granted to the class of third parties to enforce a contractual provision is very narrow, being restricted to *intended beneficiaries*.[67]

Three disconcerting conclusions flow from these observations. First, it is clear that the possibility of third-party legal action on a contractual term remains a privilege to be granted by the contracting parties, rather than a right that can be relied upon more generally. While the third party need not be identified,[68] this immediately limits the class of potential claimants under a contract. Furthermore, the possibility for a third party to sue on a contractual term rests upon the *intention* of the parties to the contract to confer a benefit upon that third party. Thus, the second conclusion is that intention is necessary (or at the very least there should not be evidence contrary to such intention). This implies that the onus is upon the

[64] These are provided per Denning LJ in *Drive Yourself Hire Co (London) Ltd v Strutt* (1954) 1 QB 250 (CA) 272. The Law Commission suggests that there was no firm rule either way by the mid-nineteenth century: Law Commission (n 60) 2.4–2.5.

[65] In the UK, see Contracts (Rights of Third Parties) Act 1999 (c31). See for a commentary, M Dean, 'Removing a Blot on the Landscape—The Reform of the Doctrine of Privity' [2000] *Journal of Business Law* 143. For additional background, see Law Commission, *Privity of Contracts* (n 60).

[66] Note especially the convergence with UNIDROIT Principles, art 5.2.1(2) of which provides that 'The existence and content of the beneficiary's right against the promisor are determined by the agreement of the parties and are subject to any conditions or other limitations under the agreement': Bonell, *Unidroit Principles in Practice* (n 44) 271.

[67] To adopt the differentiation drawn by the American Law Institute, as expressed in s 302 of the Restatement (Second) of the Law of Contracts 1981, which differentiates intended beneficiaries from incidental beneficiaries. This opens the possibility for the former category only to have a right of action under a contractual term. Similarly for the UK, s 1(1) of the Contracts (Rights of Third Parties) Act 1999 enables a third party to a contract to enforce a term of the contract in his own right, provided either that the term expressly provides for this, or that the term purports to confer a benefit on him (unless it appears that the parties to the contract did not intend the term to be enforceable by the third party).

[68] While s 308 of Restatement (Second) of the Law of Contracts does not require that an intended beneficiary is identified, the commentary notes that the lack of identification may influence the determination of whether a beneficiary is intended or incidental; and s 1(3) of the Contracts (Rights of Third Parties) Act 1999 states: 'The third party must be expressly identified in the contract by name, as a member of a class or as answering a particular description but need not be in existence when the contract is entered into'.

third party to demonstrate such intention, thus reinforcing the notion that the class of potential third-party beneficiaries is limited for any particular contract.[69] It is the third conclusion, however, that has the broadest ramifications for relying upon contract law to protect and promote human rights. Because *benefit* is the critical nexus for third-party legal action on a contractual term, contract law is effectively blind to the *burdens* imposed upon third parties by bilateral contractual agreements.[70] This is the critical point: contract law is indifferent to claims within the substantive orbit of human rights because such claims do not involve the conferral of benefits, but conversely concern remedies for injury and injustice. The overall result is that third parties suffering from human rights violations arising from contractual performance will not have an automatic right of action under contract law. This indifference of contract law is reinforced by the limitations inherent within the mechanisms of enforcement and the nature of available remedies, discussed in detail below.

C. Direct Enforcement by Contractual Parties

The doctrine of privity holds two main implications for the potential to regulate PMCs through contract law: exclusive enforcers and limited incentives. Foremost among these problems is the fact that the power of enforcement is invested almost entirely within the contracting parties, in turn raising two further problems. First, because a contract creates an internal law between the parties to it, the parties possess complete discretion as to which provisions, if any, they want to enforce. While it is conceded that some criminal justice systems allow for unfettered prosecutorial discretion, this is justified because it allows for the allocation of precious prosecutorial resources, lays the foundation for plea-bargaining and gives scope for leniency. Juxtaposed against prosecutorial discretion, however, the decision of a party to enforce a contractual term need not be based upon anything more than pure self-interest.

This leads directly to the second problem of incentives for a party possessing such discretion to enforce a contract. Indeed, enforcement might tarnish that party's reputation by association by revealing and publicising allegations of PMC misconduct that might otherwise remain obscure. A more concrete, and chilling, example is provided by an episode that

[69] This is not to include more specific limitations, such as that provided under s 313 of Restatement (Second) of the Law of Contracts, which restricts the possibility of third-party suits in the case of contracts with the government under US law.

[70] While it is impermissible under the doctrine of privity of contract for *obligations* to be imposed through contractual agreements upon third parties, this need not limit the distribution of disbenefits and other externalities.

occurred during the US State Department's contract with Blackwater, just prior to the Nisour Square massacre discussed in chapter two.[71] James Risen reports that a State Department investigation indicated that Blackwater had violated the contract in numerous ways and 'concluded that Blackwater was getting away with such conduct because embassy personnel had gotten too close to the contractor'.[72] During the course of this investigation, the head of Blackwater operations in Iraq directly threatened one of the investigators by saying that he 'could shoot, and kill [him] here in Iraq and no one would do anything about it'.[73] The lack of incentive for embassy officials, to whom Blackwater was performing the contract, to enforce the contractual terms is readily apparent when they ordered the investigators to leave Iraq, because they were 'unsustainably disruptive to day-to-day operations and created an unnecessarily hostile environment for a number of contract personnel', ending the investigation.[74]

Perhaps more unsettling is the fact that the US State Department effectively *rewarded* Blackwater with more than a billion dollars' worth of contracts after this incident,[75] indicating both the severe lack of incentive to enforce contractual terms and the absence of non-legal forms of enforcement.[76] The reasons forwarded to justify the continuing relationship between the US State Department and Blackwater suggest that it is rooted in self-interest: Blackwater has largely been successful in protecting American diplomats.[77] Because the contract serves the parties, the discretion and incentives in enforcing its terms depend largely upon whether the interests of the parties are indeed served, irrespective of the impact of

[71] J Risen, 'Before Shooting in Iraq, a Warning on Blackwater' *The New York Times* (29 June 2014) www.nytimes.com/2014/06/30/us/before-shooting-in-iraq-warning-on-blackwater.html. See also New York Times, 'State Department Documents on Blackwater Episode' *The New York Times* (29 June 2014) www.nytimes.com/interactive/2014/06/30/us/30blackwater-documents.html.

[72] Risen, 'Before Shooting in Iraq, a Warning on Blackwater' (n 71).

[73] New York Times, 'State Department Documents on Blackwater Episode' (n 71) 332–011. Corroborated, ibid, 332-016–332-017. See also, 332-002–332-005.

[74] Risen (n 71).

[75] D McCabe, 'State Department Awarded Blackwater More Than $1 Billion After Threat on Investigator's Life' *Huffington Post* (10 July 2014) www.huffingtonpost.com/2014/07/10/blackwater-state-department-contracts_n_5572355.html.

[76] Laura Dickinson notes the paucity of instances where the US government exercises its power to terminate a contract. Instead, an earlier example of PMSCs being effectively rewarded financially in the wake of being implicated in human rights abuses is provided by the expansion of CACI's contract after its involvement in the Abu Ghraib prisoner abuse scandal: Dickinson (n 35) 224 and 235.

[77] McCabe, 'State Department Awarded Blackwater More Than $1 Billion After Threat on Investigator's Life' (n 75).

that contract on others. This effect is summarised by Anne-Marie Buzatu: 'The private contractual nature of these services means that PMSC contracted security obligations run to their clients, but not to the public at large'.[78]

This episode points to the problems inherent in contract law's dependence upon contractual parties to enforce the agreement. Where the interests of both parties are sufficiently aligned, it is likely that infractions that are inconsequential to the core interests of the parties will remain unremedied. This effect may be refined with PMCs because their provision of security and other services related to coercion and organised force place their clients in a position of practical dependence in often volatile environments. A client that is reliant upon a PMC for protection may be unable to effectively monitor or control the behaviour of that PMC in the field, and is unlikely to risk displeasing that PMC if avoidable. In addition to exacerbating the lack of the third-party oversight and accountability, the alignment of interests between the PMC and its client may incentivise, or at least induce indifference towards, the disproportionate use of force if that is perceived to further their interests.

D. Limitations of Third-Party Enforcement

The second main implication of the doctrine of privity arises from the general exclusion of third parties to the contract. Laura Dickinson is optimistic that third-party beneficiary rights can be developed and implemented in order to incorporate third-party influence and participation and to open the possibility for grievance procedures for victims.[79] She views the flexibility of the contractual form as being the key to this process because '[b]eneficiaries could be defined differently depending on the context'.[80] Unfortunately, a stumbling block quickly springs up. Giving the example of the prisoner abuse scandal by L-3/CACI pursuant to a contract to perform interrogation work,[81] Dickinson suggests that the relatively high risk of physical harm posed to the detainees would warrant the availability of grievance mechanisms. Yet, as discussed above, the doctrine of privity grants only a narrow exception to allow *intended beneficiaries* the possibility of legal action on a contractual term. While the

[78] Buzatu and Buckland, 'Private Military & Security Companies' (n 38) 18. Furthermore, she suggests that this leads to asymmetric situations of security provision and that the availability of purchased security may erode the idea that the provision of security is a 'common good': Buzatu and Buckland (n 38).

[79] Dickinson (n 35) 233–34.

[80] ibid 233.

[81] See generally P Chatterjee, 'Outsourcing Intelligence in Iraq: A CorpWatch Report on L-3/Titan' (CorpWatch, 2008) www.corpwatch.org/article.php?id=15253.

'intention' component might be remedied by express contractual provisions to that effect (although in light of the discussion in the previous section, it is difficult to see why either party to the contract would desire to shoulder such obligations), it is paradoxical and even perverse to label the victims of human rights violations 'beneficiaries' to the contract that gave rise to their abuse.

Put differently, the core of Dickinson's claim is that the government entered into contract with a PMC to provide a benefit to the individuals for whom the government programme or policy was designed. This would mean that those individuals should be able to enforce the contract if its terms are breached. It is notable, then, that the workable examples provided by Dickinson involve actual benefits: contracts to clear landmines and remove other hazards.[82] But this form of PMC work is categorically different from PMC activities that jeopardise the human rights of third parties, such as the provision of interrogation or security services which involve coercive relationships or the projection of organised force. This challenges both the applicability and appropriateness of creating third-party beneficiary rights to enable the right of legal action to the victims of contractual (non-) performance.

Beyond such contradictions, Brian Bix suggests that under US law, 'courts are far less likely to allow third-party enforcement in contracts with the government'.[83] He notes that third parties who might otherwise appear to have a claim are often refused if the government is a contractual party. First, this is because a company providing services to the general public may be potentially open to massive liability, and second, because the choice over when to enforce an agreement might be part of a policy choice to be retained by government officials and not to be dispersed by third-party enforcement suits.[84] The American Law Institute is clear about the constriction of third-party beneficiaries where the government or governmental agency is involved in the contract under section 313 of the Restatement (Second) on Contract Law.[85] Overall, the doctrine of privity diminishes the likelihood that contractual provisions expressing human rights principles will be enforced by the parties themselves, and excludes the possibility of legal action for third-party victims.

[82] Dickinson (n 35) 234.

[83] Bix (n 44) 125.

[84] ibid 112.

[85] Restatement (Second) of the Law of Contracts (n 67). The commentary explains the rationale: 'Among factors which may make inappropriate a direct action against the promisor are arrangements for governmental control over the litigation and settlement of claims, the likelihood of impairment of service or of excessive financial burden, and the availability of alternatives such as insurance'. It should be noted that s 313 generally contemplates governmental contracts that 'do an act for or render a service to the public', and therefore may have limited consequences for PMSC contracts.

E. The Horizontality of Contract: Equal and Independent Parties

Beyond the limitations inherent within the core concepts of contract law are other factors that detrimentally alter the nature of responsibility. This section discusses the horizontal relationship that characterises the contractual relationships, and its consequences. Implicit within the freedom of contract ideal is the assertion that contractual parties are independent entities that are equal in standing and status inter se. The three main consequences that flow from this assertion are discussed in turn. First, contract law disturbs well-settled legal fields by introducing what appear to be new actors and by conferring the semblance of legitimacy upon them. This is evident in the discussion over the status of PMC personnel under IHL because of their (non-IHL) appellation as 'contractors'. Second, the equality among contractual parties relegates the position occupied by the State, or depending upon your perspective, elevates the status of the PMC. The formally horizontal relationship between the State and the PMC strikes a delicate balance that enables the State to exert organised violence through the PMC without being attributed or ascribed responsibility for the consequences. Third, the enforcing power of the State is diminished through the equality imposed by contract law. While the State as Leviathan enforces the criminal law,[86] the power of the State to enforce contracts arises only from its much-diminished status as a party to that contract (and relatedly, the role of even the 'minimal State' as the enforcer of contracts).[87] It is unclear why the State, with its legitimacy over coercive force leading to the possibility for it to regulate by imposition, would seek to rely instead upon its commercial influence.

F. Contract's Creation and Legitimation

While IHL provides a comprehensive and coherent framework covering all persons embroiled in situations of armed conflict, the introduction of PMC personnel through contracts has muddied once clear waters. While it is clear that IHL does (and should) not provide special status for PMC personnel,[88] this status has become the source of contention and

[86] T Hobbes, *Hobbes's Leviathan: Reprinted from the Edition of 1651* (Oxford University Press, 1929) bk II.

[87] See R Nozick, *Anarchy, State, and Utopia* (Basic Books, 1974) Preface, ix.

[88] L Cameron, 'Private Military Companies: Their Status under International Humanitarian Law and Its Impact on Their Regulation' (2007) 88 *International Review of the Red Cross* 573, 593–94.

debate.[89] The confusion introduced by PMCs into IHL is most apparent in the suggestion, reported by James Cockayne, 'that PMSC personnel should enjoy protections and privileges additional to those afforded civilians—for example it is suggested that they should enjoy the right to participate directly in hostilities without losing the protections that civilians enjoy from attack',[90] despite it being clear that such a position would contradict the fundamental tenants of IHL. The status of 'the contractor' has been the subject of much debate, and it is sufficient to note here that this confusion is largely due to the contractual status of both the PMC and its personnel, and that the semblance of legitimacy is conferred through the contract.

It needs to be noted briefly that contractual relations presuppose the independent existence of the parties. As corporations possessing legal personhood, PMCs are immediately distinguished from less structured and dependent forms of organisation, such as mercenary bands or groups.[91] This has consequences for attributing responsibility through existing mechanisms presupposing hierarchical relations, dependence and effective control. The International Court of Justice expresses this reasoning in discussing the implications of Nicaragua's contention that:

> [T]he *contras* are no more than bands of mercenaries which have been recruited, organized, paid and commanded by the Government of the United States. This would mean that *they have no real autonomy* in relation to that Government. Consequently, any offences which they have committed *would be imputable* to the Government of the United States.[92]

The implication, then, is that more temporary and less structured organisations such as mercenary groups are more dependent upon their employers, who in turn justifiably bear greater responsibility for the activities of their employees. The following section develops this point further by concretely illustrating how horizontal contractual relations frustrate attempts to impute responsibility and accountability under international law. In turn, the availability of residual enforcement mechanisms becomes a critical issue in light of the obstacles to enforcement through contract law presented above.

[89] Cameron, 'Private Military Companies' (n 88); E-C Gillard, 'Private Military/Security Companies: The Status of Their Staff and Their Obligations under International Humanitarian Law and the Responsibility of States in Relation to Their Operations' in A Alexandra, D-P Baker and M Caparini (eds), *Private Military and Security Companies: Ethics, Policies, and Civil-Military Relations* (Routledge, 2008).

[90] J Cockayne, 'Private Military and Security Companies' in *The Oxford Handbook of International Law in Armed Conflict* (Oxford University Press, 2014) 627.

[91] There were strong links existing between early PMSCs and mercenaries: C Kinsey, 'Private Security Companies: Agents of Democracy or Simply Mercenaries?' in T Jäger and G Kummel (eds), *Private Military and Security Companies: Chances, Problems, Pitfalls and Prospects* (VS Verlag fur Sozialwissenschaften, 2007).

[92] *Military and Paramilitary Activities* (1986) 1986 ICJ Rep 14 (ICJ) [114]. Emphasis added.

G. Relative Equality of Contractual Parties: State and Command Responsibility

The independent status of each contracting party and their relative equality within the contract flows as a consequence of the freedom of contract ideal, transforming the nature of responsibility. At a superficial level, the responsible entity has changed where States contract for PMC services for the simple reason that, absent the contractual relationship, the State would be acting directly and therefore would unambiguously bear responsibility. Through PMC contracts, however, this responsibility becomes blurred: (both) the State and/or the PMC may be responsible for consequences arising from the contract, depending on the factual specifics of the situation. Furthermore, both domestic and international public law mechanisms are subverted by the contractual relationship involving a private entity.

This point can be examined through the question of whether the internationally wrongful acts of a PMC can be attributed to the State. It is worth noting at the outset that Max Weber was concerned with the State retaining the monopoly over the legitimate use of force, and as such it does not necessarily preclude the State from authorising or allocating this monopoly to other entities. This can be inferred from his definition of the State as the monopoly holder over legitimate use of force including the possibility for the State to delegate its monopoly.[93] While the State may still be seen to allocate force through contracts with PMCs, States lose their hierarchical position in relation to PMCs because the State and the PMC both become essentially private parties negotiating a contract.[94] This has implications for State responsibility, because international law generally requires State action, authorisation or acquiescence to the act in question before ascribing responsibility to the State. In short, the horizontal nature of contractual relations subverts the operation of international legal mechanisms that depend upon the State occupying the position of command and control.

The commentary to Chapter II of the International Law Commission (ILC) Articles on State Responsibility stipulates that

> the general rule is that *the only* conduct attributed to the State at the international level is that of its organs of government, or of *others who have acted under the direction, instigation or control of those organs*, i.e. as *agents* of the State.[95]

[93] '[T]he right to use physical force is ascribed to other institutions or to individuals only to the extent to which the state permits it': M Weber, *From Max Weber: Essays in Sociology* (HH Gerth and C Wright Mills eds, Routledge and Kegan Paul, 1946) 78.

[94] Evidence that the State acts a private party in contractual relations is provided by para 6 of the commentary to art 4, which states that 'the breach by a State of a contract does not as such entail a breach of international law': International Law Commission, 'Report of the International Law Commission: Fifty-Third Session' (UNGA, 2001) A/56/10 87.

[95] ibid 80. Emphasis added. Note that the commentary continues by stating that, '[a]s a corollary, the conduct of private persons is not as such attributable to the State': ibid 81.

This rule is reflected within the Articles themselves: Article 4 provides the basic rule of attributing the conduct of State organs to the State; Article 5 deals the attribution to the State of the conduct of entities empowered to exercise the governmental authority; and Article 8 attributes responsibility to the State for conduct carried out on State instructions or under its direction or control.[96]

It is now possible to be more explicit about *how* the delicate balance is struck whereby the State can avoid being attributed responsibility for any internationally unlawful conduct perpetrated by a PMC contracted with that State.[97] Unless the PMC is incorporated into an organ of the State, at which point contract law ceases to be relevant, Article 4 does not have bearing upon attribution so the analysis under Articles 5 and 8 becomes critical. The existence of a contract in both instances undermines the contention that the State will be responsible for any internationally wrongful conduct committed by a PMC. This is because attribution under Article 5 depends upon the PMC being empowered to exercise governmental authority, and State instruction, direction or control are the lynchpins for Article 8. Because the commentary states that '[t]he formulation of article 5 clearly limits it to entities which are empowered by internal law to exercise governmental authority',[98] it would be a contrived argument to suggest that a contract for PMC services would fall into the ambit of Article 5. Article 8 provides more traction, in particular because it recognises the scope for States to authorise private persons to act, an example being the recruitment of 'auxiliaries' to their police and armed forces, but who remain outside the formal organisation of the State.[99] The high bar set by international jurisprudence,[100] which has to be satisfied in order to attribute the conduct of private persons acting under the instructions of, or under the direction or control, of the State makes this prospect practically impossible where contractual obligations are concerned. A cynical view of this position might be that, because of their contractual relationship, the State no longer orders the PMC, but rather connives with the PMC. As international law is blind to the prospect of States conspiring with private entities where internationally wrongful acts are concerned, the contract

[96] International Law Commission, 'Report of the International Law Commission: Fifty-Third Session' (n 94) 84–109.

[97] This discussion excludes the question of attributing responsibility to the State for its failure to take necessary measure to prevent the effects caused by the conduct of private parties: ibid 81. See for a broader discussion, Tonkin, *State Control Over Private Military and Security Companies in Armed Conflict* (n 26).

[98] International Law Commission (n 94) 94.

[99] ibid 104.

[100] See esp *Military and Paramilitary Activities* (n 92) [115]. This is analysed below in the context of the prohibition on the threat or use of force.

that regulates their relationship essentially immunises the State against the attribution of responsibility under international law.[101]

This immunising effect can also be seen in the manner in which contracts collapse the doctrine of superior responsibility under international criminal law, a doctrine which in turn reflects IHL's requirement that armed groups must be hierarchically organised.[102] The Montreux Document, reflecting existing international law, states in no uncertain terms that '[s]uperior responsibility is not engaged solely by virtue of a contract'.[103] This does not, however, preclude the possibility that superior responsibility might be engaged by a contractual relationship so further analysis is necessary. As the passive impunity issues raised by the doctrine of superior responsibility in relation to the PMC are discussed separately towards the end of this chapter, only a sketch is provided here in order to illustrate the additional difficulties introduced by contractual arrangements.

The Trial Chamber of the International Criminal Tribunal for the former Yugoslavia (ICTY) enumerated the constitutive components necessary to establish superior responsibility, foremost of which is 'the existence of a superior-subordinate relationship'.[104] The Appeals Chamber of the ICTY held that 'effective control' is the crucial ingredient of the superior-subordinate relationship,[105] and rejected influence short of the ability to prevent or punish subordinate offences.[106] It must, however, be conceded that in order to keep this doctrine applicable to civilian superiors, the ICTY accepted the replacement of the ability to impose sanctions with the ability to submit reports to the authorities that might lead to an investigation.[107] This opens the possibility for superior responsibility mechanisms to apply to the parties of a contract, insofar as the 'effective control' criterion is diluted, but the doctrine of *superior* responsibility is likely

[101] Another way of viewing this problem is through the UN Guiding Principles on Business and Human Rights. Here, States are responsible for exercising adequate oversight and for promoting respect for human rights in the business enterprises that they contract with: J Ruggie, 'Guiding Principles on Business and Human Rights: Implementing the United Nations "Protect, Respect and Remedy" Framework' (UNGA, 2011) A/HRC/17/31 10, points 5 and 6.

[102] The Commentary to API, art 43 provides: 'All armed forces, groups and units are necessarily structured and have a hierarchy, as they are subordinate to a command which is responsible to one of the Parties to the conflict for their operations. In other words, all of them are subordinate to a command and to a Party to the conflict … for it is not permissible for any group to wage a private war': ICRC, *Commentary on the Additional Protocols of 8 June 1977 to the Geneva Conventions of 12 August 1949* (Martinus Nijhoff, 1987) para 1672. See also art 4(2)(a) of the Third Geneva Convention relative to the Treatment of Prisoners of War, 12 August 1949.

[103] Montreux Document (n 36) pt I.

[104] *Prosecutor v Delalic (Trials Chamber)* [1998] ICTY Trial Chamber IT-96-21-T [346].

[105] *Prosecutor v Delalic (Appeals Chamber)* [2001] ICTY Appeals Chamber IT-96-21-A [303]. This is discussed in detail below.

[106] ibid 266.

[107] *Prosecutor v Aleksovski (Trials Chamber)* [1999] ICTY Trial Chamber IT-95-14/1T [78]. Subsequently reaffirmed in *Prosecutor v Blaskic (Trials Chamber)* [2000] ICTY Trial Chamber IT-95-14-T [302].

to require evidence of a superior-subordinate relationship that will be defeated by the horizontal nature of contractual relations.[108]

Thus, the hierarchical organisation required by IHL has been subverted by the horizontal contractual relationship both between the State and the PMC and the PMC and its personnel. This has two major consequences where PMCs are implicated in activities within the purview of international criminal law. First, the absence of 'effective control' both between the PMC and its client and within the structure of the PMC (through the employment contract) suggests that the potential to prevent or repress the commission of international crimes will be diminished where organised force is contractually allocated. Second, both the client of the PMC and senior members of the PMC would be able to point to the lack of sanctioning powers available under contract law to avert allegations of superior responsibility over the commission of any international crime. The overarching effect of horizontal contractual relationships, therefore, is that these immunise against the possibility of 'contracting' responsibility.

Given the horizontal relationship between the client and the PMC, and between the PMC and its personnel, the provision of the ICoC that 'Signatory Companies will not, and will require that their Personnel do not, invoke *contractual obligations*, [or] superior orders … as a justification' for engaging in conduct proscribed by the ICoC is especially incongruent.[109] This provision effectively attempts to equate contractual obligations (arising from consensual agreement) with the defence of superior orders (expressing a hierarchical relationship characterised by 'effective control'), evincing a fundamental misunderstanding about the limitations of contractual provisions in protecting human rights.

H. The Indifference of Contract Law

The final set of difficulties with attempts to protect human rights through contract law arises out of their ontological incompatibility. The myopic and inward-looking nature of contract law has already been discussed. In comparison, human rights law might be considered contract law's diametric opposite: human rights law expresses universal values that are

[108] It is interesting to note in this regard a suggestion made by Charles Garraway that: 'The increasing use of contractors and other civilian experts undoubtedly blurs traditional military chains of command, but where there is any superior/subordinate relationship, that relationship will be caught by the wide phrasing of article 28. It should be possible therefore to include new forms of relationships, including contractual ones': C Garraway, 'The Application of Superior Responsibility in an Era of Unlimited Information' in D Saxon (ed), *International Humanitarian Law and the Changing Technology of War* (Martinus Nijhoff, 2013) 202. The present analysis illustrates this suggestion as a paradox for the simple reason that a contractual relationship cannot be characterised by 'effective control' or possess other attributes of the superior-subordinate relationship.

[109] Swiss Federal Department of Foreign Affairs (n 37) 23. Emphasis added.

inherent within and inalienable from the individual and confers these rights without imposing concomitant duties or obligations. In arguing for the development of a global community grounded in a core of human rights, Antonio Cassese suggested that '[a]s for values, one should emphasize the existence of peremptory rules of international law (*jus cogens*) on human rights, which are at the summit of the international legal order and may not be derogated from by any state'.[110] Placing human rights as the core is justified because '[t]he doctrine of human rights has aspired from the outset to be universal, to be a doctrine that applies everywhere to everyone, irrespective of nationality, culture, tradition, ideology, or social conditions'.[111] This opposition can be seen from another perspective: purpose. At root, the function of contract law is enabling, such that it is both non-judgemental and limitless (with the tiny caveat that some impermissible choices might not be enforced). In contrast, the raison d'être of human rights law is restrictive in setting normative boundaries on acceptable treatment. In this light, it is difficult to see how contract law can provide for the adequate protection of human rights.

Before turning to demonstrate the inadequacies of contractual remedies for human rights violations that flow from this tension, it is necessary to show the possibility for reduction where contractual provisions purport to express or incorporate external (legal) obligations. This is readily evident in two of the Montreux Document's good practices. First is the suggestion that it is good practice for contracting States '[t]o determine which services may or may not be contracted out to PMSCs'.[112] Juxtapose this contractual approach against a human rights perspective: Article 9 of the Draft of a Possible Convention on Private Military and Security Companies requires State parties to 'specifically prohibit the outsourcing to PMSCs of functions which are defined as inherently State functions', and includes an enumerated non-exhaustive list of activities.[113] Second, while the Montreux Document suggests States '[t]o include contractual clauses and performance requirements that *ensure respect for relevant* national law, international humanitarian law and human rights law by the contracted PMSC',[114] the Draft Convention requires that

> [e]ach State party shall take legislative, judicial, administrative and other measures *as may be necessary to ensure* that PMSCs and their personnel *are held*

[110] A Cassese, 'A Plea for a Global Community Grounded in a Core of Human Rights' in A Cassese (ed), *Realizing Utopia: The Future of International Law* (Oxford University Press, 2012) 136.

[111] ibid.

[112] But note that this provides for the guidelines for determining any such boundaries, rather than actually imposing any concrete limitations: Montreux Document (n 36) pt II.

[113] Draft of a Possible Convention on Private Military and Security Companies (PMSCs) for Consideration and Action by the Human Rights Council 2011 (A/HRC/WG10/1/2) 9. See further arts 8–11 for specific prohibitions on PMSC activities.

[114] Montreux Document (n 36) pt I. Emphasis added.

> *accountable* in accordance with this Convention and to ensure respect for and protection of international human rights and humanitarian law.[115]

These comparisons between the contractually-orientated Document and the human rights-centric Draft Convention indicate the opposing thrusts of these legal fields.

I. Inadequacy of Contractual Remedies

Another approach to the indifference of contract law is provided by an analysis of the nature of contractual remedies in comparison with the repercussions arising from human rights violations. It is worth noting at the outset the maxim *ubi jus ibi remedium* (for the violation of every right, there must be a remedy), and that the possibility of enforcement can be considered a defining characteristic of a right.

The Montreux Document serves as a useful point of departure:

> 'Contractual clauses may also provide for the Contracting State's ability to terminate the contract for failure to comply with contractual provisions. They may also specify … that appropriate reparation be provided to those harmed by the misconduct of PMSCs and their personnel'.[116]

Two deductions can be made: first that the termination of contract is the most severe 'punishment' possible under contract law, and second that victim reparation is discretionary. These are expressions of the purpose of remedies under contract law, as Brian Bix summarises:

> The basic principle is that damages should compensate the innocent party for moneys lost due to the breach. This compensatory principle is both the *objective* and the *limit* of contract damages: the courts should try to ensure that parties are compensated, but they also are *to guard that damages do not go beyond compensation*.[117]

This principle indicates that the nature of contractual remedies is financial and that its purpose is restitution. Moreover, the restitution of contractual remedies look only to the parties: 'The basic objective of breach of contract remedies [is] to place the *nonbreaching party* in the same position it would have been in had the contract been fully performed or had the contract never been entered'.[118] Together, this explains why the provision of

[115] Draft of a Possible Convention on Private Military and Security Companies (n 113) art 7. Emphasis added.
[116] Montreux Document (n 36) pt II.
[117] Bix (n 44) 87. Emphasis added.
[118] ibid 92. Emphasis added.

compensation to victims *can only* be discretionary in the Montreux Document: the victim is not countenanced in the bilateral nature of contractual remedies.

The gross inadequacy of contractual remedies in the context of protecting human rights is revealed in comparison with the UN Basic Principles on the Right to a Remedy.[119] The scope of the obligation comprises of four duties: to prevent, to investigate, to provide access to justice and to provide remedy for victims.[120] Turning to the substantive scope of remedies within the right, the

> [a]dequate, effective and prompt reparation is intended to *promote justice by redressing* gross violations of international human rights law or serious violations of international humanitarian law. *Reparation should be proportional to the gravity of the violations and the harm suffered*.[121]

The Basic Principles require 'full and effective reparation … which include the following forms: restitution, compensation, rehabilitation, satisfaction and guarantees of non-repetition'.[122] In order to facilitate comparison with contractual remedies, below, it should be noted that under the Basic Principles, restitution seeks to restore the victim to their original situation before the occurrence of the gross violations through a broad spectrum of available actions, and that appropriate and proportional compensation should be provided for economically assessable damage.[123]

Thus, three main characteristics of human rights law remedies can be drawn out. First, remedies under human rights law serve broader purposes beyond mere economic restitution. The promotion of justice, the purpose which remedies serve, alluded to in the Basic Principles comprises of: compensatory and remedial justice, condemnation and retribution, deterrence, and restorative and reconciliatory forms of justice.[124] Second, remedies under human rights law express normative and moral dimensions, embodied through satisfaction and guarantees of non-repetition, communicating that injuries rather than mere wrongs are at stake.[125] This reinforces the need to have a wide range of available remedies under human rights law. Third, the different purpose pursued by remedies under human rights law mean that these should also be proportional and

[119] Basic Principles and Guidelines on the Right to a Remedy and Reparation for Victims of Gross Violations of International Human Rights Law and Serious Violations of International Humanitarian Law 2005.

[120] ibid 3.

[121] ibid 15. Emphasis added.

[122] ibid 18. See further Principles 19–23 for the specific content of these remedial forms.

[123] ibid 19 and 20.

[124] D Shelton, *Remedies in International Human Rights Law* (Oxford University Press, 2006) 10–16.

[125] For a critical analysis of this distinction, see S Veitch, *Law and Irresponsibility: On the Legitimation of Human Suffering* (Routledge-Cavendish, 2007) 85–92.

appropriate, leading to the possibility of punishing transgressions that censure the wrongdoer. Indeed, proportional punishment can mandate sanction under criminal law,[126] and in the case of gross human rights violations, even impose a duty to investigate and prosecute.[127] Contrast these characteristics with the goal of economic restitution underlying contractual remedies, and the inadequacy and inappropriateness of collapsing the protection of human rights into contract law become clear. In this light, it is significant that '[p]unitive damages are not available for breach of contract cases',[128] suggesting that a breach of contract carries with it insufficient injury to warrant deterrence, let alone punishment.

Until this point, the discussion has only addressed the substantive concept of remedy under human rights law and so constitutes half of the story at most. As Dinah Shelton explains:

> The word 'remedies' contains two separate concepts, the first being procedural and the second substantive. In the first sense, remedies are the processes by which arguable claims of human rights violations are heard and decided, whether by courts, administrative agencies, or other competent bodies. The second notion of remedies refers to the outcome of the proceedings, the relief afforded the successful claimant.[129]

Despite the advantage of contract law to directly impose human rights obligations touted by its advocates,[130] the denial of procedural justice can be added to the list of remedial defects. Situated within the right to an effective remedy, the limitations imposed by the doctrine of privity could be asserted to conflict with, perhaps even violate, the right to access justice.[131] Despite the existence of parallel avenues for victims to access justice which contract law does not preclude, such as through tort or criminal law, the doctrine of privity excludes the possibility for victims of human rights abuses a right to legal action under the contract. Under ordinary circumstances where contract law is confined to regulating commercial transactions, this may be unproblematic. But where contract law is elevated to the keystone of PMC regulatory mechanisms designed to protect and promote human rights in situations of armed conflict and instability, however, any restriction to the right to access justice compounds the inadequate nature of substantive remedies available under contract law.

[126] Shelton, *Remedies in International Human Rights Law* (n 124) 12–13.

[127] Principles and Guidelines on the Right to a Remedy (n 119).

[128] Bix (n 44) 98. With narrow exceptions in some jurisdictions relating to insurance claims. It should be noted that punitive damages for a breach of contract may be available if it can be characterised through an independent tort claim: ibid 94.

[129] Shelton (n 124) 7.

[130] Buzatu and Buckland (n 38) 23.

[131] Principles and Guidelines on the Right to a Remedy (n 119).

J. Denial Through Contract Law?

While something positive might be said about the possibility for contract law to circumvent the jurisdictional obstacles to PMC regulation, this section has presented several approaches towards the conclusion that there are conceptual, pragmatic and consequential arguments militating against employing contract law mechanisms to protect human rights. These concerns may once have been academic, but the reliance that developing PMC regulation places upon contractual mechanisms has magnified the importance of these issues. Yet, both this reliance upon contract law and its implications have gone unnoticed.

An argument could be advanced that contract law might usefully serve to fill the remaining gaps in the regulation of PMCs under international law that would remain even if all relevant instruments were deemed applicable to them.[132] While contractual reforms are likely to be necessary in the effort to improve oversight and accountability for PMC activities, it is worth underscoring the hazards that liealong this path. An initial objection arises from the argument that reversing privatisation is unlikely and that regulatory effort is better expended upon reform.[133] Instead, it is likely that attempts at reformation will legitimise, entrench and expand privatisation because of the effort invested in these directions, thus enhancing the system at the source of the problem.

Yet, the use of contract law as the basis to protect and promote human rights in the course of PMC operations might yield more disquieting implications: denial. This conclusion may serve as a second iteration of the interpretive denial afforded to the PMC, building upon the earlier analysis in relation to the PMC adopting the corporate form. Strained through the cloth of contract law, there is the potential that prisoner abuse or indiscriminate use of lethal force perpetrated by a PMC will be understood as a breach of contract because '[p]owerful forms of interpretive denial come for the language of legality itself'.[134] While the actions might remain the same, '[t]he harm is cognitively reframed and then allocated to a different, less pejorative class of event'.[135] In this case, a human rights violation *is the same* as a breach of contract.

The possibility for contract law to function as a mechanism for interpretive denial might culminate in the adoption of 'magical legalism', whereby the formal illegality of an activity is presented as proof that the alleged activity could not possibly have occurred.[136] While it may appear fanciful

[132] Dickinson (n 35) 237–38. It is worth noting that Dickinson does not propose contractual reform as a regulatory panacea, but rather only as one avenue to be pursued.
[133] ibid 237.
[134] Cohen (n 29) 107.
[135] ibid 106.
[136] ibid 108.

now, it is not inconceivable to think that PMCs of the near future would point to their membership of the ICoC and to provisions in their contract to conclusively prove the falsity of allegations made against them. Even if this were not appealed to outright, the inclusion of human rights obligations into contractual terms would likely facilitate the isolation of any alleged abuse perpetrated by PMCs. In such instances, the denial falls neither upon the occurrence of the event nor on shouldering responsibility for it: rather the denial is that the event was neither systematic nor routine.[137] If contractual terms protecting human rights were regularly incorporated into PMC contracts, this will allow for subsequent violations to be compartmentalised, to be viewed as exceptions to generally compliant behaviour.

IV. PASSIVE IMPUNITY: *JUS AD BELLUM* AND CORPORATE AGGRESSION

In line with the bulk of the literature on the topic,[138] this book has concentrated myopically upon impunity for PMC *conduct* up to this point. This focus is justified because PMC activity has been considered within the context of human rights, and in relation to IHL where they occur within situations of armed hostilities.[139] In the hypothetical situation where PMCs operate in accordance with their legal obligations, the question of impunity for human rights will be absolved. Yet, the issue within the context of armed conflict is more complex, however, because it is bisected into the independent legal spheres of *Jus ad Bellum* (JAB) and *Jus in Bello* (JIB). Michael Walzer differentiates these in just war theory terms:

> War is always judged twice, first with reference to the reasons … for fighting, secondly with reference to the means they adopt. The first kind of judgment is adjectival in character: we say that *a particular war is just or unjust*. The second is adverbial: we say that *a war is being fought justly or unjustly*.[140]

[137] ibid 109.

[138] eg a key compendium on PMCs focused exclusively upon their JIB ramifications: F Francioni and N Ronzitti (eds), *War by Contract: Human Rights, Humanitarian Law, and Private Contractors* (Oxford University Press, 2011). Moreover, the existing literature tackling this topic derives from moral philosophy rather than law: J Pattison, 'Just War Theory and the Privatization of Military Force' (2008) 22 *Ethics & International Affairs* 143.

[139] The focus on JIB may be justified from a victim's perspective: 'As a rule, complaints by individuals have been brought for violations of *jus in bello* … Violations for *jus ad bellum* relate to state to state relations and it is difficult for an individual to claim compensation for such violations': N Ronzitti, 'Access to Justice and Compensation for Violations of the Law of War' in F Francioni (ed), *Access to Justice as a Human Right* (Oxford University Press, 2007) 103.

[140] M Walzer, *Just and Unjust Wars: A Moral Argument with Historical Illustrations* (Basic Books, 2006) 21. Emphasis added.

In the scenario outlined above, the unblemished behaviour of the PMC within JIB will have no bearing upon JAB considerations: the possibility that they fight an unjust war justly remains. In other words, a PMC that operates in a just manner does not imply that the war that they participate in is itself just.

Within the Weberian paradigm whereby the State possesses exclusive control over organised violence, the strict separation between the political JAB decision to commence hostilities and JIB considerations pertaining to the conduct of the armed forces could be justifiable. The armed forces, as dependent functionaries of the State, are limited to JIB considerations because they possess no independent capacity to wage, or conversely refuse to wage, war. Once the political decision is made by the State apparatus, the armed forces are obliged to carry this out. While PMCs must certainly abide by JIB rules, the JAB issue is also raised for PMCs. As discussed above, PMCs are separate entities that are capable of independently concluding or rejecting contracts, much unlike the relationship of dependency between the armed forces and the State. This discretion possessed by the PMC over its participation in armed conflict constitutes de facto decisions within the JAB sphere. Moreover, JAB determinations made by the PMC are significantly more problematic because, as corporations driven by the profit-motive, only factors that affect the economic calculation will be taken into account in making that decision. In other words, when the PMC decides to join an armed conflict, this decision is not made on the moral and political grounds that appropriately govern JAB, but instead is focused on the profitability of that participation. This perspective nullifies the claim that the contracting State should be exclusively responsible for JAB issues for PMCs: unlike the armed forces which, being an organ of the State, possess no autonomy, a PMC can refuse to participate in an unjust war and consequently violate JAB where they fail to do so.

The Working Group on the Use of Mercenaries offered another approach to the JAB question posed by PMCs when it:

> [U]nderscored the paradoxical nature of the situation in which Chile finds itself. On the one hand, there is the official Chilean position to reject the war in Iraq, and on the other, the current situation in which some 1,000 Chileans are 'protecting private security in Iraq (…) and are involved in a dirty war'.[141]

In this case, the JAB decision of Chile not to participate in an unjust war was undermined by third-country PMCs which had made independent JAB determinations to participate, and employed Chilean nationals to this end. This effectively supplanted Chile's decision by deploying large numbers of its nationals into that conflict.[142] The passive impunity question,

[141] J Gómez del Prado, 'Mission to Chile' (UNHRC 2008) A/HRC/7/7/Add.4 paras 55–68.

[142] This also provides a contemporary example for the scenario underlying the laws of neutrality which restricted foreign military service that tangentially restricted mercenary activity discussed in ch 3.

situated within the JAB sphere, concerns whether PMC activity can be captured by the existing laws that govern the prohibition of the threat or use of force.[143]

While chapter three considered the narrow question of applying the crime of aggression to mercenaries, this section will first address the applicability of the international prohibition on the threat or use of force to the PMC by considering whether its conduct can be attributed to the State, building upon the analysis in the context of contract law presented above. Impunity for PMC activity in breach of JAB would occur where its actions are not attributable to the State, provided that it is also not sufficiently punished as a domestic crime of violence. As the general rules are inconclusive, the section then turns to discuss the application of the crime of aggression to the activities of the PMC, complementing the discussion in the context of mercenaries in chapter three. The question of where the criminality for aggression should lie has been tackled, but Constantine Antonopoulos only considered the bifurcated possibilities of State responsibility and individual criminal responsibility.[144] Because the PMC, as a corporation, inhabits the space between the State and the individual, the prospect for passive impunity arises insofar as corporate responsibility for aggression remains legally imperceptible. Thus, the PMC will enjoy impunity for acts of aggression insofar as their actions cannot be attributed to the State under the special rules.[145]

In turn, these issues pale into insignificance when compared with the difficulties posed by horizontal contracting whereby non-State entities, such as other companies or NGOs, engage the coercive services of PMCs for private ends.[146] In these scenarios, even the military lexicon that is

[143] The Draft Convention does provide for the prohibition of the use of force under art 8 for JAB (and also under art 18 for the use of force governed by JIB). As a draft of a proposed international document, however, the onus remains upon the State to ensure that PMCs do not violate JAB. While the Draft does stipulate these State obligations, it does not indicate where responsibility would flow in instances where a PMC either violates JAB, or commits an act of aggression: J Gómez del Prado, 'Report of the Working Group on the Use of Mercenaries as a Means of Violating Human Rights and Impeding the Exercise of the Right of Peoples to Self-Determination with the Draft of a Possible Convention on Private Military and Security Companies (PMSCs) for Consideration and Action by the Human Rights Council' (UNGA, 2010) A/HRC/15/25.

[144] C Antonopoulos, 'Whatever Happened to Crimes Against Peace?' (2001) 6 *Journal of Conflict and Security Law* 33, 36–40.

[145] Their contractors, as natural persons, will remain liable individually for the crime of aggression in theory. Yet, the focus of international criminal law on the most senior leaders suspected of being most responsible is likely to exclude the majority of PMC personnel from its purview.

[146] The question of institutional responsibility will not be covered, but see N White, 'Institutional Responsibility for Private Military and Security Companies' in Francioni and Ronzitti, *War by Contract* (n 138); N White and S MacLeod, 'EU Operations and Private Military Contractors: Issues of Corporate and Institutional Responsibility' (2008) 19 *European Journal of International Law* 965.

tenuously applied to PMCs on State contracts yields to that of security, leading to fundamental difficulties in articulating the type of activity under analysis and paving the way for interpretive denial. This shift in vocabulary focuses the analysis upon the conduct of the PMC, thereby further obscuring the anterior question as to whether they should be operating in the first place.

A. The Prohibition of the Use of Force

It is elementary that Article 2(4), which the ICJ affirmed as 'a cornerstone of the UN Charter',[147] provides that 'All Members shall refrain in their international relations from the threat or use of force against the territorial integrity or political independence of any state, or in any other manner inconsistent with the Purposes of the United Nations' subject to the 'inherent right of individual or collective self-defence' under Article 51.[148] Legally, it is also clear that this only applies to States and prohibits only inter-State violence: only States can violate JAB. Thus, from a legal perspective, the JAB assessment for PMC activity can only arise if its actions can be attributed to a State.[149] Otherwise, the spectre of violating this international prohibition would be forestalled for the simple reason that private violence is treated instead as a criminal matter for domestic laws.[150]

The rules of attribution that were developed by the ILC, introduced in the context of contract law and the protection of human rights above, have been adopted by the General Assembly.[151] To reiterate, Article 4 concerns the conduct of State organs, Article 5 the conduct of persons or entities exercising elements of governmental authority, and Article 8 conduct that is directed or controlled by a State.[152] It is interesting to note in passing that the ILC Articles may conflate role and outcome forms of responsibilities discussed in chapter one, leading to the possibility that different consequences would ensue from attribution. Through the nexus of State

[147] *Armed Activities* [2005] ICJ 908, 2005 ICJ Rep 168 [148].

[148] This analysis leaves aside the challenges raised by humanitarian intervention and the emerging Responsibility to Protect doctrine, but see C Gray, *International Law and the Use of Force* (Oxford University Press, 2008) 33–59.

[149] See generally Tonkin (n 26) 57–59; precisely addressing the question of attributing PMC conduct to the hiring State: see ibid 90–122.

[150] As Janice Thomson puts it, 'the issue [is] the extent to which the nation-state could or should be held accountable for the actions of its citizens beyond its borders': J Thomson, 'State Practices, International Norms, and the Decline of Mercenarism' (1990) 34 *International Studies Quarterly* 23, 44.

[151] UNGAR 56/83, 'Responsibility of States for Internationally Wrongful Acts'.

[152] Andrew Clapham raises the distinction between the law of State responsibility for empowered entities and entities under State control: A Clapham, *Human Rights Obligations of Non-State Actors* (Oxford University Press, 2006) 241.

control and direction, Articles 4 and 8 fall within outcome responsibility by connecting the State with the consequences of the conduct in question. Article 5, however, expresses role responsibility because attribution depends upon the governmental function played by the persons or entities in question. This raises the issue of whether it is sustainable to attribute responsibility to the State for the outcome when it is really a form of role responsibility at stake.

Continuing the analysis, Article 4 would apply de jure to the rare instances where PMC contractors were formally incorporated into the armed forces of the State, such as those Sandline/EO personnel assigned to the Papua New Guinea contract who were enrolled as 'Special Constables'.[153] Hannah Tonkin points to the possibility of the de facto incorporation of a PMC into the armed forces of a State, resting her analysis primarily upon Article 43 of API.[154] This Article defines the armed forces of a State as consisting 'of all organized armed forces, groups and units which are under a command responsible to that Party for the conduct of its subordinates', and has attained customary IHL status.[155] The lynchpin is a 'responsible command': the Commentary elaborates this point as requiring that all such armed forces, groups or units 'are subordinate to a command and to a Party to the conflict, without exception, for it is not permissible for any group to wage a private war'.[156] While Tonkin suggests that the terms of the contract might indicate whether the PMC in fact operates within a hierarchical system for these purposes, she expresses doubt for this conclusion based upon recent examples derived from US practices.[157] But beyond what might be inferred from specific examples, the above analysis in the context of contract law suggests that PMCs *cannot* fulfil Article 43 requirements. This is for the simple fact that, unlike the groups and units within the comprehension of Article 43, a PMC exists independently from the State such that it is only responsible to the State to the extent of mutual agreement (which the PMC remains free to terminate). Together, this suggests that absent de jure incorporation of a PMC as a State organ, Article 4 of the ILC Articles will not be applicable where PMCs engage in activities that would otherwise contravene the prohibition of the use of force.

[153] PW Singer, *Corporate Warriors: The Rise of the Privatized Military Industry* (Cornell University Press, 2004) 38; formal incorporation, however, has the additional benefit of frustrating the legal definition of 'mercenary': ibid 193–94.

[154] Tonkin (n 26) 86–90.

[155] r 4: J-M Henckaerts and L Doswald-Beck, *Customary International Humanitarian Law*, vol II (Cambridge University Press 2005) 14–17.

[156] ICRC, *Commentary on the Additional Protocols of 8 June 1977 to the Geneva Conventions of 12 August 1949* (n 102) 1672.

[157] Tonkin (n 26) 86–90.

Thus, it may be better to consider this relationship under Article 8 because the test consists of the twin elements of dependence and control.[158] Assuming that the State does not authorise the PMC to violate international law,[159] the ICJ imposed the 'effective control' test pronounced in *Military and Paramilitary Activities*,[160] that it subsequently reaffirmed in *Armed Activities*[161] and the *Genocide Case*.[162] The threshold of 'effective control' is extremely high, since 'United States participation, even if preponderant or decisive, in the financing, organizing, training, supplying and equipping of the *Contras*, the selection of its military or paramilitary targets, and the planning of the whole of its operation' was deemed insufficient for attributing the acts of the *Contras* to the US.[163] Given that these developed forms of hierarchical and influential relationships failed the test, it is very unlikely that the horizontal contractual nexus between the State and the PMC will suffice. At this point, mention should be made of the more lenient 'overall control' test adopted by the Appeals Chamber of the ICTY in *Tadic* which may potentially be satisfied.[164] It is clear, however, that the 'effective control' standard of the ICJ is the applicable test, not least because the ICJ affirmed that standard in two subsequent cases, but also because *Military and Paramilitary Activities* addressed the question of State responsibility, whereas *Tadic* tackled individual criminal responsibility and instead grappled with the applicable rule of IHL.[165]

There is an additional ingredient relating to the status of the corporation under Article 8 that may be relevant for the PMC. The ILC Commentary explicitly noted 'that international law *acknowledges the general separateness of corporate entities* at the national level, except in those cases where the "corporate veil" is a mere device or a vehicle for fraud or evasion' and considered only the questions that 'arise with respect *to the conduct*

[158] This is the approach adopted by the ILC, ILC, *Yearbook of the International Law Commission 2001*, vol II, pt II (n 27) 47–48, para 4.

[159] The attribution of responsibility in such instances is uncontentious. The ILC gives the example of 'State organs supplementing their own action by recruiting or instigating private persons or groups who act as "auxiliaries" while remaining outside the official structure of the State' ibid 47, para 2; this grounds Hannah Tonkin's conclusion that a State may be responsible if it exercised these elements of control over a particular PMC operation, rather than over the PMC itself: Tonkin (n 26) 120. This type of micromanagement by the State over the conduct of PMCs may be purely hypothetical.

[160] *Military and Paramilitary Activities* (n 92) [115].

[161] *Armed Activities* (n 147) [160].

[162] *Genocide Case* [2007] ICJ 91, 2007 ICJ Rep 43 [399].

[163] *Military and Paramilitary Activities* (n 92) [115].

[164] *Prosecutor v Tadic (Appeals Chamber)* [1999] ICTY Appeals Chamber IT-94-1-A [117–20]. The difference between these tests is starkly illustrated: 'In order to attribute the acts of a military or paramilitary group to a State, it must be proved that the State wields overall control over the group, not only by equipping and financing the group, but also by coordinating or helping in the general planning of its military activity. Only then can the State be held internationally accountable for any misconduct of the group': ibid 131.

[165] ILC (n 27) 48, para 5.

of companies or enterprises which are State-owned and controlled'.[166] The ILC considered that even State-owned corporate entities, which are subjected to the direct control of the State by virtue of that ownership, are to be considered as separate entities: their activities are not to be attributable to the State *unless* they exercise elements of governmental authority within the scope of Article 5.[167] Given that the PMC is not generally State-owned, but instead possess independent status as attested by their independent juridical personhood and their freedom of contract, it is unlikely that the conduct of PMCs will be attributed to the State by virtue of direction or control under Article 8.

This leads to the question whether responsibility for the PMC can be attributed to the State under Article 5 concerning the exercise of governmental authority.[168] It is interesting to note that this issue would be entirely obviated with the implementation of Article 9 of the Draft Convention because this would 'specifically prohibit the outsourcing to [PMCs] of functions which are defined as inherently State functions'.[169] As there are currently no such limitations, however, this route of attributing responsibility for PMC activities to the State remains open, especially since the Code does not incorporate any corresponding limitations. Yet, according to the ILC, this Article is directed towards parastatal entities that '*exercise elements of governmental authority* in place of State organs, as well as situations where *former State corporations have been privatized* but retain certain public or regulatory functions'.[170] Further confirmation that Article 5 is a narrow category is evident in its limitation 'to entities which are *empowered by internal law to exercise governmental authority*' and from the requirement that 'internal law in question must *specifically authorize the conduct* as involving the exercise of public authority': together this suggests that the threshold is such that toleration of the activity is insufficient.[171] Hannah Tonkin suggests, however, that the contractual nexus is sufficient because the ILC specifically provided as an example under Article 5 that 'in some countries private security firms may be contracted to act as prison guards and in that capacity may exercise public powers'.[172] This contention may be undermined in relation to PMCs, however, because the ILC clarified the way in which the powers are conferred on the entity and 'the extent to which the entity is *accountable to government* for their exercise'.[173] Although Hannah Tonkin concludes that States will be responsible for

[166] ibid 48, para 6. Emphasis added.
[167] ibid. Emphasis added.
[168] For its application to PMCs, see Tonkin (n 26) 99–113.
[169] Gómez del Prado, 'Draft Convention' (n 143).
[170] ILC (n 27) 42, para 1. Emphasis added.
[171] ibid 43, para 7. Emphasis added.
[172] ibid 43, para 2; Tonkin (n 26) 111.
[173] ILC (n 27) 43, para 6. Emphasis added.

PMC misconduct under Article 5, two factors will certainly exclude this attribution from the ambit of the Article: where the acts did not constitute an exercise of governmental authority, either in a substantive sense or at the material time.[174] Considering the narrow scope and the envisaged purpose of Article 5 to encompass parastatal entities that substitute State organs and privatised State corporations, Tonkin's conclusion is tenuous at best.[175] The difficulty of attributing the actions of the PMC to the State obviates the responsibility mechanisms operating within JAB. PMCs may 'violate' the prohibition of the use of force, but such actions will not be recognised in law as violations because their actions do not precipitate the necessary State action for this finding. PMC impunity is thus guaranteed where its actions incur into the sphere of JAB.

Beyond the difficulties revolving around attributing responsibility for the internationally wrongful conduct engaged in by PMCs is the question of how JAB binds or otherwise affects juridical persons. A recent proposal made by the UN Working Group on the Use of Mercenaries to prohibit States from outsourcing still focuses upon the use of PMCs by the State,[176] which presumably still bears primary responsibility such that the regime would suffer from the defects discussed above. In the context of the Working Group's conclusion that there is no international prohibition on outsourcing,[177] the discrepancy between what international law forbids States and what activities PMCs might be prohibited from engaging in is particularly stark. The Draft Convention prohibits the use of force in Article 8 on much narrower grounds when compared to the UN Charter: the overthrow of a government; the coercive change of internationally recognised borders; the violation of sovereignty or support of foreign occupation; and the explicit targeting of civilians or causing disproportionate harm.[178] While this is intended as an inexhaustive list to act as a starting point for further discussion,[179] this list adopts a consequentialist perspective that is problematic. In other words, while the UN Charter prohibits the threat or use of force outright subject only to the right of self-defence in Article 51, the Draft Convention aims to curtail violence directed towards specific outcomes. The implication is that private force is only prohibited to the extent that it furthers impermissible ends, significantly increasing

[174] Tonkin (n 26) 113.

[175] ILC (n 27) 42, para 1.

[176] UN Working Group on the Use of Mercenaries, 'Submission by the Working Group on the Use of Mercenaries as a Means of Impeding the Exercise of the Right of Peoples to Self-Determination' (UN Human Rights Council, 2012) A/HRC/WG.10/2/CRP.1 paras 9–12.

[177] ibid.

[178] Gómez del Prado (n 143) 28.

[179] UN Working Group on the Use of Mercenaries, 'Submission by the Working Group on the Use of Mercenaries as a Means of Impeding the Exercise of the Right of Peoples to Self-Determination' (n 176) 12.

the prospect for PMCs to enjoy passive impunity where they engage in activity that, when conducted by the State, would contravene the prohibition on the threat or use of force. Taken together, it is clear that the PMC would be able to engage in activities within the sphere of, but without violating, the rules of JAB but would amount to violating the prohibition over the use of force when conducted by the State.

B. Acts of Aggression and the Crime of Aggression

An alternative approach is to examine the imperceptibility of PMC aggression within the specific framework of unlawful acts of aggression by the State and the crime of aggression by individuals.[180] Again, the law is incapable of articulating corporate aggression per se: instead, the approach has been bifurcated with the result that this has to be attributed either to the State or the individual. The high threshold imposed by Article 3(g) of UNGA Resolution 3314 must be satisfied for attribution to the State, as the ICJ held in *Armed Activities*:

> The attacks did not emanate from armed bands or irregulars *sent by* the DRC *or on behalf* of the DRC, within the sense of [Article 3(g)] … even if this series of deplorable attacks could be regarded as cumulative in character, they still remained *non-attributable* to the DRC.[181]

Unlike the general rules governing the attribution of responsibility to the State violations of the prohibition of the use of force discussed above, the armed non-State entities must act as State proxies in lieu of direct action by the organs of the State in order to ascribe responsibility to the State for acts of aggression. Whether the contractual nexus is sufficient remains uncertain, but because of the mutual consent and horizontal relationship embodied in a contract the courts are unlikely to find that the State possesses the hierarchical position of command and control in relation to the PMC to fulfil the definition of sending by or on behalf of a State. As discussed above in the context of contract law, international law contemplates State direction and control over private entities, not State collusion. Thus, acts of aggression perpetrated by PMCs are therefore unlikely to be attributable to the State.

Article 3(g) was incorporated verbatim into Article 8 *bis* of the Rome Statute, as mentioned in chapter three, although the ICC will not exercise jurisdiction over the crime of aggression until 2017 at the earliest.[182]

[180] These are separate and distinct offences: Antonopoulos, 'Whatever Happened to Crimes Against Peace?' (n 144) 40.

[181] *Armed Activities* (n 147) [146]. Emphasis added.

[182] M Politi, 'The ICC and the Crime of Aggression: A Dream That Came Through and the Reality Ahead' (2012) 10 *Journal of International Criminal Justice* 267, 270–71.

It remains to be seen how this provision will be implemented and enforced, but individual criminal responsibility for the crime of aggression cannot capture PMC aggression for three reasons: the high threshold; the State-centric nature of the definition; and the juridical personhood of the PMC. Although the natural persons constituting the PMC and those who contract for their services will be susceptible to the new provision, corporate aggression remains legally impossible. This reinforces the notion that the law is incapable of understanding the challenge brought about by the PMC. Here are corporate entities capable of organising and projecting armed force that may equate to acts of aggression, yet the law is incapable of articulating or comprehending this possibility because of its dogmatic presuppositions of status and jurisdiction.

V. PASSIVE IMPUNITY GENERATED BY THE DOCTRINE OF COMMAND RESPONSIBILITY

It is worth noting at the outset that the focus of ICL upon those individuals who are 'most responsible' may largely exculpate PMC contractors from its purview. This is because military and political leaders fulfil that requirement more readily than PMC personnel and, in addition, are also more likely to be perceived as such. This means that although PMC contractors remain susceptible to ICL in a formal legal sense, they are simultaneously exempted from its operation in practice as a result of this focus, leading to the relative impunity for PMC contractors to its provisions.

It is within this restricted context that the applicability of the command responsibility doctrine will be explored. Command responsibility has been chosen as the exemplar of passive responsibility enjoyed by PMC contractors because of three characteristics. First, command responsibility accords primacy to role responsibility over outcome responsibility that grounds a form of passive impunity elaborated upon in chapter one. Second, command responsibility seeks to bridge the gap between collectively created harms that characterise international crimes and the individual criminal liability imposed by ICL. Third, unlike the other mechanisms developed by ICL to impose individual criminal liability for collective outcomes, command responsibility is not a mode of direct liability.

The responsibility of commanders was touched upon in chapter one to illustrate the priority of role responsibility in relation to outcome responsibility in law. This section examines the inapplicability of command responsibility to PMC contractors that generates and maintains passive impunity.[183] Despite command responsibility not being limited to de jure

[183] The present analysis seeks to illustrate the obstacles that frustrate the application of command responsibility, in contradistinction to approaches that have sought to apply the

military commanders, but also attaching to de facto military commanders and to civilians outside of the military hierarchy,[184] this section demonstrates that structural differences erect barriers against the ascription of command responsibility to PMC personnel. The command responsibility doctrine is particularly relevant to the legal creation of impunity for the PMC because of the three aforementioned characteristics, beyond those mentioned in chapter one.

The first is that a hierarchical relationship is both required and presupposed to exist within organisations which exercise violence, discussed above.[185] James Cockayne proposes that:

> Global humanitarian action may need, therefore, to deal not only with responsible command structures, but responsible enterprise more generally. Where [IHL] has operated predominantly through 'responsible command' models … 'enterprise' models … attribute responsibility and liability not through hierarchical relations but through transactional relations.[186]

He continues to suggest that the regulation of violence could be organised through modalities such as aiding, abetting, complicity, joint criminal enterprise and social influence.[187] Yet, it is unclear how these modalities of liability will be sufficient replacements for the hierarchically structured modes of responsibility. This is for the simple reason that effective control serves as the nexus through which outcome responsibility can flow unhindered from the direct perpetrators to those individuals who organised or instigated the impugned activity. In other words, the nexus of 'effective control' constrains the autonomy of the direct perpetrator, instrumentalising him in the furtherance of criminal ends. There is harmony here with Claus Roxin's conception of perpetration through an organisation where the perpetrator is the 'person who "dominates" the commission of the criminal offence in that he or she has the power to determine whether or not the relevant acts are carried out'.[188] The lack of hierarchical relationships

doctrine to PMC contractors: M Frulli, 'Exploring the Applicability of Command Responsibility to Private Military Contractors' (2010) 15 *Journal of Conflict and Security Law* 435. This chapter will exclude consideration of the cases arising in the aftermath of World War II because the contemporary law on command responsibility has evolved considerably from those contentious decisions.

184 As the ad hoc Tribunals have only used command responsibility when convicting military commanders, its extension to civilian personnel remains theoretical: B Bonafé, 'Finding a Proper Role for Command Responsibility' (2007) 5 *Journal of International Criminal Justice* 599, 616.

185 eg art 1(1) of Annex to Hague IV and art 4(2)(a) of GC III demand responsible command.

186 J Cockayne, 'The Global Reorganization of Legitimate Violence: Military Entrepreneurs and the Private Face of International Humanitarian Law' (2006) 88 *International Review of the Red Cross* 459, 488.

187 ibid.

188 G Werle, B Burghardt and C Roxin, 'Crimes as Part of Organized Power Structures' (2011) 9 *Journal of International Criminal Justice* 191, 191; indeed, the individuals who

in the PMC challenges the possibility of attributing responsibility for the misconduct of soldiers or contractors up the command chain to military commanders and civilian superiors. This highlights the command responsibility issue for modern PMCs: their structure is horizontal because they are organised along the corporate model, are bound by contract and lack recourse to military discipline and punishments as discussed above. Their activities, however, involve organised violence which has historically been organised upon a strict hierarchical relationship of military obedience that enables the application of the *respondeat superior* doctrine.[189] This presumption of hierarchy underpinned the legal development of command responsibility which has crystallised into two rules of customary IHL,[190] and constitutes a principle of ICL that is discussed below. The spectre of impunity is raised by the lack of hierarchical structure within the PMC that will prevent the doctrine of command responsibility from applying, despite their organisation and projection of violence.[191]

The second is the inapplicability of command responsibility may not create impunity per se because it is only one of a number of mechanisms that attribute individual criminal responsibility for collectively-produced harms.[192] Command responsibility, however, stands out among these mechanisms because it has evolved to impose liability *independent* of

actually carry out the crime must be fungible so that the commission of the crime is certain and is unaffected by the actions of those occupying lower positions in the organisation: Werle, Burghardt and Roxin; see also, T Weigend, 'Perpetration through an Organization' (2011) 9 *Journal of International Criminal Justice* 91.

[189] The Commentary to API, art 43 provides: 'All armed forces, groups and units are necessarily structured and have a hierarchy, as they are subordinate to a command which is responsible to one of the Parties to the conflict for their operations. In other words, all of them are subordinate to a command and to a Party to the conflict … for it is not permissible for any group to wage a private war': ICRC (n 102) 1672.

[190] r 152 relating to criminal responsibility for war crimes committed pursuant to orders, and r 153 for failure to take all necessary and reasonable measures to prevent or punish the commission of war crimes which they either knew or had reason to know about: J-M Henckaerts and L Doswald-Beck, *Customary International Humanitarian Law*, vol I (Cambridge University Press, 2009) 556–63. These find expression in API, arts 86 and 87.

[191] Indeed, the lack of formal hierarchical relationship within the modern PMC may be one characteristic that is capable of setting them apart from mercenary groups which are generally organised hierarchically. This suggests that PMCs may benefit from additional impunity mechanisms in relation to their mercenary counterparts because of their formally horizontal relationship. Personal communication with C Kinsey, 2 July 2012.

[192] Beyond traditional criminal law complicity mechanisms such as aiding and abetting, the ad hoc Tribunals have developed a tripartite theory of joint criminal enterprise while the ICC is exploring the possibility of perpetration through an organisation: A Danner and J Martinez, 'Guilty Associations: Joint Criminal Enterprise, Command Responsibility, and the Development of International Criminal Law' (2005) 93 *California Law Review* 75; S Manacorda and C Meloni, 'Indirect Perpetration versus Joint Criminal Enterprise' (2011) 9 *Journal of International Criminal Justice* 159; H van der Wilt, 'Joint Criminal Enterprise: Possibilities and Limitations' (2007) 5 *Journal of International Criminal Justice* 91; Weigend, 'Perpetration through an Organization' (n 188).

direct perpetration. As introduced in chapter one, this formulation was articulated by the ICTY Trial Chamber in *Oric*: 'the superior cannot be considered as if he had committed the crime himself, but *merely for his neglect of duty* with regard to crimes committed by subordinates'.[193] As the command responsibility doctrine is unhinged from the requirements of direct perpetration, it is capable of attributing responsibility to PMC managers, as well as the military and civilian personnel engaged with the PMC who may be aware of contractor misconduct and are in a position to prevent or punish it, but who are not directly involved with the misconduct in question. Thus, regardless of the possibilities of ascribing responsibility through other, more horizontal, modalities, impunity will be created if command responsibility cannot apply to the superiors of PMC contractors. This is because these superiors will be immunised from liability unlike the superiors of military personnel.

This feeds into the third characteristic of command responsibility: superiors are incentivised by the doctrine to monitor, oversee and control organisations that deploy coercive force, and are dissuaded from inaction to ensure subordinate compliance with IHL and human rights law. The inapplicability of command responsibility therefore would not only *create* impunity directly by absolving PMC superiors from liability, but also *foster* impunity more broadly because the structures that have been established to ensure responsibility are circumvented. In this sense, the prospect for impunity identified within the doctrine of command responsibility is far-reaching: the hierarchical organisation of violence characterised by 'effective control' is necessary not only to facilitate the flow of responsibility up the chain of command, but critically structures mechanisms of oversight aimed at ensuring compliance with IHL and human rights law. In other words, hierarchical relationships are deemed necessary for their preventive as well as their remedial function.

This section examines the modern law of command responsibility before considering the barriers to its application internally to PMC managers and externally to military and civilian superiors engaged with the PMC.

A. The Doctrine of Command Responsibility

The ICTY established the three constitutive parts of the principle of command responsibility in the landmark decision in *Delalic*:

(i) the existence of a superior-subordinate relationship;
(ii) the superior knew or had reason to know that the criminal act was about to be or had been committed; and

[193] *Prosecutor v Oric (Trials Chamber)* [2006] ICTY Trial Chamber IT-03-68-T [293]. Emphasis added.

(iii) the superior failed to take the necessary and reasonable measures to prevent the criminal act or punish the perpetrator thereof.[194]

Establishing each of these criteria is significantly more problematic for PMC contractors than for military personnel or civilian leaders. ICTY case law reveals that the major barrier arises from the first point.[195] It is important to note that the superior-subordinate relationship need neither be formalised nor permanent: the ICTY Trial Chamber in *Kunarac* recognised that 'tacit or implicit understanding' is acceptable and that 'the temporary nature of a military unit is not, in itself, sufficient to exclude a relationship of subordination'.[196] Finally, the requisite relationship is not precluded by command structures that 'are in disorder or primitive'.[197]

The lynchpin of the superior-subordinate relationship is 'effective control'.[198] Again, the ICTY Trial Chamber in *Delalic* held the opinion that 'the factor that determines liability for this type of criminal responsibility is the actual possession, or non-possession of powers of control over the actions of subordinates'.[199] This in turn requires 'that the superior have effective control over the persons committing the underlying violations of [IHL], in the sense of having the material ability to prevent and punish the commission of these offences'.[200] Furthermore, the ICTY Appeals Chamber in *Delalic* expressly rejected substantial influence short of material abilities to prevent or punish subordinate offences.[201] The tension inherent within the effective control criterion is demonstrated in *Kordic and Cerkez*, where the Trial Chamber acquitted the politician and civilian leader, Dario Kordic, of superior responsibility because the substantial influence that was factually established was an insufficient degree of control for liability to be incurred under the doctrine.[202] The military leader, Mario Cerkez,

[194] *Prosecutor v Delalic (Trials Chamber)* (n 104) [346]; reaffirmed in *Prosecutor v Halilovic (Appeals Chamber)* [2007] ICTY Trials Chamber IT-01-48-A [59]; and *Prosecutor v Perisic (Appeals Chamber)* [2013] ICTY Appeals Chamber IT-04-81-A [86].

[195] Bonafé, 'Finding a Proper Role for Command Responsibility' (n 184) 608–10.

[196] *Prosecutor v Kunarac (Trials Chamber)* [2001] ICTY Trial Chamber IT-96-23-T & IT-96-23/1-T [397 and 399], respectively.

[197] *Prosecutor v Delalic (Appeals Chamber)* (n 105) [193].

[198] 'The ability to exercise effective control in the sense of material power to prevent or punish, which the Appeals Chamber considers to be a minimum requirement for the recognition of the superior-subordinate relationship, will almost invariably not be satisfied unless such a relationship of subordination exists': ibid 303; this has been affirmed in the US Court of Appeals for the Eleventh Circuit, *Ford ex rel Estate of Ford v Garcia* (2002) 289 F3d 1283 (US Court of Appeals for the Eleventh Circuit).

[199] *Prosecutor v Delalic (Trials Chamber)* (n 104) [370].

[200] ibid 378.

[201] *Prosecutor v Delalic (Appeals Chamber)* (n 105) [266].

[202] *Prosecutor v Kordic and Cerkez (Trials Chamber)* [2001] ICTY Trial Chamber IT-95-14/2-T [840]. He was, however, convicted of direct modes of perpetration. The jurisprudence of the ICTY has indicated the preference for conviction for direct rather than command responsibility where the accused is charged under both modes of liability, see Bonafé (n 184) 611–15.

was convicted upon superior responsibility because the effective control test was satisfied as the relevant troops were under his command and he had failed to prevent the attacks or punish the attackers.[203]

While the ICTY imposed a uniform standard of effective control for military and civilian superiors in *Delalic*, these elements were subsequently diluted in *Aleksovski*, where the Trial Chamber reasoned that to 'require a civilian authority to have sanctioning powers similar to those of a member of the military would so limit the scope of the doctrine of superior authority that it would hardly be applicable to civilian authorities'.[204] In order to keep this doctrine applicable to civilians, therefore, the ability to impose sanctions was replaced by 'the possibility of transmitting reports to the appropriate authorities … [in] the likelihood that those reports will trigger an investigation or initiate disciplinary or even criminal measures'.[205] This lower standard for civilian superiors was reaffirmed by the Trial Chamber in *Blaskic*.[206] The International Criminal Tribunal for Rwanda (ICTR) Appeals Chamber also held that the effective control test applies to all superiors and that civilian superiors must exercise 'a degree of control … which is similar to the degree of control of military commanders' although, cryptically, it need not be exercised or established in the same manner.[207] The ICTR Appeals Chamber did, however, specifically overrule the Trial Chamber below 'to the extent that it suggested that the control exercised by a civilian superior must be of the same nature as that exercised by a military commander'.[208] Finally, although the Trial Chamber of the Special Court for Sierra Leone (SCSL) has elaborated upon the indicia of effective control in irregular armies, it stressed that 'the key traditional indicia of effective control remain central': this remains the case even where the exercise of these powers proves to be excessive.[209]

The effective control criterion was a point of contention during the drafting of the provision that would become Article 28 of the Rome Statute. While some delegations sought a uniform standard for military and civilian superiors akin to the jurisprudence of the ad hoc Tribunals, the US proposal ultimately succeeded, resulting in separate standards for

[203] *Prosecutor v Kordic and Cerkez (Trials Chamber)* (n 202) [843].

[204] *Prosecutor v Aleksovski (Trials Chamber)* (n 107) [78].

[205] ibid.

[206] *Prosecutor v Blaskic (Trials Chamber)* (n 107) [302].

[207] *Prosecutor v Bagilishema (ICTR Appeals Chamber)* [2002] ICTR Appeals Chamber ICTR-95-1A-A [50 and 52 respectively].

[208] ibid 55.

[209] These indicia appear to be directed towards rebel groups and are likely to be of limited utility for PMC contractors: *Prosecutor v Brima (SCSL Trial Chamber)* [2007] SCSL Trial Chamber (SCSL-04-16-T) SCSL-04-16-T [788–89].

military commanders and civilian superiors.[210] The US delegation had emphasised that:

> The main difference between civilian supervisors and military commanders lay in the nature and scope of their authority. The latter's authority rested on the military discipline system, which had a penal dimension, whereas there was no comparable punishment system for civilians in most countries. Another difference was that a military commander was in charge of a lethal force, whereas a civilian supervisor was in charge of what might be termed a bureaucracy.[211]

The American delegation noted one final difference between civilian and military superiors: timing. Civilian supervisors were only to be responsible for the activities of their subordinates during the period when the subordinates were at work, while military commanders were responsible for their forces all of the time.[212]

To date, the only application of command responsibility at the ICC has been in *Bemba*.[213] First, it had to be established that the suspect must either be a de jure or a de facto commander, depending upon whether he was formally or legally appointed.[214] It is apparent that the de jure category encompasses only commanders of a State's regular armed forces, while de facto commanders include 'regular government forces such as armed police units or irregular forces … such as rebel group, paramilitary units including, inter alia, armed resistance movements and militias that follow a structure of military hierarchy or a chain of command'.[215] Note especially that a superior-subordinate relationship is deemed to be the essential characteristic that is the common denominator between these different types of groups.

On the second part raised in *Delalic*, although the ad hoc Tribunals operated a unitary *mens rea* standard, Article 28 of the Rome Statute explicitly differentiates between: (a) military superiors who 'either knew, or owing to the circumstances at the time, *should have known* that the forces were committing or about to commit such crimes'; and (b) non-military superiors who 'either knew or, *consciously disregard information* which clearly indicated, that the subordinates were committing or about to commit such crimes'.[216] Citing the Trial Chamber in *Blaskic*, Pre-Trial Chamber II in *Bemba*

[210] UN Rome Proceedings, 'Proposal Submitted by the United States of America for Article 25'.

[211] UN Rome Proceedings, 'Committee of the Whole: Summary Record of the 1st Meeting' 67.

[212] ibid 68.

[213] *Prosecutor v Bemba (ICC Pre-Trial Chamber)* [2009] ICC Pre-Trial Chamber II ICC-01/05-01/08 [404–43].

[214] ibid 408–09.

[215] ibid 410.

[216] Emphasis added.

has clarified that the standard in Article 28(a) requires actual knowledge, or imposes an active duty upon the superior akin to negligence because he is required 'to take the necessary measures to secure knowledge of the conduct of his troops and to inquire, regardless of the availability of information'.[217] Assuming that the approach adopted in *Blaskic* is followed, a commander who has exercised due diligence in fulfilling his duties will not be liable for any resultant lack of information about the crimes of his subordinates.[218] The standard embodied in Article 28(b) for civilian supervisors remains unclear, although Pre-Trial Chamber II noted the 'intent of the drafters to take a more stringent approach towards commanders and military-like commanders compared to [civilian supervisors]'.[219] As such, the relevant standard may approximate recklessness, rather than negligence. The difference between the *mens rea* standard in Article 28(a) and (b) implies that military commanders are under an active duty to inform themselves and will be culpable where they fail to do this, while civilian supervisors are not under such a duty and will only be liable if they ignore information that is already available.[220]

On the third part raised in *Delalic*, the Trial Chamber in that case declined to formulate any general standard against which actions of superiors are to be measured because these actions are heavily contingent upon the facts of each case. The Trial Chamber did establish, however, that a commander must fulfil their legal duty 'to take all necessary and reasonable measures' to prevent the offences or to punish the perpetrators.[221] Having said this, the Trial Chamber immediately continued to hold that 'international law cannot oblige a superior to perform the impossible' such that 'a superior may only be held criminally responsible for failing to take such measures that are within his powers'.[222] This was subsequently upheld by the Appeals Chamber in *Blaskic*.[223] The Pre-Trial Chamber of the ICC in *Bemba* affirmed only that de jure and de facto command responsibility under Article 28(a) of the Rome Statute would be fulfilled where measures were taken within the 'material possibility' of the commander.[224] Taken

[217] *Prosecutor v Bemba (ICC Pre-Trial Chamber)* (n 213) [429–34]; for justifications of a 'duty of knowledge', see J Martinez, 'Understanding Mens Rea in Command Responsibility: From Yamashita to Blaškić and Beyond' (2007) 5 *Journal of International Criminal Justice* 638, 660–64.

[218] *Prosecutor v Blaskic (Trials Chamber)* (n 107) 322.

[219] *Prosecutor v Bemba (ICC Pre-Trial Chamber)* (n 213) [433].

[220] The availability of overwhelming amounts of information made possible by modern technology further confuses the issues surrounding the mental element. While Charles Garraway suggests that the current legal standards need not be adapted to accommodate for these changes, he raises more questions than answers: Garraway, 'The Application of Superior Responsibility in an Era of Unlimited Information' (n 108) 202–03.

[221] *Prosecutor v Delalic (Appeals Chamber)* (n 105) [394].

[222] ibid 395.

[223] *Prosecutor v Blaskic (Appeals Chamber)* [2004] ICTY Appeals Chamber IT-95-14-A [417].

[224] *Prosecutor v Bemba* [2009] ICC Pre-Trial Chamber II ICC-01/05-01/08 [443].

together, this implies that any lack or diminishment of material abilities to prevent or punish subordinate offences within the context of a superior-subordinate relationship would absolve the superior from being ascribed command responsibility. This implication has clear bearings upon the prospects of command responsibility applying to the PMC and its personnel, primarily because of the limited powers that can be conferred through the contractual nexus, as discussed above.

While the requirement for Article 28(b) has not been expounded upon, it is likely that the standard will be equivalent in law, but will translate in practice into a lower threshold for civilian supervisors, who are only required to transmit reports to the appropriate authorities.[225] This illustrates that command responsibility is a form of role responsibility that is divorced from outcome responsibility as discussed in chapter one. As Chantal Meloni writes, '[t]he superior's criminal responsibility flows from the neglect of a specific duty to take the measures that are necessary and reasonable in the given circumstances, in order to prevent those specific crimes or to punish the perpetrators thereof'.[226] That command responsibility imposes an autonomous form of liability for failure to act, and which is limited by his omission[227] is supported by the Trial Chamber in *Oric*[228] and subsequently reaffirmed by the Pre-Trial Chamber in *Bemba*.[229] Thus, insofar as the doctrine of command responsibility encompasses only role responsibility, reliance upon this doctrine cannot be a complete solution to allegations of impunity for outcomes that violate human rights law and IHL.

In order to apply the command responsibility doctrine to the PMC an initial differentiation must be made between what I term the internal and external dimensions: the former operates within the structure of the PMC itself between contractors, and potentially their associated military personnel; whereas the latter operates between the representatives of the entities that contract the PMC, such as State officials or corporate executives, and the PMC. In the following sections, the involvement of the PMC is demonstrated to decrease the likelihood that relevant superiors will be held liable under the doctrine of command responsibility both internally and externally. Despite the increased likelihood of a criminal outcome because this oversight mechanism will be weakened, it will be easier for PMC contractors to fulfil their obligations, thereby avoiding command responsibility in relation to their military and civilian counterparts.

225 *Prosecutor v Aleksovski (Trials Chamber)* (n 107) [78]; *Prosecutor v Blaskic (Appeals Chamber)* (n 218) [302].

226 C Meloni, 'Command Responsibility Mode of Liability for the Crimes of Subordinates or Separate Offence of the Superior?' (2007) 5 *Journal of International Criminal Justice* 619, 628.

227 ibid 629.

228 *Prosecutor v Oric (Trials Chamber)* (n 193) [293].

229 *Prosecutor v Bemba (ICC Pre-Trial Chamber)* (n 213) [405]. Emphasis added.

B. Internal Command Responsibility within PMCs

The status of PMC contractors must be assessed in order to apply the doctrine of command responsibility. The first component in *Delalic* will be difficult to satisfy because a relationship of subordination is unlikely to exist within the structure of the PMC for the reasons elaborated above in the context of horizontal contractual relationships and the lack of disciplinary or sanctioning powers. Ottavio Quirico, however, assumes that PMC contractors possess similar powers to military personnel in his analysis.[230] He cites Chia Lehnardt in support, who argues that PMCs are not ordinary companies because

> the corporate culture … and their functioning resemble those of armed forces, as the companies are often led and staffed by former troops and military commanders … It is therefore likely that the supervisory authority of senior PMC personnel in the field is very similar to that exercised by military commanders.[231]

Her conclusion, however, does not necessarily follow from the facts for three key reasons. First, there is nothing in the structure of the PMC that requires a corporate culture and function to mirror that of the armed forces. Even if there was, this would be imitation rather than replication, which is important because the adoption of the culture is not necessarily accompanied by the relevant powers. Second, there is no guarantee of consistency throughout the industry even if this were the case: 'often' is indicative because it is not 'always'. This suggests that the issue will remain for some sectors of the industry, even if it can be resolved for some PMCs. Finally, even for a PMC that is organised along military lines by former members of the armed forces, their leaders lack the legitimate disciplinary powers that military commanders would possess thereby undermining claims of 'effective control'. Thus, even if Lehnardt is correct about the nature and reach of the supervisory powers, they cannot have sufficient sanctioning powers to prevent of punish unlawful behaviour.[232] Together, these challenge the assumption made by Quirico, based on the evidence supplied

[230] O Quirico, 'The Criminal Responsibility of Private Military and Security Company Personnel under International Humanitarian Law' in Francioni and Ronzitti, *War by Contract: Human Rights, Humanitarian Law, and Private Contractors* (n 138) 435.

[231] C Lehnardt, 'Individual Liability of Private Military Personnel under International Criminal Law' (2008) 19 *European Journal of International Law* 1015, 1026. Christopher Kinsey notes, however, that 'PMCs frequently employ non-military staff in senior positions of authority'. Personal communication, 2 July 2012.

[232] She notes that 'while they cannot rely on the same disciplinary system, they have the ability to punish a crime by submitting a report to a competent state authority, thereby triggering an investigation': ibid. While this may be correct as a point of law, practice shows that investigations are rarely triggered in practice where PMC activities are reported, when they are reported. Even in the rare instances that investigations are triggered, there remain few prospects for actual punishment to be meted out. Together, this questions whether the possibility to submit reports in the context of PMC activity can suffice.

by Lehnardt, that PMC personnel operate within superior-subordinate relationships characterised by 'effective control'. As the law of command responsibility is sufficiently settled, each aspect of the doctrine will be examined in turn below.

The PMC adopts the structure of a civilian corporation for organising military services such that the relationship of subordination cannot be taken for granted. Louise Doswald-Beck indicates that identifying the person within the PMC who effectively acts as a commander surfaces as an initial difficulty that is highly contingent upon the factual circumstances.[233] In this light, it is useful to note that Sir John Hackett famously differentiated the armed forces upon their contract of 'unlimited liability',[234] in contradistinction to a civilian employment contract within the limited liability corporation. This concept underpins the differences between the nature and scope of military and civilian superiors that was underscored by the aforementioned American delegation at the Rome Conference. Military personnel are subject to the military justice system that imposes a disciplinary and penal system, with no equivalent in civilian life, such that '[i]t is the unlimited liability which sets the man who embraces this life somewhat apart'.[235] While *individual* contractors themselves may possess military backgrounds, this cannot prejudice the determination of the superior-subordinate *relationship*. *Former* military personnel have been released from service, have ended their contract of unlimited liability and are no longer subjected to the superior-subordinate relationship.

It can be inferred from *Bemba* that PMC contractors can, at most, be liable as civilian superiors rather than as military commanders. The Pre-Trial Chamber indicated that the status of de jure commanders is reserved for regular armed forces, so PMC contractors will not be satisfy this criterion unless they are formally incorporated into those forces.[236] Regarding qualification as a de facto military commander, the Pre-Trial Chamber clarified that the organisation must have a military hierarchy and chain of command.[237] As discussed above, PMCs are civilian corporations that lack the hierarchical structure and the disciplinary powers of prevention and punishment which characterise the military establishment: taken together, this is likely to preclude the possibility for PMC contractors to qualify as de facto military commanders.

The possibility remains open for the civilian standard of command responsibility to apply to PMC superiors because a lesser 'effective

[233] L Doswald-Beck, 'Private Military Companies under International Humanitarian Law' in Chesterman and Lehnardt (eds), *From Mercenaries to Market* (n 35) 135.

[234] Quoted in P Robinson, N Lee and D Carrick, *Ethics Education in the Military* (Ashgate, 2008) 49–50.

[235] ibid 50.

[236] *Prosecutor v Bemba (ICC Pre-Trial Chamber)* (n 213) 410.

[237] ibid.

control' test is imposed, per *Aleksovski*. Applying Nora Karsten's proposition that the rationale of the entity is determinative for the classification of military or non-military superiors, a military commander is a superior in an entity whose raison d'être is participation in armed conflict whereas a non-military superior does not belong to an entity with this rationale.[238] PMC contractors are likely to be classified as non-military superiors because the majority of PMCs claim to no longer offer 'tip-of-the-spear' services and because IHL bars civilians from combat functions. The application of this lower standard is the source of passive impunity for PMC contractors because this categorisation makes it easier to for them to discharge their role responsibilities, in relation to their military commander counterparts. Because the superior is liable only where he has not exercised the measures within his powers to prevent or punish the crime of his subordinates, the lower threshold of effective control, which is satisfied by the ability to transmit reports to the appropriate authorities, becomes crucial. First, by merely reporting them, the civilian supervisor will have discharged his duty, and thus have avoided the ascription of command responsibility. The military commander, however, would have to exercise all his disciplinary powers to exculpate himself from the same liability. Second, the civilian standard also elevates the *mens rea* requirement for culpability. A military commander could only be absolved for not knowing about the crimes of his subordinates after he had established that he had exercised due diligence by actively informing himself despite any possible lack of available information. The civilian supervisor, however, is not under any duty to take active steps to acquire information, such that he will only be liable where he chooses to ignore information already in his possession.

Thus, where command responsibility is held to apply to PMC contractors inter se, they will be held to the civilian standard. This has two passive impunity effects: first, it is easier for PMC contractors to discharge their (role) command responsibility; and second, the (outcome) crimes of the subordinates are more likely because of limited powers of suppression and punishment exercised by PMC supervisors. The contractual relationship between the PMC and its contractors limits the 'sanction' only to dismissal by a termination of contract, while the civilian nature of the PMC limits its supervisors to filing reports on misconduct. Considering the volume of escalation of force reports presented in chapter two and the relative lack of ensuing investigations and penal sanctions imposed, PMC contractors enjoy passive impunity from internal command responsibility.

[238] N Karsten, 'Distinguishing Military and Non-Military Superiors Reflections on the Bemba Case at the ICC' (2009) 7 *Journal of International Criminal Justice* 983, 1002.

C. External Command Responsibility

With regard to external command responsibility concerning the potential for State officials to accrue liability under the doctrine for the acts of PMC contractors, Louise Doswald-Beck has suggested that PMCs might be used to circumvent responsibility as the lack of de facto control may be sufficient to frustrate the requisite superior-subordinate relationship.[239] She suggests that

> it would be a strange result if a commander would be guilty by virtue of command responsibility because he or she put officers known to be sadists in charge of interrogations, whereas a state official who hired a PMC that has allegedly 'robust' techniques would not be

The lack of de facto control, however, might make this absurd differentiation a reality.[240]

An initial barrier to external command responsibility is that the ad hoc Tribunals have only used command responsibility to convict military commanders, especially those holding low to mid-level ranks, and consequently that the doctrine has been invoked primarily for war crimes which breach the commander's duty under IHL.[241] While it is uncertain whether these trends capture the inherent characteristics of the doctrine or whether it is no more than a quirk of the jurisprudence, these initial limitations suggest that command responsibility will neither attach to high-ranking military officers nor generally to civilian leaders for the crimes committed by PMC contractors.

The litmus test for external command responsibility of military personnel is again effective control. For military commanders,[242] the Appeals Chamber in *Hadzihasanovic* held that the relationship between the accused and the independent *El Mujahedin* detachment in question was one of cooperation, and not effective control: this was despite the established facts indicating that the detachment fought alongside military formations under the command of the accused.[243] The cooperative relationship was inferred because the detachment had signalled its continued independence from that military unit under the command of the accused.[244] Furthermore, it was not permissible to infer effective control from the absence of other authority over the detachment: this was a claim explicitly rejected

[239] Doswald-Beck, 'Private Military Companies under International Humanitarian Law' (n 233) 136.

[240] ibid.

[241] Bonafé (n 184) 616.

[242] See also Frulli, 'Exploring the Applicability of Command Responsibility to Private Military Contractors' (n 183) 456–62.

[243] *Prosecutor v Hadzihasanovic (Trials Chamber)* [2006] ICTY Trial Chamber IT-01-47-T [210].

[244] ibid 200, 210, 213, 214, 217, 221.

by the Appeals Chamber.[245] Applying this jurisprudence to the PMC reveals that its structure and organisation facilitate passive impunity by stemming the flow of external command responsibility. While the Appeals Chamber had to demonstrate the independence of the detachment from the military unit, this would not be necessary to establish for PMCs. Their independent existence is readily affirmed by their juridical corporate personhood and through their contractual nexus with the State indicating an agreement between equal and independent parties. The possibility for effective control is further undermined by the nature of the contractual relationship limiting the most severe 'sanction' to the termination of the contract, unlike the (quasi-) military structures under consideration by the ICTY.

For civilian superiors,[246] a restrictive approach is evident from the warning by the Trial Chamber in *Kordic* that 'great care must be taken in assessing the evidence to determine command responsibility in respect of civilians, lest an injustice is done'.[247] Because civilian supervisors are more readily possessed of 'tremendous influence and power',[248] but which is nevertheless short of effective control, external civilian supervisors are unlikely to be burdened with command responsibility for PMC contractors. This suggests that there is significant substance to the shocking discrepancy suggested by Doswald-Beck at the start of this section. The prospect for passive impunity is readily apparent with recourse to the PMC because civilian leaders and military commanders who would ordinarily shoulder superior responsibility when deploying ordinary armed forces would be freed from this burden when contracting a PMC towards the same ends. In turn, this possibility highlights the special characteristics of the PMC that subverts ordinary mechanisms both for ascribing responsibility and for ensuring compliance with existing legal obligations under IHL and human rights law.

D. Superior Responsibility in PMC Regulation

It is striking that the principle of superior responsibility is notably absent from the ICoC developed specifically to apply directly to PMCs,[249] but

245 ibid 217.

246 Frulli (n 183) 462–65.

247 *Prosecutor v Kordic and Cerkez (Trials Chamber)* (n 202) [840].

248 ibid 838.

249 A severely diluted provision that hints at the doctrine is included: Swiss Federal Department of Foreign Affairs (n 37) 6(d). Furthermore, a reporting requirement that may satisfy the civilian threshold for effective control has also been incorporated: ibid 24 and 28; the specific reporting requirement is extremely circumscribed, and primarily internal between the PMC and the client: reports 'will be provided to the Client and, to the extent necessary, to Competent Authorities' very much as an afterthought: ibid 63; finally, command

that it has been explicitly incorporated into both the Montreux Document and the Draft Convention which applies to States. The latter reiterate in identical terms that military and civilian officials and PMC directors and managers *may* be liable for the international crimes committed by PMC contractors 'under their effective authority and control, as a result of their failure to properly exercise control over them'.[250] The instruments differ, however, upon the role played by the contract in the doctrine. The Document, which is intended only to clarify existing obligations under international law, explicitly states that: 'Superior responsibility is not engaged solely by virtue of a contract'.[251] The Draft Convention, which is intended to be treaty-based and State-centric, provides that: 'No clause of the contract shall be interpreted as permitting evasion of responsibility on the part of supervisors'.[252] It can be deduced that contemporary international law does not consider the contractual nexus as sufficient to establish command responsibility, but equally, perhaps, that it cannot be relied upon to avoid liability.[253] As discussed above, the relationship of subordination, which is particularly difficult to establish in the civilian realm, is actively subverted by the contractual relationship. Commenting on the Document, Ottavio Quirico suggests that the capacity of PMC managers to prevent and punish under the doctrine could be satisfied by their role is assessing the IHL compliance of the activities of their PMC contractors and to suspend and remove those suspected of wrongdoing.[254] These are very tenuous powers when juxtaposed against those of military commanders who are capable of preventing and punishing wrongdoing.

Indeed, while the power of submitting reports may satisfy the criteria for civilian supervisory responsibility, the hierarchical superior-subordinate relationship as indicated by the capacity for effective control, is clearly lacking within the structure of the civilian corporation, including the PMC. Although this may be per se unproblematic in more benign contexts, this corporate structure organises lethal force in the form of the modern PMC: this in turn results in the heightened civilian standards of the command responsibility doctrine applying to a militarised (as opposed to purely civilian) organisation. The contingent nature upon which the

responsibility is likely to be obviated because of the responsibility to establish a 'corporate culture' that 'promotes awareness of and adherence … to the principles of this Code' as this suggests the lack of the requisite superior-subordinate relationship: ibid 27.

[250] Montreux Document (n 36); Gómez del Prado (n 143) 28, art 7(3). Emphasis added.

[251] Montreux Document (n 36).

[252] Gómez del Prado (n 143) 28.

[253] This latter deduction is uncertain because it might constitute an additional obligation specifically *created* by the Draft Convention. See generally the discussion above on passive impunity through contract law.

[254] Quirico, 'The Criminal Responsibility of Private Military and Security Company Personnel under International Humanitarian Law' (n 230) 436–37; referring to Montreux Document (n 36).

doctrine is included within the Document and the Draft Convention will perpetuate passive impunity for PMC contractors. Indeed, passive impunity will be generated insofar as the Document and the Draft Convention articulate the possibility for the responsibility of unlawful PMC activities to flow upwards to the managerial level of the PMC or to the civilian and military leaders engaged with the PMC without a clear indication of how this might operate in practice. This section has shown that, despite the very concrete possibility of applying the doctrine of command responsibility to the PMC, this capacity is subverted by the interaction between the characteristics of the doctrine and those of the PMC. The doctrine of command responsibility, which is already biased towards convicting lower- to mid-level military personnel, will continue to erect substantial barriers against applying to civilians, including PMC contractors, even if they fulfil roles that are very similar to those of occupied by military personnel.

Beyond these immediate conclusions, the continued ambiguity surrounding command responsibility for PMC contractors implies that customary IHL, which requires that armed forces are under responsible command, may be violated.[255] Furthermore, because responsible command is a characteristic that determines potential PMC membership in the armed forces of a State,[256] and may determine entitlement to privileged belligerency status,[257] the question of command responsibility for PMC contractors has significant ramifications beyond its direct application.

VI. CONCLUSION: THE PERPETUATION OF PASSIVE PRIVATE MILITARY COMPANY IMPUNITY

This chapter has charted an array of seemingly disparate issues that are united by their propensity to generate passive impunity for the PMC and its contractors. While the examples given above by no means comprise of an exhaustive list, especially considering the general imperceptibility of passive impunity mechanisms, they do demonstrate the operation of a range of these devices and their cumulative effect. A common denominator that can be identified is the inability of the existing legal system to recognise, let alone remedy, the challenge wrought to the regulatory system by providing or procuring military services on a private corporate basis. This lack of recognition leads, in turn, to the PMC being precluded from the very mechanisms that have been established and which are relied upon to facilitate the flow of responsibility for organised violence

[255] r 4: Henckaerts and Doswald-Beck, *Customary IHL: Rules* (n 190) 14–17. See also Hague II, art 1(1), GC III, art 4(2)(a) and API, arts 86–87.

[256] Tonkin (n 26) 86–90.

[257] M-L Tougas, 'Some Comments and Observations on the Montreux Document' (2009) 12 *Yearbook of International Humanitarian Law* 321, 331 and 338 respectively.

in order to prevent situations of impunity. This may account for the seemingly paradoxical situation whereby the organisation of the PMC can be demonstrated to breach the requirements imposed by human rights and IHL, yet are able to maintain the claim to be a law-abiding corporation providing legitimate services.

The exclusion of the PMC from the very systems that are relied upon to impute wrongdoing provides powerful forms of self-perpetuation for these passive impunity mechanisms. The implication is that the operation of these passive impunity mechanisms does not only prevent the ascription of responsibility for violations of human rights and IHL to the PMC, but goes further to impede the very possibility to reform the system. In other words, passive impunity mechanisms do not only shield the PMC from allegations of wrongdoing, but also reinforce themselves by guarding against changes to the system itself. The internal consistency of the legal system is thus reinforced because the problems introduced by the PMC remain outside its remit, thereby ensuring that the operation of passive impunity mechanisms continue into the future.

Because the established system for attributing wrongdoing is averted, there is little opportunity for the PMC to be subjected to a process through which it can be found to have done wrong, leading to three main effects. First, this opens up the possibility for denial, indeed the third iteration of interpretive denial presented in this chapter. The PMC had first neutralised mercenary and pseudo-mercenary activities into private military activities within the sphere of legitimate security company operations, and second, converted human rights violations to breaches of contract through the prism of contract law regulation. In this third iteration, the self-perpetuating nature of passive impunity mechanisms suggests both that it is simply not possible for the PMC to be found to do wrong, and that the system that effectively immunises the PMC from responsibility will be maintained. Together, this self-fulfils the prophecy of industry advocates that the PMC is a legitimate business operation that lawfully provides valuable security services, thereby providing broad denial to allegations of wrongdoing by the PMC.

Second, because the existing legal system lacks the ability to comprehend PMC-produced injuries there is no impetus to change or adapt the system in order to better cover the challenges that are introduced by PMC. Bluntly put, if the problem cannot be perceived or identified, there will be little drive to search for a solution. This has the effect of leaving PMC activity to be tangentially regulated through its nexus with the State, thereby exacerbating responsibility issues where PMCs provide martial services horizontally to non-State entities such as other corporations or private individuals. Injury suffered under such conditions will be even more difficult to redress because the lack of State action will foreclose existing remedial avenues.

Third, passive impunity mechanisms understate the injury and harm caused by PMC activity, paving the way towards industry self-regulation. Passive impunity mechanisms exclude the PMC from responsibility-ascribing mechanisms, suggesting that there will be few instances in which it will be determined to have done wrong. This exclusion thus underlies the impression that the PMC does not generate unlawful outcomes, in turn justifying lighter touch approaches to regulation. Chapter six delves into greater detail concerning the future of PMC impunity arising from the inadequacies of developing systems of regulation, so it is sufficient to note here that passive impunity mechanisms may support and reinforce the development and adoption of weak forms of industry regulation.

This last observation reiterates the cumulative nature of passive impunity mechanisms demonstrated in this chapter. The adoption of the corporate mantle by the PMC availed it of passive impunity mechanisms both in its own right as well as those that are facilitated through contract law. These contractual relations were then employed in turn to subvert the operation of important responsibility-ascribing mechanisms that are embodied by the doctrine of command responsibility. The avoidance of existing responsibility-ascribing mechanisms then justifies the development of weaker mechanisms because the nature and gravity of private military harm is distorted. This cumulative character of the passive impunity mechanisms enjoyed by the PMC is particularly astounding, suggesting that only a part of the entire process has been identified here: indeed, it may be that the whole process has not yet fully unfurled.

At the core of passive impunity mechanisms available for the PMC is the adoption of inappropriate forms of civilian organisation towards martial or violent ends. In many ways, existing international law has resolved the responsibility problem arising from the use of organised force by segregating the separate spheres of JAB and JIB to reflect the relative areas of autonomy and discretion between the State and its armed forces. It has also developed a sophisticated doctrine of command responsibility which has three broad functions: to elaborate upon the duties and responsibilities of the commander as well as the subordinates; to incentivise, perhaps even ensure oversight and compliance with IHL; and to enable the effective prevention and punishment of transgressions against IHL. The IHL requirement that armed units are bonded together under a command that is responsible to a State that is party to a conflict thus serves two purposes: first, it treats the unit as an instrument of the commander, who is ultimately responsible, within his powers, to ensure compliance with IHL; and second, it ensures that a State accrues responsibility for that unit for the purposes of international law.

Fulfilling these legal requirements would have the effect of resolving the passive impunity mechanisms described in this chapter. While IHL is not self-executing with the result that the individual often has no direct claim for breaches,[258] to the extent that IHL overlaps with human rights law the individual may have a remedy under the latter for substantive IHL claims. While this remains an imperfect system, the structure of IHL ensures that the flows of responsibility are relatively clear and established: whether or not this responsibility is called to action in reality is another matter. In the context of passive impunity, however, this realisation raises an implication that becomes especially disconcerting insofar as it points to wider defects in the ordinary legal process.

It is abundantly clear that international law requires that organised armed force is to be structured along specific lines, and these requirements are clearly pronounced.[259] In turn, these requirements serve to facilitate the flow of responsibility in order to avoid situations of alleged impunity. The clarity and purpose of these requirements raise the deeper problem of how they can be avoided or circumvented, with little voiced objection, by a form of organised armed force that specifically contradict all of the tenets embodied by these requirements. That this was possible with the introduction of the PMC suggests that it was not possible to formulate objections in legal terms or alternatively to object on points of law to the corporate organisation of armed force. Thus, the problem is deeper than the inability of the law to recognise and remedy the challenges brought forth by the PMC: instead, it may be that the law legitimates, and perhaps even legalises, a practice that would otherwise be unambiguously unlawful. Unpacking this observation, it appears that passive impunity mechanisms subsist in the space between legal orders. In the context of the PMC presented in this chapter, this tension appears to be between the restrictive ordering of human rights law and the permissive ordering of corporate and contract law. Thus, the passive impunity mechanisms enjoyed by the PMC emerge from the proclivity towards collusion that is empowered by the horizontal nature of contractual relations, insofar as these circumvent the reliance upon hierarchical relations characterised by effective control at the core of IHL.

Finally, passive impunity constitutes at most only half of the issue because it is supplemented by active impunity mechanisms discussed in the next chapter. Thus, even in rare residual situations where avenues to legal action remain open—where passive impunity mechanisms no longer thwart the possibility of a claim—there are overlapping and often interlocking mechanisms embedded within these processes that will frustrate the award of substantive remedies for severe violations of IHL and human rights law. Thus, the prospect for impunity still lurks even where passive impunity mechanisms are resolved such that responsibility processes can be initiated.

[258] Ronzitti, 'Access to Justice and Compensation for Violations of the Law of War' (n 139) 110–12.

[259] Under API, art 43, as reflected in rr 152 and 153 of customary IHL: see Henckaerts and Doswald-Beck (n 190).

5

Active Private Military Company Impunity

I. INTRODUCTION

THIS CHAPTER EXPOUNDS upon the idea of active impunity which describes situations in which the ordinary juridical process is suspended or otherwise avoided, making these largely issues of exceptionalism. In addition to the types of passive impunity which are incorporated into the very structure of the ordinary juridical process, complementary active impunity mechanisms operate to prevent the success of claims that have managed to make their way into legal fora. Thus, even in situations where the law appears on face value to be able to overcome impunity, this potential may still be thwarted by active impunity devices.

Several of the avenues through which the PMC may be exempted from the application of the law through active impunity mechanisms are demonstrated in detail. First, there is the axiomatic impossibility of corporate criminal responsibility in jurisdictions that do not provide for corporate criminal liability. The result is that corporations are immunised from the application of criminal law within these jurisdictions purely on the basis of formal, legal, status. Thus, the corporate status of PMCs provides an absolute shield against criminal law in those jurisdictions. Additionally, while PMC contractors as individuals remain criminally liable, they benefit from active impunity mechanisms in a relative sense because certain barriers are erected against their indictment when juxtaposed against their military counterparts. Second, the jurisprudence governing civil remedies has been developed by the courts to produce paradoxes that prevent the possibility of successful claims against PMCs by the direct victims of their activity.

These barriers are especially insidious because the initial amenability of PMCs to suit creates the illusion of accountability and access to remedies. Given the veneration of legal procedures, the failure of claims made in court against the PMC implies the negation of any wrongdoing on the part of that PMC. Conflating admissibility issues with questions of merit, substantive allegations are left largely unexamined as the claims fail for a variety of legalistic, usually jurisdictional, reasons. This chapter demonstrates, somewhat shockingly, how the PMC is insulated both from criminal liability and exonerated from civil liability for allegations of serious human rights abuses upon technicalities.

II. ACTIVE IMPUNITY FROM CRIMINAL LAW: *SOCIETAS DELINQUERE NON POTEST*

While the corporation in law developed independent juridical personhood and was invested with rights in parity with natural persons, it was not imbued with a critical faculty: the ability to commit crimes. William Blackstone wrote that:

> [A corporation] can neither maintain, or be made defendant, to, an action of battery or such like personal injuries; for a corporation can neither beat, nor be beaten, in it's body politic. A corporation cannot commit treason, or felony, or other crime, in it's corporate capacity: though it's members may, in their distinct individual capacities. Neither is it capable of suffering a traitor's, or felon's punishment, for it is not liable to corporal penalties.[1]

This is the doctrine of *societas delinquere non potest*, which holds as an axiom in many jurisdictions that corporations cannot commit crimes.[2] Thus, while the law invests the corporation with the benefits of independent personhood, it simultaneously imbues it with a powerful form of active impunity by suspending the application of criminal law, thereby shielding juridical persons from society's most condemnatory instrument. While some jurisdictions enable corporations to be criminally responsible,[3] the lack of international harmonisation has meant that international criminal law only applies to natural persons.[4]

[1] W Blackstone, *Commentaries On The Laws Of England*, vol 1 (Clarendon Press, 1765) 464.

[2] This position recalls the aforementioned fiction theory of the corporation which were rights-but-not-duty bearing units.

[3] The United Kingdom has extended the law on corporate manslaughter through the Corporate Manslaughter and Corporate Homicide Act 2007 (c 19). Under s 1(1):

> An organisation to which this section applies is guilty of an offence if the way in which its activities are managed or organised—
>
> (a) causes a person's death, and
> (b) amounts to a gross breach of a relevant duty of care owed by the organisation to the deceased.

Before the enactment of this legislation, corporate manslaughter was recognised in England and Wales, gathering momentum with the capsize of the *Herald of Free Enterprise*. In *R v P & O European Ferries (Dover) Ltd* [1991] 93 Cr App R 72, Turner J was guided by New Zealand law and held that 'a person who is the embodiment of a corporation and acting for the purposes of the corporation doing the act or omission which caused the death, the corporation as well as the person may also be found guilty of manslaughter', at 88–89. For a development of this area, see C Wells, *Corporations and Criminal Responsibility* (Oxford University Press, 2001) 106–26.

[4] The Rome Statute of the International Criminal Court, 17 July 1998, art 25(1) provides: 'The Court shall have jurisdiction over *natural persons* pursuant to this Statute'. Emphasis added. The failed proposals by the French to expand jurisdiction over juridical persons that mirrored the London Charter for the International Military Tribunal are discussed below.

The active impunity de jure enjoyed by the corporation is further compounded by de facto impunity arising from the difficulty of appropriately punishing abstract juridical persons. Indeed, this difficulty might at least partially justify the refusal to ascribe criminal responsibility to the corporation; Blackstone clearly associated the impossibility of corporate criminal conduct with the absurdity of physical punishment for an abstract entity. This was more famously formulated by 'Lord Chancellor Thurlow [who] said that Corporations have neither bodies to be punished, nor souls to be condemned; they therefore do as they like'.[5] What is often obscured in such claims, however, is that appropriate punishments may actually be available. Among the most severe sanctions are the charter revocation laws that exist in many jurisdictions 'that permit governments to dissolve a corporation, or seek a court order to dissolve it, if the government believes that the corporation has grossly violated the public interest'.[6] This has been expressed by Eliot Spitzer, then New York Attorney General:

> When a corporation is convicted of repeated felonies that harm or endanger the lives of human beings or destroy our environment, the corporation should be put to death, its corporate existence ended, and its assets taken and sold at public auction.[7]

The availability of charter revocation as a legal punishment for corporate misconduct, however, necessarily blurs the line between de facto and de jure impunity; because charter revocation is 'a well-kept secret'[8] and applied in extremely rare circumstances, the specific source of this impunity remains unclear. Thus, Lord Chancellor Thurlow's famous quip, in reinforcing the notion that corporations cannot be punished, may be a self-fulfilling prophecy with the unintended effect of justifying the active impunity enjoyed by corporations.

At root, the question as to whether juridical persons are capable of bearing responsibility for crime may hinge upon the applicable notions of autonomy and agency that underpin concepts of criminal responsibility. Indeed, Michael Moore has argued that the application of criminal

[5] J Poynder, *Literary Extracts from English and Other Works Collected During Half a Century Together with Some Original Matter*, vol 1 (John Hatchard, 1844) 268.

[6] J Bakan, *The Corporation: The Pathological Pursuit of Profit and Power* (Constable & Robinson, 2005) 157; see also M Ramirez, 'The Science Fiction of Corporate Criminal Liability: Containing the Machine through the Corporate Death Penalty' (2005) 47 *Arizona Law Review* 933. Charter revocation does not share the moral objections of capital punishment and may also be reversible if imposed erroneously.

[7] The difficulty with this approach is that it is contingent upon a conviction, which may be precluded by the *societas delinquere non potest* principle: G Parrish, 'Killing Corporations' *Seattle Weekly News* (14 July 1999) www.seattleweekly.com/1999-07-14/news/killing-corporations/. See also R Mokhiber, 'The Death Penalty for Corporations Comes of Age' (1998) 12 *Business Ethics* 7–8.

[8] Mokhiber, 'The Death Penalty for Corporations Comes of Age' (n 7) quoting Robert Benson.

responsibility to the corporation is fundamentally mistaken: it distorts the basic conceptual architecture of responsibility that is intrinsically associated with moral blameworthiness, and hence applies exclusively to natural persons.[9] While there is nothing intrinsically problematic with adopting this approach, it is inconsistent with the legal personhood granted to the corporation. To be coherent, Michael Moore's approach must deny parity of status between juridical and natural persons, rather than preclude juridical persons from bearing criminal responsibility. Put differently, abstract juridical persons that are considered incapable of perpetrating crime must concomitantly be understood as inanimate tools wielded by natural persons who appropriately bear the responsibility for the consequences of their use. While Michael Moore's position may be tenable under different circumstances, it lacks internal consistency with the claim that corporations are juridical *persons*, that is, units that are capable of bearing rights and obligations. The idea of the corporation as a tool is subtly resilient to the point that it has been used to justify the imposition of legal liability. As Harold Koh points out, however: '[t]he commonsense fact remains that if states and individuals can be held liable under international law, then so too should corporations, for the simple reason that both states and individuals *act through* corporations'.[10] Connecting active and passive dimensions of impunity, the prosecution of a company 'can be appropriate if the organisational structure makes it difficult to establish the criminal responsibility of a particular individual'.[11] The effect is that while corporate criminal responsibility can potentially compensate for passive impunity mechanisms that dissociate the individual responsibility of natural persons, the active impunity mechanism that suspends corporate criminal liability prevents this avenue for overcoming passive impunity, in effect constructing an impunity paradox.

In relation to PMC impunity, the Draft Convention proposed by the UN Working Group on the Use of Mercenaries specifically required would-be State Parties 'to establish the liability of legal persons and entities' which 'shall be without prejudice to the criminal liability of the natural persons who have actually committed the offences'.[12] If these provisions were implemented, corporate liability would be established as a parallel to

[9] M Moore, *Causation and Responsibility: An Essay in Law, Morals, and Metaphysics* (Oxford University Press, 2010) 246–47, 623.

[10] H Koh, 'Separating Myth from Reality about Corporate Responsibility Litigation' (2004) 7 *Journal of International Economic Law* 263, 265. Emphasis original.

[11] C Lehnardt, 'Individual Liability of Private Military Personnel under International Criminal Law' (2008) 19 *European Journal of International Law* 1015, 1033.

[12] J Gómez del Prado, 'Report of the Working Group on the Use of Mercenaries as a Means of Violating Human Rights and Impeding the Exercise of the Right of Peoples to Self-Determination with the Draft of a Possible Convention on Private Military and Security Companies (PMSCs) for Consideration and Action by the Human Rights Council' (UNGA, 2010) A/HRC/15/25, art 20(1) and (3) respectively.

individual criminal liability for the offences enumerated within the Draft Convention, thus partially overcoming the impunity paradox. Furthermore, as State Parties are required to ensure that legal persons are subjected to 'effective, proportionate and dissuasive criminal and non-criminal sanctions', it is clear that the Draft Convention envisages appropriate corporate punishments to enforce the establishment of liability to overcome impunity.[13] The crucial weakness of the Draft Convention, however, is its status as a (nascent) international instrument: the liability of legal persons remains '[s]ubject to the legal principles of the State Party' and the provision stipulates that this 'liability may be criminal, civil or administrative, or a combination of these'.[14] While these obligations under the Draft Convention would rectify active impunity in jurisdictions that recognise the criminal responsibility of legal persons, its effect will be significantly curtailed in those that do not. The explicit provision establishing the liability of legal persons suggests one avenue to overcome the active impunity enjoyed by the PMC; even in jurisdictions that limit sanctions to civil or administrative liability, this liability of legal persons can be enforced. This opens the possibility for two forms of interpretative denial. First, civil or administrative sanctions would allow PMCs to claim that they have been subjected to accountability mechanisms that have overcome impunity. Second, because criminal sanctions cannot be imposed, PMCs can claim that they have not been convicted for any criminal activity.

A. International Criminal Law and the Juridical Person

At first flush, the juridical personhood of the corporation appears to render it susceptible to the operation of international laws that apply to the person; because the corporation possesses equal status and enjoys similar rights as private individuals, they should be subjected to comparable obligations. Andrew Clapham puts aptly:

> As long as we admit that individuals have rights and duties under customary international human rights law and international humanitarian law, we have to admit that legal persons may also possess the international legal personality necessary to enjoy some rights, and conversely to be prosecuted or held accountable for violations of the relevant international duties.[15]

This parity of reasoning is supported by the effectiveness principle; again in the words of Andrew Clapham, 'if international law is to be *effective* in protecting human rights, *everyone* should be prohibited from assisting

[13] ibid art 20(4).
[14] ibid art 20(2).
[15] A Clapham, *Human Rights Obligations of Non-State Actors* (Oxford University Press, 2006) 79.

governments in violating those principles, or indeed prohibited from violating such principles themselves'.[16] These are strong justifications for ensuring parity of legal obligations for the corporate juridical person and supporting the developing mechanisms concerning the human rights obligations of corporations.[17]

These same arguments can be deployed to support the application of ICL to the corporation. Although corporations are generally incapable of bearing criminal responsibility, because ICL targets the person, their juridical personhood opens the possibility that corporations might be subjected to its principles.[18] Two points quickly stifle this potential. First, the juridical person is in this case an association of natural persons; as such, the application of ICL may constitute a form of collective punishment that had fallen out of favour in the aftermath of Nuremberg. Second, the position of the corporation is unclear within the 'schizophrenia' of ICL, as Steven Ratner points out:

> [I]nternational criminal law is … cursed by an even more profound and innate schizophrenia—that between international law and criminal law. International criminal law involves the inculpation of *individuals*, but is developed and enforced by the actions of *states*. It must address, and reconcile, the dichotomies between its two sets of constituent parts: *international law's focus upon the obligations of states versus criminal law's concern with the obligations of individuals*.[19]

While this is clearly a general structural problem of ICL, it has acute effects upon the corporation, which now share significant characteristics within the realms of both international and criminal law, but which are unambiguously regulated by neither. The transnational effects of corporations are not captured within international law, and there are the aforementioned difficulties with ascribing criminal law to the corporation.

It is clear the ICC does not possess jurisdiction over juridical persons.[20] During the negotiations, however, France submitted a proposal to include criminal organisations within the jurisdiction of the Court: 'When the crime was committed by a natural person on behalf or with the assent of a group or organization of every kind, the Court may declare that this group or organization is a criminal organization'.[21] Fines, forfeiture of proceeds,

[16] ibid 80. Emphasis added.

[17] See esp OHCHR, 'The Corporate Responsibility to Protect Human Rights: An Interpretative Guide' (2012) www.ohchr.org/Documents/Publications/HR.PUB.12.2_En.pdf.

[18] S Seck, 'Collective Responsibility and Transnational Corporate Conduct' in T Isaacs and R Vernon (eds), *Accountability for Collective Wrongdoing* (Cambridge University Press, 2011) 140–41.

[19] S Ratner, 'The Schizophrenias of International Criminal Law' (1998) 33 *Texas International Law Journal* 237, 251. Emphasis added.

[20] Art 25(1) stipulates that 'The Court shall have jurisdiction over natural persons pursuant to this Statute': Rome Statute of the International Criminal Court, 17 July 1998

[21] UN Rome Proceedings, 'Proposal Submitted by France: Article 23 Individual Criminal Responsibility: Legal Persons'. This closely mirrors the approach adopted at Nuremberg, below.

property and assets obtained by the criminal conduct and appropriate forms of reparation were to be the forms of punishment.[22] The Working Group on General Principles of Criminal Law subsequently proposed a narrower jurisdiction by restricting juridical persons to mean 'a corporation whose concrete, real or dominant objective is seeking private profit or benefit, and not a State or other public body in the exercise of State authority',[23] thus limiting this provision exclusively for the corporations. Kai Ambos writes that:

> Despite this rather limited liability, the proposal was rejected basically for several quite convincing reasons. The inclusion of collective liability would deflect from the Court's jurisdictional focus, which is on individuals. Furthermore, the Court would be confronted with serious and ultimately overwhelming problems of evidence. In addition, there are not yet universally recognized common standards for corporate liability; in fact, it is not even recognized in all major criminal law systems. Consequently, the absence of corporate criminal liability in many States would render the complementary concept unworkable.[24]

The problem with this critique is, however, that the proposed jurisdiction granted over the juridical person is both subordinate to and contingent upon the natural person. This is made explicit in the Working Paper: '*Without prejudice* to any individual criminal responsibility of natural persons … the Court *may also* have jurisdiction over a juridical person'.[25] Furthermore, the natural person must have been 'in a position of control within the juridical person', the crime must have been 'committed by the natural person acting on behalf of and with the explicit consent of that juridical person' and '[t]he natural person has been convicted of the crime charged'.[26] These restrictions upon the jurisdiction of the Court over the juridical person, when coupled with the forms of punishment, indicate that the purpose is not to depart from the individual responsibility of natural persons, but rather to facilitate restitution for criminal gain and compensation for criminal damage and injury. This proposal by France was not incorporated within the Rome Statute;[27] it is ironic that the focus upon indicting individuals for international crimes creates and perpetuates situations of impunity where these crimes are committed though corporate action.

[22] ibid.

[23] UN Rome Proceedings, 'Working Paper on Article 23' paras 5–6.

[24] K Ambos, 'General Principles of Criminal Law in the Rome Statute' (1999) 10 *Criminal Law Forum* 1, 7.

[25] UN Rome Proceedings, 'Working Paper on Article 23' (n 23) paras 5–6. Emphasis added.

[26] ibid 5(b)(c) and (d).

[27] Andrew Clapham notes that the 'discussions had become bogged down in questions of how various national penal systems would accommodate, what was for them, the alien concept of corporate criminal responsibility. The theoretical issue of the subjectivity of corporations in international law was not raised': Clapham, *Human Rights Obligations of Non-State Actors* (n 15) 246; see generally 244–47.

The source of the failure to recognise corporate criminal liability is, according to Geoffrey Robertson, Nuremberg, where the focus on individual criminal responsibility led instead to the trial of natural persons seen to represent the impugned corporate entity.[28] In this regard, the Allies had sought to indict civilian industry leaders, in particular members of the Krupp family that had dominated German armament production, for facilitating aggressive war.[29] There were, however, practical problems with indicting the senile Gustav, and objections to his substitution with Alfried: 'The upshot of this embarrassing series of prosecutorial missteps was that the Allies considered a prosecution of industrialists to be essential, but the IMT did not include any members of private German industry among its ... defendants'.[30] This meant that the industrialist trials were relegated to the subsequent trials conducted separately by the Allies pursuant to Control Council Law No 10 that governed the occupations' treatment of war criminals.[31] It is important to note, however, that these prosecutions were of individuals: the United States prosecuted 23 individuals who had served on the Farben board in *Krauch*[32] and 12 individuals who were associated with the armaments manufacturer in *Krupp*;[33] the juridical persons of I.G. Farben or the Krupp company were not indicted. Despite this, Steven Ratner recognised that '[a]lthough the universe of international criminal law does not reveal any prosecutions of corporations per se, an important precedent nonetheless shows the willingness of key legal actors to contemplate corporate responsibility at the international level'.[34]

Indeed, the infamous dictum from the Nuremberg judgment that 'Crimes against international law are committed by men, not by abstract entities, and only by punishing individuals who commit such crimes can the provisions of international law be enforced'[35] is often deployed to support the idea that ICL exclusively imposes individual criminal responsibility.[36] By tracing the origins of this understanding to its roots in the IMT at

[28] G Robertson, *Crimes Against Humanity: The Struggle For Global Justice* (Penguin, 2006) 186–91. This was the approach adopted in the aforementioned Proposal by France.

[29] A Danner, 'The Nuremberg Industrialist Prosecutions and Aggressive War' (2005) 46 *Virginia Journal of International Law* 651, 655–57.

[30] ibid 657.

[31] ibid 658–68.

[32] ibid 660–65.

[33] ibid 665–67.

[34] S Ratner, 'Corporations and Human Rights: A Theory of Legal Responsibility' (2001) 111 *Yale Law Journal* 443, 477.

[35] *United States v Goering* (1946) 6 FRD 69 (IMT) 110.

[36] There are undercurrents of reversal in the academic literature in this area: A Clapham, 'Extending International Criminal Law beyond the Individual to Corporations and Armed Opposition Groups' (2008) 6 *Journal of International Criminal Justice* 899, 899–926; B Swart et al, 'Discussion: International Trends towards Establishing Some Form of Punishment for Corporations' (2008) 6 *Journal of International Criminal Justice* 947.

Nuremberg, however, it is possible to argue that the recognition of individual criminal responsibility for international crimes was intended to create an *extension* to the restrictiveness of international law as it then stood, rather than to justify limitation to its applicability exclusively to natural persons. The context clarifies this intention: the submission to which the dictum responded was

> that international law is concerned with the actions of sovereign states, *and provides no punishment for individuals*; and further, that where the act in question is an act of state, *those who carry it out are not personally responsible*, but are protected by the doctrine of the sovereignty of the State.[37]

Seen in this light, the assertion that international crimes are committed by natural persons is designed to circumvent the 'Act of State' defence.[38] This deployed the juridical personhood of the State as a shield against individual criminal liability that would effectively give rise to impunity for their perpetration. This view is reinforced by Chief Prosecutor Robert Jackson's opening address:

> Of course, the idea that a state, any more than a corporation, commits crimes is a fiction. Crimes always are committed only by persons. While it is quite proper to employ the fiction of responsibility of a state or corporation for the purpose of imposing a collective liability, *it is quite intolerable to let such a legalism become the basis of personal immunity*.[39]

Prior to the Nuremberg Trials, individual liability for international law obligations was a contentious matter,[40] and the only unambiguous actors on the international plane were the States themselves. Thus, this dictum reaffirms an exception to this orthodox position by recognising individual responsibility for violations of international law. This individual criminal responsibility was envisaged to be borne by the leadership echelon possessed of 'broad discretion and exercised great power. Their responsibility is correspondingly great and may not be shifted to that fictional being, "the State", which can not be produced for trial, can not testify, and can not be sentenced'.[41] Moreover, Jackson's interest in effecting this shift

[37] *United States v Goering* (n 35) 110. Emphasis added.

[38] Q Wright, 'The Law of the Nuremberg Trial' (1947) 41 *American Journal of International Law* 38, 70–71.

[39] Office of the United States Chief of Counsel for Prosecution of Axis Criminality, *Nazi Conspiracy and Aggression*, vol 1 (United States Government Printing Office, 1946) 167–69 www.loc.gov/rr/frd/Military_Law/pdf/NT_Nazi_Vol-I.pdf. Emphasis added.

[40] The IMT cited the US Supreme Court judgment of Stone CJ to this effect in *Ex p Quirin* (1942) 317 US 1 (US Supreme Court) 27–28. The prohibitions available for certain acts were historically limited to States, which held the legal obligation to prevent their nationals from perpetrating those prohibited actions: see A Cassese, *International Criminal Law* (Oxford University Press, 2008) 4–5.

[41] Office of the United States Chief of Counsel for Prosecution of Axis Criminality, *Nazi Conspiracy and Aggression*, vol 1 (n 39) 169.

away from criminalising the State arises from the desire to avert future warfare:

> An International Law which operates only on states can be enforced only by war because the most practicable method of coercing a state is warfare … The only answer to recalcitrance was impotence or war. Only sanctions which reach individuals can peacefully and effectively be enforced: Hence, the principle of the criminality of aggressive war is implemented by the Charter with the principle of personal responsibility.[42]

In summary, two crucial points emerge: first the 'abstract entities' mentioned can be understood as States, rather than corporations (or other associations or bodies); and second that the dictum may be interpreted as expanding, rather than constricting, the categories of actors which are capable of being held responsible for violations of international law. Seen from this perspective overcoming impunity may have been the lynchpin of early developments in ICL, which is supported by the Charter of the IMT itself.[43] Although Article 6 provides that the IMT was established to try and punish persons who 'whether as individuals or as members of organizations' committed the specified crimes of the Charter. Article 9, however, enables the declaration by the IMT of 'that the group or organization of which the individual was a member was a criminal organization'. Article 10 clarified the purpose; the determination of criminal organisation was a short-cut that enabled national authorities to prosecute individuals for their membership of such criminal organisations. The centrality of individual criminal responsibility at Nuremberg, however, remains unequivocal.[44] Whether the focus of ICL on individual criminal responsibility need necessarily impair the recognition of corporate criminal liability can be questioned; indeed corporate criminal responsibility could facilitate rather than impair the fulfilment of the purposes of ICL. The subordinate and contingent relationship between juridical and natural persons as evinced in the balance struck by the aforementioned Rome Conference proposal by France illustrates that this relationship is not zero-sum, but can instead be complementary. Building upon Nuremberg, however, was the fact that corporate criminality was not a significant issue raised before the ICTY and ICTR;[45] this resulted in a dearth of precedent for corporate criminal responsibility during the drafting stages of the Rome Statute, which has essentially ended the question.

[42] ibid 168.

[43] Charter of the International Military Tribunal—Annex to the Agreement for the prosecution and punishment of the major war criminals of the European Axis ('London Agreement') 8 August 1945.

[44] Agreement for the Prosecution and Punishment of major War Criminals of the European Axis, and Establishing the Charter of the International Military Tribunal (I.M.T) 1951, 82 UNTS 279.

[45] Robertson, *Crimes Against Humanity* (n 28) 187.

It is ironic that ICL, which had emerged as an expansion of international law to encompass individual criminal liability as a departure from the exclusive liability of States, subsequently justified its restriction to natural persons upon this same expansion. It is particularly striking that the jurisdiction of ICL exclusively over natural persons has not been developed in a principled manner, but has rather been premised upon the prosecutorial preferences at Nuremberg and the inherited legal dogma concerning the nature and status of juridical persons. The individual criminal responsibility obsession of ICL obfuscates the crucial role played by collectives that both characterises and perpetrates international crime. While the notion of collective responsibility has been delegitimised in the aftermath of Nuremberg, a principled distinction may be justified where a collective has been ascribed separate and independent status as a juridical person. This is especially pressing where the corporation shields individual natural persons from criminal indictment, and complementarily, where the corporation segregates role responsibilities and generates irresponsibility that effectively precludes the conviction of those natural persons who are capable of bearing criminal responsibility. Corporate criminal responsibility needs to be developed because it can articulate and capture the additional dimension of organisation that characterise international crimes, as well as the simultaneously individual and collective nature of the corporate juridical person.

B. In the Docket of the United States Federal Courts

Turning away from the corporate immunity provided by international criminal law towards the PMC, the treatment of PMC contractors under US domestic law is particularly instructive for the legal structuring of impunity for three reasons. First, there is jurisdiction: the US is a significant home and hiring State for PMCs; has been involved with the administration of territory where PMCs have been active; and is the jurisdiction in which many PMCs are incorporated. This means that US federal courts have greater potential to hear cases concerning PMC misconduct. Second, and partly as a result of the first point, US federal courts have specifically pronounced judgment in a number of PMC cases which set precedent for future cases and which indicate how PMCs are likely to be treated. Moreover, because of the respectability of the US federal justice system, their judgments may have an influential comparative effect where courts in other jurisdictions hear PMC-related cases. Third, both criminal and civil legislation is appearing in the US that apparently seek to improve PMC accountability.

Despite these advantages, PMCs and their contractors continue to benefit from active impunity mechanisms. While the following sections elucidate the process of suspending the ordinary application of law, it should be stressed at the outset that PMCs and their contractors are often simply omitted from legal suits; for example, detainee abuse litigation arising out of Iraq and Afghanistan indicted only military and (political) civilian superiors.[46]

C. Active Impunity: Suspension of US Criminal Law for the PMC

The aforementioned *societas delinquere non potest* principle constitutes a mechanism of active impunity that absolves corporations from criminal responsibility, accounting for the complete absence of the PMC itself from criminal suits. Active impunity mechanisms also operate to alleviate PMC contractors from the ordinary legal process. As contractors are natural persons who are fully capable of bearing criminal responsibility, any absence of contractors relative to military personnel from criminal dockets signals the potential for active impunity. These are complementary to the passive impunity mechanisms associated with additional difficulties of securing a conviction where PMC contractors have been indicted, as embodied by *Paul Slough*, below.[47]

Active impunity from criminal law can be divided into jurisdictional and substantive barriers to its operation. The former category involves the exclusion of PMC contractors upon their status either as non-military personnel, or contingent upon the juridical status of their employers. The initial discrepancy within *military*, rather than federal, jurisdiction needs to be noted. US military personnel are charged with crimes under the Uniform Code of Military Justice (UCMJ).[48] The Supreme Court in *Reid* established a presumption against civilians being tried under military

[46] *In re: Iraq and Afghanistan Detainees Litigation* (2007) 479 FSupp2d 85 (US District Court for the District of Columbia). While it is not clear from the facts of the case whether PMC contractors were factually involved in the alleged abuses claimed by the plaintiffs, the presence of Janis Karpinski (commander of the 800th Military Police Brigade implicated in the Abu Ghraib scandal) as a defendant suggests that the suit omitted PMCs and their contractors in its focus upon military and political leaders. At any rate, the suit failed on numerous grounds.

[47] *US v Paul Slough* [2009] US District Court for the District of Columbia Criminal Action No: 08-0360, 677 FSupp2d 122; *US v Paul Slough* [2011] US Court of Appeals for the District of Columbia No 10-3006, 641 F3d 544.

[48] See generally K Huskey and S Sullivan, 'United States: Law and Policy Governing Private Military Contractors after 9/11' in C Bakker and M Sossai (eds), *Multilevel Regulation of Military and Security Contractors: The Interplay Between International, European and Domestic Norms* (Hart Publishing, 2012) 359–62.

jurisdiction, at least for capital crimes in peacetime.[49] Indeed, crimes committed by civilians are generally excluded from military jurisdiction; in *Solorio*, the Supreme Court upheld its consistent jurisprudence that the military *status* of the accused constituted the sole factor for the exercise of court martial jurisdiction over an offence.[50] Civilian exclusion from UCMJ jurisdiction is thus structurally in-built. While this is both necessary and justifiable where civilian and military roles are strictly segregated, it can no longer be tenable where PMC contractors fulfil inherently governmental functions.[51] In these situations, the exclusion of PMC contractors from UCMJ jurisdiction instead constitutes an active impunity mechanism thwarting trial for civilian misconduct hinged exclusively upon their non-military status. Framed differently, the civilian status of PMC contractors immunises them from suit under military law, despite their activities within the military sphere. Indeed, Katherin Chapman has argued that the UCMJ should supply the criminal law for PMCs as military courts would have fewer practical difficulties with evidence and investigation will be functioning adequately, and that possible constitutional issues can be overcome.[52]

Although the UCMJ was expanded in 2006 to encompass individuals 'accompanying an armed force in the field',[53] Kristine Huskey and Scott Sullivan note three remaining limitations: its constitutionality has not yet been challenged; there must be a direct connection or relationship of dependence between the civilian and the activities of the armed forces; and the civilian must be in the vicinity of actual hostilities.[54] In other words, even if the UCMJ overcomes constitutional challenge *à la Reid*, it may fail to cover PMC contractors who are not sufficiently integrated into military activities, who fulfil supporting roles, or who operate in non-conventional theatres, thereby immunising them from suit solely upon their civilian status.

[49] As the Court noted, subjecting civilians to the jurisdiction of military tribunals will deprive them of constitutionally protected rights in the Fifth and Sixth Amendments: *Reid v Covert* (1957) 354 US 1 (US Supreme Court) 3. As *Reid* concerned the conviction of a wife of a US serviceman for his murder, the facts are readily distinguished from those commonly found in cases concerning PMC contractors in situations of armed conflict who operate in parallel to military personnel.

[50] *Solorio v US* (1987) 483 US 435 (US Supreme Court) 439.

[51] See esp the discussion surrounding the term in the document preceding the Draft Convention: Gómez del Prado, 'Report of the Working Group on the Use of Mercenaries' (n 12) 82–84; see also art 9 of the Draft Convention which would prohibit the delegation or outsourcing of inherently State functions: ibid 29. Despite the continuing debate, it is fairly settled that interrogation, for example, is an inherently governmental task.

[52] K Chapman, 'The Untouchables: Private Military Contractors' Criminal Accountability under the UCMJ' (2010) 63 *Vanderbilt Law Review* 1047, 1066–79.

[53] Public Law 109-364 120 Stat 2083.

[54] Huskey and Sullivan, 'United States: Law and Policy Governing Private Military Contractors after 9/11' (n 48) 360–61.

Returning to federal jurisdiction, the Military Extraterritorial Jurisdiction Act 2000 (MEJA)[55] established federal court jurisdiction over civilians alleged to have committed criminal offences overseas. This jurisdiction applied only to individuals 'while employed by or accompanying the Armed Forces outside the United States … or while a member of the Armed Forces'.[56] The obvious limitation was that this only applied to contractors working for the Department of Defense such that jurisdiction of individuals under contract to other federal agencies remained barred. This flaw was partially rectified by the 2004 extension to MEJA,[57] but jurisdiction remains excluded for PMC contractors who are altogether unassociated with the Department of Defense.[58] The active impunity mechanism is clear; susceptibility to MEJA jurisdiction hinges arbitrarily upon the status of the entity contracting the PMC. Even after the 2004 extension, discrepancy in MEJA liability exists for contractors performing parallel functions contingent upon who they work for, potentially leading to discrepancies of jurisdiction within PMCs that perform a range of contracts.[59]

The substantive barrier persists within the categories of crime indicted under MEJA jurisdiction. With the notable exception of *Paul Slough*,[60] the cases enabled by MEJA have fallen short of the spectre of international crimes and instead concern offences within the sphere of domestic criminal law and which would not necessarily be remiss within civilian life.[61] Crucially, this is not due to a lack of serious allegations; the evidence

[55] Public Law 106–523 114 Stat 2488. The definitions of the terms used in the Act, however, curtail its jurisdiction to 'to the extent such employment relates to supporting the mission of the Department of Defense overseas'. See generally C Doyle, 'Civilian Extraterritorial Jurisdiction Act: Federal Contractor Criminal Liability Overseas' www.fas.org/sgp/crs/misc/R42358.pdf.

[56] ibid, per s 3261 (A)(1) and (2).

[57] National Defense Authorization Act. Public Law 108-375 118 Stat 1811, s 1088.

[58] See generally Huskey and Sullivan (n 48) 355–56.

[59] In the new indictment, *US v Paul Slough (Renewed Indictment)* [2013] District Court for the District of Columbia CR-08-360 (RCL) the defence lawyers have argued that MEJA should not apply because the contractors were under State Department contracts: E Tucker and F Frommer, 'New Charges in Blackwater Shootings' *Huffington Post* (17 October 2013) www.huffingtonpost.com/huff-wires/20131017/us--blackwater-prosecution/?utm_hp_ref=business&ir=business. Similarly in the UK, PMC contractors working for the MOD may be tried under military law: C Kinsey, personal communication 2 July 2012.

[60] *US v Paul Slough* (n 47). It should be noted, however, that the entire case went forward without having adequately addressed whether the federal courts have jurisdiction in the first place. This is because of the definitional technicality of the terms used in the Act which curtail its reach. The Blackwater guards were contracted to the US State Department, and there may be a question mark hanging over whether this is sufficient to satisfy the requirement in MEJA that 'such employment relates to supporting the mission of the Department of Defense overseas': J Stewart and S Gray, 'The Blackwater Trial: Part 2—Legal Issues' http://justsecurity.org/16807/blackwater-trial-part-2-legal-issues/.

[61] Examples of MEJA conviction include non-violent crime such as the possession of child pornography, and violent crimes such as abusive sexual contact and assault and attempted murder: Huskey and Sullivan (n 48) 357–58.

presented in chapter two illustrated a range of PMC misconduct attaining the mantle of international crime. This suggests that although MEJA constitutes a step towards overcoming impunity for PMC contractors committing crimes abroad, its effect is limited to improving accountability for crimes within the domestic sphere and to reconciling conflicts internal to the military establishment.[62]

The failure of criminal law to apply to PMC contractors is poignantly illustrated by the lack of criminal prosecutions for the PMC contractors involved with the torture and abuse of detainees at Abu Ghraib mentioned in chapter two. As the Court of Appeals for the DC Circuit found in *Saleh*:

> [A] number of American servicemen have already been subjected to criminal court-martial proceedings in relation to the events at Abu Ghraib and have been convicted for their respective roles. While the federal government *has jurisdiction to pursue criminal charges* against the contractors should it deem such action appropriate, and although extensive investigations were pursued by the Department of Justice upon referral from the military investigator, *no criminal charges eventuated against the contract employees.*[63]

The active impunity for the L-3/Titan and CACI contractors is starkly illuminated when their treatment under the criminal law is juxtaposed against that received by the US military personnel involved. The criminal law has effectively been suspended from applying to contractors *because* of their status as contractors. As both the military personnel and the contractors were performing parallel roles,[64] it is startling that no criminal charges have been initiated against any contractor, especially since jurisdiction to prosecute exists.

A recent case at the US District Court for the District of Columbia succinctly captures the problem of holding PMC contractors accountable for allegations of serious human rights abuse.[65] *Paul Slough* concerned the

[62] The Eleventh Circuit confirmed the conviction of a PMC contractor for abusive sexual contact with an Army National Guard Specialist in *US v Maldonado* (2007) 215 FedAppx 938 (US Court of Appeals for the Eleventh Circuit). This suggests that MEJA is more likely to be deployed where contractor violence is directed towards the military or other contractors, rather than external persons. A prime example of a criminal conviction for intra-contractor violence is Danny Fitzsimons, although his case was held within Iraqi jurisdiction: C Davies, 'Briton Danny Fitzsimons Jailed in Iraq for Contractors' Murders' *The Guardian* (28 February 2011) www.guardian.co.uk/world/2011/feb/28/danny-fitzsimons-jailed-iraq-murders.

[63] *Saleh v Titan* (2009) 580 F3d 1 (United States Court of Appeals for the DC Circuit) 2. Citations omitted. Emphasis added. Interestingly, the Court continued to note that available contractual remedies were not pursued, undermining regulatory mechanisms based upon the contract.

[64] Judge Roberts for the District Court, found that Titan contractors 'were fully integrated into the military units to which they were assigned' and 'performed their duties under the direct command … of military personnel': *Ibrahim v Titan* (2005) 391 FSupp2d 10 (US District Court DC) 10.

[65] The defendants were indicted under the Military Extraterritorial Jurisdiction Act (MEJA) 2000 Public Law 106–523 114 Stat 2488. MEJA was intended to extend federal

now infamous Blackwater Nisour Square incident, briefly mentioned in chapter two, in which 17 Iraqi civilians were killed and many more injured.[66] In that case, the Memorandum Opinion handed down by Judge Urbina dismissed the indictment against all of the defendants on the basis of tainted evidence: the compelled statements were held to violate the Fifth Amendment against self-incrimination under the rule in *Garrity*.[67] While the case appears to be a straightforward affirmation of constitutional rights, the main legal flaw arose out of the circularity which immunised the Blackwater personnel from legal suit:

> The issue was that the guards, as government contractors, were obligated to give an immediate report of what they had done, but the Constitution prevents the government from requiring a defendant to testify against himself, so those statements could not be used in a prosecution.[68]

In other words, active impunity is the combined effect of the obligation that required government contractors to immediately report the incidents in which they were involved, and the constitutional requirements of due process that excluded the admissibility of these very incident reports as evidence in court. At the very least, active impunity subsists in a significantly higher threshold for conviction for private military contractors because a large body of directly relevant evidence is eliminated from consideration. This type of active impunity is reminiscent of Rule 70 of the ICTY under which information provided on a confidential basis to the Prosecutor could not be disclosed without the prior consent of the provider of the information and could not be given in evidence without disclosure to the accused. Sir Geoffrey Nice, who was lead prosecutor in the Milosevic trial, reported that the defence team in that trial took advantage of this Rule to submit unfavourable evidence precisely to prevent its use in the trial by the prosecution.[69] PMC contractors appear to have de facto immunity

court jurisdiction to overseas civilians who commit criminal offences, but applied only to individuals 'while employed by or accompanying the Armed Forces outside the United States … or while a member of the Armed Forces' per s 3261 (A)(1) and (2). Thus, persons who were contracted to other US agencies were excluded from MEJA, which was extended by the National Defense Authorization Act 2004, Public Law 108-375 118 Stat 1811, by s 1088: see generally, Doyle, 'Civilian Extraterritorial Jurisdiction Act' (n 55).

[66] *US v Paul Slough* (n 47). For an alternative perspective, see 'Blackwater Incident: What Happened' *BBC* (8 December 2008) http://news.bbc.co.uk/1/hi/7033332.stm.

[67] *Garrity v New Jersey* (1967) 385 US 493 (US Supreme Court). The Supreme Court held that the Fifth Amendment privilege against self-incrimination bars the government from using statements compelled under a threat of job loss in a subsequent criminal prosecution.

[68] M Wald, 'U.S. Lawyers Knew about Legal Pitfalls in Blackwater Case' *New York Times* (2 January 2010) www.nytimes.com/2010/01/02/us/02legal.html?_r=4&ref=blackwater_usa; see also J Risen, 'Efforts to Prosecute Blackwater Are Collapsing' *New York Times* (20 October 2010) www.nytimes.com/2010/10/21/world/21contractors.html?scp=6&sq=nisour%20square%20blackwater&st=Search.

[69] G Nice, 'Can there be War without War Crimes?' (King's College London, 16 May 2012).

from suit, despite their overt susceptibility to indictment and conviction de jure.[70] This event thus clearly satisfies Louis Joinet's definition of impunity. Thus, this formal legal openness to try private military contractors in US courts is highly deceptive; while there is no formal bar to prosecution various legal obligations conspire to create an impunity paradox in practice.

The UN Working Group on the Use of Mercenaries commented on this outcome the following week.[71] The Chairperson Rapporteur (and former UN Special Rapporteur), Shiasta Shameem commented:

> We respect the independence of the United States judiciary and the requirements for due process, but are very concerned that the recent decision to dismiss the case against Blackwater guards may lead to a situation where no one would be accountable for grave human rights violations ... After such a decision, the Iraqi Government and the families of victims correctly feel they have no recourse to justice for the alleged human rights abuses that took place in Nissour Square ... Credible oversight and accountability of private security companies working on the behalf of the United States and other governments remain essential to avoid these alleged violations to be unpunished in future.[72]

An unarticulated message in this passage is that it is the very law itself which obstructs justice. The law provides an insurmountable barrier, in the name of due process protection in this instance, to the allocation of responsibility and attribution of accountability for severe breaches of human rights.

At the time of writing, the holding of the District Court in this case remains uncertain. The DC Circuit has remanded the case on the basis that the question of tainted evidence was not treated with the appropriate levels of differentiation, and has reinstated the charges.[73] The Supreme Court has declined involvement, having denied the petition for certiorari, so the outcome of the saga remains to be seen.[74] At the time of writing, the US Justice Department is bringing fresh charges against four of

[70] This type of immunity has not been raised as a form of defence: M Frulli, 'Immunity for Private Military Contractors: Legal Hurdles or Political Snags?' in F Francioni and N Ronzitti (eds), *War by Contract: Human Rights, Humanitarian Law, and Private Contractors* (Oxford University Press, 2011) 466–69.

[71] OHCHR, 'Mercenaries: UN Experts Say That the Nissour Square Killings in Iraq Should Not Remain Unpunished.' *UN Working Group on the Use of Mercenaries* (7 January 2010) www.ohchr.org/EN/NewsEvents/Pages/DisplayNews.aspx?NewsID=9705&LangID=E.

[72] ibid.

[73] *US v Paul Slough* (n 47); J Risen, 'Appeals Court Revives Case Against Blackwater Guards' *New York Times* (22 April 2011) www.nytimes.com/2011/04/23/us/23blackwater.html.

[74] *Paul Slough v US* [2012] US Supreme Court 11-591, 132 SCt 2710; Associated Press, 'Supreme Court Won't Get Involved in Prosecution of Blackwater Guards for 2007 Shooting' *Huffington Post* (4 June 2012) www.huffingtonpost.com/2012/06/04/blackwater-trial-supreme-court_n_1567846.html.

the former Blackwater contractors which, US Attorney Ronald Machen asserts, 'demonstrates our commitment to upholding the rule of law even in times of war and to bringing justice to the memories of those innocent men, women and children who were gunned down in Baghdad more than six years ago'.[75] Much will depend upon the defence lawyers' objection concerning the applicability of MEJA to the contractors, who were working for the State department. As Kristine Huskey and Scott Sullivan note, the extension of MEJA to encompass civilian contractors of 'other Federal agencies' and 'any provisional authority' remains limited 'to the extent such employment relates to supporting the mission of the Department of Defense'.[76]

The Nisour Square incident was the catalysing event that galvanised the international community to develop adequate regulatory mechanisms for the PMC industry.[77] This atrocity was the public tip of a very large iceberg of alleged criminal activity and deniable operations engaged in by Blackwater alone: its contractors have reportedly participated in clandestine CIA raids on such a regular basis such that there 'was a feeling that Blackwater eventually became an extension of the [CIA]'.[78] There is strong evidence from other cases before US federal courts that this was not a solitary and aberrant event:[79] instead, the use of disproportionate force by PMCs may have become routine.[80] Despite the indictment

[75] Tucker and Frommer, 'New Charges in Blackwater Shootings' (n 59); yet, '[t]he government has exercised its prosecutorial discretion in dismissing the charges against Mr. Ball based on its assessment of the admissible evidence against him' according to an email written by spokesman William Miller: Al Jazeera, 'Blackwater Faces New Charges in Iraq Killings' *Al Jazeera* (18 October 2013) www.aljazeera.com/news/americas/2013/10/blackwater-faces-new-charges-iraq-killings-2013101805946849805.html.

[76] Huskey and Sullivan (n 48) 356.

[77] In that sense, it may be symbolic that the Montreux Document was concluded a year and a day after Nisour Square.

[78] J Risen and M Mazzetti, 'Blackwater Guards Tied to Secret C.I.A. Raids' *New York Times* (11 December 2009) www.nytimes.com/2009/12/11/us/politics/11blackwater.html?ref=blackwater_usa.

[79] See eg *Abtan*, which also arose out of Nisour Square, and *Albazzaz* concerning an earlier event taking place in Watahba Square in Baghdad. These were consolidated and settled out of court 6 January 2010: *In re XE Services Alien Tort Litigation* (2009) 655 FSupp2d 569 (US District Court Eastern District of Virginia, Alexandria Division). The possibility to settle clearly distinguishes civil suits such as ATCA from criminal trials.

[80] See ch 2 above. The issue of role responsibility potentially underlies the disproportionate use of force by PMCs. Authors who document the operation of PMCs in the field highlight the primacy of protecting the principle as the overarching role played by contractors. Seen in this context, the (disproportionate) use of force by contractors, so long as it enabled the fulfilment of this role, will be selected regardless of countervailing (outcome responsibility) considerations related to the human rights of bystanders: J Ashcroft, *Making A Killing: The Explosive Story of a Hired Gun in Iraq* (Virgin Books, 2010); B Shepherd, *The Circuit* (Pan, 2009). While Blackwater is reportedly the worst on this front, J Broder and J Risen, 'Blackwater Tops Firms in Iraq in Shooting Rate' *New York Times* (27 September 2007) www.nytimes.com/2007/09/27/world/middleeast/27contractor.html, it is by no means the only PMC engaged in these excesses as exemplified by the UK PMC Aegis: J Serralvo, 'Privatized

and conviction of PMC contractors for crimes arising from extraterritorial actions under the extended jurisdiction of MEJA, these have generally concerned lesser offences than the serious violations of human rights, and possibly international crimes perpetrated against civilians alleged above and in chapter two.[81] Thus, while the *lacunae* of the criminal law gradually appear to be filled, their capacity to overcome impunity for the full spectrum of PMC activity remains questionable. *Paul Slough*, and the precedent it will set, still hangs in the balance. Perhaps more revealing in terms of active impunity is the perceptible skew of the criminal law that is exemplified by its successful operation in only relatively minor offences. As only a small fraction of the reported allegations of gross breaches of human rights and use of disproportionate force see the light of a criminal trial, the question mark remaining over *Paul Slough* is magnified. Yet, even if convictions are secured, justice would be achieved only in a narrow sense. Again, this is only one drop in an ocean of contractor misconduct that will never be remedied. In another sense, the *Paul Slough* saga has been six years and counting, such that most of the damage that impunity can do has already been done. The outrage and backlash in the aftermath of *Nisour Square* necessitated a more rapid response, giving credence to the legal maxim, 'justice delayed is justice denied'.

III. ACTIVE IMPUNITY: FORECLOSING CIVIL REMEDIES

The suspension of criminal law to the PMC *qua* corporation, and the severe limitations found in its application to PMC contractors demonstrated above, makes it necessary to consider whether civil remedies are capable of taking up the slack to overcome impunity for allegations of gross violations of human rights.[82] In pursuing this question, however, the strong possibility that interpretive denial lurks within the stark contrast

Military Firms Impunity in Cases of Torture: A Crime of Humanity?' (2012) 14 *International Community Law Review* 117; Human Rights First, 'Private Security Contractors at War: Ending the Culture of Impunity' www.humanrightsfirst.org/wp-content/uploads/pdf/08115-usls-psc-final.pdf; S Rayment, '"Trophy" Video Exposes Private Security Contractors Shooting up Iraqi Drivers' *The Telegraph* (27 November 2005) www.telegraph.co.uk/news/worldnews/middleeast/iraq/1504161/Trophy-video-exposes-private-security-contractors-shooting-up-Iraqi-drivers.html.

[81] These cases often deal with violence between contractors and non-violent offences such as child pornography: Huskey and Sullivan (n 48) 357–58. A prime example of a criminal conviction for intra-contractor violence is Danny Fitzsimons, although his case was held within Iraqi jurisdiction, Davies, 'Briton Danny Fitzsimons Jailed in Iraq for Contractors' Murders' (n 62).

[82] A Atteritano, 'Liability in Tort of Private Military and Security Companies: Jurisdictional Issues and Applicable Law' in Francioni and Ronzitti (eds), *War by Contract* (n 70); and Huskey and Sullivan (n 48) 362–77.

between content and form must be kept in mind.[83] Conduct that potentially amounts to international crimes is framed here only within the legal parameters of civil actions. This effectively neutralises the recognition of the criminal nature of the harms claimed at the outset because the harms are subtly, yet definitively, re-categorised at most as civil wrongs.

The very recourse to civil remedies, however, indicates another form of active impunity at play. The profit-orientated nature of the corporation suggests that it is adept at maximising rewards in balancing against risks. In criminal law where the risks are not all financial, and potentially involve imprisonment, greater deterrence is achieved because the balance against material reward can be more difficult to maximise. The deterrent effect of civil remedies, on the other hand, is curtailed for the corporation because the prospect of financial penalties can easily be balanced against potential financial reward. Corporations can see the levy of a fine as merely a cost of doing business: provided that the reward will be greater than the fine, that conduct remains profitable even in face of the imposed fine. While civil suits may pose reputational risks to the corporation, the impact of such risks is largely interpreted in financial terms, usually through reduced profits later.[84] While large fines, in absolute terms, may be more beneficial to the claimants, civil remedies must also include sufficiently large relative fines to be effective. The relative nature of the fines is critical to the effectiveness of the deterrent and must be capable of significantly offsetting the potential profit for any given activity in a particular industry. This relativity becomes especially important for the PMC industry because of the lucrative contracts awarded by the State itself, which continues to be the industry's most significant patron.[85] The effectiveness of a fine on a PMC is thus contingent upon both the absolute size of the fine and the relative size of the fine against the size of the contracts awarded to it by the State.[86]

[83] S Cohen, *States of Denial: Knowing About Atrocities and Suffering* (Polity, 2001) 7–8, 105–09.

[84] In this context, the fact that the PMC industry is reliant primarily upon large contracts with States, international organisations and other corporations, largely insulates it from the potential consumer backlash that reputational risks raise in other types of industry.

[85] For a recent snapshot of the industry by the UN Working Group on the Use of Mercenaries, focusing on US contracts in Iraq and Afghanistan, see Working Group on the Use of Mercenaries, 'Report of the Working Group on the Use of Mercenaries as a Means of Violating Human Rights and Impeding the Exercise of the Right of Peoples to Self-Determination' (UNGA, 2013) A/68/339 29–35.

[86] To date, there have not been any successful civil claims made against any PMC for allegations of torture and ill-treatment, and the chance for future successes is slim as demonstrated in this chapter. As such, the closest comparison is with the out of court settlement in *Al-Quraishi v Nakhla Voluntary Dismissal* [2012] US District Court District of Maryland, Greenbelt Division PJM 08-1696 as discussed below. The parent company of L-3 Services, implicated in torture and abuse at Abu Ghraib and elsewhere in Iraq, settled the case with 71 former inmates for $5.28 million: P Yost, 'Abu Ghraib Settlement: Defense Contractor Engility Holdings Pays $5M To Iraqi Torture Detainees' *Huffington Post* (8 January 2013)

Crudely put, even if civil remedies were to be successfully imposed upon a PMC, their deterrent effect will be neutralised if the State continues to award it sufficiently large contracts. Taken further, any future contracts by the State with a PMC against which claims have succeed may be interpreted as condoning, and even encouraging, that company's poor record of behaviour.[87] Thus, the lack of public or policy interest in holding PMCs and their contractors to account,[88] is further compounded with the State incentivising recidivism through the continual award of substantial contracts to PMCs which are implicated of wrongdoing.[89]

The discussion will now focus on the two main federal avenues opened to claimants seeking civil remedies for egregious human rights abuses: the Alien Tort Claims Act (ATCA) and the Torture Victim Protection Act (TVPA). At the time of writing, these laws have been the subject of intense litigation such that their interpretation has settled to some degree. To fully expose the intricacies of the active impunity mechanisms at play, however, it is necessary to follow the flow of judicial decisions rather than to begin with the authoritative cases. Redress through the vagaries of state tort law, while showing some promising signs, is beyond the scope of this chapter.[90]

A. The Alien Tort Claims Act 1789

The 1789 Alien Torts Claims Act (ATCA) is a unique piece of legislation in the US which enables the federal courts to assert jurisdiction over

www.huffingtonpost.com/2013/01/08/abu-ghraib-settlement-defense-contractor-pays_n_2435226.html. Yet, in relation to the $450 million-a-year contract that L-3 had with the US military in 2006, the settlement amount pales in comparison. While this settlement positively amounts to some compensation for the victims, it is relative small compared to the size of the company's contracts with the US alone. In contracting with L-3, the US is nullifying any deterrent effect of this settlement. Finally, considering the subsequent closure of avenues to such claims in *Al-Shimari v CACI (District Court rehearing)* [2013] US District Court for the Eastern District of Virginia, Alexandria Division 1:08-cv-827 (GBL/JFA) it is unlikely that settlements will be a source of compensation in the future. At the time of writing, the plaintiff-appellants have entered an appeal to Fourth Circuit: *Al-Shimari v CACI (Appeal)* [2013] US Court of Appeals for the Fourth Circuit No. 13-1937(L); No 13-2162.

[87] As a successful claim is unlikely given the overlapping layers of legalised impunity, this may extend perhaps to an out of court settlement, or even credible claims of misconduct against a PMC.

[88] Lehnardt, 'Individual Liability of Private Military Personnel under International Criminal Law' (n 11) 1034.

[89] Reliance upon the implication of wrongdoing here is intentional, given the obstacles that systematically prevent the plaintiffs from succeeding in their claims as demonstrated below.

[90] The question hanging over state tort claims concerns the application and extension of *Boyle* preemption. The Supreme Court held: 'In a few areas involving "uniquely federal interests", state law is pre-empted and replaced … by federal law of a content prescribed … by the courts': *Boyle v United Technologies Corp* (1988) 487 US 500 (US Supreme Court) 500.

international wrongs occurring extraterritorially.[91] Although lying dormant for most of its history, it has since 1980 in *Filartiga*[92] been used to challenge human rights abuses. Gradually, the ATCA developed into the centrepiece legislation for human rights violations claims against corporations for the past decade having been initiated by the Ninth Circuit decision in *Doe*.[93] Especially because corporations were immune from criminal indictment, ATCA offered the potential to alleviate at least some of the active impunity enjoyed by corporations, including PMCs.

ATCA was designed as a mechanism for ascribing tort liability for international wrongs, giving effect to a 'general doctrine recognized in Western systems of tort law … that a violation of a criminal or regulatory standard that protects particular individuals entails tort liability for the damage done'.[94] In doing so, tort law is opened up to claims for violations of international criminal law, potentially providing an alternative mechanism to avert impunity for alleged violations. It should be emphasised, however, that ATCA *does not* ascribe criminal responsibility. While this confers the dual benefit of circumventing the doctrine of *societas delinquere non potest* thus making corporations amenable to suit, and may be preferable in terms of settlement and remuneration for the victims, it fails to carry both the rigour and stigma associated with the process of criminal law. To reiterate, the use of ATCA for human rights violations thus opens up the possibility for interpretative denial of the outcome:[95] the law re-categorises the harm as a civil wrong in tort, despite the fact that the yardstick of substantive law that is applied is that of international criminal law. Seen in this context, an interpretative denial mechanism in favour of corporate defendants is structurally in-built into the law; because juridical persons cannot stand criminal trial, their wrongs, even if attaining the substantive mantle of international crime, are limited to being a civil wrong in tort only. But interpretative denial can go further than this; the possibility of settlement, which is not possible with criminal trials, may forestall the

The *Boyle* principle, which initially applied to contractors providing goods, was extended to service contractors by the Eleventh Circuit in *Hudgens v Bell Helicopters* (2003) 328 F3d 1329 (US Court of Appeals for the Eleventh Circuit). Because *Hudgens* concerned maintenance contractors, its applicability to PMC contractors remains uncertain.

[91] 28 U.S.C. § 1350. Post *Sosa*, this is known as the Alien Tort Statute (ATS), but for consistency, ATCA will be used throughout. It reads: 'The district courts shall have original jurisdiction of any civil action by an alien for a tort only, committed in violation of the law of nations or a treaty of the United States'. For its application to PMC regulation, see generally Atteritano, 'Liability in Tort of Private Military and Security Companies: Jurisdictional Issues and Applicable Law' (n 82) 477–83.

[92] *Filartiga v Pena-Irala* (1980) 630 F2d 876 (US Court of Appeals for the Second Circuit).

[93] *John Doe v UNOCAL Corporation* (2002) 395 F3d 932 (US Court of Appeals for the Ninth Circuit).

[94] G Fletcher, *Tort Liability for Human Rights Abuses* (Hart Publishing, 2008) 57.

[95] Cohen, *States of Denial* (n 83) 7–8, 105–09.

trial process altogether, pre-empting unfavourable outcomes for corporate defendants by entirely averting *any* finding of wrongdoing.[96]

There are, however, numerous difficulties associated with using ATCA for these purposes. It is not obvious that ATCA is the appropriate tool to arraign corporations for the alleged human rights abuses of aliens.[97] The rationale of the sentence-long 1789 Act is shrouded in mystery both because the legislative history of the provision had been lost and because it had not been litigated since its inception for almost two centuries until *Filartiga*.[98] The result is that ATCA law is predominantly judicial, which in turn has generated ambiguity over its scope, substance and reach. Consensus developed that ATCA is a jurisdictional statute; the Supreme Court in *Sosa*, however, elaborated further 'that the First Congress did not pass the [ATCA] as a jurisdictional convenience to be placed on the shelf for use by a future Congress or state legislature that might, someday, authorize the creation of causes of action'.[99] The Supreme Court held that content of ATCA was to be the 'ambient' law at that time, as expressed within Blackstone's trilogy of 'common law criminal offences based on individual assaults with international overtones … "violation of safe conducts, infringement of the rights of ambassadors, and piracy"'.[100] The point is, however, that the common dominator of the Blackstonian trilogy was the protection of 'effective diplomatic and commercial relationships among countries. Maintaining the basic grid of communication was essential for the flourishing of international trade and peaceful relations among countries'.[101] From the foregoing, it can be argued that alleged human rights violations do not fall within the appropriate ambit of ATCA.[102] Although Judge Kaufman famously pronounced in *Filartiga* that 'for the purposes of civil liability, the torturer has become—like the pirate and slave trader before him—*hostes humani generis*',[103] George Fletcher points out that this status of pirates may have been a pragmatic response to overcome the fact that 'no single state could claim jurisdiction',[104] and

[96] Settlements may be beneficial to the victims and may be implicitly tantamount to the acceptance of guilt. That no verdict is imposed, however, can be a ready source of denial of wrongdoing. Notably, the parent company of L-3 Services settled out of court a class action suit involving allegations of torture and other ill-treatment at Abu Ghraib and other sites in Iraq: *Al-Quraishi v Nakhla Voluntary Dismissal* (n 86); further reported in Yost, 'Abu Ghraib Settlement' (n 86).

[97] See generally J Ku, 'The Curious Case of Corporate Liability under the Alien Tort Statute: A Flawed System of Judicial Lawmaking' (2010) 51 *Virginia Journal of International Law* 353.

[98] *Filartiga v Pena-Irala* (n 92).

[99] *Sosa v Alvarez-Machain* (2004) 542 US 692 (US Supreme Court) 719.

[100] Fletcher, *Tort Liability for Human Rights Abuses* (n 94) 136–40.

[101] ibid 154.

[102] The Supreme Court opened a crack in the door by holding that new causes of actions could be recognised under international law: *Sosa v Alvarez-Machain* (n 99) 732–33.

[103] *Filartiga v Pena-Irala* (n 92) 890.

[104] Fletcher (n 94) 155.

that 'slave trading, which was permitted under the Constitution at least until 1808, could not have been seen as a violation of international law in 1789'.[105] The point is that piracy in *Filartiga*, percolated through slave trading into torture, provided the somewhat tenuous link that enables ATCA to be deployed in contemporary human rights abuses. Although *Filartiga* remains good law, this background raises fundamental questions about the appropriateness of suing for the violations of human rights under ATCA, especially where private actors and corporations are involved.[106] The Supreme Court in *Sosa* recognised the difficulties inherent within the substantial reach of ATCA. Justice Souter for the majority famously held that 'judicial power should be exercised on the understanding that the door is still ajar subject to vigilant doorkeeping, and thus open to a narrow class of international norms today'.[107] The threshold remained high, however, with the Supreme Court requiring 'any claim based on the present-day law of nations to rest on a norm of international character accepted by the civilized world and defined with a specificity comparable to the features of the 18th-century paradigms we have recognized'.[108] This would prove to be a point of contention in claims against private actors and corporations. Justice Scalia's concurring opinion joined by Justices Rehnquist and Thomas, however, objected to any expansion of ATCA beyond the original Blackstonian trilogy: 'The question is not whether that door will be left ajar, but whether this Court will open it' absent Congressional action.[109] In this context, while it is currently undisputed that ATCA can be used to sue for gross violations of human rights, a highly restrictive approach would be justified because any expansion of ATCA beyond protecting diplomatic and commercial relationships 'could seriously threaten international investment and trade both in developing countries and in the United States'.[110] The majority position arguably strikes a compromise: the limitations placed upon the substance of the claim or the status of the defendant may thwart accountability and perpetuate impunity for

[105] ibid 156.

[106] As Fletcher notes, the Supreme Court in Sosa 'did not want to confront the question of principle underlying the Blackstonian trilogy': ibid.

[107] *Sosa v Alvarez-Machain* (n 99) 729.

[108] ibid 725; 732–33; Retrospective responsibility is revealed to be entrenched into the legal process: P Cane, *Responsibility in Law and Morality* (Hart Publishing, 2002) 31. New actors perpetrating old wrongs can thus be immunised from retrospective legal responsibility based upon the tautology that such liability had not historically been recognised as wrongs that could be perpetrated by the actor.

[109] *Sosa v Alvarez-Machain* (n 99) 746, Requirement for Congressional action: ibid 744.

[110] G Hufbauer and N Mitrokostas, 'International Implications of the Alien Tort Statute' (2004) 7 *Journal of International Economic Law* 245, 247. This article contends that either the Supreme Court must narrow the scope of the ATCA or Congress must make such amendments in the interests of international trade and commerce; this balance was arguably struck by Justice Souter in *Sosa v Alvarez-Machain* (n 99) 729.

severe harm; the high threshold may prevent the overextension of ATCA and protect it from the critique of the minority view.

B. Corporate Liability Under ATCA

While ATCA has been used for the past 30 years by victims suing for alleged corporate human rights abuses by private parties,[111] including corporations and more specifically PMCs, the continued liability of corporations to the provision is hotly contested.[112] Unfortunately, while the Supreme Court originally granted certiorari on the question of corporate liability under ATCA, and focused upon this question for the first round of briefings, the Court did not directly address this question.[113] The continuing uncertainty mandates a careful analysis of the Circuit split on whether corporations are liable as defendants under ATCA.

On the one hand, Judge Cabranes for a majority of the Court of Appeals for the Second Circuit in *Kiobel* held that corporations were immune from suit under the ATCA.[114] The reasoning was premised upon the principle of individual criminal liability for offences under international law as espoused at Nuremberg that was further supported by the Rome Statute not adopting the proposal to grant the ICC jurisdiction over juridical persons.[115] Judge Cabranes concludes that 'modern international tribunals make it abundantly clear that, since Nuremberg, the concept of corporate liability for violations of customary international law has not even begun to "ripen" into a universally accepted norm of international law'.[116] This is a narrow and formalistic interpretation of ATCA: because there

[111] *Filartiga v Pena-Irala* (n 92).

[112] Ku, 'The Curious Case of Corporate Liability under the Alien Tort Statute' (n 97); Koh, 'Separating Myth from Reality about Corporate Responsibility Litigation' (n 10).

[113] *Kiobel v Royal Dutch Petroleum* [2013] US Supreme Court 10-1491, 133 S.Ct. US 1659. It should be noted that the opinions appear to assume that corporations are liable to be sued under ATCA. See for an overview, I Wuerth, 'Kiobel v. Royal Dutch Petroleum Co.: The Supreme Court and the Alien Tort Statute' (2013) 107 *American Journal of International Law* 601.

[114] *Kiobel v Royal Dutch Shell* (2010) 621 F3d 111 (United States Court of Appeals for the Second Circuit). For a background of the facts, see generally Human Rights Watch, 'The Price of Oil: Corporate Responsibility and Human Rights Violations in Nigeria's Oil Producing Communities' (Human Rights Watch 1999) 1-56432-225-4.

[115] *Kiobel v Royal Dutch Shell* (n 114) 118–20. Interestingly, however, Cabranes J claims that the proposal of the Rome Statute to grant jurisdiction over juridical persons to the ICC was 'soundly rejected'. The discussion, in ch 4, concerning the commentary of the negotiations for the Rome Statute illustrates that the exclusion of juridical persons from the ICC's jurisdiction are more for policy and evidentiary reasons and should therefore not be applied as evidence that criminal jurisdiction over juridical persons is or should be barred per se, especially in other courts.

[116] ibid 137, and 149. Cited approvingly in the partial dissent of Judge Kavanaugh in *Doe v Exxon Mobil* [2011] US Court of Appeals for the DC Circuit 09-7125, 654 F3d 11, 82–83.

was no customary international law norm recognising corporate liability for violations of international law, corporations could not be held liable under ATCA. Aligned to this position is the claim by *amicus curiae* filed by corporations in *Kiobel* on appeal to the Supreme Court 'that the companies are committed to *voluntarily complying* with human rights norms—but that standards set by the United Nations ... *are mere guidelines that are not enforceable as legal norms*'.[117] Peter Weiss points to a tautology inherent within this claim: 'What they are really saying is that there are legal norms against torture and such, but that *they can't be enforced against corporations because they have never been enforced under international law*'.[118] Implicit within this claim is a form of interpretative denial; corporations cannot be held liable for human rights because only States have human rights obligations.[119] While the exclusion of corporations from liability for international wrongs may have been justified where the State possessed the Weberian monopoly over the use of force, this has been undermined by the capacity of corporations, such as PMCs, to deploy organised force, or which are otherwise capable of perpetrating serious international wrongs.

On the other hand, critics of this decision have noted that it overturns the uncontentious application of ATCA to corporations since 1997.[120] Indeed, '[p]rior to the *Kiobel* court's ruling ... no appellate court had ever held that corporations were not subject to suit under the [ATCA]'.[121] Two Circuits continued to hold that corporations are proper defendants under ATCA after the ruling in *Kiobel*. The DC Circuit in *Doe v Exxon Mobil* expressly

[117] P Weiss, 'Should Corporations Have More Leeway to Kill Than People Do?' *New York Times* (24 February 2012) www.nytimes.com/2012/02/25/opinion/should-corporations-have-more-leeway-to-kill-than-people-do.html. Emphasis added.

[118] ibid. Emphasis added.

[119] Kaufman J held in the first ATCA case that only 'deliberate torture perpetrated under color of official authority violates universally accepted norms of international law and human rights': *Filartiga v Pena-Irala* (n 92) 878. This is further supported by the centrality of State action in the definition of certain international crimes, the best example of which is torture. Art 1 of the Convention against Torture provides that 'the term "torture" means any act by which severe pain or suffering ... is intentionally inflicted on a person ... *when such pain or suffering is inflicted by or at the instigation of or with the consent or acquiescence of a public official or other person acting in an official capacity*': Convention against Torture and Other Cruel, Inhuman or Degrading Treatment or Punishment 1984 (A/RES/39/46). Emphasis added. In terms of the ATCA, however, the State action requirement was removed in *Kadic* where the Second Circuit affirmed that the prohibition of genocide and war crimes provided for by international law applied to individuals, who were amenable to suit under ATCA without demonstrating State action: *Kadic v Karadzic* (1995) 70 F3d 232 (US Court of Appeals for the Second Circuit) 241–43. As discussed below, however, this may apply only within the jurisdiction of the Second Circuit.

[120] O Murray, D Kinley and C Pitts, 'Exaggerated Rumours of the Death of an Alien Tort? Corporations, Human Rights and the Remarkable Case of Kiobel' (2011) 12 *Melbourne Journal of International Law* 57, 59.

[121] T Giannini and S Farbstein, 'Corporate Accountability in Conflict Zones: How Kiobel Undermines the Nuremberg Legacy and Modern Human Rights' (2010) 52 *Harvard International Law Journal Online* 119, 121.

disagreed with the *Kiobel* ruling of the Second Circuit, with Judge Roberts writing for the majority on this point that 'neither the text, history, nor purpose of the [ATCA] supports corporate immunity for torts based on heinous conduct allegedly committed by its agents in violation of the law of nations'.[122] The DC Circuit concurred with the Eleventh Circuit which had also upheld corporate liability for ATCA claims in *Sinaltrainal*[123] and *Romero*.[124] These Eleventh Circuit cases, however, did not consider in detail the question whether corporations are proper defendants for the purposes of ATCA. The Seventh Circuit unanimously concurred with the holding of the DC Circuit a few days later in *Flomo*,[125] where Judge Posner found that

> [t]he factual premise of the majority opinion in the *Kiobel* case is incorrect. At the end of the Second World War the allied powers dissolved German corporations that had assisted the Nazi war effort, along with Nazi government and party organizations—and did so on the authority of customary international law.[126]

Returning to *Kiobel* at the Second Circuit itself, the concurring opinion of Judge Leval's forcefully underscored the broad and deep ramifications of excluding corporate liability under ATCA raised by the majority judgment and is worth setting out in full:

> Adoption of the corporate form has always offered important benefits and protections to business—foremost among them the limitation of liability to the assets of the business, without recourse to the assets of its shareholders. The new rule offers to unscrupulous businesses advantages of incorporation never before dreamed of. So long as they incorporate (or act in the form of a trust), businesses will now be free to trade in or exploit slaves, employ mercenary armies to do dirty work for despots, perform genocides or operate torture prisons for a despot's political opponents, or engage in piracy—all without civil liability to victims. By adopting the corporate form, such an enterprise could have hired itself out to operate Nazi extermination camps or the torture chambers of Argentina's

[122] *Doe v Exxon Mobil* (n 116). Roberts J was also in explicit agreement with the Eleventh Circuit. It should, however, be noted that Judge Kavanaugh's partial dissent explicitly rejected corporate liability under ATCA: 'Customary international law does not recognize corporate liability': ibid 72–73; this in turn is premised upon his reading of *Sosa* on the question of whether in ATCA cases, customary international law 'extends the scope of liability for a violation of a given norm to the perpetrator being sued': *Sosa v Alvarez-Machain* (n 99) 732, note 20. Going into greater detail, Judge Kavanaugh considers both the substantive content and the categories of defendant to be determined on a 'norm specific basis'. This leads to his conclusion that customary international law must specifically impose corporate liability for aiding and abetting torture, extra-judicial killing, or prolonged detention for the claim to succeed: *Doe v Exxon Mobil* (n 116).

[123] *Sinaltrainal v Coca-Cola Co* (2009) 578 F3d 1252 (US Court of Appeals for the Eleventh Circuit).

[124] *Romero v Drummond Co* (2008) 522 F3d 1303 (US Court of Appeal for the Eleventh Circuit).

[125] No 10-3675. 11 July 2011.

[126] ibid 6-7.

> dirty war, immune from civil liability to its victims. By protecting profits earned through abuse of fundamental human rights protected by international law, the rule my colleagues have created operates in opposition to the objective of international law to protect those rights.[127]

Judge Leval's point needs to be reiterated. Excluding corporate liability under ATCA goes further than immunising corporations: it facilitates profit-making through the violation of human rights. Thus, Judge Leval continues by arguing that ATCA 'confers on U.S. courts jurisdiction to entertain civil suits for violations of the law of nations', relying on *Sosa*. His opinion concurs with the majority in dismissing the complaint only upon the factual failure of the claim to meet the tests concerning aiding and abetting under ATCA, when combined with the requirement for specific facts capable of supporting a plausible inference.[128] The majority judgment of the Second Circuit in *Kiobel* can be considered not only as the minority view but one that is contrary to both the protection and promotion of human rights as well as, arguably, prior jurisprudence.

In this light, that the Second Circuit's decision in *Kiobel* was the source of the Circuit split that sparked Supreme Court review is somewhat startling. The Supreme Court did not directly address the question of corporate liability under ATCA, instead making the unusual move of putting the case to the next term in order to solicit supplemental briefs concerning the extraterritorial application of the statute.[129] The majority dismissed *Kiobel*, holding that the presumption against extraterritoriality applied to ATCA and that nothing in the statute rebuts that presumption.[130] Yet, early indications[131] and the ruling handed down for the TVPA in *Mohamad*,[132] a case that was heard by the Supreme Court in conjunction with *Kiobel*, suggested that the Court was likely to adopt the Second Circuit approach and exclude corporations from liability under ATCA. Peter Weiss framed the dilemma before the Court as 'whether to accept an argument that,

[127] *Kiobel v Royal Dutch Shell* (n 114) 150.

[128] ibid 153–54 and 188–96, relying on; *Presbyterian Church of Sudan v Talisman Energy* (2009) 582 F3d 244 (US Court of Appeals for the Second Circuit); *Ashcroft v Iqbal* (2009) 129 SCt 1937 (US Supreme Court) respectively.

[129] *Kiobel v Royal Dutch Petroleum (Order in Pending Case)* [2012] US Supreme Court 10-1491.

[130] *Kiobel v Royal Dutch Petroleum* (n 113).

[131] R Barnes, 'Court Skeptical about Overseas Corporate Abuse Suits' *Washington Post* (29 February 2012) www.washingtonpost.com/politics/court-skeptical-about-overseas-corporate-abuse-suits/2012/02/28/gIQA9bx1gR_story.html.

[132] The Supreme Court held that '[a]s used in the TVPA, the term "individual" encompasses only natural persons. Consequently, the Act does not impose liability against organizations': *Mohamad v Palestinian Authority* [2012] US Supreme Court 11-88, 132 SCt 1702, 1703. See also R Barnes, 'Supreme Court Says Torture Victim Law Applies Only to People, Not Organizations' *Washington Post* (18 April 2012) www.washingtonpost.com/politics/supreme-court-says-torture-victim-law-applies-only-to-people-not-organizations/2012/04/18/gIQAZHfWRT_story.html. The Court, however, did not restrict the types of individuals amenable to suit under the TVPA, thus leaving open the possibility for corporate officers or employees to suit. This case is discussed below in the context of the TVPA.

in effect, leaves corporations less culpable than individuals are for human rights violations committed abroad—or whether to hold that if a 200-year-old law can be used to hold individual violators to account, it can be used against corporate violators as well'.[133] This potential for corporate liability under ATCA to be excluded underscores the active dimension of impunity: accountability for serious human rights abuses should not be contingent upon the formal legal status of the alleged violator.

While the opinions of the Justices in *Kiobel* imply that corporations are amenable to suit under ATCA, the Supreme Court erected an additional obstacle against corporate liability under the statute. The majority of the Court held, ambiguously, that

> even where the claims touch and concern the territory of the United States, they must do so with sufficient force to displace the presumption against extraterritorial application. *Corporations are often present in many countries, and it would reach too far to say that mere corporate presence suffices.*[134]

Critically, this establishes a higher threshold for corporate defendants under ATCA than would be applicable for individuals, generating active impunity that shields the corporation, relative to the individual. The incongruity is readily apparent in the stark contrast between *Kiobel*'s 'mere corporate presence' in the United States as insufficient grounds for an ATCA claim against a corporation, and the Second Circuit's consistent jurisprudence in *Filartiga* and *Kadic* that mere physical presence in the United States is enough to base an ATCA claim against an individual.[135]

C. Distinguishing Direct Perpetration by PMCs from the Corporate Complicity Jurisprudence Under ATCA

There is another significant obstacle to a successful claim against a corporation under ATCA: complicity.[136] As George Fletcher observes:

> Unlike the early days of *Filartiga*, *Tel-Oren*, *Karadzic*, and indeed *Sosa*—*where the violators themselves were sued as defendants*, the business of suing under the ATCA has become a search for defendants who can actually compensate victims … This has directed attention to the *corporate defendants who play an indirect role* in most systematic human rights abuses.[137]

[133] Weiss, 'Should Corporations Have More Leeway to Kill Than People Do?' (n 117).

[134] *Kiobel v Royal Dutch Petroleum* (n 113). Citations omitted, and emphasis added.

[135] The only jurisdictional link with the defendant, Americo Norberto Pena-Irala, was that he was personally present on the territory of the United States (pending administrative deportation) that allowed service of process: *Filartiga v Pena-Irala* (n 92) 878–79. Similarly, Radovan Karadzic was personally served summons while physically in the United States as an invitee of the United Nations: *Kadic v Karadzic* (n 119) 237.

[136] For an excellent overview of the relevant complicity issues, see Fletcher (n 94) 161–71.

[137] ibid 161. Emphasis added.

This seismic shift in litigation strategy has led to the question of corporate liability under ATCA becoming subsumed exclusively beneath the role of PMCs as the *accessories*, rather than the *direct perpetrators*, of human rights abuses. George Fletcher succinctly describes this litigation model:

> The resulting relationship is triangular—among P, D, and C. The plaintiff-victim P sues the corporate defendant C for having *contributed* to the defendant D's human rights violation. Thus P seeks to collect from C for *facilitating* the wrongs of D.[138]

Unfortunately, these relationships in the model are far from clear-cut in reality. This in turn raises significant questions concerning the justifiability of immunising corporations from accessory liability. Consider a systematic practice in Indonesia documented by Human Rights Watch as an example:

> The Indonesian military makes itself available to provide security services for private interests. Different military units can earn money by forming private security companies, and individual commanders charge a fee to loan out their troops as private guards … More famously, [the Indonesian military] provides security to large multinational companies … The reliance of major companies, particularly in the extractive sector, on state security forces (military and/or police) to protect their installations in remote and dangerous locations around the world can be rife with problems if the arrangements are not carefully managed. In Indonesia, questions surrounding company payments for military security are acute because of the armed forces' record of corruption and human rights violations.[139]

This example blurs the boundaries of the accessory liability model, insofar as the model suggests that corporations only facilitate or otherwise contribute towards breaches of human rights that are primarily perpetrated by the State. Instead, the corporation can be seen as the instigator of the human rights violations, in such relationships, and the State is relegated to a tool serving the purposes of the corporation. The culpability of the corporation is elevated by its instigation of the human rights violations in question, which mere accessory liability fails to adequately reflect.

Furthermore, this Indonesian example can be directly related back to ATCA jurisprudence. This is precisely the relationship and behaviour alleged by the plaintiffs in *Doe*:

> that Exxon's security forces were comprised of members of the Indonesian military … retained these soldiers as guards for its natural gas facility even though Exxon was aware that the Indonesian military had committed human rights abuses in the past, and knew that performance of the security contract would lead to human rights violations by Indonesian soldiers against the residents of Aceh.[140]

[138] ibid. Emphasis added.

[139] Human Rights Watch, 'Too High a Price: The Human Rights Cost of the Indonesian Military's Economic Activities' (Human Rights Watch, 2006) vol 18, no 5(C) 45–46. Citations omitted.

[140] *Doe v Exxon Mobil* (n 116).

Situated in the context reported by Human Rights Watch, above, Exxon was not merely *complicit* in the human rights abuses suffered by the claimants, but rather the *instigator*. This relationship may more appropriately be recognised as the corporate *modus operandi*: it underlies the ATCA claims raised in *Bowoto* and *Kiobel* in Nigeria, as well as *Doe v UNOCAL* in Burma.[141]

Beyond conflating the distinction between corporations that aid and abet human rights violations and those that initiate those violations, the dominance of the post-*Sosa* litigation model of suing complicit corporations has another neglected effect: the question of corporate liability has been collapsed into the (now presumed) role of corporations as mere accessories. Conflating corporate liability with accessory liability can, in turn, undermine ATCA claims where the corporation is itself the actual direct perpetrator of the alleged human rights abuses at stake. This has happened to some extent with the Supreme Court's limitation of 'mere corporate presence' in *Kiobel*.[142] While this limitation might indeed be justifiable for corporations sued for complicity under ATCA, the same cannot be said for corporations that are implicated for direct perpetration. Again, the invocation of Second Circuit jurisprudence, in the form of *Filartiga* and *Kadic*, serves to underline the point.[143] In both instances, the case was initiated against the direct perpetrator of the alleged human rights violations and it is difficult to show how corporations might somehow be treated differently on this ground.

Yet, the minority position of the DC Circuit in *Doe*, involving a claim of corporate complicity, suggested that 'for plaintiffs to maintain their claims, customary international law must impose liability against corporations for *aiding and abetting* torture, extra-judicial killing, or prolonged detention. It does not.'[144] Without contesting the requisite level of specificity imputed into customary international law, this reasoning reveals that the accessory liability of corporations, rather than corporate liability per se, constitutes a partial barrier to ATCA claims against corporations. The underlying assumption is that corporations are capable of causing serious human rights violations either negligently or recklessly, and only in an indirect or complicit manner.

Equating corporate liability with complicity has clear implications for the amenability of PMCs to suit under ATCA. In its control over physical

[141] For the situational context of these claims, see Human Rights Watch, 'The Price of Oil' (n 114). For the fact of the claims, see; *Bowoto v Chevron* (2010) 621 F3d 1116 (US Court of Appeals for the Ninth Circuit) 1116; *Kiobel v Royal Dutch Petroleum* (n 113) 'It is undisputed that the Myanmar Military provided security and other services for the Project, and that Unocal knew about this': *John Doe v UNOCAL Corporation* (n 93) 936–38.

[142] *Kiobel v Royal Dutch Petroleum* (n 113).

[143] *Filartiga v Pena-Irala* (n 92); *Kadic v Karadzic* (n 119).

[144] Judge Kavanaugh's partial dissent in *Doe v Exxon Mobil* (n 116). Emphasis added.

force and its coercive relationship over individuals, the PMC has departed from the hitherto purely civilian nature of the corporation. As described in chapter two, the PMC has crafted a category of military corporations that, plotted by their position high along the severity of harm and proximity to harm axes, are capable of perpetrating immense harm in a direct manner. Thus, the PMC can be clearly distinguished from the 'standard' ATCA (or TVPA, discussed below) claim against civilian corporations. Claims against PMCs can, but need not, rest on complicity:[145] the PMC can directly perpetrate serious human rights violations on its own. This potential for direct perpetration categorically differentiates the ATCA claims made against PMCs, such as in the context of CACI and L-3 Services in Abu Ghraib torture and prisoner abuse discussed below.

The active impunity effects provided by focusing upon corporate complicity to the PMC is twofold. First, relative insulation against liability under ATCA is provided by the failure to recognise the potential for PMCs to directly perpetrate human rights abuses. This relative insulation is compounded by the interpretative restrictions placed upon ATCA that are premised upon corporate complicity. Second, and more powerfully, there is a fundamental difference between immunising complicit corporations and perpetrator corporations. Implicit within accessory liability in the former scenario is that the direct perpetrators will remain amenable to ATCA claims. While this avenue might establish culpability rather than compensation for the victims, there is an alternate route to justice. Yet, this is not the case with the latter scenario: an absolute bar to justice will be erected where direct perpetrator corporations, such as the PMC, are immunised.

There are strong reasons to justify using ATCA to hold PMCs accountable, foremost of which 'is the opportunity to provide legal redress, empowerment, and justice for tort victims'.[146] While these purposes may be achieved by suing corporate officers or employees under ATCA,[147] in lieu of corporate liability, the quest for compensation that has defined contemporary ATCA litigation would be frustrated. Suing the PMC under ATCA would obviate the contemporary triangular litigation model because PMCs are in a position to compensate victims. As George Fletcher puts it,

> [i]n the post-*Sosa* period, the focus has fallen on the corporate defendants who are in a position to pay damages for the enormous harm done … The point of these suits should be as much to do well (by making money) as to do good (to make the right moral point).[148]

[145] Strangely, even in analyses specifically addressing PMC misconduct, the focus remains on complicity rather than direct perpetration: see T Garmon, 'Domesticating International Corporate Responsibility: Holding Private Military Firms Accountable under the Alien Tort Claims Act' (2003) 11 *Tulane Journal of International and Comparative Law* 325, 350–53.

[146] J Lam, 'Accountability for Private Military Contractors Under the Alien Tort Statute' (2009) 97 *California Law Review* 1459, 1496.

[147] This possibility remains with the TVPA: see *Mohamad v Palestinian Authority* (n 132).

[148] Fletcher (n 94) 163.

Seen in this light, while individual liability under ATCA may satisfy only the latter point, liability of direct corporate perpetrators will be capable of fulfilling both of Fletcher's aims in addition to averting active impunity for PMCs. As the following section will illustrate, however, amenity of corporations to suit under ATCA does not neutralise PMC impunity because corporate liability under ATCA constitutes only the first obstacle.

D. State Action Requirement

In light of the Circuit split over corporate liability, it is not surprising that the few cases where PMCs were sued under ATCA occurred within the jurisdiction of the DC Circuit, which under *Doe*, accepted corporate liability. Yet, the law of the DC Circuit presents a different barrier for claims against PMCs and their contractors: the State action requirement.[149] This in turn is the subject of another Circuit split which the Supreme Court in *Sosa* recognised, but did not rule upon.[150]

The original requirement that torture must be State-sanctioned to violate international law was imposed by the Second Circuit in *Filartiga*.[151] This requirement was also subsequently lifted by the Second Circuit in its seminal decision of *Kadic*.[152] The result, in effect, was that the Second Circuit set the precedent requiring State action under ATCA which became widely adopted in the jurisprudence. It was not until 15 years later, however, that the Second Circuit recognised this flaw and overturned the State action requirement within its own jurisdiction. Critically, this subsequent retraction has left the legacy that non-State actors may be liable for violations of the law of nations (or treaty of the United States) under ATCA within the jurisdiction of the Second Circuit, but this result remains uncertain under the jurisprudence of other Circuits which appear largely to adhere faithfully to the initial State action requirement established in *Filartiga*.[153]

The State action requirement persists within the DC Circuit because of precedent in *Sanchez–Espinoza*.[154] In effect, the DC Circuit had directly imported the *Filartiga* requirement from the Second Circuit, but crucially

[149] See generally ibid 125–28.

[150] Comparing the DC Circuit case of *Tel-Oren* with the Second Circuit case of *Kadic*: *Sosa v Alvarez-Machain* (n 99) 733, note 20.

[151] *Filartiga v Pena-Irala* (n 92) 878.

[152] Judge Newman held that: 'We do not agree that the law of nations, as understood in the modern era, confines its reach to state action. Instead, we hold that certain forms of conduct violate the law of nations whether undertaken by those acting under the auspices of a state or only as private individuals': *Kadic v Karadzic* (n 119) 239.

[153] eg Judge Lee for the Eastern District of Virginia is explicitly unconvinced by *Kadic*: *Al-Shimari v CACI* (2009) 657 FSupp2d 700 (US District Court for the Eastern District of Virginia, Alexandria Division) 728.

[154] *Sanchez-Espinoza v Reagan* (1985) 770 F2d 202 (US Court of Appeals for the DC Circuit).

failed to update by incorporating the subsequent development in *Kadic*. Judge Edwards wrote a concurring opinion in the DC Circuit case of *Tel-Oren*, that

> The Second Circuit [in *Filartiga*] surveyed the law of nations and concluded that *official torture* constituted a violation. Plaintiffs in the case before us do not allege facts to show that official or state-initiated torture is implicated in this action.[155]

This was then cited approvingly by then-Judge Scalia in *Sanchez–Espinoza*:

> We are aware of no treaty that purports to make the activities at issue here *unlawful when conducted by private individuals*.... As for the law of nations-so-called 'customary international law,' arising from 'the customs and usages of civilized nations,' we conclude that this also *does not reach private, non-state conduct* of this sort.[156]

This provided binding precedent for the DC Circuit.

Yet, as Aaron Garfield notes, the State action requirement for ATCA liability is highly incongruous because:

> The question is *not* whether the [ATCA] can be applied against private actors, *but why it should be applied to anything but private actors*. None of the 18th-century paradigms discussed in *Sosa* envisage any state action. All three norms, as well as the general principle they illustrate, *can only be violated by private actors*.[157]

Indeed, the State action requirement may have been accidentally imported into ATCA jurisprudence when the Second Circuit translated the maritime pirate into the torturer as an enemy of mankind in the specific context of *Filartiga*.[158] Where the maritime pirate is distinguished by his extreme private status, torture as defined by the UN Convention against Torture, requires a nexus with the State.[159] As the frame of reference for ATCA is the law of nations, the position of international law is crucial. With regard

[155] *Tel-Oren v Libyan Arab Republic* (1984) 726 F2d 774 (US Court of Appeals for the DC Circuit) 791. While this is not a court holding, it has been widely cited in ATCA judgments. Emphasis added.

[156] *Sanchez–Espinoza v Reagan* (n 154) 206–07 Emphasis added.

[157] A Garfield, 'Bridging a Gap in Human Rights Law: Prisoner of War Abuse as War Tort' (2005) 37 *Georgetown Journal of International Law* 725, 755. Emphasis added.

[158] *Filartiga v Pena-Irala* (n 92) 890.

[159] Art 1 defines 'torture' as being contingent upon severe pain or suffering 'inflicted by or at the instigation of or with the consent or acquiescence of a public official or other person acting in an official capacity': Convention against Torture and Other Cruel, Inhuman or Degrading Treatment or Punishment (n 119). The Appeals Chamber of the ICTY held the definition of the crime of torture under art 1 of CAT to reflect customary international law: *Prosecutor v Kunarac (Appeals Chamber)* [2002] ICTY Appeals Chamber IT-96-23-A & IT-96-23/1-A [146]. A convincing riposte to this position is offered by George Fletcher: 'In offering an affirmative account of torture, the element of state action is strikingly unnecessary. So long as there is a relationship of domination between the torturer and the victim, it is not clear why the official status of the torturer should matter. According to the [UN Convention against Torture] and Filartiga, however, only official state torture constitutes a violation of international law': Fletcher (n 94) 125–27.

to acts of torture in the context of armed conflict, however, the requirement for State action has been severely undermined by the Trial Chamber of the ICTY in *Kunarac* which concluded that 'the presence of a state official or of any other authority-wielding person in the torture process is not necessary for the offence to be regarded as such'.[160]

The reasoning of the Trial Chamber in *Kunarac* was that the three conventions that have specifically defined torture are *human rights* instruments. The Trial Chamber held that the precedent set in *Furundzija* had erred when it drew upon human rights law to determine the definition of torture for *international humanitarian law*, and concluded that there were important structural differences between HRL and IHL.[161] First, the purpose of HRL is to protect individuals against the State while the aim of IHL is to diminish the effects of armed hostilities upon its victims.[162] Second, that international criminal law that is applied by the ICTY is a penal law regime that pits the prosecutor against the defendant, while HRL holds the State as the defendant.[163] The Trial Chamber continued to distinguish provisions directed against the State and those addressed to individuals; while HRL norms generally fall into the former, IHL norms are mixed.[164] The Trial Chamber concluded that individual criminal responsibility is engaged with the violation of the Articles of the ICTY Statute, such that 'the participation of the state becomes secondary and, generally, peripheral'.[165] Indeed, the Appeals Chamber subsequently affirmed that 'the public official requirement is not a requirement under customary international law in relation to the criminal responsibility of an individual for torture outside of [CAT]'.[166] The criminalisation of torture thus diverges depending upon the body of law being applied. Under human rights law, it is criminalised per se but requires State action; under international humanitarian law, it is criminalised as a war crime, a crime

[160] *Prosecutor v Kunarac (Trials Chamber)* [2001] ICTY Trial Chamber IT-96-23-T & IT-96-23/1-T para 496. This drew a firm distinction between the position of human rights instruments, exemplified by CAT. Article 1 defines torture as an official act: Convention against Torture and Other Cruel, Inhuman or Degrading Treatment or Punishment (n 119). See generally *Prosecutor v Kunarac (Trials Chamber)* [465–97].

[161] *Prosecutor v Kunarac (Trials Chamber)* (n 160) paras 466 and 468 respectively. Upheld by the Appeals Chamber: *Prosecutor v Kunarac (Appeals Chamber)* (n 159) [144–48].

[162] *Prosecutor v Kunarac (Trials Chamber)* (n 160) [470]. The Trial Chamber specifically referred to the ATCA jurisprudence of the Second Circuit in *Kadic v Karadzic* (n 119) 240–41 and 244–45 where it clarified that international human rights law was the legal corpus that was being applied in *Filartiga*, and that in the human rights context, the international law prohibition of torture only exists by State action or under the colour of law. It is significant that the Second Circuit departed from *Filartiga* by removing the State action requirement in *Kadic*.

[163] *Prosecutor v Kunarac (Trials Chamber)* (n 160) [470].

[164] ibid 489.

[165] ibid 493.

[166] *Prosecutor v Kunarac (Appeals Chamber)* (n 159) [148].

against humanity, or as a grave breach which is not contingent upon the status of the perpetrator.[167] Alexander Zahar and Goran Sluiter praise this decision as 'decisive and a model of accurate reasoning' and conclude that the decision 'must now be regarded as settled law'.[168]

This convincing distinction between torture alleged under the human rights paradigm and that of the laws of armed conflict suggest that the State action requirement, where it applies, should appropriately be limited to the former; any extension into the latter category would signal active impunity for non-State actors. But even exclusively within the human rights arena, the requirement of State action constitutes a powerful form of active impunity for corporations by prima facie immunising them from ATCA liability on purely formalistic grounds. It is particularly noteworthy that this form of active impunity is further reinforced by the availability of sovereign immunity from suit for State actors which may be extended to cover certain categories of private actors, including PMCs.

E. An Overview of Active Impunity Under ATCA

By combining the question of corporate liability with the State action requirement under ATCA, it is now possible to illustrate how active impunity is structured for corporations that violate human rights in a direct manner such as PMCs. Prior to, and now complementing, the general extraterritoriality limitation imposed by the Supreme Court in *Kiobel*, there are two factors creating different impunity paradoxes depending upon the Circuit. Under the jurisdiction of the Second Circuit, corporate liability remains entirely foreclosed under ATCA under *Kiobel* despite the removal of State action requirement per *Kadic*. This means that although private actions are capable of violating the law of nations, there is an absolute bar for claims against corporations per se. While this potentially leaves corporate officers and employees amenable to suit the corporation is immunised, thus failing to articulate the core role played by the corporation in any claim.

This situation is exactly inverted within the jurisdiction of the DC Circuit. Corporate liability under ATCA is unproblematic; *Doe* established that corporations are prima facie amenable to suit. Instead, corporate action is immunised under the State action requirement that immunises private actions. The result is that corporate liability under ATCA is permissible, but the statute cannot be breached by private actions alone without the

[167] *Prosecutor v Kunarac (Trials Chamber)* (n 160) [495–96]; for the various applicable criteria, see Cassese, *International Criminal Law* (n 40) 149–52.

[168] A Zahar and G Sluiter, *International Criminal Law* (Oxford University Press, 2007) 125–26.

colour of law. This does leave the narrow possibility of corporate liability for violations of the law of nations (or a treaty of the US) through the mode of complicity liability as an accessory. This has the effect of immunising corporations that violate human rights directly for lack of requisite State action.

In addition, there is another impunity paradox subsisting between the State actor requirement and the government contractor defence. George Fletcher describes that:

> The difficulty with insisting on an element of state action … is that state action, particularly by the US government, invites a claim of sovereign immunity under the Foreign Torts Claims Act … The US government is not in general liable for torts that occur abroad.[169]

Liability under ATCA has been constructed by the courts to entirely preclude claims against corporations, including PMCs, for direct human rights abuses even when these are not forestalled by their corporate juridical personhood. Private actors are immunised from suit under ATCA because of the State actor requirement; yet, the liability of State actors is foreclosed by sovereign immunity which may be extended to cover these private actors. This confluence of factors is best illustrated by the convoluted ATCA claims against PMCs. It should not come as a surprise that there have not been any successful ATCA cases brought against PMCs to date: the interlocking exclusionary mechanisms that frustrate claims are intricate and impermeable.

Before dissecting the ATCA claims that have been brought against PMCs, the overarching active impunity mechanism provided by the Supreme Court in *Kiobel* must be underscored. The Court crafted an elegantly simple, yet impenetrable, shield against future ATCA claims made against PMCs by generally excluding extraterritorial claims.[170] Considering that

[169] Fletcher (n 94) 127.

[170] Judge Bybee, writing for the majority of the Ninth Circuit, held that the ATCA did not apply to the case because the impugned conduct occurred exclusively in Columbia: *Mujica v AirScan Inc* [2014] US Court of Appeals for the Ninth Circuit 10-55515 25–35. In dissent, Judge Zilly, objected to the majority decision by writing that: 'In focusing on the [ATCA] "claims," and not the underlying "conduct," the Kiobel Court carefully left open the door through which foreign victims of heinous acts by U.S. nationals could hold such individuals or corporate entities accountable. The majority now unnecessarily slams the door shut': ibid 80. Interestingly, both the majority and dissent quote Judge Martin, in dissent at the Eleventh Circuit, saying: 'The United States would fail to meet the expectations of the international community were we to allow U.S. citizens to travel to foreign shores and commit violations of the law of nations with impunity': *Cardona v Chiquita Brands* [2014] US Court of Appeals for the Eleventh Circuit 12-14898, 760 F3d 1185. This suggests that the practical ramifications of the case are fully appreciated, but that the legalistic 'touch and concern' test must prevail. See for an overview, J Stempel, 'U.S. Court Refuses to Hold Occidental Liable in Colombia Bombing' *Reuters* (12 November 2014) www.reuters.com/article/2014/11/12/us-occidental-colombia-bombing-idUSKCN0IW27020141112.

both the role of the PMC and the functions it provides are the support of military operations, its activity is likely to be predominantly extraterritorial. Thus, *Kiobel* clarifies PMC immunity against ATCA by removing the illusion that a successful claim will be possible. In those rare situations where a claim is not pre-empted by extraterritoriality, the impunity paradoxes subsisting within Circuit jurisprudence remain in place to deflect those claims.

F. PMCs Under ATCA

The two cases of *Ibrahim*[171] and *Saleh*[172] that emerged from the Abu Ghraib scandal in Iraq, mentioned in chapter two, illustrate how active impunity operates within ATCA claims against PMCs. These class action suits alleged that the intelligence firms providing detention and translation services to the military, L-3/Titan and CACI, had tortured and severely abused the Iraqi plaintiffs or their relatives.[173] Judge Robertson ruled for the US District Court of the DC in both cases, holding in *Ibrahim*, that:

> Plaintiffs' allegations describe conduct that is abhorrent to civilized people, and surely actionable under a number of common law theories. After *Tel–Oren* or *Sanchez–Espinoza*, however, it is not actionable under the [ATCA]'s grant of jurisdiction, as a violation of the law of nations.[174]

The claim, which would have been foreclosed within the jurisdiction of the Second Circuit that does not allow corporate liability under ATCA, floundered within the jurisdiction of the DC Circuit because State action was lacking. The plaintiffs in *Saleh* subsequently sought to exploit the possibility, 'that torture by private parties would be actionable under the [ATCA] if the private parties were acting under color of law'.[175] In other words, there was potential that State-*sanctioned* private activity would fall within the scope of ATCA. This argument was rejected outright by Judge Robertson because *Sanchez–Espinoza* remains binding Circuit precedent.[176] In a critique of the cases, however, Jenny Lam argued that '[*Sanchez–Espinoza* and *Tel-Oren*] did not consider the possibility of private individuals acting under color of law and therefore should not have been treated as binding circuit precedent in *Saleh*'.[177]

171 *Ibrahim v Titan* (n 64).
172 *Saleh v Titan* (2006) 436 FSupp2d 55 (US District Court of the District of Columbia).
173 P Chatterjee, 'Outsourcing Intelligence in Iraq: A CorpWatch Report on L-3/Titan' (CorpWatch 2008) www.corpwatch.org/article.php?id=15253.
174 *Ibrahim v Titan* (n 64) 15.
175 *Saleh v Titan* (n 172) 57.
176 ibid 58.
177 Lam, 'Accountability for Private Military Contractors Under the Alien Tort Statute' (n 146) 1480.

These two cases were consolidated on appeal as *Saleh*, where a majority of the DC Circuit affirmed the dismissal of all claims against Titan/L-3, and also dismissed all claims against CACI by reversing the judgment of the District Court.[178] The DC Circuit considered the ATCA claim in depth. Referring to *Sosa*, where the Supreme Court was guardedly open to new classes of action, it noted that judicial restraint should be exercised.[179] The DC Circuit found that the claims made were 'stunningly broad' as the plaintiffs alleged that 'any "abuse" inflicted or supported by Titan's translator employees … is condemned by settled consensus of international law'.[180] While torture that was committed by a State was recognised to violate international law, this could not be extended to encompass private actors. There are three active impunity mechanisms involved.

First, for the claim to succeed, the plaintiffs asserted that the private actions took place under colour of law, rather than making the direct claim that the defendants were State actors, in order to avoid a paradox. While establishing that the defendants were State actors would have grounded an ATCA claim, it would simultaneously immunise them from liability. As Judge Messitte accomplishes in *Al-Quraishi*,[181] below, it is possible to distinguish the State actor category from that of acting under the colour of law. Instead, the paradox between the aforementioned State actor requirement and the defence of sovereign immunity to action under the colour of law was accepted in *Saleh*. Judge Silberman acknowledged that,

> as the district court recognized, appellants are caught between Scylla and Charybdis: they cannot artfully allege that the contractors acted under color of law for jurisdictional purposes while maintaining that their action was private when the issue is sovereign immunity.[182]

Second, the superiority of Congress for creating causes of action was acknowledged to forestall judicial recognition of novel categories of action. Alleged acts of torture by private parties fell into the *lacunae* between existing legislation:

> Through acts such as the Torture Victim Protection Act, the Military Commissions Act, the federal criminal torture statute, the War Crimes Act, the Foreign Claims Act, and the Uniform Code of Military Justice, Congress has created an extensive body of law with respect to allegations of torture. *But Congress has declined to create a civil tort cause of action that plaintiffs could employ*.[183]

[178] *Saleh v Titan* (n 63). The Court's conclusion on ATCA appears to be unanimous; the dissenting opinion of Judge Garland does not question ATCA.
[179] ibid 14–15.
[180] ibid 15.
[181] *Al-Quraishi v Nakhla* [2010] US District Court District of Maryland, Greenbelt Division PJM 08-1696, 728 FSupp2d 702.
[182] *Saleh v Titan* (n 63) 15–16.
[183] ibid 13. Note 9. Citations omitted and emphasis added.

While the lack of applicable legislation per se may not have been fatal to the claim, because of potential flexibility in judicial interpretation, a third mechanism came into play.[184] The judicial restraint established in *Sosa* ensured that the courts could not readily expand the causes of action under ATCA to fill the *lacuna*, thus foreclosing the novel category of action alleged by the claimants.[185] This unsatisfactory decision of the DC Circuit in *Saleh* stands because the Supreme Court denied the petition for certiorari.[186]

This result is, however, only one outcome of several possible impunity permutations in ATCA claims against PMCs. The first and most imperceptible, is the exclusion of corporate liability per the Second Circuit in *Kiobel* discussed above.[187] Second, although this first obstacle was cleared in *Saleh* because the claim was made within the DC Circuit, the claim was undermined by the State action requirement just as the District Court in *Saleh* had held. This was also the justification that Judge Shanstrom adopted to dismiss the claim in *Manook* which concerned another claim against a PMC.[188] Third, where this State action requirement is satisfied, the claim fails upon the defence of sovereign immunity as the Court of Appeals in *Saleh* had held. Thus, despite the initial appearance of ATCA as an avenue to redress human rights abuses perpetrated by PMCs, its jurisprudence instead structures subtle multilayered active impunity mechanisms. Hinting at these mechanisms, George Fletcher concludes:

> '[t]he important point is that torture inflicted by private parties could well be considered a violation of the law of nations. And even if the government and its officials are not liable under the ATCA, those who supply them with services and otherwise assist in their violations are liable, in tort, as accomplices for violations of the law of nations'.[189]

Yet, even this proposition potentially provides an active impunity mechanism for PMCs by imposing liability through complicity in a State-centric paradigm, an approach that may become increasingly problematic. In addition to the fact, discussed above, that the PMC should be recognised as being capable of perpetrating human rights abuses directly, rather than simply playing the role of accessories, PMCs are increasingly providing services for other non-State entities in turn, such as international organisations, other corporations and commercial interests, and charities.[190]

[184] A progressive court might have navigated the obstacles given recourse to creative interpretation; see Judge Peter Messitte's skilful example below.

[185] *Saleh v Titan* (n 63) 14–15.

[186] The petition was denied 27 June 2011: *Saleh v Titan* [2011] US Supreme Court 09-1313, 131 SCt 3055.

[187] *Kiobel v Royal Dutch Shell* (n 114).

[188] *Manook v Research Triangle Institute International* (2010) 693 FSupp2d 4 (US District Court for the District of Columbia) 17–19.

[189] Fletcher (n 94) 127.

[190] A Katz, 'Annual Report of the Working Group on the Use of Mercenaries as a Means of Violating Human Rights and Impeding the Exercise of the Right of Peoples to Self-Determination' (UNHRC, 2013) A/HRC/24/45 8–9.

ATCA liability may also be excluded upon the limited *substantial* reach of ATCA: only a limited and restrictive class of international wrongs can be entertained after *Sosa*. This was raised in *Al-Shimari*, again concerning the Abu Ghraib scandal, where 'the Court is unconvinced that a suit against private civilian interrogators falls within the class of hybrid international norms in existence when the [ATCA] was enacted'.[191] That the DC Circuit neglected to consider the aforementioned reasoning and development in *Kunarac*, which had the effect imposing individual criminal liability for acts of torture in the context of the armed conflict irrespective of State action or action under the colour of law, suggests that both *Saleh* and *Al-Shimari* were wrongly decided. Indeed, incorporating the principles expounded in *Kunarac* into *Saleh* would have circumvented the paradox between State action and State immunity. In the context of *Al-Shimari*, this would have enabled the court to recognise that individual responsibility for acts of torture in situations of armed conflict could fall within the narrow category of international acts contemplated within ATCA in the aftermath of *Sosa*.

A final mechanism of active impunity is revealed through ATCA claims against Blackwater. *In re XE* consolidated five cases that arose out of Nisour Square and other incidents that allege shootings or beatings in Iraq.[192] Because ATCA claims are civil law remedies, however, Blackwater was ultimately able to avoid (potentially) negative limelight by settling out of court, without definitive ascription or admission of guilt or wrongdoing.[193] Although the summary execution claims were dismissed because State action was required for ATCA liability,[194] Judge Ellis for the District Court had opened the possibility for Blackwater to be liable under ATCA for war crimes claims: 'the [ATCA] recognizes a cause of action alleging war crimes, and claims arising under this cause of action are cognizable *against non-state actor defendants, including corporations*',[195]

[191] *Al-Shimari v CACI* (n 153) 728. Consolidated with *Al-Quraishi* on Appeal, considered below. The Court granted the motion to dismiss the ATCA claims, but allowed state law claims to proceed.

[192] *In re XE Services* (n 79) 573–76.

[193] *In re XE Services* (n 79). The company was reported to say that the settlement 'enables Xe's new management to move the company forward free of the costs and distraction of ongoing litigation': J Risen, 'Former Blackwater Guards Charged With Murder' *The New York Times* (8 January 2010) www.nytimes.com/2010/01/08/world/asia/08blackwater.html. The relative merits of civil and criminal law mechanisms to tackle impunity are beyond the scope of this book.

[194] *In re XE Services* (n 79) 592–94. Referring to the Second Circuit exception in *Kadic*, genocide, war crimes per Common Article 3 of the Geneva Conventions and torture within genocide and war crimes do not require State action for ATCA liability. Summary execution, however, does not fall within the *Kadic* exception, underscoring the force of the State action requirement as an active impunity mechanism.

[195] ibid 588. Emphasis added. The plaintiffs were required to establish factually the alleged war crimes claims to sustain the action. Judge Ellis justified this approach by 'applying the principles of *Sosa*, the [ATCA] confers subject-matter jurisdiction over properly stated claims of war crimes' despite the Fourth Circuit not having confronted this question squarely: ibid 583.

subsequently granting leave for the plaintiffs to rectify defects associated with these claims.[196] Blackwater then settled out of court, but not without further controversy.[197]

To reach this conclusion, Judge Ellis relied on harmonious jurisprudence from the Eleventh, Second and Ninth Circuits because the binding Fourth Circuit had not then confronted this question squarely. This conclusion was reversed for a period by controlling jurisprudence of the Fourth Circuit in *Al-Shimari* and *Al-Quraishi*,[198] before being barred by the extraterritoriality exclusion provided by the Supreme Court in *Kiobel*, detailed below. In other words, while Blackwater settled out of court to avoid an adverse verdict in this case,[199] subsequent Fourth Circuit and Supreme Court jurisprudence would have prevented such ATCA liability from being incurred both on appeal and into the future.

It is particularly noteworthy that this is not the only instance where subsequent appellate jurisprudence frustrates an ATCA claim made against a PMC, such that settlement would have been unnecessary. Yet, the stark disjuncture between a civil settlement and the violent force suffered by the victims in the cased combined under *In re XE* indicates a residual and final active impunity mechanism. This in turn underscores the need for functional criminal law sanctions capable of establishing culpability and imposing appropriate punishment that complement compensatory civil law mechanisms.

G. Overcoming Active Impunity Under ATCA?

The District Court case of *Al-Quraishi*,[200] which also arose from the Abu Ghraib scandal, has showed signs of reversal. Judge Messitte appeared to successfully navigate the active impunity obstacles provided by ATCA jurisprudence detailed above. He denied the defendant PMC's motion to

[196] *In re XE Services* (n 79) 592.

[197] *In re XE Services Dismissal Order* (US District Court Eastern District of Virginia, Alexandria Division). The victims claimed that they were led into thinking that this settlement would be their last chance for compensation because they were led to believe that the company was going to file for bankruptcy: L Sly, 'Iraqis Say They Were Forced to Take Blackwater Settlement' *Los Angeles Times* (11 January 2010) http://articles.latimes.com/2010/jan/11/world/la-fg-iraq-blackwater11-2010jan11. For the general situation concerning claims against Blackwater at that time, see also Risen, 'Former Blackwater Guards Charged With Murder' (n 193).

[198] *Al-Shimari v CACI* [2011] US Court of Appeals for the Fourth Circuit No 10-1891; No 10-1921, 658 F3d 413; *Al-Quraishi v Nakhla* (2011) 657 F3d 201 (US Court of Appeals for the Fourth Circuit).

[199] The company was reported to say that the settlement 'enables Xe's new management to move the company forward free of the costs and distraction of ongoing litigation'; Risen, 'Former Blackwater Guards Charged With Murder' (n 193).

[200] *Al-Quraishi v Nakhla* (n 181).

dismiss, holding inter alia that the defendants were liable under ATCA,[201] and that they were not entitled to sovereign immunity.[202] The reasoning underlying this conclusion must be analysed in detail because it reveals the potential of ATCA to assert accountability for PMC misconduct. This potential in turn unveils the active impunity mechanisms that have suspended PMC liability under that statute.

Judge Messitte applied *Sosa* principles during his examination of whether private parties are liable under ATCA to adopt a nuanced approach. In light of Aaron Garfield's observation above,[203] the earliest ATCA cases grounded the claim that private parties may be sued under the Act.[204] Judge Messitte noted in particular the Supreme Court's differentiation between both the type of violation concerned and the year when they occurred in their analysis of *Tel-Oren* and *Kadic*: this supports the requirement that the liability of private actors needs to be assessed on a case-by-case basis.[205] Judge Messitte further relied on Supreme Court precedent in *Argentine Republic* that '[ATCA] by its terms does not distinguish among classes of defendants',[206] in order to proceed to examine whether liability existed under the law of nations for each alleged violation.[207] The conclusion upon assessing liability for war crimes was that '[t]he weight of authority thus shows that a claim of war crimes may be asserted against private actors apart from any of state action'.[208] The three cases (*Tel-Oren*, *Saleh* and *Sanchez–Espinoza*) cited only excluded private liability for *torture* under ATCA, but do not touch upon the question of war crimes. Liability for torture, however, necessitated State action or commission under colour of law. This was factually satisfied because the defendants fulfilled a public function; they operated alongside military personnel, who under different circumstances would have performed these functions.[209] As an alternative colour of law argument, the defendants were alleged to have conspired with military personnel, who are unequivocally State actors, to commit the alleged instances of torture.[210]

[201] ibid 741–60. The state law claims made in this case are beyond the scope of this chapter, not least for its current uncertainty. At any rate, the Fourth Circuit held that 'the plaintiff's state law claims are preempted by federal law and displaced by it': *Al-Quraishi v Nakhla* (n 198) 203; and *Al-Shimari v CACI* (n 198). The Fourth Circuit, sitting en banc, subsequently reversed the majority decision of the panel below and dismissed the appeal, allowing the case to proceed to discovery stage for the state law claims: *Al-Shimari v CACI* [2012] US Court of Appeals for the Fourth Circuit (en banc) No 09-1335; No 10-1891; No 10-1921.

[202] *Al-Quraishi v Nakhla* (n 181).

[203] Garfield, 'Bridging a Gap in Human Rights Law' (n 157) 755.

[204] *Al-Quraishi v Nakhla* (n 181).

[205] ibid 743.

[206] *Argentine Republic v Amerada Hess Shipping* (1989) 488 US 428 (US Supreme Court) 438. This case, however, concerned the liability of foreign States, rather than of private parties.

[207] *Al-Quraishi v Nakhla* (n 181).

[208] ibid 747.

[209] ibid 751.

[210] ibid.

Under this alternative, however, finding that the defendants were operating under the colour of law would risk raising the shield of sovereign immunity that exempts liability under ATCA. Judge Messitte held that the activity under colour of law can extend beyond official behaviour to encompass individual action.[211] This is crucial because it prised open a gap in the impunity paradox. The defendants may have operated under colour of law, but in their *individual capacity*, which prevents their claim to immunity under the government contractor defence. The final significant hurdle for present purposes is the question of corporate liability under ATCA. Judge Messitte relies on *Presbyterian Church* which held that '[a] private corporation is a juridical person and has no per se immunity under US domestic or international law'.[212] He continues by citing other cases to ground the contention that corporations, as juridical persons, are indistinguishable from individual natural persons.[213] Conspicuous for its absence, however, is the aforementioned conflicting case of *Kiobel* where the Second Circuit withheld corporate liability under ATCA.[214]

The significance of *Al-Quraishi* is that the District Court revealed the possibility of imposing ATCA liability upon PMCs for actions alleged amounting war crimes and torture based upon the identical factual situation examined in *Saleh* and *Ibrahim*. This potential underscores the array of active impunity mechanisms operating within ATCA jurisprudence. Juxtaposing *Al-Quraishi* directly against *Saleh* and *Ibrahim* demonstrates that, while accountability for PMC misconduct *is possible* under ATCA, the statute is structured to give several interlocking avenues that prevent PMC liability and that have become embodied within the jurisprudence.

H. Broadening and Deepening Active Impunity: The Supreme Court Decision in *Kiobel*

To fully explicate the powerful and pervasive active impunity device provided by the Supreme Court decision in *Kiobel* the progress of *Al-Quraishi* and *Al-Shimari* in the Fourth Circuit, alluded to in the discussion of *In re XE* above, need to be discussed in detail. In *Al-Shimari*, Judge Lee at the District Court dismisses only those claims made under ATCA jurisdiction

[211] ibid 753.

[212] *Presbyterian Church of Sudan v Talisman Energy* (2003) 244 FSupp2d 289 (US District Court Southern District of New York) 319.

[213] *Al-Quraishi v Nakhla* (n 181).

[214] *Kiobel v Royal Dutch Shell* (n 114). The argument by analogy to the TVPA will be considered in section III.H.

for two reasons.[215] First, 'the Court doubts that the content and acceptance of the present claims are sufficiently definite under *Sosa* because the use of contractor interrogators is a modern, novel practice'.[216] Second, Judge Lee was also 'unconvinced that [ATCA] jurisdiction reaches private defendants such as CACI'.[217] In other words, CACI were immunised from ATCA liability by virtue of the novel and private character of PMCs, which as discussed in chapter two, define the PMC industry. Given the similarity of facts between *Al-Quraishi* and *Al-Shimari*, the skill with which Judge Messitte charted a course through the active impunity mechanisms is presented in stark contrast.

On appeal, the Fourth Circuit issued judgments that dismissed both *Al-Quraishi* and *Al-Shimari* on the same day and for the same reasons.[218] Yet, a short window of opportunity emerged when the Fourth Circuit reheard *Al-Quraishi* and *Al-Shimari* together en banc, and remanded the cases back to the District Court for lack of jurisdiction.[219] It was during this period, when the prospect of a successful claim might have been possible, that *Al-Quraishi* was settled.[220] The claimants in *Al-Shimari*, however, were less fortunate with timing: the Supreme Court closed this window in *Kiobel* by exempting extraterritorial action from the purview of ATCA just under 10 months after the Fourth Circuit's en banc panel prised it open.[221] Absent a Fourth Circuit reversal in *Al-Shimari*, the *Al-Quraishi* settlement would turn out to be the last opportunity for the victims to secure some measure of compensation for corporate torture at Abu Ghraib. Given the Supreme Court's unambiguous exclusion 'of seeking relief for violations of the law of nations occurring outside the United States' from

[215] 'The Court holds that the [ATCA] does not confer original jurisdiction over civil causes of action against government contractors under international law because such claims are fairly modern and therefore not sufficiently definite among the community of nations, as required under Sosa': *Al-Shimari v CACI* (n 154) 726. See generally ibid 704–05, and 725–28.

[216] *Al-Shimari v CACI* (n 153) 727.

[217] ibid 728; explicitly questioning the authority of *Kadic v Karadzic* (n 119).

[218] *Al-Quraishi v Nakhla* (n 198); *Al-Shimari v CACI* (n 198). The reasoning largely follows *Saleh v Titan* (n 63). At fn 37, the UN Working Group on the use of Mercenaries succinctly explained that 'In a review of the Al-Shimari decision by the full 4th Circuit Court of Appeals, it was determined that the case could go forward, since the defendants' objections to liability were actually defences, not immunities from suit': UN Working Group on the Use of Mercenaries, 'Submission by the Working Group on the Use of Mercenaries as a Means of Impeding the Exercise of the Right of Peoples to Self-Determination' (UN Human Rights Council, 2012) A/HRC/WG.10/2/CRP.1.

[219] *Al-Shimari v CACI and Al-Quraishi v Nakhla (Fourth Circuit rehearing)* [2012] US Court of Appeals for the Fourth Circuit (en banc) No 09-1335; No 10-1891; No 10-1921.

[220] *Al-Quraishi v Nakhla Voluntary Dismissal* (n 86).

[221] The difference in treatment by the District Courts may also have been influential. Recall that Judge Messitte was a lot more accepting of the ATCA claims *Al-Quraishi v Nakhla* (n 181); whereas Judge Lee refused to accept the ATCA claim: *Al-Shimari v CACI* (n 153).

the purview of ATCA,[222] the Fourth Circuit is unlikely to find grounds to hear an appeal. Despite the material difference of Abu Ghraib prison being within the jurisdiction of the US at the material time, the impugned actions still occurred outside of the territory of the United States, which remains the paramount factor expressed by the Supreme Court.

As Katherine Hawkins poignantly notes, *Al-Shimari* is the last of the cases against CACI and that the 'evidence of CACI's role in the torture Abu Ghraib will never see the light of day unless the Fourth Circuit reverses the district court's decision, and allows the case to proceed to trial'.[223] The insult of interpretative denial here cannot be clearer:[224] the axiomatic impossibility of an ATCA claim against a PMC shrouds its substantive wrongs. Despite strong substantive allegations,[225] it is fairly certain that *Al-Shimari*'s dismissal will stand because of *Kiobel*. The intricately interwoven active impunity mechanisms in the jurisprudence of ATCA described above no longer form the front line against ATCA claims, but will instead remain as residual obstacles barring claims which occur on the territory of the United States. In the somewhat perverse aftermath of *Al-Shimari*, CACI applied for and was granted, a Bill of Costs that required the victim-plaintiffs to pay costs of $13,731.61,[226] strongly disincentivising victims from making future claims against PMCs.[227] Contextualising this within the (officially undisclosed) settlements awarded by Blackwater in *In re XE*, where one victim who lost his left eye received only $10,000, and another who lost an eye and the use of his leg received $30,000 in settlement,[228] this order adds injury to existing juridical insult and torturous injury.

Yet, the Supreme Court's exclusion of events taking place extraterritorially was borne of its own motion: the Court, asked one question, answered

[222] *Kiobel v Royal Dutch Petroleum* (n 113).

[223] K Hawkins, 'CACI's Forgotten Role in Abu Ghraib (I)' *Huffington Post* (29 August 2013) www.huffingtonpost.com/katherine-hawkins/cacis-forgotten-role-in-a_b_3830280.html3; K Hawkins, 'CACI's Forgotten Role in Abu Ghraib (II)' *Huffington Post* (9 September 2013) www.huffingtonpost.com/katherine-hawkins/cacis-forgotten-role-in-a_1_b_3847081.html.

[224] Cohen (n 83) 107.

[225] A Taguba, '"Taguba Report": Article 15-6 Investigation of the 800th Military Police Brigade' (2004); G Fay, 'Fay Report: AR 15-6 Investigation of the Abu Ghraib Detention Facility and 205th Military Intelligence Brigade' (2004).

[226] *Al-Shimari v CACI Bill of Costs Order* [2013] US District Court for the Eastern District of Virginia, Alexandria Division 1:08-CV-00827-GBL-JFA.

[227] While formally, the Bill of Costs may be standard court procedure, commentators have noted that 'few large companies exercise that right in cases where they are sued by individuals on tortious civil rights or human rights grounds'. This may substantiate the allegation made by an attorney for the plaintiffs that it appears to be an attempt to intimidate the plaintiffs: M Censer, 'CACI Seeking Payment from Former Abu Ghraib Prisoners' *The Washington Post* (16 August 2013) www.washingtonpost.com/blogs/capital-business/post/caci-seeking-payment-from-former-abu-ghraib-prisoners/2013/08/12/4c573550-035d-11e3-a07f-49ddc7417125_blog.html.

[228] Sly, 'Iraqis Say They Were Forced to Take Blackwater Settlement' (n 197).

another.[229] *Kiobel* was brought to the Supreme Court because of the Circuit split sparked by the Second Circuit below holding that corporations are not liable under ATCA. Yet, when it came to consider the case, the Supreme Court directed the parties to file supplemental briefs addressing the question: 'Whether and under what circumstances the [ATCA] allows courts to recognize a cause of action for violations of the law of nations occurring within the territory of a sovereign other than the United States'.[230] This change in tack signalled the potential restriction in the *substantial* scope of the Act beyond the original question of mere *jurisdiction*. Put differently, in the aftermath of the Supreme Court's decision in *Kiobel*, the only relevant question became whether the alleged wrongful conduct took place outside of the territory of the United States.[231]

In one of the first lower court decisions since *Kiobel*, Judge Proctor (generally agreeing with Justices Alito and Thomas' concurring opinion) largely forecloses ATCA claims as they have been used by human rights campaigners since *Filartiga*. He held that,

> where a complaint alleges activity in both foreign and domestic spheres, an extraterritorial application of a statute arises *only* if the event on which the statute *focuses* did not occur abroad. Of course, [ATCA] *focuses* on the torts of extrajudicial killings and war crimes (violations of the law of nations), [and] the tort at issue occurred abroad, in Colombia, and *not* in the United States.[232]

In contrast, had the Supreme Court only decided upon the initial question of corporate liability under ATCA, the most far-reaching conclusion would have been to concur with the Second Circuit below in exempting corporations from the remit of ATCA. Together, this suggests that the Supreme Court restricted the scope of ATCA more than was justified. In turn, this creates a powerful active impunity mechanism insofar as it immunises all allegations of misconduct, regardless of severity, on the narrow question of

229 *Kiobel v Royal Dutch Petroleum* (n 113).

230 *Kiobel v Royal Dutch Petroleum* (n 113). Filed 5 March 2012.

231 *Balintulo v Daimler AG* [2013] US Court of Appeals for the Second Circuit No 09-2778-cv(L) 20: The Second Circuit was unambiguous about the necessity for the impugned action to occur within US territory: 'As we have now made clear, Kiobel forecloses the plaintiffs' claims because the plaintiffs have failed to allege that any relevant conduct occurred in the United States. The plaintiffs resist this obvious impact of the Kiobel holding on their claims. The Supreme Court's decision, they argue, does not preclude suits under the [ATCA] based on foreign conduct when the defendants are American nationals, or where the defendants' conduct affronts significant American interests identified by the plaintiffs. Curiously, this interpretation of Kiobel arrives at precisely the conclusion reached by Justice Breyer, who, writing for himself and three colleagues, only concurred in the judgment of the Court affirming our decision to dismiss all remaining claims brought under the [ATCA]': *Balintulo v Daimler AG*. Citations omitted. This would entirely exclude the potential for using ATCA against PMCs for which the US is the home or hiring State.

232 *Giraldo v Drummond Co* [2013] US District Court for the Northern District of Alabama, Southern Division 2:09-CV-1041-RDP 17. Citations omitted.

geographical location. The potential for interpretative denial is clear: under ATCA harm or damage suffered outside of the United States is not wrong.[233]

I. Torture Victims Protection Act 1991

The other pertinent avenue for civil claims to be made against PMC misconduct in US courts is provided for by the Torture Victims' Protection Act (TVPA) which establishes a civil action against 'Any individual, who under actual or apparent authority, or color of law, of any foreign nation … subjects an individual to torture … or … subjects an individual to extrajudicial killing'.[234] First introduced as a bill in 1986, it was catalysed by Congressional concern over the mistreatment of American soldiers in the 1991 Gulf War.[235] The TVPA was 'enacted … to give the benefits of the *Filartiga* decision to US citizens as well as foreigners'.[236]

The analysis of the TVPA is considerably more straightforward than that of ATCA because its content has been defined by Congress without substantive reference to the contentious content of the law of nations. That Congress did not simply extend ATCA to encompass US claimants, but instead enacted the TVPA illustrates that Congress did not seek parity between the two Acts.[237] Indeed, the TVPA differs from ATCA on substance—the former is restricted to torture and summary execution while the latter encompasses any violation of the law of nations or US treaty—and is more procedurally limited than ATCA.[238] Furthermore, as the DC Circuit held in *Saleh*, the TVPA did not 'include as possible defendants either American government officers or private US persons whether or not acting in concert with government employees'.[239] This constitutes the first active impunity mechanism within the TVPA: US persons are categorically immune from TVPA liability. In *Manook*, the only case to date where the TVPA was directly invoked against a PMC,[240] the claim was

[233] Recall the difference between harms and wrongs on the one hand, and injuries on the other which are contingent upon legal recognition: S Veitch, *Law and Irresponsibility: On the Legitimation of Human Suffering* (Routledge-Cavendish, 2007) 86.

[234] Pub.L. 102-256, 106 Stat. 73. This was consolidated with the ATCA under 28 U.S.C. para1350 (2006).

[235] B Emmons, 'Tortured Language: "Individuals," Corporate Liability and the Torture Victim Protection Act' (2011) 96 *Minnesota Law Review* 675, 683–84.

[236] Fletcher (n 94) 122. This is because only aliens are entitled to claim under ATCA.

[237] See eg *Al-Quraishi v Nakhla* (n 181).

[238] ibid.

[239] As further evidence for this proposition, the DC Circuit noted that 'President George H.W. Bush stated: "I am signing the bill based upon my understanding that the [TVPA] does not permit suits for alleged human rights violations in the context of United States military operations abroad"' *Saleh v Titan* (n 63) 16.

[240] The relative lack of PMC cases emerging under the TVPA may be explained by its limited substantial reach of torture and summary execution, and its limited jurisdiction which only enables US residents to sue.

denied because the '[d]efendants were not acting under color of law', and citing approvingly the DC Circuit in *Saleh*, held that US persons could not be defendants under the TVPA.[241] Adopting this reading of the TVPA, the District Court held that the defendant in *Manook* was not liable because the Research Triangle Institute is a private US person under the TVPA.[242]

This reasoning, however, is inconsistent with the second active impunity mechanism operating within another body of TVPA jurisprudence that prevents corporate liability under the Act. As with ATCA, the question whether juridical persons were encumbered with TVPA liability was the subject of a Circuit split. In *Mohamad v Rajoub*, the DC Circuit held that TVPA liability was limited to natural persons,[243] in stark contrast to the Circuit's ATCA position. Similarly, the Fourth Circuit in *Aziz* held that that the TVPA excluded corporate defendants from liability.[244] The Ninth Circuit concurred in *Bowoto*, where corporate liability was excluded upon strictly literal interpretation of the statute that applied Congressional guidance on the interpretation of common legislative terms.[245] The Ninth Circuit noted, however, that this conclusion conflicted with Eleventh Circuit jurisprudence in *Aldana*,[246] but emphasised that corporate liability was not contended in that case.[247] Importantly, the Eleventh Circuit has since developed corporate liability consistently under the TVPA in *Romero* and *Sinaltrainal*.[248] While the Supreme Court denied certiorari in *Bowoto*,[249] it had ruled conclusively a week earlier in *Mohamad* that '[t]he text of the TVPA convinces us that Congress did not extend liability to organizations, sovereign or not'.[250] While the defendant was a non-sovereign organisation in that case, rather than a juridical person such as a corporation,

[241] *Manook v Research Triangle Institute International* (n 188) 20; quoting approvingly the DC Circuit in Saleh: *Saleh v Titan* (n 63) 16.

[242] *Manook v Research Triangle Institute International* (n 188) 20.

[243] *Mohamad v Rajoub* (2011) 634 F3d 604 (US Court of Appeals for the DC Circuit).

[244] *Aziz v Alcolac* (2011) 658 F3d 388 (US Court of Appeals for the Fourth Circuit).

[245] As Judge Schroeder concluded: 'We agree with the district court that Congress's use of the word "individual" throughout the statute indicates that it did not intend for the TVPA to apply to corporations. Indeed, Congress has directed courts to presume the word "individual" in a statute refers to natural persons and not corporations. In the Dictionary Act, Congress provided definitions for a number of common statutory terms that courts are to apply "unless the context indicates otherwise." One term defined is "person," which the Dictionary Act defines as being broader than a reference to an individual. The Act defines "person" to include "corporations, companies, associations, firms, partnerships, societies, and joint stock companies, as well as individuals." The Dictionary Act therefore speaks of "corporations" and "individuals" as distinct terms, and we must therefore presume those terms have different meanings': *Bowoto v Chevron* (n 141) 1126–27. Citations omitted.

[246] *Aldana v Del Monte Fresh Produce* (2005) 416 F3d 1242 (US Court of Appeals for the Eleventh Circuit).

[247] *Bowoto v Chevron* (n 141) 1126.

[248] *Romero v Drummond Co* (n 124); *Sinaltrainal v Coca-Cola Co* (n 123).

[249] *Bowoto v Chevron* [2012] US Supreme Court 10-1536, 132 SCt 1968.

[250] *Mohamad v Palestinian Authority* (n 132) www.supremecourt.gov/opinions/11pdf/11-88.pdf.

the Supreme Court is unambiguously clear that the TVPA only imposes liability on natural persons.[251]

The Supreme Court was arguably bound by Congressional intention and offered several consistent grounds for this position. First, the text of the TVPA imposes liability upon 'individuals' in contradistinction to 'persons', emphasising that 'this Court routinely uses "individual" to denote a natural person, and in particular to distinguish between a natural person and a corporation'.[252] Second, the term 'individual' is employed once to denote a perpetrator and four times to denote the victim; because only a natural person is capable of being a victim of torture or extra-judicial killing, the Supreme Court adopted a presumption that the term is used consistently throughout the legislation to limit its scope to natural persons.[253] Third, clear Congressional intent could be gleaned from the legislative history of the statute.[254] Although the Supreme Court held that it was not necessary to rely on the statute's history, this was decisive in Justice Breyer's concurring opinion. He said that the 'word "individual" is open to multiple interpretations … to include natural persons, corporations, and other entities … [t]he legislative history of the statute … makes up for whatever interpretative inadequacies remain after considering language alone'.[255]

What is particularly striking, however, is that 'the [TVPA] would be rendered toothless by a construction of the "individual" that limits liability to natural persons' which the plaintiffs argued would foreclose effective remedy for victims and their families.[256] The Supreme Court itself noted the difficulties that this interpretation created for plaintiffs, especially because '[p]ersonal jurisdiction may be more easily established over corporate than human beings. And natural persons may be more likely than organizations to be judgment proof'.[257] Because these limitations were imposed by Congress, however, the courts are prevented from extending the liability of the TVPA, despite the validity of countervailing arguments and its consequences for perpetuating impunity.

That *Manook* was not open to appeal on the TVPA claim is inconsequential because the controlling authority of *Mohamad*, pre-empting corporate liability, would lead the appeals court to the same result. The different

[251] ibid 1703.
[252] ibid 1707.
[253] ibid 1708. This approach arguably lacks nuance, however, as there is not necessarily any correspondence between the individual as perpetrator and the individual as victim beyond their linguistic commonality.
[254] ibid 1709–10.
[255] ibid, Justice Breyer, concurring opinion: ibid 1711.
[256] *Mohamad v Palestinian Authority* (n 132).
[257] In this regard, the Court noted that only 2 TVPA plaintiffs have ever recovered successfully: ibid.

grounds upon which the claims in *Manook* and *Mohamad* were denied, however, indicates the interlocking active impunity mechanisms built into the TVPA. In the former, while corporate liability was accepted, the claim was pre-empted on the American nationality of the defendant. In the latter, the exclusive focus upon liability of only natural persons foreclosed the claim such that the foreign nationality requirement need not be considered. Here, again, is the operation of an interlocking active impunity mechanism. The first stage excludes all claims that are not made against natural persons under *Mohamad*. The small class of claims capable of proceeding then confront the second stage, where under *Manook*, US persons are exempt from liability under the statute. Thus, the TVPA only imputes liability to a small class of defendants: non-US natural persons found to have committed torture or extra-judicial killing. The alternating rationale for excluding the TVPA claim is reminiscent of the differing reasons proffered against ATCA dissected above. It is not surprising, therefore that the Supreme Court echoed its own approach in that jurisprudence by adopting the more restrictive of the options available. A more powerful active impunity mechanism for the TVPA is provided in *Mohamad* because non-American groups, organisations and corporations, presumably including PMCs, remain liable under *Manook*. Under the Torture Victim Protection Act, only acts of torture or extra-judicial killing perpetrated by non-US natural persons can constitute a wrong recognised by that law.

IV. CONCLUSION: ACTIVE PRIVATE MILITARY COMPANY IMPUNITY AND INTERPRETATIVE DENIAL REVISITED

One of the enduring problems with active impunity mechanisms is the fact that these may be conflated with the failure of a claim as a result of a defect on substantive grounds. Unlike passive impunity mechanisms which preclude the possibility of initiating or engaging processes for determining and ascribing responsibility, active impunity mechanisms allow these to function and instead subvert the operation of these processes. In other words, active impunity mechanisms are conflated with the merits of the claim. Insidiously, it is not possible to determine, definitively, whether a particular claim has fallen because of an inherent flaw within the claim itself or because of the operation of interlocking active impunity mechanisms. This has lingering effects, because even where active impunity mechanisms are identified and have been demonstrated to operate within a particular context, the received message from the official dismissal of a claim is likely to be rather that the claim itself was deficient. With unsuccessful claims as the basis of argument, it is difficult to suggest that the defect lies instead within the very system that rendered those determinations. This effect makes it even more difficult to demonstrate the existence of active impunity mechanisms, thus perpetuating the effect further.

Situating this chapter again within Stanley Cohen's concept of interpretative denial, the effects of the active impunity mechanisms that are available to the PMC can be illustrated. The various legal exclusionary mechanisms that obstructed the array of cases brought against PMCs have a powerful exonerating effect—they have done no wrong. While this is, correctly, the effect of a solemn court judgment, its application in such contexts is somewhat perverse for two reasons.

First, the claims did not discuss in depth, and were not dismissed, for lack of substantive merit. Rather, the success of the claims was obstructed by artificial legal barriers associated with formal personhood, circumscribed jurisdiction and the vagaries of legal interpretation. The vindication in these cases, therefore, was not that its conduct was clean; instead, the exemption was because of limitations in the relevant law. This strongly suggests that any deficiency present in these cases concerned the legal process and the structure of the law, and not in the substance of the claim. Yet, the interpretation of the cases failing is that there was no wrong.

Second, a more nuanced version of this effect is present with the reduction in the ontological significance within civil claims. This is true for ATCA, but especially for the TVPA which only encompasses torture and extra-judicial killings, because substantive wrongs that otherwise amount to gross human rights abuses and international crimes are neutralised into mere civil wrongs. That the civil claims presented above do not constitute criminal indictments actually develops in two interesting directions. As mentioned above, civil claims allow the defendant to settle in order to obvert a negative judgment. The prospect of risking only financial penalties can collapse serious human rights violations into just another cost of doing business, and even a variable that can prove profitable.

Yet more insidiously, however, is the fact that civil suits expose the victim-plaintiff to considerable costs where their claims fail. A purely financial balancing, eerily akin to that undertaken by corporations between profit and risk, may feature prominently into the decision whether a victim will file a claim in pursuit of justice. Where, as in the example provided above which illustrated that the costs awarded in one case were of the same magnitude as a settlement for serious permanent injury sustained in another, a claim may not be financially feasible let alone desirable. Given the obstacles strewn in the path of civil claims against PMCs, that none have been successful to date and that the jurisprudence has since been constricted, two settlements have been the most favourable outcome for the victims to date. The prospect of facing a substantial Bill of Costs, roughly equivalent to what might be awarded in a settlement, significantly disincentivises victims to become plaintiffs against PMCs. In turn, this would stymie the already scarce flow of claims: in the atrophy of these apparently receptive legal avenues will be the subtle transformation of the mechanisms of active impunity mechanisms into those of passive impunity. In other words, if an avenue for legal redress becomes sufficiently well barricaded, the ordinary operation of legal processes might suppress attempts to utilise that avenue.

Even without exploring such implications, the active impunity mechanism demonstrated in this chapter serve to strongly reinforce the axiom that corporations cannot be incorporated to pursue criminal ends, further reinforcing interpretative denial. Applying Stanley Cohen's idea of 'magical legalism',[258] the PMC cannot commit crimes because the law does not recognise corporate criminal responsibility. This might be extended to the civil claims, that the PMC can do no wrong because those laws do not apply. If this suspension of common sense engendered by such syllogism were the only effect, then perhaps the harm of these active impunity mechanisms might be limited.

Interpretative denial, unfortunately, has severe ramifications upon the future of PMC impunity. If active impunity mechanisms insulate the PMC against legal findings of wrongdoing, whether criminal or civil, the implication is that both it and its activities are benign. This in turn implies that relatively lax regulation, oversight and accountability, such as industry self-regulation, would be sufficiently rigorous. In other words, the active impunity mechanisms that exclude the PMC from criminal liability and exonerate it from civil liability provide the foundation for building weak industry regulation into the future.

[258] Cohen (n 83) 108.

6

The Future of Private Military Impunity

I. INTRODUCTION

THIS CHAPTER CONSIDERS the future of PMC impunity that will be structured by the industry-specific regulatory mechanisms that have recently been, or are currently being, tabled on the international plane. The dynamic nature and uncertain trajectory of these developments, however, requires this chapter both to extrapolate from the current structures of impunity examined in previous chapters and to identify structural deficits that are emerging within these developing regulatory regimes. This is necessary to demonstrate that, in addition to the existing impunity mechanisms currently enjoyed by the PMC identified in earlier chapters, novel forms of impunity are likely to be introduced by and will persist within the very regulatory mechanisms that are being tailored to regulate the PMC industry.

Such a trajectory sets the future of PMC impunity fundamentally apart from the structures of impunity that the PMC has enjoyed to date because the emerging forms of PMC regulation are intended and designed specifically to address and redress the unique legal challenges raised by the PMC. As such, they simultaneously possess the prospect of remedying the deficiencies inherent within seeking to apply general rules to the specific characteristics of the PMC, as well as the potential to entrench impunity within the very systems designed to contain PMC excesses if the regulation is poorly designed or implemented. The purpose of this chapter is therefore to critically highlight the deficiencies lurking within emerging PMC regulatory mechanisms in order to illuminate the potential for impunity to persist into the future. The ongoing development of PMC regulation offers the important opportunity for improvement if its weaknesses can be identified and addressed in a timely manner.

The weight placed in this chapter upon the impunity-generating potential of PMC industry-specific regulation is not, emphatically, to detract from the likelihood that more general forms of impunity identified in earlier chapters will continue: rather the purpose is to highlight new directions in which impunity may be created and maintained into the future.

In this context, it is useful to situate these emerging impunity mechanisms within the continuing chain of developments which imbue the PMC with impunity. In line with the progression of this book, PMC activity has been able to continue in an under-regulated fashion as a direct consequence both of the law's failure to marginalise or criminalise mercenary activity, and the adoption of the corporate form that further legitimates and insulates the PMC.[1] That the law did not register PMC activity as particularly perilous paved the way for industry advocates to advance the acceptability of light-touch self-regulatory mechanisms in response to allegations of impunity for serious violations of international humanitarian and human rights law. Perversely completing the cycle, the relatively speedy development of these lighter forms of self-regulation, when compared with the drawn-out participatory processes involved with framing an international convention, makes it possible to detract attention from the imperative of developing more robust regulatory mechanisms. Even where rigorous regulation may be developed, the urgency to implement them is diffused because of the ready availability of countervailing self-regulation mechanisms. Indeed, the speed with which lighter forms of PMC industry regulation are accepted and adopted may even enhance their legitimacy in relation to competing modes of regulation, despite the persistence of structural and substantive flaws.

The approach of this chapter is to consider the future of PMC impunity inherent within the developing industry-specific regulation along four dimensions: content and contortion; competition and capture; composition and competence; and compliance and consequence. These proposed criteria can be envisaged as expanding concentric circles, gradually moving outwards from the core of abstract principles that inform the regulatory regime to increasingly practical concerns affecting its implementation. Thus, the chapter first sets out the development, nature and characteristics of each trajectory of PMC regulation on the international plane as the basis upon which the analysis of each criterion can take place. It is then necessary to highlight the potential imbalance between prospectively setting standards and retrospectively enforcing them which constitutes a major challenge that confronts voluntary self-regulation regimes. Thus, the chapter embarks on an exploration of the temporal dimensions of the concept of responsibility before turning to outline the historical progression towards self-regulation for the PMC industry within the United Kingdom. The regulatory relevance of these four dimensions is then laid

[1] See chs 3 and 4 respectively. Even the UN Working Group on the Use of Mercenaries has acknowledged that PMC activities fall outside of the UN Mercenary Convention's definitions, and thus remain beyond its regulatory scope: A Nikitin, 'Report of the Working Group on the Use of Mercenaries as a Means of Violating Human Rights and Impeding the Exercise of the Right of Peoples to Self-Determination' (UNHRC, 2009) A/HRC/10/14 paras 40–41.

out before the chapter is able to turn to analysing the emerging mechanisms that seek to regulate the PMC industry along the four dimensions.

The emphasis throughout this chapter is placed upon voluntary self-regulation initiatives developed for the PMC industry, in particular the International Code of Conduct (ICoC), for three main reasons. First, there has been significant interest and uptake among States, other potential clients and the PMC industry itself. This suggests that these initiatives are actively shaping the practice of the PMC industry and defining the relationships between the industry and those engaged with it. Second, this positive reception, when combined with its relative speed and the perceived inclusiveness of the process, may have the effect of crowding out competing modes of PMC regulation. In doing so, these initiatives are implicitly setting the standards and limitations of regulation to the extent that there are now signs that membership will be a prerequisite for business and may soon even be reflected in the domestic legislation of some States.[2] Third, the pseudo-international nature of these initiatives may destabilise or distend both the content and scope of existing legal obligations in a subtle manner that is favourably permissive for the industry.

The result is that the ICoC may realistically dominate the field as the primary mode of PMC industry regulation. With the characteristics of self-regulation in mind, this chapter then turns to consider strategies for improving the ICoC and to shed light on its deficiencies. In particular, this chapter proposes to incentivise more robust oversight by considering possible avenues of imposing collective due diligence responsibilities onto the Association that oversees adherence to the ICoC.

While the discussion in this chapter focuses upon the ramifications relating to PMC-specific regulation, the analysis undertaken here may become more generalisable and can provide an evaluative framework for emerging forms of regulation in other sectors. The approach of this chapter may be especially useful to gauge the appropriateness of industry self-regulation in corporate sectors, and can be adapted to assess the efficacy of such regulation on activities that have potentially adverse impacts on the protection of human rights.

II. REGULATION OF PMCs ON THE INTERNATIONAL PLANE

An argument advanced by Allison Stanger is that strategic outsourcing is the key to harnessing the power of the private sector to tackle contemporary

[2] Indeed, framing the ICoC in domestic legislation may be a possible avenue to circumvent the critical weakness of the ICoC Association in enforcement: R Shah, 'Beating Blackwater: Using Domestic Legislation to Enforce the International Code of Conduct for Private Military Companies' (2014) 123 *Yale Law Journal* 2559.

global issues, and as such, outsourcing per se is unproblematic so long as there is adequate oversight and regulation.[3] This perspective provides an alternative approach by focusing the analysis on the question of whether the mechanisms designed for regulating the PMC industry are capable of neutralising the issues and concerns that surround security and military outsourcing.

There are currently two competing paradigms for the regulation of PMCs on the international plane, although neither can truly be said to be an inter*national* mechanism. The more prominent International Code of Conduct (ICoC) fails this signifier because it is an agreement conducted between the *companies* themselves (rather than States), while the incomplete UN *Draft* Convention process has been stalled in an UN open-ended intergovernmental working group.[4]

A. Irresponsible Regulation: Neglecting the Temporal Dimension of Responsibility

To begin to consider these mechanisms, it is necessary to expound upon a neglected form of impunity that arises within the temporal dimensions of responsibility because this may reveal the systemic bias within PMC regulation regimes. This section will illustrate that the two temporal forms of responsibility, prospective and retrospective, inform different aspects of the regulatory mechanism, namely standard-setting respectively and accountability. For a regulatory mechanism to be fair and effective, it must employ and balance measures from both temporal forms of responsibility. This is necessary to allay allegations either that the regulation imposes excessive responsibility or conversely facilitates impunity. Without a clear

[3] A Stanger, *One Nation Under Contract: The Outsourcing of American Power and the Future of Foreign Policy* (Yale University Press, 2011) 10–11.

[4] Henceforth 'Draft Convention'. The Draft Convention can be found in J Gómez del Prado, 'Report of the Working Group on the Use of Mercenaries as a Means of Violating Human Rights and Impeding the Exercise of the Right of Peoples to Self-Determination with the Draft of a Possible Convention on Private Military and Security Companies (PMSCs) for Consideration and Action by the Human Rights Council' (UNGA, 2010) A/HRC/15/25. The mandate of the Working Group can be found in Human Rights Council, 'Open-Ended Intergovernmental Working Group to Consider the Possibility of Elaborating an International Regulatory Framework on the Regulation, Monitoring and Oversight of the Activities of Private Military and Security Companies' (UN Human Rights Council, 2010) A/HRC/RES/15/26. The mandate of the Working Group was renewed pursuant to Human Rights Council, 'Open-Ended Intergovernmental Working Group to Consider the Possibility of Elaborating an International Regulatory Framework on the Regulation, Monitoring and Oversight of the Activities of Private Military and Security Companies' (UN Human Rights Council, 2013) A/HRC/RES/22/33. It should be noted that the Draft Convention is only one of the avenues for regulation to be considered by the Working Group. At the time of writing in November 2014, the Working Group has concluded its third session.

understanding of the temporal dimension of responsibility and how these are expressed within regulation, however, a regulatory regime that is heavily skewed towards either form may imbue the PMC with the aura of responsibility, while it simultaneously generates irresponsibility.

HLA Hart's typology of responsibility, discussed in chapter one, has been criticised for not according sufficient importance to the temporal dimension of responsibility. The assumption of retrospectivity—that responsibility is synonymous with accountability—which permeates the concept of responsibility,[5] may be challenged by differentiating between the possession of an excuse and it subsequent deployment. In John Gardner words: 'At an earlier time we might say that the wrongdoer *has* an excuse; only at the later time can she *offer* it'.[6] This questions the common assumption that responsibility is, or indeed can be, fixed at the material time of commission because the ascription of responsibility (if it occurs) necessarily takes place *after* the fact. Furthermore, the process of ascribing responsibility may be affected by intervening factors including the deployment of an excuse or defence above, or through re-categorising the cognitive significance of an event through interpretative denial or interpretive assertion mechanisms.[7]

It was Peter Cane who developed the most sophisticated analysis by differentiating between 'historic' and 'prospective' forms of responsibility:[8]

> In a temporal sense, responsibility looks in two directions. Ideas such as accountability, answerability and liability look backwards to conduct and events in the past. They form the core of … 'historic responsibility'. By contrast, the ideas of roles and task look to the future, and establish obligations and duties—'prospective responsibilities' … Accounts of legal responsibility tend to focus on historic responsibility at the expense of prospective responsibility.[9]

In adopting this framework, 'historic responsibility' will be substituted with 'retrospective responsibility' for three reasons: first to underscore the temporal element; second to accommodate Gardner's earlier observation that the ascription of responsibility for past actions may be contingent upon intervening factors; and third to use the antonym of 'prospective responsibility' to prevent ambiguity.

Peter Cane further divides prospective responsibilities into two categories: 'productive' responsibilities directed to the production of good outcomes, and 'preventive' responsibilities aimed at the prevention of

[5] Responsibility and accountability are often used synonymously: K Ainley, 'Excesses of Responsibility: The Limits of Law and the Possibilities of Politics' (2011) 25 *Ethics & International Affairs* 407, 410. Explicitly at fn 8.

[6] J Gardner, 'The Mark of Responsibility' (2003) 23 *Oxford Journal of Legal Studies* 157, 161. Emphasis original.

[7] S Cohen, *States of Denial: Knowing About Atrocities and Suffering* (Polity, 2001) 107–09.

[8] P Cane, *Responsibility in Law and Morality* (Hart Publishing, 2002) 31–39.

[9] ibid 31.

bad outcomes. Simply put, the standard-setting forms of responsibility may either be directed towards the production of virtuous outcomes or be aimed at prohibiting harmful results. Because Peter Cane emphasises prospective forms of responsibility to counterbalance the law's predisposition towards retrospective responsibility, he does not elaborate upon this latter category. Instead, for retrospective responsibility, we look to James Crawford and Jeremy Watkins who draw a distinction between 'responsibility as answerability' and 'responsibility as liability'.[10] The former connotes the calling to account for conduct which is accompanied by the possibility of riposte to assail the charges.[11] Although there is some scope for confusion with Hart's categories,[12] the latter suggests responsibility through the violation of an existing obligation which is thus open to some form of censure.[13] This proposition can be contextualised within Gardner's question related to the point in time when responsibility is affixed: within this context liability responsibility appears to be the result of answerability responsibility where attempts at justification or reinterpretation have failed.

The prospect for impunity subsists within different aspects of these temporal dimensions of responsibility. Taking retrospective responsibility mechanisms first, the availability of defences illustrate that the notion of responsibility is temporally flexible and may be imposed or alleviated at a later point in time.[14] Retrospective responsibility is thus susceptible to active impunity mechanisms that suspend legal liability, as well as interpretative denial mechanisms which downplay the registered severity of harm. These mechanisms operate to disavow retrospective responsibility by altering the very processes of accountability. Conversely, prospective responsibility affects an anterior notion of responsibility that is broadly tied to denial mechanisms. As prospective responsibility mechanisms delineate obligations and set the benchmarks of conduct, the subsequent breach of these obligations is entirely precluded where these have not been adequately established beforehand. Impunity is generated because the lack of established standards forestalls the possibility of subsequent accountability processes.

This refined model of the temporality in the concept of responsibility is useful for analysing the appropriateness and utility of competing PMC regulatory regimes. Forms of *legal* regulation are generally predisposed towards *retrospective* responsibility whereas *self-regulation* mechanisms in

[10] J Crawford and J Watkins, 'International Responsibility' in S Besson and J Tasioulas (eds), *The Philosophy of International Law* (Oxford University Press, 2010) 283–84.
[11] ibid 283.
[12] HLA Hart, *Punishment and Responsibility: Essays in the Philosophy of Law* (Oxford University Press, 2008) 222–27.
[13] Crawford and Watkins, 'International Responsibility' (n 10) 284.
[14] Gardner, 'The Mark of Responsibility' (n 6) 161.

the form of declaratory of codes of conduct tend to emphasise *prospective* responsibility. Both retrospective and prospective forms of responsibility are complementary and have to be embodied within a regulatory mechanism to ensure its appropriateness and robustness. The tension between show trials on one hand, and impunity on the other, may be used to demonstrate the temporal dimensions of responsibility.[15] Over-emphasis upon retrospectivity runs the risk of becoming a show trial because accountability is asserted over all other factors, including consideration of prior standards against which one is measured. Show 'trials are either staged (Lenin's show trials) or scripted (Stalin's) and often decisions are made in advance by the State'.[16] While Gerry Simpson asserts that such trials constitute the perversion of the legal process,[17] an alternative view is that show trials lie at the extremes of accountability where prospective responsibility considerations are absent. The particular jeopardy of being held to (criminal) account for actions without the existence of clearly delineated obligations is entrenched within the universal rule against retroactive punishment.[18] On the other hand, a sense of impunity may arise from an excessive skew towards prospective responsibility. Obligations and duties may be clearly defined, but no consequence attaches to their breach because there are no accountability mechanisms to provide sanction that give rise to the classic conception of impunity.

Over-reliance on prospective responsibility mechanisms may result in laudable catalogues of obligations and standards that ground claims of improved regulation. These may simultaneously detract from adequate retrospective accountability mechanisms for their enforcement that lead in turn to impunity. This is consistent with the form of passive impunity that subsists between role and outcome responsibilities. Prospective responsibility mechanisms clearly define role responsibilities by establishing obligations and duties whereas retrospective responsibility mechanisms correspond with outcome responsibilities because they are concerned with the consequences. Despite the assertion of a form of responsibility in both instances, impunity may arise in situations where these different forms of responsibility are not balanced in the same instance.

Finally, the more subtle effect of prospective responsibilities needs to be reiterated because these delineate the sphere within which retrospective

[15] Other scholars have focused on different aspects of the tension between show trials and impunity: M Koskenniemi, *Politics of International Law* (Hart Publishing, 2011) 171–97; G Simpson, *Law, War and Crime: War Crimes Trials and the Reinvention of International Law* (Polity, 2007) 11–29.

[16] Simpson, *Law, War and Crime* (n 15) 109. See ch 3 above concerning the Luanda mercenary trials and Hugh Byatt's opinion that this was a show trial conducted for political purposes: H Byatt, 'Sentences Passed on British Mercenaries in Angola, Part, The Trial of British Mercenaries in Angola June/July 1976', FCO 45/2000.

[17] Simpson (n 15) 105–31.

[18] Enshrined eg in ICCPR, art 15 and ECHR, art 7.

responsibilities subsequently operate. Retrospective responsibilities can only be assessed and affirmed where prior obligations, and their relevant standards, have been established. Thus, prospective responsibilities may generate passive impunity because of the definitional role it plays. There can be no retrospective accountability mechanisms for adherence to obligations that do not exist, short of show trials.

B. The Path to Self-regulation in the United Kingdom

The failure to establish a prospective policy for the PMC industry created early problems for the UK, as Sarah Percy notes:

> The UK, despite being closely associated with the world of private security, since at least the 1970s, has had little policy engagement with private actors selling military and security services before they appeared on the international stage. Indeed, the UK government has an unfortunate pattern of dealing with the problems caused by private force in civil wars abroad after they occur.[19]

In the wake of the 'Arms to Africa' scandal the UK commissioned two reports, one from the House of Commons Foreign Affairs Committee[20] and the subsequent response from the FCO,[21] but neither resulted in any specific legislative action. Industry self-regulation was briefly discussed as an option for regulating PMCs by the Foreign and Commonwealth Office (FCO) and was conceived to operate through a trade association comprised of members of the industry.[22] The benefits identified included 'an assurance of respectability' provided by the member companies and that it 'would help establish standards of behaviour within the industry'.[23]

[19] Although this example demonstrates problems associated with a lack of policy formation, this highlights the problems associated where prospective standards are not established: S Percy, 'Private Security Companies and Civil Wars' (2009) 11 *Civil Wars* 57, 66; for broader political ramifications, see ibid 65–70.

[20] United Kingdom Foreign and Commonwealth Office, *Private Military Companies: Options for Regulation* Green Paper (2001–02, HC 577).

[21] House of Commons Foreign Affairs Committee, *Private Military Companies* (2001–02, HC 922); the regulatory framework within the UK is explained in detail in A Bohm, K Senior and A White, 'The United Kingdom' in C Bakker and M Sossai (eds), *Multilevel Regulation of Military and Security Contractors: The Interplay Between International, European and Domestic Norms* (Hart Publishing, 2012).

[22] United Kingdom Foreign and Commonwealth Office, *Private Military Companies* (n 20) 76. It has been suggested that the independent formation of the British Association of Private Security Companies (BAPSC), which sought to promote the commercial and political interests of the industry, had influenced this direction as it provided a model upon which a government-backed self-regulation scheme could be based (although ultimately the UK chose to partner with the Aerospace Defence and Securities Industry (ADS) Group. Another factor influencing this predisposition towards self-regulation is its relatively low cost: Bohm, Senior and White, 'The United Kingdom' (n 21) 320–21.

[23] United Kingdom Foreign and Commonwealth Office (n 20) 76.

The drawbacks, however, appeared to carry more weight in the report: 'The lack of legal backing would mean that the Government might be compelled to watch while a company pursued a course that was plainly contrary to the public interest'.[24] When the United Kingdom House of Commons Foreign Affairs Committee considered the efficacy of a voluntary code of conduct, it stated:

> We agree that a voluntary code of conduct would help to establish standards of behaviour in the industry ... The development of such a code of conduct should be welcomed, particularly while legislation is being drafted. However, *we conclude that a voluntary code is insufficient to regulate the private military industry, because it would not enable the Government to prevent the activities of disreputable companies which were detrimental to the United Kingdom's interests.*[25]

Implicit within this statement are two important points related to responsibility. The first is the establishment of industry standards—a form of prospective responsibility imposing obligations and duties—through a voluntary code of conduct. It is not immediately obvious what standards PMCs should be measured against or what obligations they might bear. Although PMCs operate within the context of armed hostilities, they have neither taken on the rights and obligations of IHL because they are neither States and nor are they prima facie parties to the conflict. Conversely, PMCs may potentially agree to be held to *higher* standards than the bare minimum dictated by IHL. The second is the recognition that establishing standards is insufficient on its own. Prospective responsibility mechanisms need to be complemented by retrospective responsibility mechanisms capable of ensuring adherence and enforcing accountability to those standards.

It became evident that the UK was set on government-backed system of self-regulation despite repetitive consultations expressing discord and disagreement as to the best way forward.[26] William Hague, then the Foreign Secretary, declared that the UK would regulate the industry 'through a trade association based on a voluntary code of conduct agreed with and monitored by the Government' and would '[u]se their leverage as a key buyer of [PMC] services to promote compliance with the code', and '[s]eek an international agreement on standards consistent with the UK code'.[27] The prospective bias of this approach was implicit within its 'aim of *promoting high standards* in the [PMC] industry internationally, and

[24] ibid.

[25] House of Commons Foreign Affairs Committee, *Private Military Companies* (n 21) 137. Emphasis original. Given the transnational dimension of these companies' operations, it might be similarly difficult to suppress unlawful activity as well.

[26] Bohm, Senior and White (n 21) 310–11; for a good overview of these developments, see ibid 316–24.

[27] W Hague, 'Private Military and Security Companies' HC Deb 16 September 2010, cols 59 WS.

reducing the risk that the activities of [PMCs] might give rise to human rights or humanitarian law concerns'.[28] After this statement of intent, Henry Bellingham, then the Minister for Conflict Issues, confirmed the UK preference for 'a robust code and monitoring regime for U.K.-based [PMCs]'.[29] Whether the possible inclusion of complementary retrospective responsibility mechanisms will constitute part of the regime remains to be seen.[30] Two major weaknesses of the UK approach have been highlighted. First, this remains a *voluntary* system of regulation. Although it has been predicted to cover the majority of the industry, the unregulated minority will continue to be unregulated and it is precisely this part of the industry that is likely to engage in illicit activities into the future and which requires close regulation.[31] Second, there are oversight and enforcement difficulties with self-regulation. Funding the trade association inspectorate through membership fees risks both insufficient resources for its purposes and acts as a disincentive for it to exclude members for misconduct—a sanction which may have limited effect upon the PMC at any rate.[32]

In the context of highlighting the deficiencies inherent in relying upon voluntary self-regulation alone, it is noteworthy that Hannah Tonkin specifically draws upon the approach adopted by the UK as opening the door for home State responsibility for harmful PMC activities abroad:

> Notwithstanding the existence of [home state] obligations, a number of key states—most notably the UK—continue to close their eyes to [PMCs] operating from their territory ... State inaction ... would represent a conscious failure to prevent harmful [PMC] activities overseas, and in certain circumstances this could give rise to the responsibility of the home state under international law.[33]

Furthermore, the UK would not be able to claim ignorance of the risks posed by PMC activity abroad, considering that it had produced two

[28] ibid. Emphasis added. While William Hague continued by underlining that the UK would ensure effective monitoring of the code to hold the PMC industry accountable, codes of conduct bias prospective over retrospective responsibility which is demonstrated below.

[29] UK Foreign and Commonwealth Office, 'Promoting High Standards in the Private Military and Security Company Industry' (9 March 2011) www.fco.gov.uk/en/news/latest-news/?id=619162882&view=PressS.

[30] There is the possibility that, with governmental backing, the standards of the code might be overseen and enforced through legislative means. This avenue appears unlikely, however, both because legislation itself was proposed and rejected as a regulatory solution and because the UK seems to be predisposed to using its financial influence as a consumer of security services as stated above.

[31] Bohm, Senior and White (n 21) 321–23.

[32] Not to mention its violation of the principle of *nemo iudex sua causa*: ibid 323–24. These difficulties also apply to the International Code of Conduct discussed below.

[33] H Tonkin, *State Control Over Private Military and Security Companies in Armed Conflict* (Cambridge University Press, 2011) 259; Nigel White arrives at a similar conclusion for home State responsibility: N White, 'Regulatory Initiatives at the International Level' in Bakker and Sossai (eds), *Multilevel Regulation of Military and Security Contractors: The Interplay Between International, European and Domestic Norms* (n 21) 27.

official papers that specifically drew attention to these risks as well as posing a range of alternative regulatory solutions.[34] Furthermore, the UK as a home State for many PMCs

> is in a good position to prevent human rights violations arising from the commercial export of security services because it is able to regulate the [PMC] 'at the source' by virtue of the effective territorial control it exercises over the centre of management of the company.[35]

Given its position of control and the obligations accrued by virtue of being the home State,[36] the trajectory of the UK towards implementing a system of self-regulation for the PMC industry is deeply unsatisfactory.[37] While the UK commitment to promoting high standards in the industry is a laudable objective, its current approach severely understates the requisite accountability mechanisms that purport to enforce adherence to these standards. Any replication of the UK approach onto the international plane risks magnifying the issues raised here, and also has the potential to introduce new challenges through the possibility of altering accepted international norms or establishing new ones.

C. The Montreux Document Process

The Montreux Document,[38] concluded precisely a year after the Nisour Square incident, constituted the first step in international standard-setting for the industry by concretely delineating prospective responsibilities.[39] The Document, initiated by the Swiss Federal Department of Foreign Affairs with cooperation from the ICRC, was the outcome of extensive

[34] House of Commons Foreign Affairs Committee (n 21); United Kingdom Foreign and Commonwealth Office (n 20).

[35] F Francioni, 'The Role of the Home State in Ensuring Compliance with Human Rights by Private Military Contractors' in F Francioni and N Ronzitti (eds), *War by Contract: Human Rights, Humanitarian Law, and Private Contractors* (Oxford University Press, 2011) 105.

[36] This is overlooking the additional obligations of the UK as a hiring State of PMC services: see generally C Hoppe, 'Positive Human Rights Obligations of the Hiring State in Connection with the Provision of "Coercive Services" by a Private Military or Security Company' in Francioni and Ronzitti (eds), *War by Contract* (n 35).

[37] The Working Group specifically stated that codes of conduct were insufficient on their own, Gómez del Prado (n 4) 20.

[38] Henceforth 'the Document'. Montreux Document on Pertinent International Legal Obligations and Good Practices for States Related to Operations of Private Military and Security Companies during Armed Conflict 2008. For a commentary about the negotiation process and analysis, see J Cockayne, 'Regulating Private Military and Security Companies: The Content, Negotiation, Weaknesses and Promise of the Montreux Document' (2008) 13 *Journal of Conflict and Security Law* 401; and M-L Tougas, 'Some Comments and Observations on the Montreux Document' (2009) 12 *Yearbook of International Humanitarian Law* 321.

[39] White, 'Regulatory Initiatives at the International Level' (n 33) 12–13.

consultations made through five intergovernmental meetings and four expert meetings over the course of almost three years.[40] It was finalised and endorsed by 17 States at the time,[41] but its ranks have since swelled to 50 States and three international organisations.[42]

The Document is the product of a participatory process between the initial 17 States, with the consultation of civil society and the PMC industry that lends the perception that the Document was developed upon a broad and suitable range of perspectives.[43] This basis for the Document's legitimacy was jeopardised, however, by the tensions which emerged within the final negotiations concerning the language of human rights in particular.[44] Non-governmental organisations, which championed the inclusion of stronger human rights language, were subsequent excluded from the final processes because 'the final document would be an intergovernmental statement negotiated in the conventional intergovernmental fashion'.[45] In particular, James Cockayne reported that:

> Human rights advocacy organizations increasingly voiced concern through 2008 that the conservative approach was 'trading away' the Document's human rights language, in an effort to secure the support of the widest possible group of states—and in particular the United States—on IHL issues.[46]

The constriction of participants to the final Document magnifies the critiques concerning composition and process levelled by José Gómez del Prado, then a member of the UN Working Group on the Use of Mercenaries:

> The [Montreux Process] has been presented to the UN General Assembly and Security Council but has not followed, in its discussions and in the adoption of the Declaration, the criteria and the *universal approach* of the world body.

[40] Cockayne, 'Regulating Private Military and Security Companies' (n 38) 402.

[41] It should be noted that this group of 17 also included States with little experience with PMCs, like Germany, who participated because of their interest in the legal dimensions: C Seiberth, *Private Military and Security Companies in International Law A Challenge for Non-Binding Norms: The Montreux Document and the International Code of Conduct for Private Security Providers* (Intersentia, 2013) 125.

[42] As of 27 June 2014. See: www.eda.admin.ch/eda/en/fdfa/foreign-policy/international-law/international-humanitarian-law/private-military-security-companies/participating-states.html.

[43] See Montreux Document (n 38) Preface.

[44] Cockayne (n 38) 421–22.

[45] ibid 422.

[46] He continues by writing that: 'Some human rights advocacy organizations began to query whether they had been brought into the negotiation purely as a triangulating tactic, since their inclusion served to represent the ICRC perspective as more "moderate", facilitating increased state support for that position': ibid. Note also the subtle structural change reported by Cockayne that further undermines the purported human rights orientation of the Document: 'the language of the document was subtly repositioned to move it away from an orientation based on victims' rights to a remedy for harms they suffer, towards a more legalist orientation based on actors' formal legal responsibilities to provide a remedy': ibid 424.

> The process has been carried out in *secrecy* without the involvement of any UN human rights special procedure or relevant UN departments. The selection of participants remains a mystery.[47]

This makes the attempt of the relatively small and unrepresentative group of States to clarify the international legal obligations and best practices concerning the PMC industry potentially problematic.

The major shortcoming of the Document, as Gómez del Prado has pointed out, is its over-emphasis upon prospective responsibility: 'The document is a *promotional declaration of intentions* and lacks any binding mechanisms'.[48] He noted further that '[n]othing in the document indicates that states should ensure that *existing laws are enforced*, including criminal laws as well as bans on torture and cruel treatment and that [PMCs] *be held accountable* for serious crimes'.[49] The Document is clearly restricted to pronouncing prospective responsibilities because it does not provide for enforcement mechanisms to ensure accountability. Yet, even in this role the Document is limited because its Preface makes clear that it is 'not a legally binding instrument and does not affect existing obligations of States under [international law]' and so 'should not be interpreted as limiting, prejudicing or enhancing … existing obligations … or as creating or developing new obligations under international law'.[50]

While the Document is clearly skewed in favour of establishing prospective responsibilities, it can still play a potentially important role in overcoming impunity. Indeed, despite a little hesitation about the Document's legitimacy,[51] Nigel White suggests that '[a]s a piece of soft law, adopted outside any formal organisational structures, its claim to identify existing obligations while proposing good practice may seem to be wholly constructive'.[52] This is echoed by James Cockayne, who indicates its significance both as 'an important statement of *lex lata* regarding states' existing duties to protect [HRL] and to ensure respect for [IHL], when dealing with [PMCs]' and because it 'provides soft standards in the form

[47] J Gómez del Prado, 'Private Military and Security Companies and the UN Working Group on the Use of Mercenaries' (2008) 13 *Journal of Conflict and Security Law* 429, 443. Emphasis original. He goes on to demonstrate the disproportional regional representation of the Document's participating States.

[48] ibid 445. Emphasis added.

[49] ibid 447. Emphasis added.

[50] Montreux Document (n 38) Preface, paras 3 and 4.

[51] For the background of negotiations for the Montreux Document, see esp Cockayne (n 38) 417–27; Seiberth, *Private Military and Security Companies in International Law* (n 41) 123–29.

[52] N White, 'The Privatisation of Military and Security Functions and Human Rights: Comments on the UN Working Group's Draft Convention' (2011) 11 *Human Rights Law Review* 133, 134.

of 73 "good practices", which may lay the foundation for further practical regulation'.[53] When these sections of the Document are framed in Peter Cane's terminology, these responsibilities can be further divided into 'preventive' responsibilities in the first part of the Document on pertinent international legal obligations, and 'productive' responsibilities in the second part relating to good practices. Making this division reveals both the bias of legal responsibilities towards fixing the minimum preventive responsibilities, but simultaneously shows the progressive potential for extra-legal regulatory mechanisms to exceed legal standards by proposing productive responsibilities. Amnesty International hinted at this latter point when it considered that implementing the good practices section 'would constitute real progress in preventing violations of [IHL] and [HRL]'.[54] The specific contribution of non-legally binding instruments may therefore be the generation of productive responsibilities aimed at fostering virtuous behaviour which may compensate for the law's bias towards only framing preventive responsibilities.[55]

Indeed, the preventive responsibilities that are based upon legal standard in the first part of the Document are a significant weakness of the Document. Again, Amnesty International raised this point by saying that the 'international law section … does not elaborate with enough detail and precision the applicable international law, so limiting its utility either as guidance to States and [PMCs] on their existing legal obligations'.[56] This may indicate a broader problem associated with legal preventive responsibilities: because only the minimum standards are stipulated, their application to novel situations is severely circumscribed. As Corinna Seiberth has suggested, 'Its approach in affirming existing international law is conservative with respect to state responsibility and incomplete by omitting extraterritorial jurisdiction of human rights and due diligence obligations'.[57] This suggests that the Document has failed in its objective to provide 'a clarification of pertinent legal obligations under [IHL] and [HRL]'.[58] Conversely, the Document demonstrates the weakness of establishing productive responsibilities. For example, while the Document

[53] Cockayne (n 38) 403–04.

[54] Amnesty International, 'Amnesty International Public Statement on the Montreux Document on Pertinent International Legal Obligations and Good Practices for States Related to the Operations of Private Military and Security Companies during Armed Conflict' (2008) IOR 30/010/2008, 2.

[55] Some commentators suggest that the greatest potential of the Document lies in the best practices section: Seiberth (n 41) 158.

[56] Amnesty International, 'Amnesty International Public Statement on the Montreux Document on Pertinent International Legal Obligations and Good Practices for States Related to the Operations of Private Military and Security Companies during Armed Conflict' (n 54) 2.

[57] Seiberth (n 41) 159. See generally ibid 156–60.

[58] Montreux Document (n 38).

recommends home States to establish an authorisation system,[59] the UK has entirely disregarded this and instead opted for a government-backed system of self-regulation.[60]

D. International Code of Conduct

The Document was the outcome of the Swiss Initiative,[61] but its principles were subsequently endorsed within the International Code of Conduct (ICoC).[62] The ICoC was signed by the first 58 member companies in a ceremony in Geneva on 9 November 2010,[63] but membership has subsequently swelled to 708 companies,[64] indicating its popularity with the industry. The stated aim of the ICoC is 'to both clarify international standards for the private security industry operating in complex environments, as well as to improve oversight and accountability of these companies', and it 'sets-out human rights based principles for the responsible provision of private security services'.[65] The ICoC thus expresses a policy commitment to respect human rights, and provides a point of departure for due diligence assessments in this regard.[66]

The development of the ICoC adopted a two-stage process. Drafting of the core document started in 2009 and progressed through a series of workshops involving a range of stakeholders, with the final version of the Code being approved in September 2010.[67] The ongoing process to

[59] ibid 54–67.

[60] Bohm, Senior and White (n 21) 325.

[61] The subtle change in the language of the Document from an orientation based upon victim's rights to a remedy towards the formal legal responsibility of actors to provide remedies has been noted by Andrew Clapham, who suggests that this has opened up a space for the subsequent development of a global code of conduct to complement the Document: Cockayne (n 38) 424–25.

[62] Swiss Federal Department of Foreign Affairs, 'International Code of Conduct for Private Security Service Providers' (2010) para 3. For an overview of the ICoC, see Seiberth (n 41) 161–90. Nigel White notes that reference is also made to the Ruggie Framework in the Preamble of the ICoC: White (n 33) 13–14. Finally, there are a number of 'private' codes of conduct purporting to regulate the PMC industry which are generally sponsored by trade associations: see C Hoppe and O Quirico, 'Codes of Conduct for Private Military and Security Companies: The State of Self-Regulation in the Industry' in Francioni and Ronzitti (n 35). The present code may be tentatively distinguished by the participation of select States, NGOs and other parties, although the dominance of PMCs in its development raises significant questions.

[63] A description of the ICoC can be found on its website at: www.icoc-psp.org/About_ICoC.html. For an excellent overview, see Seiberth (n 41) ch 5.

[64] As of 1 September 2013. For the full membership list, see: www.icoc-psp.org/uploads/Signatory_Companies_-_August_2013_-_Composite_List2.pdf.

[65] www.icoc-psp.org/About_ICoC.html.

[66] Seiberth (n 41) 165–66. A subtle shift needs to be noted at this point: because the ICoC concerns corporate respect for human rights law, its scope is limited to setting the boundaries of corporate (role) responsibilities.

[67] ibid 161–62.

operationalise the ICoC has sought to develop an oversight mechanism in the form of a Draft Charter. This was developed by a multi-stakeholder steering committee and was ready for public consultation in 2012. The final version was endorsed as the Articles of Association for the International Code of Conduct Association (ICoCA) in February 2013.[68]

While this staggered process may have been necessary to develop the ICoC in a timely and effective manner, it may be the source of a considerable weakness. This is because the companies that signed up to the ICoC, at least prior to the conclusion of the ICoCA, endorsed the commitments embodied within the Code without an awareness of the precise contours of their responsibilities. This suggests two cynical possibilities arising from the fact that the companies were able to sign up to the ICoC without details of the actual accountability mechanism itself: that the PMCs thought it unlikely that a rigorous mechanism could be developed; or that they would be able to dilute the rigour of the enforcement mechanism through their participation in its development.[69] At least in this sense, the credibility of the ICoC would have increased if it were open for signature after the conclusion of both the standards and the oversight mechanism. As it stands, this two-stage process hints at a scramble for industry legitimacy because the ICoC was endorsed by many of its member companies when the scope of their liabilities remained unclear.

The stated purposes of the ICoC, and the fact that it was concluded largely by a consortium of the PMCs for the companies themselves means that it only 'articulates principles' and possesses no legal effect of any kind.[70] This confirms the prospective standard-setting orientation of the ICoC, reinforced by the fact that it was envisaged to be complemented by an oversight and enforcement mechanism. Thus the ICoC, like the Document, is clearly restricted to establishing prospective responsibilities. This is evident in the declaratory nature of the vast majority of its provisions which explicitly state their obligations as 'Signatory Companies will …, and will require that their Personnel will'.[71] Where the provisions are not so overt, the prospective orientation of the responsibility is instead expressed as agreements to existing obligations or responsibilities.[72]

In this vein, Nigel White has noted that the ICoC has 'well-developed and quite specific rules on the use of force' and certain enumerated human

[68] ibid 162.

[69] A third possibility, that the companies signed up 'blind' to the ICoC, is possible but unlikely because corporations are generally sensitive to the scope of their liabilities and seek to avoid potentially open-ended undertakings.

[70] Swiss Federal Department of Foreign Affairs, 'International Code of Conduct for Private Security Service Providers' (n 62) 13 and 14.

[71] ibid 17–21, 23–26, 28–31, 32–35, 37–57, 59–61, 63–67 and 69.

[72] eg ibid 22, 27, 36, 38, 68.

rights protections.[73] This may have been possible because of the prospective orientation of the ICoC, suggesting a glimmer of hope for establishing productive responsibilities beyond bare legal requirements. That said, the scope of the ICoC has been undermined by its partial exclusion of certain human rights, most notably any reference to the right to life.[74] White also questions the possibility for the ICoC to delineate certain prospective responsibilities.[75] Pointing to the exceptions within the ICoC's restrictions on the use of firearms, he suggests that violations to the right of life would be allowed under the ICoC in circumstances *beyond* those prescribed by HRL documents.[76] This led him to conclude that 'it is highly questionable whether a non-binding code can imbue [PMCs] with such a right'.[77] This highlights the peril that increased permissiveness might be introduced by attempts to delineate prospective responsibilities that differ from widely accepted standards, a peril that may be exacerbated where question marks hang over the legitimacy of the processes or participants involved in framing those standards.

The shortcomings of the ICoC in reflecting at least the minimum human rights law requirements indicate the boundaries of non-orthodox processes for generating prospective responsibilities. Perhaps mindful of this challenge, the ICoC was initiated through the Swiss Federal Department of Foreign Affairs with the support of the Democratic Control of Armed Forces and the Geneva Academy of International Humanitarian Law, but 'it was clear from the outset that *the process should be industry-driven*'.[78] A multi-stakeholder process was adopted to broaden the range of participants, and included representatives from prominent PMCs, other industry associations including ISOA and BAPSC, members of civil society and

[73] White (n 33) 15; Swiss Federal Department of Foreign Affairs (n 62) 28–42.

[74] White (n 33) 15. Note the ambiguity of legal obligations in the observation that 'PMSCs may use force within the boundaries of self-defence, but they may not use offensive or preventive force. The ICoC is not explicit about the limitation to personal self-defence with respect to the use of force. It states that companies should take all "reasonable steps to avoid the use of force" and that it shall be in conformity with applicable law': Seiberth (n 41) 172. This subtle alteration in legal standards appears to extend the use of force by PMCs beyond that which is acceptable under international law.

[75] The prospective responsibility angle provides a different way of assessing the comprehensiveness of the ICoC, rather than focusing exclusively upon whether human rights law guarantees are adequately encapsulated. See Seiberth (n 41) ch 5 for a useful overview of how the ICoC measures up to human rights standards. Seiberth suggests that '[t]he authority and effectiveness of the Code depends on how closely it sticks to the scope of binding international law as its foundation', but a distinction can arguably be made between productive and preventive responsibilities: ibid 166.

[76] This allegation applies also to the sections on the use of force and firearms and on detention and apprehending persons. In particular, '[t]he language of the Code does not require a clear warning before use of firearms, and it allows PMSCs to use force beyond circumstances of self-defence': Seiberth (n 41) 180–81.

[77] White (n 33) 15; Swiss Federal Department of Foreign Affairs (n 62) 31.

[78] Seiberth (n 41) 161. Emphasis added.

government representatives.[79] Yet, despite this apparent breadth of participants, José Gómez del Prado's criticism of secret processes and mysterious selection of the participants in the context of the Swiss Initiative framing the Montreux Document reverberates with regard to the ICoC: the selection of participants and their impact upon the Code, or the processes by which it was concluded, remain opaque.[80]

While legitimacy problems challenge parallel processes such as the Document and the ICoC, a distinction should be drawn between their development of preventive and productive responsibilities. Examples, like the one above that seek to expand the categories of permissible violation to the right of life, suggest that the ICoC may erode established human rights protections and should be rejected. But this should not, however, prejudice the development of productive responsibilities through these parallel extra-legal processes because their ability to articulate precise and progressive responsibilities may instead improve standards in a way that legal obligations cannot. Human rights guarantees should serve as a floor, treatment below which cannot be tolerated, but equally should not act as a ceiling that prevents attempts to raise the standards of protection.

E. ICoC Draft Charter and Association

While the subtle shift in standards introduced by the ICoC has attracted criticism, the primary weakness of the ICoC is its lack of accountability mechanisms.[81] The ICoC included a commitment for 'external independent mechanisms for effective governance and oversight' to be established, which led to the development of a Draft Charter as 'a concrete step towards ensuring Signatory Companies are held accountable to the principles and standards set out in the [ICoC]'.[82] The efficacy of the ICoC as a form of PMC regulation critically depends upon the robustness of these oversight and accountability mechanisms,[83] but these may be severely hindered by the internal composition of its decision-making board,[84]

[79] ibid.

[80] A broad spectrum of participation and representation cannot by itself guarantee plurality of opinions and perspectives because the interests and outlook may overlap and converge.

[81] Note the converging opinion of the UN Working Group on the Use of Mercenaries: A Minty, 'Report of the Open-Ended Intergovernmental Working Group to Consider the Possibility of Elaborating an International Regulatory Framework on the Regulation, Monitoring and Oversight of the Activities of Private Military and Security Companies on Its Second Session' (UNGA, 2012) A/HRC/22/41 para 17.

[82] Swiss Federal Department of Foreign Affairs (n 62) 7(b); also 5, 8, 9, 11 and 12; Swiss Federal Department of Foreign Affairs, 'Draft Charter of the Oversight Mechanism for the International Code of Conduct for Private Security Service Providers' 16 January 2012.

[83] White (n 33) 16.

[84] In potential contravention to the principle of natural justice *nemo iudex sua causa* preventing persons from judging in a case in which they have an interest.

the lack of transparency relating to its processes and lack of available disciplinary measures.[85]

As the current focus is upon the temporal division of responsibilities, it will overlook the issues raised by the participants and procedures in favour of analysing the absence of punitive measures that arguably characterise retrospective accountability. In common with other forms of self-regulation,[86] the most serious sanctions available under the ICoC are suspension and termination of membership.[87] At a fundamental level, this places the imposition of sanctions in direct opposition to the effectiveness of the oversight mechanism because the costs of running the mechanism will be met by the membership fees.[88] A more subtle issue arises from the fact that these sanctions are not actually available for alleged violations of human rights, but rather for assertions that a member company 'has failed to provide an effective internal grievance procedure'.[89] This reveals the strict segregation of responsibility under the ICoC oversight mechanism, suggesting that the worst transgression within the ICoC framework is the failure of a company to provide access to a grievance mechanism (a role responsibility). Where material breaches of the ICoC are alleged (a causal responsibility), including violations of human rights, third-party claimants are instead provided with facilitation and mediation processes. On one hand, these processes can be interpreted as non-punitive within the ICoC framework because continuing membership is not threatened. On the other hand, this division may strike a fair balance between ensuring

[85] These difficulties have been noted in United Kingdom Foreign and Commonwealth Office (n 20) 76. See also the analysis of the UN Working Group on the Use of Mercenaries: F Patel, 'Report of the Working Group on the Use of Mercenaries as a Means of Violating Human Rights and Impeding the Exercise of the Right of Peoples to Self-Determination' (UNHRC, 2012) A/HRC/21/43 paras 19–23. See generally Seiberth (n 41) ch 6.

[86] For a comparison, see Seiberth (n 41) 214–22.

[87] Swiss Federal Department of Foreign Affairs, Draft Charter (n 82) s IX.F. For the ICoC Articles of Association, art 13.2.7, see ICoC, 'International Code of Conduct for Private Security Service Providers' Association: Articles of Association' www.icoc-psp.org/uploads/ICoC_Articles_of_Association.pdf. It is difficult to describe these sanctions as 'punitive', questioning whether reliance can be placed on the ICoC process to regulate the activities of the PMC industry in which excesses can readily attain the mantle of criminal activities.

[88] The relative lack of resources available to the oversight mechanism has already been argued to undermine its effectiveness: Seiberth (n 41) 223–24. This will operate as a material disincentive to further restrictions to its membership.

[89] Paras 66 and 67 of the ICoC undergird this requirement, which is given effect in the Draft Charter, Swiss Federal Department of Foreign Affairs (n 82) X.A.2. The UN Working Group on the Use of Mercenaries puts this distinction in a different way: 'The draft Code only permits the review of complaints about a company's lack of internal grievance procedures—it does not provide any means of addressing the substance of a third party complaint': UN Working Group on the Use of Mercenaries, 'Submission by the Working Group on the Use of Mercenaries as a Means of Impeding the Exercise of the Right of Peoples to Self-Determination' (UN Human Rights Council, 2012) A/HRC/WG.10/2/CRP.1 para 33(b). Art 13 of the Articles of Association detailing the 'Complaints Process' is largely devoted to grievance procedures: ICoC, 'International Code of Conduct for Private Security Service Providers' Association: Articles of Association' (n 87).

access to grievance procedures and the possibility of providing material compensation to the victims of ICoC violations.

An overall conclusion may be drawn from the perspective of available sanctions: the ICoC is concerned about establishing processes for reviewing compliance and not for providing avenues of punishment and prevention for human rights abuse. The result is that a PMC's membership of the ICoC signals that it has in place the necessary review and grievance procedures, but crucially says nothing about its actual compliance with human rights in its operations. The major problem then arises where ICoC membership is used as a benchmark to guarantee the standard and quality of PMCs, or as a prerequisite for awarding contracts, as both the US[90] and UK[91] have proposed. Because the retrospective accountability mechanism of the ICoC is detached from causal responsibilities, ICoC membership is in no way jeopardised by activities that infringe upon human rights, even those that are recurrent or systematic, and so cannot be used appropriately as a legitimating or regulatory device.

Approaching the regulation question through the perspective of prospective responsibility has demonstrated that non-legally binding and self-regulatory mechanisms can play an important role in overturning impunity insofar as they reaffirm existing (generally preventive) standards and are able to progressively develop (generally productive) good practices. Indeed, the ICoC's independence from legal mechanisms may even be advantageous in this respect. Self-regulatory mechanisms are capable of articulating precise preventive responsibilities to diminish the potential for excesses of responsibility,[92] and may foster virtuous behaviour that is capable of raising the level of applicable standards. These effects are magnified within the ICoC for two reasons. First, because the ICoC is concluded between the PMCs themselves, it can operate directly upon the relevant actors without involving intermediaries, such as the State. Second,

[90] Office of the Spokesperson, 'State Department to Incorporate International Code of Conduct into Worldwide Protective Services Contracts' (*U.S. Department of State*, 16 August 2013) www.state.gov/r/pa/prs/ps/2013/08/213212.htm. See also the reliance placed upon the ICoC 'to improve private security contractor (PSC) compliance with applicable laws and respect for human rights, and to provide additional tools for identifying, avoiding, and remediating impacts that PSCs may have on communities and other stakeholders': 'Human Rights Committee Consideration of Reports Submitted by States Parties under Article 40 of the Covenant: Fourth Periodic Report United States of America' (UN International Covenant on Civil and Political Rights, 2012) CCPR/C/USA/4 para 544.

[91] M Simmons, 'Written Statement to Parliament: International Code of Conduct for Private Security Providers Association' (*UK Foreign and Commonwealth Office*, 15 October 2013) www.gov.uk/government/speeches/international-code-of-conduct-for-private-security-providers-association.

[92] Ainley, 'Excesses of Responsibility' (n 5).

provided that the minimum standards set by the law are met, the ICoC is free to articulate higher standards and develop new practices that have not been subject to legal regulation.[93]

The exclusive focus upon prospective responsibilities, however, renders both the ICoC and the Document toothless and empty: without complementary accountability mechanisms their fulfilment relies upon the vagaries of good faith.[94] Where the ICoC is concerned, the accountability mechanism which has been created suffers from serious defects: these are thrown into sharp relief when juxtaposed against the UN Working Group's proposal of a specialised international court to enforce their code and serve as a forum for disputes,[95] as well as the actual enforcement mechanism envisaged in the Draft Convention itself.

F. International Law Mechanisms: The UN Working Group Draft Convention

In 2000, Kofi Annan recommended that '[c]onsideration should also be given to an international convention regulating the actions of private and corporate security firms, which we see involved in internal wars in growing numbers'.[96] This recommendation was urged in the context of protecting the vulnerable, noting inter alia that '[i]nternational conventions have traditionally looked to states to protect civilians, but today this expectation is threatened in several ways … Second, non-state combatants, particularly in collapsed states, are often ignorant or contemptuous of humanitarian law'.[97] His recommendation for a specific convention addressing the PMC industry is central to this goal, because '[t]o strengthen protection, we must assert the centrality of international humanitarian and human rights law. We must strive to end the culture of impunity'.[98] The UK House of Commons Foreign Affairs Committee echoed Kofi Annan two

[93] Examples of this in the Code can be found in the 'Specific Commitments Regarding Management and Governance': Swiss Federal Department of Foreign Affairs (n 62) G.

[94] The UN Working Group on the Use of Mercenaries recognised the need for 'punitive measures to be included in this code for companies which breach the standards', but does not indicate that these penalties need to be legally imposed: Nikitin, 'Report of the Working Group on the Use of Mercenaries as a Means of Violating Human Rights and Impeding the Exercise of the Right of Peoples to Self-Determination' (n 1) 50.

[95] ibid 60.

[96] K Annan, 'We the Peoples: The Role of the United Nations in the Twenty-First Century' (2000) para 212.

[97] ibid 210.

[98] ibid 211. This is also an excellent expression of the orthodox legal approach to PMC impunity.

years later when, having overviewed existing international legal instruments, it stated that:

> A new international agreement to regulate the activities of PMCs would complement and make more effective legislation at a purely national level. *We recommend that the Government, as it considers national regulatory measures, also develop a new draft international convention to regulate PMCs which might replace the existing* [UN Mercenary Convention].[99]

In a precursor report to the Draft Convention, the UN Working Group on the Use of Mercenaries affirmed that the UN Mercenary Convention would be of limited application for regulating PMC activities and elaborated upon the characteristics that such a new convention should possess.[100] This report indicated that the Draft Convention would implement legal standards that would be supported by retrospective accountability mechanisms,[101] thereby balancing prospective and retrospective responsibilities. The Working Group considered that the Montreux Document usefully identified existing IHL and HRL obligations and that its good practices could be a useful tool to develop guidelines.[102] So while IHL and HRL norms constitute the prospective standards for the Draft Convention,[103] these remain limited to its preventive limb leaving little space in a legal treaty to foster virtuous practices.

The strength of the Draft Convention lies in its accountability mechanisms.[104] In a precursor report, the Working Group stipulated that enforcement mechanisms are required for any type of PMC regulation to ensure individual and corporate accountability under all circumstances.[105] The Working Group specifically proposed an international court of arbitration to provide a formal dispute mechanism relating to issues arising from PMC activities. Furthermore, it specifically promulgated that 'a "[PMC] Code" could also be established, which would run in conjunction with the court and is the "law" which it considers'.[106] This arrangement would have the additional benefit of providing binding obligations to PMCs and their contractors directly.[107] The proposition demonstrates

[99] House of Commons Foreign Affairs Committee (n 21) 25. Emphasis original.

[100] Nikitin (n 1) 40 and 38, respectively.

[101] ibid 40–51, 59–61, respectively.

[102] ibid 43. The Working Group, however, continued by elaborating key weaknesses in the Montreux Process and the resultant Document.

[103] Nigel White has noted that unlike the Montreux Document, the Draft Convention is not limited to situations of armed conflict, and thus accords primacy to HRL over IHL: White, 'The Privatisation of Military and Security Functions and Human Rights' (n 52) 136. This is especially important considering that a threshold of intensity has to be satisfied before IHL is engaged, which constitutes a limiting factor for the Document.

[104] In this regard, the preamble states: 'Taking into account the adoption of codes of conduct, but considering that self-regulation of [PMCs] is not sufficient to ensure the observance of [IHL] and [HRL] by the personnel of these companies': Gómez del Prado (n 4) 20.

[105] Nikitin (n 1) 59.

[106] ibid 60.

[107] ibid.

how the prospective responsibilities enumerated in the aforementioned Document and the ICoC could be complemented by a rigorous, albeit non-legal, enforcement mechanism. Such a process would be able to remedy the failings of accountability within the ICoC process and improve the transparency and impartiality aspects of the mechanism. Importantly, the Working Group emphasised that the civil nature of this enforcement mechanism would mean that it was an inappropriate venue to try alleged crimes, which would require either an additional criminal law convention or an additional protocol to the Rome Statute.[108] In this light, the inadequacy of the ICoC mechanism alone, which falls short of even civil standards, is clearly deficient for criminal matters.

The actual enforcement mechanisms provided for by the Draft Convention comprise of international supervision and national regulation.[109] On the international level, the Draft Convention provides for an Oversight Committee following the general model of UN human rights treaties.[110] In addition to the usual powers possessed by such committees, the Oversight Committee would also operate an inquiry procedure,[111] and appoint a conciliation commission.[112] This substantially increases its role from receiving and considering the reports submitted by States Parties, and to making observations and recommendations in reply.[113] Perhaps the most progressive enforcement mechanism available under the Draft Convention is the power of the Oversight Committee to receive petitions, albeit optional for States Parties. This enables aggrieved individuals and groups to make claims that their rights provided for under the Draft Convention have been violated.[114] Finally, in order to complement the Oversight Committee, a raft of articles require would-be States Parties to the Draft Convention to provide effective domestic regulation and enforcement: to enact specific offences under their domestic law; to establish jurisdiction over offences; and to fulfil obligations related to prosecution or extradition and mutual assistance.[115] The provisions of the Draft Convention would therefore be overseen and enforced by the State, and not a consortium of PMCs themselves under the ICoC.

[108] ibid 60–61.

[109] Gómez del Prado (n 4) V; see commentary at White (n 33) 22–24.

[110] White (n 33) 22. For the weaknesses of this form of enforcement mechanism, see esp G Robertson, *Crimes Against Humanity: The Struggle For Global Justice* (Penguin, 2006) 55–63, although certain defects noted by Robertson have been rectified in the Draft Convention.

[111] Gómez del Prado (n 4) arts 33 and 34.

[112] ibid arts 35 and 36.

[113] ibid arts 31 and 32.

[114] ibid art 37. Nigel White suggests that this type of committee 'can be successful if the Committee performs its tasks with impartiality and bases its decisions on accepted interpretations if international law': White (n 33) 23.

[115] Gómez del Prado (n 4) arts 19–28.

The relative weakness of the Draft Convention, as a legal mechanism, is that it only defines preventive responsibilities associated with existing IHL and HRL standards, thereby relinquishing the opportunity to raise standards associated with PMC activity. This may be a lost opportunity, if there is truth in industry lobbyist Doug Brooks' claims that 'PMCs have often been exemplary in their behaviour ... and their capacities ... [t]he fact that PMCs often use elite troops from the best-trained militaries in the world allows them to field extremely competent forces'.[116] Of course, establishing an international convention insisting that PMCs adhere to the existing levels of protection afforded by IHL and HRL seeks to set a minimum level of protection and would not in itself prevent PMCs from upholding higher standards.

G. International Law Mechanisms: The UN Intergovernmental Working Group

The UN Human Rights Council has established an open-ended Intergovernmental Working Group with

> the mandate to consider the possibility of elaborating an international regulatory framework, including, inter alia, the option of elaborating a legally binding instrument on the regulation, monitoring and oversight of the activities of private military and security companies, including their accountability, taking into consideration the principles, main elements and draft text as proposed by the [UN Working Group on the Use of Mercenaries].[117]

The broad and inclusive mandate of the Intergovernmental Working Group is noteworthy because it is not teleological in seeking to develop and operationalise the Draft Convention, but is rather open to all possibilities.

The largest obstacle facing the Draft Convention is its chances of conclusion and adoption in the face of the Montreux Document and the ICoC.[118] Although the Draft Convention was supported by Russia, China and most of the developing countries on the Human Rights Council, it has received

[116] D Brooks, 'Messiahs or Mercenaries? The Future of International Private Military Services' (2000) 7 *International Peacekeeping* 129, 135.

[117] Human Rights Council, 'Open-Ended Intergovernmental Working Group' (n 4) 4.

[118] The objection to the Draft Convention is well-articulated by: 'A number of delegations [which] stated their view that it was premature to consider negotiations on a legally binding instrument at this stage. They noted the need to reinforce existing PMSC-specific initiatives, namely the Montreux Document and International Code of Conduct, and to carefully assess their impact, before embarking on new initiatives which might divert attention and resources, and result in a convention with only a few ratifications': Minty, 'Report of the Open-Ended Intergovernmental Working Group to Consider the Possibility of Elaborating an International Regulatory Framework on the Regulation, Monitoring and Oversight of the Activities of Private Military and Security Companies on Its Second Session' (n 81) 58.

opposition from the US, UK and the EU.[119] Most telling is the approach of the UK, which 'concurred with the Working Group on the importance of better regulating the activities of [PMCs] in order to raise standards and help prevent human rights abuses', but simultaneously 'reiterated its opposition to the draft convention which it viewed as impractical'.[120] That the Document and the ICoC are the basic documents under consideration at the Institute of International Humanitarian Law Round-Table is another sign that the Draft Convention is being sidelined.[121]

This rift in regulatory models is problematic because: 'States connected to the [PMC] industry are more likely to stick with and entrench the Montreux process, and those opposed to [PMCs] as a modern form of mercenarism are more likely to support the Draft Convention process'.[122] The development of alternative 'soft law' regulation such as the Document and the ICoC divert both attention and urgency away from more stringent and robust mechanisms such as the Draft Convention.[123] Furthermore, because the Document and the ICoC are supported by the States that are most involved with PMC activity[124] their participation in the parallel process would undermine both the relevance and efficacy of the Draft Convention if and when it does comes into force.[125] Given the

[119] White (n 52) 150. The UK and US have voted their opposition to the open-ended Working Group to elaborate upon a legally binding instrument Human Rights Council, 'Open-Ended Intergovernmental Working Group' (n 4). A binding treaty is considered by the latter as superfluous given the existing standards and developing initiatives seeking to regulate the PMC industry.

[120] Human Rights Council, 'Human Rights Council Holds Interactive Dialogue on Human Rights and International Solidarity and on Mercenaries' (2011) www.ohchr.org/en/NewsEvents/Pages/DisplayNews.aspx?NewsID=11367&LangID=E. Christopher Kinsey notes that this is a recurring issue for the UK both because of the continuing use of Gurkhas and because of the practice for UK officers to enlist in foreign militaries.

[121] While Faiza Patel is to speak on the Draft Convention, only the Document and the Code are referenced as basic documents on the PMC issue: International Institute of Humanitarian Law, 'XXXVth Round Table: Private Military and Security Companies' www.iihl.org/iihl/Documents/Draft%20Agenda%20Internet%20Sanremo%202012%20%20%2831%2005%202012%29-1.pdf.

[122] White (n 52) 150; this rift may reflect ideological and political differences between these States: White (n 33) 18.

[123] The proliferation of soft law reactions to the problem of PMC regulation also leads to the fragmentation of standards that frustrate uniformity. A recent example is provided by the US DoD requiring contractors to meet certifiable standards that govern their operations. While laudable in itself, the initiative has not spread beyond the Pentagon such that the State Department, which is heavily dependent upon the PMC industry, has not adopted these standards: C Davenport, 'Pentagon Imposes Strict Standards on Private Security Firms' *The Washington Post* (26 November 2014) www.washingtonpost.com/business/economy/pentagon-imposes-strict-standards-on-private-security-firms/2014/11/26/4b018ff8-7421-11e4-9c9f-a37e29e80cd5_story.html?wprss=rss_business.

[124] Gómez del Prado, 'Private Military and Security Companies and the UN Working Group on the Use of Mercenaries' (n 47) 443.

[125] Christopher Kinsey notes that a similar rift emerged in the 1960s and 1970s over mercenaries between European and African States that undermined the efficacy of the Mercenary Conventions discussed above in ch 3. Personal communication 2 July 2012.

limited international support given to the UN Mercenary Convention, the availability of the alternative claims to regulation presented by the Document and especially the ICoC, will further diminish participation in the Draft Convention process. Unlike the UN Mercenary Convention which failed widespread ratification despite not facing competing processes, the development of the Draft Convention faces substantial competition.[126] At the time of writing, the mandate of the Intergovernmental Working Group has been renewed for an additional two year period, reflecting the only consensus reached that 'there is a need for further discussion in the open-ended intergovernmental working group'.[127]

III. INCENTIVISING ROBUST SELF-REGULATION

The competing modes of PMC regulation suggest that a divided approach to the problem will persist into the future. Nigel White has, however, indicated points of cooperation between the Montreux and ICoC processes on one hand and the UN Draft Convention on the other by drawing on the former to develop the standards for the industry and adopting the enforcement mechanisms of the latter.[128] Given the sluggish pace of the UN Intergovernmental Working Group, the support of the Document by States involved with PMCs, and the enthusiasm espoused by the industry itself of the ICoC, a more effective route to regulation may be to develop incentives towards robust self-regulation. Such an endeavour necessarily risks elevating self-regulation over other avenues of oversight and accountability, but this concession might be justified considering the present unlikelihood of concluding a firm and broadly supported international instrument designed to regulate the PMC industry.

It is interesting to note that, while there are numerous benefits conferred on PMC members of self-regulatory bodies such as the ICoCA, there are few incentives for these bodies to regulate their members in a robust manner and motivation compounds the list of issues they face. The tension between continued membership as a source of revenue on the one hand and suspension or termination as a sanction on the other has already been noted, but the conflicting interests go further than this. A large membership confers the appearance of legitimacy to the regulatory body, but this strains its ability to properly oversee the activities of all of its members. This ability is further constrained by limited resources in a practical sense.

[126] This is not to neglect the potential of the ICoC to regulate the industry, especially because it is capable of bypassing the structural State-centric weakness of the Draft Convention by directly addressing the PMC itself: White (n 33) 29.

[127] Minty (n 81) 76. See also, Human Rights Council, 'Renewal of the Mandate of the Open-Ended Intergovernmental Working Group' (n 4).

[128] White (n 33) 30.

It is also difficult to identify the incentive for such a regulatory body to reprimand any of its members harshly as because these regimes are voluntary this would risk the displeasure of the membership, and even defection from the regime. From a cynical perspective, it could be argued that the very attractiveness of a voluntary self-regulatory regime is that the membership possess the upper hand in relation to the regulatory body, and derive a range of benefits from membership with few associated costs.

A tension also appears in relation to the reputation of a self-regulatory body: in that it must strike a balance between the public impression that it is a regulator looking out for the public interest, and the perception of the industry that it is a trade association functioning in its service. These reputational costs, however, are unlikely to be weighed equally. Public concern over the misbehaviour of its membership may be deflected, for example, because the company involved is likely to bear a large share of the blame and will decay over time at any rate. From this perspective, however, a flight from the regulatory body may even be triggered if its members believe that it is not functioning in favour of the industry. At the very least, developing incentives for more robust self-regulation could provide a counter-balance for the narrower situation at present where the semblance of industry regulation in the form of the ICoC creates a mirage of oversight and accountability from the third-party perspective.

A. Collective Responsibility of Self-regulatory Bodies

With the main objective of regulation to overcome impunity for PMC activity, the proposal is to create a system of incentives and disincentives that encourage rigorous oversight by the self-regulatory body. This might be achieved by imposing responsibility directly upon the self-regulatory bodies themselves, thereby assigning costs to those bodies for lax oversight and accountability. The proposal advanced here is a variant of regulatory negligence, and the negligence framework is particularly apt because the regulatory body appropriately bears role responsibilities associated with fulfilling supervisory obligations. There are, however, obstacles that need to be overcome before such responsibilities may be imposed upon self-regulatory bodies even if the arguments in favour are compelling.

The very idea of regulatory negligence is primarily an administrative law concept. As such, it is targeted against public powers that cause and manage harm, and the focus is placed upon accountability for public authorities in instances of failure.[129] While it may be argued that self-regulatory bodies assume public functions insofar as they seek to regulate activities

[129] F Kristjanson and S Moreau, 'Regulatory Negligence and Administrative Law' (2012) 25 *Canadian Journal of Administrative Law and Practice* 103, 104.

which would otherwise be managed by public bodies, this creates a formalistic obstacle against extending the concept to non-profit associations (which is the status that the ICoCA holds in Switzerland). This problem mirrors the issues raised by the PMC industry itself in privatising the provision of military activities, but is unlikely to be overcome by a parity of argumentation.

A similar obstacle is raised by the orientation of liability of non-profit associations, which is restricted to a discrete number of grounds that are intended to govern the direct actions of these associations. Non-profit associations are envisaged to act in a direct manner, rather than engage in regulatory work, so the law governing their activities is likely to be tailored towards establishing their responsibility in action rather than omission. This potentially leaves a liability gap in the regulation of non-profit associations where these are given an oversight function. Alternatively, this type of organisation has been inappropriately co-opted to perform regulatory functions without undergoing necessary adjustments.

Another major obstacle arises within the legal meaning of negligence under the common law. It is important to note that the very possibility of examining the conduct of regulatory bodies through the lens of negligence was made possible by the wide net cast by the Privy Council, which had rejected the narrower frame of breach of statutory duty.[130] As Keith LJ duly acknowledged, adopting the duty of care standard over that of statutory duty has 'far-reaching implications as regards the potential liability in negligence of a wide variety of regulatory agencies … and also to some extent by non-governmental bodies'.[131] The difficulty is surmounting the duty of care threshold, and it is unfortunate that *Yuen Kun Yeu* does not provide a precedent for success because the foreseeability of harm must be accompanied by sufficient proximity.[132] While it is clear that the criterion of foreseeability alone would be far too broad,[133] the requirement for proximity is too narrow when the principle is extended to regulators who are one step removed from the harm.[134] Retaining the requirement for proximity effectively insulates regulators from bearing a duty of care because their failure of adequate oversight may have contributed to, rather than directly caused, the harm in question.

[130] H Mclean, 'Negligent Regulatory Authorities and the Duty of Care' (1988) 8 *Oxford Journal of Legal Studies* 442, 449.

[131] *Yuen Kun Yeu v Attorney General of Hong Kong* (1987) [1988] AC 175 (PC) 190.

[132] ibid 190–92.

[133] ibid 190.

[134] Per Keith LJ: '[O]ne has to ask whether, as between the alleged wrongdoer and the person who has suffered damage there is a sufficient relationship of proximity or neighbourhood such that, in the reasonable contemplation of the former, carelessness on his part may be likely to cause damage to the latter': ibid.

This leads to broader objections against the development of regulatory negligence: that another party had contributed more directly to the negative outcome, implying that the failure of the regulatory body is not the main source of the wrong.[135] This objection seemingly adopts a zero-sum approach to responsibility by alternately pinning responsibility for the wrong upon either the direct violator (the PMC in our context) or the regulator (the ICoCA), and might be reconciled by a complementary approach where responsibility is attributed jointly and severally.

Instead, there is a significant advantage to developing regulator responsibility: deterrence.[136] Liability can be a useful reminder to the regulator that she has a role to fulfil in the prevention of harm and to incentivise her to discharge this obligation with care. In turn, this may have knock-on effects that further decrease the probability of harm because more care may be elicited from the actors by the regulator.[137] The objection to responsibility that is raised by the relative distance between the regulator and the harm may be overturned by the reliance placed upon the regulatory body by the public and by potential victims. The existence of a regulatory body suggests that it can be relied upon to prevent certain categories of harm, and the breach of this trust can be a powerful argument in favour of asserting regulator liability.[138]

The relative distance between the regulator and the harm may also justify one of the rare instances where segregating role and outcome responsibilities is appropriate. Indeed, the responsibilities of a regulator are the paragon example of role responsibility because these concern obligations of oversight and supervision attached to the particular function. As regulatory bodies are one step removed from the harm, it would be inappropriate to ascribe causal responsibility to the regulator who lacks proximity to, and who is not the primary cause of, that harm. The imposition of role responsibilities upon regulators can be the source of incentives to maximise the robustness of oversight and be a source of liability for failure, but this is not the same as saying that the regulator was responsible in a causal sense for the harm.[139]

It is clear that this approach cannot remedy the full spectrum of concerns hanging over the PMC industry because this proposal is targeted

[135] I Giesen, 'Regulating Regulators through Liability: The Case for Applying Normal Tort Rules to Supervisors' (2006) 2 *Utrecht Law Review* 8, 13.

[136] ibid 14–15.

[137] ibid.

[138] ibid 16.

[139] In the PMC context, self-regulatory bodies such as the ICoCA occupy very different positions from States, which both regulate and consume PMC services, and the PMC itself which is causally connected to the harm. This accounts for the difficulty in analysing State and PMC responsibility exclusively within the framework of due diligence, but justifies this approach with regard to regulators.

only at the narrow issue of incentivising self-regulatory bodies to fulfil the function assigned to them. While the accountability of regulators does not remedy the broader limitations of self-regulation it may produce broader effects. A more thorough and careful regulator, for example, may be less attractive to proponents of laissez faire regulation who may then seek alternatives. More specifically, recurrent harms that continue to occur despite the diligence of the ICoCA may reveal the shortcomings of the voluntary trade association approach to regulating the PMC industry.

IV. THE FUTURE OF IMPUNITY IN PMC REGULATION

It could be argued that the development of the Document and the ICoC as a regulatory alternative has in fact created an intractable problem favouring the persistence of impunity for PMC activities.[140] From this cynical perspective, partial and incomplete initiatives such as the Montreux Document and the International Code of Conduct may function to subvert the development of uniform and comprehensive regulation through transparent and inclusive processes. The availability of an alternative avenue of regulation diffuses the urgency of developing regulation and provides a retort to claims that the PMC industry operates unregulated despite the significant shortcomings of that regime.

It is important to note that this result need not have been foreseen, let alone intended, by those who sought to develop PMC regulation along these lines. The selection of participants involved with the Montreux Process and the development of the ICoC may have been due to considerations of experience with the industry, and to ensure applicability and relevance moving forward. Similarly, the relative speed through which the Document and the ICoC were developed may be explained by the desire to close any regulatory gaps quickly and efficiently. Yet, these initiatives have created a clear rift in the international community's response to the PMC industry, and their relative pace may be interpreted as an attempt to stall other developments towards more uniform and robust regulation for the PMC industry. Impunity for PMC activity will persist into the future as a direct result of this division in the international community's response, which entrenches selective regulation and frustrates other attempts to overcome the problem.

[140] The tension reported by the Intergovernmental Working Group captures this problem: some delegations expressed the primacy of the ICoC, while other delegations highlighted the regulatory gaps, the weaknesses in human rights protections and the lack of criminal accountability in existing attempts to regulate the PMC industry: Minty (n 81) 29–32.

A. The Future of PMC Impunity: Repetition of Existing Regulatory Problems

Before proceeding to analyse the future of PMC impunity and to present the four dimensions of regulation proposed in this chapter, it is important to acknowledge that perhaps the most significant regulatory problem is the replication of past deficiencies. Nowhere is this possibility better illustrated than in the reflection of the limitations of national trade association in the ICoC.[141] Indeed, a strong criticism of PMC industry codes of conduct is that they have failed to constrain unlawful behaviour in the past. The three companies canvassed in chapter two neatly underscore the different types of shortcomings that appear inherent within voluntary self-regulatory regimes, suggesting that impunity may be generated despite these codes signalling the appearance of improved regulation and responsibility.

Taking Blackwater first, the company had been a member of the International Peace Operations Association (IPOA)[142] since 2004. Blackwater quit its membership in 2007, in the wake of investigations relating to contracts with the US State Department as a result of Nisour Square and other incidents. The company left the association in a nonchalant manner, indicating in its accompanying statement: 'We have decided to take a hiatus from the [association] … We, like many other organizations engaged in this type of work, are pursuing other aspects and methods of industry outreach and governance'.[143] Three flaws of self-regulation are revealed in this one move: that membership is retained only when it is expedient to the member; that no negative repercussions need ever arise with membership; and that membership is neither a guarantor of good behaviour nor an avenue of remedy when things go wrong. In this vein, it is particularly interesting to note that Academi (the direct successor of Blackwater), along with DynCorp and its deep records of human rights abuse allegations charted in chapter two, are currently members of both the IPOA and the ICoC.[144]

The recurrent issue is the voluntary nature of self-regulatory mechanisms. One important aspect of the problem was revealed above with

[141] The inadequacies of voluntary and non-legally enforceable corporate codes of conduct that purport to protect human rights have been underlined in other contexts: Robertson, *Crimes Against Humanity* (n 110) 189–91.

[142] The organisation was subsequently renamed the International Stability Operations Association (ISOA) in October 2010.

[143] A Cole, 'Blackwater Quits Security Association' *Wall Street Journal* (11 October 2007) http://online.wsj.com/news/articles/SB119207104012555696?mod=googlenews_wsj&mg=reno64-wsj&url=http%3A%2F%2Fonline.wsj.com%2Farticle%2FSB119207104012555696.html%3Fmod%3Dgooglenews_wsj.

[144] This continues to be the case at the time of writing in November 2014.

Blackwater leaving IPOA to avoid possible scrutiny by the association. Voluntary regulation can always be avoided whenever the costs of membership outweigh the benefits that it confers—a calculation that undermines the ability of voluntary regulation to protect fundamental human rights. Voluntary regulation attracts precisely those regulatees who want to be seen in the image projected by the particular association, and to benefit from the reputational boost this provides. It fails, however, to capture other actors who do not wish to be burdened by such obligations, do not see the benefits of submitting to such regulation, or are formally operating in different service sectors.

This last point is illuminated by the example given in chapter two concerning CACI and Titan (now L-3 Communications) which are formally companies that provide professional and communications services. Yet, despite nominally operating within the communications sector, these companies became embroiled within a prisoner abuse scandal, inflicting violence in a direct manner that justifies their substantive categorisation as PMCs. The disjuncture between what these companies say they do, and what they actually do, may emerge as critical gap in the coverage of voluntary self-regulation regimes for the PMC industry. These companies are not members of ISOA, which claims 'to be the world's only association serving the stability sector exclusively',[145] perhaps because they do not perceive themselves as operating within this sector. The restricted nature of self-regulation regimes is reproduced in the ICoC because the instrument only applies to 'business activities [that] include the provision of Security Services either on its own behalf or on the behalf of another, irrespective of how such Company describes itself'.[146] Thus, being confined to the relevant sector, comprehensive coverage eludes the trade association model of voluntary regulation (including ISOA and ICoC).

Despite, or perhaps because of, the weaknesses of voluntary self-regulation it often receives strong support, standing in stark contrast to the low levels of ratification enjoyed by legal forms of regulation. If the UN Mercenary Convention was the harbinger of the Draft Convention, it not only suggests that it will receive little international interest and support, but also that the support it will receive will come from countries with tangential interests in regulating the PMC industry. This represents a different aspect of future PMC impunity where those involved with the industry champion the weaker regulation, leaving those with limited direct interest in the industry to advocate for stricter regulation. Repeating previous iterations of private force regulation, gaps persist because those

[145] The Association describes itself in these terms on its website: www.stability-operations.org/?page=Membership

[146] See Swiss Federal Department of Foreign Affairs (n 62) 5, B Definitions: Private Security Companies and Private Security Service Providers.

most involved lack the interest and incentives to close them, while those committed to strong regulation often have little actual engagement with, and therefore impact upon, these activities.

As the future of PMC impunity is not restricted to the repetition of previous and existing issues, however, this chapter continues by exploring possible characteristics grouped around four dimensions upon which emerging regulatory regimes might usefully be analysed. These begin with possible flaws within the foundations of the regulation and move towards issues that arise from its implementation, suggesting that improvements will be easier to make in the later categories but will have a lesser impact overall.

B. The Future of PMC Impunity: Regulatory Content and Contortion

By setting out its prospective responsibilities, the core of a regulatory regime is its content and any deficiencies at this level cannot be compensated at a later stage.[147] The discussion in chapter four provides an example of where the regulatory reaction to PMC activity was railroaded into *Jus in Bello* considerations. As the concern over PMC conduct translated into the content of PMC regulation, this effectively framed the parameters of the debate and the scope of ensuing regulation. The crystallisation of this content effectively excludes other factors from the regulatory calculation, illustrated in this case by the difficulty with which *Jus ad Bellum* issues can be expressed, let alone deliberated, in terms of PMC regulation. The potential for impunity to remain for activities beyond the purview of the regulatory content is clear, demonstrating the peril of overly restrictive content.

Beyond these broad issues of framing, inclusion and exclusion, the content of regulation may be afflicted by two interrelated issues. The content of developing regulatory regimes may be afflicted by contortion when compared with the underlying normative framework. Human rights law provides a consistent level of protection where PMCs are concerned, and an example of this contortion is provided by subtle alterations of these protections in the Montreux Document and the International Code of Conduct. As discussed above, some of these provisions are too permissive

[147] In the literature on industry self-regulation, this process approximates 'industrial morality': 'One of the critical first steps on the path to industry self-regulation is the development of an industry-wide normative framework, a set of industrial principles and practices that defines right conduct as it spells out the industry's public commitment to moral restraint and aspiration': N Gunningham and J Rees, 'Industry Self-Regulation: An Institutional Perspective' (1997) 19 *Law and Policy* 363, 376–80.

with the use of force while others are criticised for diluting other protections. Such contortion gives the appearance that the content of human rights law has been faithfully reproduced in the regulation while simultaneously changing the substance of the protections the regulatory regime can in fact offer.

The precision with which the content is articulated will determine the residual amount of ambiguity within the regulation, but this is affected by the indeterminate nature of human rights provisions. Ordinary legal processes compensate this generality by providing relatively authoritative and consistent interpretations that refine the content of human rights laws. It is difficult to see how self-regulatory regimes will be able to promulgate clear interpretations of voluntary codes of conduct, let alone ones that are both widely accepted and consistent with those pronounced by international or judicial bodies. Even if a self-regulatory instrument successfully replicates the content of human rights law, the protection it purports to provide can still diverge from international standards because of divergent interpretations.

It is therefore paramount that new forms of regulation accurately reflect the provisions of fundamental human rights as a bare minimum, and to take care not to alter or dilute its protections.[148] Close attention is necessary to avoid any divergence that would effectively create a parallel system of regulation.

C. The Future of PMC Impunity: Regulatory Competition and Capture

It is arguable that alternative forms of regulation create competing, rather than complementary or cooperating, systems whether or not their content differs. The very possibility to choose between regulatory regimes may provide incentives for regulators to dilute protection because 'regulators see themselves as being in competition with one another and they will not want to take such a restrictive approach that key businesses move their … operations to regulatory environments that they find more supportive of their business activities'.[149] From the regulatee perspective, the availability of vying modes of regulation reduces the effectiveness of local

[148] John Ruggie recognised the peril in listing out a set of rights that businesses should respect when he was developing the framework for Business and Human Rights: 'Briefly, business can affect virtually all internationally recognized rights. Therefore, any limited list will almost certainly miss one or more rights that may turn out to be significant in a particular instance, thereby providing misleading guidance': J Ruggie, 'Protect, Respect and Remedy: A Framework for Business and Human Rights' (UNGA, 2008) A/HRC/8/5 para 6.

[149] R Brownsword and M Goodwin, *Law and the Technologies of the Twenty-First Century: Text and Materials* (Cambridge University Press, 2012) 294.

regulators because it would be possible to migrate to more favourable alternatives.[150] These pressures combine to reduce the reach and efficacy of regulatory regimes, and the concessions made to appear like an acceptable option for both regulators and regulatees sparks a vicious cycle that drive down standards and protections. An example may be provided by the UK's path to self-regulation of the PMC industry. Once the option was made available, it was unlikely to be restrictive to prevent the flight of the valuable PMC industry from the UK, but also to provide an attractive environment for foreign PMCs to relocate to. The possibility of regulatee defection to more hospitable climes renders strict regulation increasingly irrelevant, highlighting the tension that regulators face. On the one hand, the public expects high levels of protection and rigorous oversight, but on the other hand, regulatees will only acquiesce to relatively unrestrictive regimes. The leverage provided by regulatory competition may transform into regulatory capture by the regulatees:[151]

> Where the regulatory environment is, indeed, bottom-up in its nature, then there is an analytical sense in which regulators are captured by their regulatees—because, quite simply, in such a self-regulatory environment, agents act as both regulators and regulatees. Moreover, it is the fact that regulatees have 'ownership' of their regulatory environment that is seen as key to its effectiveness. In other words, self-regulation implies ownership/capture.[152]

The capture and ownership of voluntary self-regulation by the regulatees appears to be a logical conclusion of such competition. This is problematic because the regulatees will submit to regulation insofar as it confers more benefits than costs, making this an extremely weak form of oversight especially where human rights are concerned.

The ICoCA demonstrates a different form of regulatory capture in that it attempts to crowd out alternative avenues for victims. This is evident from the articles of association which allow the Secretariat to inform the complainant 'of fair and accessible grievance procedures that may offer an effective remedy, including any such grievance procedure provided by a relevant Member company',[153] and where these are challenged as being unsatisfactory, 'the Board may suggest that the complaint be referred to another, identified fair and accessible grievance procedure that may offer an effective remedy, and/or recommend that the Member company take

[150] ibid 345.

[151] 'In general, then, where there are concerns about regulatory capture, we are presupposing a regulatory environment that is more top-down, in which there is a clear separation between regulators and regulatees and, in which, in all probability, there are conflicting interests on the part of regulators and regulatees. In such a setting, we will talk about regulatory capture where, at one or more stages of the regulatory cycle, regulatees are able to exert undue influence over regulators': ibid 298.

[152] ibid.

[153] ICoC (n 87) art 13.2.2.

corrective action within a specified period'.[154] Finally, a claim is closed if the Board of the ICoCA is satisfied that a member company has taken corrective action or if the claim has been referred elsewhere.[155] Thus, it is clear that the ICoC attempts to control the entire claims process of would-be victims, by mandating that its member companies establish internal grievance mechanisms that are overseen by the ICoCA. The Association takes it upon itself to give advice concerning accessible fora to claimants, thereby sending them down a parallel process over which it maintains a degree of control. Insofar as the ICoCA itself has been captured by its member companies, this ability to channel the course of claims may be a subtle source of PMC impunity into the future.

D. The Future of PMC Impunity: Composition and Competence of the Regulators

Related to issues of regulatory competition and capture is the question of who plays what roles in the process. Particular issues are raised with whether the regulators have the requisite experience and resources to maintain meaningful oversight and whether they are suitably placed with regard to regulatees. Implied within the capture and ownership of a regulatory mechanism by the regulatees is a challenge concerning the composition of the oversight body. As Roger Brownsword and Morag Goodwin suggest, there is an assumption that regulators and regulatees are clearly separated and likely to have conflicting interests.[156]

The concept of natural justice provides a framework to consider the composition of the oversight body and consists of rule against bias (*nemo iudex in causa sua*) and the right to a fair hearing (*audi alteram partem*). Summing up the rule against bias, Hewart CJ famously said: 'It is not merely of some importance, but of fundamental importance that justice should not only be done, but should manifestly and undoubtedly be seen to be done',[157] and the rule protects against direct,[158] and apparent,[159] bias. The components of the right to a fair hearing comprise of: the prior notice of the hearing, the opportunity to be heard, fair conduct of the hearing, the right to legal representation, and the decision and reasons for it. The processes available under the ICoC in particular appear to fall far short

[154] ibid, art 13.2.5.
[155] ibid, art 13.2.6.
[156] Brownsword and Goodwin, *Law and the Technologies of the Twenty-First Century* (n 149) 298.
[157] *R v Sussex Justices, ex p McCarthy* (1924) 1 KB 256 (King's Bench) 259.
[158] *Dimes v Grand Junction Canal* (1852) 3 HLC 759 (HL) 793; *R v Bow Street Metropolitan Stipendiary Magistrate, ex p Pinochet Ugarte (No 2)* (2000) 1 AC 119 (HL) 142–43.
[159] *Porter v Magill* (2002) 2 AC 357 (HL) 495.

of these criteria, with clear deficits where the rule against bias is concerned. This is because the multi-stakeholder approach adopted by the ICoC, in which industry, government and civil society are represented, results in indistinct boundaries between regulators and regulatees. While the ICoC's articles of association stipulate 'fair and accessible' procedures that possibly satisfy the first three aspects of the right to a fair hearing, it is difficult to envisage the provision of legal representation for the simple fact that self-regulation is an extra-legal process. Even the provision of a professional representative would arguably fall short of this right because the procedural rules are unlikely to be sufficiently clear.

Aggravating this apparent collusion of the regulators are possible limitations in their competence. Corinna Seiberth points to 'a danger of watering down initial promises for lack of financial resources', and that the objective to keep costs down 'might result in oversight mechanisms that provide only limited scrutiny [which] might jeopardise the good intentions for effective implementation of the Code'.[160] And while the draft budget provides for field visits, these are projected to be at relatively low levels: 10 visits for 100 member companies and 15 for 150, begging the question whether this will provide sufficient oversight.[161] To the challenge of resources could be added a conjecture concerning the professional experience and its relation to regulatory competence. This can be inferred from the imbalance within the structure of the ICoC, where representatives from civil society who are likely to possess relevant experience with monitoring and oversight are outnumbered by those representing the industry and government.

E. The Future of PMC Impunity: Compliance and Consequence of Regulation

The final set of considerations revolves around the outcome of the regulatory process, and in particular with the questions of compliance and the consequences that these raise. Compliance with regulation implies that regulatees adhere to the requirements imposed by the regulatory regime. This usually involves effective monitoring arrangements, and may be accompanied by sanctions and other guarantees of non-repetition as well as the possibility of rehabilitation.

From the regulatee perspective, the questions of compliance may be decided through a calculation weighing the costs and benefits. In the balance are likely to be broader issues of regulatory content (easy to abide by

160 Seiberth (n 41) 223–24.
161 ibid 224.

low standards), regulator capture and competence (less onerous to satisfy partial regulators) which makes compliance contingent upon the specific configuration of the regulatory regime.

The major factor for the regulatee, however, is likely to be the consequences that flow from non-compliance. These are relatively minor where self-regulation is concerned, which suggests that the balance tips in favour of compliance. Where self-regulation adopts diluted standards and allow for regulatees to influence its processes, the scales tip even further because the costs are few. If these suppositions hold, the implication is that self-regulatory regimes will enjoy high levels of regulatee compliance, but raises the question of whether such compliance satisfies the ideals and expectations of regulation.

Adopting a different meaning of consequence, one that is broader than the immediate ramifications of non-compliance, might suggest that self-regulation is merely a mirage of regulation. The assessment from the end-point perspective suggests that self-regulatory processes may make little difference to PMC behaviour and accountability for the reasons given above. Indeed, high levels of regulatee compliance in the absence of coercive pressures may confirm this suspicion because it implies that it is an empty process. A cynic might go so far as to observe that the actual consequence of this illusion is to crowd out alternative forms of regulation in order to perpetuate impunity into the future.

V. CONCLUSION

This chapter sought to discuss the future of PMC impunity by extrapolating from the contemporary trends in both the analysis of the industry and the regulatory mechanisms currently being tabled on the international plane. By dividing the concept of responsibility into its prospective and retrospective dimensions, the chapter provides a different perspective for assessing the strengths and weaknesses of developing regulatory regimes. In doing so, it suggests that self-regulation may be a useful avenue for advancing the standards of protection but may unfortunately be marred by difficulties in assuring that those standards are adhered to. This stands in contrast to more traditionally legal forms of regulation which emphasise enforcement, perhaps at the expense of progressively developing protections.

The outline of the competing forms of PMC-specific regulation plays out these different biases, and the brief account provided has pointed out salient aspects of the various strengths and weaknesses from the responsibility perspective. Indeed, adopting the approach that law creates structures of impunity hints at potential iatrogenic effects in which the regulatory measures adopted to address a problem create and perpetuate those very problems.[162] Rather than resolve the impunity issue, these instruments may instead entrench these effects both by channelling the focus and because they dissociate responsibilities. This leads to the possibility that impunity for the PMC industry will be structurally built into the very regimes that are designed to overcome these allegations. Yet, the existence of these regulatory instruments, in grounding assertions the PMCs are and will be held responsible, will make the industry unassailable against future allegations of impunity because of the appearance that they are regulated.

Even if this is too strong a conclusion, the prospects that the PMC will enjoy impunity for their activities into the future remain high. The regulatory developments at the international plane replicate important features of existing attempts to regulate both the PMC industry itself and its mercenary predecessors. The implication that can be drawn is that existing flaws will be adopted into new forms of regulation and will fail to provide the structure of responsibility and accountability necessary to combat allegations of impunity.

The four dimensions advanced in this chapter against which forms of regulation can be measured reveal significant shortcomings in the preferred avenue of trade association self-regulation embodied by the ICoC process. While further research is necessary to refine these criteria, the initial assessment provides a more detailed framework through which to critique the robustness of industry self-regulation for PMCs. Beyond merely providing another means with which to critique developing regulation, however, this framework may help to identify points of improvement and a means against which alterations can be measured.

This trajectory may indicate the peril of adopting a purely reactive approach towards regulation. Percy has argued that regulators should consider the direction of the PMC industry rather than to respond to the challenges raised by previous manifestations of private force,[163] but even this approach remains reactionary. The analysis in this chapter suggests that further factors are at play which will continue to undermine the efficacy of industry regulation because PMC activities continue to dictate the parameters and possibilities of regulation. Where industry takes the lead and regulators are left to seek compromises, the structural deficits identified through the four different sets of regulatory issues are likely to remain intact.

[162] Adapted from criminological iatrogenesis: B Bowling, 'Transnational Criminology and the Globalisation of Harm Production' (British Criminology Society Conference 2010, 'Human Rights Human Wrongs: Dilemmas and Diversities in Criminology').

[163] See generally S Percy, 'Regulating the Private Security Industry: A Story of Regulating the Last War' (2012) 94 *International Review of the Red Cross* 941.

7

Conclusion

THIS BOOK HAS demonstrated that the law and its processes fulfil a central function in the creation and maintenance of the impunity experienced by the PMC and its contractors. Not only have legal processes been shown to dissociate responsibility for its atrocities away from the PMC, but the law has also been shown to shield it from being held accountable for its activities. This conclusion has challenged what I termed the orthodox legal approach to the question of PMC impunity which is an approach that is premised upon the assumption that legal processes operate to overcome impunity. This orthodox approach has sought to resolve the question of PMC impunity by increasing both the substantial scope and the applicable reach of the law. That approach, however, has been demonstrated to exhibit inadequacies and shortcomings that have been strikingly illustrated by the recidivist practices of the PMC. The book has shown that it was not the absolute absence of law that facilitated PMC impunity because its activities were potentially governed by a range of existing laws. Instead, it was shown that PMC impunity arose because those laws were neither unambiguously applicable nor clearly binding upon the PMC. This meant that the laws which were expected to govern the PMC did not regulate its activities with any degree of certitude, thereby enabling the PMC to avoid responsibility. The contemporary debate surrounding whether or not the PMC could be considered subject to these existing laws underscored these uncertainties.

I have argued that the law itself has contributed towards PMC impunity by showing the inherent characteristics of the law that inhibit the very processes of responsibility. There are, I have argued, two versions of legalised impunity: the weak version, which suggested that the law presented an obstacle that hindered the process of overcoming PMC impunity; and the strong version, which indicated that the law is itself instrumental towards the generation of PMC impunity. By demonstrating that the law is the source of, rather than the solution to, PMC impunity this book has challenged the validity of the response adopted by the orthodox legal approach. Instead, this book has shown that the orthodox approach, which fuels the development of ever more comprehensive laws in an attempt to rein in PMC activity, may instead have the perverse effect of creating and entrenching exactly those situations of impunity that it has sought to overcome.

The contribution of this book has been to show how the law and its processes have created and maintained the structures of impunity that benefit the PMC, rather than to fulfil its assumed function of assigning responsibility and imposing accountability on the PMC. An original approach was adopted which took the existence of impunity as its point of departure because the purpose was to understand how the legal mechanisms of impunity operated. To pursue this radical approach, the concept of impunity was examined in order to develop a theoretical framework that sought to demonstrate the relationship between law and impunity. The role of the law in structuring impunity for the PMC was revealed by uniting the disparate concerns about the weaknesses and inadequacies of juridical processes with the observations of how applicable laws could be circumvented or suspended. In the passive dimension of impunity, legal processes were demonstrated to compartmentalise and isolate different forms of responsibility, which were further magnified by the over-reliance upon the law where it failed to fulfil this role. These processes were demonstrated to be unable to ascribe appropriate meaning to actions or events and were revealed to be instrumental in the denial of wrongdoing. Furthermore, these were complemented by the active dimension of impunity which withheld the application of the law in specific situations, immunised certain categories of actors from the law in others, or which even suspended the entire legal order. This demonstrated that impunity was integral to the functioning of the law itself where international crime and international human rights and humanitarian laws were concerned.

This book has argued that the law has been incapable of comprehending the range of challenges posed by the PMC. This, in turn, has limited its ability to subject the industry to appropriate forms of scrutiny and has frustrated its attempts at regulation. The existing typologies of the industry reveal how the law has failed to recognise the PMC's characteristic combination of civilian status with direct participation in hostilities which are considered to be mutually exclusive under IHL. In spite of the general IHL prohibition of civilians participating in armed conflict, the PMC has been able legally to organise lethal force along the civilian corporate model because the law had previously failed to marginalise the individual mercenary or criminalise the broader practices of mercenarism. While the law had imposed certain limits upon organised private violence, the prohibition of mercenary activities was never the actual aim pursued by the law; rather, this was the tangential effect arising from the restriction of other activities. In the early modern era, the laws of neutrality that limited the ability of individuals to participate in foreign wars had impacted upon mercenary activities. The purpose of these laws, however, was not to restrict mercenaries but rather to prevent States from becoming embroiled in foreign conflicts. Similarly, although mercenaries were denied the right of privileged belligerency under IHL, this provision cut against both the humanitarian grain of that body of law and the historical treatment of mercenaries. The laws that sought to broadly criminalise mercenary practices were historically and geographically limited within the post-colonial context and apply only where such activities frustrate the right of peoples to self-determination. This context renders these laws largely inapplicable to the contemporary activities of the modern PMC. Additionally there have been notable the problems of defining the mercenary with the effect that the laws built from such unstable foundations have proved impossible to apply in practice. In fact, the laws that limit mercenary activity have pursued other aims or have become obsolete because the conditions they were intended to address no longer exist, with the result that the modern PMC could readily exclude itself from these provisions.

This implied the lawfulness of organised private forces, and a close examination of the law revealed that the mutually exclusive combination of civilian status and military activity that characterised the PMC has not been registered by the law. Another indication of the law's failure to register the challenges raised by the PMC is that legal doctrine governing armed conflict continued to presume the hierarchical organisation of the armed forces. This was the foundation of the command responsibility doctrine that enabled responsibility for breaches of IHL to flow up the chain of command in order to hold superiors liable for the actions of their subordinates. The formally horizontal nature of PMC organisation, however, effectively neutralised the application of this doctrine to PMC contractors, thereby immunising them from this form of liability, despite their control over organisation of lethal force. These effects are further compounded by the corporate juridical personhood adopted by the PMC, which was in turn made possible by the failure of the law to marginalise mercenaries or to criminalise mercenarism. This distinct legal personality exempted the PMC both from international criminal law and from domestic criminal law within jurisdictions where corporate criminal responsibility is not recognised. This corporate exception to criminal law was premised upon the basis that corporations could do no harm. While this might rarely be true even for civilian corporations, the corporate status of the PMC was shown to unjustifiably immunise it from the criminal law even when its activities clearly implicate it. The position of the PMC at the interstices of the civilian and the military has continued to confound the ordinary juridical processes which has led to its exemption from legal, and especially criminal, liability.

Even where PMCs appear to be amenable to legal action for civil remedies by their victims, the detailed analysis of the jurisprudence showed that impunity paradoxes have been developed by US federal courts to prevent successful claims by the victims. In particular, two promising pieces of legislation that have facilitated claims against human rights violations in other contexts were closely examined. This analysis demonstrated that despite the possibility of initiating a case against the PMC, success in such claims was entirely foreclosed by the way the courts had developed the jurisprudence. A contribution of this book, therefore, is the identification and analysis of this insidious form of impunity that lurked within the functioning of ordinary legal processes. The analysis revealed that even where the law had the initial appearance of overcoming PMC impunity it had instead been interpreted and structured by the courts to absolutely prevent the PMC from being held accountable. This remained true even in situations where misconduct, including serious violations of human rights, had been factually established and where the victim lacked alternative avenues of remedy. These laws are likely to become even more limited as early indications have suggested that the courts are likely to develop the jurisprudence in a manner that would further restrict, or entirely prevent, human rights claims made by victims against PMCs.

The law was also demonstrated to exhibit biases that foster PMC impunity. The traditional distinction made between the body of laws that regulate recourse to armed force and those that regulate the conduct within hostilities has limited the consideration of PMC impunity exclusively within concerns over its conduct. The law would consider the question of PMC impunity solved where its conduct is in compliance with its HRL and IHL obligations. This has neglected the potential for PMC impunity to arise where its activities violate the prohibition of the threat or use of force because the law recognises this as an obligation that exclusively attaches to States. Similarly, the law is incapable of recognising PMC activity that would amount to corporate aggression because the crime of aggression has been framed by ICL to impose individual criminal responsibility. The private and corporate status of the PMC was shown to frustrate the application of the laws that regulate recourse to armed force. The result is that the PMC can deploy organised violence with impunity because the law does not register these types of activities as wrongs that a corporation can commit.

Legalised impunity for the PMC may be extrapolated from the regulatory mechanisms that are currently being developed specifically for the industry. These forms of regulation were shown to exhibit strong biases and large blind spots. I have sought to demonstrate that these new regulatory mechanisms diverge in their conceptualisation of responsibility which had focused either on its retrospective character associated with accountability or on its prospective character involved with setting standards. The imbalance between these forms of responsibility was argued to guarantee the future of PMC impunity within the very regulatory mechanisms that have been developed to regulate its activity. In order to ameliorate the weaknesses inherent within the currently favoured model of self-regulation, the assertion of collective responsibility for the self-regulatory body was forwarded. Finally, four dimensions were proposed along which the rigour and robustness of developing forms of regulation could be measured.

The hope is the issues I have identified in this book will help to combat the situations of impunity that the PMC has enjoyed since its inception. By arguing that the solution is not necessarily more law, but should include an examination of how those laws are interpreted and applied, it has suggested that the issues are more deeply rooted than they might have initially appeared. Both the proposed framework upon which to organise the issues and the perspective from which to reconsider them is meant to provide a more nuanced approach to resolving PMC impunity. Similarly, the detailed excavation I undertook in this book was intended to showcase the specific factors through which the law created and maintained situations of impunity enjoyed by the PMC. By detailing the source of the problem, the hope is both that better solutions can be crafted to this hitherto intractable problem and that there will be fewer opportunities for situations of impunity to remain in the future.

While the scope of this book has been largely confined to the problems introduced by the modern PMC, I would like to suggest that this is by no means a limitation of either the theoretical framework or the approach adopted in this book. Indeed, it may be that the PMC has simply provided a visible example of the law's intertwined relationship with impunity that was the easiest to identify. The natural trajectory for future work in this vein would be to apply these methods to examine other emerging actors and activities to see if similar effects are exhibited. In the context of contemporary developments in the legal regulation of armed hostilities, it appears that the prospect of autonomous weapons systems will introduce analogous issues and trigger similarly inadequate responses. But the next iteration of innovation may create even more intractable problems. If autonomous weapons systems provide any indication, orthodox legal responses will appear to be even more remote than their reaction to the introduction of Private Military Companies because artificial entities are engaged in the business of life and death. In situations such as these, it may well be worth considering in earnest the limitations of the law, and the hope is that the methods introduced here may go some way to meeting those needs.

Selected Bibliography

Abrahamsen R and Williams M, *Security Beyond the State: Private Security in International Politics* (Cambridge University Press, 2010)

Acheson D, 'Law and Conflict: Changing Patterns and Contemporary Challenges—Panel: Cuban Quarantine: Implications for the Future: Remarks' (1963) 57 *American Society of International Law Proceedings* 13

Agamben G, *State of Exception* (University of Chicago Press, 2005)

Ainley K, 'Excesses of Responsibility: The Limits of Law and the Possibilities of Politics' (2011) 25 *Ethics & International Affairs* 407

Al Jazeera, 'Blackwater Faces New Charges in Iraq Killings' *Al Jazeera* (18 October 2013)

Al-Shalchi H, 'Libya Military Court Jails Accused Foreign Mercenaries' *Reuters* (4 June 2012)

Ambos K, 'General Principles of Criminal Law in the Rome Statute' (1999) 10 *Criminal Law Forum* 1

Amnesty International, '"Disappearances" and Political Killings: Human Rights Crisis of the 1990s: A Manual for Action' Swiss Federal Department of Foreign Affairs (1994) ACT 33/01/94

——, 'Amnesty International Public Statement on the Montreux Document on Pertinent International Legal Obligations and Good Practices for States Related to the Operations of Private Military and Security Companies during Armed Conflict' (2008) IOR 30/010/2008

Annan K, 'We the Peoples: The Role of the United Nations in the Twenty-First Century' (UNGA, 2000) A/54/2000

Antonopoulos C, 'Whatever Happened to Crimes Against Peace?' (2001) 6 *Journal of Conflict and Security Law* 33

Apuzzo M, 'Trying to Salvage Remains of Blackwater Case' *The New York Times* (11 May 2014)

——, 'Blackwater Jurors Urged to Give Iraqis Justice' *The New York Times* (27 August 2014)

——, 'Former Blackwater Guards Convicted in Iraq Shooting' *The New York Times* (22 October 2014)

Arango T and Schmidt M, 'Iraqis Say No to Immunity for Remaining American Troops' *New York Times* (4 October 2011)

Arendt H, *On Violence* (Harcourt Publishers, 1970)

——, *Eichmann in Jerusalem: A Report on the Banality of Evil* (Penguin, 1994)

Armstrong S, *War Plc: The Rise of the New Corporate Mercenary* (Faber and Faber, 2008)

Ashcroft J, *Making A Killing: The Explosive Story of a Hired Gun in Iraq* (Virgin Books, 2010)

Associated Press, 'Blackwater Trial: Supreme Court Refuses Guards' Appeal' *Huffington Post* (4 June 2012)

Atteritano A, 'Liability in Tort of Private Military and Security Companies: Jurisdictional Issues and Applicable Law' in F Francioni and N Ronzitti (eds), *War by Contract: Human Rights, Humanitarian Law, and Private Contractors* (Oxford University Press, 2011)

Avant D, *The Market for Force: The Consequences of Privatizing Security* (Cambridge University Press, 2005)

Bakan J, *The Corporation: The Pathological Pursuit of Profit and Power* (Constable & Robinson, 2005)

Bakker C and Sossai M (eds), *Multilevel Regulation of Military and Security Contractors: The Interplay Between International, European and Domestic Norms* (Hart Publishing, 2012)

Ballesteros E, 'Report on the Use of Mercenaries as a Means of Violating Human Rights and Impeding the Exercise of the Right of Peoples to Self-Determination' (1995) E/CN.4/1995/29

——, 'Report on the Use of Mercenaries as a Means of Violating Human Rights and Impeding the Exercise of the Right of Peoples to Self-Determination' (2001) E/CN.4/2001/19

——, 'Report on the Use of Mercenaries as a Means of Violating Human Rights and Impeding the Exercise of the Right of Peoples to Self-Determination' (2003) E/CN.4/2004/15

Barlow E, *Executive Outcomes: Against All Odds* (Galago, 2008)

Barnes R, 'Court Skeptical about Overseas Corporate Abuse Suits' *Washington Post* (29 February 2012)

——, 'Supreme Court Says Torture Victim Law Applies Only to People, Not Organizations' *Washington Post* (18 April 2012)

Barnett A, 'Scandal-Hit US Firm Wins Key Contracts' *The Guardian* (13 April 2003)

Baxter R, 'So-Called Unprivileged Belligerency: Spies, Guerrillas, and Saboteurs' (1951) 28 *British Year Book of International Law* 323

BBC, 'Abu Ghraib Inmates Sue US Firms' *BBC* (1 July 2008)

——, 'Blackwater Incident: What Happened' *BBC* (8 December 2008)

——, 'Iraq War in Figures' *BBC* (14 December 2011)

——, 'US Flag Ceremony Ends War in Iraq' *BBC* (15 December 2011)

Beaumont P, 'Abu Ghraib Abuse Firms Are Rewarded' *The Guardian* (16 January 2005)

Berman N, 'Privileging Combat—Contemporary Conflict and the Legal Construction of War' (2004) 43 *Columbia Journal of Transnational Law* 1

Best G, *Humanity in Warfare: Modern History of the International Law of Armed Conflicts* (Methuen, 1980)

Bilefsky D and Simons M, 'Netherlands Held Liable for 300 Deaths in Srebrenica Massacre' New York Times (16 July 2014)

Bix B, *Contract Law: Rules, Theory, and Context* (Cambridge University Press, 2012)

Black I, 'Syria's Bashar Al-Assad Vows to Display Captured Foreign Mercenaries' *The Guardian* (16 May 2012)

Blackstone W, *Commentaries On The Laws Of England*, vol 1 (Clarendon Press, 1765)

Bohm A, Senior K and White A, 'The United Kingdom' in C Bakker and M Sossai (eds), *Multilevel Regulation of Military and Security Contractors: The Interplay Between International, European and Domestic Norms* (Hart Publishing, 2012)

Bolkovac K and Lynn C, *The Whistleblower: Sex Trafficking, Military Contractors, and One Woman's Fight for Justice* (Palgrave Macmillan, 2011)

Bonafé B, 'Finding a Proper Role for Command Responsibility' (2007) 5 *Journal of International Criminal Justice* 599

Bonell M, *Unidroit Principles in Practice: Caselaw and Bibliography on the Unidroit Principles of International Commercial Contracts* (Transnational Publishers, 2006)

Bottomley S, 'The Birds, the Beasts, and the Bat: Developing a Constitutionalist Theory of Corporate Regulation' (1999) 27 *Federal Law Review* 243

Bovens M, *The Quest for Responsibility: Accountability and Citizenship in Complex Organisations* (Cambridge University Press, 1998)

Bowling B, 'Transnational Criminology and the Globalisation of Harm Production', *Human Rights Human Wrongs: Dilemmas and Diversities in Criminology* (Proceedings of the Annual Conference of the British Society of Criminology, 2010)

Bradford W, 'Breach of Neutrality (Opinion of 6 July 1795)' (1852) 1 *Official Opinions of the Attorneys General of the United States* 57

Bradley C, 'Attorney General Bradford's Opinion and the Alien Tort Statute' (2012) 106 *American Journal of International Law* 509

Broder J and Risen J, 'Blackwater Tops Firms in Iraq in Shooting Rate' *New York Times* (27 September 2007)

Brooks D, 'Messiahs or Mercenaries? The Future of International Private Military Services' (2000) 7 *International Peacekeeping* 129

—— and Chorev M, 'Ruthless Humanitarianism: Why Marginalizing Private Peacekeeping Kills People' in A Alexandra, D-P Baker and M Caparini (eds), *Private Military and Security Companies: Ethics, Policies and Civil-military Relations* (Routledge, 2008)

—— and Shevlin J, 'Reconsidering Battlefield Contractors' (2005) 6 *Georgetown Journal of International Affairs* 103

Brown K, 'With Troop Exit, a Civilian Phase for the U.S. in Iraq' *Bloomberg* (24 October 2011)

Brownlie I, 'Volunteers and the Law of War and Neutrality' (1956) 5 *International & Comparative Law Quarterly* 570

——, Principles of Public International Law (Oxford University Press, 2008)

Brownsword R and Goodwin M, *Law and the Technologies of the Twenty-First Century: Text and Materials* (Cambridge University Press, 2012)

Burmester HC, 'The Recruitment and Use of Mercenaries in Armed Conflicts' (1978) 72 *American Journal of International Law* 37

Buzatu A-M and Buckland B, 'Private Military & Security Companies: Future Challenges in Security Governance' (DCAF, 2010) DCAF Horizon 2015 Working Paper No 3

Byatt H, 'Sentences Passed on British Mercenaries in Angola, Part, The Trial of British Mercenaries in Angola June/July 1976' (1976) FCO 45/2000

Cameron L, 'Private Military Companies: Their Status under International Humanitarian Law and Its Impact on Their Regulation' (2007) 88 *International Review of the Red Cross* 573

—— and Chetail V, *Privatizing War: Private Military and Security Companies under Public International Law* (Cambridge University Press, 2013)

Cane P, *Responsibility in Law and Morality* (Hart Publishing, 2002)

Cassel D, 'Lessons from the Americas: Guidelines for International Response to Amnesties for Atrocities' (1996) 59 *Law and Contemporary Problems* 197

Cassese A, 'Mercenaries: Lawful Combatants or War Criminals?' (1980) 40 *ZaöRV* 1

——, 'When May Senior State Officials Be Tried for International Crimes? Some Comments on the Congo v Belgium Case' (2002) 13 *European Journal of International Law* 853
——, *International Criminal Law* (Oxford University Press, 2008)
——, 'A Plea for a Global Community Grounded in a Core of Human Rights' in A Cassese (ed), *Realizing Utopia: The Future of International Law* (Oxford University Press, 2012)
Censer M, 'CACI Seeking Payment from Former Abu Ghraib Prisoners' *Washington Post* (16 August 2013)
Centeno M, 'Limited War and Limited States' in D Davis and A Pereira (eds), *Irregular Armed Forces and their Role in Politics and State Formation* (Cambridge University Press, 2003)
Cesner R and Brant J, 'Law of the Mercenary: An International Dilemma' (1976) 6 *Capital University Law Review* 339
Chapman K, 'The Untouchables: Private Military Contractors' Criminal Accountability under the UCMJ' (2010) 63 *Vanderbilt Law Review* 1047
Chatterjee P, 'Outsourcing Intelligence in Iraq: A CorpWatch Report on L-3/Titan' (CorpWatch, 2008)
——, 'Military Contractors' Mercenary Motives' *The Guardian* (31 August 2011)
——, 'CIA "Rendition" Contractors Data Cache To Be Released' *CorpWatch* (22 May 2012)
Cherif Bassiouni M, 'Searching for Peace and Achieving Justice: The Need for Accountability' (1996) 59 *Law and Contemporary Problems* 9
Chomsky N, *Understanding Power: The Indispensable Chomsky* (Vintage, 2003)
Chulov M and Smith D, 'Libya: Gaddafi's Army of Mercenaries Face Backlash' *The Guardian* (2 September 2011)
Clapham A, *Human Rights Obligations of Non-State Actors* (Oxford University Press, 2006)
——, 'Extending International Criminal Law beyond the Individual to Corporations and Armed Opposition Groups' (2008) 6 *Journal of International Criminal Justice* 899
Cleaver G, 'Subcontracting Military Power: The Privatisation of Security in Contemporary Sub-Saharan Africa' (2000) 33 *Crime, Law & Social Change* 131
Coady CAJ, 'Objecting Morally' (1997) 1 *Journal of Ethics* 375
——, *Morality and Political Violence* (Cambridge University Press, 2008)
Coalition Provisional Authority, 'CPA Order 17: Status of the Coalition Provisional Authority, MNF—Iraq, Certain Missions and Personnel in Iraq' 27 June 2004
Cobain I and Quinn B, 'How US Firms Profited from Torture Flights' *The Guardian* (31 August 2011)
Cobbett's Parliamentary History, 'Debate in the Lords on the Duke of Richmond's Motion for an Address to Countermand the March of the German Troops' (1776) 16 George III
Cockayne J, 'The Global Reorganization of Legitimate Violence: Military Entrepreneurs and the Private Face of International Humanitarian Law' (2006) 88 *International Review of the Red Cross* 459
——, 'Make or Buy? Principle-Agent Theory and the Regulation of Private Military Companies', *From Mercenaries to Market: The Rise and Regulation of Private Military Companies* (Oxford University Press, 2007)

——, 'Regulating Private Military and Security Companies: The Content, Negotiation, Weaknesses and Promise of the Montreux Document' (2008) 13 *Journal of Conflict and Security Law* 401
——, 'Private Military and Security Companies', *The Oxford Handbook of International Law in Armed Conflict* (Oxford University Press, 2014)
Coffee J, '"No Soul to Damn: No Body to Kick": An Unscandalized Inquiry into the Problem of Corporate Punishment' (1981) 79 *Michigan Law Review* 386
Cohen S, *States of Denial: Knowing About Atrocities and Suffering* (Polity, 2001)
Cole A, 'Blackwater Quits Security Association' *Wall Street Journal* (11 October 2007)
Comiteau L, 'Dutch Blamed for Srebrenica Dead' *BBC* (5 July 2011)
Commission on Wartime Contracting, 'Transforming Wartime Contracting: Controlling Costs, Reducing Risks. Final Report to Congress' (2011)
Committee of Privy Counsellors, *Report of the Committee of Privy Counsellors Appointed to Inquire into the Recruitment of Mercenaries* (Cmnd 6569, 1976)
Cooperstein T, 'Letters of Marque and Reprisal: The Constitutional Law and Practice of Privateering' (2009) 40 *Journal of Maritime Law and Commerce* 221
Cotton J, 'The Rights of Mercenaries as Prisoners of War' (1977) 77 *Military Law Review* 143
Craswell R, 'Promises and Prices' (2011) 45 *Suffolk University Law Review* 735
Crawford J and Watkins J, 'International Responsibility' in S Besson and J Tasioulas (eds), *The Philosophy of International Law* (Oxford University Press, 2010)
Danner A, 'The Nuremberg Industrialist Prosecutions and Aggressive War' (2005) 46 *Virginia Journal of International Law* 651
—— and Martinez J, 'Guilty Associations: Joint Criminal Enterprise, Command Responsibility, and the Development of International Criminal Law' (2005) 93 *California Law Review* 75
Davenport C, 'Pentagon Imposes Strict Standards on Private Security Firms' *Washington Post* (26 November 2014)
Davies C, 'Briton Danny Fitzsimons Jailed in Iraq for Contractors' Murders' *The Guardian* (28 February 2011)
Davis J, *Fortune's Warriors: Private Armies and the New World Order* (Douglas & McIntyre, 2002)
Dean M, 'Removing a Blot on the Landscape—The Reform of the Doctrine of Privity' [2000] *Journal of Business Law* 143
De Schutter O, 'The Responsibility of States' in S Chesterman and A Fisher (eds), *Private Security, Public Order* (Oxford University Press, 2009)
Dewey J, 'The Historic Background of Corporate Legal Personality' (1925) 35 *Yale Law Journal* 655
Dickinson L, 'Public Law Values in a Privatized World' (2006) 31 *Yale Journal of International Law* 383
——, 'Contract as a Tool for Regulating Private Military Companies' in S Chesterman and C Lehnardt (eds), *From Mercenaries to Market: The Rise and Regulation of Private Military Companies* (Oxford University Press, 2007)
——, *Outsourcing War and Peace: Preserving Public Values in a World of Privatized Foreign Affairs* (Yale University Press, 2011)
Dinstein Y, *The Conduct of Hostilities under the Law of International Armed Conflict* (Cambridge University Press, 2004)

——, *War, Aggression and Self-Defence* (Cambridge University Press, 2005)
——, *The Conduct of Hostilities under the Law of International Armed Conflict* (Cambridge University Press, 2010)
——, *War, Aggression and Self-Defence* (Cambridge University Press, 2011)
Dörmann K, 'The Legal Situation of "Unlawful/Unprivileged Combatants"' (2003) 85 *International Review of the Red Cross* 45
Doswald-Beck L, 'Private Military Companies under International Humanitarian Law' in S Chesterman and C Lehnardt (eds), *From Mercenaries to Market: The Rise and Regulation of Private Military Companies* (Oxford University Press, 2007)
Doyle C, 'Civilian Extraterritorial Jurisdiction Act: Federal Contractor Criminal Liability Overseas' Congressional Research Service (15 February 2012) R42358
Druzin B, 'Restraining the Hand of Law: A Conceptual Framework to Shrink the Size of Law' (2014) 117 *West Virginia Law Review* 100
Duker W, 'The President's Power to Pardon: A Constitutional History' (1976) 18 *William and Mary Law Review* 475
Emmons B, 'Tortured Language: "Individuals," Corporate Liability and the Torture Victim Protection Act' (2011) 96 *Minnesota Law Review* 675
Fabre C, 'In Defence of Mercenarism' (2010) 40 *British Journal of Political Science* 539
Fahim K and Baume M de la, 'Head of French Security Company Killed in Libya' *New York Times* (12 May 2011)
Fainaru S and al-Izzi S, 'U.S. Security Contractors Open Fire in Baghdad' *Washington Post* (27 May 2007)
Fallah K, 'Corporate Actors: The Legal Status of Mercenaries in Armed Conflict' (2006) 88 *International Review of the Red Cross* 599
Fay G, 'Fay Report: AR 15-6 Investigation of the Abu Ghraib Detention Facility and 205th Military Intelligence Brigade' (2004)
Feinman J, 'Critical Approaches to Contract Law' (1982) 30 *UCLA Law Review* 829
Fifield A, 'Contractors Reap $138bn from Iraq War' *Financial Times* (18 March 2013)
Fletcher G, *Tort Liability for Human Rights Abuses* (Hart Publishing, 2008)
Ford D, *Flying Tigers: Claire Chennault and His American Volunteers, 1941-1942* (HarperCollins-Smithsonian Books, 2007)
Francioni F, 'The Role of the Home State in Ensuring Compliance with Human Rights by Private Military Contractors' in F Francioni and N Ronzitti (eds), *War by Contract: Human Rights, Humanitarian Law, and Private Contractors* (Oxford University Press, 2011)
—— and Ronzitti N (eds), *War by Contract: Human Rights, Humanitarian Law, and Private Contractors* (Oxford University Press, 2011)
Frulli M, 'Exploring the Applicability of Command Responsibility to Private Military Contractors' (2010) 15 *Journal of Conflict and Security Law* 435
——, 'Immunity for Private Military Contractors: Legal Hurdles or Political Snags?' in F Francioni and N Ronzitti (eds), *War by Contract: Human Rights, Humanitarian Law, and Private Contractors* (Oxford University Press, 2011)
Gardner J, 'The Mark of Responsibility' (2003) 23 *Oxford Journal of Legal Studies* 157
Garfield A, 'Bridging a Gap in Human Rights Law: Prisoner of War Abuse as War Tort' (2005) 37 *Georgetown Journal of International Law* 725
Garmon T, 'Domesticating International Corporate Responsibility: Holding Private Military Firms Accountable under the Alien Tort Claims Act' (2003) 11 *Tulane Journal of International and Comparative Law* 325

Garraway C, 'The Application of Superior Responsibility in an Era of Unlimited Information' in D Saxon (ed), *International Humanitarian Law and the Changing Technology of War* (Martinus Nijhoff, 2013)
Gattini A, 'A Historical Perspective: From Collective to Individual Responsibility and Back' in A Nollkaemper and H van der Wilt (eds), *System Criminality in International Law* (Cambridge University Press, 2009)
Geiser U, 'Mercenary Companies to Face Ban' *swissinfo.ch* (23 January 2013)
Ghebali V-Y, 'The United Nations and the Dilemma of Outsourcing Peacekeeping Operations' in A Bryden and M Caparini (eds), *Private Actors and Security Governance* (LIT & DCAF, 2006)
Giannini T and Farbstein S, 'Corporate Accountability in Conflict Zones: How Kiobel Undermines the Nuremberg Legacy and Modern Human Rights' (2010) 52 *Harvard International Law Journal Online* 119
Giesen I, 'Regulating Regulators through Liability: The Case for Applying Normal Tort Rules to Supervisors' (2006) 2 *Utrecht Law Review* 8
Gill T and Fleck D (eds), *The Handbook of the International Law of Military Operations* (Oxford University Press, 2011)
Gillard E-C, 'Private Military/Security Companies: The Status of Their Staff and Their Obligations under International Humanitarian Law and the Responsibility of States in Relation to Their Operations' in A Alexandra, D-P Baker and M Caparini (eds), *Private Military and Security Companies: Ethics, Policies, and Civil–Military Relations* (Routledge, 2008)
Gillespie A, *History of the Laws of War: Combatants and Captives*, vol 1 (Hart Publishing, 2011)
Glanz J and Lehren A, 'Growing Use of Contractors Added to Iraq War's Chaos—Iraq War Logs—WikiLeaks Documents' *New York Times* (23 October 2010)
Glanz J and Rubin A, 'From Errand to Fatal Shot to Hail of Fire to 17 Deaths' *New York Times* (3 October 2007)
Goff P, 'Mercenaries Bill Passed' *beehive.govt.nz* (1 July 2004)
Gómez del Prado J, 'Private Military and Security Companies and the UN Working Group on the Use of Mercenaries' (2008) 13 *Journal of Conflict and Security Law* 429
——, 'Report of the Working Group on the Use of Mercenaries as a Means of Violating Human Rights and Impeding the Exercise of the Right of People to Self-Determination' (UNHRC, 2008) A/HRC/7/7
——, 'Mission to Chile' (UNHRC, 2008) A/HRC/7/7/Add.4
——, 'Report of the Working Group on the Use of Mercenaries as a Means of Violating Human Rights and Impeding the Exercise of the Right of Peoples to Self-Determination with the Draft of a Possible Convention on Private Military and Security Companies (PMSCs) for Consideration and Action by the Human Rights Council' (UNGA, 2010) A/HRC/15/25
——, 'Mission to Iraq' (UNHRC 2011) A/HRC/18/32/Add.4
Gray C, *International Law and the Use of Force* (Oxford University Press, 2008)
Green L, 'The Status of Mercenaries in International Law' (1978) 9 *Manitoba Law Journal* 201
Green P and Ward T, *State Crime: Governments, Violence and Corruption* (Pluto Press, 2004)

Greenwood C, 'The Scope of Application of Humanitarian Law' in T Gill and D Fleck (eds), *The Handbook of the International Law of Military Operations* (Oxford University Press, 2011)
Groome D, 'Adjudicating Genocide: Is the International Court of Justice Capable of Judging State Criminal Responsibility' (2007) 31 *Fordham International Law Journal* 911
Guardian, 'US Embassy Cables: Afghan Government Asks US to Quash "Dancing Boys" Scandal' *The Guardian* (2 December 2010)
Guissé EH and Joinet L, 'Progress Report on the Question of Impunity of Perpetrators of Human Rights Violations pursuant to Sub-Commission Resolution 1992/23' (UNESC 1993) E/CN.4/Sub.2/1993/6
Gul S, 'The Secretary Will Deny All Knowledge Of Your Actions: The Use of Private Military Contractors and Implications for State and Political Accountability' (2006) 10 *Lewis and Clark Law Review* 287
Gunningham N and Rees J, 'Industry Self-Regulation: An Institutional Perspective' (1997) 19 *Law and Policy* 363
Hague W, 'Private Military and Security Companies' HC Deb 16 September 2010, cols 59 WS
Hamilton A et al, *The Federalist Papers* (Oxford University Press, 2008)
Hansard Parliamentary Debates (Cornelius Buck, 1854)
Harper C, 'From Impunity to Reconciliation', *Impunity: An Ethical Perspective* (World Council of Churches Publications, 1996)
—— (ed), *Impunity: An Ethical Perspective* (World Council of Churches Publications, 1996)
Hart HLA, *Punishment and Responsibility: Essays in the Philosophy of Law* (Oxford University Press, 2008)
Harvey D, *A Brief History of Neoliberalism* (Oxford University Press, 2007)
Hawkins K, 'CACI's Forgotten Role in Abu Ghraib (I)' *Huffington Post* (29 August 2013)
——, 'CACI's Forgotten Role in Abu Ghraib (II)' *Huffington Post* (9 September 2013)
Hedley S, 'Keeping Contract in Its Place—Balfour v Balfour and the Enforceability of Informal Agreements' (1985) 5 *Oxford Journal of Legal Studie* s 391
Henckaerts J-M and Doswald-Beck L, *Customary International Humanitarian Law*, vol II (Cambridge University Press, 2005)
——, *Customary International Humanitarian Law*, vol I (Cambridge University Press, 2009)
Hobbes T, *Hobbes's Leviathan: Reprinted from the Edition of 1651* (Oxford University Press, 1929)
Hodge N, 'Panel's War-Waste Records Sealed as Work Ends' *The Wall Street Journal* (30 September 2011)
Hoe A, *David Stirling: The Authorised Biography of the Founder of the SAS* (Warner Books, 1992)
Holmqvist C, *Private Security Companies: The Case for Regulation* (SIPRI, 2005)
Honore T, *Responsibility and Fault* (Hart Publishing, 2022)
Hoover M, 'The Laws of War and the Angolan Trial of Mercenaries: Death to the Dogs of War' (1977) 9 *Case Western Reserve Journal of International Law* 323
Hopkins N, 'Defence Cuts: More Compulsory Redundancies to Come' *The Guardian* (1 September 2011)

——, 'War in Whitehall and an Uncertain Future for Armed Forces' *The Guardian* (1 September 2011)
——, 'MoD Spent £600m on Consultants' *The Guardian* (17 November 2011)
——, 'Ministry of Defence to Cut Further 3,000 Civilian Jobs' *The Guardian* (26 January 2012)
Hoppe C, 'Positive Human Rights Obligations of the Hiring State in Connection with the Provision of "Coercive Services" by a Private Military or Security Company' in F Francioni and N Ronzitti (eds), *War by Contract: Human Rights, Humanitarian Law, and Private Contractors* (Oxford University Press, 2011)
—— and Quirico O, 'Codes of Conduct for Private Military and Security Companies: The State of Self-Regulation in the Industry' in F Francioni and N Ronzitti (eds), *War by Contract: Human Rights, Humanitarian Law, and Private Contractors* (Oxford University Press, 2011)
Horwitz M, 'Santa Clara Revisited: The Development of Corporate Theory' (1985) 88 *West Virginia Law Review* 173
House of Commons Foreign Affairs Committee, *Private Military Companies* (2001–02, HC 922)
Hufbauer G and Mitrokostas N, 'International Implications of the Alien Tort Statute' (2004) 7 *Journal of International Economic Law* 245
Human Rights First, 'Private Security Contractors at War: Ending the Culture of Impunity' (2008)
Human Rights Watch, 'The Price of Oil: Corporate Responsibility and Human Rights Violations in Nigeria's Oil Producing Communities' (1999) 1-56432-225-4
——, 'Hopes Betrayed: Trafficking Women and Girls to Post-Conflict Bosnia and Herzegovina for Forced Prostitution' (2002) vol 14, no 9 (D)
——, 'Too High a Price: The Human Rights Cost of the Indonesian Military's Economic Activities' (2006) vol 18, no 5(C)
——, 'Libya: Stop Arbitrary Arrests of Black Africans' *Human Rights Watch* (4 September 2011)
Huskey K and Sullivan S, 'United States: Law and Policy Governing Private Military Contractors after 9/11' in C Bakker and M Sossai (eds), *Multilevel Regulation of Military and Security Contractors: The Interplay Between International, European and Domestic Norms* (Hart Publishing, 2012)
Ibbetson D, *A Historical Introduction to the Law of Obligations* (Oxford University Press, 1999)
ICC, 'The Crime of Aggression' (11 June 2010) RC/Res.6
——, 'Depository Notification: Adoption of Amendments on the Crime of Aggression' (11 June 2010) C.N.651.2010.TREATIES-8
'ICC Finds Congo's Lubanga Guilty' *BBC* (14 March 2012)
ICoC, 'International Code of Conduct for Private Security Service Providers' Association: Articles of Association' (2013)
——, 'The International Code of Conduct for Private Security Service Providers: Signatory Companies' (2013)
ICRC, *Commentary on the Additional Protocols of 8 June 1977 to the Geneva Conventions of 12 August 1949* (Martinus Nijhoff, 1987)
ILC, *Yearbook of the International Law Commission 1991*, vol II, pt II (UN, 1994)
——, *Yearbook of the International Law Commission 1995*, vol II, pt II (UN, 1998)
——, *Yearbook of the International Law Commission 2001*, vol II, pt II (UN, 2007)

International Institute of Humanitarian Law, 'XXXVth Round Table: Private Military and Security Companies' 31 May 2012

International Law Commission, 'Report of the International Law Commission: Fifty-Third Session' (UNGA, 2001) A/56/10

Ireland P, 'Capitalism without the Capitalist: The Joint Stock Company Share and the Emergence of the Modern Doctrine of Separate Corporate Personality' (1996) 17 *The Journal of Legal History* 41

Isaacs T and Vernon R (eds), *Accountability for Collective Wrongdoing* (Cambridge University Press, 2011)

Isenberg D, 'A Government in Search of Cover: Private Military Companies in Iraq' in S Chesterman and C Lehnardt (eds), *From Mercenaries to Market: The Rise and Regulation of Private Military Companies* (Oxford University Press, 2007)

——, 'It's Déjà Vu for DynCorp All Over Again' *The Huffington Post* (6 December 2010)

Jäger T and Kümmel G, 'PSMCs: Lessons Learned and Where to Go from Here' in T Jäger and G Kümmel (eds), *Private Military and Security Companies: Chances, Problems, Pitfalls and Prospects* (VS Verlag fur Sozialwissenschaften, 2007)

Johnson R, 'Violation of the Neutrality Act of 1818 (Opinion of 28 April 1849)' (1852) 5 *Official Opinions of the Attorneys General of the United States* 92

Johnston J, 'Blacklisted Contractor Continues Receiving Government Money through Haiti Contracts' *The Hill* (2 December 2011)

Joinet L, 'Question of the Impunity of Perpetrators of Violations of Human Rights (Civil and Political Rights): Final Report Prepared by Mr. L. Joinet, pursuant to Subcommission Resolution 1995/35' (UNESC, 1996) E/CN.4/Sub.2/1996/18

——, 'Question of the Impunity of Perpetrators of Violations of Human Rights (civil and Political Rights): Revised Final Report Prepared by Mr. L. Joinet, pursuant to Subcommission Decision 1996/119' (UNESC, 1997) E/CN.4/Sub.2/1997/20/Rev.1

Jørgensen N, 'Criminality of Organisations under International Law' in A Nollkaemper and H van der Wilt (eds), *System Criminality in International Law* (Cambridge University Press, 2009)

Joyner C, 'Redressing Impunity for Human Rights Violations: The Universal Declaration and the Search for Accountability' (1997) 26 *Denver Journal of International Law and Policy* 591

Kahneman D, *Thinking, Fast and Slow* (Penguin, 2012)

Kaldor M, *New and Old Wars: Organized Violence in a Global Era* (Polity, 2001)

Karsten N, 'Distinguishing Military and Non-Military Superiors Reflections on the Bemba Case at the ICC' (2009) 7 *Journal of International Criminal Justice* 983

Katz A, 'Annual Report of the Working Group on the Use of Mercenaries as a Means of Violating Human Rights and Impeding the Exercise of the Right of Peoples to Self-Determination' (UNHRC, 2013) A/HRC/24/45

Kelley M, 'Falsehoods in Iraq Shooting Unpunished' *USA Today* (2 April 2009)

Kennedy D, *The Dark Sides of Virtue: Reassessing International Humanitarianism* (Princeton University Press, 2005)

Kinsey C, *Corporate Soldiers and International Security: The Rise of Private Military Companies* (Routledge, 2006)

——, 'Private Security Companies: Agents of Democracy or Simply Mercenaries?' in T Jäger and G Kummel (eds), *Private Military and Security Companies: Chances, Problems, Pitfalls and Prospects* (VS Verlag fur Sozialwissenschaften, 2007)

Kleffner J, 'The Collective Guilt of Organised Armed Groups for System Crimes' in A Nollkaemper and H van der Wilt (eds), *System Criminality in International Law* (Cambridge University Press, 2009)

Klein N, *The Shock Doctrine: The Rise of Disaster Capitalism* (Penguin, 2008)

Koh H, 'Separating Myth from Reality about Corporate Responsibility Litigation' (2004) 7 *Journal of International Economic Law* 263

Koskenniemi M, *Politics of International Law* (Hart Publishing, 2011)

Kristjanson F and Moreau S, 'Regulatory Negligence and Administrative Law' (2012) 25 *Canadian Journal of Administrative Law and Practice* 103

Kritsiotis D, 'Mercenaries and the Privatization of Warfare' (1998) 22 *Fletcher Forum of World Affairs* 11

Krygier M, 'Compared to What?' (2009) 34 *Australian Journal of Legal Philosophy* 241

Ku J, 'The Curious Case of Corporate Liability under the Alien Tort Statute: A Flawed System of Judicial Lawmaking' (2010) 51 *Virginia Journal of International Law* 353

Kwakwa E, 'The Current Status of Mercenaries in the Law of Armed Conflict' (1990) 14 *Hastings International & Comparative Law Review* 67

Lam J, 'Accountability for Private Military Contractors Under the Alien Tort Statute' (2009) 97 *California Law Review* 1459

Lardner R, 'Military Spending Waste: Up To $60 Billion In Iraq, Afghanistan War Funds Lost To Poor Planning, Oversight, Fraud' *Huffington Post* (30 August 2011)

Law Commission, *Privity of Contracts: Contracts for the Benefit of Third Parties* (Law Com No 242, 1996)

Lee C, 'Neutrality (Opinion of 10 December 1795)' (1852) 1 *Official Opinions of the Attorneys General of the United States* 61

Legare H, 'Violation of Neutrality and Act of Congress of 1818 (Opinion of 8 January 1842)' (1852) 3 *Official Opinions of the Attorneys General of the United States* 741

Lehnardt C, 'Private Military Companies and State Responsibility' in S Chesterman and C Lehnardt (eds), *From Mercenaries to Market: The Rise and Regulation of Private Military Companies* (Oxford University Press, 2007)

——, 'Individual Liability of Private Military Personnel under International Criminal Law' (2008) 19 *European Journal of International Law* 1015

Lindroos-Hovinheimo S, 'Is Law Necessarily Unjust' (2009) 6 *No Foundations—Journal of Extreme Legal Positivism* 69

Liu H-Y, 'Leashing the Corporate Dogs of War: The Legal Implications of the Modern Private Military Company' (2010) 15 *Journal of Conflict and Security Law* 141

——, 'Mercenaries in Libya: Ramifications of the Treatment of "Armed Mercenary Personnel" under the Arms Embargo for Private Military Company Contractors' (2011) 16 *Journal of Conflict and Security Law* 293

——, 'Refining Responsibility: Differentiating Two Types of Responsibility Issues Raised by Autonomous Weapons Systems' in Nehal Bhuta and others (eds), Autonomous Weapons Systems—Law, Ethics Policy (Cambridge University Press 2015)

Lobel J, 'The Rise and Decline of the Neutrality Act: Sovereignty and Congressional War Powers in United States Foreign Policy' (1983) 24 *Harvard International Law Journal* 1

Lockwood G, 'Report on the Trial of Mercenaries: Luanda, Angola-June, 1976' (1976) 7 *Manitoba Law Journal* 183

Lynch T and Walsh AJ, 'The Good Mercenary?' (2000) 8 *Journal of Political Philosophy* 133
MacCormick N, 'Argumentation and Interpretation in Law' (1995) 9 *Argumentation* 467
Machiavelli N, *The Prince* (P Bondanella tr, Oxford University Press, 2005)
Mallison T and Mallison S, 'The Juridical Status of Irregular Combatants under the International Humanitarian Law of Armed Conflict' (1977) 9 *Case Western Reserve Journal of International Law* 39
Manacorda S and Meloni C, 'Indirect Perpetration versus Joint Criminal Enterprise' (2011) 9 *Journal of International Criminal Justice* 159
Manson K and Wright R, 'Somali Pirates Spawn Lucrative Security Trade' *Financial Times* (8 February 2012)
Marston G, 'United Kingdom Materials on International Law 1982' (1982) 53 *British Yearbook of International Law* 337
Martinez J, 'Understanding Mens Rea in Command Responsibility: From Yamashita to Blaškić and Beyond' (2007) 5 *Journal of International Criminal Justice* 638
Matthias A, 'The Responsibility Gap: Ascribing Responsibility for the Actions of Learning Automata' (2004) 6 *Ethics and Information Technology* 175
McCabe D, 'State Department Awarded Blackwater More Than $1 Billion After Threat On Investigator's Life' *Huffington Post* (10 July 2014)
McDougall C, *The Crime of Aggression under the Rome Statute of the International Criminal Court* (Cambridge University Press, 2013)
Mclean H, 'Negligent Regulatory Authorities and the Duty of Care' (1988) 8 *Oxford Journal of Legal Studies* 442
Meikle J, 'British Contractor Jailed in Iraq for Colleagues' Murders' *The Guardian* (28 February 2011)
Meloni C, 'Command Responsibility Mode of Liability for the Crimes of Subordinates or Separate Offence of the Superior?' (2007) 5 *Journal of International Criminal Justice* 619
Melzer N, 'Fifth Expert Meeting on the Notion of Direct Participation in Hostilities' (ICRC, 2008)
——, 'Interpretive Guidance on the Notion of Direct Participation in Hostilities Under International Humanitarian Law' (ICRC, 2009) Publication Ref 0990
Mendes E, *Peace and Justice at the International Criminal Court: A Court of Last Resort* (Edward Elgar Publishing, 2010)
Miller C, 'Contractors Outnumber Troops in Iraq' *Los Angeles Times* (4 July 2007)
Milliard T, 'Overcoming Post-Colonial Myopia: A Call to Recognize and Regulate Private Military Companies' (2003) 176 *Military Law Review* 1
Minty A, 'Report of the Open-Ended Intergovernmental Working Group to Consider the Possibility of Elaborating an International Regulatory Framework on the Regulation, Monitoring and Oversight of the Activities of Private Military and Security Companies on Its Second Session' (UNGA, 2012) A/HRC/22/41
Mitchell D, 'Libyan Extraction: How Companies Get Employees out of Global Hotspots' *CNN* (3 March 2011)
Mockler A, *New Mercenaries* (Sidgwick & Jackson, 1985)
Mokhiber R, 'The Death Penalty for Corporations Comes of Age' (1998) 12 *Business Ethics* 7
Moore M, *Causation and Responsibility: An Essay in Law, Morals, and Metaphysics* (Oxford University Press, 2010)

——, *Placing Blame* (Oxford University Press, 2010)
Moreno-Ocampo L, 'Statement to the United Nations Security Council on the Situation in Libya, pursuant to UNSCR 1970' (ICC, 4 May 2011)
Mourning P, 'Leashing the Dogs of War: Outlawing the Recruitment and Use of Mercenaries' (1981) 22 *Virginia Journal of International Law* 589
Murray O, Kinley D and Pitts C, 'Exaggerated Rumours of the Death of an Alien Tort? Corporations, Human Rights and the Remarkable Case of Kiobel' (2011) 12 *Melbourne Journal of International Law* 57
Nadelmann E, 'Global Prohibition Regimes: The Evolution of Norms in International Society' (1990) 44 *International Organization* 479
Nagan W and Hammer C, 'The Rise of Outsourcing in Modern Warfare: Sovereign Power, Private Military Actors, and the Constitutive Process' (2008) 60 *Maine Law Review* 429
Neff S, *War and the Law of Nations: A General History* (Cambridge University Press, 2005)
Newell V and Sheehy B, 'Corporate Militaries and States: Actors, Interaction, and Reactions' (2006) 41 *Texas International Law Journal* 67
New York Times, 'Blackwater's Impunity' *The New York Times* (16 May 2008)
——, 'Status of the Forces Agreement' *New York Times* (21 October 2011)
——, 'State Department Documents on Blackwater Episode' *New York Times* (29 June 2014)
——, 'A Verdict on Blackwater' *New York Times* (22 October 2014)
Nikitin A, 'Report of the Working Group on the Use of Mercenaries as a Means of Violating Human Rights and Impeding the Exercise of the Right of Peoples to Self-Determination' (UNHRC, 2009) A/HRC/10/14
——, 'Mission to South Africa' (UNHRC, 2011) A/HRC/18/32/Add.3
Nollkaemper A and van der Wilt H (eds), *System Criminality in International Law* (Cambridge University Press, 2009)
Nozick R, *Anarchy, State, and Utopia* (Basic Books, 1974)
Ntoubandi F, 'South Africa: The Regulatory Context of Private Military and Security Services' in C Bakker and M Sossai (eds), *Multilevel Regulation of Military and Security Contractors: The Interplay Between International, European and Domestic Norms* (Hart Publishing, 2012)
O'Brien K, 'What Should and What Should Not Be Regulated?' in S Chesterman and C Lehnardt (eds), *From Mercenaries to Market: The Rise and Regulation of Private Military Companies* (Oxford University Press, 2007)
O'Cinneide C, 'Strapped to the Mast: The Siren Song of Dreadful Necessity, the United Kingdom Human Rights Act and the Terrorist Threat' in M Gani and P Mathew (eds), *Fresh Perspectives on the 'War on Terror'* (ANU Press, 2008)
Office of the Spokesperson, 'State Department to Incorporate International Code of Conduct into Worldwide Protective Services Contracts' (*US Department of State*, 16 August 2013)
Office of the United States Chief of Counsel for Prosecution of Axis Criminality, *Nazi Conspiracy and Aggression*, vol Opinion and Judgment (United States Government Printing Office 1946)
OHCHR, 'Mercenaries: UN Experts Say That the Nissour Square Killings in Iraq Should Not Remain Unpunished.' *UN Working Group on the Use of Mercenaries* (7 January 2010)

——, 'The Corporate Responsibility to Protect Human Rights: An Interpretative Guide' (2012)
——, 'The use of mercenaries as a means of violating human rights and impeding the exercise of the right of peoples to self-determination' UN Commission on Human Rights Resolution 2005/2, 7 April 2005
Ortiz C, 'The Private Military Company: An Entity at the Centre of Overlapping Spheres of Commercial Activity and Responsibility' in T Jäger and G Kümmel (eds), *Private Military and Security Companies: Chances, Problems, Pitfalls and Prospects* (VS Verlag fur Sozialwissenschaften, 2007)
Østensen ÅG, *UN Use of Private Military and Security Companies: Practices and Policies* (DCAF, 2011) 3
Parrish G, 'Killing Corporations' *Seattle Weekly News* (14 July 1999)
Patel F, 'Report of the Working Group on the Use of Mercenaries as a Means of Violating Human Rights and Impeding the Exercise of the Right of Peoples to Self-Determination' (UNHRC, 2012) A/HRC/21/43
Pattison J, 'Just War Theory and the Privatization of Military Force' (2008) 22 *Ethics & International Affairs* 143
Penrose M, 'Impunity—Inertia, Inaction, and Invalidity: A Literature Review' (1999) 17 *Boston University International Law Journal* 269
Percy S, 'Mercenaries: Strong Norm, Weak Law' (2007) 61 *International Organization* 367
——, *Mercenaries: The History of a Norm in International Relations* (Oxford University Press, 2007)
——, 'Private Security Companies and Civil Wars' (2009) 11 *Civil Wars* 57
——, 'Regulating the Private Security Industry: A Story of Regulating the Last War' (2012) 94 *International Review of the Red Cross* 941
Pérez AB de, 'Mission to Equatorial Guinea' (UNHRC, 2011) A/HRC/18/32/Add.2
Politi M, 'The ICC and the Crime of Aggression: A Dream That Came Through and the Reality Ahead' (2012) 10 *Journal of International Criminal Justice* 267
Poynder J, *Literary Extracts from English and Other Works Collected During Half a Century Together with Some Original Matter, vol 1* (John Hatchard, 1844)
Preparatory Commission for the International Criminal Court, 'Historical Review of Developments Relating to Aggression' (UN Working Group on the Crime of Aggression, 2002) PCNICC/2002/WGCA/L.1
Punch M, 'Suite Violence: Why Managers Murder and Corporations Kill' (2000) 33 *Crime, Law & Social Change* 243
——, 'Why Corporations Kill and Get Away with It: The Failure of Law to Cope with Crimes in Organisations' in A Nollkaemper and H van der Wilt (eds), *System Criminality in International Law* (Cambridge University Press, 2009)
Quinn B, 'Computer Sciences Corporation Could Retain £1bn in Health Contracts' *The Guardian* (6 March 2012)
Quirico O, 'The Criminal Responsibility of Private Military and Security Company Personnel under International Humanitarian Law' in F Francioni and N Ronzitti (eds), *War by Contract: Human Rights, Humanitarian Law, and Private Contractors* (Oxford University Press, 2011)
Radin MJ, 'Market-Inalienability' (1986) 100 *Harvard Law Review* 1849
——, *Contested Commodities: Trouble with Trade in Sex, Children, Body Parts and Other Things* (Harvard University Press, 2001)

Ralby I, Tonkin H and Wilmshurst E, 'Regulation of Private Military Security Companies in Armed Conflict: Meeting Summary International Law Programme' (Chatham House, 2011)
Ramirez M, 'The Science Fiction of Corporate Criminal Liability: Containing the Machine through the Corporate Death Penalty' (2005) 47 *Arizona Law Review* 933
Rasor D, 'Out of Iraq: What Will the War Service Industry Do Now?' *Truthout* (26 October 2011)
Ratnam G and Gienger V, 'Iraq-U.S. Accord Wipes Out Contractor Immunity (Update1)' *Bloomberg* (20 November 2008)
Ratner S, 'The Schizophrenias of International Criminal Law' (1998) 33 *Texas International Law Journal* 237
——, 'Corporations and Human Rights: A Theory of Legal Responsibility' (2001) 111 *Yale Law Journal* 443
Rayment S, '"Trophy" Video Exposes Private Security Contractors Shooting up Iraqi Drivers' *The Telegraph* (27 November 2005)
Richards D, 'Twenty-First Century Armed Forces—Agile, Useable, Relevant' (Annual Defence Lecture, Chatham House, 17 September 2009)
Risen J, 'End of Immunity Worries U.S. Contractors in Iraq' *New York Times* (1 December 2008)
——, 'Former Blackwater Guards Charged With Murder' *The New York Times* (8 January 2010)
——, 'Efforts to Prosecute Blackwater Are Collapsing' *New York Times* (20 October 2010)
——, 'Appeals Court Revives Case Against Blackwater Guards' *New York Times* (22 April 2011)
——, 'Before Shooting in Iraq, a Warning on Blackwater' *The New York Times* (29 June 2014)
—— and Mazzetti M, 'Blackwater Guards Tied to Secret C.I.A. Raids' *New York Times* (11 December 2009)
Roberts A, *The Wonga Coup: Simon Mann's Plot to Seize Oil Billions in Africa* (Profile Books, 2006)
——, 'Transformative Military Occupation: Applying the Laws of War and Human Rights' (2006) 100 *American Journal of International Law* 580
Robertson G, *Crimes Against Humanity: The Struggle For Global Justice* (Penguin, 2006)
Robins N, *The Corporation That Changed the World: How the East India Company Shaped the Modern Multinational* (Pluto Press, 2006)
Robinson P, Lee N and Carrick D, *Ethics Education in the Military* (Ashgate, 2008)
Rogin J, 'McCaskill: The Afghan Oversight Office Is Rudderless' *Foreign Policy* (2 November 2011)
Romano R, 'Metapolitics and Corporate Law Reform' (1984) 36 *Stanford Law Review* 923
Ronzitti N, 'Access to Justice and Compensation for Violations of the Law of War' in F Francioni (ed), *Access to Justice as a Human Right* (Oxford University Press, 2007)
Rosemann N, 'The Privatization of Human Rights Violations—Business' Impunity or Corporate Responsibility? The Case of Human Rights Abuses and Torture in Iraq' (2005) 5 *Non-State Actors and International Law* 77

Rowlands, E, 'Angola (Mercenaries)' HC Deb 12 July 1976, vol 915 cols 44-49
Ruggie J, 'Protect, Respect and Remedy: A Framework for Business and Human Rights' (UNGA, 2008) A/HRC/8/5
——, 'Guiding Principles on Business and Human Rights: Implementing the United Nations "Protect, Respect and Remedy" Framework' (UNGA, 2011) A/HRC/17/31
Rumsfeld D, 'DOD Acquisition and Logistics Excellence Week Kickoff—Bureaucracy to Battlefield. U.S. Department of Defense, Office of the Assistant Secretary of Defense (Public Affairs)' (2001)
Rush R, 'Neutrality (Opinion of 27 July 1816)' (1852) 1 *Official Opinions of the Attorneys General of the United States* 190
Sandel M, *Justice: What's the Right Thing to Do?* (Penguin, 2010)
Sapone M, 'Have Rifle With Scope, Will Travel: The Global Economy of Mercenary Violence' (1999) 30 *California Western International Law Journal* 1
Sassòli M, 'The Implementation of International Humanitarian Law: Current and Inherent Challenges' (2007) 10 *Yearbook of International Humanitarian Law* 45
Sayapin S, 'The Definition of the Crime of Aggression for the Purpose of the International Criminal Court: Problems and Perspectives' (2008) 13 *Journal of Conflict and Security Law* 333
Scahill J, 'Blackwater Founder Remains Free and Rich While His Former Employees Go Down on Murder Charges' *The Intercept* (22 October 2014)
Schmidt M, 'Immunity Gone, Contractor in Iraq Sentenced to Prison' *New York Times* (28 February 2011)
Schooner S, 'Contractor Atrocities at Abu Ghraib: Compromised Accountability in a Streamlined, Outsourced Government' (2005) 16 *Stanford Law & Policy Review* 549
Schwellenbach N and Leonnig C, 'U.S. Policy a Paper Tiger Against Sex Trade in War Zones' *Washington Post* (18 July 2010)
Seck S, 'Collective Responsibility and Transnational Corporate Conduct' in T Isaacs and R Vernon (eds), *Accountability for Collective Wrongdoing* (Cambridge University Press, 2011)
Seiberth C, *Private Military and Security Companies in International Law A Challenge for Non-Binding Norms: The Montreux Document and the International Code of Conduct for Private Security Providers* (Intersentia, 2013)
Serralvo J, 'Privatized Military Firms Impunity in Cases of Torture: A Crime of Humanity?' (2012) 14 *International Community Law Review* 117
Shah R, 'Beating Blackwater: Using Domestic Legislation to Enforce the International Code of Conduct for Private Military Companies' (2014) 123 *Yale Law Journal* 2559
Shameem S, 'Report on the Question of the Use of Mercenaries as a Means of Violating Human Rights and Impeding the Exercise of the Right of Peoples to Self-Determination' (UNGA, 2005) A/60/263
——, 'Mission to Afghanistan' (UNHRC, 2010) A/HRC/15/25/Add.2
——, 'Mission to the United States of America' (UNHRC, 2010) A/HRC/15/25/Add.3
Shays C and Thibault M, 'Reducing Waste in Wartime Contracts' *Washington Post* (29 August 2011)
Shearer D, *Private Armies and Military Intervention* (Oxford University Press, 1998)

Sheehy B, Maogoto J and Newell V, *Legal Control of the Private Military Corporation* (Palgrave Macmillan, 2009)

Shelton D, *Remedies in International Human Rights Law* (Oxford University Press, 2006)

Shepherd B, *The Circuit* (Pan, 2009)

Simmons, M, 'Written Statement to Parliament: International Code of Conduct for Private Security Providers Association' (*UK Foreign and Commonwealth Office*, 15 October 2013)

Simpson G, *Law, War and Crime: War Crimes Trials and the Reinvention of International Law* (Polity, 2007)

——, 'Men and Abstract Entities: Individual Responsibility and Collective Guilt in International Criminal Law' in A Nollkaemper and H van der Wilt (eds), *System Criminality in International Law* (Cambridge University Press, 2009)

Singer PW, 'The Ultimate Military Entrepreneur' (2003) Spring *Military History Quarterly* 6

——, *Corporate Warriors: The Rise of the Privatized Military Industry* (Cornell University Press, 2004)

Slavin E, 'U.S. Pursuing Legal Protections for Contractors Still in Iraq' *Stars and Stripes* (14 December 2011)

Sly L, 'Iraqis Say They Were Forced to Take Blackwater Settlement' *Los Angeles Times* (11 January 2010)

Solis G, *The Law of Armed Conflict: International Humanitarian Law in War* (Cambridge University Press, 2010)

Spicer T, *An Unorthodox Soldier: Peace and War and the Sandline Affair* (Mainstream Publishing, 2000)

Stahn C, 'Complementarity, Amnesties and Alternative Forms of Justice: Some Interpretative Guidelines for the International Criminal Court' (2005) 3 *Journal of International Criminal Justice* 695

Stanger A, *One Nation Under Contract: The Outsourcing of American Power and the Future of Foreign Policy* (Yale University Press, 2011)

Stempel J, 'U.S. Court Refuses to Hold Occidental Liable in Colombia Bombing' *Reuters* (12 November 2014)

Stewart J and Gray S, 'The Blackwater Trial: Part 2—Legal Issues' *Just Security* (27 October 2014)

Stratton A, 'Libya Campaign May Cost UK £260m' *The Guardian* (23 June 2011)

Swart B and others 'Discussion: International Trends towards Establishing Some Form of Punishment For Corporations' (2008) 6 *Journal of International Criminal Justice* 947

Swissinfo.ch, 'Mercenary Services Outlawed by Parliament' *swissinfo.ch* (24 September 2013)

Swiss Federal Department of Foreign Affairs, 'International Code of Conduct for Private Security Service Providers' 9 November 2010

——, 'Draft Charter of the Oversight Mechanism for the International Code of Conduct for Private Security Service Providers' 16 January 2012

Taguba A, '"Taguba Report": Article 15-6 Investigation of the 800th Military Police Brigade' (2004)

Talijaard R, 'Implementing South Africa's Regulation of Foreign Military Assistance Act' *Private Actors and Security Governance: Geneva Centre for the Democratic Control of Armed Forces* (LIT & DCAF, 2006)

Tallgren I, 'The Sensibility and Sense of International Criminal Law' (2002) 13 *European Journal of International Law* 561
Taulbee J, 'Myths, Mercenaries and Contemporary International Law' (1985) 15 *California Western International Law Journal* 339
Thomson J, 'State Practices, International Norms, and the Decline of Mercenarism' (1990) 34 *International Studies Quarterly* 23
——, *Mercenaries, Pirates, and Sovereigns: State-Building and Extraterritorial Violence in Early Modern Europe* (Princeton University Press, 1994)
Tickler P, *The Modern Mercenary: Dog of War, or Soldier of Fortune?* (Patrick Stephens, 1987)
Tilly C, 'War Making and State Making as Organised Crime' in P Evans, D Rueschemeyer and T Skocpol (eds), *Bringing the State Back in* (Cambridge University Press, 1985)
——, *Coercion, Capital and European States, A.D.990-1990* (Blackwell, 1992)
Tonkin H, *State Control Over Private Military and Security Companies in Armed Conflict* (Cambridge University Press, 2011)
Tougas M-L, 'Some Comments and Observations on the Montreux Document' (2009) 12 *Yearbook of International Humanitarian Law* 321
Tucker E and Frommer F, 'New Charges in Blackwater Shootings' *Huffington Post* (17 October 2013)
Turns D, 'Weapons in the ICRC Study on Customary International Humanitarian Law' (2006) 11 *Journal of Conflict and Security Law* 201
UK Foreign and Commonwealth Office, 'Promoting High Standards in the Private Military and Security Company Industry' (9 March 2011)
UN Human Right Council, 'Open-Ended Intergovernmental Working Group to Consider the Possibility of Elaborating an International Regulatory Framework on the Regulation, Monitoring and Oversight of the Activities of Private Military and Security Companies' (UNHRC, 2010) A/HRC/RES/15/26
——, 'Human Rights Council Holds Interactive Dialogue on Human Rights and International Solidarity and on Mercenaries' *UNHCR* (13 September 2011)
——, 'UNHCR Fears for the Safety of Refugees Caught in Libya's Violence' *UNHCR* (22 February 2012)
——, 'Open-Ended Intergovernmental Working Group to Consider the Possibility of Elaborating an International Regulatory Framework on the Regulation, Monitoring and Oversight of the Activities of Private Military and Security Companies' (UNHRC, 2013) A/HRC/RES/22/33
UN Human Rights Committee, 'Compilation of General Comments and General Recommendations Adopted by Human Rights Treaty Bodies' (UN International Human Rights Instruments, 1997) HRI/GEN/1/Rev.3
——, 'General Comment No 31: The Nature of the General Legal Obligation Imposed on States Parties to the Covenant' (UN International Covenant on Civil and Political Rights, 2004) CCPR/C/21/Rev.1/Add. 13
——, 'Human Rights Committee Consideration of Reports Submitted by States Parties under Article 40 of the Covenant: Fourth Periodic Report United States of America' (UN International Covenant on Civil and Political Rights, 2012) CCPR/C/USA/4
UN Secretary General, 'Secretary-General Reflects on "Intervention" in Thirty-Fifth Annual Ditchley Foundation Lecture' 28 June 1998 SG/SM/6613

United Kingdom Foreign and Commonwealth Office, *Private Military Companies: Options for Regulation* Green Paper (2001–02, HC 577)
UN Rome Proceedings, 'Proposal Submitted by the United States of America for Article 25' (16 June 1998) A/CONF.183/C.1/L.2
——, 'Proposal Submitted by France: Article 23 Individual Criminal Responsibility: Legal Persons' (16 June 1998) A/CONF.183/C.1/L.3
——, 'Proposal Submitted by the Comoros and Madagascar' (3 July 1998) A/CONF.183/C.1/L.46
——, 'Working Paper on Article 23' (3 July 1998) A/CONF.183/C.1/WGGP/L.5/Rev.2
——, 'Committee of the Whole: Summary Record of the 1st Meeting' (20 November 1998) A/CONF.183/C.1/SR.1
UN Working Group on the Use of Mercenaries, 'Report of the Working Group on the Use of Mercenaries as a Means of Violating Human Rights and Impeding the Exercise of the Right of Peoples to Self-Determination' (UNGA, 2007) A/62/301
——, 'Alarming Rise in Mercenary Activities Calls for Attention' *UN Working Group on the Use of Mercenaries* (1 November 2011)
——, 'Submission by the Working Group on the Use of Mercenaries as a Means of Impeding the Exercise of the Right of Peoples to Self-Determination' (UNHRC, 2012) A/HRC/WG.10/2/CRP.1
——, 'Mission to Honduras' (UNHRC 2013) A/HRC/24/45/Add.1
——, 'Mission to Somalia' (UNHRC 2013) A/HRC/24/45/Add.2
——, 'Report of the Working Group on the Use of Mercenaries as a Means of Violating Human Rights and Impeding the Exercise of the Right of Peoples to Self-Determination' (UNGA, 2013) A/68/339
Van Buren P, 'Immunity: Disastrous Decisions in 2007 Return to Haunt 2012' *Huffington Post* (4 November 2011)
Van der Wilt H, 'Joint Criminal Enterprise: Possibilities and Limitations' (2007) 5 *Journal of International Criminal Justice* 91
Van Deventer H, 'Mercenaries at Geneva' (1976) 70 *American Journal of International Law* 811
Veitch S, *Law and Irresponsibility: On the Legitimation of Human Suffering* (Routledge-Cavendish, 2007)
Vergakis B, 'Piracy Definition in Dispute as Piracy Trial Looms' *Huffington Post* (16 April 2012)
Vinuales J, 'Impunity: Elements for an Empirical Concept' (2007) 25 *Law and Inequality: A Journal of Theory and Practice* 115
Wald M, 'U.S. Lawyers Knew about Legal Pitfalls in Blackwater Case' *New York Times* (2 January 2010)
Walzer M, Just and Unjust Wars: A Moral Argument with Historical Illustrations (Basic Books, 2006)
Wayne L, 'America's For-Profit Secret Army' *New York Times* (13 October 2002)
Weber M, *From Max Weber: Essays in Sociology* (HH Gerth and C Wright Mills eds, Routledge and Kegan Paul, 1946)
Weigend T, 'Perpetration through an Organization' (2011) 9 *Journal of International Criminal Justice* 91
Weiss P, 'Should Corporations Have More Leeway to Kill Than People Do?' *New York Times* (24 February 2012)

Wells C, *Corporations and Criminal Responsibility* (Oxford University Press, 2001)
Werle G, Burghardt B and Roxin C, 'Crimes as Part of Organized Power Structures' (2011) 9 *Journal of International Criminal Justice* 191
White N, 'Institutional Responsibility for Private Military and Security Companies' in F Francioni and N Ronzitti (eds), *War by Contract: Human Rights, Humanitarian Law, and Private Contractors* (Oxford University Press, 2011)
——, 'The Privatisation of Military and Security Functions and Human Rights: Comments on the UN Working Group's Draft Convention' (2011) 11 *Human Rights Law Review* 133
——, 'Regulatory Initiatives at the International Level' in C Bakker and M Sossai (eds), *Multilevel Regulation of Military and Security Contractors: The Interplay Between International, European and Domestic Norms* (Hart Publishing, 2012)
—— and MacLeod S, 'EU Operations and Private Military Contractors: Issues of Corporate and Institutional Responsibility' (2008) 19 *European Journal of International Law* 965
Whyte D, 'Lethal Regulation: State-Corporate Crime and the United Kingdom Government's New Mercenaries' (2003) 30 *Journal of Law and Society* 575
Wilmshurst E, 'Chatham House International Law Discussion Group Private Military and Security Companies' *Chatham House* (22 January 2008)
Wilson J and Maguire K, 'American Firm in Bosnia Sex Trade Row Poised to Win MoD Contract' *The Guardian* (29 November 2002)
Wright Q, 'The Law of the Nuremberg Trial' (1947) 41 *American Journal of International Law* 38
Wuerth I, 'Kiobel v. Royal Dutch Petroleum Co.: The Supreme Court and the Alien Tort Statute' (2013) 107 *The American Journal of International Law* 601
Yost P, 'Abu Ghraib Settlement: Defense Contractor Engility Holdings Pays $5M To Iraqi Torture Detainees' *Huffington Post* (8 January 2013)
Zahar A and Sluiter G, *International Criminal Law* (Oxford University Press, 2007)
Zarate J, 'The Emergence of a New Dog of War: Private International Security Companies, International Law, and the New World Disorder' (1998) 34 *Stanford Journal of International Law* 75

Index

www.ingramcontent.com/pod-product-compliance
Ingram Content Group UK Ltd.
Pitfield, Milton Keynes, MK11 3LW, UK
UKHW021238300926
15471UKWH00013B/432

9 781509 918393